THIRTIETH ANNIVERSARY EDITION

In Nine Languages, Bought by 20,000 People a Month

What Color Is Your Parachute?

"This book is the recognized bible for anyone looking for a job . . ."
United Kingdom, *Careers '98*

"With more than five million copies in print worldwide, *Parachute,* now in its 26th annual edition, remains the gold standard of career guides."
Fortune Magazine, 1/15/96

"*Parachute* remains the most complete career guide around. . . . It covers all the ground less ambitious books do, as well as some the others don't, mostly in the realm of the psyche. . . . The book is a sentimental favorite, if only because I actually knew people who carved out career niches for themselves by following its advice."
Barbara Presley Noble, *New York Times,* 2/13/95

"Richard deserves sainthood for all the people he's helped during the last 27 years."
Bob Rosner, *Working Wounded,* February 1998

"This is . . . the Cadillac of job-search books."
Kerri S. Smith, *Rocky Mountain News,* 11/5/95

"*What Color Is Your Parachute?* Just the title of this book intrigues me. After reading it from cover to cover (and working through a dozen of Richard Bolles's flower exercises) I realized that it should be required reading for anyone who wants to successfully carve out their own career niche. Revised and updated annually, *Parachute* (a word coined by the author when he was referring to career transitions back in the late 1960s) is about taking chances, gaining confidence, and making changes in your career and life. Complete with exercises on self-assessment and career planning, it is . . . valuable to those who are securely employed but unhappy with what they're doing. Richard Bolles has also crafted a magnificent Web site -- JobHuntersBible.com, the companion for his wit, words, and wisdom, which includes information (and lots of links) on one of his newest works -- *Job Hunting on the Internet.*"
Michael Landes, *The Back Door Guide to Short Term Job Adventures,* Fall 1999

"This is the best-selling job hunter's book in the world, and has been for 25 years. It is revised and updated annually, is popular not just in the U.S. but in many other countries around the world, and is available in seven languages. Bolles has helped millions of people change jobs, find new careers or get back on their feet. This book is not just for the person who's out of work. It is even more valuable to those who are employed but not really happy with what they're doing. . . ."
PeopleSuccess.com, July 5, 1999

This is an annual. That is to say,
it is substantially revised each year,
the new edition appearing each November.
Those wishing to submit additions,
corrections, or suggestions for the
2001 edition should submit them prior
to February 1, 2000, using the form
provided in the back of this book.
(Forms reaching us after that date will,
unfortunately, have to wait for the
2002 edition.)

What Color Is
Your Parachute?

Other Books by Richard N. Bolles

The What Color Is Your Parachute? Workbook

Job-Hunting on the Internet,
　　1999 edition, revised and enlarged

The Career Counselor's Handbook
　　(with Howard Figler as co-author)

The Three Boxes of Life,
　　And How to Get Out of Them

How to Find Your Mission in Life

Job-Hunting Tips for the So-Called Handicapped

2000 Edition

What Color Is Your Parachute?

A Practical Manual
for
Job-Hunters
& Career-Changers

by

Richard Nelson Bolles

Ten Speed Press

PUBLISHER'S NOTE

This publication is designed to provide accurate and authoritative information in regard to the subject matter covered. It is sold with the understanding that the publisher is not engaged in rendering professional career services. If expert assistance is required, the service of the appropriate professional should be sought.

The drawing on page 90–91 is by Steven M. Johnson, author of *What the World Needs Now.*

Copyright © 2000, 1999, 1998, 1997, 1996, 1995, 1994, 1993, 1992, 1991, 1990, 1989, 1988, 1987, 1986, 1985, 1984, 1983, 1982, 1981, 1980, 1979, 1978, 1977, 1976, 1975, 1972, 1970
by Richard Nelson Bolles.

Distributed in Australia by Simon and Schuster Australia, in Canada by Ten Speed Press Canada, in New Zealand by Southern Publishers Group, in South Africa by Real Books, in Southeast Asia by Berkeley Books, and in the United Kingdom and Europe by Airlift Books.

Library of Congress Catalog Card Information on file with the publisher.
ISBN 1-58008-123-1, paper
ISBN 1-58008-125-8, cloth

Published by Ten Speed Press, P.O. Box 7123, Berkeley, California 94707
www.tenspeed.com

Typesetting by Star Type, Berkeley
Cover design by Thomjon Borges
Printed in the United States of America

2   3   4   5   —   2000   1999

Contents

continued

interview. The fear behind employers' questions. How to deal with handicaps. How to end the interview: the six essential questions. The importance of thank-you notes. How and when to negotiate salary. How to win at salary negotiation. Fringe benefits. What to do when interviews never lead to a job. Reasons job-hunters get rejected. Who gets hired the most often.

This is dedicated to the one I love
(my wife, Carol)

We tell these stories time and again,
And you know we'll keep telling them
In the time to come - -
So long as it is not yet our time.

Yes, but that day will come
When our time is up,
And we are out of time.
Then to whatever realm we go,
The memories of us will linger here
In the hearts of those we left behind,
And we will at last
Be timeless.

Time is our addiction and obsession. And we tend to measure it by the amount of change we see. Okay, looking back over the past thirty years, the changes in our culture since 1970 have indeed been tremendous. I think of FedEx, fax machines, pagers, cell-phones, ATMs, e-mail, the Internet, and many other technological innovations.

But we would not be able to deal with change if there were not also constancy in our lives: things that don't change, but remain dependable, predictable, and trustworthy. In marking the passage of time, we need to note what has stayed the same. For, that is the ground on which we stand, from which we turn to deal with change.

This is the ground which Archimedes had in mind when he said, "Give me a place to stand and I will move the earth." This is the ground the Old Testament had in mind, when Elijah was to behold all the fury of Nature's elements. He was told to "stand upon the mount."

We need a place to stand. An unchanging place, in our lives. Hence, in looking back over the past thirty years, Constancy must be our preoccupation, as much as Change is.

So, what does stay constant over the years?

Well, our skills, for one. If you were good at analyzing things twenty years ago, you almost certainly still are.

And our values and character, for another. If you prized honesty twenty years ago, you probably still do.

And our faith, for another. Eternity is by definition unchanging at its core.

And I would add: the general nature of the job-hunt (see my diagram on page 19). Hasn't changed much in thirty years. People were sending out resumes then. People are sending out resumes now. Only difference: now they use e-mail.

Even so, many employers were tired of resumes thirty years ago. Many employers are tired of resumes now. Even e-mailed ones.

(In the current issue of USA Today, *as I write - - July 15, 1999 - - is the headline "Enough already with the e-resumes." It reports that "some companies are getting thousands of resumes dumped into e-mail boxes each day. Others are fed up with mass e-mailed resumes and yearn for a more personal touch." One employer is quoted as saying, "It bogs down your mailbox and your server. There's so much volume, and it's so inappropriate, and it's only going to get worse." Manpower, for example, reports receiving 80,000 e-mailed resumes a month, with that number expected to double by the end of the year.)*

Yes, the general nature of the job-hunt hasn't changed much in thirty years. It's still all about human nature. And it's all about knowing yourself, your gifts, and what you have to offer to the world. And it's all about deciding whether you want to take the easy way and find "just a job," or whether you want to do the hard work necessary to figure out and identify a job that really fits you.

Change and constancy. They must be our themes when we consider the passage of time. Not surprisingly, they are our themes also with regard to the history of this book. The book is revised every year, and one year it manifests Change; while another year it manifests Constancy.

Last year Change was the theme. I dramatically rewrote this entire book, taking out two hundred pages, boiling the book down to its simplest essence.

This year, Constancy is the theme. Being immensely pleased with the reader feedback to last year's dramatic revision, I have decided to leave well enough alone - - contenting myself with hardly touching the book for this 2000 year edition, except for the necessary updating of information, addresses, etc.

Well, there you have it: my own personal meditation upon what these past thirty years have wrought. The passage of Time. Change and Constancy.

To hold the two together in this book, to hold the two together in your life, that more than ever seems to me to be the essence of job-hunting wisdom, not to mention the essence of wisdom about Life.

And now, to close this Preface, I want to voice my annual heartfelt litany of gratitude:

• My thanks first of all to my 6,000,000 readers, and most especially to the two thousand or so who send me letters over the course of a year. I rarely can answer them any more, but I do read every one of the letters that come in, and feel that no author could possibly ask for more loving, and appreciative readers -- not in a million years. Thank you so much for writing me, for updating me on new ideas that you have discovered, or for letting me know when and how this book has helped you.

• My thanks also to those intellectual leaders in the field who have been such good friends to me over the years, kind and helpful: John Holland, the late John Crystal, Sidney Fine, Harvey Belitsky, Dick Lathrop, Daniel Porot, Arthur Miller, Tom and Ellie Jackson, Nathan Azrin, Bernard Haldane, and Howard Figler. (Howard and I have just written, and Ten Speed has published, a new book entitled, *The Career Counselor's Handbook,* by Figler and Bolles.)

• My thanks to my longtime publisher (for 27 years now) Phil Wood, and to all the folks over at Ten Speed Press in Berkeley, who help get this book out, each year: Kirsty Melville, Jason Rath, Anna Erickson, Hal Hershey, Jackie Wan, and Linda Davis, our caring typesetter. My most especial gratitude and appreciation to Bev Anderson, my layout artist for the past 28 years -- a genius if ever there was one.

• My thanks to my friends who have helped me with this work over these many years, and particularly with my annual two-week workshop each August: Verlyn Barker, Daniel Porot, David Swanson, Jim Kell, Carol Christen, Brian McIvor, Susie Page, Mary Ann Kaczmarski, Rita Morin, Ellen Wallach, Erica Chambré, Norma Wong, and a host of others, including the late John Crystal, and the late Bob Wegmann.

• My thanks also to my family, who have given me so much encouragement and love over the years -- my beloved wife, Carol, with her compassion, wit, and wisdom; my four grown children, Stephen, Mark, Gary, Sharon -- and their families; my stepdaughter, Serena; my sister, Ann Johnson and her family, and last but hardly least, my ninety-six-year-old aunt, Sister Esther Mary, of the Community of the Transfiguration (Episcopal) in Glendale, Ohio, who has taught me to serve the Lord, from my youth up.

• Surely, no litany of thanks would be complete without my thanking The Great Lord God, Father of our Lord Jesus Christ, and source of all grace, wisdom, and compassion, Who has given me this work of helping so many people of different faiths, tongues, and nations, with their job-hunt, and the meaning of their life. I am grateful beyond measure for such a life, such a mission, and such a privilege.[1]

Dick Bolles
P. O. Box 379
Walnut Creek
California 94597-0379
7/16/99

1. Let me forewarn any agnostic readers that some readers at amazon.com (five, in fact) have complained there is too much religion in this book. In actual fact, there are (only?) five sentences which mention faith or God anywhere in the body of this book. Oh true, there is also an optional Epilogue about faith and mission in the back of the book, but it is back there where no one need stray except those who want to read it.

Why is faith in this book, at all? Well because of a little known fact, which is that this, the most popular job-hunting book in the world, is written by a man who has been an ordained Episcopal minister for the past 46 years.

Oh, and faith is also in this book (the Epilogue at least) because many many readers have begged for it to be in. (According to Gallup polls, 94% of the American people believe in some form of God.)

My Annual Grammar & Language Footnote

Throughout this book, I often use the apparently plural pronoun "they," "them," or "their" after *singular* antecedents -- such as, "You must approach *someone* for a job and tell *them* what you can do." This sounds strange and even *wrong* to those who know English well. To be sure, we all know there is another pronoun -- "you" -- that may be either singular or plural, but few of us realize that the pronouns "they," "them," or "their" were also once treated as both plural and singular in the English language. This changed, at a time in English history when agreement in *number* became more important than agreement as to sexual *gender*. Today, however, our priorities have shifted once again. Now, the distinguishing of sexual *gender* is considered by many to be more important than agreement in *number*.

The common artifices used for this new priority, such as "s/he," or "he and she," are -- to my mind -- tortured and inelegant. Casey Miller and Kate Swift, in their classic, *The Handbook of Nonsexist Writing*, agree, and argue that it is time to bring back the earlier usage of "they," "them," and "their" as both singular and plural -- just as "you" is/are. They further argue that this return to the earlier historical usage has already become quite common *out on the street* -- witness a typical sign by the ocean which reads "*Anyone* using this beach after 5 p.m. does so at *their* own risk." I have followed Casey and Kate's wise recommendations in all of this.

As for my commas, they are deliberately used according to my own rules -- rather than according to the rules of historic grammar. My own rules are: I write conversationally, and put in a comma wherever I would normally stop for a breath, were I speaking the same line.

The same conversational rule applies to my use of *italics*. I use *italics* wherever, were I speaking the sentence, I would put *emphasis* on that word or phrase. Rarely, I also use italics where there is a digression of thought, and I want to maintain the main thought and flow of the sentence. All in all, I write as I speak.

P.S. Over the last twenty-eight years, a few critics (very few) have claimed that *Parachute* is too complicated in its vocabulary and grammar for anyone except a college graduate. An index in England that analyzes a book to tell you what grade in school you must have finished in order to understand it, rated my book a 6.1, which means you need only have finished sixth grade in an English school in order to understand it.

Here in the U.S., a college instructor phoned me to tell me that my book was rejected by the authorities as a proposed text for his college course, because the book's language/grammar was not up to college level. "What level was it?" I asked. "Well," he replied, "when they analyzed it, it turned out to be written on an eighth-grade level." Sounds about right to me.

R.N.B.

CHAPTER ONE

A Hunting
We Will Go

Okay, this is it.
The moment of truth has arrived
For You. It's time
To go out, and look for a job,
Out there in *the job-market,*
Which all your friends speak of
In hushed tones, as a battlefield littered with the bodies
Of the unemployed,
Who tried and failed to find a job
Before you.

It's a very strange market, out there,
One area in sunny prosperity,
Another in deep Depression,
As Asian markets crash and burn.
Five million people unemployed now
In the U.S. alone.
So that even in good times
The battlefield is littered with new bodies.
Those just laid off,
Who had worked at one
Place, for *years*
And thought their jobs
Would always be secure there,
But then got downsized
Without any warning,
In a merger, takeover, makeover,
Or whatever,
Completely beyond their control.

And now You
Laid off, or merely discontent
With your lot in life
Are about to go out there
On that battlefield
And look for work.
You've heard of course
All the horror stories:
You've heard
Of former college profs with two degrees

Working now at the local deli;
 Of union workers who went out on strike
  Only to find, this time,
   Their jobs were not waiting for them,
    For no one told them that if they strike
     They might strike out
      In this *new world*.
       You've heard the stories
        Of people pounding the pavements
        For weeks and months,
         Even in good times,
          Without finding anything.
          Of college graduates
           With shiny degrees
            Who cannot find any work
             They're trained in.
            Of friends who went back to school
           To learn the *hot* trade of the moment, but
          Can find no work in that *hot* trade,
         And now are
        Unemployed, angry, and depressed.

       With 'welfare-to-work'
        Programs
         Everywhere
        There are inevitably some sad stories
       That newspapers *love*
      To run
     Of people thrown off welfare
    Who can't find any job.
   Misery always sells papers,
  We read them,
  And we are depressed.
  For them.
  And for ourselves.
  Anyway, now it is our turn
   To hunt.

    And what is it we do,
     When our job-hunting time has come?

We procrastinate,
That's what we do.
We're *busy winding things up,* we say.
Or, just waiting until we feel a little less
'Burnt-out,' and more 'up' for the task
Ahead, we say; though actually,
If the truth were known,
We're hoping for *a miracle,*
You know the one I mean:
A rescuer, suddenly appearing
On a white horse,
Coming, coming to save us.
We don't know
His name: is it
Our former employer,
Or the government,
Our union,
Our relatives or friends?
We are unclear; we only know
The world owes us
A job.
It shouldn't be up to us
To have to go hunting for it
So hard, ourselves,
Although of course we know
It is precisely up to
Us.

So, we make up a glorious resume
-- By ourselves or with some help.
How it sparkles, how it shines,
How quickly it will get us
A job.
And then we post it
On the Internet
Or mail it out
By the hundreds,
By the bushels,
Waiting for that inevitable
E-mail, or call,

From some bright-eyed employer-type
Who, seeing our glorious history,
Has cried out *"This is exactly the person*
That we have been looking for!"

But there is one small problem: the e-mail
Or the phone call
Never comes.
And we are left to wait
And wait
And wait
While the world goes out of its way,
It seems,
To tell us how little
It cares
Whether we find work,
Or not.

We seek out family and friends' advice,
And the first thing
That they say to us, is,
"Have you gone on the Internet?"
"Have you tried the job-posting sites?"
"Oh, you have? How many hours?"
"Weeks, you say? And . . . nothing?" .
"Oh!"
They search for some of the older ways
To recommend
To you:
"Have you tried employment agencies?"
"Why, no," we say,
So down we go.
Down, down, down
To the ante-room, and all those hopeful
Haunted faces.
Our first bout, here,
With *The Dreaded Application Form.*
"Previous jobs held.
List in reverse chronological order."
We answer the questions, then we sit

And wait.
The interviewer, at last, calls us in;
She (or he) of the over-cheerful countenance,
Who we know will give us good advice.
"Let's see, Mr. or Ms.,
What kind of a job are you looking for?"
"Well," say we,
"You can see, there, what I've done.
What do you think?"
She studies, again, our application form;
"It seems to me," she says, *"that with your background*
-- It is a bit unusual --
You might do very well in sales."
"Oh sales," say we. *"Yes, sales,"* says she, *"in fact*
I think I could place you almost immediately.
We'll be in touch. Is this your phone?
I'll call you tomorrow night, at home."
We nod, and shake her hand, and that
Is the last time we ever hear
From her.

We're reduced to the want ads,
By our miserable plight,
But we are dumbfounded
Right there, at the sight
Of those little boxes
Describing jobs that are built
As little boxes
For the soul.
We call on the employers,
We tell them, of course, that we're job-hunting now,
"And your ad looked just right for me . . ." O wow!
Look at that face change, are we in the soup!
As we wait for the heave-ho, the ol' Alley-oop!
" *'Over-qualified'?* you say?
Two hundred before me
Have been here already,
And you have only five
Vacancies? No,
Of course I understand."

We pound the pavements,
 Knocking on doors,
  Visiting companies,
   Getting rejected
    At place after place,
     Getting discouraged,
      Day after day,
       Getting depressed - -
       How pathetic, this is,
       This Neanderthal thing
       So cheerfully named,
       The Job Hunt.

     Weeks drag by,
     Months drag by,
     And we are reeling
      From rejection shock,
       And ever we are thinking:
        The job-hunt seems the loneliest task in the world.
       Is it this difficult for other job-hunters
      Or career-changers?

 Well, friend, the answer is YES.

  Are other people this discouraged,
   And desperate and depressed,
  And frustrated, and so low in self-esteem after
 A spell of job-hunting?

The answer, again - - unhappily - - is

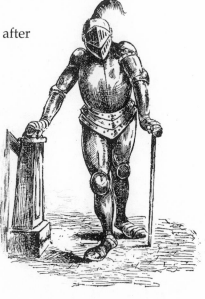

         YES.

         YES.

            YES.

*Well, yes, you do have
great big teeth; but, never mind
that. You were great to at least
grant me this interview.*

Little Red Riding Hood

CHAPTER TWO

Rejection Shock

Chapter 2

OUR NEANDERTHAL
JOB-HUNTING SYSTEM

Sure, the preceding account of the job-hunt is rather bleak.

But it has happened, is happening, and will continue to happen to countless millions of job hunters around the world, in just the fashion described.

Why?

Because our whole job-hunting system is Neanderthal.

Year after year this system condemns man after man, woman after woman, to go down the same path, face the same problems, make the same mistakes, endure the same frustrations, go through the same loneliness, and end up feeling as though there is something wrong with *them*.

It knows only one goal: to go after *known vacancies*. And it offers only three ways to do this: sending out or posting one's **resume**, answering newspaper **ads** or job postings, and going to employment **agencies**. Strategies which have spectacularly low success rates.

Consequently, year after year this system forces millions of us to remain unemployed after months and months of job-hunting, or -- if we find a job -- to end up *underemployed*, in the wrong field, at the wrong job, doing the wrong tasks, well below the peak of our abilities.

It doesn't matter what you do: you can send your resume out

by the bushels, hang it from every tree on the Internet, read every ad, go to every agency, contact every search firm -- only to discover after a lengthy period of time that none of this works for you, and you are still unemployed.

REJECTION SHOCK

When -- and if -- this happens to you, you will find yourself feeling as though you're experiencing some kind of "Rejection Shock." It's a kind of personal psychological Shock, character- ized by a slow or rapid erosion of your self-image, and the con- viction that there is something wrong with you, leading to lower expectations, depression, desperation, and despair. This can assume, consequently, all the proportions of a major crisis in your life, your personal relations and your family, leading to withdrawal (often), estrangement (frequently), where divorce is often a consequence and even suicide is not unthinkable. My first introduction to this was when the front page of our local newspaper described a job-hunter who put a plastic bag over his head, leaving a suicide note that said "Even a genius can't find a job." (He was a member of Mensa.)

It's bad enough not to be able to find a job. But add to that, this feeling of Rejection, and . . . *Yuck!* Most of us *hate* rejection. We dedicate a large part of our lives to avoiding it -- when dat- ing, when proposing new ideas, and so forth. We'll even reject others first, if we think they're about to reject us. We'll do any- thing to avoid rejection, and I mean *anything.* As we grow older, we become pretty good at throwing Rejection out of our lives.

But then, along comes the job-hunt. Eight times in our life- time (usually) we have to go through this painful process. And, except at its very end, it is **nothing but** a process of rejection. My friend Tom Jackson (in his *Guerrilla Tactics in the Job Market*) has aptly captured this, in this depressingly accurate descrip- tion of a typical job-hunt, as you go to employer after employer, asking, "Will you hire me?":

NO NO NO NO NO NO NO NO NO NO NO NO NO NO
NO NO NO NO NO NO NO NO NO NO NO NO NO NO
NO NO NO NO NO NO NO NO NO NO NO NO NO NO
NO NO NO NO NO NO NO NO NO NO NO NO NO NO
NO NO NO NO NO NO NO NO NO NO NO NO NO **YES**.

Rejection shock, indeed! The job-hunt makes a root canal look like a walk in the park.

When we turn to industry personnel experts or human resources people and say, "Show me a better way," it becomes obvious that many of them in their quiet meditative moments are just as baffled by the job-hunt as we are.

This is never more clear than when they themselves are out of a job -- as increasingly happens in these days of mergers, hostile takeovers, and downsizings -- and they have to join the many who are out 'pounding the pavements.' You would think that they would absolutely be in their element, and know precisely what to do. Yet the average hiring executive who yesterday was interviewing to screen out or hire others, and today is out job-hunting, is often just as much at a loss as anyone else, in knowing how to go about the job-hunt systematically, methodically and successfully.

Very often the best they can suggest for themselves is what they suggested, in the past, to others: 'the numbers game,' they call it. Just a fancy name for our old friends: resumes, ads, and agencies.

THE NUMBERS GAME

You can guess where the term came from. It came from the world of gambling, where if you place sufficient bets on enough different numbers, one of them is bound to pay off, for you.

Ah, I see you have grasped immediately what the analogue of this is, in the job-hunt. Resumes, you say? Ah yes, resumes.

You play them just like a bunch of bets: place enough of them, and one is bound to pay off. According to a study some time back, it pays off on the 1470th bet -- that is to say, there is one job offer tendered and accepted (and only one) for every 1,470 resumes that are floating around out there in the whole world of work. It's as though sending out 1,469 gets job-hunters nowhere. It's the 1,470th that pays off, and gets a job. Hence, "the numbers game."

In its original evolution, someone must have worked it all out, *backwards*. The logic of the numbers in a job-hunt would have gone like this:

For the job-hunter to get a job he or she really likes, they need to have two or three job offers -- in the end -- to choose from.

In order to get those two or three offers, the job-hunter probably would have to interview at six to nine different companies, that have *known vacancies.*

In order to get those six to nine 'high-chance' interviews, the job-hunter must have contacted 'x' number of companies, by sending them some kind of mail -- resumes and/or cover letters -- that will cause those companies to invite the job-hunter in.

And what is 'x'? Well, some experts will tell you it's 100 -- that you must send out 100 resumes to get one job interview. Others will tell you it takes 200 resumes sent out, to get one job interview. And still others will tell you it takes 500, on up to 1200 or more.

Consequently, the consensus is that you should send out between 500 and 1000 resumes, though some experts say there is no limit: send out 10–15 resumes a day, they say, until you get the interviews that result in the three job offers you need.

That's how it all got worked out, *backwards.* (And a backwards system, it remains.)

WHERE
THE NUMBERS GAME
CAN BE FOUND

You like?

Many of the books you can pick up in the job-hunting section of your local bookstore -- or online at such sites as amazon.com -- *will sell you this game,* for twenty bucks or so.

Many of the job-hunting resources listed in your local Yellow Pages directory under 'Career and Vocational Counseling' or 'Resume Service' *will sell you this game,* for a hundred bucks or so.

Many of the executive counseling firms you can go to, the ones with the big fee up-front -- *will sell you this game,* with a little psychological testing and interview-role-playing thrown in, for three thousand bucks or so.

Many of the welfare-to-work programs *sell this game* to their clients, at varying costs to their funding sources.

And the Internet with its thousands of job-posting sites and resume-posting sites *will sell, sell, sell you nothing else but this game,* for just the modest cost of a computer, modem, and Internet Service Provider.

In all of the above, there may be a few clever variations here and there, especially in the vocabulary they use to describe what they are selling, so that you will think they are selling you something entirely new.

But if it all comes down to *known job vacancies,* if it all comes down to resumes, ads/postings, and agencies, I assure you you have happened upon The Little Ol' Game We've All Come to Know and Love So Well: Numbers.

THE INTERNET
NUMBERS

How bad are the numbers? How much are they stacked against us, as we go out job-hunting? For an answer to that question, we turn to the latest darling of 'the Numbers game,' namely, the Internet. Fortunately for us, the Internet *loves* numbers. It counts *everything*.

Let's look at the resume numbers, then. Job-hunters have thronged to the Internet to post their resume, sometimes on a number of sites. What we want to know is: *how many* job-hunters, and (more importantly) *how many* employers, ever meet on these sites?

On the site of the National Business Employment Weekly (www.nbew.com/) Peter Weddle has put up a fascinating Guide to some of these major resume-posting sites on the Web, giving us a great deal of information about each. With the kind permission of the NBEW, I have constructed a chart, summarizing the numbers that Peter gathered *from the sites themselves*. It is on page 16.

They were for the period January 1998 in every case, in order that the statistics might be comparable -- *so don't think this is the current traffic on these sites*. This was just one moment frozen in time, so that we could see what the numbers are . . . typically.

As you will see in the chart, the numbers are depressing.

One site had 59,283 resumes, but only 1,366 employers even *looked* at them during the 90 days previous to this survey; another had 85,000 resumes, but only 850 employers even looked at them over a period of three months; another had 40,000 resumes, but only 400 employers looked at them; another had 26,644 resumes, but only 41 employers looked at them.

Here are the gory details with the number of job *listings* or job *postings* thrown in, gratis -- since, in the absence of the other figure, these *sometimes* indicate the relative employer involvement on that site:

Number of Resumes Here	Charge for Posting Your Resume?	Employers Searching Here in Last 90 Days	Name of the Site and Its URL
275,000	No	(Figure Not Available) Only 25,000 Job Listings	The Monster Board www.monster.com
200,000+	No	(Figure Not Available) Only 10,000 Job Listings	NationJob Network www.nationjob.com
150,000	No	(Figure Not Available) Only 45,000 Job Listings	JobTrak www.jobtrak.com
125,000	No	(Figure Not Available) Only 4,034 Job Listings	CareerSite www.careersite.com
120,989 Technical jobs	No	(Figure Not Available) 100,000 Job Listings	PassportAccess www.passportaccess.com
85,000	No	**850** employers 37,502 Job Listings	Net-Temps www.net-temps.com
76,441	No	(Figure Not Available) 109,862 Job Listings	Online Career Center www.occ.com
70,000	No	(Figure Not Available) Only 3,500 Job Listings	Career.Com www.career.com
59,283	No	**1,366** employers 24,312 Job Listings	Westech Virtual Job Fair www.VJF.com
56,945	Yes	(Figure Not Available) 121,826 Job Listings	GUARANTEED Job Search Success www.joblynx.com
55,000	No	(Figure Not Available) 70,000+ Job Listings	CareerMosaic www.careermosaic.com
40,000	No	**400** employers Only 1,000 Job Listings	Town Online Working www.townonline. com/working
38,000	No	(Figure Not Available) 12,734 Job Listings	E.span www.espan.com
30,723	No	(Figure Not Available) Only 3,627 Job Listings	HotJobs www.hotjobs.com
30,000	No	**15** employers (new) Only 350 Job Listings	US RESUME www.usresume.com
26,644	No	**41** employers 40,000 Job Listings	America's Employers www.americasemployers.com

What depressing numbers! 85,000 job-hunters (in one example) playing 'the Numbers Game' faithfully, by posting their resume on one of these sites, as they have been told to do; and only 850 employers even *look* at those 85,000 resumes, over a three-month period. That's less than 10 employers per day!

The moral of this, for job-hunters building their online resume? *If you build it, they will not come.* In most cases. There are always, of course, the lucky ones.

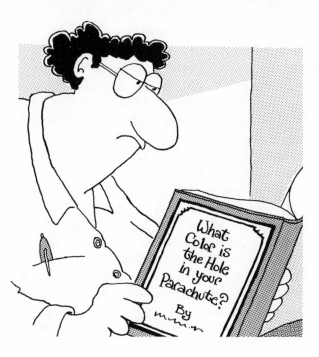

The latest self-help book for pessimists

EMPLOYERS' FAVORITE WAYS OF HIRING

From this we see that employers and job-hunters search in entirely different ways! You can understand this if you look at a diagram of our job-hunting system in the U.S. and in most of the developed world, on page 19.

What makes our job-hunting system Neanderthal, you ask? Well, let's start with the left-hand (red) arrow in the diagram. This indicates the way a *typical* employer likes to find a new employee. Starting at the bottom of the diagram, and working up, we see that **their preferred method is first of all to hire from within, moving or promoting an employee whose work they already know and like.**

Only if that doesn't work, do they then move on up to their next favorite method: asking their friends and colleagues if there is someone whose work *they* like, that they could recommend for the job that employer is trying to fill. At this point, they're also open to job-hunters who offer proof of what they can do -- via a 'portfolio' in the case of an artist, or anything similar in the case of other professions.

Only if that doesn't work, do they then move on up to their next favorite method: turning to a search firm (in the case of higher-level employees) or an employment agency (in the case of lower-level employees), and asking them to find somebody for them.

Only if none of the above methods work, do they then reluctantly move on up to their least favorite methods: looking at job-hunters' resumes, or posting a 'help-wanted ad' in the newspapers or on the Internet.

Now compare the left-hand (red) arrow to the right-hand (gray) arrow in the diagram. The latter indicates the way a typical job-hunter likes to find a new employer. Starting at the top of the diagram, we see that **a job-hunter's preferred methods *are in exactly the reverse order from that of employers.*** The methods that employers like the least are the ones which job-hunters like the most! Now, that's Neanderthal!

OUR NEANDERTHAL JOB-HUNTING SYSTEM

6 "I will place an ad to find some-one."

The way a typical job-hunter likes to hunt for a job (starts here)

Newspaper Ads

Resumes

5 "I will look at some resumes which come in, unsolicited."

Employment Agency for Lower Level Jobs

4 "I want to hire someone for a lower level job, from a stack of potential candidates that some agency has screened for me."

This is called 'a private employment agency,' or -- if it is within the company -- 'the human resources department,' formerly the 'personnel department.' Incidentally, only 15% of all organizations have such an internal department.

Search Firm for Higher Level Jobs

3 "I want to hire someone for a higher level job, from among outstanding people who are presently working for another organization; and I will pay a recruiter to find this outstanding candidate for me."

The agency, thus hired by an employer, is called 'a search firm' or 'headhunter'; only employers can hire such agencies.

A Job-Hunter Who Offers Proof

2 "I want to hire someone who walks in the door and can show me samples of their previous work."

"I want to hire someone whose work a trusted friend of mine has seen and recommends."

That friend may be: mate, best friend, colleague in the same field, or colleague in a different field.

From Within

1 *Employer's Thoughts:*

"I want to hire someone whose work I have seen." (Promotion from within of a full-time employee, or promotion from within of a part-time employee; hiring a former consultant for a regular position (formerly on a limited contract); hiring a temp for a regular position; hiring a volunteer for a regular position.)

The way a typical employer prefers to fill vacancies (starts here)

We could of course improve the numbers, and the efficiency of the job-hunt, if employers would just adopt the resume as their favorite way of finding applicants. *Then we'd have a match between employers' favorite approach and job-hunters' favorite approach.*

So, why don't they? Well, we begin with:

LIES, DAMN LIES, AND STATISTICS

That's how someone once declined the word "lies." "Lies" and "resumes" got married to each other a while back. In 1992, it was discovered that one-third of all 15 to 30-year-olds believed it was okay to lie on a resume.[1] *Heaven only knows what the statistic is today!* Nor is this trend restricted to the young. People in high places - - executives, superintendents of schools, and the like - - have falsely claimed doctorates, and otherwise lied on their resumes. (And been caught.) Experts now estimate that one-third to one-half of all job-hunters lie on their resumes.[2]

They lie by: inflating their title or responsibilities, omitting their firings or failures, inflating their results, inflating their credentials, hiding jobs where they did terribly, and a lot of other subterfuges.

Now if you were an employer, how much faith would you put in a piece of paper where you know there are lies on one-third to one-half of it? Not much.

MOUNTAINS OF MAIL

Ah, but still they come - - unbidden, unrestrained - - over the Internet and through the mails, mostly because everyone's been told this is the best way to apply for a job. The myth dies hard.

Some companies receive as many as 250,000 resumes a year; even small companies may receive as many as ten to fifteen a week. As experts have noted, companies feel at times as though they're floating on a sea of resumes.

---

1. In a survey of 6,873 high school and college students, done by the Josephson Institute of Ethics, reported in *USA TODAY*, 11/13/92.

2. *The San Francisco Chronicle*, 10/10/92.

Resume: An ingenious device that turns a human being into an object (an eight and a half by eleven inches piece of paper). This transformation device is then often used to try and convince people we have never met to invest thousands of dollars in us, by hiring us for a job we have not yet specifically identified.

Michael Bryant

Consequently, employers' first intent is not *selection*, but *elimination*. (Of course, if you're agriculturally-minded or Biblically-oriented, you may prefer the phrase: *winnowing the crop*.) The Human Resources department, if they have one (only 15% of businesses do), or some hapless secretary or clerk, is given the task of getting the stack down to *manageable size*. "See who you can eliminate."

Whose resume gets selected for this dubious honor? Well, first of all, resumes that don't *feel* good -- rough paper, etc. The first impression a resume gives is to the fingers of the 'Eliminator,' even before their eyes see what's on the paper. So, the fingers vote to eliminate you even before the eyes do. It is to cry. *"I was eliminated by crummy paper."*

Secondly, resumes that the Eliminator's eyes don't like, format-wise, even before they read the content thereof. It is to cry, even more. *"I was eliminated by poor typography."*

And: resumes so poorly written that employers can't tell anything about the person behind them. Or: resumes so slickly written (by a professional service) that employers can't tell anything about the person behind them.

Not to mention, resumes that have a $206-a-week clerk applying for the CEO's job; or a $100,000-a-year executive applying for the mail room. Or people attempting a dramatic career change.

The theme at the receptionist's desk or in the human resources office of a company, is: Elimination. This is why you can send out bushels of resumes, and never once get called in for an interview. This is why millions remain unemployed, in the U.S. alone. It's all about 'numbers.'

RESUMES

Well I know you believe everything I've said so far, but you're going to put together a resume anyway, aren't you? After all, your best friend got their job through a resume, and you know that you can too! Gonna write the thing, gonna hang the thing on the Internet, or mail it out, and see if it will pay off for you too, by golly!

And even if it doesn't, you *love* the thought of having a resume out there on the Internet or sitting on some employer's desk. Right?

> "Resumes make sense: there is no way a harried executive or department head can set aside the time to interview every inquiry about employment that is made to his or her organization; there is not enough time."
>
> *(Anon.)*

Okay. There are lots of instructions *out there,* about how to do that. They are:

• **In print:** There are dozens of books on resumes, available at any large bookstore (Borders, SuperCrown, Barnes & Noble, B. Dalton, and amazon.com, for example), and also at any small bookstore or your local library. Browse. You'll be amazed. My personal favorites are:

Richard Lathrop, *Who's Hiring Who?* Ten Speed Press, Box 7123, Berkeley, CA 94707. Richard describes and recommends "a qualifications brief" -- the idea that in approaching an employer you should offer him or her a written proposal of what you will do in the future, rather than "a resume" or summary of what you did in the past. The most popular 'resume' book, according to our mail.

Yana Parker, *The Damn Good Resume Guide*. 1996. Ten Speed Press, Box 7123, Berkeley, CA 94707. Describes, in ten steps, how to write functional and chronological resumes. Employers' comments upon resumes which actually got people jobs, are especially helpful. The next most popular resume book (according to our mail). Yana's other resume resources, available from Ten Speed Press, Box 7123, Berkeley, CA 94707, are: *The Resume Workbook*. (1998); *The Resume Catalog: 200 Damn Good Examples*. (1996); *Blue Collar & Beyond: Resumes for Skilled Trades and Services*. (1995); *Ready-To-Go Resumes* software. (1995); *Resume Pro: the Professional's Guide*. (1993). For further information about any of these, you can contact her at Damn Good Resume Service, P.O. Box 3289, Berkeley, CA 94703, 510-658-9229, or on her Website (www.damngood.com)

David Swanson, *The Resume Solution; How To Write (and Use) A Resume That Gets Results*. 1991. JIST Works, Inc., 720 North Park Ave., Indianapolis, IN 46202-3431. (Dave has been on staff at 19 of my two-week workshops.)

Tom Jackson, and Ellen Jackson, *The New Perfect Resume*. 1996, revised. Anchor Press/Doubleday, Garden City, NY 11530. This is Tom's best-selling book, and with good reason. This edition is completely updated with 100+ resume samples and with some good career advice.

• **On the Internet:** There are many sites giving explicit, detailed instructions on how to write a resume, and how to post it on the Internet. So many, in fact, that you need a list of them all. I think the best list by far, is by Gary Will (`http://members.xoom.com/worksearch/reswri.htm`). He lists the best articles on the Internet, rates them, summarizes them, links to them, and gives you his evaluation of them. My favorite sentence on his dazzling site: "If you plan things just right, you will have a perfect resume by the time you're old enough to retire." *(Amy Lindgren)*

All right, we've spent enough time on resumes; let's look at the rest of the numbers game, and see if any of it *might* be useful to you. It's dicey, the odds are stacked against you -- but no one has the right to tell you not to at least *try* it.

The main parts of this game, as you will recall, are:
- resumes
- ads
- agencies

We've tackled resumes. Now, let's briefly look at the other two, to see what's involved.

ADS OR
JOB POSTINGS

Ads are found in various places, masquerading under various names: "classifieds," "help wanted," "job listings," "job postings," and plain old "ads." Keep in mind the fact that ads (on the Internet or off) do not give you a complete picture of the job-market, by any means. A study conducted in two sample cities -- one large, one smaller -- revealed that "85% of the employers in San Francisco, and 75% in Salt Lake City, did not hire any employees through want ads" in a typical year. Yes, that said *any* employees, during the whole year.

So, what you get with ads are only "descriptions of vacancies that some employers couldn't fill any other way" (see page 19).

These days, there are three places where you can find such ads:

On the Internet. This is where *certain kinds of jobs* -- high tech, financial, healthcare, computer, engineering, government and academic jobs -- are increasingly (and sometimes exclusively) to be found. On the Internet, want ads are called "job-postings" or "job-listings." How to find them, if you have Internet access? Well, there are lots of ways, but the simplest is to go to my site (`www.jobhuntersbible.com`), and thence to its sub-section called (not surprisingly) "Job Postings." That section has reviews of, and links to, the major job listing sites on the Internet, together with an evaluation of how helpful such sites are, in general.

In Newspapers: This, of course, is where people without Internet access go, to find job ads. Experts advise you, for the sake of thoroughness, to study the job ads in your local daily or weekly newspaper each issue, and to study all of them, from A to Z -- because ads are generally alphabetized by job title, and sometimes the work you're looking for is buried under a title you would never guess. Increasingly, lots of newspapers post their ads on the Web as well; the Parachute site above will take you to these, again under "Job Postings."

In Newsletters, Clearinghouses or Registers: Each occupation, interest or specialty tends to have a newsletter, or association, or clearinghouse, or register of "Jobs Available." I have listed on page 26ff a sampling of the kind of things you can

Newsletters, Registers, Clearinghouses, of Job Listings

Here are some *examples* (only) of the type of thing you can find for almost any profession, interest, or specialty -- either in print, or on-line, or both; I have chosen to list here the kinds of Registers not easy to categorize:

• For Nonprofit Organizations Doing Public or Community Service: ACCESS, Networking in the Public Interest, 1001 Connecticut Ave., N.W., Suite 838, Washington, D.C. 20036. 202-785-4233. Fax: 202-785-4212. Amy Kincaid, Executive Director. Listings of job opportunities in the nonprofit sector, ranging from entry level to Executive positions, are disseminated through a publication called Community Jobs: The National Employment Newspaper For The Nonprofit Sector. ($25 for three monthly issues). (www.communityjobs.org/)

• For Jobs in the Experiential/Adventure (Outdoor) Education Field: Jobs Clearinghouse. Association for Experiential Education, 2305 Canyon Blvd., Suite #100, Boulder, CO 80302-5651. 303-440-8844. Fax: 303-440-9581. Timmy Comstedt, Manager. Monthly listings of full-time, part-time, seasonal jobs and internships, in the U.S. and abroad, in the experiential/adventure education field. (3 months for $24, or one issue for $9). Write, call or fax for details, if you are interested.

• For Jobs Outdoors: Environmental Opportunities, P.O. Box 4379, Arcata CA 95518. 707-826-1909. Fax: 707-826-2495. Sanford Berry publishes a monthly newsletter (called Environmental Opportunities), listing environmental jobs and internships. Each issue contains sixty to one hundred full-time positions in a variety of disciplines.

• For Jobs in Horticulture: Ferrell's JOBS IN HORTICULTURE, 2214 Douglas Drive, Carlisle, PA 17013-1025. 1-800-428-2474. A semi-monthly guide to opportunities. The rate for individuals is $24.95 for six issues (3 months' worth), or $45 for 12 issues (6 months' worth). For students, the rate is only $19.95. (www.hortjobs.com/)

• For Jobs Working with Horses: Equimax U.S.A. Inc., HC 65, Box 271, Alpine, TX 79830. phone: 915-371-2610 or 800-759-9494; fax: 915-271-2612; e-mail: 73051.1264@compuserve.com For singles or couples interested in jobs where they would be working with horses. Founded by Seth Burgess, who discovered his interest in horses after reading Parachute twenty years ago. Offers a List of Jobs and also a List of

Candidates. Job List subscription with 12 automatic updates, weekly, bi-weekly, or monthly (your choice) costs $45. (www.equimax.org)

• For Jobs as Caretakers: The Caretaker Gazette, P.O. Box 5887, Carefree AZ 85377-5887. phone: 602-488-1970; email: caretaker@uswest.net. For those interested in jobs serving as housekeepers or caretakers or extra hands, sometimes with owners on premises, sometimes not. Lists jobs around the world. $27 for 1-year subscription. (www.angelfire.com/wa/caretaker)

• For the Blind: Job Opportunities for the Blind, 1800 Johnson St., Baltimore, MD 21230. 1-410-659-9314. A listing and referral service for blind workers, together with info about working with the blind. Operated by the National Federation For the Blind, in partnership with the U.S. Department of Labor. (www.blind.net/bons0003.html)

• For Jobs Outside the U.S.: International Employment Hotline, a monthly newsletter which lists international employment opportunities, founded by Will Cantrell, now published by the Carlyle Corporation. International Employment, 1088 Middle River Road, Stanardsville, VA 22973. They also publish International Career Employment Weekly, $4.95 per issue. phone: 1-800-291-4618; e-mail: cc@internationaljobs.org .

• For Jobs in the Christian Church: Intercristo is a national Christian organization that lists over 19,000 jobs, covering hundreds of vocational categories within 1300 or more Christian Service organizations in the U.S. as well as overseas. Their service is called Christian Placement Network. In 1997-1998, 9,000 people used the Network, and one out of every twenty-five of them found a job thereby (which, of course, means that 24 out of 25 didn't). But if those odds don't bother you, or the fact that some readers feel a large number of the listings are in very conservative church settings, then contact them at 19303 Fremont Ave. North, Seattle, WA 98133 (phone their machine at 1-800-426-1342, or a live person at 1-206-546-7330). The cost of being listed there, for three months, is $45.95. If you prefer quicker action, three months on their Website costs $59.95, but you get an instant listing of jobs that match your criteria. From that same Website you can order (for about $75) the self-guided Birkman Career Assessment Tool, which matches you to job-titles in the non-profit sector (only). You must have an IBM-compatible PC in order to use the disk this will come on. Ann Brooks is their Executive Director. (www.jobleads.org)

turn up. To find other lists, if you have Internet access go to my favorite search engine, Metacrawler, and in the search window, type the word "jobs" plus your interest or specialty, and see what it turns up. (`www.metacrawler.com`)

Now, suppose that in one of these places you find an ad that looks interesting to you; what do you do about it?

RULES FOR ANSWERING ADS

If you see an ad for which you might qualify, even three-quarters, send off your resume, OR your resume and a covering letter, OR just a covering letter.

● **Keep in mind that you may be competing with a vast number of other people, responding to that same ad.** Number of resumes typically received by an employer as a result of their ad: 20 to 1,000. Ads on the Internet may receive a response within the hour. Ads in newspapers receive a response within 24 to 96 hours, with the third day usually being the peak day.

● **Keep in mind that your most likely fate is that you will be screened out.** Typically only 2 to 5 out of every 100 responses make it past the screening process when received. In other words, 95 to 98 out of every 100 responses are screened out.

● **In spite of the overwhelming odds, answering ads does pay off for some job-hunters.** Indeed, some find their perfect job this way. But in view of the high odds *against that*, most experts say if you're going to play this game, there are certain tips to keep in mind as you draft your response (your covering letter):

● **The goal of your response is to get invited in for an interview, nothing more.** Whether you get hired or not is the task of that interview, not the task of your response to their ad.

● **Keep your response brief.** Just quote all of the ad's specifications, then list what experience or qualifications you have that exactly match each of those specifications, and leave it at that. List them as a series of points, with perhaps "bullets" (●) as they are called, in front of each point.

● **If there's some skill you don't have, like *experienced with motorboats* respond at least with *interested in motorboats.*** Of course, that's only if it's true!

● **If the ad doesn't mention salary requirements, don't you either.** Why give another excuse for getting your response screened out? If the ad does request that you state your salary requirements, some experts say ignore the request, because many employers put it in there only to be able to screen you out without ever having to waste time on an interview. If you omit any mention of it, the employer may suppose you accidentally overlooked it. Other experts say, Naw, don't get cute. Answer the request, but do so by stating a range that's at least three to five thousand dollars wide, and add "depending on the nature and scope of duties and responsibilities," or words to that effect. e.g., *"My salary requirements are between fifteen and twenty thousand dollars, depending upon the amount of responsibility I would have."*

● **Volunteer nothing else.** Period. Every unnecessary point you add to your response may be the very thing that gets you screened out. So, if there is anything else you want to tell them, save it for the interview -- *if* you get invited in.

● **Your final sentence in your letter ought to leave the control in your hands.** Essentially this means putting the initiative in their hands, but reserving for yourself a backup strategy. Not "I hope to hear from you," but "I look forward to hearing from you, and will call your office next week just to be sure you received this." (A woman did this with a friend of mine a week ago; good thing. He hadn't received her letter.) Be sure to include your phone number, fax number, and e-mail address (if you have one), as every employer has their preferred way of getting in touch with you, if you interest them.

Things to Beware Of In Ads or Job Postings

FAKE ADS

(Positions advertised which don't exist) -- usually posted by placement firms or agencies posing as employers, in order to get you to send in your resume (to a box number, usually) in order to fatten their "resume bank" for future clout with employers. Also run by swindlers so they can get your Social Security number and/or the number of your driver's license (these two numbers alone enable them to take you to the cleaners with merchants, etc.). It's often a 900 number they ask you to call.

BLIND ADS

(No company name, just a box number). These, according to most insiders, are particularly unrewarding to the job-hunter's time. But many job-hunters are skilled at answering them with just the information asked for, and they do get a job as a result. However, if by chance you are presently working, there is always the danger that this ad was placed by your own company unbeknownst to you. If that is the case, you can get fired on the spot -- just for answering it. I know of actual cases where this has happened.

PHONE NUMBERS

In ads: most experts say, "Don't use them except to set up an appointment." Period. ("I can't talk right *now*. I'm calling from work.") They counsel that you should beware of saying more, lest you get screened out prematurely over the telephone. Other experts, however, think it is useful to use the phone number if you can talk to the actual person you would be working for (not the human resources department or a receptionist).

If you get such a person, use the call to inquire for more information *about the job* (without talking about yourself or your own qualifications). Ask, "Could I meet with you or at least send you my resume?" If the employer says yes to the appointment, arrange the time there and then. On the other hand, if they prefer your resume, thank them for their time and then ask to be turned over to their secretary, so that from the latter you can get the exact spelling of this employer's name, title, and address. Thence send a covering letter plus resume. In the covering letter you can say something like, "Thank you for our phone conversation, and thank you for encouraging me to send you my resume." In the remainder of the covering letter, then, highlight the parts of the phone talk you want them to recall.

PHRASES

Which need lots of translating, like:

"Energetic self-starter wanted" (= You'll be working on commission)

"Good organizational skills" (= You'll be handling the filing)

"Make an investment in your future" (= This is a franchise or pyramid scheme)

"Much client contact" (= You handle the phone, or make 'cold calls' on clients)

"Planning and coordinating" (= You book the boss's travel arrangements)

"Opportunity of a lifetime" (= Nowhere else will you find such a low salary and so much work)

"Management training position" (= You'll be a salesperson with a wide territory)

● **Make certain the spelling in the letter and resume is absolutely errorless.** "Almost perfect" won't do. Spelling errors will often cause your letter and resume to be put at the bottom of their pile of prospects (if they're desperate) or dismissed completely if they're not. So, before sending it, show your letter and resume to at least two friends or workmates or family whom you know to be excellent spellers. If a spelling error is found, *retype* the entire letter (using 'white-out' for a boo-boo is a no-no).

● **Consider sending your answer by FedEx**, if you're not resorting to e-mail -- or even if you are. Until everyone is doing this (and they're not yet), your response will stand out in the mind of the employer, believe me.

● **Beware of 'cute' strategies.** Some magazine articles counsel cute strategies -- such as mailing your resume in a box, or wearing a sign-board outside the offices of the place you're interested in, or putting "Personal and Confidential" on your envelope as if it were from a friend, etc. Trouble is: some employers have seen these strategies a hundred times, and are decidedly irritated when they see them yet again. Other employers aren't. In other words, it's a risk. You decide whether the risk is worth taking.

● **Stay 'on' an ad that you like.** Some job-hunters go on the Internet or read their local newspaper every day specifically noting ads that a) they would like to respond to, but b) they don't have all the credentials, qualifications or experience that the ad calls for. (They may send their resume and a covering letter in immediately, anyway.) But, they don't stop there. They watch to see if that ad stops running, *and then starts running again some days or weeks later.* That's a sign that the employer is having trouble finding a person with the qualifications he or she was asking for. At this point you can contact them (again) and bargain. Here's how one job-hunter reported her success with this strategy: "The particular ad I answered the first time it ran required at least an associate degree, which I did not have. What I did have was almost ten years' experience in that particular field. When the ad reappeared a month later I sent a letter saying they obviously had not found what they were looking for in the way of a degree, so why not give me a chance; they already had my resume. Well, it worked. I got the interview, I made them an offer that was $6,000 less than they were going to pay a degreed person, but still a $6,000 increase for me, over my prior position. I got the job. Needless to say, everyone was happy. I have recommended this same procedure to three of my friends, and it worked for two out of three of them, also."

EMPLOYMENT AGENCIES

From our youth up, we are taught (out on the street) that there are two places to turn to when you're out of work: want ads (on or off the Internet) and employment agencies. We just dealt with the first of these. Now let us look at the second.

Employment agencies seem very attractive when one is "up against it." We all like to think that somewhere out there is someone who knows where all the vacancies are. But, sad to relate, no place in the country has even a clue as to where all the jobs are.

The best that anyone can offer us is clues about where *some* vacancies are. Places having such information are called employment agencies. The Yellow Pages of your phone book will give you their names.

Basically, you will discover there are four kinds of agencies you can turn to: Government/State Employment Agencies; private agencies; temp agencies; and agencies retained by employers.

• **Government/State Employment Agencies**: This is the United States Employment Service, known in different States by different names: "Job Service," "Employment Development Department," the State Unemployment Office, and so on. (`www.doleta.gov/uses/`) There are almost 2,000 such offices nationwide, and your acquaintances will be able to tell you where the nearest one is; it's where people go to file for unemployment benefits. Most offices serve not only entry-level workers, but also professionals. Their services are free. They of course have lists of job vacancies, and some also maintain a list of which jobs are most in demand. Ask if yours does.

Your local office will have access also to **America's Job Bank**, a nationwide electronic database of job openings. (`www.ajb.dni.us/html/seekers.html`) On their computer or yours you can access AJB's list of openings in any of 48 states, typically totaling 680,000 vacancies daily, 7 million yearly.

Although USES has seen its staff and budget greatly reduced over the past twenty years, they still offer services beyond job-listings, providing special assistance to youths aged 16 to 22, veterans, people with disabilities, economically disadvantaged people, and older workers. About one-tenth of these offices also offer job-search workshops.

Effectiveness? According to one study, USES placed only 13.7% of those who looked for a job there; that means of course that 86.3% of the job-hunters who went there failed to find a job.

• **Private Agencies**: There are at least 8,000 private employ-ment or placement agencies in the U.S. The exact number is un-known, since new ones are born, and old ones die, every week. You will find them listed in the Yellow Pages, under "Employ-ment Agencies"; *some* few of them are also on the Internet. (**www.ajb.dni.us/html/skr_pub_nav_07.html**) Many pri-vate employment agencies specialize in particular kinds of openings, as your Yellow Pages listings will usually make abundantly clear: e.g., executives, financial, data processing, or other specialties.

A private employment agency has a contract -- it is the appli-cation form filled out by the job-hunter!!! Fees are always charged -- the only question is: do they charge you, or the em-ployer? Be sure to ask which is the case. In 80% of executives' cases, it is the employer who pays the fee.

When it is the job-hunter who must pay the fee, many if not most states have laws governing those fees. In New York, for example, a fee cannot exceed 60% of one month's salary, i.e., a $15,000-a-year job will cost you $750. The fee may be paid in weekly installments of 10% (e.g., $75 on a $750 total).

Some agencies ask you to agree that you will let them have 'exclusive handling' of you, usually on the application form. Experts say, don't grant it -- if you do, and then find a job inde-pendently of them, you may still have to pay them a fee.

Private employment agencies are usually a volume business, meaning they live by the numbers game: they need to turn over the most clients in the least amount of time. *If you are a career-changer, you will usually be given little attention; you take too much of their time to place you. Possible exception for you to investigate: a new, or suddenly expanding agency, which needs job-hunters badly if it is ever to get employers' business.*

The agency's loyalty in the very nature of things must lie with those who pay the bills (which in most cases is the employer), and those who represent repeat business (again, employers).

Effectiveness? Some time back, a spokesman for the Federal Trade Commission announced that the average placement rate for employment agencies was only 5% of those who walked in the door. That means a 95% failure rate, right?

• **Temp Agencies**: These are simply private employment agencies which specialize in placing people in temporary, or short-contract, jobs. However, with temp agencies the question of fee is simple: it is always the employer who pays -- directly to the agency. The agency pockets part of the money, as their fee, and gives you, the temp worker, the rest. Temp agencies have multiplied like rabbits in the last ten years, and there is an agency for almost any specialty or career you can think of (including doctors, etc.) *Haven't heard of one for ministers, priests and rabbis, yet, though.*

They are listed in your Yellow Pages, under the heading "Employment – Temporary." They are also to be found under the heading "Employment Agencies." Look in both places.

For executives, there is *The Directory of Executive Temporary Placement Firms,* available from Kennedy Information, Kennedy Place, Route 12 South, Fitzwilliam, NH 03447. phone: 800-531-1026; fax: 603-585-9555. It lists 225 such firms and costs $29.90.

Effectiveness? Higher than the typical private employment agency, though in certain geographical areas and with certain specialties and with certain agencies you can list yourself with them, but never get sent out on a job. If you want a fascinating look "inside the belly of the whale," use your Internet access (if you have it) to go to "The Red Guide to Temp Agencies." Though it's only for New York City, it's where temp workers report their experience with some 65 different agencies, "the morning after." (**www.panix.com/~grvsmth/redguide/**)

• Agencies Hired by Employers:

These are called Executive Recruiters or Executive Search Firms; sometimes also "Headhunters." (In the old days, these firms searched only for executives, hence their now-somewhat-outdated title; though, currently, 64% of executive positions are still filled through recruiters.)

These recruiting agencies are retained by employers. *The very existence of this thriving industry testifies to the fact that employers are as baffled by our country's Neanderthal job-hunting 'system' as we are. As I emphasize throughout this book, employers don't know how to find decent employees, any more than job-hunters know how to find decent employers.*

So, what do employers want executive recruiting agencies or firms to do? They want these firms to search for and find executives, financial officers, computer engineers, salespeople, technicians, or whatever, *who are already employed somewhere else, and have a good track record.* Then they want these agencies to lure those people away from where they are working, and get them to come work for the employer who hired them.

For the average job-hunter, this is the old *good news and bad news* dilemma. The good news is, these places are aware of, and are trying to fill, actual vacancies. The bad news is, their primary targets are people who are already employed.

Experts are totally divided as to whether or not the unemployed should waste any time contacting these executive recruiters.

Those who recommend you do, point out that the term "executive recruiter" has become very loosely used, these days. Yesterday's employment agency is often today's executive recruiter. (Employment agencies typically have to operate under more stringent state or federal regulations, hence the migration of some employment agencies to this different, less supervised, genre known as Executive Search.) Whatever they call themselves, these new Recruiters are hungry for the names of job-hunters, before they turn to offer their services to employers -- and in many cases will interview a job-hunter who approaches them politely, and with respect for how busy they are. I have known so-called Recruiters in some of the smaller firms who truly extended themselves on behalf of very inexperienced job-hunters (even *gave* them a copy of *Parachute*).

Look in the Yellow Pages under the heading "Executive Search Consultants." Also, Kennedy Information has a famous Directory of Executive Recruiters, available from Kennedy Information, Kennedy Place Route 12 South, Fitzwilliam, NH 03447. phone: 800-531-1026; fax: 603-585-9555. It lists 3,756 search firms at 5,830 office locations in North America. Cost: $44.95. Updated annually. Kennedy also has an online database for North America as well as an International database, searchable on their Web site (`www.kennedyinfo.com/js/jobseek.html`) for a fee.

Effectiveness? As long as you don't put all your eggs or hopes in this one basket, and as long as you remain realistic that, if you're unemployed or looking for a non-executive position, this pursuit of executive recruiters isn't very likely to lead *anywhere*, you really have nothing to lose -- except some stationery and stamps.

HOW WELL DOES IT ALL WORK?

Well, let's face facts. In spite of the numbers being stacked against us,

For many folks, this Numbers Game works *exceedingly well*. They end up with just the job they wanted, and they are ecstatically happy about the whole thing -- especially if they were just wandering aimlessly about before they discovered this plan. This works just beautifully, by contrast -- *for many people.*

For others, this Numbers Game works *passably well.* They end up with a job of sorts, and a salary of sorts, even though in retrospect they realize it is not really the kind of work they had been looking for and hoping for, and the salary is *way* below what they really needed or wanted. But: a job is a job is a job, and better than ending up unemployed. (Parenthetically, the one thing that the job-hunting system/Numbers game does exceedingly well is to scare people, to the point where they are more than willing to lower their expectations and their self-esteem, and settle for a job far below their initial expectations.)

For the rest of the job-hunting folk who use this 'system,' it just doesn't work at all: they remain unemployed. (In the U.S., as I write, that number is 6,739,000 job-hunters -- and this is during supposedly 'wonderful' economic times in the U.S., with low inflation and 'low' unemployment.) *People trying to change careers have particular difficulty with the Numbers game.*

This week, next week, next month, thousands of job-hunters will send out 400, 500, 600, 800, 1000 resumes or more, post their resume on a dozen Internet job sites, answer one hundred newspaper ads or job postings on the Internet, visit twenty employment agencies, and still not get *one single invitation to come in for an interview.* It happens all the time. It has happened to me. It may happen to you.

CONCLUSION

'The Numbers Game' it is. You play the numbers, in this great Neanderthal job-hunting system of ours.

If it works for you, and you get a fine job, great! But if it doesn't, you may be interested in the other plan -- you know, the one they had saved up for you, in case all of this didn't work?

Small problem: with most of the personnel experts in our country, there is no other plan.

And that

is

that.

*I*t ain't what you don't know
that gets you in trouble;
it's what you know for sure
that ain't so.

Mark Twain

You Can Do It!

Chapter 3

"I DON'T HAVE A PARACHUTE
OF ANY COLOR."

From the preceding chapter, two facts have stood out -- like Mount Everest:

(1) The traditional job-hunt is Neanderthal, a matter of playing the numbers and hoping they pay off for you; but, in the end, a big fat gamble.

(2) Most so-called 'experts' -- such as corporations' human resources people -- haven't the foggiest idea how to search for a job except using this system: resumes, ads/job postings, and agencies, as they prove when they themselves are out of a job.

Now, on with our story.

THE CREATIVE MINORITY

Fortunately for all of us, there have always been a creative minority among human resource 'experts' -- starting with John Scott of the Bell Telephone Laboratories, back in 1921 -- who refused to accept the idea that the job-hunt has to be as bad as it is, or as much of an out-and-out gamble, as it is; and sat down to figure out *how it could be done better.*

Even in days before studies were conducted and statistics were gathered, members of the creative minority intuitively grasped three fundamental truths about the job-hunt:

1. **There are always jobs (vacancies) out there, waiting to be filled.**

2. **Whether you can find these jobs or not, depends on what job-search method you are using.**

3. **If you're job-hunting, and coming up 'empty,' you need to change the method you are using.** The jobs (vacancies) are still out there, waiting for you to find them.

What they knew intuitively as far back as 1921, we now know more certainly, because in the interim the job-hunt has been studied *to death!* Particularly in the U.S., though its lessons apply to other developed countries throughout the world.

So let us take a detailed look at these three truths through modern-day glasses.

THE FIRST FUNDAMENTAL TRUTH ABOUT THE JOB-HUNT

There are always jobs (vacancies) out there, waiting to be filled.

New jobs are always being created. Each month, in the U.S.,[1] the government tells us exactly how many. It's called the monthly unemployment report, and it's issued on the first Friday of each month.

---

1. People all over the world read and use this book, not only in English but in its many other translations. If you live in another country, I want to make clear that throughout this book, I use the U.S. as but an example of the kind of thing that happens in most countries throughout the world. It is just that most studies of the job-hunt have been done in the U.S., and when we need statistics, it is from the U.S. that they are most available.

As I write, two million new jobs were created in the last twelve months in the U.S. -- jobs that never existed previously.

In addition to these two million new jobs that never existed before, companies and employees were of course also playing musical chairs with the jobs that already existed.

That is to say, among the 129,275,000 jobs that already existed a year ago in the U.S., a number of them fell vacant during the year -- and for the following reasons:

People got promoted -- thus leaving vacant the job they previously held.

People retired -- thus leaving vacant the job they held.

People quit -- thus leaving vacant the job they held.

People decided to move -- thus leaving vacant the job they held.

People got injured or fell sick -- sometimes for a long time, thus leaving vacant for long- or short-term periods, the job they held.

People died -- thus leaving vacant the job they held.

And of course, **people got fired or laid off** -- often due to downsizing, mergers, and hostile takeovers. That should have meant there were less jobs, and that is the case, initially. But studies of such companies reveal they often start hiring again within a very short time (comparatively), as they realize they 'cut too close to the bone,' or need new people with new skills.

For all these reasons, there are always jobs (vacancies) out there.

HOW MANY VACANCIES?

Well, just exactly how many? Since the U.S. keeps statistics on *everything*, we actually know the number. Adding up the new jobs that get created each year, and the old jobs that fall vacant each year, for however brief a time, there were 21,000,000 vacancies waiting to be filled, just in the last six months.

Since you may cordially disbelieve this number, let me tell you how we know it. Since October 1, 1997, every U.S. employer who hires somebody new must report that fact to a designated State agency within twenty days of the date of the hire. Each State then submits its New Hire Reports to the National Directory of New Hires, a component of the Federal Parent Locator Service (FPLS). Adding up all these numbers, the National Directory of New Hires (NDNH) reported 21 million people got newly hired in the U.S. during the six-month period 10/1/97 – 3/31/97.[2]

That works out to almost one million vacancies a week -- either due to 'musical chairs' among existing jobs, or the creation of new jobs in the U.S. -- vacancies that have to be filled by *someone*. Believe me, there are always jobs out there, waiting to be filled.

THERE ARE VACANCIES
EVEN DURING RECESSIONS

You may say to yourself, but hey! these are good times in the U.S. -- the best in fifty years. What about other times in the U.S. when things won't be so hotsy-totsy? What about other countries, going through hard times even now? What happens to this claim that there are always jobs out there?

Well, it is perfectly true that *new* jobs don't get created at the same rate in hard times as in good times. But the other factor -- the 'revolving chairs' *among the jobs that already exist* -- holds true even during recessions or 'hard times.' People still get promoted, retire, quit, move, get sick for long stretches, or die -- leaving their job vacant. Even in the hardest of times.

---

2. The NDNH is *online* at
www.acf.dhhs.gov/programs/cse/newhire/employ/employ.htm

For example: in the U.S. there have been nine recessions since World War II. During one of these, the National Federation of Independent Business conducted a survey to discover how many vacancies there were among *small* businesses. They discovered there were one and a half million, at that moment, *even during that recession.* Add to that the number from large businesses, and you have a formidable number of jobs available, even during hard times.

Each year *millions* of people become unemployed, and then successfully find jobs, good jobs, sometimes great jobs, even during hard times.

So, write it on your bathroom mirror when you are job-hunting or trying to change careers: "In good times or in bad, there are *always* jobs out there." *Say it again, Sam.*

THE SECOND FUNDAMENTAL TRUTH ABOUT THE JOB-HUNT

Whether you can find these jobs or not, depends on what job-search method you are using.

We come now to our second fundamental truth about the job-hunt. To illustrate this point, let us step outside the world of work for a moment, and take an example from everyday life.

Suppose you moved to a big city, and found a really nice apartment to rent, but you decided you didn't want (or need) a telephone. And now let us suppose that some months later someone comes looking for you. They *think* you live in this city, but they're just not sure. However, being resourceful they go and look in the telephone book, because they assume that anyone who lives in the big city *must* have a telephone. But when they look, there is no mention of you. They call information to ask if you have an unlisted number. Nope. All their efforts turn up nothing. Nada. Zip.

So, what do they conclude? Well, you know what they conclude. They conclude you don't live in that city. And why did they reach this conclusion? Because they thought if you were there, you must be in the phone book. And if you weren't listed, you must not live in that city. But of course you are there. **They were just using the wrong search method.**

In exactly the same way, job-hunters turn to want ads, job-postings, or employment agencies, to find those jobs that do exist. But they often come up empty -- **because they're using the wrong search method**.

If you're going to find a job, your success does not depend on a good job-market. Everything depends on what search method you're using, to find those jobs that *are* out there, in good times or bad.

THE FIVE WORST WAYS TO TRY TO FIND A JOB

So, let's review what search methods are available to you, listing them in order, from *worst* success rate to *best* success rate:[3]

1. **Using the Internet**. If you are seeking a technical or computer-related job, or a job in engineering, finances, or healthcare, I estimate the success rate to be 10%. For the other 10,000 job titles that are out there: 1%.

That is, out of every 100 job-hunters who use the Internet (job-postings and resume-postings) as their search method, exactly one of them will find a job thereby. 99 job-hunters out of

---

3. Where no study or survey was available, I made my own personal estimate, based on twenty-seven years of experience with thousands of job-hunters. But there are plenty of studies, done over the past twenty years. Here are the ones which are particularly helpful:

Steven M. Bortnick and Michelle Harrison Ports, "Job search methods and results: tracking the unemployed, 1991," *Monthly Labor Review,* December 1992. Studied the success of job-seekers who had been looking for a job, over a period of 8 weeks.

John Bishop, John Barron and Kevin Hollenbeck, *Recruiting Workers: How recruitment policies affect the flow of applicants and quality of new workers.* The Ohio State University, The National Center for Research in Vocational Education, Sept. 1983. They discovered that "informal search methods" (such as described here in *Parachute*) are more effective than "formal search methods," such as employment agencies.

Carl Rosenfeld, "Job Search of the Unemployed, May 1976," *Monthly Labor Review,* November 1977. A Bureau of Labor Statistics study, which -- unlike the first study cited above -- interviewed job-hunters at only one moment in time.

Bureau of the Census, "Use and Effectiveness of Job Search Methods," *Occupational Outlook Quarterly,* Winter, 1976. A study of ten million job-seekers. Incidentally, I don't think the date of the study matters much. Job-hunting is all about human nature, and human nature doesn't change much over the years.

100 will not find the jobs that *are* out there - - if they use only this method to search for them.

2. **Mailing out resumes to employers at random**. This search method has a 7% success rate.

That is, out of every 100 job-hunters who use this search method, 7 will find a job thereby. 93 job-hunters out of 100 will not find the jobs that *are* out there - - if they use only this method to search for them.

(I'm being generous here with my percentages. One study revealed there is actually only one job-offer made and accepted, for every 1470 resumes floating around out there in the world of work. Another study puts the figure even higher: one job offer for every 1700 resumes floating around out there. If this sounds like good odds to you, thou shouldest clear the cobwebs out of thy brain. Would you take an airplane, if you knew only one out of 1700 got through, to its destination?)

3. **Answering ads in professional or trade journals**, appropriate to your field. This search method also has a 7% success rate.

That is, out of every 100 job-hunters who use this search method, 7 will find a job thereby. 93 job-hunters out of 100 will not find the jobs that *are* out there - - if they use only this method to search for them.

4. **Answering local newspaper ads**. This search method has a 5–24% success rate.

That is, out of every 100 job-hunters who use this search method, between 5 and 24 will find a job thereby. 76–95 job-hunters out of 100 will not find the jobs that *are* out there - - if they use only this method to search for them.

(The fluctuation between 5% and 24% is due to the level of salary that is being sought; the higher the salary being sought, the fewer job-hunters who are able to find a job using this search method).

5. **Going to private employment agencies or search firms for help**. This method has a 5–24% success rate, again, depending on the level of salary that is being sought.

Which is to say, out of every 100 job-hunters who use this method, between 5 and 24 will find a job thereby. 76–95 job-hunters out of 100 will not find the jobs that are out there - - if they use only this method to search for them.

(It should be noted that the success rate of this method has risen slightly in recent years, *in the case of women* but not of men: in a recent study, 27.8% of female job-hunters found a job within two months, by going to private employment agencies.)

THE THIRD
FUNDAMENTAL TRUTH
ABOUT THE JOB-HUNT

If you're job-hunting, and coming up 'empty,' you need to change the search method you have been using.

I'm sure you noticed that our old friends from the Numbers game - - resumes, ads, and agencies - - all appear on the *Five Worst* List. Ouch![4]

Therefore: if you've just been using resumes, ads, and agencies to find a job - - on or off the Internet - - and this has turned up *nothing*, it's time to change your search method.

---

4. Incidentally, there are at least four other search methods for trying to find the jobs that are out there, that technically fall into the "Least Effective" category. These are:

a. Going to **places where employers pick out workers**. This has an 8% success rate - - that is, out of every 100 people who use this method, 8 will find a job thereby. 92 will not. (15% of U.S. workers are union members, and it is claimed that those among them who have access to a union hiring hall, have a 22% success rate - - that is, 22 out of every 100 find a job using this method. What is not stated, however, is how long it takes to get a job at the hall, and how long a job typically lasts - - in the trades, that may be for just a few days.)

b. Taking **a Civil Service examination**. This has a 12% success rate - - that is, out of every 100 people who use this method, 12 will find a job thereby. 88 will not.

c. Asking **a former teacher or professor** for job-leads. This also has a 12% success rate - - that is, out of every 100 people who use this method, 12 will find a job thereby. 88 will not.

d. Going to **the state/Federal employment service office**. This has a 14% success rate - - that is, out of every 100 people who use this method, 14 will find a job thereby. 86 will not.

THE FIVE BEST WAYS
TO TRY TO FIND A JOB

1. **Asking for job-leads from: family members, friends, people in the community, staff at career centers** -- especially at your local community college or the high-school or college where you graduated. You ask them one simple question: do you know of any jobs at the place where you work -- or elsewhere? This search method has a 33% success rate.

That is, out of every 100 people who use this search method, 33 will find a job thereby. 67 job-hunters out of 100 will not find the jobs that *are* out there -- if they use only this method to search for them.

2. **Knocking on the door of any employer, factory, or office that interests you, whether they are known to have a vacancy or not.** This search method has a 47% success rate.

That is, out of every 100 people who use this search method, 47 will find a job thereby. 53 job-hunters out of 100 will not find the jobs that *are* out there -- if they use only this method to search for them.

3. **By yourself, using the phone book's Yellow Pages** to identify subjects or fields of interest to you in the town or city where you are, and then calling up the employers listed in that field, to ask if they are hiring for the type of position you can do, and do well. This method has a 69% success rate.

That is, out of every 100 job-hunters or career-changers who use this search method, 69 will find a job thereby. 31 job-hunters out of 100 will not find the jobs that *are* out there - - if they use only this method to search for them.

4. **In a group with other job-hunters, using the phone book's Yellow Pages to identify subjects or fields of interest to you in the town or city where you are, and then calling up the employers listed in that field, to ask if they are hiring for the type of position you can do, and do well.** This method has an 84% success rate.

That is, out of every 100 people who use this method, 84 will find a job thereby. 16 job-hunters out of 100 will not find the jobs that *are* out there - - if they use only this method to search for them.

5. **The Creative Approach to Job-Hunting or Career-Change.** This method has an 86% success rate.

That is, out of every 100 job-hunters or career-changers who use this search method, 86 will find a job or new career thereby. 14 job-hunters out of 100 will not find the jobs that *are* out there - - if they use only this method to search for them.

WHAT IS 'THE CREATIVE APPROACH' TO JOB-HUNTING OR CAREER-CHANGE?

Since the Creative Approach has the very best success rate, of all the job-search methods available to you, let us see how it got invented and what it involves.

The creative minority began by asking themselves what makes our present job-hunting system so Neanderthal. There were, it seemed to them, three fatal assumptions:

Fatal Assumption No. 1: *"The job-hunter should remain somewhat loose (i.e., vague) about what he or she wants to do, so they will be able to take advantage of whatever vacancies may become available."* Good grief, said the creative minority, this is why we have such a great percentage of people in this country who are *underemployed.* If you don't state just exactly what you want to do, first of all to yourself, and then to the employers you meet, you are - - in effect - - handing over that decision to others. And others, vested with such awesome responsibility for your life, will either duck the responsibility, or define you as only capable of doing such and such level of work (a safe, no risk diagnosis).

Fatal Assumption No. 2: *"The job-hunter should spend his or her time only on those organizations which have already indicated they have a vacancy."* Nonsense, said the creative minority. The job-market isn't like some high-school prom, where the job-hunters have to sit on the edge of the dance-floor, like shy wallflowers, while the employers are whirling around out in the center of the floor, enjoying all the initiative. In many cases, the dancing employers (if we may pursue the metaphor) are stuck with partners who are stepping on their toes, constantly. So, often-times the employer is *praying* someone will pay no attention to the silly ritual, and come to his or her rescue by cutting in. And (to pursue the metaphor further), people who cut in are usually pretty good dancers.

Fatal Assumption No. 3: *"Employers only see people who can write well."* That's pretty ridiculous, when it's put that way. But, say the creative minority, isn't that exactly the assumption that our present job-hunting system is based on? To get hired, you must get an interview. To get an interview, under this system, you must first let them look at your resume -- either by mail, or by posting it on the Internet. But the resume is only as good as your writing ability makes it. If the resume is poorly written, it will of course behave like a Fun House mirror, which distorts dramatically what you are really like. But, *no allowance is made for this possibility by the companies that see your resume, except one time out of a thousand.* Your resume is assumed to be an accurate mirror of who you are. You could be Einstein, but if you don't write well, you will not get an interview. Employers only see people who can write well. Ridiculous? You bet it is. But that's why I say our present job-hunting system is Neanderthal.

THE THREE SECRETS
OF SUCCESSFUL JOB-HUNTING

Once the fatal assumptions of the Numbers Game were brought into the bright light of day, it was of course easy for the creative minority to design a new job-hunting approach - - and one that worked. The prescription almost wrote itself, since it was just the opposite of the three fatal assumptions.

Success Secret #1: **You must decide just exactly what you have, to offer to the world.** This involves identifying, for yourself and others, what your favorite (transferable) skills are - - *in order of priority or importance to you.*

Success Secret #2: **You must decide just exactly where you want to use your skills.** This involves identifying your favorite subjects or fields of interest, as well as your geographical preferences, which you then explore through *research* (in books or on the Internet), and personal *informational interviewing.*

Success Secret #3: **You must go after the organizations that interest you the most, whether or not they are known to have a vacancy.** 'Going after them' means using your contacts -- anybody you know -- to get an appointment there; specifically, to get an appointment with the one individual there who actually has the power to hire you for the job that you most want to do. (Of course, you must have done a little research on them first, to find out just exactly who that is.)

(Incidentally, the word "organizations" is used very broadly throughout this book, to mean small businesses, large corporations, associations, foundations, agencies, the government and any other place that offers employment to people.)

For any job-hunter who is having trouble finding a job by the usual route -- resumes, ads, and agencies -- this prescription of the creative minority is *a lifesaver.*

For any job-hunter who wants more than 'just-a-job' this prescription of the creative minority is *crucial.*

But, for the job-hunter who is trying to strike out in a new direction, or who of necessity must seek a different line of work than they have done in the past, this prescription of the creative minority is *a matter of life and death.*

YOU CAN DO IT!

When you are looking for work, you will get advice from every side, and what it usually adds up to is: *you don't stand a chance. Give up . . . now! That isn't a kind world waiting for you out there, anymore. There isn't a single job out there for you to find . . . trust us, we've looked. And even if there is, it will be at a vastly reduced income for you. Take our advice, and just retreat to your bed, pull the covers over your head, and turn the electric blanket up to nine.*

All in all, a sort of *music to get depressed by.*

You must pay no attention to this advice, of course.

And you must not give up hope.

Even if you already began your job-search -- have sent out resumes or curricula vitae by the bushel, searched want ads by the hour, visited federal/state, and private employment agencies from A to Z, hung out on the Internet, looking at all those job-posting and resume sites for days or weeks -- all without turning up a single thing.

This says nothing about whether or not you can find a job.

There *is* a way. You *can* find a job, and a job which you love. You *can* flourish. The prescription of the creative minority is the key: What, Where, and How.

1. What: You must decide just exactly what you want to do.

2. Where: You must decide just exactly where you want to do it.

3. How: You must go after the organizations that interest you the most, whether or not they are known to have a vacancy.

Successful job-hunting is a learned skill. You have to study it. You have to practice it. You have to master it, just like any new skill. And master it thoroughly, because you'll need it all the rest of your life.

CONCLUSION

Okay, so where are we?

You're job-hunting or trying to change careers.

You've tried 'the system' everyone says is the way to do it: resumes, ads, and agencies, only to discover it is no system at all. It's just 'a Numbers Game.' It's pathetic. It's Neanderthal.

You're intrigued by the Creative Minority's alternative prescription of What, Where, and How.

You want to try it. Even if it takes work, because you know that it has a success rate that is twelve times that of resumes, in turning up jobs.

You're ready. But you want some guidance.

Good.

That's what the remainder of this book is about.

Concerning the creative job-hunting method, a reader (a student graduating from the University of Texas at Austin) wrote recently: "I can't begin to tell you how grateful I am that you wrote this book. I will be graduating this May and will be gainfully employed by an employer of my choice thereafter. I have the job I want, in the field I love (aviation) while my friends are still sending out resumes! To this day, I have never written nor used such a useless piece of paper! I think I'll put all of my friends out of their misery by telling them to quit wasting time on resumes, and buy them all a copy of your book!"

*F*orget *"what's available out there."*
Go after the job you really want the most.

— David Maister

CHAPTER FOUR

The Creative Approach To
Job-Search
and Career-Change

What

DO YOU HAVE,
TO OFFER TO THE WORLD?

You Must Figure Out Which of Your Skills
You Most Delight to Use

Chapter 4

Panel 1: WELL, HERE IT IS, ANOTHER FRESHLY-TYPED RESUME AND JOB APPLICATION.

Panel 2: AND I THROW IT DIRECTLY INTO THE TRASH.

Panel 3: CARSON! YOU DIDN'T EVEN MAIL THAT ONE OFF! / I KNOW.

Panel 4: BUT AFTER SO MANY REJECTIONS, IT'S JUST NICE TO CUT OUT THE MIDDLE MAN.

Wild Life by John Kovalic, © 1989 Shetland Productions. Reprinted with permission.

"I CAN'T FIND A JOB"

When a job-hunter tells me: *"I can't find a job",* that tells me nothing, until they tell me *how* they have been looking for it. The search method one uses, is everything! Everything!

The best job-search method, by far, has turned out to be the so-called **creative job-hunting approach**, as we saw in the previous chapter. This method leads to a job for 86 out of every 100 job-hunters who *faithfully* follow it. Such an effectiveness-rate - - 86% - - is astronomically higher than all other individual job-hunting methods.[1] That's why when nothing else is working for you, this is the method that you will thank your lucky stars for.

This is also the method you must turn to, if you've decided you would like to find a new career - - and you'd prefer not to have to take years out of your life to go back to school and get retrained with a new degree, etc., etc. (Or, even if you do want to go back to school, and need to know what to study or major in.)

---

1. I emphasize that this is for individual job-hunters or career-changers, working by themselves. Group strategies, such as Nathan Azrin's 'job-club' concept, Chuck Hoffman's Self-Directed Job-Search, Dean Curtis's Group Job Search program, etc., where you work essentially as a very well-disciplined class, have also achieved success-rates in the 85-90% range, usually by using telephone approaches to employers, with endless group feedback and coaching.

As I mentioned in the previous chapter this method does take time and effort. Most people like to avoid *effort*. I overheard a conversation in New York City's Central Park between two college students. We'll call them Jim and Fred. In half a minute they perfectly illustrated the amount of effort that altogether-too-many people put into their life-planning:

Jim: Hey, what are you majoring in?

Fred: Physics.

Jim: Physics? Man, you shouldn't major in physics. Computer science is the thing these days.

Fred: Naw, I like physics.

Jim: Man, physics doesn't pay much.

Fred: Really? What does?

Jim: Computer science. You should switch to computer science.

Fred: Okay, I'll look into it tomorrow.

Many career choices (and career-changes) in our culture are made in this fashion -- on impulse and whim, in a moment, in the twinkling of an eye. A casual conversation with someone. A decision to just follow in our parents' footsteps. An article on a news broadcast. An invitation from our father or a friend to come work where they do. Letting 'the job-market' rather than your heart dictate what you should go into.

> When you choose a career, you have got to know what it is **you** want to do, or else someone is going to sell you a bill of goods somewhere along the line that can do irreparable damage to your self-esteem, your sense of worth, and your stewardship of the talents that God gave you.

No, no! If you are going to follow the prescription of the Creative Minority, you must come to this task with your sleeves rolled up, prepared to do The Exercises thoroughly. Just remember: the benefits far outweigh the pain. Here are a couple of comments from readers (courtesy of amazon.com):

"It changed my life. The exercises take some time and thought, but they really led me to a rewarding and fun career I would never have considered without them."

"The exercises took quite a bit of effort, yet the results have permanently shaped the way I think about what I want to do with my life, no matter what my job at the time happens to be. I find myself returning to the insights gained from "Parachute" every few years and am amazed that the essential qualities I identified through the book remain consistent, no matter where I'm working or what I'm doing."

TRAVELS WITH FARLEY by Phil Frank © 1982. Field Enterprises, Inc. Courtesy of Field Newspaper Syndicate.

TREATING EACH JOB-HUNT AS THOUGH IT WERE A CAREER-CHANGE

I didn't invent this method. The Creative Minority did. But let me tell you what I especially like about it (besides the fact that it works so well).

I like the fact that it treats every job-hunt as though *it might be* a career-change.

Traditionally, we have been taught that if you want just a plain-old job-hunt, there is one method for *that*. But if you want to change careers, that's another kettle of fish, entirely.

Not so, with the Creative Minority! They say: **if you want to do a successful job-hunt, you must go through the same process you would if you wanted to change careers.**

Why do I like this philosophy? Because, first of all, **it makes sense to me**. Career-change seems to me to be the more radical process -- therefore more complicated, and time-consuming than just job-hunting. Now if the Creative Minority appear and tell me they've found a more effective method of job-hunting, I would expect it to be more complicated, and time-consuming than the traditional job-hunt -- or about as complicated and time-consuming as a career-change is. The two are of equal complexity; it is not surprising the two processes are virtually the same. This makes vast sense to me.

I like it secondly, because **it leaves open the door of possibilities.** Suppose you're halfway through your job-hunt and you suddenly realize you don't want the same old same old, that you had before. You suddenly realize you want to change careers. With the Creative Minority's process, no problem! You don't have to go back and redo everything. They were treating your job-hunt as though it were a career-change, from the beginning.

Experts say that we should count on having anywhere between three and six careers during our lifetime. The job-hunt is a time when many of us[2] suddenly decide "the time is now" -- for any of the following reasons:

• **We got fired,** and we can't find our old work any more. In this changing life, and changing world, jobs do vanish. You must not necessarily expect that you will be able to find exactly the same kind of work that you did in the past.

• **We are not earning enough,** and we need a new career that pays us more money -- more of what we're worth.

---

2. How many? Well, the U.S. keeps the best statistics; they may be *indicative,* at least, of what happens in other countries.

In the U.S., a survey found that 45% of all U.S. workers said they would change their careers if they could.

And each year about 10% of all U.S. workers actually do. In the most recent year surveyed, that equated to 10 million workers who changed careers that year. Of these: 5.3 million changed careers *voluntarily,* and in 7 out of 10 cases their income went up;1.3 million changed careers *involuntarily,* because of what happened to them in the economy, and in 7 out of 10 cases, their income went down; and 3.4 million changed careers for a *mixture* of voluntary and involuntary reasons, such as needing to go from part-time to full-time work, etc. (There is no record of what happened to *their* income.)

- **We've been asked to do the work of three,** and we feel stressed out, angry, exhausted, burnt out, and grumpy; we want a job or career that is a little easier on us, so we'll have time to smell the flowers.
- **We had been hardly stretched at all** by our previous work, and we'd like something that offers a real challenge and 'stretches' us.
- **We've been doing this work for ten, fifteen years, but it was a bad choice from the beginning,** and now we've decided to set it right.
- **We had a dream job, but our much-beloved boss moved on,** we now find ourselves working for 'a jerk,' and the dream job has turned into 'the job from hell.' We not only want a new employer, we've decided to go for a new career.
- **We've reached mid-life, and are ready for the famous 'mid-life change.'** [3]
- **We're looking more and more for 'our mission in life,'** and while we don't yet know what that is, we do know for sure that what we're presently doing *isn't it.* (Indeed, most of us are engaged in a life-long search for, and journey toward, *meaning* - - a process in which career-change plays an important part.)

For any or all of these reasons, we may decide to change careers. The job-hunt is often the time that we make that change.

How nice, then, that the Creative Minority came up with a process that treats every job-hunt as though it is to be a career-change.

We're ready for the process. The process is ready for us.

ARLO & JANIS reprinted by permission of NEA Inc.

WHAT IS
CAREER-CHANGE?

It's important to begin by understanding exactly what a career-change is. This is murky territory, because the word 'career' is used in so many different ways in everyday language.

(1) It is used, first of all, to mean *work* in contrast to *learning* or *leisure*. Thus when clothing ads speak of "a career outfit," they are referring to clothes which are worn primarily at work, rather than during learning-activities or leisure-activities.

(2) It is used, secondly, to sum up *a person's whole life in the world of work*. Thus when people say of someone at the end of their life, "He or she had a brilliant career," they are referring to *all* the occupations this person ever held, and all the work this person ever did.

(3) Thirdly, in its most common sense -- the one used here -- it is used as a synonym for the word *'field'* or *'job,'* as in the phrase 'a career-change,' where what is actually meant is a 'job/field change.'[4]

Okay, so much for the word 'career.' Now when we make a 'career-change,' what exactly is it that we're changing? Well, let's take a look-see.

$$\text{CAREER} = \boxed{\begin{array}{c} \text{Occupation} \\ \hline \text{FIELD} \end{array}}$$

As you see here, **basically a career is made up of two parts: (the name of) an occupation, and a field.** To explain this, let's momentarily 'freeze' the name of the occupation, and say it is: 'secretary.' (*I choose this because more than once in the past, I worked as a secretary myself*).

---

3. Despite the *myth* that career-change is primarily a mid-life phenomenon, in point of fact people can and do change careers at *all* ages. In the study referred to in footnote 2, only one out of ten career-changers was actually in mid-life.

4. Incidentally, 'career' comes from the Latin *carrus*, referring to a racetrack where horses wildly *careen* while competing in a race. We might observe that the wild way in which people often *careen* into a new career today, accidentally preserves the original meaning of the word.

Now, suppose you were just starting out in this occupation of 'secretary.' The next question you would have to ask yourself would be: where you would like to work as 'secretary'? Do you want to be a secretary with . . . a law firm? . . . a gardening store? . . . an airline? . . . a church? . . . a photographic laboratory? . . . a bank? . . . a chemical plant? . . . the Federal government? . . . or what?

All these places are *fields*. Law, Gardening, Air travel, Religion, Photography, Banking, Chemistry, Government - - they are all *fields*. What field you choose makes a big difference.

Let's take another example. Let's 'freeze' the name of the occupation as 'management consultant.'

Suppose you were just going into this career: where would you like to be a management consultant? With . . . a computer firm? . . . an automobile company? . . . a grocery store chain? . . . a leisure company? . . . an HMO? . . . or what? Again, these are all *fields*. Management, Computers, Automobiles, Food, Leisure, Healthcare. The field makes a big difference. *(You will realize that all these fields can be studied in college, or other schools where they are called "Majors," "Subjects," or just plain "Fields." Many can also be picked up, on the job - - through apprenticeship, experience, and finding a mentor there.)*

Memorize this equation, please; it will help you a lot, down the line: **a career = occupation + field**. You must define both, for your job-hunt to succeed.

Failure to do this can cause much damage to your job-hunt or career-change plans. For example, if you have defined your career goal as that of being a management consultant - - but nothing is turning up, you know what your problem is. You have only defined your **occupation**, and that by itself isn't enough.

You must also define what **field** you want to be a management consultant in, if your job-hunt is to be successful. *Until* you've decided what field you want to do management consulting in, your job-hunt has too broad a target. That's why you can't find a job.

The Creative Minority's process enables you to decide both **occupation** and **field** (or the building-blocks thereof), because it treats every job-hunt as though it were a career-change.

As I said, that's what I like about it.

Used by permission of Johnny Hart and Creators Syndicate, Inc.

THE THREE STEPS
TO JOB-HUNTING SUCCESS

But now that I have told you what I like about it, let us get on with it.

I am going to use my rich skills at overkill, to not simply *walk you through* the steps of creative job-hunting/career-change, but to gently *drum this process into your head,* until you can hear the steps in your sleep.

I want to do this, because it is essential that you *master* this approach, and master it *for life.* You are in all likelihood going to be out job-hunting again, you are in all likelihood going to be changing careers again. Job-hunting/career-change is a repetitive activity in our lives these days. You never know when you'll need it again. "Sometime. Come soon."

So, to recapitulate from our previous chapter, the creative approach to job-hunting/career-change has three parts to it. And these parts are easiest to remember as *What, Where* and *How:*

---

1. What: You must decide just exactly what you have to offer to the world. This involves identifying your gifts, or talents -- which is to say, your favorite skills, *in order of priority or importance to you.* Experts call these **your transferable skills**, because they are transferable to any field/career that you choose, regardless of where you first picked them up, or how long you've used them in some other field.

Once you know your skills, you have the building-blocks of your occupation; with these building-blocks, you can define an occupation that you love to do.

2. Where: **You must decide just exactly where you want to use your skills.** This involves identifying your *favorite subjects* or fields of interest, as well as your geographical preferences, which you then explore through *research* (in books or on the Internet), and personal *informational interviewing*. *Where* is primarily a matter of the **fields of knowledge** *you have already acquired*, which you most enjoy using. But it also has to do with your preferred working conditions, what kinds of data or people or things you enjoy working with, where you'd most like to live, etc.

Once you know your favorite subjects, you have the building blocks of your field; with these building-blocks, you can define a field that you would love to do your occupation in. Also, you can now put occupation and field together, to define a career that you would love to do.

3. How: **You must go after the organizations that interest you the most, whether or not they are known to have a vacancy.** 'Going after them' means using your contacts -- anybody you know -- to get an appointment there; specifically, to get an appointment with the one individual there who actually has the power to hire you for the job that you most want to do. (Of course, you must have done a little research on them first, to find out just exactly who that is, not to mention other valuable information about the organization's goals, etc.)

Once you have mastered these techniques, you know how to get into your new career that you love.

THE CRUCIAL IMPORTANCE
OF 'WHAT'

Now, faced with this three-fold prescription from the Creative Minority, our immediate instinct is to leap over *What* and *Where*, and go directly to *How* -- *how* do we find vacancies, *how* do we do our resume, *how* do we conduct a job-interview?

There are, indeed, thousands of job-hunting books and job-hunting workshops devoted solely to How: how to do resumes, interviews, salary negotiation -- thereby encouraging job-hunters to think this is all there is, to successful job-hunting.

This is a *huge* mistake.

Your Favorite Transferable Skills Are the Key to Job-Hunting Success

Search for work you only half-care about, and you'll search for it with only half your being; but search for work you are desperately anxious to find, and you'll hunt for it with all of your being.

The more you are searching for the thing that you most love to do, the more you will transform not only your job-hunt, but also your life. This begins with identifying skills you are passionate about using!

'. . . and give me good abstract-reasoning ability, interpersonal skills, cultural perspective, linguistic comprehension, and a high sociodynamic potential.'

THAT BOGEY-WORD: SKILLS

Now, many people just "freeze" when they hear the word 'skills.' It begins with high school job-hunters: "I haven't really got any skills," they say.

It continues with college students: "I've spent four years in college, and still I haven't picked up any skills."

And through our first years in the world of work. "I'm an unskilled worker."

And through the middle years, especially when a person is thinking of changing his or her career: "I just know I'll have to go back to college, and get retrained, because I don't have any skills in this new field, except maybe at entry level."

'Skills' is one of the most misunderstood concepts in the English language -- a misunderstanding that is shared, I might add, by altogether too many employers, personnel or human resources departments, and other so-called 'vocational experts.'

Their misunderstanding is revealed in their use of the terms "skilled and unskilled." To be blunt about it, **there is no such thing as 'unskilled.'** Everyone has skills, and has used them since childhood. They are enshrined in the reputation we get among our friends and family: "A whiz at remembering things," "Great with his hands," "Very outgoing with people," "Can fix anything that's broken," "A wonderful eye for color," and that sort of thing.

But there is such a thing as being deeply unaware of our skills. I know a woman who could walk into a room, look at twenty people there, walk out of the room and from memory perfectly describe every person she had seen in those fifteen seconds, down to the articles of jewelry they were wearing. Ironically, she said she was 'unskilled' -- she thought everyone could do that.

Many of us have skills we are unaware of. By inventorying your skills -- both those you are aware of and those you aren't, you will automatically put yourself way ahead in the job-hunt. Such inventory will also facilitate any career-change you care to make -- without your buying into the folly called 'I can only change careers if I go back to school.'

Maybe in order to change careers you will need some retraining, but very often it is possible to make a dramatic career-change without any retraining. It all depends. And you won't really *know* if you need further training, until you have inventoried your favorite skills and fields of knowledge *that you already possess.*

DEFINING 'TRAITS'

The skills you need to inventory are *your transferable skills.*

Now, many people think transferable skills are such things as: *has lots of energy, gives attention to details, gets along well with people, shows determination, works well under pressure, is sympathetic, intuitive, persistent, dynamic, dependable,* etc. But no matter how widespread this misconception, these are not functional/transferable skills, but the *style* with which you do your transferable skills.

To illustrate, let's take *"gives attention to details."* Suppose one of your transferable skills is "researching"; in such a case, *"gives attention to details"* describes the manner or style with which you do 'researching.'

So these things many job-hunters mistake for transferable skills -- *has lots of energy, gives attention to details, gets along well with people, shows determination, works well under pressure, is sympathetic, intuitive, persistent, dynamic, dependable* -- are actually your **traits.** (They may also be called your 'self-management skills,' 'temperaments,' or 'type.' Popular tests such as the *Myers-Briggs* measure this sort of thing.[5])

---

5. The Myers-Briggs Type Indicator, or 'MBTI,' measures what is called *psychological type.* For further reading about this, see:

Paul D. Tieger & Barbara Barron-Tieger, *Do What You Are: Discover the Perfect Career for You Through the Secrets of Personality Type.* 1992. Little, Brown & Company, Inc., division of Time Warner Inc., 34 Beacon St., Boston MA 02108. For those who cannot obtain the MBTI, this book includes a method for readers to identify their personality types. This is a very popular book.

David Keirsey and Marilyn Bates, *Please Understand Me: Character & Temperament Types.* 1978. Includes the Keirsey Temperament Sorter -- again, for those who cannot obtain the MBTI® (Myers-Briggs Type Indicator) -- registered trademarks of Consulting Psychologists Press.

A publication list of other readings about psychological type can be obtained from the Center for Application of Psychological Type, 2720 N.W. 6th St., Gainesville, FL 32609. 904-375-0160.

DEFINING
'TRANSFERABLE SKILLS'

All right, then, if what we often mistake as transferable skills are actually 'traits,' then what exactly are transferable skills? Here is a brief crash course on the subject, setting forth the seven principles of transferable skills:

1. Transferable skills are the secret of job-hunting success, because they are the most basic unit -- the atoms -- of whatever career, occupation, or job you choose.

You can see this from this diagram:

Skills as the Basic Unit of Work

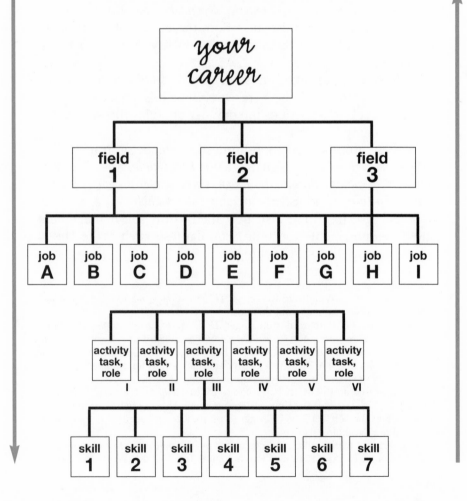

2. Transferable skills are the secret of changing careers without necessarily going back to school, because they allow you to build a picture of a new career from the ground up.

Look at the previous diagram. The creative approach to career-change essentially starts at the top on the left, works down to the bottom, then goes back up the other side to the top.

That is, you take your present or previous career, and you break it down *(through field and tasks -- whether you liked them or not)* to its most basic atomic level: skills.

Then you construct a new career, beginning with the basic level, your favorite skills, and going on up through your favorite tasks to your favorite field.

Down one side of the diagram, up the other side. Voila! a new career. Your favorite transferable skills are the foundation on which all else rests.

3. Transferable skills are almost always verbs.

Specifically, they are action verbs, in the gerund form (ending with -ing), and they may be thought of as 'focussed energies' that act upon some object.

4. Transferable skills divide into three basic families.

Transferable skills are customarily divided into three *families*, according to what kind of object they act upon -- whether it be some kind of **Data** (Information), or **People** or **Things.**

Within each of these three families there are *simple* skills, and there are higher, or *more complex* skills. The families can be diagrammed as three inverted pyramids, with the simpler skills at the bottom in each, and the more complex or higher skills above them, in order:

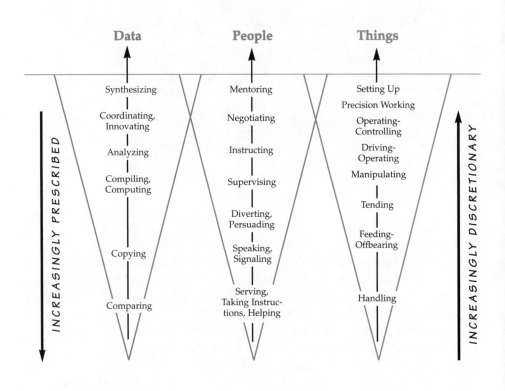

5. When you inventory your transferable skills, you should always claim the *highest* skills you legitimately can on the basis of your past performance.

On *each* transferable skills pyramid, you want to claim the highest skill you legitimately can, based on what you have in the past proven you can do.[6]

As a general rule - - to which there are exceptions - - each skill that is higher on a triangle depends upon your being able to do all the skills listed below it on that triangle. So you probably can claim the skills below the highest skill you claim, on each inverted pyramid. Always check to see if this is so.

6. If you desire a more detailed official explanation of what each of these skills is, I refer you to the *U.S. Dictionary of Occupational Titles*, 1991 revised fourth edition, pp. 1005–1006 in vol. II, available in any public library in the U.S.

6. The higher your transferable skills, the more freedom you will have on the job.

Simpler skills can be, and usually are, heavily *prescribed* by the employer, so if you claim *only* the simpler skills, you will have to '*fit in*' -- following the instructions of your supervisor, and doing exactly what you are told. The *higher* the skills you can legitimately claim, the more you will be given freedom to carve out the job the way you want to -- so that it truly fits *you*.

7. The higher your transferable skills, the less competition you will face, because jobs which use such skills are rarely found through the search-methods the average job-hunter or career-changer uses.

Not for you the way of classified ads, resumes, and agencies. No, if you claim higher skills, then to find jobs which use them you *must* follow the creative job-hunting method described in the next two chapters.

The essence of this creative approach to job-hunting or career-change is that you may approach *any organization that interests you, whether or not they have a known vacancy* -- using your contacts to get in, there. Naturally, at whatever places you visit -- and particularly those which have not advertised any vacancy -- you will find far fewer job-hunters that you have to compete with, than would be the case if you were just answering ads or job postings.

In fact, if the employers you visit happen to like you well enough, they may even create for you a job that does not presently exist. *In which case, you will be competing with no one, since you will be the sole applicant for that newly created job.* While this doesn't happen most of the time, it is astounding how many times it *does* happen.

The reason it does is that the employers often have been *thinking* about creating a new job within their organization, for quite some time -- but with this and that, they just have never gotten around to *doing* it. Until you walk in, with a clear idea of exactly what skills you have. Then they decide they don't want to let you get away, since *good employees are as hard to find as are good employers.*

At this point, they suddenly remember the job they have been thinking about creating for many weeks or months, now.

So, they dust off their *intention*, create the job on the spot, and offer it to you! And if that new job is not only what *they* need, but is exactly what *you* were looking for, then you have: Match-match. Win-win.

From our country's perspective, it is interesting to note that by this job-hunting initiative of yours, you have helped *accelerate* the creation of more jobs in your country. How nice to help your country, as well as yourself!

And so, the paradoxical moral of all this: The less you try to 'stay loose' and open to *anything,* the more you define in detail your skills with *Data/Information* and/or *People* and/or *Things,* and at the highest level you legitimately can, **the more likely you are to find a job.** *Just the opposite of what the typical job-hunter or career-changer starts out believing.*

SOME QUICK STRATEGIES
FOR IDENTIFYING YOUR
TRANSFERABLE SKILLS

Ten Tips For The Impatient Job-Hunter

1

✳ Take the job-label off yourself (*"I am an auto-worker,"* etc.) and define yourself instead as *"I am a person who can . . ."* Then think of how you would finish that sentence. What tasks? What skills can you do? Make a list.

2

✳ Think of some other line (or lines) of work that you could do, can do, and would enjoy doing. Perhaps it's something you've already done, in a very small way, in your spare time (*like: make dresses, repair sailboats, etc.*) Then: what skills does it take to do that? Add these to your list.

3

✳ Ask yourself: "What am I good at? What does everyone tell me?" What skills does it take, etc., etc. Add these to your list.

4

✳ What turns you on? If a thing turns you on, you'll be good at it; if it doesn't, you won't. What energizes you? List the work, and tasks, that energize you, that give you your power in life. What skills are you using at such times? On the list you're keeping, put them down, and put a plus in front of them. Then: what exhausts you with very little effort and for very little reason? What skills are you using at such a time? List them, too, but this time put a minus sign in front of them. Skills that exhaust you usually do so for a reason: you don't like to use them. Avoid them.

5

✳ Ask yourself: "What have I done in the past that I really loved doing?" What are your hobbies? Astronomy? Aerospace? Airplanes? Bicycling? Birding? Boating or kayaking? Books? Cars? Caves? Collecting coins, or stamps, or dolls, or anything else? Cooking? Crafts? Dance? Electronics? Fishing? Flowers or gardening? Genealogy? Horses? Hunting? Juggling? Magic? Martial arts or other physical stuff? Minerals or rocks? Models? Motorcycles? The outdoors? Pets? Photography? Puppetry? Trains? Travel? Woodworking? Or what? Ask yourself, "What *did* I like about these things? What do I *still* like doing?" See what kinds of skills any of these might point to, for you. Add them to your list.

6

✳ Ask yourself: do I primarily like to use my skills with People, or my skills with Things, or my skills with Information? And, which ones? Add them to your list.

7

✳ What natural sensitivities do you have, that you don't think everyone else necessarily has? This could be things your eyes pick up (e.g., colors, facial expressions, bodies showing injury); *or* things your ears pick up (e.g., birdsongs); *or* things your nose picks up (e.g., faint odors in the air); *or* things your mouth picks up (e.g., peculiar tastes); *or* things your body picks up (e.g., air currents, temperature changes); *or* things your brain picks up (e.g., connections, disharmony, remembering details), etc., etc. Add them to your list.

8

✳ What skills, when you even hear their name, do you instinctively feel you possess? Here is a list to choose from. Put a check mark in front of each skill that you believe you possess. Put a star in front of each skill that you enjoy doing. And put a circle in front of each skill that you believe you do well.

The ones, at the end, that have a check mark *and* a star *and* a circle are the ones you should pay particular attention to. Add them to your list.

A List of 246 Skills as Verbs

achieving	acting	adapting	addressing	administering
advising	analyzing	anticipating	arbitrating	arranging
ascertaining	assembling	assessing	attaining	auditing
budgeting	building	calculating	charting	checking
classifying	coaching	collecting	communicating	compiling
completing	composing	computing	conceptualizing	conducting
conserving	consolidating	constructing	controlling	coordinating
coping	counseling	creating	deciding	defining
delivering	designing	detailing	detecting	determining
developing	devising	diagnosing	digging	directing
discovering	dispensing	displaying	disproving	dissecting
distributing	diverting	dramatizing	drawing	driving
editing	eliminating	empathizing	enforcing	establishing
estimating	evaluating	examining	expanding	experimenting
explaining	expressing	extracting	filing	financing
fixing	following	formulating	founding	gathering
generating	getting	giving	guiding	handling
having responsibility	heading	helping	hypothesizing	identifying
illustrating	imagining	implementing	improving	improvising
increasing	influencing	informing	initiating	innovating
inspecting	inspiring	installing	instituting	instructing
integrating	interpreting	interviewing	intuiting	inventing
inventorying	investigating	judging	keeping	leading
learning	lecturing	lifting	listening	logging
maintaining	making	managing	manipulating	mediating
meeting	memorizing	mentoring	modeling	monitoring
motivating	navigating	negotiating	observing	obtaining
offering	operating	ordering	organizing	originating
overseeing	painting	perceiving	performing	persuading
photographing	piloting	planning	playing	predicting
preparing	prescribing	presenting	printing	problem solving
processing	producing	programming	projecting	promoting
proof-reading	protecting	providing	publicizing	purchasing
questioning	raising	reading	realizing	reasoning
receiving	recommending	reconciling	recording	recruiting
reducing	referring	rehabilitating	relating	remembering
rendering	repairing	reporting	representing	researching
resolving	responding	restoring	retrieving	reviewing
risking	scheduling	selecting	selling	sensing
separating	serving	setting	setting-up	sewing
shaping	sharing	showing	singing	sketching
solving	sorting	speaking	studying	summarizing
supervising	supplying	symbolizing	synergizing	synthesizing
systematizing	taking instructions	talking	teaching	team-building
telling	tending	testing & proving	training	transcribing
translating	traveling	treating	trouble-shooting	tutoring
typing	umpiring	understanding	understudying	undertaking
unifying	uniting	upgrading	using	utilizing
verbalizing	washing	weighing	winning	working
writing				

9

❋ Weigh what problems your skills in the past have helped solve for an employer. For example, did your skills help that employer with: making customers want to return, the quality of service, the quality of the merchandise, the timeliness of deliveries, bringing costs down, inventing new products, *or what*? If so, which skills enabled you to do this? Add these to your skills list.

10

❋ Ask yourself: "Among all the people I've met, or know, or have read about, whose job would I most love to have?" Then: what skills does it take to do that? Do you have them? Add them to your list.

HOW TO IDENTIFY
YOUR TRANSFERABLE
SKILLS
IN GREATER DETAIL

If none of this works for you, or if it represents a good beginning, but you want to go deeper, then turn to The Exercises on p. 267, and do the skills analysis described there.

It involves writing seven stories from your life -- times when you were really enjoying yourself -- and then seeing what skills you used there.

Here is a specific example of such a story, so you can see how it is done:

"I wanted to be able to take a summer trip with my wife and four children. I had a very limited budget, and could not afford to put my family up, in motels. I decided to rig our station wagon as a camper.

"First I went to the library to get some books on campers. I read those books. Next I designed a plan of what I had to build, so that I could outfit the inside of the station wagon, as well as topside. Then I went and purchased the necessary wood. On weekends, over a period of six weeks, I first constructed, in my driveway, the shell for the 'second story' on my station wagon. Then I cut doors, windows, and placed a six-drawer bureau within that shell. I mounted it on top of

the wagon, and pinioned it in place by driving two-by-fours under the station wagon's rack on top. I then outfitted the inside of the station wagon, back in the wheelwell, with a table and a bench on either side, that I made.

"The result was a complete homemade camper, which I put together when we were about to start our trip, and then disassembled after we got back home. When we went on our summer trip, we were able to be on the road for four weeks, yet stayed within our budget, since we didn't have to stay at motels.

"I estimate I saved $1900 on motel bills, during that summer's vacation."

Ideally, each story you write should have the following parts, as illustrated above:

I.) Your goal: what you wanted to accomplish: *"I wanted to be able to take a summer trip with my marriage partner and four children."*

II.) Some kind of hurdle, obstacle, or constraint that you faced (self-imposed or otherwise): *"I had a very limited budget, and could not afford to put my family up, in motels."*

III.) A description of what you did, step by step (how you set about to ultimately achieve your goal, above, in spite of this hurdle or constraint): *"I decided to rig our station wagon as a camper. First I went to the library to get some books on campers. I read those books. Next I designed a plan of what I had to build, so that I could outfit the inside of the station wagon, as well as topside. Then I went and purchased the necessary wood. On weekends, over a period of six weeks, I . . ." etc., etc.*

IV.) A description of the outcome or result: *"When we went on our summer trip, we were able to be on the road for four weeks, yet stayed within our budget, since we didn't have to stay at motels."*

V.) Any measurable/quantifiable statement of that outcome, that you can think of: *"I estimate I saved $1900 on motel bills, during that summer's vacation."*

The Exercises on page 267ff will take you through this whole process of analyzing seven stories, identifying your transferable skills, and prioritizing them, as below.

PRIORITIZING YOUR FAVORITE SKILLS

There are three steps to skill-identification. You may think of them as: *Inventory, Prioritize, Flesh Them Out.*

Once you have inventoried the transferable skills that you possess, it is *crucial* for you to move on to the second step (Prioritize), by deciding which ones are your favorites. And you must then put your top six most favorite skills -- whether with **Data** or **People** or **Things** -- in exact order of priority, on the following diagram:

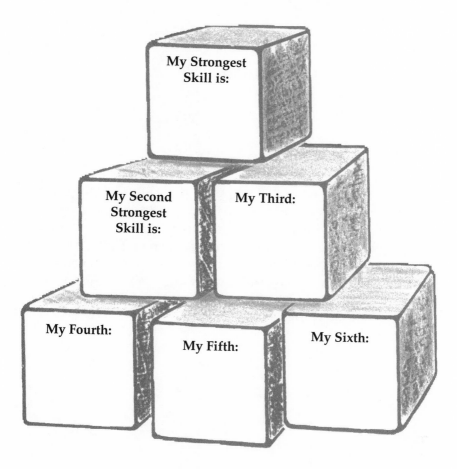

'FLESHING OUT'
ONE-WORD
DEFINITIONS
OF SKILLS

Once you have identified your favorite transferable skills, and put them in order of priority for you as to which ones you enjoy the most, it is time to move on to the third step in skill-identification: *fleshing out* your description of your six favorites, with more than just one word.

Suppose you've listed:

That's a fine start at defining your skill, but unfortunately it doesn't yet tell us much. Organizing what? *People,* as at a party? *Nuts and bolts,* as on a workbench? Or *lots of information,* as on a computer? These are three entirely different skills. The one word *organizing* doesn't tell us which one is *yours.* So, you must *flesh out* each of your favorite transferable verbs with some object -- some kind of **Data/Information**, or some kind of **People**, or some kind of **Thing** -- such as:

"I'm good at organizing information."

Finally, if you can, add some adverb or adjective phrase. Why? Well,

"I'm good at organizing information *painstakingly and logically*"
and
"I'm good at organizing information *in a flash, by intuition,*"

are two *entirely different* skills. The difference between them is spelled out not in the verb, and not in the object, but in the adjectival or adverbial phrase there at the end.

So, now, what do we end up with? Something like this, in the case of each of your six favorite skills:

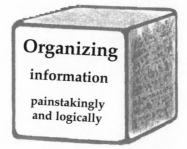

Now, that's a good skill-identification -- because it makes you stand out, from 19 other 'organizers'!

When you are face-to-face with a person-who-has-the-power-to-hire-you, you want to be able to explain what makes you different from nineteen other people who can basically do the same thing that you can do. It is often the **adjective** or **adverb** that will save your life, during that explanation.

CONCLUSION

When you have done this with all six of your favorite transferable skills, Voila! You are finished defining **WHAT**.

In case you've read this whole section, but haven't yet actually gone and done The Exercises, and you feel "Oh, I just can't do all those stories," you may be interested in how a woman job-hunter in England, avoided writing the stories, but found another way (the PIE method she refers to, is fully described in the next chapter):

"I have a Ph.D. in Chemistry, but the last thing I wanted to do on graduating was to work in a laboratory or a research group. I read your book, and tried - - but failed - - to write the stories; it required too much soul-searching! Consequently, it took me nine months before I decided on a new career path. It was Daniel Porot's PIE method that got me there - - Practice Interviewing, Informational Interviewing, Employment Interviewing. It helped build my confidence enormously, and I felt I had the power - - rather than being the victim of the employment market. I followed your ideas and advice, and have just been offered my first permanent position. I am overjoyed, because I chose this new career looking at my interests and skills, rather than my qualifications. Now I am a Clinical Research Scientist in a hospital. I feel now at long last, at 27 years of age, I am finally on the right track to finding my mission in life."

"WHILE YOU'RE WAITING FOR YOUR SHIP TO COME IN, WHY DON'T YOU DO SOME MAINTENANCE WORK ON THE PIER ?"

A Friendly Word to Procrastinators

If two weeks have gone by, and you haven't even *started* doing the inventory described in this chapter and in the Exercises, then - - I hate to tell you this - - you're going to have to get someone to help you.

Your life in the world of work will consume 80,000 hours of your time on this earth. Yet, most of us spend more time planning next summer's vacation, which will consume only 224 hours of our time on this earth, than we do in trying to figure out what we want to do with those 80,000 hours.

So, don't procrastinate any longer! Choose a helper for your job-hunt - - a friend rather than family, if possible. A tough friend - - you know, *taskmaster*. Ask them if they're willing to help you. Assuming they say yes, put down in *both* your appointment books a regular *weekly* date when you will guarantee to meet with them, and they will guarantee to meet with you, check you out on what you've done already, and be very stern with you if you've done little or nothing since last week's meeting.

If you have no friend who will help you, then you're probably going to want to think about professional help. (See pages 305–335, in Appendix B.) Go talk to several career-counselors. Choose the one you like best, and *get on with it.*

You've only one life to live, my friend. The time to make sure it is the life you really most want, is now.

I have learned this
At least, by my experiment:
If one advances confidently
In the direction of his dreams,
And endeavors to live
The life he has imagined,
He will meet with a success
Unexpected in common hours.

—Henry David Thoreau

CHAPTER FIVE

The Systematic Approach To
Career-Change
And Job-Hunting

Where

DO YOU MOST WANT TO USE THOSE SKILLS?

You Must Figure Out
Just Exactly What Field
and What Kinds of Places
You Would Most Delight to Work In

Chapter 5

YOU'LL LIKE THIS JOB, EXCEPT EVERY NOW AND THEN, WHEN THEY DUMP A LOT OF PAPER WORK ON YOU.

THE THREE STEPS
TO JOB-HUNTING
(AND CAREER-CHANGING)
SUCCESS:
WHAT, WHERE AND HOW

We come now to the second part of the creative approach to job-hunting and career-change. In case two weeks (or two months!) have passed since you last looked at the previous chapter, let me briefly summarize.

In the previous chapter we dealt with the first part of the creative approach, What, viz:

1. What: You must decide just exactly what you have to offer to the world. This involves identifying your gifts, or talents -- which is to say, your favorite skills, *in order of priority or importance to you.*

In this chapter, the one you are presently reading, we come to the second question:

2. Where: You must decide just exactly where you want to use your skills. This involves identifying your *favorite subjects* or fields of interest, as well as your geographical preferences, which you then explore through *research* (in books or on the Internet), and personal *informational interviewing*. **Where** is primarily a matter of the **fields of knowledge** *you have already acquired*, which you most enjoy using.

But it also has to do with your preferred working conditions, what kinds of data or people or things you enjoy working with, where you'd most like to live, etc.

Once you know your favorite subjects, you have the building blocks of your field; with these building-blocks, you can define a field that you would love to do your occupation in.

Also, you can now put occupation and field together, to define a career that you would love to do.

So: in the previous chapter, you did the homework on your favorite **skills** -- *or at least saw how it is done.*

But, as we have seen, it is not sufficient to simply say *I love using my skills.* You must define for yourself Where you want to use those skills, that is, in what field. And the building blocks of your field are your favorite knowledges.

THE FIVE
STEPS TO
'WHERE'

You approach Where through a series of five steps, each taken in turn. They are:

• STEP #1

What are the names of my favorite subjects or interests?

• STEP #2

What field do these interests point me toward?

• STEP #3

What occupation in this field do I especially like?

• STEP #4

What **career** would give me a chance to do this occupation in this field -- combining my most enjoyable skills with my greatest interests?

• STEP #5

What are the names of organizations that hire people who choose this career, and match my particular values?

Now let us see how you find the answers to these questions, step by step (all five of them).

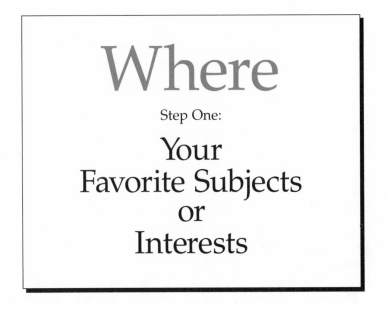

Where

Step One:

Your
Favorite Subjects
or
Interests

The thing we are looking for here -- 'Favorite **knowledges**' -- has two other names. They are sometimes called 'favorite **subjects**.' And they are sometimes called "your **interests**."

All three terms are pretty interchangeable, and refer to the fact that each of us knows a little bit about a lot of things. Among all the things we know something about, we naturally have preferences. Some subjects interest us; some don't.

Take my case. I know a little bit about accounting, but I'm basically not interested in the subject.

I know a lot about fundraising, but again, I'm basically not interested in the subject.

On the other hand, I know a lot about job-hunting, and I am interested in the subject. Very.

You see the point, I'm sure. One of my interests (there are others) is: job-hunting. Another way of saying it, is: job-hunting is one of my favorite subjects.

Now, turning from my life to yours, the question at hand is: What subjects or bodies of knowledge are *you* interested in? Even better, which subjects *turn you on?*

SOME QUICK STRATEGIES FOR IDENTIFYING YOUR FAVORITE SUBJECTS OR INTERESTS

Ten Tips For The Impatient Job-Hunter or Career-Changer[1]

1

* What are your favorite hobbies or interests *(Computers? Gardening? Spanish? Law? Physics? Department stores? Hospitals? etc., etc.)*? Start a list.

2

* What do you love to talk about? Ask yourself: if you were stuck on a desert island with a person who only had the capacity to speak on a few subjects, what would you pray those subjects were?

If you were at a get-together, talking with someone who was covering two of your favorite subjects at once, which way would you hope the conversation would go? Toward which subject?

If you could talk about *something* with some world expert, all day long, day after day, what would that subject or field of interest be? Add any ideas that these questions spark in you, to your list.

3

* What magazine articles do you love to read? I mean, what subjects? You get really interested when you see a magazine article that deals with. . . . *what subject?* Add any ideas to your list.

4

* What newspaper articles do you love to read? You get really interested when you see a newspaper special report that deals with. . . . *what subject?* Add any ideas, here, to your list.

---

1. I am indebted to Daniel Porot of Geneva, Switzerland, for many of these suggestions.

5

* If you're browsing in a bookstore, what sections of the bookstore do you tend to gravitate towards? What subjects there do you find really fascinating? Add any ideas, here, to your list.

6

* What sites on the Internet (if you have Internet access) do you tend to gravitate towards? What subjects do these sites deal with? Do any of these really fascinate you? Add any ideas, here, to your list.

7

* If you watch TV, and it's a 'game show,' which categories would you pick? If it's an educational program, what kinds of subjects do you stop and watch? Add them to your list.

8

* When you look at a catalog of courses that you could take in your town or city (or on TV), which subjects really interest you? Add any ideas, here, to your list.

9

* If you could write a book, and it wasn't about your own life or somebody else's, what *would* be the subject of the book? Add it to your list.

10

* There are moments, in most of our lives, when we are so engrossed in a task, that we lose all track of time. *(Someone has to remind us that it's time for supper, or whatever.)* If this ever happens to you, what task, what subject, so absorbs your attention that you lose all track of time? Add it to your list.

DON'T DECIDE
YOUR FUTURE
BEFORE YOU'VE FIRST
INVENTORIED
YOUR PAST

The quick exercises above may yield a very satisfying list of your favorite subjects, or interests. That's if your knowledge of yourself is very very clear.

But in most cases our self-knowledge could use a little more work. A weekend would do.

In a weekend, you can cast a wider net, and inventory *all* the fields you know anything about -- whether or not they are your favorites. *(You can, of course, stretch the inventory over a longer period of time, if you prefer. It's up to you as to just how you do it.)*

On the following page, fill out each column. *You can copy this chart on to a larger piece of paper (or to a spreadsheet on your computer) if you need more room.*

Here are three points to keep in mind, as you fill this out.

1. **Every column/category on the chart is worth thinking about.**

2. **It is only necessary that you love talking about a subject, and know *something* about it -- it is not necessary that you have a *mastery* of it.** Your degree of *mastery* is irrelevant -- unless you want to work at a level in the subject or field that demands and requires mastery.

3. **It doesn't matter *how* you picked up the knowledge.** As John Crystal used to say, it doesn't matter whether you learned it in college, or sitting at the end of a log. It can be a subject that you just picked up a lot of knowledge about as you went along the way in life -- say, *antiques,* or *cars,* or *interior decorating,* or *music* or *movies* or *psychology,* or *the kind of subjects that come up on television 'game shows.'* Let's take *antiques* as an example. Suppose it's one of your favorite subjects, yet you never studied it in school. You picked up your knowledge of antiques by going around to antique stores, and asking lots of questions. And you supplemented this by reading a few books on the subject, and you subscribe to an antiques magazine. You've also bought a few antiques, yourself. That's enough, for you to put antiques on your list of subjects or interests.

Subjects I Know Something About

Which column you decide to put a subject in, below, doesn't matter at all. The columns are only a series of pegs, to hang your memories on. Which peg, is of no concern. Jot down a subject anywhere you like.

Column 1	Column 2	Column 3	Column 4	Column 5
Studied in High School or College or Graduate School	Learned on the Job	Learned from Conferences, Workshops, Training, Seminars	Learned at Home: Reading, TV, Tape Programs, Study Courses	Learned in My Leisure Time: Volunteer Work, Hobbies, etc.
Examples: Spanish, Typing, Accounting, Computer Literacy, Psychology, Geography	*Examples: Publishing, Computer graphics, How an organization works, How to operate various machines*	*Examples: Welfare rules, Job-hunting, Painting, How to Use the Internet*	*Examples: Art Appreciation, History, Speed Reading, A Language*	*Examples: Landscaping, How to sew, Antiques, Camping, Stamps*

PRIORITIZING YOUR FAVORITE KNOWLEDGES OR INTERESTS

Once you have made an inventory of the subjects you *know something about*, the next step is to pick out your favorites from among them all. You must not skip over this step.

The quickest way to pick out your favorites is to look at the chart and your other lists, and simply let your instinct or intuition tell you which is your favorite subject -- or your *three* favorites.

The Game of Paper and Bowl

Sometimes playing a game will help your intuition.

(1) Go to your chart, and copy each subject by itself on a little slip of paper.

(2) Then get a bowl (of any size), and play this pretend game: you have to give away all those subjects to others, except for three that you may keep for yourself.

(3) One by one drop into the bowl any piece of paper that has a subject written on it that you are willing to give to someone else.

(4) If you come to a piece of paper that has a subject on it you aren't sure you want to let go of, hold on to it.

(5) Keep going, until you are left with only the subjects you just can't bear to give away; they may be one to twenty en toto.

(6) At this point, empty the bowl, and now from those subjects that remain in your hand, drop into the empty bowl the subject you are *least reluctant* to let go of. Repeat, with the pieces of paper that remain in your hand. Keep going, until you are down to just three pieces of paper in your hand. All the subjects in the bowl (now) are worth jotting down on a piece of paper. But the ones that remain in your hand are the subjects or interests you care the most about.

If you'd prefer a more step-by-step left-brain approach, then from the chart and other list(s), randomly pick out what you think are your top ten favorites (in no particular order), and then turn to the Prioritizing Grid on page 279. Using that Grid and comparing those ten just two at a time, you will be able to put them in exact order of your own personal preference: "this is my favorite," "this is my next favorite," and so on, and so forth.

Put your top three on the following diagram:

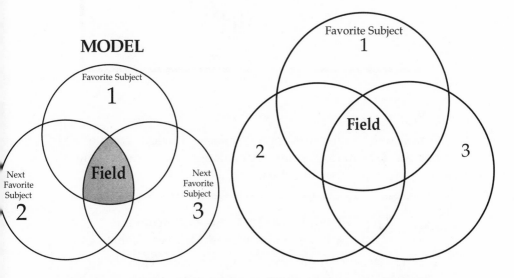

As I said earlier, your favorite Subjects form the building blocks for defining your favorite Field. Since you now know your three favorite Subjects, you are ready to define your "Field."

Where

Step Two:

Your Favorite Field

THE JOB-MARKET VS. YOUR HEART

The way in which most people choose a field is from a list of what **the job-market** wants. Magazines, newspapers and the Internet just *love* lists like these:

The Top Ten Fields In Terms of Percentage-Growth Between Now And The Year 2006

Computer and data processing services (experts think this field will have grown 108% between 1996 and 2006), Health services (68%), Management and public relations (60%), Miscellaneous transportation services (60%), Residential care (59%), Personnel supply services (53%), Water and sanitation (51%), Individual and miscellaneous social services (50%), Offices of health practitioners (47%), Amusement and recreation services (41%).[2]

The Top Ten Fields In Terms of Pay (Median Earnings)

Engineering, mathematics, computer and information sciences, pharmacy, architecture/environmental design, physics, accounting, economics, health/medical technologies, and physical therapy.[3]

We are brainwashed, from our youth up, to thus let the job-market determine what field we should go into. Unfortunately, choosing a field in this manner often puts us into a field we learn to cordially hate as we grow older. It's like putting on a suit that's three sizes too small for us. The 'fit' is terrible!

The Creative Minority's prescription for how you choose a field starts at the opposite end: it begins, not with the job-market, but with you!

You! What are your passions? What is your mission on earth? What are your dreams? Talk to yourself! Tell yourself what your interests are. And *then* choose a field that honors and uses those interests.

You should be the guiding light in how you choose a field -- not the job-market, with its alleged needs.

If you choose a field you love, will there be jobs you can do, in that field? Of course -- but we can figure those out later!

If you choose a field you love, will there be vacancies in that field? Of course -- but we can scout those out later!

For now, choose a field you love! Choose a field that fits you, by identifying your interests -- the subjects to which your heart is drawn -- as you have just done; and then letting the top three point to a field that uses them all.

Begin with your heart! Find a field you love, and you will hunt for a job in it with every fibre of your being. **Passion is the key to perseverance, and perseverance is the key to finding a job.**

That's the prescription for finding work you can love. That's the prescription for finding your mission in life. That's the prescription for job-hunting success. So say the Creative Minority, with their 86% success rate!

2. http://stats.bls.gov/news.release/ecopro.table4.htm

3. Source: "Earnings of college graduates, 1993: Fields of study is a major determinant of the wide variations in earnings." *Monthly Labor Review,* December 1995.

COMBINING
INTERESTS
TO FORM
A FIELD

How do we put three interests of yours together to form or define a field? Let's take an example of an actual job-hunter/career-changer, whom we'll call Larry.

After doing the exercises above, Larry discovered that his three favorite interests or favorite subjects were: psychiatry, plants, and carpentry.

So far, so good. Now, how did he define a field, from these? The same way you will. There are seven steps to be followed:

1. **You're going to have to go talk with people.** Printed resources usually won't 'cut it' for this part of the process. You're going to have to talk with people, either face-to-face, or on the phone, or through an Internet newsgroup.

2. **Choose an expert in each of your favorite three knowledges.** How did Larry choose who to talk to? He took his favorite knowledges or interests, above -- psychiatry, plants, and carpentry -- and tried to think of an expert in each subject.

For psychiatry, the expert was obviously a psychiatrist, or a professor of psychiatry at a nearby university.

For plants, the expert was obviously a gardener or landscape artist.

And for carpentry, the expert was obviously a carpenter.

3. **Get names for each of those 'expert' categories.** Having chosen the *occupational categories*, Larry had to then go find names of actual psychiatrists, gardeners, and carpenters. How did he do that? Combination of the telephone company's Yellow Pages, and anyone from among the people he already knew, who was either a psychiatrist, or gardener, or carpenter.

4. **Plan to go talk to them**. Face-to-face is best, but you can use the phone or Internet mailing lists, of course.

5. **Decide to visit first the expert with the largest overview.** This is often, but not always, the same as asking: who took the longest to get their training? The particular answer here, from among psychiatrists, gardeners and carpenters: *the psychiatrists.*

6. **Visit two or three of these experts, in each category. Don't take just one person's word for anything.** Larry went to see three psychiatrists -- the head of the psychiatry department at

the nearest university, plus two in active practice,[4] and (showing them his three-circles diagram, below) he asked them:

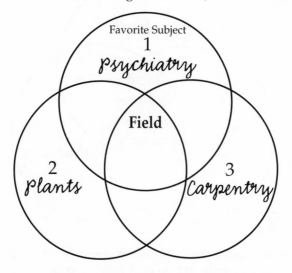

Do you have any idea how to put these three interests of mine -- carpentry, plants, and psychiatry -- together into one field or career? He knows it may be a career that already exists, *or* it may be he will have to create this career for himself.

7. **If the experts don't know, ask them for a referral.** Experts are good for two things: the actual information you're looking for; or the suggestion of the name of another expert -- who might know what they don't.

In Larry's case, he kept going until he found how you can put all three of his interests together in one field. A psychiatrist eventually told him:

"There is a branch of psychiatry that uses plants to help heal people, particularly those who have been catatonic.

"That would combine your interest in plants and psychiatry. As for your carpentry interests, I suppose you could use that to build the planters for your plants."

Voila! Larry had found his field, even though it didn't have a *precise* name in his mind, as yet:

---

4. If there were no psychiatrists at any academic institution near him, then he would do all his research with psychiatrists in private practice -- getting their names from the phone book -- and asking them for, and paying for, *a half session.* This, if there is no other way.

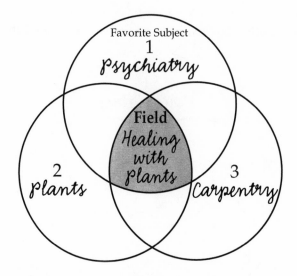

And so can you, if you just follow these seven steps.

When you know the name of a field that uses your three favorite subjects or three greatest interests, put the name of that Field in the center of your three-circles diagram here (or on page 264).

Put Your Three Favorite Subjects
and the Field They Point To
Here:

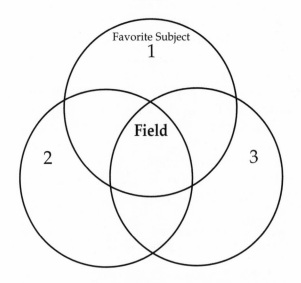

A Sampler of Internet Resources about Fields

Once you've identified a field, you want to find out more about it. There is the Internet, of course. Go to my Web site, if you have Internet access (`www.jobhuntersbible.com`), and then to the subdivision of my Net-Guide called "Research." There, under the subheading, "Research Sites: Career Fields," you will find a list of sites that may help you find information about the field you have chosen.

A Sampler of Print Resources about Fields

There are also resources in print that you can turn to, in your local libraries. They include:

Occupational Outlook Handbook. Department of Labor, NTC Publishing Group, 225 W. Touhy Ave., Lincolnwood, IL 60646.

Occupational Outlook Handbook for College Graduates. Superintendent of Documents, U.S. Government.

Dictionary of Holland Occupational Codes.

Dictionary of Occupational Titles.

Encyclopedia of Associations, Vol. 1, National Organizations of the U.S.; Vol. 2, Geographic and Executive Indexes; Vol. 3, New Associations and Projects. Gale Research, Inc., 835 Penobscott Bldg. Detroit, MI 48226-4094. Lists 25,000 organizations, associations, clubs and other nonprofit membership groups that are in the business of giving out information. There is a companion series of books: *Regional, State and Local Organizations,* a five-volume set, which lists over 50,000 similar organizations on a regional, state or local level. There is another companion volume, also: *International Organizations.* This lists 4,000 international organizations, concerned with various subjects.

Newsletters in Print. Gale Research, Inc., 835 Penobscott Bldg. Detroit, MI 48226-4094. Detailed entry on 10,000 newsletters in various subject fields, or categories. It includes newsletters that are available only online, through a computer and modem.

Standard and Poor's Industry Surveys. Good basic introduction, history, and overview of any industry you may be interested in.

Standard Industrial Classification Manual. 1991. Reprint of material originally published by the U.S. Government Printing Office. Available from: Gordon Press, P.O. Box 459, Bowling Green Station, New York, NY 10003. Gives the Standard Industrial Classification code number for any field or industry -- (often called the SIC code) which is the number used by most business references in their indices. Soon to be replaced.

U.S. Industrial Outlook. Reprinted from material published by the U.S. Department of Commerce. Available from JIST Works, 720 N. Park Ave., Indianapolis, IN 46202. Covers 350 manufacturing and service industries. Gives the trends and outlooks for each industry that you may be interested in. Updated annually.

Information Industry Directory. Gale Research, Inc., 835 Penobscott Bldg. Detroit, MI 48226-4094. Lists 30,000 computer-based information systems and services, here and abroad. Their companion volume, *Gale Directory of Databases.* Gale Research, Inc., 835 Penobscott Bldg. Detroit, MI 48226-4094, lists trade shows, conventions, users' groups, associations, consultants, etc., worldwide.

Professional's Job Finder, by Daniel Lauber. Planning/Communications, 7215 Oak Ave., River Forest, IL 60305. Lists over 3,003 associations, directories, journals, trade magazines, newsletters, computerized job-listings, online services, job-matching services, salary surveys, etc. -- *categorized* very helpfully by fields, industries and occupations -- where contacts may be found, or job-leads advertised. Very thorough.

Non-Profits' and Education Job Finder, by Daniel Lauber. Planning/Communications, 7215 Oak Ave., River Forest, IL 60305. Lists over 2,222 associations, directories, journals, trade magazines, newsletters, computerized job-listings, online services, job-matching services, foundations, grants, and salary surveys, etc. -- dealing with education and all of the non-profit sector -- where contacts may be found, or job-leads advertised.

Government Job Finder, by Daniel Lauber. Planning/Communications, 7215 Oak Ave., River Forest, IL 60305. Lists over 2,002 associations, directories, journals, trade magazines, newsletters, computerized job-listings, online services, job-matching services, salary surveys, etc. -- dealing with local, state or federal government work in the U.S. and abroad -- where contacts may be found, or job-leads advertised. Very thorough. Also, free updates are available online for all three of these books at:

    `http://jobfindersonline.com`

National Recreational Sporting and Hobby Organizations of the U.S. Columbia Books, Inc., 777 14th St. NW, Washington, DC 20005.

Research Center Directory. Gale Research, Inc., 835 Penobscott Bldg. Detroit, MI 48226-4094. Also: *Research Services Directory.* The two volumes together cover some 13,000 services, facilities, and companies that do research into various subjects, such as feasibility studies, private and public policy, social studies and studies of various cultures, etc.

Step Three:

Your Favorite Occupation

WHAT CAN YOU DO IN YOUR CHOSEN FIELD?

Look at your circle diagram. Think about the field you've written there. Enjoy the thought of working in it.

Now, what you may well be thinking next is: "Well, I see what field it is that I would love to work in, but I know there is no job in that field that *I* would be able to do."

An understandable fear! But, dear friend, let me say it gently: you don't know any such thing. **There is some place for your skills, in any field you choose.**

A field is like a meadow, a large meadow. No matter what field you choose, lots of people are out standing in it.

Let us take Movies, Cinema, or the Film Industry as our example.

Suppose you love Movies, and want to choose this field for your next career. Your first instinct will be to think that this means if you don't have skills as an actor or actress, or a screen writer, or a director, or movie critic, there's nothing for you in this field.

Not true. There are many other skills needed in this field called Movies. The closing credits at the end of any movie will show you what those skills are -- and their occupational name:

Researchers *(especially for movies set in another time)*, Travel experts *(to scout locations)*, Interior designers *(to design sets)*, Carpenters *(to build them)*, Painters *(for backdrops, etc.)*, Artists, computer graphics designers *(for special effects)*, Costume designers, Make-up artists, Hair stylists, Photographers *(camera operators)*, Lighting technicians, Sound mixers and sound editors, Composers *(for soundtrack)*, Conductors, Musicians, Singers, Stunt people, Animal trainers, Caterers, Drivers, First aid people, Personal assistants, Secretaries, Publicists, Accountants, etc., etc.

And so it is with any field.

No matter what your transferable skills are, they can be used in any meadow or field that you choose.

PUTTING A NAME
TO YOUR SKILLS

Now, and only now, that you have identified a field where you could happily use your favorite skills, is it time to put an occupational name to those skills you identified (*in the previous chapter*) as your favorite transferable skills.

Here's how you go about doing that.

1. **On one piece of paper, write down your six favorite transferable skills, plus your chosen field.** Put the skills on the top half of the paper, the field that you just identified, on the bottom half. Under the name of the field, add your three favorite interests. Thus, in Larry's case, the bottom half of his paper would read:

Healing with Plants
  (Psychiatry)
  (Plants)
  (Carpentry)

Every field gives you a broad choice between jobs with *people*, jobs with *data*, or jobs with *things*. Let's take the field of agriculture as an example. Within agriculture:

You could be driving tractors and other farm machinery -- and thus be working primarily with **things**; or

You could be gathering statistics about crop growth for some state agency -- and thus be working primarily with **information**/data/ideas; or

You could be supervising a crew on a farm, and thus be working primarily with **people**.

Many jobs combine two or more of these factors, as for example teaching in an agricultural college -- thus working with both **information** and **people**.

You have to decide, after looking at your favorite transferable skills, which of these three would be your priority in your chosen field. Write it at the top of the paper.

2. **At the very top of the paper, now write down whether - - broadly speaking - - you want to work primarily with people, or primarily with information/data/ideas, or primarily with things.**

3. **Choose at least ten friends, family, or professionals whom you know, to show this paper to.** These people should be from as many different backgrounds, education, and occupations, as possible. Try to include, when you can, people from the field that interests you.

4. **Show this piece of paper to them.** Tell them you are looking for names of occupations that would use these skills. Ask each one of them to look at the paper, to look at the skills in particular, and tell you what job or jobs these suggest to them.

5. **Jot down *everything* these ten people tell you.**

6. **If none of it looks valuable, choose five additional people you know in the business world and non-profit sector or your (new) chosen field.** Go show them your paper; ask them the same questions, as before.

7. **Once you've got some worthwhile ideas, go home, and study what they have said.**

SOME QUICK STRATEGIES
FOR IDENTIFYING
YOUR OCCUPATION

Seven Tips For The Impatient Job-Hunter
or Career-Changer

If you're just too shy or too busy (I did not say, 'lazy') to do the above research, here are some quick strategies that may - - or may not - - be helpful, in putting a name to an occupation that you would love - - precisely because it would use your favorite transferable skills.

1

* After looking over your list of favorite transferable skills, ask yourself: which occupational family sounds as though it might match your favorite transferable skills. There are traditionally twenty such families, as follows:

OCCUPATION FAMILIES

1. Executive, Administrative, and Managerial Occupations
2. Engineers, Surveyors, and Architects
3. Natural Scientists and Mathematicians
4. Social Scientists, Social Workers, Religious Workers, and Lawyers
5. Teachers, Counselors, Librarians, and Archivists
6. Health Diagnosing and Treating Practitioners
7. Registered Nurses, Pharmacists, Dieticians, Therapists, and Physician Assistants
8. Health Technologists and Technicians
9. Writers, Artists, and Entertainers
10. Technologists and Technicians, Except Health
11. Marketing and Sales Occupations
12. Administrative Support Occupations, Including Clerical
13. Service Occupations
14. Agricultural, Forestry, and Fishing Occupations
15. Mechanics and Repairers
16. Construction and Extractive Occupations
17. Production Occupations
18. Transportation and Material Moving Occupations
19. Handlers, Equipment Cleaners, Helpers, and Laborers
20. Other

2

❋ If you want a longer list, we begin with the fact that experts can name at least 12,741 different occupations out there, with 8,000 alternative names, adding up to a grand total of more than 20,000.[5] Twenty thousand occupations to choose from! Most of us would find it impossible to choose between 20,000 of *anything*. In fact, we have trouble choosing between 20 items on a restaurant menu!

So of course, experts have produced shorter lists of occupations for you to look at. Some U.S. experts have hacked the 20,000 down to just 1,222 options, because (they say) you can find 95% of the 133 million workers in the U.S. in a mere 1,222 of those 20,000 occupations. (The other 18,778 job titles are filled by just 5% of the workforce.)[6]

And 50% of the 131 million workers in the U.S. are to be found in just 50 occupations (they say). See if any of these sound as though they might match your favorite transferable skills:

The Top Fifty Most Common Occupations

Automobile mechanics, carpenters, electricians, light- or heavy-truck drivers, construction laborers, welders & cutters, groundskeepers & gardeners, electrical and electronic engineers, freight, stock, and material movers or handlers, guards and police, production occupations, supervisors, farmers, commodities sales representatives, laborers, lawyers, farm workers, stockhandlers & baggers, insurance sales, janitors & cleaners, managers & administrators, supervisors & proprietors, machine operators, teachers -- university, college, secondary and elementary school, stock & inventory clerks, accountants & auditors, underwriters and other financial officers, secretaries, receptionists, childcare workers, registered nurses, typists, bookkeepers, textile sewing machine operators, nursing aides, orderlies & attendants, hairdressers & cosmetologists, waiters & waitresses, maids and housemen, cashiers, general office clerks, administrative support occupations, sales workers, computer operators, miscellaneous food preparation occupations, production inspectors, checkers & examiners, cooks, real estate salespeople, and assemblers. *You will note that many of these do not require extensive training or schooling.*

3

✳ If you want to be sure that your occupation is one that is in great demand, here are the Top Ten Occupations In Terms of Number of New Workers Needed By The Year 2006. See if any of these sound as though they might match your favorite transferable skills: Cashiers, Systems analysts, General managers and top executives, Registered nurses, Salespersons in retail, Truck drivers (light and heavy), Home health aides, Teacher aides and educational assistants, Nursing aides, orderlies and attendants, Receptionists and information clerks.[7] *You will note that many of these do not require extensive training or schooling.*

---

5. A description of 20,000 job-titles in the U.S. can be found in any U.S. library, in a volume known as the U.S. *Dictionary of Occupational Titles*. It is known more familiarly as the *D.O.T.*, and is published by the Bureau of Labor Statistics. Some other countries, notably Canada, have similar volumes.

While vocational experts always recommend using this directory, our readers have found it a *terribly unhelpful* book for the end of the twentieth century. As one reader, a chemist, wrote: "While it claims to be updated to 1991, I found that *every* description I looked up was last updated in 1977! [That's over twenty years ago!] I read the description of my present occupation and it sounds quite good. I only wish I was doing what it described. That may have been what a chemist did 20 years ago but with most companies de-emphasizing research it is hardly what they do today." If you want to dabble in the D.O.T. despite this warning, be sure to supplement what you learn there by talking to people actually doing what you'd like to do. They'll tell you what the job or career is really like.

Incidentally, the D.O.T. is currently being updated and supplanted by O*NET (see the next footnote) The Occupational Information Network. For details, if you have Internet access, go to `http://www.doleta.gov/almis/onetnew1.htm`

6. This is the strategy of the U.S. Department of Labor, with O*NET. This O*NET system will eventually replace the D.O.T.'s 12,741 job-titles, with just 1,222 of its own.

7. `http://stats.bls.gov/news.release/ecopro.table7.htm`

4

✳ If you feel, like Rodney Dangerfield, that you get no respect, and you're looking for an occupation that would give that to you, you might like to know what are The Top Ten Occupations In Terms of Prestige. See if any of these sound as though they might match your favorite transferable skills: Physician (Prestige Score: 82), College professor (78), Judge (76), Attorney (76), Astronomer (74), Dentist (74), Bank officer (72), Engineer (71), Architect (71), and Clergy (70).[8] *You will note that most of these require extensive training or schooling.*

5

✳ If you've got bills and debts on your mind, here are the Top Ten Occupations In Terms of Pay. See if any of these sound as though they might match your favorite transferable skills: Physicians (Median salary: $148,000), Dentists ($93,000), Lobbyists ($91,000), Veterinarians ($63,069), Management consultants ($61,900), Lawyers ($60,500), Electrical engineers ($59,100), School principals ($57,300), Aeronautical engineers ($56,700), Airline pilots ($56,500), and Civil engineers ($55,800).[9] *You will again note that most of these require extensive training or schooling.*

6

✳ And, finally, if you like to be 'on the cutting edge,' here is someone's idea of 'The Ten Hottest Occupations.' (No criteria were given, for what makes them the 'hottest.') See if any of these sound as though they might match your favorite transferable skills:

Computer animator, On-line content producer, *Mutual fund manager,* Industrial environmentalist, *Family doctor,* Management consultant, *Intellectual property lawyer,* Priest, rabbi, minister, *Interactive ad executive,* and Physical therapist.[10] *In some cases, extensive training or schooling is first required.*

---

8. Source: The National Opinion Research Center.

9. Source: *Money* Magazine, and *The Bureau of Labor Statistics*

10. Or so *P.O.V. Magazine* says (quoted in *USA Today*, April 11, 1996).

7

❋ Remember, one person's *best career* is another person's *poison*. Before you pick an occupation from a list, you have to first define for yourself what kind of work would make a good 'occupational-fit' for you -- in terms of skills used, tasks undertaken, field of interest worked with, preferred people environment, and so forth. You have to define all that, and until you do, you don't know whether you will thrive in those occupational waters, or sink like a stone.

If these tips give you some useful clues, great! But if not, you know what you must do: go back and do the research suggested prior to the tips here. And do it thoroughly, until you find the name of an occupation that *sounds* as though it matches your favorite transferable skills.

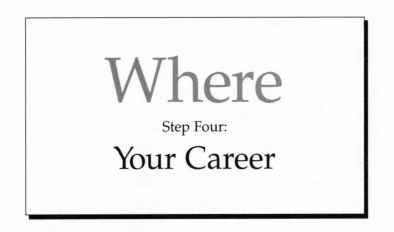

Where

Step Four:

Your Career

PUTTING OCCUPATION
AND FIELD TOGETHER

When you've found the name of an occupation that sounds interesting to you *(you may call your occupation by any name you please -- though one-word or two-word titles are preferred)* you're ready at last to define a career for yourself. Or two. Or three.

Our definition of a career, as you recall, is this equation: **a career = occupation + field**.

In Step Three, just completed, you got some idea of your favorite **occupation** -- based on your skills.

In Step Two, before that, you got some idea of your favorite **field - -** based on your interests and special knowledges.

Voila! You are now ready to put them together: **a career = occupation + field**.

Occupation:

Field:

Once you have a heart, look at both occupation and field, and see if there's some immediately-obvious way you can put them together. For example, if you love to work with numbers, and your favorite field is health, you would obviously want to think about working in the accounting department of a hospital.

WHAT'S
IN A NAME?

All you know at the moment about this occupation or career you have tentatively chosen, is how it *sounds*. What you need to find out, now, is what the job is really like, beneath the high-sounding title.

Where do you begin such exploration? Everyone will tell you: go to the Internet, go to libraries, go to directories. Ah, the wisdom of this world - - if only it were accurate!

The bad news, unfortunately, is that the most dependable and up-to-date information on jobs and careers is *not* found in any of these three ways. It's found by going and talking to *people*.

The reason for this is that last week's absolutely true certifiably guaranteed 100% accurate information *(on the Internet or in printed resources)* about jobs and careers is, today, completely outdated.

Things are just moving too fast. Books can't keep up. They're outdated before they're in print. Even the Internet can't keep up, except on a very few sites.[11] So, if you want to find out if this new career or job *fits* you, **you must go talk to people actually doing the work that interests you.**

This "Bizarro" cartoon by Dan Piraro is reprinted by permission of Chronicle Features, San Francisco, CA.

And if *talking to people face-to-face* is a problem for you, be-cause you're shy, I have a word to say at the end of this chapter, about how to deal with shyness.

TALKING TO WORKERS, 'TRYING ON' JOBS

When you go talk to people, you are hoping they will give you some idea of what the work feels like, from the inside.

You want to get beneath the career title -- say, *psychiatrist working with plants* -- and get some feel for what the day-to-day work is like.

_____

11. Examples of what I wish there were more of, are to be found at: http://www.temp24-7.com/ and at http://www.disgruntled.com/ and at http://ivillage.com/work/

For this purpose you must, as I said, go talk to people actually doing the work that interests you. In the particular example here, you must go talk to actual *psychiatrists who use plants, in their healing work.*

What are you doing, with such research? Well, in effect, you are mentally *trying on jobs* to see if they fit you.

It is exactly analogous to your going to a clothing store and trying on different suits (or dresses) that you see in their window.

Why do you try them on? Well, the suits or dresses that look *terrific* in the window don't always look so hotsy-totsy when you see them on *you*. Lots of pins were used, on the backside of the figurine in the window. On you, without the pins, the clothes may not hang quite right, etc., etc.

Likewise, careers that look terrific in the window of books or your imagination don't always look so great when you see them up close and personal, in all their living glory, and imagine yourself in that career, day after day, month after month, year after year.

You want to find a career that looks terrific in the window, *and* on you. Toward that end, you are trying to find out what *this* career feels like. Here is how you go about it.

• **Get the names of people who actually do the work you are interested in (defined on page 118, on your heart diagram). Use the Yellow Pages, ask your friends.**

• **Make an appointment with them. Ask for only 10 minutes of their time (and keep to it).** If they are very busy, or a professional, offer to pay them for their time. ("How much would you charge for me to take ten minutes of your time, to learn about the work you do?") When you are face to face with them, here are some questions you should ask:

• **How did you get into this work?**

• **What do you like the most about it?**

• **What do you like the least about it?**

• **Where else could I find people who do this kind of work?**

(You should always ask them for more than one name, so that if you run into a dead end at any point, you can easily visit the other people they suggested.)

If it becomes apparent to you, during the course of this ten-minute visit, that this career, occupation, or job definitely *doesn't* fit you, then the last question (above) gets turned into a slightly different query:

• **Do you have any ideas as to who else I could go talk to, about my skills and interests (favorite subjects), so I can find out what other careers or work these might point to?** If they can't think of anyone, ask them if they know who *might* know. And so on. And so forth. Then go visit the people whose names they give you.

"THEY SAY I HAVE TO GO BACK TO SCHOOL, BUT I HAVEN'T THE TIME OR THE MONEY"

If you decide you do like this career you've just been exploring with these people, be sure to add the following question, before you leave their presence: "What kind of training do you have to have, before getting into this line of work?"

Many times, unfortunately, you will hear *bad news*. They will tell you something like: "In order to be hired for this occupation, you have to have a master's degree and ten years' experience." If you're willing to do that, if you have the time, and the money, fine! But what if you don't?

Then, this is what you do: you search for *the exception:*

• **Yes, but do you know of anyone in this field who got into it without that master's degree, and ten years' experience?**

• **And where might I find him or her?**

• **And if you don't know of any such person, who might know some names?**

You will need to check and cross-check any information that people tell you or that you read in books (even this one).

Keep clearly in mind that there are people *out there* who will tell you something that absolutely *isn't* so, with every conviction in their being -- because they *think* it's true. Sincerity they have, one hundred percent. Accuracy is something else again.

Therefore, no matter how many people tell you that such-and-so are the rules about getting into a particular occupation, and there are no exceptions -- believe me, there *are* exceptions *(except where a profession has rigid entrance examinations, as in, say, medicine or law.)*

Rules are rules. But somewhere in this vast world, *somebody* found a way to get into this career you dream of, without going through all the hoops that everyone else is telling you are *absolutely essential.*

You want to find out who these people are, and go talk to them, to find out *how they did it.*

Okay, but suppose you are determined to go into a career that everyone says takes *years* to prepare for; and you can't find *anyone* who took a shortcut? What then?

Even here, you can get *close* to the profession *without* such long preparation. Every professional speciality has one or more paraprofessional positions, which require much less training. For example, instead of becoming a doctor, you can go into paramedical work; instead of becoming a lawyer, you can go into paralegal work, etc., etc.

Keep up this information gathering until you find the names of at least *two* careers, or jobs, that really fit you.

Never, ever, put all your eggs in one basket. The secret of surviving out there in the jungle is *having alternatives.*

Be careful. Be thorough. Be persistent. This is your life you're working on, and your future. Make it glorious. Whatever it takes, find out the name of your ideal career, your ideal occupation, your ideal job -- *or jobs.*

INFORMATIONAL INTERVIEWING

There is a name for this process I have just described: of testing a career by going to talk to people who are actually doing the work you would like to do.

It is called Informational Interviewing.[12] But it is sometimes, incorrectly, confused with other names. Some even think this

---

12. I invented the term many years ago (over the strong protests, I might add, of my mentor at that time, John Crystal, who wanted the word 'interviewing' reserved only for 'the hiring interview'). But the *idea* goes way back in the history of the creative minority. The first one to propose it, at least in embryonic form, was Alphonso William Rahn, an engineer at Western Electric Company. In 1936 he published a book (now out of print) called, *Your Work Abilities.* In it he suggested each job-hunter write a paper describing what functions he knew how to perform; and then show it to everyone. ("Will you take three minutes to read these specifications of what I can do, in case my services might be helpful to you or your associates, either now or later?")

gathering of information is the same as 'Networking.' But it is not.

To avoid this confusion, I have summarized in the chart on the next pages just exactly what Informational Interviewing is, and how it differs from the other ways in which *people* can help and support you during your job-hunt or career-change.

Those other ways are: Networking, Support Groups, and Contacts. I have also thrown in, at no extra charge, a first column in that chart, dealing with an aspect of the job-hunt that never gets talked about: namely, the importance *before your job-hunt ever begins,* of nurturing the friendships you have let slip, over time -- by calling them or visiting them and re-establishing relationships *before* you ever need anything from them, as you most certainly may, later on in your job-hunt.

The Job-Hunter's or Career-Changer's

The Process ⬇	1. Valuing Your *Community* Before the Job-Hunt	2. Networking
What Is Its Purpose?	To make sure that people whom you may someday need to do you a favor, or lend you a hand, know long beforehand that you value and prize them *for themselves.*	To gather a list of contacts *now* who might be able to help you with your career, or with your job-hunting, at some future date. And to go out of your way to *regularly* add to that list. *Networking is a term often reserved only for the business of adding to your list; but, obviously, this presupposes you first listed everyone you* already *know.*
Who Is It Done With?	Those who live with you, plus your family, relatives, friends, and acquaintances, however near (geographically) or far.	People in your present field, or in a field of future interest that you yourself meet; also, people whose names are given to you by others.
When You're Doing This Right How Do You Go About It? (Typical Activities)	You make time for them in your busy schedule, long before you find yourself job-hunting. You do this by: (1) Spending 'quality time' with those you live with, letting them know you really appreciate who they are, and what kind of person they are, (2) Maintaining contact (phone, lunch, a thank-you note) with those who live nearby, (3) Writing friendly notes, regularly, to those who live at a distance -- *thus letting them all know that you appreciate them* for themselves.	You deliberately attend, for this purpose, meetings or conventions in your present field, or the field/career you are thinking of switching to, someday. You talk to people at meetings and at 'socials,' exchanging calling cards after a brief conversation. Occasionally, someone may suggest a name to you as you are about to set off for some distant city or place, recommending that while you are there, you contact them. A phone call may be your best bet, with follow-up letter after you return home, unless *they* invite *you* to lunch during the phone call. Asking *them* to lunch sometimes 'bombs.' (See below.)
When You've Really Botched This Up, What Are The Signs?	You're out of work, and you find yourself having to contact people that you haven't written or phoned in ages, suddenly asking them out of the blue for their help with your job-hunt. *The message inevitably read from this is that you don't really care about them at all, except when you can* use *them. Further, you get perceived as one who sees others only in terms of what they can do for you, rather than in a relationship that is 'a two-way street.'*	It's usually when you have approached a very busy individual and asked them to have lunch with you. If it is an aimless lunch, with no particular agenda -- they ask during lunch what you need to talk about, and you lamely say, "Well, uh, I don't know, So-and-So just thought we should get to know each other" -- you will not be practicing *Networking.* You will be practicing *antagonizing.* Try to restrict your *Networking* to the telephone.

Guide To Relationships With Others

3. Developing A Support Group	4. Informational Interviewing	5. Using Contacts
To enlist some of your family or close friends specifically to help you with your emotional, social, and spiritual needs, when you are going through a difficult transition period, such as a job-hunt or career-change -- so that you do not have to face this time all by yourself.	To screen careers *before* you change to them. To screen jobs *before* you take them, rather than afterward. To screen places *before* you decide you want to seek employment there. To find answers to *very specific questions* that occur to you during your job-hunt.	It takes, let us say, 77 pairs of eyes and ears to find a new job or career. Here you recruit those 76 other people (don't take me literally -- it can be any number you choose) to be your eyes and ears -- once you know what kind of work, what kind of place, what kind of job you are looking for, *and not before.*
You try to enlist people with one or more of the following qualifications: you feel comfortable talking to them; they will take initiative in calling you, on a regular basis; they are wiser than you are; and they can be a hard taskmaster, when you need one.	Workers, workers, workers. You *only* do informational interviewing with people actually doing the work that interests you as a potential new job or career for yourself.	Anyone and everyone who is on your 'networking list.' (See column 2.) It includes family, friends, relatives, high school alumni, college alumni, former co-workers, church/synagogue members, places where you shop, etc.
There should be three of them, at least. They may meet with you regularly, once a week, as a group, for an hour or two, to check on how you are doing. One or more of them should also be available to you on an "as needed" basis: the Listener, when you are feeling 'down,' and need to talk; the Initiator, when you are tempted to hide; the Wise One, when you are puzzled as to what to do next; and the Taskmaster, when your discipline is falling apart, and you need someone to encourage you to 'get at it.' It helps if there is also a Cheerleader among them, that you can tell your victories to.	You get names of workers from your co-workers, from departments at local community colleges, or career offices. Once you have names, you call them and ask for a chance to talk to them *for twenty minutes.* You make a list, ahead of time, of all the questions you want answers to. If nothing occurs to you, try these: (1) How did you get into this line of work? Into this particular job? (2) What kinds of things do you like the most about this job? (3) What kinds of things do you like the least about this job? (4) Who else, doing this same kind of work, would you recommend I go talk to?	Anytime you're stuck, you ask your contacts for help *with specific information.* For example: When you can't find workers who are doing the work that interests you. When you can't find the names of places which do that kind of work. When you have a place in mind, but can't figure out the name of 'the person-who-has-the-power-to-hire-you.' When you know that name, but can't get in to see that person. At such times, you call every contact you have on your Networking list, if necessary, until someone can tell you the specific answer you need.
You've 'botched it' when you have no support group, no one to turn to, no one to talk to, and you feel that you are in this, all alone. You've 'botched it' when you are waiting for your friends and family to notice how miserable you are, and to prove they love you by taking the initiative in coming after you; rather than, as is necessary with a support group, *your* choosing and recruiting them -- asking them for their help and aid.	You're trying to use this with people-who-have-the-power-to-hire-you, rather than with *workers.* You're claiming you want information when really you have some other hidden agenda, with this person. *(P.S. They usually can smell the hidden agenda, a mile away.)* You've botched it, whenever you're telling a lie to someone. The whole point of informational interviewing is that it is a search for Truth.	Approaching your 'contacts' too early in your job-hunt, and asking them for help only in the most general and vague terms: "John, I'm out of work. If you hear of anything, please let me know." *Any what thing?* You must do all your own homework *before* you approach your contacts. They will not do your homework for you.

WHAT IF I GET OFFERED A JOB ALONG THE WAY, WHILE I'M GATHERING ALL THIS INFORMATION?

You probably won't. Let me remind you that during this information gathering, you are *not* talking primarily to employers. You're talking to workers.

Nonetheless, an occasional employer *may* stray across your path during all this Informational Interviewing. And that employer *may* be so impressed with the carefulness you're showing, in going about your career-change and job-search, that they want to hire you, on the spot. So, it's *possible* that you might get offered a job while you're still doing your information gathering. Not *likely*, but *possible*. And if that happens, what should you say?

Well, if you're desperate, you will of course say *yes*. I remember one wintertime when I had just gone through the knee of my last pair of pants, we were burning old pieces of furniture in our fireplace to stay warm, the legs on our bed had just broken, and we were eating spaghetti until it was coming out our ears. In such a situation, *of course* you say yes.

But if you're not *desperate*, if you have a little time to be more careful, then you respond to the job-offer in a way that will buy you some time. You tell them what you're doing: that the average job-hunter tries to screen a job *after* they take it. But you are doing what you are *sure* this employer would do if they were in your shoes: you are examining careers, fields, industries, jobs, organizations *before* you decide where you can do your best and most effective work.

And you tell them that since your Informational Interviewing isn't finished yet, it would be premature for you to accept their job offer, until you're *sure* that this is the place where you could be most effective, and do your best work.

But, you add: "Of course, I'm tickled pink that you would want me to be working here. And when I've finished my personal survey, I'll be glad to get back to you about this, as my preliminary impression is that this is the kind of place I'd like to work in, and the kind of people I'd like to work for, and the kind of people I'd like to work with." In other words, *if you're not desperate yet*, you don't walk immediately through any opened doors; but neither do you allow them to shut.

GETTING INTO
YOUR NEW CAREER

Once you've found a career that really fits you, your next problem is: how do you move into it, from your previous job or work history?

We're talking about **career-change** here. Everyone knows what that is, in a foggy, general sort of way.

But with our equation in hand -- **a career = occupation + field** -- we can now see in more detail just exactly what is involved.

We can see that **a career-change is a change in either occupation or field -- or both.**

Types of Career Change Visualized

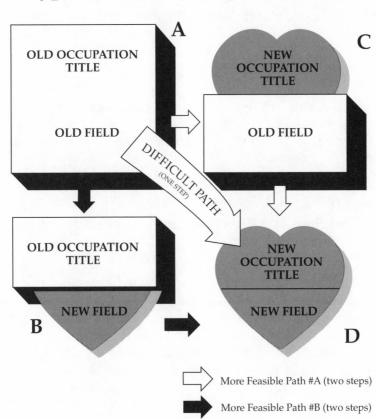

Thus, there are (technically) three kinds of career-change you can choose between:

(1) **You can change just your field** but not your occupation. This is a move from A to B, in the previous diagram. *In spite of its simplicity, this is a career-change. You may become much happier just by moving into a new* field.

(2) **You can change just your occupation**, but not your field. This is a move from A to C, in the diagram. *In spite of its simplicity, this is a career-change. You may become much happier just by changing your* occupation, while you remain in the same field where you are presently working.

(3) **You can change both your occupation and your field.** This is a move from A to D, in the diagram. *This is career-change as people most commonly define it.* You may decide you can only be happy if you change both occupation and field.

HOW TO CHANGE BOTH OCCUPATION AND FIELD

If you decide you want to change both your occupation and your field *(and why not, after all the thought you've put into the earlier exercises in this chapter?)* there are three ways you can go about doing that:

a) **In A Single Bound.** The move can be made all at once (The Difficult Path) -- going from A to D, in a single bound.

b) **One Step At A Time.** The move can be made in two steps (More Feasible Path #A), as indicated by the two white arrows, where you first change only your occupation, but not your field.

c) **One Step At A Time.** The move can be made in two steps (More Feasible Path #B), as indicated by the two red arrows, where you first change only your field, but not your occupation.

To illustrate all of this, let us suppose your present (or most recent career) is that of **an accountant** at a **television** station. You're fed up with it. You want to change careers. You've decided you would like to be **a reporter** who covers the **medical** field. So, your goal is to change both occupation and field.

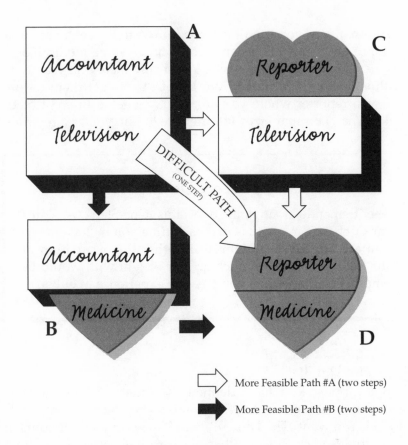

More Feasible Path #A (two steps)

More Feasible Path #B (two steps)

Now of course you could try to make this career-change In A Single Bound -- zowie! Both field and occupation are changed! It's hard, because when asked by your prospective employer what experience you've had in your new career, you may have great difficulty. That's why we call this The Difficult Path.

But there are the other two ways to go, the One-Step-At-A-Time method, that I mentioned above.

Thus, in the diagram above, you can first move from A to C: ask the television station where you already work as an accountant to hire you as a reporter instead, or go to another television station and ask to be hired as a reporter. You'd stay there one year, two, or three; then you'd move from C to D: you'd try to get a job as a reporter at some medical journal, newspaper, or Internet site.

Alternatively, you can first move from A to B: stay an accountant, but get a new job, as an accountant, at some medical journal, newspaper, or Internet site. You'd stay there one year, two, or three; then you'd move from B to D: try to get them to hire you as a reporter where you are, or try to get a different medical journal, newspaper, or Internet site to hire you as a reporter.

"What Experience Do You Have?"

The tremendous advantage of this One-Step-At-A-Time career-change method, is that **each time you make a move, you are already experienced in either the occupation or the field**. This carries much greater weight with would-be employers, than when you have no experience in either.

CHANGING CAREERS
IN A SINGLE BOUND

But suppose you have defined the career of your dreams, and you just can't wait! You want to get there In A Single Bound. You want 'The Difficult Path.' How do you sell yourself to a would-be employer, when you are inexperienced in both occupation *and* field? Good question!

In that case, you must dive beneath occupation and field.

You recall (from the diagram on page 72) that every **occupation** is composed of a series of **tasks** or assignments; and every task or assignment, in turn, requires that you have certain **skills**, to do it well.

Hence, skills must be your preoccupation, rather than titles. Titles are not easily perceived by would-be employers as transferable, but skills are.

You also recall that every **field** is composed of several **interests** or **special knowledges**, such as you inventoried earlier in this chapter.

Hence, your knowledges must be your preoccupation, rather than fields. Fields are not easily perceived by would-be employers as transferable, but special knowledges are.

So, with your focus on skills and on knowledges, how do you prepare for 'The Difficult Path'?

- **You go and chat with three or more people who are already in that job or career.**
- **You ask them:** What tasks or assignments do you have to do, in this job or career? **You follow up on this, immediately, by asking them:** What skills does it take to do such tasks or assignments? *Jot down their answers.*
- **You turn then to your other focus, and ask them:** What do you have to know a lot about, what knowledges are you expected to possess, in order to do this job or career? *Jot down their answers.*
- **Throw in a bonus question (for yourself):** What assets or personal qualities are required, in order to be successful in this job or career? *Jot down their answers.*

After interviewing all three people who are already in the job or career you aspire to,

- **You will end up with three lists: 'Skills Needed'; and, 'Knowledges Needed'**, plus your bonus list of 'Personal Qualities Required for Success in this Field.'
- **Compare these lists with the skills and knowledges that you already possess** (as you found out in this chapter and the previous one). On the 'Skills Needed' list, and the 'Knowledges Needed' list, put a check beside each one that you already possess.
- **Now, when you approach a would-be employer, for this new job or career, you can present yourself as someone who is indeed *experienced*.** Of course you are brand new to both **occupation** and **field**, but you *are* experienced where it really counts -- in the **skills** and special **knowledges** needed to do that job, and succeed in that career. And you can try to show that employer how your skills and knowledges will help the employer get more customers, or make more profits, or accomplish more of their goals. Add in, here, the personal qualities you have, that you know are needed for success in this field. And if it's the right employer, you have a chance, of making a career-change in a single bound.

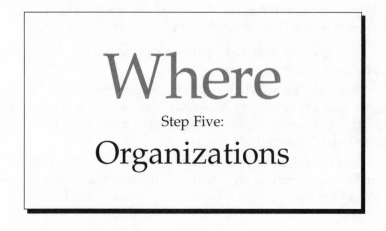

Where

Step Five:

Organizations

NAMES OF ORGANIZATIONS:
TOO MANY OR TOO FEW

You've got your career clearly in mind.

Now is the time to look for places where you can do this kind of work.

Keep in mind that here, as throughout your job-search, you are not looking for names of places that have a vacancy.

You are merely looking for names of places that *interest you*, regardless of whether or not they have a vacancy.

That certainly involves using the Yellow Pages.

It may also involve talking to all your contacts (see page 175).

Or, it may involve picking a pretty street in your town, where you would love to work, and looking at every building up and down both sides of that street, to see what kinds of places are there. (I know job-hunters and career-changers who have actually done this -- and found a great place!)

In any and all ways that may occur to you, you search for names of organizations that interest you.

As you do this search, one of two things will happen:

a) you'll be turning up **too many** names of places where you could conceivably work, or

b) you'll be turning up **too few** names of places which hire people in the career that interests you.

Hence, you either need to cut down the territory, or widen it. Let's look at the first scenario, first.

CUTTING DOWN THE TERRITORY

If you end up with too many names of places that could theoretically hire you in the career that interests you, what should you do? The answer is: **cut the territory down, by narrowing your search** *categories.* [13]

Your Flower Diagram

Your search categories are determined by the information you supply for the petals of a Flower Diagram, that you will find in Appendix A.

You can find directions, beginning on page 263, for filling out that Diagram. To do so, you do some brief, helpful, and interesting exercises, that many readers find to be the most interesting part of this book -- whether they need to cut the territory down, or not.

So, interrupt your journey through this chapter to go to Appendix A, and deal with that Flower.

Once you have the Flower filled out, you are ready to come back here, and proceed with this exercise of cutting the territory down.

---

13. If you resist this idea of *cutting the territory down* -- if you feel you could be happy *anywhere* just as long as you were using your favorite skills -- then almost no organization in the country can be ruled out. In the U.S. alone there are currently over 16 million employers, hence 16 million job-markets, out there. (And a *proportional* number in other countries.) So if you aren't willing to cut the territory down, then you'll have to go visit them all. Good luck! We'll see you in about 43 years.

Let's take an example, to see how you go about cutting the territory down. Suppose you discovered that the career which interests you the most is *metalworking*. You tell yourself you want to be a welder. Well, that's a beginning. You've cut the 16 million U.S. job-markets down to:

I want to work in a place that hires welders.

But the territory is still too large. There might be thousands of places in the country, that use welders. You can't go visit them all. So, you've got to cut the territory down, further. Suppose that on your geography *petal* you said that you really want to live and work in the San Jose area of California. That's helpful: that cuts the territory down further. Now your goal is:

I want to work in a place that hires welders, within the San Jose area.

But, the territory is still too large. There could be 100, 200, 300 organizations which fit that description. So you look at your Flower Diagram for further help, and you notice that under *preferred working conditions* you said you wanted to work for an organization with fifty or less employees. Good, now your goal is:

I want to work in a place that hires welders, within the San Jose area, and has fifty or less employees.

This territory may still be too large. So you look again at your Flower Diagram for further guidance, and you see that on the Things *petal* you said you wanted to work for an organization which works with, or produces, *wheels.* So now your statement of what you're looking for, becomes:

I want to work in a place that hires welders, within the San Jose area, has fifty or less employees, and makes wheels.

Using your Flower Diagram, you can thus keep cutting the territory down, until the *'targets'* of your job-hunt are no more than 20 places. That's a manageable number of places for you to *start with.* You can always expand the list later, if none of these 20 turn out to be very promising or interesting. For the time being, you've succeeded in cutting down the territory.

WIDENING THE TERRITORY

Sometimes your problem will be just the opposite: you can't turn up enough names of places that interest you.

What should you do? The answer is: **widen the territory, by broadening your search** *categories.*

Let's take an example. Suppose in your new career you want to be a teacher.

Where do teachers work? Schools, you say.

And finding that schools in your geographical area have no openings, you might say, *"Well, there are no jobs for people in this career."* But that is not true.

The correct answer to "where do teachers work?" is:
• Schools
• Corporate training and educational departments in organizations
• Organizations whose business it is to run workshops
• Foundations
• Private Research Firms
• Firms which offer educational consultants to other places
• Teachers' associations
• Professional and trade associations or societies
• Military bases
• State and local councils on higher education
• Training academies, such as fire and police

And the list can be further widened. You could work:
• at places that would employ you full-time
• at places that would employ you part-time (maybe you'll end up deciding to hold down two or even three part-time jobs, which altogether would add up to one full-time job, in order to give yourself more variety);
• at places that take temporary workers, on assignment for one project at a time;
• at places that take consultants, one project at a time;
• at places that operate with volunteers, etc.
• at places that are nonprofit;
• at places that are for profit;
• and, don't forget, places which you yourself would start up, should you decide to be your own boss.

All this, for teachers. It is the same with almost any occupation: there are *many* places where you could work. As you talk to people about your job-hunt they will accidentally volunteer information not only about organizations, but also about *kinds* of organizations -- as above. Listen keenly, and keep notes.

Keep widening your territory! And ask for *names* of organizations in each category that you discover.

You may also want to look at directories, that give you names.

If it's smaller organizations that you're looking for, your best directory for names is going to be the Yellow Pages of your local phone book. Look under every related heading that you can think of.

Also, see if the Chamber of Commerce publishes a business directory; often it will list not only small companies but also local divisions of larger companies, with names of department heads; and sometimes will even include the (SIC) industry codes. You won't likely lack for names, believe me -- unless it's a very small town you live in, in which case you'll need to cast your net a little wider, to include other towns or villages that are within commuting distance.

Other directories are listed on page 141ff.

Once you have about 20 names of organizations or businesses that might hire you for the kind of work you are dying
to do, take the three that look most interesting to you, and
do some research on them, *before* approaching them for a hiring
interview.

Every worker in the world takes the measure of their
organization, and decides whether or not they would enjoy working there. Trouble is, most job-hunters or career-
changers do so, *after* they are hired there.

For example, a U.S. survey found that 57% of those who
found jobs through the Federal/State employment service
were not working at that job just 30 days later; obviously,
many of them found out during those 30 days that they
wouldn't enjoy continuing to work there. That's a little
late to find that out! You want to be wiser than that.

RESEARCHING PLACES
BEFORE YOU APPROACH
THEM

Why is it important for you to research a company or organization ahead of time? There are three reasons:

**You want to distinguish yourself from all those other job-
hunters who walk in on a place and say, "Uh, what exactly do
you guys do here?"** Using contacts, the Internet, and books --
you want to demonstrate that you cared enough about the
place, to learn something about it before you walked in.

**You want to know if they need someone with your skills
and knowledge.** You want to know what kind of work they do
there. And what their needs or problems or challenges are. And
what kind of goals are they trying to achieve, what obstacles
are they running into. Then you will be better able to talk about
how your skills and knowledges could help them, once you
reach the interview.

You want to know if *you* would enjoy working there. You
don't want to ignorantly take a job that you'd soon have to quit

because of something about them, that you didn't know or bother to find out, before you started there.

By doing this research of a place ahead of time, you are choosing a better way, by far. Essentially, you are *screening out* places *before* you commit to them. How sensible! How smart!

Okay, so what do you do to try to find out? Well, just ask yourself **what you wish you had known about previous jobs, before you took them**. In that moment after you quit or were fired, as you looked back, what did you wish you had known before you took that job? This will give you your research topics for a future job. For example, you may have wished you had known:

What the real goals of the place were, instead of the folderol they put in their annual report.

What 'the corporate culture' was like, there: cold and clammy, or warm and appreciative.

What kinds of timelines they conducted their work under, and whether they were flexible or inflexible.

What the job was really like.

Whether the skills you care the most about, in yourself, would really get used. Or was all that talk about 'your skills' just window dressing to lure you there -- and you, with rich people skills, ended up spending your time pushing paper?

More about the boss, and what she or he was like, to work for. Ditto for your immediate supervisor(s).

What your co-workers were like: easy to get along with, or difficult? And who was which?

How close the company or organization was to having to lay off people, or on how tight a budget they were going to ask your department to operate.

So, that's what you want to research before you get a job offer at this new place (if you get a job offer there).

Of course **you can't find all of this out** *before* **the interview. But if you're lucky, you will discover some of it.** The rest of it you must try to find out *during* the interview. So, the above topics are your Research Agenda, and they are also your Interview Agenda -- the things you will try to notice or discover during the hiring interview there, should you succeed in 'getting in.'

There are six ways you can discover this information ahead of time. I list the methods here, starting with the quickest and progressing to those which take more time (in order). Most job-hunters or career-changers will start with the easiest level, and progress to the next level *only if* they didn't find out what they wanted at lower levels.

- **Easiest Research:** Friends and Neighbors. Ask *everybody* you know, if they know anyone who works at the organization that interests you. And, if they do, ask them if they could arrange for you and that person to get together, for lunch, coffee or tea. At that time, tell them why the place interests you, and indicate you'd like to know more about it. *(It helps if your mutual friend is sitting in, with the two of you, so the purpose of this little chit-chat won't be misconstrued.)*

This is the vastly preferred way to find out about a place. However, obviously you need some alternatives up your sleeve, in case you run into a dead end here. So we press on.

- **Research Level #2:** The Internet. Go to my Web site, if you have Internet access (`www.jobhuntersbible.com`), and then to the sub-division of my NetGuide called "Research." There you will find a comprehensive list of sites that can help you find out information about companies. Also, you can go to a search engine (try Metacrawler: `www.metacrawler.com`) and type in the name of the organization you're trying to find out more about. See what it turns up. You will find the Internet is better than printed resources if it's a small company that you're looking for.

- **Research Level #3:** What's In Print. There are three repositories for stuff in print:

1) The organization itself may have stuff in print, about its business, purpose, etc. The CEO or head of the organization may have given talks. The organization may have copies of those talks. In addition, there may be brochures, annual reports, etc., that the organization has put out, about itself. How do you get a hold of these? The person that answers the phone is the person to check with, in small organizations. In larger organizations, the publicity office, or human relations office, are the places to check. Human resources may also have some stuff.

(continued on page 142)

A Sampler of Print Resources

You may find these print resources at your local public library (of course), but don't forget other libraries that may be near you, such as a business library or a local university, college, or community college library.

Many public libraries have very efficient database search capabilities, through their computers, and can dig up, copy and mail to you copies of reports on local companies (for a modest cost). For example, one Pennsylvania job-hunter got the Cleveland (Ohio) Library to send him copies of annual reports on a Cleveland-based company. So, if there's an organization or company that interests you in some other city, you might want to try contacting the nearest large public library to that organization's home base, and see what that librarian can turn up for you. (*Please* write and thank them, afterward.)

In addition to public libraries in other cities, there are special libraries located at various places in the U.S. These are listed in:

• *Directory of Special Libraries and Information Centers.* Gale Research, Inc., 835 Penobscott Bldg. Detroit, MI 48226-4094. It lists 22,000 research facilities, on various subjects, maintained by libraries, research libraries, businesses, nonprofit organizations, governmental agencies, etc. Detailed subject index, using over 3,500 key words.

Some of the following books are inexpensive enough for you to purchase, *if you want to* -- from your local bookstore or via the Internet. Browse them, first, if you can.

Other books or directories are *hideously* expensive, in which case *thank God* for your local library.

Indexes/Indices

There are *(mercifully)* indexes/indices to all these directories:

• Klein's *Guide to American Directories;* and

• *Directories in Print.* Gale Research, Inc., 835 Penobscott Bldg. Detroit, MI 48226-4094. It contains over 15,000 current listings of directories, indexed by title or key word or subject (over 3,500 subject headings).

See also:

• *Encyclopedia of Business Information Sources.* Gale Research, Inc., 835 Penobscott Bldg. Detroit, MI 48226-4094. Identifies electronic, print and live resources dealing with 1,500 business subjects. Their companion volume is entitled *Business Organizations, Agencies and Publications Directory*, listing over 24,000 entries, such as federal government advisory organizations, newsletters, research services, etc.

For Researching Large Companies

• Company/college/association/agency/foundation *Annual Reports.* Get these directly from the personnel department or publicity person at the company, etc., or from the Chamber or your local library.

• *The Almanac of American Employers.* Focuses on the 500 largest, fastest growing, most successful corporate employers; available in most public libraries. Covers companies of 2,500+ employees. Plunkett Research, Ltd., P.O. Drawer 8270, Galveston, TX 77553. 409-765-8530.

2) The public library may have files on the organization - - newspaper clippings, articles, etc. You never know; and it never hurts to ask the librarian.

3) The public library has books and directories that may give you information about the organization. This is more likely to be the case if it is a large organization you are trying to research, and not (for example) "a mom-and-pop store." In the latter case, the Internet is usually a better bet, as I mentioned above. In any event, give both a try.

• **Research Level #4:** Getting Information from People at the Organization. If you just can't find out what you want to know from print resources, the Internet, or your friends, you can always go directly to organizations that interest you and ask questions about the place. This is called "Informational Interviewing," as we saw earlier (p. 122) but in this application of it, I must caution you about several things:

At this point in your job-hunt, be careful how you think of yourself. You are not yet "job-hunter," wanting to be hired there. You are still "job-researcher," trying to learn whether or not there would be a fit between you and that organization.

You must first approach the people at that organization whose business it is to give out information - - receptionists, public relations people, 'the personnel office,' etc., before tackling anybody else in the organization. Gather all the printed material they have, about that place, and leave. You can come back at another time, after you've 'digested' what you picked up, there.

You must then read whatever is in print about that organization. You never want to ask questions of anyone at that organization, until you know what questions they have already answered in print (or on their Web site, if they have one). Read all that stuff, before bothering *them*. You should also have visited the library to see what information about the organization is there.

You must then approach *subordinates* to the boss, with your remaining questions, rather than the top person in the place - - unless the boss is the only one who would know the answer.

This is Informational Interviewing, not a plea to be hired.

(continued on page 144)

* *America's Fastest Growing Employers: The Complete Guide to Finding Jobs with over 275 of America's Hottest Companies*, by Carter Smith with Peter C. Hale. Adams Media, 260 Center St., Holbrook, MA 02343.
* *Corporate and Industry Research Reports.* Published by R.R. Bowker/Martindale-Hubbell, 121 Chanlon Rd., New Providence, NJ 07974. Can be very helpful.
* *Corporate Jobs Outlook!* A newsletter published every 60 days, available in most public libraries. Covers companies of 500 to 2,500 employees. Plunkett Research, Ltd., P.O. Drawer 8270, Galveston, TX 77553. 409-765-8530.
* *Corporate Technology Directory.* Lists companies by the products they make or the technologies they use. Corporate Technology Information Services, Inc., 12 Alfred St., Suite 200, Woburn, MA 01801-9998.
* *Directory of American Research and Technology: Organizations Active in Product Development for Business.* R.R. Bowker, 121 Chanlon Rd., New Providence, NJ 07974.
* *Directory of Corporate Affiliations.* National Register Publishing Co., Inc.
* *Dun & Bradstreet's Million Dollar Directory.* Very helpful.
* *Dun & Bradstreet's Million Dollar Directory - Top 50,000 Companies.* Very helpful. An abridged version of Dun's *Million Dollar Directory Series.*
* *Dun & Bradstreet's Reference Book of Corporate Managements.*
* *F & S Indexes* (recent articles on firms).
* *F & S Index of Corporations and Industries.* Lists "published articles" by industry and by company name. Updated weekly.
* Fitch Corporation Manuals.
* *Fortune* Magazine's 500; they also publish interesting articles during the rest of the year, on major corporations, such as *"America's Most Admired Corporations."* Visit your local library, and browse back issues.
* *Hoover's Company Profiles on CD-ROM.* Hoover's, Inc., 1033 La Posada Drive, Suite 250, Austin, TX 78752, 512-374-4500. 2,500 profiles of companies. Includes all the companies in Hoover's books, plus 1,100 more. For Windows or DOS computers.
* *Hoover's Handbook of American Business.* Hoover's, Inc., 1033 La Posada Drive, Suite 250, Austin, TX 78752, 512-374-4500. Profiles of over 500 major U.S. companies. A special section on the companies that have created the most jobs in the last 10 years and those that have eliminated the most jobs. Expensive; see your local library.
* *Hoover's Handbook of World Business.* Hoover's, Inc., 1033 La Posada Drive, Suite 250, Austin, TX 78752, 512-374-4500. 250 profiles of major European, Asian, Latin American, and Canadian companies who employ thousands of Americans both in the U.S. and abroad.
* *How To Read A Financial Report: Wringing Cash Flow and Other Vital Signs Out of the Numbers*, by John A. Tracy, CPA. John Wiley & Sons, Business Law/General Books Division, 605 Third Avenue, New York, NY 10158-0012. Also Chichester, Brisbane, Toronto and Singapore.
* *Macmillan's Directory of Leading Private Companies.*
* *Moody's Industrial Manual* (and other Moody manuals).
* Periodicals worth perusing in your public library, in addition to *Fortune*, mentioned above, are *Business Week, Dun's Review, Forbes,* and the *Wall Street Journal.*

Bothering the boss with some simple questions about the place, when someone else there could have answered your question quite handily, is committing *job-hunting suicide*. Bosses have better things to do with their time, than answering elementary questions from a job-researcher. For detailed instructions on how to do this, see page 125.

If you run into a brick wall at the place that interests you the most, go visit similar organizations -- and use them to find out about 'norms' in that field, which may apply then to the organization you're most interested in.

Job-Hunters Who Are Tricksters

I regret to report that there is no honest, open-hearted job-hunting *technique* that cannot be twisted by those with clever, devious spirits, into some kind of *trick*. This has happened with Informational Interviewing. *Some* job-hunters have thought, "Okay, I know I'm just looking for information at this point in my job-hunt. But wouldn't this be a great *trick* to use to get in to see the hiring person -- asking them for some of their time, claiming you need *information*, and then hitting them up for a job?"

In case *you*, even for a moment, are tempted to follow in their footsteps, let me gently inform you what one New York employer told me he said to such a trickster: "You came to see me to ask for some information. And I gladly gave you my time. But now, it is apparent you really want a job here, and you think you've found a clever 'trick' that would get you in my door. You've essentially lied. Let me tell you something: on the basis of what I have just seen of your style of doing things, I wouldn't hire you if you were the last person on earth."

In this Age of Rudeness, Lies, Manipulation, and Getting Ahead At Any Cost, *you* will want, above all else, to be a beacon of integrity, truth, and kindness throughout your job-hunt or career-change -- including the time you are doing Informational Interviewing. *That's* the kind of employee employers are *dying* to find.

(continued on page 146)

• Registers of manufacturers for your state or area (e.g., *California Manufacturers Register*).
• *Standard and Poor's Corporation Records.*
• *Standard and Poor's Industrial Index.*
• *The Adams Jobs Almanac,* by the Editors of Adams Media. Adams Media, 260 Center St., Holbrook, MA 02343. Gives a sampling of the major companies in thirty-one industries, together with the kinds of positions they are usually looking for -- when they're looking. Has a state-by-state index of the major employers, plus an introductory session on career outlooks and job-hunting. This same publisher has a *JobBank Series* for individual cities, which you can find in your local bookstore.
• *Thomas' Register.* Thomas Publishing Co. There are 27 volumes in the Thomas register. All the manufacturers there are, for 52,000 products and services, plus catalogs, contacts, and phone numbers.
• *Walker's Manual of Western Corporations.* Walker Western Research Co., 1452 Tilia Ave., San Mateo, CA 94402.
• *Ward's Business Directory, 6 vols.* Gale Research, Inc., 835 Penobscott Bldg. Detroit, MI 48226-4094. Updated yearly. Despite the titles, helpful in identifying smaller companies, as well as large.

For Researching Smaller Companies

Hoover's Handbook of Emerging Companies, Hoover's, Inc., 1033 La Posada Drive, Suite 250, Austin, TX 78752, 512-374-4500. Lists and profiles of 250 smaller, emerging companies with high growth rates. A *sampler* for those seeking employment at smaller companies.

Chamber of Commerce data on an organization or field that interests you (visit the Chamber in the appropriate city or town).

Better Business Bureau report on a particular organization that you may be interested in (call the BBB in the city where the organization is located). These reports sometimes only tell you if there are outstanding, unresolved complaints against a company; if the company has scrambled to settle a complaint in the past, their record will now look pretty good. Still, it's a useful thing to know -- if there are or have been such complaints.

People Who Know People

Most of these are consultants within specific fields; often they know companies within their field, and individuals within those companies, by name:

Consultants and Consulting Organizations Directory. Gale Research, Inc., 835 Penobscott Bldg. Detroit, MI 48226-4094. Lists over 15,000 firms, individuals and organizations engaged in consulting work. Consultants are usually experts in their particular field, and hence may be useful to you in your information search about that job or career-change that you are contemplating.

Dun's Consultants Directory.

American Society for Training and Development Directory: Who's Who in Training and Development, 1640 King St., Box 1443, Alexandria, VA 22313-2043.

Contacts Influential: Commerce and Industry Directory. Businesses in particular market area listed by name, type of business, key personnel, etc. Contacts Influential, Market Research and Development Services, 321 Bush St., Suite 203, San Francisco, CA 94104, if your library doesn't have it.

• **Research Level #5:** Temporary Agencies. Many job-hunters and career-changers have found that a useful way to explore organizations is to let yourself be sent out by an agency that places workers for short periods, in short-term jobs -- often called 'temp agencies.'

An amazing number of companies use temp agencies. Whereas temp workers only comprised 10% of some companies' workforce in 1989, temps now represent from 25 to 60% of their total workforce.[14] Hence, you get access through a temp agency to a lot of places, where you can do your research on the spot.

This strategy for exploring places does not appeal to everyone. Some job-hunters and career-changers mentally balk at the very idea of enrolling with a temp agency, because they remember the old days when such agencies were solely for clerical workers and secretarial help. But these days there are temp agencies *(at least in the larger cities)* which send out: accountants, industrial workers, assemblers, drivers, mechanics, construction people, engineering people, software engineers, programmers, computer technicians, production workers, managers and executives, nannies (for young and old), health care/dental/medical people, legal specialists, insurance specialists, sales/marketing people, underwriting professionals, financial services people, as well as the professions temp agencies have always handled -- data processing, secretarial, and office services.

So, check your Yellow Pages, under 'Temporary Agencies,' or 'Employment Agencies,' make some phone calls, and if you discover a temp agency which loans out people with your particular skills and expertise, register with them, and let them send you out. (If they don't ever send you out, go seek another agency.) Hopefully, within the space of just a few weeks, you will get a chance to see a number of organizations from the inside.

It may be the agency won't send you to exactly the place you hoped for; but sometimes by working in parallel organizations, you can develop contacts *over there* in the organization of greatest interest to you.

• **Research Level #6:** Volunteer Work. If you don't wish to research a number of places, because your research turned up

---

14. *San Francisco Chronicle,* 6/30/94.

one place that interests you above all others -- a useful way to research that place is to volunteer your services there, for two or three weeks, at no cost to them, with the proviso that they can terminate you as a volunteer at any time.

Of course, some places will turn your offer down, cold. But others will be interested in your offer. After all, you offer them three sterling advantages: (1) You cost nothing. (2) If you turn out to be a *pain*, they won't have to endure you for long. (3) It will be easy for them to tell you to go.

You also get three advantages: (1) You will learn about the place -- and maybe decide you would never want to actually work there. (2) You give them a chance to see you in action, and if they like you, they *may* want to hire you. I say *may*. Don't be mad if they simply say at the end, "Thanks very much for helping us out." That's what *usually* happens. (3) This is a very good strategy for career-changers, in particular, even if it doesn't lead to a hire. If you are trying to move into a new field, volunteering at this place (in that field) will often get you a very good letter of reference, at the end. So, when you then approach other places, and they say, Have you had any experience in this field?, you can hand them the letter of reference, and say, "Yes, I have."

SEND A THANK-YOU NOTE

After *anyone* has done you a favor, during this Informational Interviewing phase of your job-hunt, you must *be sure* to send them a thank-you note by the very next day, at the latest. Such a note goes to *everyone* who helps you, or who talks with you. That means friends, people at the organization in question, temporary agency people, secretaries, receptionists, librarians, workers, or whoever.

Ask them, at the time you are face to face with them, for their calling card (if they have one), or ask them to write out their name and work-address, on a piece of paper, for you. You *don't* want to misspell their name. It is difficult to figure out how to spell people's names, these days, simply from the sound of it. What sounds like "Laura" may actually be "Lara." What sounds like "Smith" may actually be "Smythe," and so on. Get that name and address, *but get it right*, please. And let me reiterate: write them the thank-you note that same night, or the very next day at the latest. A thank-you note that arrives a week later, completely misses the point.

Ideally it should be handwritten, but if your handwriting is the least bit difficult to read (ranging on up to *indecipherable*), by all means type it. It can be just two or three sentences. Something like: *"I wanted to thank you for talking with me yesterday. It was very helpful to me. I much appreciated your taking the time out of your busy schedule, to do this. Best wishes to you,"* and then your signature. *Do* sign it, particularly if the thank-you note is typed. Typed letters without any signature seem to be multiplying like rabbits in the world of work, these days; the absence of a signature is usually perceived as making your letter *real* impersonal. You don't want to leave that impression.

You care about people. Show it.

Wild Life by John Kovalic, © 1989 Shetland Productions. Reprinted with permission.

STARTING YOUR OWN BUSINESS

We have been talking about how you research an organization, prior to persuading them to hire you.

All of this changes, of course, when there is no employer you need to approach, or persuade, because you have decided you want to be your own boss.

You've studied your skills and interests, and decided they point toward starting your own business. In which case, there's no one you have to persuade. You can just . . . go . . . do . . . it!

It takes a lot of guts to try something new. It's easier, however, if you keep three principles in mind:

1. There is always some risk, in trying something new. Your job is not to avoid risk -- there is no way to do that -- but to make sure ahead of time that the risks are *manageable*.

2. You find this out before you start, by first talking to others who have already done what you are thinking of doing; then you evaluate whether or not you still want to go ahead and try it. *Don't ever overlook this step!!*

3. Have a Plan B, already laid out, *before you start*, as to what you will do if it doesn't work out; i.e., know where you are going to go, next. Don't wait, *puh-leaze!* Write it out, now. *This is what I'm going to do, if this doesn't work out:* ....

The things you want to keep in mind if you're going to be working for yourself are as follows:

Twelve Tips for the Impatient About-to-be-self-employed

1. **If you're sharing your life with someone, sit down with that partner or spouse and ask what the implications are** *for them* **if you try this new thing.** Will it require all your joint savings? Will they have to give up things? If so, what? Are they willing to make those sacrifices? And so on.

2. **Move slowly, if you can.** Experts say that if you have a job, *don't* quit it. Better by far to move *gradually* into self-employment, doing it as a moonlighting activity first of all, while you are still holding down that regular job somewhere else. That way, you can test out your new enterprise, as you would test a floorboard in an old run-down house, stepping on it cautiously without at first putting your full weight on it, to see whether or not it is strong enough to support you.

3. **Decide if you want to go into a business you already know.** Maybe your new business should be something that you've been doing for years - - albeit in the employ of someone else. Now, you want to strike out on your own, and be *an independent contractor*, or *free-lancer* or someone who *contracts out your services*.[15] Fine.

4. **Decide if you'd prefer to start a business you haven't ever done before.** Experts say that the underlying theme to 90% of businesses started up these days is they sell goods or services that save people time. Mail order, delivery services (home deliveries of local restaurants' dinners, or home delivery of grocery orders from any downtown supermarket, evening delivery of laundry or dry-cleaning at the office or in the evening at people's homes, etc.), services rendered at the office (daytime or evening office cleaning services), services rendered at the home (such as home repairs - - especially in the evening or on week-

---

15. If you decide to launch yourself on this path, be sure to talk to people who have been free-lancers, until you know the name of every pitfall and obstacle in *free-lancing*. Where do you find such people? Well, free-lancers are *everywhere*. Independent screenwriters, copy writers, artists, songwriters, photographers, illustrators, interior designers, video people, film people, consultants, and therapists, are only *some* examples of the type of people who must free-lance, in the very nature of their job. Talk with enough of them, even if they're not free-lancing in the same business you have in mind, until you learn all the pitfalls of free-lancing.

ends -- of TVs, radios, audio systems, laundries, dishwashers, etc., automobile repair or cleaning, fixing or replacement of screens or storm doors at the home, care for the elderly in their own homes, or childcare, etc.).

Don't like any of these? Then look around your own community, and ask yourself what service or product already offered in that community could stand a lot of *improving?* Make a list. There may be something on that list that *grabs* you. If so, go do it.

5. **Decide if you have some invention that could be the basis for your own business.** If you have come up with something really wonderful, made a mock-up -- it's been sitting in your drawer, or the garage -- but you've never attempted to duplicate or manufacture it before, now might be a good time to try. Think out very carefully just how you are going to get it manufactured, advertised, and marketed, etc. There are firms out there which claim to specialize in promoting inventions such as yours, for a fee. However, according to the Federal Trade Commission, in a study of 30,000 people who paid such promoters, not a single inventor ever made a profit after giving their invention to such firms.[16] You're much better off, *of course*, doing your own research as to how one gets an invention marketed. Through the copyright office, your library, and the Internet, locate other inventors, and ask how they succeeded in marketing their own invention. Of course one of the first things they're going to tell you is to go get your invention copyrighted or trademarked or patented, before you ever give it into the hands of someone else.

6. **Decide if you'd like to be working at home.** Three hundred years ago, of course, nearly everybody worked at home or on their farm. Only when the industrial revolution came, did the idea of working *away from* home become the rule. In recent times, however, the idea of working at home has been finding new life, due to congestion on the highways, and the development of new technologies. If you're thinking about working out of your own home, apartment, or condo, you would be joining the more than 23.8 million home-based workers who already do this in the U.S., plus the estimated 25 million additional workers who are *thinking* about doing it.

---

16. *San Francisco Chronicle,* 1/26/91.

"YES, THE BUSINESS HAS BECOME BIGGER, BUT FRED STILL LIKES TO WORK AT HOME."

The major problems of home businesses are obvious: conflict between your business and personal life, interruptions, and the like. Bring carloads of self-discipline, and perseverance, if you decide to go this route.

7. **Decide if you'd prefer to buy a franchise.** Franchises exist because some people want to *buy in* on an already established business -- and they have money in their savings, or can get a bank loan. Fortunately, there are a lot of such franchises. Your library or bookstore should have books that list many of these, in this country and elsewhere.

You will learn that some *types* of franchises have a failure rate *far* greater than others, while others should be avoided like the plague, because they charge too much for you to *get on board*, and often don't do the advertising or other commitments that they promised they would.

There is hardly a franchising book that doesn't warn you eighteen times to go talk to people who have *already* bought that same franchise, before you ever decide to go with them. And I mean *several* people, not just one. If you don't like what you hear, but want something in that same field, go talk to *other* franchises that are competitors to *this one*. Maybe there's something better, that your research will uncover.

If you don't want to do any of this homework first, *'cause it's just too much trouble,* but decide to just 'sign up,' you will deserve what you get, believe me.

8. **Decide if you'd like to run a business from cyberspace, from your favorite leisure spot.** It is possible to define a business -- given cellular phones, regular or Internet telephony, fax machine, e-mail, and the Internet -- that can be run from a ski resort or wherever your preferred environment in the whole world is. If you can run a business with these tools, you can operate anywhere -- because these tools, like skills, can make your business independent of one particular place.

9. **Decide if you'd like a special place to be the site of your business.** For example, your dream may be: *I want a horse ranch, where I can raise and sell horses.* Or *I want to run a bed-and-breakfast place.* Stuff like that.

10. **No matter what business you want to start, you *must* go talk to people already doing that business.** If you can't find an exact match, break your idea down into its parts, take two at a time, and go research *that*.

For example, let's suppose your dream is -- here we take a ridiculous case -- to use computers to monitor the growth of plants at the South Pole. And suppose you can't find anybody who's ever done such a thing. The way to tackle this seemingly insurmountable problem, is to break the proposed business down into its parts, which in this case are *computers, plants,* and *the South Pole* -- and then combine any two of these parts together, to define a parallel business. In this case, that would mean finding someone who's *used computers with plants here in the States,* or someone who's *used computers at the South Pole* or someone who has *worked with plants at the South Pole,* etc. From those in parallel businesses, you can learn the pitfalls that wait for you, and how to overcome them.

11. **The secret of success is learning what is: A — B = C.** It is *mindboggling* how many people start a new business, at home or elsewhere, without ever talking to anybody else in the same kind of business.

One job-hunter told me she started a homemade candle business, without ever talking to anyone else who had tried a similar endeavor. Her business went belly-up within a year and a half. She concluded: no one should go into such a business. I concluded: she hadn't done her homework, before she started.

To avoid her fate, you need to go talk to people who started up the same kind of business you are thinking about, and find out from them what skills and knowledges are needed to run this kind of business. Make a list. We'll call that list '**A**.'

Then you need to sit down and figure out which of those skills and knowledges you have, using the inventory you did in this chapter and the previous one. Make a list. We'll call this list '**B**.'

Then subtract **B** from **A**, and this yields **C**: the skills and knowledges needed, that you don't have. You'll have to learn them, or go out and hire them.

Doubtless at this point you would like an example of this whole process. Okay. Our job-hunter is a woman who has been making harps for some employer, but now is thinking about going into business for herself, not only *making* harps at home, but also *designing* harps, with the aid of a computer. After interviewing several homebased harpmakers and harp designers, and finishing her own self-assessment, her chart of A — B = C came out looking like the next page.

A − B = C

Skills and Knowledges Needed to Run This Kind of Business Successfully	Skills and Knowledges Which I Have	Skills and Knowledges Needed, Which I Have to Learn or Get Someone to Volunteer, or I Will Have to Go Out and Hire
Precision-working with tools and instruments	Precision-working with tools and instruments	
Planning and directing an entire project	Planning and directing an entire project	
Programming computers, inventing programs that solve physical problems		Programming computers, inventing programs that solve physical problems
Problem solving: evaluating why a particular design or process isn't working	Problem solving: evaluating why a particular design or process isn't working	
Being self-motivated, resourceful, patient, and persevering, accurate, methodical, and thorough	Being self-motivated, resourceful, patient, and persevering, accurate, methodical and thorough	
Thorough knowledge of: Principles of electronics	*Thorough knowledge of:*	*Thorough knowledge of:* Principles of electronics
Physics of strings	Physics of strings	
Principles of vibration	Principles of vibration	
Properties of woods	Properties of woods	
Computer programming		Computer programming
Accounting		Accounting

From this she learns that if she decides to try her hand at becoming an independent harpmaker and harp designer, she needs to learn or hire someone who knows: *computer programming, knowledge of the principles of electronics, and accounting* if she is to be successful. Her choices here: school, or co-opting a friend, or hiring on a part-time basis.

12. **You must do this research at least twenty-five miles away from where you intend to put your own business.** Why twenty-five miles away? Well, actually, that's a minimum. You want to interview businesses which, if they were in the same town with you, would be your rival. And if they were in the same town with you, wouldn't likely tell you how to get started. After all, they're not going to train you just so you can then take business away from them.

But, when a guy, a gal, or a business is twenty-five miles away -- even better, fifty miles away -- you're not as likely to be perceived as a rival, and therefore they're much more likely to tell you what you want to know about their own experience, and how *they* got started, and where the landmines are hidden.

What's the landmine they're *most* likely to tell you about? Job-hunting. Yes, yes, I know. The whole idea of working for yourself is that you can avoid the job-hunt. *Technically*, that's true. But in another sense, it's not. In many businesses you have to hunt, and hunt, and hunt for new clients or customers (think of them as short-term employers). And you have to do it continuously.

If this is the one aspect of running your own business that you have no stomach for, you should plan to start out by *hiring, co-opting, or getting* someone to do this for you -- someone who, in fact, 'eats it up.' There are such, out there; you will have to find and link up with one of them.

But, by observing **A – B = C**, you can succeed in whatever form of self-employment you choose.

Internet Resources about Self-Employment

Once you've decided you want to be self-employed, go to my Web site, if you have Internet access

(www.jobhuntersbible.com)

and then to the division of my NetGuide called "Research." There, under the sub-heading "Resources for Those Seeking Self-Employment," you will find a list of sites with information about various aspects of self-employment.

A Sampler of Print Resources about Self-Employment

There are also resources in print that you can turn to, in your local libraries or bookstores. Below are the *kind* of books you will find at your local bookstore or public library:

Paul and Sarah Edwards, *Finding Your Perfect Work: The New Career Guide to Making a Living, Creating a Life*. A Jeremy P. Tarcher/Putnam Book, 200 Madison Avenue, New York, NY 10016. 1996. The book features an alphabetical directory of self-employment careers. *Incidentally, they advertise this as "The What Color Is Your Parachute for the Next Decade." For the record, that's the fifth book I've seen, with that claim.*

Paul and Sarah Edwards, *Working from Home: Everything You Need to Know about Living and Working under the Same Roof*. 3rd ed. J.P. Tarcher, Inc., 200 Madison Avenue, New York, NY 10016. Now revised and expanded. 440 pages. Has a long section on computerizing your home business, and on telecommunicating.

Barbara Brabec, *Homemade Money: Your Homebased Business Success Guide*: 4th ed. Betterway Books, 1507 Dana Avenue, Cincinnati, OH 45207. 1992. A very fine book, with an A to Z business section, and a most helpful summary of which states have laws regulating (or prohibiting) certain home-based businesses; it is updated regularly. Barbara also publishes a newsletter, *National Home Business Report*. If you wish more information, you can ask for her catalog, by writing to National Home Business Network, P.O. Box 2137, Naperville, IL 60567.

Arden, Lynie, *The Work-at-Home Sourcebook*. 5th ed. 1994. Live Oak Publications, P.O. Box 2193, 1515 23rd St., Boulder, CO 80306.

Nicholas, Ted, *How To Form Your Own Corporation Without A Lawyer For Under $75.00*. 1996. Upstart Publishing Company, Dearborn Financial Publishing, Inc., 155 N. Wacker Dr., Chicago, IL 60606-1719. For mail orders, write: Nicholas Direct, Inc., 1511 Gulf Blvd., P.O. Box 877, Indian Rocks Beach, FL 34635. This is a classic in the field, with over a million copies sold, through fifteen revisions.

Robert Laurance Perry, *The 50 Best Low-Investment, High-Profit Franchises*. 1990. Prentice-Hall, Order Dept., 200 Old Tappan Road, Old Tappan, NJ 07675. 1-800-223-2348. Since there is a disturbing trend in franchises these days toward higher and higher start-up fees, up in the $150,000 category or higher, Perry attempts to list ones which people can afford; most of them are less than $20,000, some less than $5,000.

PURSUING
YOUR DREAM

Whether you are among the 10% of job-hunters who want to start their own business, or the 90% who are content to work for someone else, hold on to your dreams.

The concept of "a dream job" or "a dream career" has been dying a horrible, rattling death, in the culture of the '90s. In many places, both in this country and around the world, people consider themselves lucky if they have any job.

But dream jobs still exist. They are found by luck, or they are found by the kind of persevering research described in this chapter. Just the right tasks, in just the right place -- that match your favorite skills and your interests.

But dream jobs only begin with this. They are sustained and maintained, over time, by the attitude you bring to them.

> "We who lived in concentration camps can remember the men who walked through the huts comforting others, giving away their last piece of bread. They may have been few in number, but they offer sufficient proof that everything can be taken from a man but one thing: the last of the human freedoms -- to choose one's attitude in any given set of circumstances . . ."
>
> Victor Frankl

If you demand that your dream job be one which is permanent, allows you to 'lean on the oars,' in a predictable setting, with raises and promotions as your reward, then your likelihood of being happy in this world of work is not very great.

Attitude is everything! Attitude has to do with the way you act, but -- even more -- with how you think about things.

So, what attitudes help to make a job into 'your dream job'? These four:

- **1. Think of every job you get as** temporary. 90% of the workforce (in the U.S. at least) is not self-employed; so, you are probably going to end up working for someone else. And how long that job lasts will be up to them, and not just you. If they so will it, your job may end at any time, and without warning. This has always been true to some degree, but now it is even more true than ever -- due to the nature of today's job market.

So, when you go job-hunting, you must think to yourself, "I am essentially a 'temp' worker, hunting for a job that is basically a temporary job, whose length I do not know. I'm going to have to be mentally prepared to start job-hunting again, at any time."

At your 'dream job,' you must take one day at a time, and take it with gratitude. It may not last forever, but while it does last, savor it and enjoy it.

- **2. Think of every job you get as** a seminar. Almost every job today is moving and changing so fast, in its very nature, that you must think of this job you are looking for, as one that will inevitably be a learning experience for you. Think of it as enrolling in a seminar.

If you would make it your 'dream job,' you must love to learn new tasks and procedures, and at the hiring, emphasize this to the employer, and emphasize that you are a faster learner (if it's true).

- **3. Think of every job you get as an** adventure. Most of us love adventures. An adventure is a series of unfolding events that are unpredictable. That's today's jobs, all right! Power plays! Ambition! Rumors! Poor decisions! Strange alliances! Betrayals! Rewards! Sudden twists and turns that no one could have predicted ahead of time, will unfold before your very eyes.

If you would make this your 'dream job,' go to meet the unpredictableness of it all with high spirits, and a sense of excitement rather than dread.

- **4. You must think of every job you get as one where the** satisfaction **must lie in the work itself.** Despite your best research during your job-hunt, you may end up in a job where your bosses fail to recognize or acknowledge the fine contribution that you make, leaving you feeling unloved and unappreciated. So if this is to be your 'dream job,' you must choose one that gives you satisfaction in the very doing of it.

PURSUING
YOUR DREAM
IN STAGES

With these four attitudes, you can not only find but, more importantly maintain, 'your dream job.'

Just remember, sometimes that dream job will be found in *stages*, even as we saw in the section on career-change (p. 128).

One retired man we know, who had been a senior executive with a publishing company, found himself bored to death in retirement, after he turned 65. He contacted a business acquaintance, who said apologetically, "We just don't have anything open that matches or requires your abilities; right now all we need is someone in our mail room." The 65-year-old executive said, "I'll take that job!" He did, and over the ensuing years steadily advanced once again, to just the job he wanted: as a senior executive in that organization, where he utilized all his prized skills, for some time. He retired as senior executive for the second time, at the age of 85.

It is amazing how often people do get their dreams, whether in stages or directly. The more you don't *cut* the dream down, because of what you *think* you know about *the real world*, the more likely you are to find what you are looking for.

Most people don't find their heart's desire, because they decide to pursue just half their dream - - and consequently they hunt for it with only *half a heart.*

If you decide to pursue your whole dream, your best dream, the one you die to do, I guarantee you that you will hunt for it *with all your heart.* It is this *passion* which often is the difference between successful career-changers, and unsuccessful ones.

This letter is from a reader, who pursued her dream, and found it:

"I was a woman who majored in Humanities and then floated around after college in several jobs, which were just jobs. To be honest, I was in my early twenties (which I have nicknamed the decade of terror), and had no idea what I wanted to do. Only, I longed for self-expression and passion in my work. I purchased your book, did some informational interviews, even saw a career counselor, all to no avail.

"Five years later, now, I have come back to your book (the new edition, of course), and identified my values, skills and talents. With my values and skills in mind, I went to the library to research government and non-profit careers, and found myself much interested in the latter. I copied a list of them and began contacting the organizations whose values were closely related to mine: helping people in the community.

"One organization in particular called me back the next day, and asked if I could interview for a professional position with them. I did, explored further to be sure I understood what the job entailed, interviewed a second time, and in less than one month was offered the position of my dreams!

"Thanks to you and your advice on the most successful ways to find employment - - previously, over a period of four months, I had applied for at least fifty jobs from the want ads, with no hits - - I am now happily employed doing the kind of work I like best, and I did so in record time."

A Word to Those Who Are Shy

The late John Crystal[17] had to often counsel the shy. They were *frightened* at the whole idea of going to talk to people for information, never mind for hiring. So John developed a system to help the shy. He suggested that before you even begin doing any Informational Interviewing, you first go out and talk to people about *anything* just to get good at *talking to people*. Thousands of job-hunters and career-changers have followed his advice, over the past twenty-five years, and found it really helps. Indeed, people who have followed John's advice in this regard have had a success rate of 86% in finding a job - -and not just any job, but *the* job or new career that they were looking for.

Daniel Porot, the job-hunting expert in Europe, has taken John's system, and brought some organization to it. He observed that John was really recommending three types of interviews: this interview we are talking about, just for practice. Then Informational Interviewing. And finally, of course, the hiring-interview. Daniel decided to call these three the *'The PIE Method,'* which has helped thousands of job-hunters and career-changers in both the U.S. and in Europe. Porot's "PIE Chart" follows on the next pages:

---

17. John also was the inventor of WHAT, WHERE, and HOW - - which I have used as the basic framework for Chapters 4, 5, and 6, here.

| | **Pleasure** | **Information** | **Employment** |
Initial:	**P**	**I**	**E**
Kind of Interview	Practice Field Survey	Informational Interviewing or Researching	Employment Interview or Hiring Interview
Purpose	To Get Used to Talking with People to Enjoy It; To "Penetrate" Networks	To Find Out If You'd Like a Job, Before You Go Trying to Get It	To Get Hired for the Work You Have Decided You Would Most Like to Do
How You Go to the Interview	You Can Take Somebody with You	By Yourself or You Can Take Somebody with You	By Yourself
Who You Talk To	Anyone Who Shares Your Enthusiasm About a (for You) Non-Job-Related Subject	A Worker Who Is Doing the Actual Work You Are Thinking About Doing	An Employer Who Has the Power to Hire You for the Job You Have Decided You Would Most Like to Do
How Long a Time You Ask for	10 Minutes (and DON'T run over -- asking to see them at 11:50 may help keep you honest, since most employers have lunch appoint-ments at noon)	Ditto	
What You Ask Them	Any Curiosity You Have About Your Shared Interest or Enthusiasm	Any Questions You Have About This Job or This Kind of Work	You Tell Them What It Is You Like About Their Organization and What Kind of Work You Are Looking For.

Initial:	Pleasure **P**	Information **I**	Employment **E**
What You Ask Them *(continued)*	If Nothing Occurs to You, Ask: 1. How did you start, with this hobby, interest, etc.? 2. What excites or interests you the most about it? 3. What do you find is the thing you like the least about it? 4. Who else do you know of who shares this interest, hobby or enthusiasm, or could tell me more about my curiosity? a. Can I go and see them? b. May I mention that it was you who suggested I see them? c. May I say that you recommended them? *Get their name and address*	If Nothing Occurs to You Ask: 1. How did you get interested in this work and how did you get hired? 2. What excites or interests you the most about it? 3. What do you find is the thing you like the least about it? 4. Who else do you know of who does this kind of work, or similar work but with this difference: _____? 5. What kinds of challenges or problems do you have to deal with in this job? 6. What skills do you need in order to meet those challenges or problems? *Get their name and address*	You tell them the kinds of challenges you like to deal with. What skills you have to deal with those challenges. What experience you have had in dealing with those challenges in the past.
AFTERWARD: That Same Night	SEND A THANK-YOU NOTE	SEND A THANK-YOU NOTE	SEND A THANK-YOU NOTE

Why is it called *'PIE'*? [18]

P is for the *warmup* phase. John Crystal named this warmup 'The Practice Field Survey.'[19] Daniel Porot calls it **P** for *pleasure.*

I is for 'Informational Interviewing.'

E is for the employment interview with the-person-who-has-the-power-to-hire-you.

How do you use this **P** for *practice* to get comfortable about going out and talking to people *one-on-one?*

This is achieved by choosing a topic -- *any* topic, however silly or trivial -- that is a pleasure for you to talk about with your friends, or family. To avoid anxiety, it should not be a topic that is connected to any present or future career that you are considering. Rather, the kinds of topics that work best, for this exercise, are:

• a hobby you *love,* such as skiing, bridge playing, exercise, computers, etc.

• any leisure-time enthusiasm of yours, such as a movie you just saw, that you liked a lot

• a long-time curiosity, such as how do they predict the weather, or what do policemen do

• an aspect of the town or city you live in, such as a new shopping mall that just opened

• an issue you feel strongly about, such as the homeless, AIDS sufferers, ecology, peace, health, etc.

There is only one condition about choosing a topic: it should be something you *love* to talk about with other people: a subject you know nothing about, but you feel a great deal of enthusiasm for it, is far preferable to something you know an awful lot about, but it puts you to sleep.

18. Daniel has summarized his system in a new book published here in the U.S.: it is called *The PIE Method for Career Success: A Unique Way to Find Your Ideal Job,* 1996, and is available from its publisher, JIST Works, Inc., 720 North Park Avenue, Indianapolis IN 46202-3431. Phone 317-264-3720. Fax 317-264-3709. It is a fantastic book, and I give it my highest recommendation.

19. If you want further instructions about this whole process, I refer you to "The Practice Field Survey," pp. 187–196 in *Where Do I Go From Here With My Life?* by John Crystal and friend. Ten Speed Press, Box 7123, Berkeley, CA 94707.

Enthusiasm

Throughout the job-hunt and career-change, the key to 'interviewing' is not found in memorizing a dozen rules about what you're supposed to say.

No, the key is just this one thing: now and always, be *sure* you are talking about something you feel *passionate about.*[20]

Enthusiasm is the key -- to *enjoying* 'interviewing,' and conducting *effective* interviews, at any level. What this **P** exercise teaches us is that shyness always loses its power and its painful self-consciousness -- *if* and *when* you are talking about something *you love.*

For example, if you love gardens you will forget all about your shyness when you're talking to someone else about gardens and flowers. *"You ever been to Butchart Gardens?"*

If you love movies, you'll forget all about your shyness when you're talking to someone else about movies. *"I just hated that scene where they . . ."*

If you love computers, then you will forget all about your shyness when you're talking to someone else about computers. *"Do you work on a Mac or an MS-DOS machine?"*

That's why it is important that it be your enthusiasms -- here, your hobbies -- later, in Informational Interviewing, your *favorite* skills and your *favorite* subjects -- that you are exploring and pursuing in these conversations with others.

Having identified your enthusiasm, you then need to go talk to someone who is as enthusiastic about this thing, as you are. *For best results with your later job-hunt, this should be someone you don't already know.* Use the Yellow Pages, ask around among your friends and family, *who do you know that* loves *to talk about this?* It's relatively easy to find the kind of person you're looking for.

You love to talk about skiing? *Try a ski-clothes store, or a skiing instructor.* You love to talk about writing? *Try a professor on a nearby college campus, who teaches English.* You love to talk about physical exercise? *Try a trainer, or someone who teaches physical therapy.*

Once you've identified someone you think shares your enthusiasm, you then go talk with them. When you are face-to-face with your *fellow enthusiast,* the first thing you must do is relieve their understandable anxiety. *Everyone* has had someone visit them who has stayed too long, who has worn out their welcome. If your *fellow enthusiast* is worried about you staying too long, they'll be so preoccupied with this that they won't hear a word you are saying.

So, when you first meet them, ask for *ten minutes of their time, only.* Period. Stop. Exclamation point. And watch your wristwatch *like a hawk,* to be sure

20. This is what the late Joseph Campbell used to call 'your bliss.'

you stay no longer. *Never* stay longer, unless they *beg* you to. And I mean, *beg, beg, beg.*[21]

Once they've agreed to give you ten minutes, you tell them why you're there -- that you're trying to get comfortable about talking with people, for information -- and you understand that you two share a mutual interest, which is . . .

Then what? Well, a topic may have its own unique set of questions. For example, I love movies, so if I met someone who shared this interest, my first question would be, "What movies have you seen lately?" And so on. If it's a topic you love, and often talk about, you'll *know* what kinds of questions you begin with. But, if no such questions come to mind, no matter how hard you try, the following ones have proved to be good conversation starters for thousands of job-hunters and career-changers before you, no matter what their topic or interest.

So, look these over, memorize them *(or copy them on a little card that fits in the palm of your hand),* and give them a try:

Questions Shy People Can Practice With

Addressed to the person you're doing the Practice Interviewing with:

- How did you get involved with/become interested in this? (*"This"* is the hobby, curiosity, aspect, issue, or enthusiasm, that you are so interested in.)
- What do you like the most about it?
- What do you like the least about it?
- Who else would you suggest I go talk to that shares this interest?
- Can I use your name?
- May I tell them it was you who recommended that I talk with them?
- *Then, choosing one person off the list of several names they may have given you, you say,* Well, I think I will begin by going to talk to this person. Would you be willing to call ahead for me, so they will know who I am, when I go over there?

---

21. A polite, "Oh do you have to go?" should be understood for what it is: politeness. Your response should be, "Yes, I promised to only take ten minutes of your time, and I want to keep to my word." This will almost always leave a *very* favorable impression behind you.

Incidentally, during *this* Practice Interviewing, it's perfectly okay for you to take someone with you -- preferably someone who is more outgoing than you feel you are. And on the first few interviews, let them take the lead in the conversation, while you watch to see how they do it.

Once it is *your turn* to conduct the interview, it will by that time usually be easy for you to figure out what to talk about.

Alone or with someone, keep at this Practice Interviewing until you feel very much at ease in talking with people and asking them questions about things you are curious about.

In all of this, *fun* is the key. If you're having fun, you're doing it right. If you're not having fun, you need to keep at it, until you are. It may take your seeing four people. It may take ten. Or twenty. You'll know.

Summary of This Chapter

There is no limit to what you can find out about Where you'd like to work -- careers, and places which hire for those careers -- if you go out and talk to people. When you find places that interest you, it is irrelevant whether they happen to have a vacancy, or not. In this dance of life, called the job-hunt, you get to decide first of all, through your research, whether or not *you* want them. Only after you have decided that, is it appropriate to ask -- as in the next chapter -- if they also want you.

You're a bunch of jackasses. You work your rear ends off in a trivial course that no one will ever care about again. You're not willing to spend time researching a company that you're interested in working for. Why don't you decide who you want to work for and go after them?

Professor Albert Shapiro,
*The late William H. Davis Professor
of The American Free Enterprise System
at Ohio State University*

CHAPTER SIX

The Systematic Approach To
Career-Change
And Job-Hunting

How

DO YOU OBTAIN SUCH A JOB?

You Must Identify
The Person Who Has The Power to Hire You,
and Show Them How Your Skills
Can Help Them With Their Goals

Chapter 6

'I'll tell you why I want this job. I thrive on challenges.
I like being stretched to my full capacity. I like solving problems.
Also, my car is about to be repossessed.'

Okay, so you've decided *what* skills you most enjoy using.

And you've decided *where* you would like to use them.

Now you've come to the point of it all: *how* do you find such a job? As we saw in chapter 3, the jobs are always out there *but* finding them can be slow and painstaking work.

You must be mentally (and financially) prepared for your job-search to last a lot longer than you think it will. Even the shortest job-hunt lasts between two and eighteen weeks, depending on a variety of factors -- what kind of job you are looking for, where you are living, how old you are, how high you are aiming, and what the state is of the local economy.

Be mentally prepared for it to take eighteen weeks or longer. Experienced outplacement people have long claimed that your search for one of the jobs that are out there will probably take one month for every $10,000 of salary that you are seeking. This may be pure drivel, but you get the picture, don't you?

You, of course - - the Impatient Job-Hunter - - want to know how to do your job-search *faster.* Okay, here are some tips.

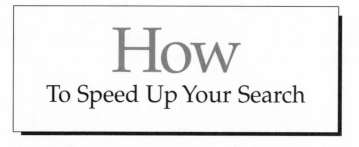

How
To Speed Up Your Search

Tips for the Impatient Job-Hunter

Here are twelve ways to speed up your job-search:

1

❋ **Treat your job-hunt as a full-time job, just like any other - - 'punch in' at 9, and 'punch out' at 5**. Don't buy the world's idea that you are 'unemployed.' As of this minute, you have a full-time job (without pay). Your new job-title is "Job-hunter" (or "Career-changer").

The swiftness with which you complete your job-search is usually directly proportional to time you spend on it.

Studies have revealed the depressing fact that two-thirds of all job-hunters spend only 5 hours a week (or less) hunting for a job.[1]

If you would speed it up, you must spend 35 hours a week working at it from 9 to 5 every weekday (giving yourself one hour off for lunch or 'flake-out' time). That should cut down, dramatically, the number of weeks it takes you to find work.

To illustrate, let us imagine a woman job-hunter who devotes only 5 hours a week to her search; and it turns out, in the end, to take 30 weeks, before she finds a job. That means it took a total of 150 hours.

---

1. According to the U.S. Census Bureau, discussed in "Job Search Assistance Programs: Implications for the School," authored by the late Robert G. Wegmann, and first appearing in *Phi Delta Kappan,* December 1979, pp. 271ff.

Now let us suppose that same job-hunter were to be hurled back in time, but this time she knew it was going to take 150 hours. Therefore she decides to give 35 hours a week to the task, in order to 'eat up' the 150 hours faster. As you can figure out for yourself, her 150 hour job-hunt should then take little more than 4 weeks, before she found work - - other things being equal.[2]

2

* **Find some kind of support group**, so that you don't have to face the job-hunt all by yourself. Ever. You'd be amazed how much the support of others can keep you going and speed up your job-hunt. Here are the kinds of support groups you can choose from:

a. **Your mate or partner, grandparent, brother or sister, or best friend.** A loving 'taskmaster' is what you need. Someone who will make a regular weekly appointment to meet with you, check you out on what you've done that week, and be very stern with you if you've done little or nothing since you last met. You want understanding, sympathy, and discipline. If your mate, brother or sister, or best friend, can offer you all of these, run - - do not walk - - to enlist them immediately.

b. **Job-hunting groups that already exist in your city or town**, such as "Forty Plus" clubs, "Experience Unlimited" groups, job-hunt classes at your local Federal/state employment offices, or at the local Chamber of Commerce, or at your local college or community college, or at your local Adult Education center, or at your local church, synagogue, or place of worship.[3] The likelihood that such help is available in your community increases dramatically for you if you are from cer-

---

2. Of course, there are some factors beyond a job-hunter's control, that may prolong the job-hunt, such as how long it takes an interviewing-committee to schedule the next round of interviews at the place that interests you (you will often be invited back two or three times before they make up their mind about you), etc. Nonetheless, the main point of our illustration still remains.

3. A U.S. listing of *some* of these kinds of places is to be found in the *National Business Employment Weekly*, on its pages called "Calendar of Career Events." It's available on many newsstands, $3.95 an issue, or you can order six issues for $19 directly from: National Business Employment Weekly, P.O. Box 435, Chicopee, MA 01021-0435. Their phone is: 800-JOB-HUNT. (That's 562-4868) ext. 193.

tain groups held to be disadvantaged, such as low income, or welfare recipients, or youth, or displaced workers, etc. Ask around.

c. **A local career counselor.** I grant you that career counselors aren't usually thought of as 'a support group.' But many of them do have group sessions; and even by themselves they can be of inestimable support. If you can afford their services, and none of the above suggestions have worked, this is a good fall-back strategy. Before choosing such a counselor, however, *please* read pages 306–315 in the back of this book. It will tell you how to locate such counselors, and how to evaluate them.

d. **A job-hunting group that doesn't currently exist, but that you could help form.** Some enterprising job-hunters, unable to locate any group, have formed their own by running an ad in the local newspaper, near the "help wanted" listings. *"Am currently job-hunting, would like to meet weekly with other job-hunters for mutual support and encouragement. Propose using 'What Color Is Your Parachute?' as our guide."* Enlist your priest, minister, rabbi or religious leader, at your local church, synagogue or religious centre, to help find a place to meet.

3

✳ **Enlist your contacts. Tell them what kind of work you're looking for, and ask for their help in getting leads. It takes about eighty pairs of eyes, and ears, to speed up your job-search. Your contacts *are* those eyes and ears.**

This subject of contacts is widely misunderstood. It is often defined as "business contacts," leading many job-hunters to say, "I don't have any contacts." Oh yes you do.

Every person you know, is a contact.
Every member of your family.
Every friend of yours.
Every person in your address book.
All the people whose e-mail addresses you have.
Every person on your Christmas-card list or its equivalent.
Every person in your church, synagogue, mosque, or religious assembly.
Every co-worker you've ever had.

Every doctor, or medical professional you know.

Every one who does personal work on you: your barber, hairdresser, manicurist, physical trainer, body worker, and the like.

Every person you know at your gym or in your athletic pursuits. Every leisure partner you walk with, play golf or tennis with, etc.

The waiters, waitresses, and manager of your favorite restaurants.

Every merchant you know, every gas station attendant.

The tellers, manager and friends at the place where you bank.

Every person you meet in line at the supermarket or bank.

Every professor, teacher, etc. you once knew or maybe still know how to get a hold of.

Every person who comes to do repairs or maintenance work for you.

Every person you know at any group you belong to.

Every person you met at any party.

Every person you meet, stumble across, or blunder into, during your job-hunt, whose name, address, and phone number you have the grace to ask for. (Always have the grace to ask for it.)

4

✳ **Expand your contacts.** There are five ways to 'grow' your contact list:

(1) **Attend lectures.** Some job-hunters make it a point to join the crowd that gathers 'round a speaker at the end of a talk, and -- with notepad poised -- ask such questions as: "Is there anything special that people with my expertise can do?" And here they mention their *generalized* job-title: computer scientist, health professional, chemist, writer, or whatever. Very useful information has thus been turned up. You can also go up to the speaker afterwards, and ask if you can contact him or her for further information -- "and at what address (e-mail or otherwise)?"

(2) **Attend conventions in your chosen field.** These likewise afford rich opportunities to make contacts. Says one college

graduate: "I snuck into the Cable Advertisers Convention at the Waldorf in N.Y.C. That's how I got my job."

(3) **Leave a message on your answering machine, if you have one.** One job-hunter used the following message: " Hi! This is Sandra. Being recently laid-off, I'm busy right now, out looking for a job in the accounting department of some hospital. Leave me a message after the beep, and if you happen to have any leads or contacts for me, be sure to mention that too, along with your phone number. Thanks a lot."

(4) **Study the *things* that you like to work with, and then write to the manufacturer of that *thing* to ask them for a list of places in your geographical area which use that *thing*.** For example, if you like to work on a particular machine, you would write to the manufacturer of that machine, and ask for names of organizations in your geographical area which use that machine. Or if you like to work in a particular environment, think of the supplies used in that environment. Let's say you love darkrooms. You think of what brand equipment or supplies is usually used in darkrooms, and then you contact the sales manager of the company that makes those supplies, to ask where his (or her) customers are. Some sales managers will not be at all responsive to such an inquiry; but others graciously will, and thus you may gain some very helpful leads.

As you expand your contacts list, you may find it helpful to set up a file with 3×5 cards, putting on each the name of one contact of yours, with address, phone number, and anything you know about where they work or who they know that may be of use at a later date.

Go back over those cards frequently. This is the way you stay in touch with the eighty pairs of eyes and ears that you need to speed up your job-search.

5

⁕ **Go after any place that interests you. Pay no attention to whether or not there is a known vacancy at that place.** If you base your job-hunt just on places where there is a known vacancy -- advertised in newspapers or posted on the Internet -- you will prolong your search forever! Vacancies often develop at places long before any notice is put out that that vacancy exists.

Moreover, when bosses or managers are thinking of creating a new position, this intention often lies in their mind for quite some time before they get around to doing anything about it. If you contact them during that opportune quiet period, you come as the answer to their prayers.

Be prepared always to tell them what makes you different from nineteen other people who can do the same thing that you do.

And don't be put off by rejection. If they have nothing to offer you, ask them if they know of anyone else who might be hiring. Thank them kindly for any leads they may give you.

Keep going until you find someone who is hiring at a place that you like.

6

✶ **Go after organizations with twenty or less employees.** There is a natural tendency for job-hunters to focus their job-hunt only on large, well-known organizations, and when they can't find a job at any of these places, they assume that no one is hiring. Indeed, some job-hunters just read the newspaper and if they read that large organizations are laying off lots of people through mergers and downsizings, they just assume things are bad everywhere. This is a very common, and very costly, mistake.

The fact is, small companies -- with 100 or less employees -- have been creating two out of every three new positions since 1970, even in the worst of times. For example, while the Fortune 500 companies in the U.S. were cutting 3.7 million jobs from their payrolls during the 1980s, smaller companies created 19 million new jobs.[4] You can therefore speed up your job-search by concentrating on small firms in your field that are within commuting distance, and have one hundred or less employees. (Personally, I would *begin* with firms that have twenty or less employees.) The way to locate these is through the Yellow Pages listings in your field.

Look in particular for small businesses that seem to be on their way up -- growing, and expanding.[5] The way to locate

---

4. *The San Francisco Chronicle*, 2/1/93.

these is by reading the business news in your daily newspaper, and talking to everyone you can, including the local Chamber of Commerce, to find out which small businesses are growing and expanding -- companies like Apple Computer which started out in a garage, or ASK Group, of Mountain View, California, which started out in a spare bedroom. Target any place that interests you.

7

✳ **Don't just send a resume to a place that interests you; visit the place**. If you want to speed up your job-search, you should physically go to any place that interests you, which might hire someone with your skills. Studies show that 47.7% of job-hunters who knock on doors find a job thereby, while only .06% of those who send resumes do.

Said one job-hunter: *"The very first real job I got was by knocking door-to-door, asking if they needed a draftsman. I got a favorable response at the fifth, but not the last, place I knocked; interviewed a few days after; and was working within the week. I was incredibly lucky, as were they: their current draftsman had given notice that day I knocked. I worked there two years and then went on to a much better position at the invitation of friends I had made at that first job."*

In their pioneering study of the job-hunt some years ago, *The Job Hunt: Job-Seeking Behavior of Unemployed Workers in a Local Economy*, A. Harvey Belitsky and Harold A. Sheppard discovered that going face-to-face at a workplace, even without any introduction or leads, was *the* most effective job-search method if you were a blue-collar worker. Blue-collar and other workers take note.

---

5. "The lion's share of job creation over time," says Bennett Harrison, author of *Lean and Mean: The Changing Landscape of Corporate Power in the Age of Flexibility*, "is contributed by a tiny fraction of new firms." In 1985 there were 245,000 businesses started up, but just 735 of them accounted for 75% of the employment gains between 1985 and 1988. *Paying attention to the business section of your local newspaper, over time, should help you identify which ones are doing the lion's share of hiring. If you lump all small businesses together, the picture is not so rosy. If you're interested in the virtues and defects of small businesses, order the 1998 report,* **Small Consolation**, *from the Economic Policy Institute, at 1-800-EPI-4844, or visit* `http://epinet.org.small.html`

8

* **Visit at least 2 employers each weekday, face-to-face.** Studies have shown that the average U.S. job-hunter only contacts six employers a month. That adds up to little more than one employer per week.[6]

They further learned that if a job-hunter contacted two employers a week, the job-search typically lasted up to a year; if ten employers a week, the search typically ended with a job within six months or less; *and,* at twenty employers a week, the search time typically dropped to 90 days or less.[7]

So, determine to visit two employers per weekday, one in the morning and one in the afternoon (at least). Do this for as many weeks (or months) as your job-hunt may last. Thus you will greatly shorten the length of your job-hunt.

9

* **When all other approaches fail, canvass by telephone.** If you've tried all other ways to speed up your job-search, and failed, telephoning is your fall-back strategy.[8]

The strategy experts suggest is: call up, one by one, every single company or organization in the Yellow Pages (in your area) that looks interesting to you, to ask them if they might be hiring, for the kind of work you do. Call as many as 100 or 200 per day! It is almost guaranteed to turn up something, just by the sheer weight of numbers.

---

6. A survey cited by the late Robert G. Wegmann in "Job Search Assistance: A Review," in the *Journal of Employment Counseling,* December 1979, p. 212.

7. Goodrich & Sherwood Co., reported in "How to Succeed in Rotten Times," Oct. 1992.

8. Some experts hold the opposite view: never, never use the telephone, they say, because it only makes it easier for the employer to screen you out over the phone.

Nonetheless, all the *successful* group job-search programs that I have studied over the years, from Nathan Azrin's Job Club to Dean Curtis's Welfare Reform programs, based on the Dave Perschau/Chuck Hoffman model, have attributed their great success rates precisely to their heavy use of the telephone.

Nathan had job-hunters make at least 10 phone calls a day; Chuck had them make 100 phone calls in the morning, and 100 in the afternoon. Both were successful, Chuck's program the more so. The implication is clear: the more phone calls you make, the faster you're likely to find a job.

Personally, I infinitely prefer knocking on their doors to phoning them up. But if you're 'striking out' with every other method, and you're really desperate to speed things up, telephoning does work. Naturally, you first have to get over your distaste for the idea -- most people *hate* doing (not to mention receiving) telephone solicitations. But this is on behalf of your own job-search, rather than selling a product.

Here's how to do it, according to job-search veterans:

Plan how many calls a day you're going to try to make, and stick to that goal. Some experts advise you to make 200 calls a day. Others advise fewer calls, making them only to places that *really* interest you, and only after researching each place, before you call.

Stand up when you make your phone calls; your voice is more forceful that way.

Have a mirror in front of you, on the wall, at eye level, so you can watch yourself in it, to see if you are smiling as you talk.

If you're only making a few calls that day, call before 8 a.m. shortly before noon, or after 5 p.m. If it's managers you're seeking, and if they're hardworking, they're likely to be there at those times -- without an intervening receptionist. Of course if you're trying to make 100, 200 phone calls a day, this rule goes out the window.

When you are connected, ask to speak with 'the manager.' In smaller organizations this is the person who will usually know the hiring plans there.

If someone suggested you call this manager, use their name as a reference when you call. Something like this: "Hi! Your name was given to me by . . . ." Alternatively, try to start the call with any connection there may be between you and the caller. "I just read that you . . . and as it turns out I. . . ." (e.g., "I just read that you grew up in Wisconsin, and as it turns out, so did I." *If you can't find a connection, don't invent one.*)

Try to keep your 'little speech' down to fifteen seconds or less. When the manager comes on the line, address them by name, introduce yourself by name, and then *briefly* (in one sentence) describe your greatest personal strength or top skill, a *brief* description of your experience, and then ask if there is a job opening for someone with your skills and background. For example, *"I am an experienced writer, with three published books, and I wonder if you have any job openings for someone with my experience?"* If *"yes,"* set up an interview time, repeat it, and repeat your name; if *"no,"* ask if they know of anyone else who might be hiring a person with your background.[9]

Write all this out ahead of time. Before you make your call, set down the objective of that call in writing and the key points (above) you want to make during the conversation. *Write out every word.* This is your *script*; don't try to *wing it.* When you're talking to the manager, unabashedly read what you wrote out -- but try not to *sound* like you're reading it. Rehearse it several times until it starts to sound (and feel) natural.

If the conversation goes more than one minute, add other tidbits about yourself: if you've done something in the community, written articles for the local paper, served on a volunteer committee, etc., work that into the conversation.

Know how to deal with an interviewer's turndown or objections. Try responding with:

I understand . . .

I can appreciate your position . . .

I see your point . . .

---

9. I am again indebted to Dean Curtis, for this advice.

Of course! However . . .

Thank the manager before signing off, whether they have a job lead for you, or not.

10

❋ **To speed up your job-search be willing to look at different kinds of jobs**: full-time jobs, part-time jobs, unlimited contract jobs *(formerly called 'permanent jobs')*, short-term contract jobs, temporary jobs, working for others, working for yourself, etc. Short jobs often turn into longer jobs, if they are pleased with the quality of your work.

11

❋ **Zero in on several organizations, not just one.** One place may stand out above all the rest, a boss so wonderful you would die to work for them. To get a job there would be the dream of your life.

Well, maybe you'll get that dream-come-true. But - - *big question* - - what are your plans if you don't? If you would speed up your job-search, you've *got* to have other plans **now** - - not when that first target runs out of gas, three months down the road. You must go after more than one organization. (I recommend five, at least.)

I have studied successful and unsuccessful job-hunters for over a quarter of a century, now, and the single greatest thing I have learned is that *successful* job-hunters *always have alternatives.* Alternative ways of describing what they want to do. Alternative ways of going about the job-hunt (not just resumes, agencies, and ads). Alternative job prospects. Alternative 'target' organizations that they go after. Alternative ways of approaching employers. And so on, and so forth.

So, if you would speed up your search, be sure you have more than one employer that you are pursuing at any one time.

12

✳ **Even if all your attempts to speed up your job-search don't seem to be paying off, don't give up.** One job-hunter out of every three becomes an unsuccessful job-hunter *simply because* they abandon their search prematurely. And if you ask them why they abandoned it, they say, "I didn't think it was going to be this hard; I didn't think it was going to take this long."

In other words, what 'does in' so many job-hunters is some *unspoken* mental quota in our head, which goes something like this: *I expect I'll be able to find a job after about 30 phone calls, 15 calls in person, and three interviews.* We go about our job-hunt, fill or exceed those quotas, and then give up. Don't let this happen to you.

Keep going until you find a job. **Persistence** is the name of the game. *Persistent* means being willing to go back to places that interested you, at least a couple of times in the following months, to see if by any chance their 'no vacancy' situation has changed.

The one thing an individual needs above everything else is hope, and hope is born of persistence.

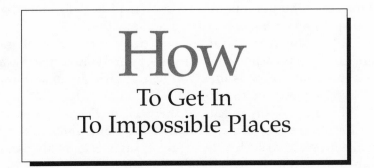

How
To Get In
To Impossible Places

Okay, so you try all these tips for speeding up your job-search, and you're frustrated *because* . . .

You've found a place where you'd *really* like to work. But, the person you'd have to see, in order to get hired there, is in an office castle with fifty-foot walls, with a ring of fire around it, three knights in full-armor guarding it, totally surrounded by a wide moat whose deep waters are filled with hungry alligators.

And you want to know how to get a hiring-interview with this person. Right? Well, it isn't as difficult as it might at first seem . . . if you are determined. Here are the rules:

Find Out How Large The Place Is

Most discussions of job-interviewing proceed from a false assumption: they *assume* you are going to approach a large organization -- you know, the ones where you need a floor-plan of the building, and an alphabetical directory of the staff -- with a large site on the Internet. But, actually many job-hunters don't want to work for a behemoth like that. They want a small organization.

This distinction is important, because the techniques for getting in a small organization vs. a large organization vary greatly.

Getting Into A Small Organization Is 'A Piece of Cake'

We said earlier that a job-hunter is well-advised to concentrate on small organizations. But there is more to be said on the subject.

From a job-hunter's point of view, small organizations have five distinct advantages over large organizations:

1. With a small organization, **you don't need to wait until there's a *known* vacancy, because they rarely advertise vacancies even when there is one.** You just go over there and ask if they need someone with your skills and knowledge.

2. With a small organization, **there is no Personnel or Human Resources Department to screen you out.** Only 15% of all organizations have such a department; small organizations usually belong to the 85% who don't.

3. With a small organization, **there's no problem in identifying the person-who-has-the-power-to-hire-you.** It's *the boss.* Everyone there knows who it is. They can point to his or her office door, easily. It's what we call "The One-Minute Research Project."

4. With a small organization, **you do not need to first approach them through the mail; the boss is much more 'available.'** And if, by chance, he or she is well-protected from intruders, it is relatively easy to figure out how to get around *that.* Contacts are the answer, as we shall see.

5. With a small organization, **there is a greater likelihood that they will be willing to create a new position for you,** *if you quietly convince them that you are too good to let slip out of their grasp.*

Add to these five advantages, the fact that small organizations often are 'job-creating machines' - - representing 80% of all private businesses, employing one-fourth of all workers in the private sector, and creating two-thirds of all new jobs[10] - - and you will see why many job-hunting experts say:

Go after the small organizations - - *especially* if you've been pursuing large organizations previously, and getting nowhere. You can thus overcome a lot of barriers, in one fell swoop.

---

10. This statistic, first popularized by David Birch of M.I.T., and 'bandied about' for many years, was widely debated during the '90s by economists such as Nobel laureate Milton Friedman, Harvard economist James Medoff, Steven J. Davis, a labor economist at the University of Chicago, John Haltiwanger at the University of Maryland, and Scott Schuh at the Federal Reserve. Critics often concede that small companies do create a lot of jobs in the economy, but then *sniff,* "Small businesses are not the places you see *the best* jobs," as one economist put it. (The emphasis is mine.) 'Best jobs' mean - - to these critics - - jobs with high pay, high benefits, government-mandated health and safety regulations, and union representation. (*San Francisco Chronicle*, 3/29/93). See footnote 5 for more commentary (page 179).

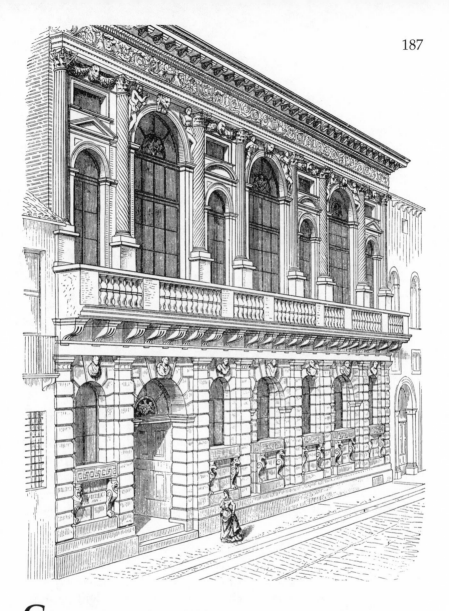

Getting Into A Large Organization Takes A Plan

In getting in to 'impossible places,' it's the large organizations that are the problem - - the ones, as I mentioned above, where you need a floor-plan of the building, and an alphabetical directory of the staff.

There are problems in approaching such giants for a hiring-interview, not the least of which is that many of them are not creating new jobs - - they're playing downsizing, merger and takeover games these days, with thousands laid off as a consequence.

If you approach these places by mail (or resume), you're very likely to be politely dismissed or get no answer at all. And if you go knock on their door, you're very likely to end up in the human resources or personnel department, whose basic job *all too often* is to screen you out. Oops!

Still, there is a way to get in. It begins with three basic truths:

1. You don't want to just get into the building. **You want to see *a particular person* in that building, and only that person**: namely, the person–who–has–the–power–to–hire–you for the job you are interested in. Most job-hunters don't even *try* to find out who that person is, before approaching a large organization.

Rather, they approach each large organization in what can only be described as a haphazard, scatter-shot fashion - - sending the organization their resume or c.v.[11] with some cover letter (or posting same on the Internet) - - and hoping it will haphazardly fall into the hands of 'the right person.'

It usually doesn't. It falls into the hands of 'the screening-out committee,' and it only takes them eight seconds (it's been timed) to scan your resume and reject you.

If you want to get in there, you have to find out ahead of time *who* at that organization has the power to hire you for the position you have in mind.

---

11. C.v. stands for *curriculum vitae*, a term for *resume* that is favored outside the U.S., as well as in academic circles within the U.S.

2. **You want to get an interview with the person–who–has–the–power–to–hire–you** *through personal contacts,* **and not by sending your resume.** Once you have identified *who* at that organization has the power to hire you for the position you have in mind, you then need to discover what mutual friend the two of you might have in common, who could help you get in there, for an appointment. This intermediary is what I earlier called 'a contact' (page 175). Thus, the person–who–has–the–power–to–hire–you will see you because that mutual friend has made the appointment for you, and recommended you.

It is astonishing how often this approach works -- it has, in fact, an 86% effectiveness rate for getting a hiring-interview and, subsequently, a job, even in 'impossible places.'

But let's talk about the 14% of the time when it doesn't work. You will, of course, be furious that you can't get in to see that person, despite the techniques recommended in this section.

But, could I ask you a question: *"Why* do you want to work for such a person? I mean, never mind that you're taking this very personally, with *Rejection, rejection, rejection* flashing on and off in your brain. But, stop and think for a minute: haven't they *(by these actions)* told you something important about *the way they do things?* And having gained that information, isn't it time for you to reassess *whether you really want to work at a place so guarded, so impenetrable, so 'un-user-friendly'?"*

3. **But after you have had an interview with the person–who–has–the–power–to–hire–you, your resume may be useful.** There's an old saying among the creative minority: "A resume is something you never send ahead of you, but always leave behind you."

Which is to say, after you've concluded an interview there, it may be useful to send your resume to the interviewer the next day at the latest. Reason? It helps the employer to remember you. If they had a very busy schedule the day you were there, you may be just a blur in their mind by next morning. Your resume, together with a thank-you note, helps to correct that.

Also it helps your interviewer explain to others in that organization why they are considering you.

Why send the resume the next day; why not just hand it to the interviewer as you leave? Because, when you say truthfully to the interviewer as you leave: "I don't have my resume with me, but I will mail it to you tonight for sure"-- this gives you the chance to go home and edit (and then reprint) your resume so that it is 'individualized' for this particular place, highlighting all the skills or knowledges that the interview revealed they are most interested in.

But do be sure to mail or fax it that night or early the next morning, at the latest! (And since faxes are often blurred, mail them a neat 'hard copy' the same day.)

Incidentally, there is an exception to the rule -- "A resume is something you never send ahead of you, but always leave behind you." You may need to send the resume on ahead when you're contacting some employer who is halfway across the country. Normally, however, this is not the way to try to get in to large organizations.

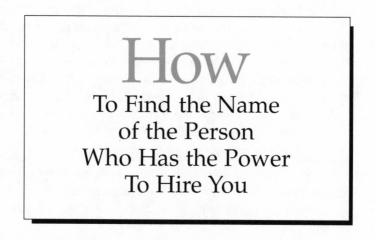

How
To Find the Name
of the Person
Who Has the Power
To Hire You

Okay, let's say the place you're interested in is a large organization called *Mythical Corporation*.

And let's say you know the kind of job you'd like to get there. How do you find out the name of the person–who–has–the–power–to–hire–you there *for that position?*

First Stab at It: You go on the Internet or you go to your local public library, and search the directories there.

On the Internet, go to

`www.jobhuntersbible.com`

and then to the section entitled **Research**, which lists helpful sites such as Hoover's.

If you don't have Internet access, go to the library and ask the friendly librarian for help.

This may give you just the information you want.

But if they don't, there is another way.

One small problem: this takes time, persistence, and lots of determination. It is not a method for everybody, by any means. But, everyone always wants to know, just how do you find information that seems impossible to find. So this is not so much a battle plan, as it is an answer to your curiosity.

Okay, here's how it goes.

Find an insider at your target organization.

You want first of all to find 'an insider' at Mythical Corporation -- not necessarily the person who has the power to hire. Just *someone* who works there.

You go about locating this 'insider' by approaching all the people you know, and asking each of them, "Do you know anyone who works, or used to work, at Mythical Corporation?"

You ask that question again and again of *everyone* you know, or meet, until you find someone who says, "*Yes, I do.*"

Bingo! You've found the insider.

Explore how to get in touch with this insider.

When someone has said, "Yes I do know someone there," you then ask them the following questions:

- "What is the name of the person you know who works, or used to work, at Mythical Corporation?"
- "Do you have their phone number and/or address?"
- "Would you be willing to call ahead, to tell them who I am?"

Once you've been connected, you then either phone the insider or make an appointment to go see them ("I won't need more than 10 minutes of your time.") Once you are talking to them, after the usual polite chit-chat you ask them the question you are dying to know.

Ask the insider who in their organization would have the power to hire you -- that is to say, someone with your skills and interests.

Because they are inside the organization that interests you, they are usually able to give you the exact answer to the question that has been puzzling you: "What is the name of the person who would have the power to hire me at Mythical Corporation, for this kind of position (which you then describe)?" If they answer that they do not know, ask who would know.

Keep going until you find out not only that hiring person's name, address, phone, and e-mail address, but also whatever your insider can tell you about that person's job, that person's interests, and their style of interviewing.

Enlist the insider's help in getting an interview with the person–who–has–the–power–to–hire–you.

Once you have the name you want, you explore whether or not this 'insider' could help you get an appointment with the person–who–has–the–power–to–hire–you there. You explore it with this series of questions, asked each in turn:

• "Given my background, and the kind of job I am looking for *(which you here describe)*, would you recommend that I go see them?"

• "Do you know them, personally? If not, could you give me the name of someone who does?"

• "If you know them personally, what can you tell me about him -- or her?"

• "Do you have their phone number and/or address?"

• "May I tell them it was you who recommended that I talk with them?"

• "Would you be willing to call ahead, to tell them who I am, and to help set up an appointment?"

• Before leaving, you can also ask them about the organization, in general.

But suppose the 'insider' you talked to, knows the name of the person who has the power to hire you but doesn't know them well enough to get you an interview, what then?

Well, then you go back to your other contacts outside that organization -- now armed with the name of the person you are trying to get in to see -- and try to find another 'insider.' Approaching as many of your friends as necessary, you ask each of them, "Do you know Ms. or Mr. See, at Mythical Corporation or do you know someone who might?" You keep asking, until you find someone who says, *"Yes, I do."*

Then of course, over the phone or -- better -- in person, you ask this new 'insider' the same familiar questions, above.

Always remember to thank them. Always write them a thank-you note, *that night.*

All of this does take time and work, but when you've gotten an appointment in this fashion, set up by 'a mutual friend,' you will find it is indeed possible to 'get in' to impossible places.

This technique works also, of course, for a small organization. It is based on a universal human principle: Everyone has friends, including any person–who–has–the–power–to–hire–you. You are simply approaching them through *their* friends.

My favorite (true) story about using this technique concerns a job-hunter I know, in Virginia. He decided he wanted to work for a particular health-care organization in that State, and not knowing any better, he approached them by visiting their Human Resources Department. After dutifully filling out a job application, and talking to someone there in that department, he was told there were no jobs available. Stop. Period. End of story.

Approximately three months later he learned about this technique of approaching your favorite organization by using contacts, and insiders. He explored his contacts diligently, got the name of an insider, and that person got him an interview with the person–who–had–the–power–to–hire–him for the position he was interested in. The employer and he hit it off, immediately. The appointment went swimmingly. "You're hired," said the person–who–had–the–power–to–hire–him. "I'll call Human Resources and tell them I just hired you, and you'll be down to fill out the necessary stuff."

Our job-hunter never once mentioned that he had previously approached that same organization through that same Human Resources Department, and been turned down cold.

Wild Life by John Kovalic, © 1989 Shetland Productions. Reprinted with permission.

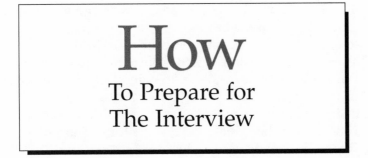

How
To Prepare for
The Interview

When you are asking for the interview with the boss, tell them you only need twenty minutes; and be prepared to stick to your word about this. Don't stay one minute longer! This will always impress an employer tremendously! *(The only exception is if the employer at the end of the twenty minutes begs you to stay longer. And I mean, begs!)*

Research the organization ahead of time, before going in for an interview. In the employer's mind, this will put you way ahead of the other people they may be interviewing.

An employer said to me, "I'm so tired of job-hunters who come in, and say, *'Uh, what do you guys do here?'* that the next time someone walks in who already knows something about us, I'm going to hire him or her, on the spot." And he did, within the week.

So, when you first set up the appointment, ask them right then and there if they have anything *in writing* about their organization; if so, request they mail it to you, so you'll have time to read it before the interview. Or, if the interview is the next day, offer to come down today and pick it up, yourself.

Visit also your local library, and ask the librarian for help in locating any newspaper articles or other information about that organization.

Finally, ask all your friends if they know anyone who is working there, or used to work there; if they do, ask them to put you in contact with them, *please.* Tell them you have a job-interview there, and you'd like to know anything they can tell you about the place.

All organizations, be they large or small, profit or nonprofit, love to be loved. If you have gone to all this trouble, to learn so much about them - - before you ever walk in their doors, they will be impressed, believe me, because most job-hunters never go to this trouble. *They* walk in knowing little or nothing about the organization. This drives employers *nuts.*

An IBM college recruiter was wont to ask a graduating senior, "What do the initials IBM stand for?" The senior didn't know, and the interview was over.

Picture how you're going to conduct the interview. The most important rule you will need to pay attention to is the 50/50, 2 minute max rule.

The 50/50 rule means that throughout the interview you will listen half the time, speak half the time. Reason? It seems they did a study at M.I.T. to see why people got hired. Turned out, job-hunters who talked half the time, and let the employer talk the other half of the time, were the ones who got hired. People who didn't follow that mix, were the ones who didn't get hired. My hunch as to *why* this is so, is that if you talk too much about yourself, you come across as one who is self-absorbed, and blind to the needs of the organization; while if you talk too little, you come across as one who is trying to hide something about their history.

The 2 minute max rule means that when you are asked a question, you try never to speak for more than two minutes, in answering it. Twenty seconds may be sufficient. Reason? Studies have confirmed that this makes a *very good* impression on an interviewer.[12] People who ramble on and on don't get hired.

Be aware ahead of time of what the employer will be listening for. They want any evidence they can find that you would be a good employee, were they to hire you.

They are scared, of course, that they will hire a bad employee. So, think out before the interview how a bad employee would behave in the position you're seeking: such things as - - *comes in late, takes too much time off, follows his or her own agenda*

---

12. This one was conducted by my colleague, Daniel Porot, in Geneva, Switzerland.

"I'm hoping to find something in a meaningful, humanist, outreach kind of bag, with flexible hours, non-sexist bosses, and fabulous fringes."

instead of the employer's, etc. Then emphasize to the employer how much you are the very opposite.

Let me emphasize, here, what are the marks of a good employee in almost any job (this is what the employer will be listening for).

A good employee these days is one who: wants more than a paycheck; is dependable, self-motivated, with drive, energy, and enthusiasm; is self-disciplined, and good at managing their own time; gives 150%; is punctual, arriving at work on time or early, and staying until quitting time, or later; loves to learn, is very trainable, is flexible, and can respond to novel situations, or adapt when circumstances at work change.

Most employers will also be listening for any signs that you are a person who can handle people well; that you use language effectively; can work with a computer; are committed to teamwork; are project-oriented, and goal-oriented; have creativity and are good at problem solving; you are able to identify opportunities, markets, coming trends. And, above all, they are listening to see if you have a good attitude, integrity, and would be loyal to that organization.

So, plan to demonstrate or claim as many of these as you *legitimately* can, during the hiring interview.

Just be sure that whatever you claim is illustrated by your job-hunt. For example, if you claim you are very *thorough* in all your work, be sure your job-hunt looks truly thorough. (Hint: research the company, before going in there for the job-interview.)

Employers know this simple truth: Most people job-hunt the way they live their lives.

Plan **to take into the interview-room with you any evidence you can, of past accomplishments.** A portfolio, photographs, documents, etc. If you are an artist, craftsperson or anyone who produces a product, try to bring a sample of what you have made or produced -- either in 'the flesh,' or in photos, or videotapes.

Determine **ahead of time not to bad-mouth your previous employer(s) or place(s) of work.** Employers often feel as though they are a fraternity or sorority. During the interview you want to come across as one who displays courtesy toward all members of that fraternity or sorority. Bad-mouthing a previous employer only makes this employer worry that were they to hire you, you would end up bad-mouthing *them.*

If you know the previous employer is going to give you a very bad recommendation, just say something simple like, "I usually get along with everybody; but for some reason, my past employer and I just didn't get along. Don't know why. It's never happened to me before. Hope it never happens again."

If you think the employer will not only bad-mouth you, but claim you did somzething bad that you didn't do, you can add: "When I left there, false claims were made against me; I thought *I* should tell you that, rather than wait for you to discover it and wonder why I hadn't mentioned it." (Point this out only at the end of the interview, or interviews, after the employer has indicated they really want you.)

Determine not to drag out all the dirty laundry from the past, all the injustices done to you, all the wrong treatment you suffered. Be gracious toward your past employers, even as this employer hopes you would be gracious to them.

Decide what image you're going to try to convey: job-beggar, or resource person? The attitude with which you enter the interview room is important. Do not go wimpishly, as one coming to beg a favor. Go helpfully, as one offering them resources they need. Go as resource person, not job-beggar.

I cannot tell you the number of employers I have known over the years, who can't figure out how to find the right employee. That even includes employers who are 'human resource experts!' It is absolutely mind-boggling. But it's the nature of our Neanderthal job-hunting system.

You're having trouble finding the employer. The employer is having trouble finding you. You may pass each other in the dark. *What a great country!*

By coming there you solve this problem. You are not just answering your own prayers; you are answering the employer's as well -- if that employer was looking for You, needed you, your skills, your knowledge, but didn't know how to find you -- and suddenly, here you are!

Of course, you don't know for sure that they need you; that remains for this hiring-interview to uncover.

But at least by choosing them only after you've done all the homework described in our previous two chapters, there's a good chance you are in the right place -- whether they have an announced vacancy or not.

Decide you're going to make them both an 'oral proposal' and a 'written proposal.' Determine to make clear during the interview that you are concerned what *you can do for them*, to help them with *their* problems. You will see immediately what a switch this is from the way most job-hunters approach an employer! *("How much do you pay, and how much time off will I have?")* Will he or she be glad to see you, with this different emphasis? In most cases, you bet they will. They *want* a resource person, and a problem-solver. Determine to summarize, orally, at the end of the interview what it is you have to offer them; send a written summary of that, the next day.

How
To Conduct An Interview

Okay, you're in. The interview is about to begin. And now you're starting to sweat bullets. Face-to-face at last with the person-who-actually-has-the-power-to-hire-you. Stop sweating! There are six comforting thoughts you can console yourself with:

COMFORTING THOUGHT #1:

In a hiring-interview, you're still doing research.

Your natural question, as you approach any job-interview, often is, "How do I convince this employer to hire me?" Wrong question. It implies that you have already made up your mind that this would be a grand place to work at, and this boss a grand person to work for, so that all that remains is for you to sell yourself. This is rarely the case.

In most cases, despite your best attempts to research the place thoroughly, you don't know enough about it yet, to say that. You have *got* to use the hiring-interview as a chance to gather further information about this place, and this boss.

If you understand *this* about an interview, you will be ahead of 98% of all job-hunters -- who all too often go to the hiring-interview as a lamb to the slaughter. Or you may prefer the metaphor of a criminal on trial before a judge.

You *are* on trial, of course, in the employer's eyes.

But, so is that employer and that organization on trial, in *your* eyes.

You are studying everything about this employer, at the same time that they are studying everything about you.

Two people, both sizing each other up. You know what this should remind you of. Dating, of course.

Well, the job interview is every bit like 'the dating game.' Both of you have to like each other, before you can even discuss the question of *'going steady,'* i.e., a job. So, you're sitting there, sizing each other up. *Great!*

The importance of your doing your own weighing of this person, this organization, and this job, *during* the hiring-interview, cannot be overstated. The tradition in the U.S., and throughout the world for that matter, is to find a job, take it, and *then* try to figure out during the first three months that you're in the job, whether you like it or not -- and quitting if you decide you don't.

By using the hiring-interview to screen the organization *before you go to work there* you can save yourself time, money, grief, and guilt.

If you learn enough in the hiring-interview to 'quit' the job even before it's offered to you, instead of *quitting three months after you've taken the job*, the employer will thank you, your Mother will thank you, your spouse or partner will thank you, and of course you will thank yourself, for being so intelligent and mature.

The end of the matter: don't think of this as a hiring-interview. Think of it as 'further research.'

COMFORTING THOUGHT #2:

Hiring-interviews are not a science.

As you go to the interview, do remember that the person-who-has-the-power-to-hire-you is sweating too. Why? Because, the hiring-interview is not a very reliable way to choose an employee.

In a survey conducted among a dozen top United Kingdom employers,[13] it was discovered that the chances of an employer finding a good employee through the hiring interview was only 3% *better* than if they had picked a name out of a hat. In a further ironic finding, it was discovered that if the interview were conducted by someone who would be working directly with the candidate, the success rate dropped to 2% *below* that of

---

13. Reported in the *Financial Times Career Guide 1989* in the United Kingdom.

picking a name out of a hat. And if the interview were conducted by a so-called personnel expert, the success rate dropped to *10% below* that of picking a name out of a hat.

No, I don't know how they came up with these figures. But they are totally consistent with what I know of the whole hiring process. I have watched so-called personnel or human resources experts make *wretchedly* bad choices about hiring for their own office, and when they would morosely confess this to me some months later, over lunch, I would gently tease them with, "If you don't even know how to hire well, yourself, how do you keep a straight face when you're called in as a hiring consultant by another organization?" And they would ruefully reply, "We act as if it were a science."

Well, let me tell you, dear friend, the hiring-interview is *not* a science. It is a very very hazy art, done badly by most of its employer-practitioners, even when they have a kind heart and carloads of good intentions.

COMFORTING THOUGHT #3:

Oftentimes the employer is as scared as you are.

So, you are sitting there with sweaty palms, but you are probably assuming that the person–who–has–the–power–to–hire–you is sitting there *enjoying* this whole masochistic process. Well, sure, sometimes that's true. But more often than not, the employer is sitting there scared.

So, you have not one but two individuals (*you* and *the employer*) sitting there, scared to death. It's just that the employer has learned to *hide* his or her fears better than you have, because they've had more practice.

But he or she is, after all, a human being just as you are. He or she may *never* have been hired to do *this. This* just got thrown in with all their other duties. And they may *know* they're not very good at it.

So, what is going on in an employer's head, while they're interviewing you? Oh, things like this:

A. That you won't be able to do the job: that you lack the necessary skills or experience, and the hiring-interview didn't uncover this.

B. That if hired, you won't put in a full working day, regularly.

C. That if hired, you'll be frequently "out sick," or otherwise absent whole days.

D. That if hired, you'll only stay around for a few weeks or at most a few months, and then quit without advance warning.

E. That it will take you too long to master the job, and thus it will be too long before you're profitable to that organization.

F. That you won't get along with the other workers there, or that you will develop a personality conflict with the boss himself (or herself).

G. That you will do only the minimum that you can get away with, rather than the maximum that they hired you for.

H. That you will always have to be told what to do next, rather than displaying initiative -- always in a responding mode, rather than an initiating mode (and mood).

I. That you will have a work-disrupting character flaw, and turn out to be: dishonest, or totally irresponsible, a spreader of dissention at work, lazy, an embezzler, a gossip, a sexual harasser, a drug-user or substance abuser, a drunk, a liar, incompetent, or -- in a word -- bad news.

J. *(If this is a large organization, and your would-be boss is not the top person)*: that you will bring discredit upon them, and upon their department/section/division, etc., for ever hiring you in the first place -- making them lose face, possibly also costing your would-be boss a raise or promotion.

K. That you will cost a lot of money, if they make a mistake by hiring you. Currently, in the U.S. the cost to an employer of a bad hire can run $50,000 or more, including relocation costs, lost pay for the period for work not done or aborted, and severance pay -- if *they* let you go.

No wonder the employer is scared . . . anxious . . . worried . . . or whatever word you prefer.

Moreover, the hiring interview has become *everything*. In the old days, an employer might have gotten useful information to guide them in the hiring decision outside the interview, from your previous employers. No more. In the past decade, as job-hunters started filing lawsuits left and right alleging 'unlawful discharge,' or 'being deprived of an ability to make a living,' most Previous Employers adopted the policy of refusing to volunteer *any* information about Previous Employees, except name, rank and serial number -- i.e., the person's job-title and dates of employment. And that is even more true today.

So, the interviewer is completely on his own -- or her own -- in trying to figure out whether to hire you or not. They're just as nervous as you are.

COMFORTING THOUGHT #4:

You don't have to memorize a lot of answers to difficult interview questions. Books on interviewing, of which there are many, often publish lists of the kind of questions they think employers might ask you, such as:

- Tell me about yourself.
- Why are you applying for this job?
- What do you know about this job or company?
- How would you describe yourself?
- What are your major strengths?
- What is your greatest weakness?
- What type of work do you like to do best?
- What are your interests outside of work?
- What accomplishment gave you the greatest satisfaction?
- What was your worst mistake in previous jobs?
- Why did you leave your last job?
- Why were you fired (if you were)?
- How does your education or experience relate to this job?
- Where do you see yourself five years from now?
- What are your goals in life?
- How much did you make at your last job?

Well, the list goes on and on. It sometimes totals eighty-nine questions -- or more.

You are then told that you should prepare for a hiring-interview by writing out, practicing, and memorizing some clever answers to *all* these questions -- answers which these books furnish for you. They're sometimes very clever; but let me tell you, my friend, your preparation for the hiring-interview doesn't need to be so complicated.

Beneath the dozens and dozens of possible questions like those above, there are really only *five basic questions* that underlie all the rest.

Five. Just five. Whether they're ever put into words or not, the person-who-has-the-power-to-hire-you wants to know:

1. **"Why are you here?"** *They mean by this, "Why are you knocking on my door, rather than someone else's door?"*

Then, the person-who-has-the-power-to-hire-you wants to know:

2. **"What can you do for us?"** *They mean by this, "If I were to hire you would you be part of the problems I already have, or would you be a part of the solution to those problems? What are your skills, and how much do you know about some subject or field that is of interest to us here?"*

Then, the person-who-has-the-power-to-hire-you wants to know:

3. **"What kind of person are you?"** *They mean by this, "Do you have the kind of personality that makes it easy for people to work with you, and do you share the values which we have at this place?"*

Then, the person-who-has-the-power-to-hire-you wants to know:

4. **"What distinguishes you from nineteen other people who have the same skills as you have?"** *They mean by this, "Do you have better work habits than the nineteen others, do you show up earlier, stay later, work more thoroughly, work faster, maintain higher standards, go the extra mile, or . . . what?"*

Lastly, the person-who-has-the-power-to-hire-you wants to know:

5. **"Can I afford you?"** *They mean by this, "If we decide we want you here, how much will it take to get you, and are we willing and able to pay that amount -- governed as we are by our budget, and our inability to pay you as much as the person who would be above you, on the organizational chart?"*

Since there are really only five basic questions on the employer's mind, and not eighty-nine, there are really only five answers you need to know.

But, you had *better* know those five. If you've done your homework, you will. If you haven't, you won't. Period. End of story.

You, of course, have the right -- nay, the duty -- to be asking yourself the same five questions, though in a slightly different form:

1. **What does this job involve?**

2. **Do my skills truly match this job?**

3. **Are these the kind of people I would like to work with, or not?** *Do not ignore your intuition if it tells you that you would not be comfortable working with these people!!*

4. **If we like each other, and both want to work together, can I persuade them there is something unique about me, that makes me different from nineteen other people who can do the same tasks?**

5. **Can I persuade them to hire me at the salary I need or want?**

And that's it!

You don't, necessarily ask these questions out loud, except perhaps the first one. But finding answers to them should be your goal during the interview.

To get at them, you might begin your part of the interview by reporting to them just exactly how you've been conducting your job-hunt, and what impressed you so much about *their* organization during your research, that you decided to come in and talk to them about a job. Then you can devote your attention, during the remainder of the interview, to exploring the five questions above, in your own way.[14]

If the job you want doesn't really exist there -- yet -- but you hope they'll *create* such a job for you, then your five questions get changed into five *statements*, that you make to this person-who-has-the-power-to-hire-you. You tell them:

1. **What you** like **about this organization.**

2. **What sorts of** needs **you find intriguing in this field and in this organization** (don't ever use the word "*problems*," as most employers prefer synonyms, such as '*needs*' -- unless you first hear the word '*problems*' coming out of their mouth).

3. **What** skills **seem to you to be needed in order to meet such needs.**

---

14. Additional questions you may want to ask, to elaborate upon these five:
    What significant changes has this company gone through in the last five years?
    What values are sacred to this company?
    What characterizes the most successful employees this company has?
    What future changes do you see in the work here?
    Who do you see as your allies, colleagues or competitors in this business?

IT'S WHAT I'VE ALWAYS HEARD.. TIMING IS EVERYTHING..

4. **Evidence** **from your past experience that demonstrates you have the very skills in question, and that you perform them in the manner or style you claim.** And, finally:

5. **What is** unique **about the way** *you* **perform those skills.** As I said before, every prospective employer wants to know *what makes you different* from nineteen other people who can do the same kind of work as you do. You *have* to know what that is. And then not only talk about it, but actually demonstrate it, by the way you conduct your part of the hiring-interview. *e.g.,* *"I am very thorough in the way I would do the job for you"* = be thorough in the way you have researched the place before you go in for the hiring-interview.

Try to put your finger on the 'style' or 'manner' in which you do your work, that is distinctive and sets you apart from the others who might be approaching this employer.

COMFORTING THOUGHT #5:

The employer doesn't *really* care about your past.

In most cases, as I have been emphasizing, the person-who-has-the-power-to-hire-you is *scared* not about the past but about the future. No employer cares about your past. In fact, in the U.S., employers can only legally ask you questions that are related to the requirements and expectations of the job. They cannot ask about such things in your past (or present) as your creed, religion, race, age, sex or marital status.

The employer cares only about your future . . . with *them*. But that future is difficult to predict, so they usually try to guess your future behavior by asking about your past behavior on the job.

Do not be fooled by questions about your past. There is a fear about the future, that lies beneath all of an employer's questions. Let me illustrate:

Employer's Question	The Fear Behind The Question	The Point You Try To Get Across	Phrases You Might Use To Get This Across
"Tell me about yourself"	The employer is afraid he/she isn't going to conduct a very good interview, by failing to ask the right questions. Or is afraid there is something wrong with you, and is hoping you will blurt it out.	You are a good employee, as you have proved in the past at your other jobs. (Give the briefest history of who you are, where born, raised, interests, hobbies, and kind of work you have enjoyed the most to date.) *Keep it to two minutes, max.*	In describing your past work history, use any *honest* phrases you can about your work history, that are self-complimentary: "Hard worker." "Came in early, left late." "Always did more than was expected of me." Etc.
"What kind of work are you looking for?"	The employer is afraid that you are looking for a different job than that which the employer is trying to fill. E.g., he/she wants a secretary, but you want to be an office manager, etc.	You are looking for precisely the kind of work the employer is offering (but don't say that, if it isn't true). Repeat back to the employer, in your own words, what he/she has said about the job, and emphasize the skills you have to do *that*.	If the employer hasn't described the job at all, say, "I'd be happy to answer that, but first I need to understand exactly what kind of work this job involves." *Then* answer, as at left.
"Have you ever done this kind of work before?"	The employer is afraid you don't possess the necessary skills and experience to do this job.	You have skills that are transferable, from whatever you used to do; and you did it well.	"I pick up stuff very quickly." "I have quickly mastered any job I have ever done."

Employer's Question	The Fear Behind The Question	The Point You Try To Get Across	Phrases You Might Use To Get This Across
"When did you leave your last job?" *-- or* **"How did you get along with your former boss and co-workers?"**	The employer is afraid you don't get along well with people, especially bosses, and is just waiting for you to 'bad-mouth' your previous boss or co-workers, as proof of that.	Say whatever positive things you possibly can about your former boss and co-workers (*without telling lies*). Emphasize you usually get along very well with people -- and then let your gracious attitude toward your previous boss(es) and co-workers prove it, right before this employer's very eyes (and ears).	If you left voluntarily: "*My boss and I* both felt I would be happier and more effective in a job where [here describe your strong points, such as] I would have more room to use my initiative and creativity." If you were fired: "Usually, I get along well with everyone, but in this particular case the boss and I just didn't get along with each other. Difficult to say why." *You don't need to say any more than that.* If you were laid off and your job wasn't filled after you left: "My *job* was terminated."
"How is your health?" *-- or* **"How much were you absent from work during your last job?"**	The employer is afraid you will be absent from work a lot, if they hire you.	You will not be absent. If you have a health problem, you want to emphasize that it is one which will not keep you from being at work, daily. Your productivity, compared to other workers', is excellent.	If you were *not* absent a lot at your last job: "I believe it's an employee's job to show up every work day. Period." If you *were* absent a lot, say why, and stress that it was due to a difficulty that is now *past*.

Employer's Question	The Fear Behind The Question	The Point You Try To Get Across	Phrases You Might Use To Get This Across
"Can you explain why you've been out of work so long?" -- or "Can you tell me why there are these gaps in your work history?" *(Usually said after studying your resume.)*	The employer is afraid that you are the kind of person who quits a job the minute he/she doesn't like something at it; in other words, that you have no 'stick-to-it-iveness.'	You love to work, and you regard times when things aren't going well as challenges, which you enjoy learning how to conquer.	"During the gaps in my work record, I was studying/doing volunteer work/doing some hard thinking about my mission in life/finding redirection." (Choose one.)
"Wouldn't this job represent a step down for you?" -- or "I think this job would be way beneath your talents and experience." -- or "Don't you think you would be underemployed if you took this job?"	The employer is afraid you could command a bigger salary, somewhere else, and will therefore leave him/her as soon as something better turns up.	You will stick with this job as long as you and the employer agree this is where you should be.	"This job isn't a step down for me. It's a step up -- from welfare." "We have mutual fears: every employer is afraid a good employee will leave too soon, and every employee is afraid the employer might fire him/her, for no good reason." "I like to work, and I give my best to every job I've ever had."
And, lastly: **"Tell me, what is your greatest weakness?"**	The employer is afraid you have some character flaw, and hopes you will now rashly blurt it out, or confess it.	You have limitations just like anyone else but you work constantly to improve yourself and be a more and more effective worker.	Mention a weakness and then stress its positive aspect, e.g., "I don't like to be oversupervised, because I have a great deal of initiative, and I like to anticipate problems before they even arise."

As the interview proceeds, you want to quietly notice *(but not comment on)* the time-frame of the questions the employer is asking.

Because, when the interview is going well for you, the time-sequence of the employer's questions will usually move -- however slowly -- through the following stages.

1. **Distant past**: *e.g., "Where did you attend high school?"*

2. **Immediate past**: *e.g., "Tell me about your most recent job."*

3. **Present**: *e.g., "What kind of a job are you looking for?"*

4. **Immediate future**: *e.g., "Would you be able to come back for another interview next week?"*

5. [*Optional*: **Distant future**: *e.g., "Where would you like to be five years from now?"*]

The more the interviewer's questions move from the past to the future, the more favorably the interview is going for you. On the other hand, if the interviewer's questions stay firmly in the past, the outlook is not so good. *Ah well, y' can't win 'em all!*

If the time-frame of the interviewer's questions moves firmly into the future, then experts suggest you ask -- now -- some essential questions *about the organization.*

The research you're doing here concerns what you can do for the company, not what the company can do for you. Don't ask -- at this point -- about their health plan, days off, vacation time, benefits or salary; page 221 will tell you when.)

What is the job, specifically, that I am being considered for?
If I were hired, what duties would I be performing?
What responsibilities would I have?
What would you be hiring me to accomplish?
Would I be working with a team, or group? To whom would I report?
Whose responsibility is it to see that I get the training I need, here, to get up to speed?
How would I be evaluated, how often, and by whom?
What were the strengths and weaknesses of previous people in this position?
Why did *you* yourself decide to work here?
What do you wish you had known about this company before you started here? What particular characteristics do you think have made you successful in your job here?
May I meet the person I would be working for (if it isn't you)?

Remember, as job-expert Nathan Azrin has said for years, *The hiring process is more like choosing a mate, than it is like deciding whether or not to buy a new car.*

'Choosing a mate' is of course a metaphor: it means that *the mechanisms* by which human nature decides to hire someone, are *similar to* the mechanisms by which we decide whether or not to marry someone.

In hiring, as in dating, both people are scared of making a mistake.

COMFORTING THOUGHT #6:

No matter what handicap you have, it will not keep you from getting hired. It will only keep you from getting hired at *some* places.

Most of us think that when we go job-hunting we have some special handicap (hidden or obvious), that's going to keep us from getting a job. Forever.

The handicaps that bother us are such things as:

I have a physical handicap
I have a mental handicap
I never graduated from high school
I never graduated from college
I am just graduating
I just graduated a year ago
I graduated too long ago
I am a self-made man
I am a self-made woman
I am too handsome
I am too beautiful
I am too ugly
I am too thin
I am too fat
I am too young
I am too old
I am too new to the job-market
I am too near retirement
I have a prison record
I have a psychiatric history
I have never held a job before
I have held too many jobs before
I have only had one employer
I am Hispanic
I am Black
I am Asian
I am a foreigner
I have not had enough education
I have had too much education
I am too much of a generalist

I am too much of a specialist
I am a clergyperson
I am just coming out of the military
I've only worked for volunteer organizations
I have only worked for large employers
I have only worked for small employers
I am too shy
I am too assertive
I come from a very different kind of background
I come from another industry
I come from another planet

I guess the true meaning of the above comprehensive list is that there are about three weeks of your life when you're employable.

Many of us think we need a special book to teach us how to job-hunt with our handicap. Actually, all we really need is to keep firmly in mind this one simple truth:

> There are two kinds of employers out there: those who will be put off by your handicap, and therefore won't hire you;
>
> AND
>
> Those who will not be put off by your handicap, and therefore will hire you, if you are qualified for the job.

You are not interested in the former kind of employer, no matter how many of them there are -- except as a source of referrals.

You are only looking for the second kind of employer.

So: if the employer you are talking to in a particular interview is obviously bothered by your (supposed) handicap, you want to quietly bring that interview to a conclusion, and ask them -- in parting -- if they know of anyone else who might be interested in your skills. Keep going, until you find that second kind of employer.

It doesn't matter what skills-you-don't-have, as long as the skills-that-you-do-have exactly match those-needed-in-the-job.

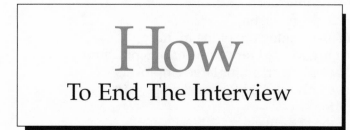

How
To End The Interview

At some point this interview has to come to a close. Not that you may not be back for further interviews. But this interview should end with you asking six, maybe seven, questions. In most cases, if you don't ask for this information, the employer won't volunteer it, believe me:

#1. **"Given my skills and experience, is there work here that you would consider me for?"** This is if you haven't honed in on a specific job, from the beginning. Otherwise you begin with #2.

#2. **"Can you offer me this job?"** It is astonishing how many job-hunters have secured a job simply by being bold enough to ask for it, at the end of the interview, either with the words above or something similar. I don't know *why* this is so. I only know *that* it is so.

So, if after hearing all about this job at this place, you decide you'd really like to have it, *ask for it.* The worst thing the employer can say is "No," or "We need some time to think about all the interviews we're conducting with various people." In which case you move on to #3. (Or #7, if they turn you down flat.)

#3. **"Do you want me to come back for another interview?"** If the employer is seriously considering you, this interview will very likely be only the first in a series; there usually is a second round of interviews, and often a third and fourth.

You, of course, want to be in those subsequent rounds. Indeed, many experts say the *only* purpose you should have in mind for the first interview at a particular place, is to be invited back for a second interview.

If you've secured *that,* say they, the first interview was a ringing success.

#4. **"When may I expect to hear from you?"** You *never* want to leave control of the ensuing steps in this process in the hands of the employer. You want it in your own hands. Even if the employer says, *"We need time to think about this,"* or *"We will be calling you for a second interview,"* you don't want to leave that as just a good intention on the employer's part. You want to nail it down.

#5. **"What would be the latest I can expect to hear from you?"** The employer has probably given you their *best* guess, in answer to your previous question. Now you want to know *what is the worse case* scenario? One employer, when I asked him the *worse case* scenario replied, *"Never!"* I thought he had a great sense of humor. Turned out he wasn't joking.

#6. **"May I contact you after that date, if for any reason you haven't had a chance to get back to me by that time?"** Some employers will not appreciate this question; you'll know that's the case if you get some retort like, *"Don't you trust me?"*

Most employers, however, appreciate your offering them what is in essence a safety-net. They know they can get busy, become overwhelmed with other things, forget how long a time has elapsed. It's reassuring, in such a case, that you offer them a backup fail-safe strategy -- particularly if they really are interested in you. (If they dislike this question, it may be a clue that they're not really interested in you, and are just 'blowing you off' -- as they say.)

[#7. **Optional: "Can you think of anyone else who might be interested in hiring me?"** This question is asked *only* if they replied *"No,"* to your first question, above.]

When you've got the answers to the first six questions here, jotting down any answers you may need to, you stand up, thank them sincerely for their time, give a firm handshake, and leave.

In the following days, rigorously keep to this covenant, and don't contact them (except with a thank-you note) until after the *latest* deadline you two agreed upon, in answer to question #6, above.

If you do contact them after that date, and if they tell you things are still up in the air, you ask questions #4, #5, and #6, all over again. And so on, and so forth.

Incidentally, it is entirely appropriate for you to insert a thank-you note into the running stream after *each* interview or telephone contact. That will help them remember you, without your bugging them.

BACK HOME:
THE IMPORTANCE OF
THANK-YOU NOTES

You're home that night. Putting your feet up. Relaxing. The job-hunt is over for the day. *Oops,* no it's not. You've still got work to do: thank-you notes.

Every expert on interviewing will tell you three things:

(1) **Thank-you notes *must* be sent after *every* interview**, by every job-hunter, that same day or the next morning at the latest;

(2) **Most job-hunters ignore this advice** -- indeed, it is the most overlooked step in the entire job-hunting process; and

(3) **Therefore you will stand out from all the other interviewees** if you remember to send a thank-you note to the person who interviewed you (and to their secretary, or anyone else you made contact with while you were there).

If you need any additional encouragement, here are seven reasons for sending a thank-you note to the employer who interviewed you:

You are giving evidence that you have good people skills. Sending a thank-you note backs up any claim you made to that effect, during the interview. From this they know: you *are* good with people, 'cause you remember to thank them.

It helps the employer to remember you. If they had a very busy schedule the day you were there, you may be just a blur in their mind by next morning. The thank-you note helps to correct that.

It gives the interviewer something to show to other members of the committee, if more than one person is going to be involved in the hiring decision.

It gives you a chance to emphasize your interest in further talks, if the first interview went well. "I'd love to talk further with you, at your convenience."

It gives you an opportunity to correct any wrong impression you left behind you. You can correct any wrong impressions, add anything you forgot to tell them, and underline the main two or three points that you want to stand out in their minds as they weigh whether or not to hire you.

It may cause them to give you the job. One baseball team hired a woman for a public relations job *solely* because she was the only one (out of 35 job-hunters interviewed) who sent them a thank-you note.

If you don't get the job, it gives you a chance to ask them for further leads that they may hear of from other colleagues, who might need someone with your skills.

Says one human resources manager: "A prompt, brief, faxed business letter thanking me for my time along with a (brief!) synopsis of his/her unique qualities communicates to me that this person is an assertive, motivated, customer service-oriented salesperson who utilizes technology and knows the rules of the 'game.' These are qualities I am looking for . . . At the moment I receive approximately one letter . . . for every fifteen candidates interviewed."

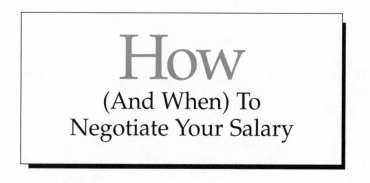

How
(And When) To
Negotiate Your Salary

When the interviewing process is almost all over, and it's gone well, it's time to deal with the question that is inevitably on the employer's mind: *how much is this person going to cost me?* and also on yours: *how much does this job pay?*

The rules are simple:

(1) **Before you go to the interview, figure out how much you need to make from this job, if it's offered to you.** The job-hunter's nightmare is that you just love the prospect of working here, but: *What if their highest figure is so far below your lowest figure, that you will starve if you accept it?*

Let's say you need $14 an hour, just to survive, but the highest they're willing to pay is $8 an hour.

You see the problem. You've *got* to know, beforehand, just how much you need to make, at a minimum.

You can deal with this in one of two ways: a) take a wild guess - - and risk finding out after you take the job that it's simply impossible for you to live on that salary *(the favorite strategy in this country, and most others)*; or, b) do some figuring, so you'll know what you're talking about. Exercises to help you do this are on pages 299–301.

(2) **In the interview, never discuss salary until the end, after they've definitely said they want you.**

The left-brained way of putting this is:

Never Discuss Salary

Until *all* of the following conditions have been fulfilled:
- Until you're in the final interview at that place, for that job.
- Until they've gotten to know you, at your best, so they can see how you stand out above the other applicants.
- Until you've gotten to know them, as completely as you can, so you can tell when they're being firm, or when they're flexible.
- Until you've found out exactly what the job entails.
- Until they've had a chance to find out how well you match the job-requirements.
- Until you've decided, "I'd really like to work here."
- Until they've said, "We want you."
- Until they've said or implied, "We've *got* to have you."

The right-brained way of putting the same thing is:[15]

When To Negotiate Salary

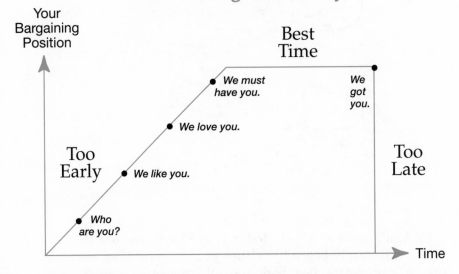

Why is it to your advantage to delay salary discussion? Because, if you really *shine* during the hiring-interview, they may -- at the end -- mention a higher salary than they originally had in mind when the interview started.

So, don't raise it earlier. And if it is the employer who raises the salary question too early in the process, your gentle reply should be: "I'll gladly come to that, but could you first help me to understand what this job involves?" *or* "Until you've decided you definitely want me, and I've decided I definitely could help you with your tasks here, I feel discussion of salary is a bit premature." That will work, in most cases.

Of course if they're asking you too early because they're determined to give the job to the one who's willing to work for the lowest salary, you'll have to decide how badly you want the job; and if the answer is, "Very badly," you're going to have to give a reply -- hopefully in terms of a *range* -- and just pray.

(3) **You'll have to *negotiate* for your salary, because the employer will rarely begin by telling you the most they are willing to pay.** Salary negotiation would never happen if *every* employer in *every* hiring-interview mentioned, right from the start, the top figure they are willing to pay for that position.

Some employers do start there. And that's the end of any salary negotiation with them!

But most employers don't. Hoping they'll be able to get you for less, they start *lower* than they're ultimately willing to go. This creates *a range*. And that range is what salary negotiation is all about.

For example, if the employer wants to hire somebody for no more than $12 an hour, they may start *the bidding* at $8 an hour. In which case, their range is from $8 to $12 an hour. Or if they want to pay no more than $20 an hour, they may start the bidding at $16 an hour. In which case their range runs from $16 to $20 an hour.

If a range *is* thus involved, you have every right to try to negotiate the highest salary possible *within that range.*

The employer is trying to save money. You're trying to get the most money you can, for the sake of your loved ones as well as yourself. Nothing is wrong with either goal. But if the employer starts low, salary negotiation is proper, and expected.

(4) **To win at salary negotiation, don't be the first one to mention a figure.** Experienced interviewers will always try to get you to mention a figure before they do, by asking some innocent-sounding question, such as: "What kind of salary are you looking for?" *Well, how kind of them to ask me what I want --* you may be thinking. No, no, no. Kindness has nothing to do with it.

They are hoping *you* will be the first to mention a figure, because they know a weird truth about salary negotiation, borne out by many years' experience. It is: *whoever mentions a salary figure first, generally loses salary negotiation, in the end.*

So of course, you will *always* want to respond to that innocent-sounding question with some reply like: "Well, you created this position, so you must have some figure in mind, and I'd be interested in knowing what that is."

(5) **To win at salary negotiation, know what a top salary offer would be, in this field.** Okay, the employer mentions a figure: how do you tell whether it's the *starting bid*, or their *top* offer?

Well, you can't really tell. But you can make a guess *if* you have some idea of what jobs pay in that field or industry -- generally speaking. And that means research.

Oh, come on! I can hear you say. *Isn't this more trouble than it's worth?* Well, sure, if you think it is. But if you're determined to get this job, salary research can pay off *handsomely.*

Let's say it takes you from one to three days to run down this sort of information on the three or four organizations that interest you the most. And when you finally get to salary negotiation, you realize their bid is low for the industry. So, you quote the industry figures, and ask for (let's say) a salary that is $2 an hour more than they originally intended to pay you. And they agree to give you that, because you know what the industry standard is. What does that add up to?

Well, if you work a forty-hour week for 50 weeks a year, $2 an hour would add up to $4,000 more for you each year, than you would otherwise have gotten. In just the next three years, you would be earning $12,000 extra, or more, because of your salary research. *Not bad pay, for one to three days' work!*

I know *many* job-hunters and career-changers to whom this has happened.

So, to put this another way: if you don't do this research, it'll cost ya!

Okay then, how do you do it? Well, there's a simple rule: **abandon books, and go talk to people**.

I'll give some examples from various industries, so you can see how it goes:

> First Example: *Working at your first entry-level job, say at a fast-food place.*

They pay what they pay. You can walk in, ask for a job application, and interview with the manager. He or she will usually tell you the pay, outright. It's usually *inflexible.* But at least you'll find how easy it is to discover what the pay is. (Incidentally, filling out an application, or having an interview there, doesn't commit you to take the job -- but you probably already know that. You can always decline an offer from *any place.* That's what makes this research harmless.)

> Second Example: *Working at a place where you can't discover what the pay is, say at a construction company.*

If that construction company where you would hope to get a job is difficult to research, go visit a different construction company in the same town - - one that isn't of much interest to you - - and ask what they make there. Fill out one of their applications, and talk to the hiring person about what kinds of jobs they have (or might have in the future), at which time prospective wages is a legitimate subject of discussion. Then, having done this research on a place you don't care about, go back to the place that really interests you, and apply. You still don't know exactly what they pay, but you do know what their competitor pays - - which will usually be close.

> Third Example: *Working in a one-person office, say as a secretary.*

Here you can often find useful salary information by perusing the *Help Wanted* ads in the local paper for a week or two. Most of the ads probably won't mention a salary figure, but a few *may*. Among those that do, note what the lowest salary offering is, and what the highest is, and see if the ad reveals some reasons for the difference. It's interesting how much you can learn about salaries, with this approach.

Another way to do salary research is to find a *Temporary Work Agency* that places secretaries, and let yourself be farmed out to various offices: the more, the merrier. It's relatively easy to do salary research when you're *inside* the place. (Study what that place pays *the agency*, not what the agency pays *you.*) If it's an office where the other workers *like* you, you'll be able to ask questions about a lot of other jobs there besides secretarial ones, including salary issues. It's like *summertime,* where the research is easy.

Before you finish your research, before you go in to that organization for your final interview, you want to discover what the range is, for that job. In any organization which has more than five employees, that range is relatively easy to figure out. It will be less than what the person above you makes, and more than what the person below you makes, viz:

If The Person Who Would Be Below You Makes	And The Person Who Would Be Above You Makes	The Range For Your Job Would Be
$37,000	$42,000	$38,000–$41,000
$22,000	$27,000	$23,000–$26,000
$10,000	$13,500	$10,500–$12,500

One teensy-tiny little problem: *how* do you find out the salary of those who would be above and below you? Well, first you have to find out their *names* or the names of their *positions.* If it is a small organization you are going after - - one with twenty or less employees - - finding this information out should be *duck soup.* Any employee who works there is likely to know the answer, and you can usually get in touch with one of those employees, or even an ex-employee, through your contacts. Since two-thirds of all new jobs are created by companies of that size, that's the size organization you are likely to be researching, anyway.

If you are going after a larger organization, then you have our familiar life-preserver to fall back on, namely, every contact you have (family, friend, relative, business, or church acquaintance) who might know the company, and therefore, the information you seek. You are looking for Someone Who Knows Someone who either is working, or has worked, at the particular place or places that interest you, who therefore has or can get this information for you.

If you absolutely run into a blank wall on a particular organization (everyone who works there is pledged to secrecy, and they have shipped all their ex-employees to Siberia), then seek out information on their nearest *competitor* in the same geographic area. *For example,* let us say you were researching Bank X, and they were proving to be inscrutable about what they pay their managers. You would then try Bank Y as your research base, to see if the information is easier to come by, there. You make an assumption, and that is that the two are probably similar in their pay scales, and that what you learned about Bank Y was applicable also to Bank X.

Also experts point out that in researching salaries, you should take note of the fact that most governmental agencies have civil service positions *which match or almost match* those in private industry. Their job descriptions and pay ranges are available to the public. Go to the nearest City, County, Regional, State or Federal Civil Service office, find the job description nearest what you are seeking in private industry, and then ask for the starting salary.

Also, if you have access to the Internet, you can go to the site run by Mary Ellen Mort called JobStar

(`http://jobstar.org/`)

which has the most extensive collection of salary surveys by industry or position, that exists on the Web.

When all this research is done, when you are in the actual hiring-interview, and the employer mentions the figure *they* have in mind, you are then ready to respond: "I understand of course the constraints under which all organizations are operating in the late '90s, but I believe my productivity is such that it would *justify* a salary in the range of . . ." -- *and here you mention a figure near the top of their range.*

It will help a lot if during this discussion, you are prepared to show in what ways you will *make money* or in what ways you will *save money* for that organization, such as would justify the higher salary you are seeking. Hopefully, this will succeed in getting you the salary you want.[16]

---

16. Daniel Porot, in Europe, suggests that if you and an employer really hit it off, and you're *dying* to work there, but they cannot afford the salary you need, consider offering them part of your time. If you need, and believe you deserve, say $25,000, but they can only afford $15,000, you might consider offering them three days a week of your time for that $15,000 (15/25 = 3/5). This leaves you free to take other work those other two days.

Once all salary negotiation is concluded to your satisfaction, do remember to ask to have it summed up in a letter of agreement -- or employment contract -- that they give to you. It may be you cannot get it in writing, but do try! The Road to Hell is paved with oral promises that went unwritten, and -- later -- unfulfilled.

Many executives unfortunately 'forget' what they told you during the hiring-interview, or even deny they ever said such a thing.

Also, many executives leave the company (willingly or unwillingly) and their successor or a new top boss may disown any *unwritten* promises: *"I don't know what caused them to say that to you, but they clearly exceeded their authority, and of course we can't be held to that."*

There's also the matter of raises, down the road. You should plan on asking for one annually, unless they are regularly offering one to you without your having to ask.

When you ask for a raise, a year from now -- or *whenever* -- you will need to justify it. Toward this end, once you are in the job, plan to keep track of your accomplishments there, on a weekly basis -- jotting them down, every weekend, in your own private journal. Career experts, such as Bernard Haldane, recommend you do this without fail. You can then *summarize* these accomplishments annually on a one-page sheet, for your boss's eyes, when raise or promotion is the subject under discussion.[17]

---

17. In any good-sized organization, you will often be amazed at how little attention your superiors pay to your noteworthy accomplishments, and how little they are aware at the end of the year that you really are *entitled* to a raise. Noteworthy your accomplishments may be, but no one is taking notes . . . unless *you* do.

Fringe Benefits

During your salary negotiation, do not forget to pay attention to so-called fringe benefits. 'Fringes' such as life insurance, health benefits or health plans, vacation or holiday plans, and retirement programs typically add another 30% to many workers' salaries. That is to say, if an employee receives $800 salary per month, the fringe benefits are worth another $240 per month.

If your job is at a higher level, benefits may include but not be limited to: health, life, dental, disability, malpractice insurance; insurance for dependents; sick leave; vacation; personal leave/personal days; educational leave; educational cost reimbursement for coursework related to the job; maternity and or parental leave; health leave to care for dependents; bonus system or profit sharing; stock options; expense accounts for entertaining clients; dues to professional associations; travel reimbursement; fee sharing arrangements for clients that the employee generates; organizational memberships; parking; automobile allowance; relocation costs; sabbaticals; professional conference costs; time for community service; flextime work schedules; fitness center memberships.

You should therefore remember to ask what benefits are offered, and -- if they want you badly enough -- negotiate for the benefits you want.

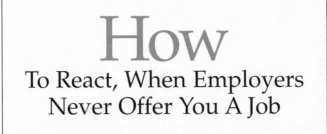

How

To React, When Employers Never Offer You A Job

WHEN IT'S NOT YOUR FAULT

I hear regularly from job-hunters who report that they followed all the advice in this chapter, and were quite successful at getting interviews -- but they still didn't get hired. And they want to know what they're doing wrong. Well, unfortunately, the answer *sometimes* is: Nothing.

A few -- very few -- employers play games, and invite you in for an interview despite the fact that they have already hired someone for the position in question!

You are cheered, of course, by the ease with which you get these interviews. But unbeknownst to you, the manager who is interviewing you *(we'll say it's a he)* has a personal friend he already agreed to give the job to. Of course, there's one small hurdle to get over, namely that the State or the Federal government gives funds to this organization, and has mandated that this position be advertised and open to all.

So this manager must pretend to comply. He chooses ten candidates, including his favorite, and pretends to interview them all with an open mind. Then he does what he always intended to do: he rejects the first nine out of hand and chooses his favorite. You're automatically rejected -- even if you are a better candidate. This tenth person is, after all, his *friend*. The manager ends this charade by claiming he followed the mandated hiring procedures *to the letter*.

I don't know *how often* this happens, but I know it does happen -- first of all, because more than one employer has actually confessed it to me. And, secondly, because at one point in my life it actually happened to me.

If you are one of the nine allegedly interviewed in this charade, you will always be baffled as to *why* you got turned
down. *"What did I do wrong,"* you'll cry. The answer may be:
Nothing.

WHEN IT IS YOUR FAULT

But, ah, what if no games are being played? You are getting
rejected at place after place, because there is something really
wrong with the way you are coming across, during these hiring-
interviews.

And, it doesn't have to be a big thing. For example, you could
have all the skills in the world, have researched this organization to death, have practiced *interviewing* until you are a master
at giving precisely the 'right answers,' be absolutely the perfect
person (skillwise) for this job, and yet lose the hiring-interview
because . . . *your breath smells terrible.*

You're ready to fight dragons, and you're getting destroyed
by a mosquito?!

Yes, and there are a lot of other 'mosquitoes' that can fly in --
often during the first 30 seconds to two minutes of your interview -- and cause *the person-who-has-the-power-to-hire-you* to
start thinking, *"I sure hope we have some other candidates besides
this one"*: These 'interview-killers' fall into five basic categories:

1. **Nervous mannerisms**: *it is a turn-off for employers if --*
• you give a limp handshake, *or*
• you slouch in your chair, or endlessly fidget in your seat,
during the interview, *or*
• you continually avoid eye contact with the employer, *or*
• you crack your knuckles, *or* are constantly playing with
your hands, or your hair.

2. **Lack of self-confidence**: *it is a turn-off for employers if --*
• you are continuously being extremely self-critical,
• you are downplaying your achievements or abilities,
• you are speaking so softly you cannot be heard, or so
loudly you can be heard two rooms away,
• you are giving one-word-answers to all the employer's
questions,

- you are constantly interrupting the employer,
- or you are giving answers in an extremely hesitant fashion.

3. **Inconsiderateness toward other people**: *it is a turn-off for employers if - -*
- you show a lack of courtesy to the receptionist, secretary, and (at lunch) to the waiter or waitress,
- you display extreme-criticalness toward your previous employers and places of work,
- you drink strong stuff (ordering a drink if and when the employer takes you to lunch is always a bad idea, as it raises the question in the employer's mind, *Do they normally stop with one, or do they normally keep on going?* Don't. . . . do. . . . it!)

4. **Your values**: *it is a turn-off for employers, if they see in you - -*
- any signs of dishonesty or lying, on your resume or in the interview;
- any signs of irresponsibility or tendency to goof off;
- any sign of arrogance or excessive aggressiveness; any sign of tardiness or failure to keep appointments and commitments on time, including the hiring-interview;
- any sign of not following instructions or obeying rules;
- any sign of constant complaining or blaming things on others;
- any sign of laziness or lack of motivation;
- any sign of a lack of enthusiasm for this organization and what it is trying to do; *or*
- any sign of instability, inappropriate response, and the like.
- the other ways in which you evidence your *values*, such as: what things impress you or don't impress you in the office; what you are willing to sacrifice in order to get this job *and* what you are *not* willing to sacrifice in order to get this job; your enthusiasm for work;
the carefulness with which you did or didn't research this company before you came in;
and blah, blah, blah.

5. **Your appearance and personal habits**: interview after interview has revealed that if you are a male, *you are much more likely to get the job if:*

- you have freshly bathed, have your face freshly shaved or your hair and beard freshly trimmed, have clean fingernails; and are using a deodorant;
- you have on freshly laundered clothes, and a suit rather than a sports outfit, pants with a sharp crease, and shoes freshly polished;
- you do not have bad breath, do not dispense gallons of garlic, onion, stale tobacco, or the odor of strong drink, into the enclosed office air; but have brushed and flossed your teeth, plus used a mouthwash if necessary;
- you are not wafting tons of after-shave cologne fifteen feet ahead of you, as you enter the room.

If you are a female, interview after interview has revealed that *you are much more likely to get the job if* – –
- you have freshly bathed, have not got tons of makeup on your face; have had your hair newly 'permed' or 'coiffed'; have clean or nicely manicured fingernails, that don't stick out ten inches from your fingers; and are using a deodorant;
- you wear a bra, have on freshly cleaned clothes, a suit or sophisticated-looking dress, shoes not sandals, and ones which don't call *a lot* of attention to themselves;
- you do not have bad breath, do not dispense gallons of garlic, onion, stale tobacco, or the odor of strong drink, into the enclosed office air; but have brushed and flossed your teeth, plus used a mouthwash if necessary;
- you are not wafting tons of perfume fifteen feet ahead of you, as you enter the room.

Remember, since the hiring process is more like choosing a mate, than deciding whether or not to buy a new house, the employer is simply trying to determine if they like you. In which case, these 'mosquitoes' can kill you, no matter how qualified you may otherwise be.

P.S. In the U.S. at least, *many* an employer watches to see if you smoke, either in the interview or at lunch. (*In a race between two equally qualified people, the nonsmoker will win out over the smoker 94% of the time, according to a study done by a professor of business at Seattle University.*)

Some experts counsel job-hunters who smoke to try to hide it during the interview. Personally, I think all such attempts to deceive the employer are ill-advised. So what if you do pull it off? It will come out that you smoke, after you are hired, and the employer who hates smoking can always manage to fire you, on one pretext or another. My advice: don't try to hide it.

But, I do think it is legitimate to *delay* revealing it until the employer has decided they really want you. Once a job-offer has been made, *then* I think it is crucial for you to tell the employer you smoke, and offer an easy way out: "If this is a truly offensive habit to you, and one you don't want in any of your employees, I'd rather bow out gracefully now, than have it become an issue between us down the road." Such consideration, thoughtfulness, and graciousness on your part may go a long way to soften the employer's resistance to the fact that you are a smoker. Many places, in fact, allow employees who smoke to go outside for a 'smoke break' at stated intervals.

You may take this list of 'interview-killers' to heart, or just ignore it. If you do decide to ignore it, and then -- despite interview after interview -- you continue not to get hired, you might want to rethink your position on all of this.

It may indeed be the mosquitoes, not the dragons, that are killing you. And if that is the case, you can fix any or all of these things; they're all within your control. Once fixed, your next interviews may go much much better.

But if they don't, then I would recommend you go to a career counselor who charges by the hour, and put yourself in their tender knowledgeable hands. Role-play an interview, and see what advice they have to give you.

CONCLUSION

We have covered now the techniques of successful job-hunters. We have seen that the three secrets of successful career-change or systematic job-hunting are: WHAT, WHERE and HOW.

If you are having great trouble in finding work, you must not merely read these chapters and exercises, but *do it all*.

Here is one job-hunter's experience with all of this:

"Before I read this book, I was depressed and lost in the futile job-hunt using Want Ads Only. I did not receive even one phone call from any ad I answered, over a total of 4 months. I felt that I was the most useless person on earth. I am female, with a 2½-year-old daughter, former professor in China, with no working experience at all in the U.S. We came here seven months ago because my husband had a job offer here.

"Then, on June 11th of this year, I saw your book in a local book-store. Subsequently, I spent 3 weeks, 10 hours a day except Sunday, reading every single word of your book and doing all of the exercises. After getting to know myself much better, I felt I was ready to try the job-hunt again. I used Parachute throughout as my guide, from the very beginning to the very end, namely, salary negotiation.

"In just two weeks I secured (you guessed it) two job offers, one of which I am taking, as it is an excellent job, with very good pay. It is (you guessed it again) a small company, with 20 or so employees. It is also a career-change: I was a professor of English; now I am to be a controller!

"I am so glad I believed your advice: there are jobs out there, and there are two types of employers out there, and truly there are!

"I hope you will be happy to hear my story."

With a little bit of luck, these techniques should work for you as they have worked for her.

You have a precious kind of knowledge, now: how to get hired. And to paraphrase something Dick Lathrop first said many years ago, in his book *Who's Hiring Who:*

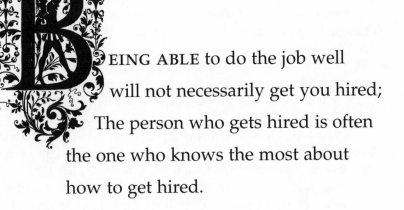

EING ABLE to do the job well will not necessarily get you hired; The person who gets hired is often the one who knows the most about how to get hired.

Epilogue

How To Find Your Mission In Life

God and One's Vocation

Foreword

As I started writing this section, I toyed at first with the idea of following what might be described as an "all-paths approach" to religion. But, after much thought, I decided not to try that. This, because I have read many other writers who tried, and I felt the approach failed miserably. An "all-paths" approach to religion ends up being a "no-paths" approach, even as a woman or man who tries to please everyone ends up pleasing no one. It is the old story of the "universal" vs. the "particular."

Those of us who do career counseling could predict, ahead of time, that trying to stay universal is not likely to be helpful, in writing about religion. We know well from our own field that truly helpful career counseling depends upon defining the **particularity** or uniqueness of each person we try to help. No employer wants to know only what you have in common with everyone else. He or she wants to know what makes you unique and individual. As I have argued throughout this book, the identification and inventory of your uniqueness or *particularity* is crucial if you are ever to find meaningful work.

This particularity invades and carries over to *everything* a person does; it is not suddenly "jettisonable" when he or she turns to religion. Therefore, when I or anyone else writes about religion I believe we **must** write out of our own particularity -- which *starts*, in my case, with the fact that I write, and think, and breathe as a Christian -- as you might expect from the fact that I have been an ordained Episcopalian minister for the last forty-five years. Understandably, then, this article speaks from a Christian perspective. I want you to be aware of that, at the outset.

Balanced against this is the fact that I have always been acutely sensitive to the fact that this is a pluralistic society in which we live, and that I owe a great deal to my readers who may have religious convictions quite different from my own. It has turned out that the people who work or have worked here in my office with me, over the years, have been predominantly of other faiths, mainly Jewish. Furthermore, **Parachute's** more than 6 million readers have not only included Christians of every variety and persuasion, Mormons, Christian Scientists, Jews, members of the Baha'i faith, Hindus, Buddhists, adherents of Islam, but also believers in 'new age' religions, secularists, humanists, agnostics, atheists, and many others. I have therefore tried to be very courteous toward the feelings of all my readers, *while at the same time* counting on them to translate my Christian thought forms into their own thought forms. This ability to thus translate is the indispensable *sine qua non* of anyone who wants to communicate helpfully with others, these days.

In the Judeo-Christian tradition from which I come, one of the indignant Biblical questions is, "Has God forgotten to be gracious?" The answer was a clear No. I think it is important *for all of us* also to seek the same goal. I have therefore labored to make this section gracious as well as helpful.

R.N.B

TURNING POINT

For many of us, the job-hunt offers a chance to make some fundamental changes in our whole life. It marks a turning point in how we live our life.

It gives us a chance to ponder and reflect, to extend our mental horizons, to go deeper into the sub-soil of our soul.

It gives us a chance to wrestle with the question, "Why am I here on Earth?" We don't want to feel that we are just another grain of sand lying on the beach called humanity, unnumbered and lost in the 5 billion other human beings.

We want to do more than plod through life, going to work, coming home from work. We want to find that special joy, "that no one can take from us," which comes from having a sense of Mission in our life.

We want to feel we were put here on Earth for some special purpose, to do some unique work that only we can accomplish.

We want to know what our Mission is.

THE MEANING
OF THE WORD
'MISSION'

When used with respect to our life and work *Mission* has always been a religious concept, from beginning to end. It is defined by Webster's as "a continuing task or responsibility that one is destined or fitted to do or specially called upon to undertake," and historically has had two major synonyms: *Calling* and *Vocation*. These, of course, are the same word in two different languages, English and Latin. Both imply God. To be given a Vocation or Calling implies *Someone who* calls. To have a Destiny implies *Someone who determined the destination for us.* Thus, the concept of Mission lands us inevitably in the lap of God, before we have hardly begun.

I emphasize this, because there is an increasing trend in our culture to try to speak about religious subjects without reference to God. This is true of "spirituality," "soul," and "Mission," in particular. More and more books talk about Mission as though it were simply "a purpose you choose for your own life, by identifying your enthusiasms."

This attempt to obliterate all reference to God from the originally-religious concept of Mission, is particularly ironic because the proposed substitute word -- enthusiasms -- is derived from two Greek words, 'en theos,' and means "God in us."

In the midst of this "redefining culture" we find an oasis called "the job-hunting field." It is a field that was raised on a firm concept of "God." That's because most of its inventors, most of its leaders over the years -- the late John Crystal, Arthur Miller, Ralph Mattson, Tom and Ellie Jackson, Bernard Haldane, Arthur and Marie Kirn, myself and many others -- have been people who believe firmly in God, and came into this field because we think about Him a lot, in connection with meaningful work.

Nor are we alone. Many many job-hunters also think about God a lot. In the U.S., 94% of us believe in God, 90% of us pray, 88% of us believe God loves us, and 33% of us report we have had a life-changing religious experience - - and these figures have remained virtually unchanged for the past fifty years, according to opinion polls conducted by the Gallup Organization. (*The People's Religion: American Faith in the 90s.* Macmillan & Co. 1989).

What is not so clear is whether we think about God in connection with our work. Often these two subjects -- spiritual beliefs and Work -- live in separate mental ghettos within the same person's head.

But unemployment offers us a chance to fix all that: to marry our work and our religious beliefs together, to talk about Calling, and Vocation, and Mission in life -- to think out why we are here, and what plans God has for us.

That's why a period of unemployment can absolutely change our life.

THE SECRET OF
FINDING YOUR MISSION
IN LIFE:
TAKING IT IN STAGES

> I will explain the steps toward finding your mission in life
> that I have learned in my seventy years on Earth. Just remem-
> ber two things. First, I speak from a Christian perspective, and
> trust you to translate this into your own thought-forms.
>
> Secondly, I know that these steps are not the only Way --
> by any means. Many people have discovered their Mission by
> taking other paths. And you may, too. But hopefully what I
> have to say may shed some light upon whatever path you take.

I have learned that if you want to figure out what your Mission in
life is, it will likely take some time. It is not a *problem* to be solved in a
day and a night. It is a *learning process* which has steps to it, much like
the process by which we all learned to eat. As a baby we did not
tackle adult food right off. As we all recall, there were three stages:
first there had to be the mother's milk or bottle, then strained baby
foods, and finally -- after teeth and time -- the stuff that grown-ups
chew. Three stages -- and the two earlier stages were not to be disparaged. It was all Eating, just different forms of Eating -- appropriate to
our development at the time. But each stage had to be mastered, in
turn, before the next could be approached.

There are usually three stages also to learning what your Mission in life is, and the two earlier stages are likewise not to be disparaged. It is all "Mission" - - just different forms of Mission, appropriate to your development at the time. But each stage has to be mastered, in turn, before the next can be approached.

Of course, there is a sense in which you never master any of these stages, but are always growing in understanding and mastery of them, throughout your whole life here on Earth.

As it has been impressed on me by observing many people over the years (admittedly through *Christian spectacles*), it appears that the three parts to your Mission here on Earth can be defined generally as follows:

(1) *Your first Mission here on Earth* is one which you share with the rest of the human race, but it is no less your individual Mission for the fact that it is shared: and it is, **to seek to stand hour by hour in the conscious presence of God, the One from whom your Mission is derived**. *The Missioner before the Mission*, is the rule. In religious language, your Mission here is: *to know God, and enjoy Him forever, and to see His hand in all His works.*

(2) Secondly, once you have begun doing that in an earnest way, *your second Mission here on Earth* is also one which you share with the rest of the human race, but it is no less your individual mission for the fact that it is shared: and that is, **to do what you can, moment by moment, day by day, step by step, to make this world a better place, following the leading and guidance of God's Spirit within you and around you**.

(3) Thirdly, once you have begun doing that in a serious way, *your third Mission here on Earth* is one which is uniquely yours, and that is:

a) **to exercise that Talent which you particularly came to Earth to use -- your greatest gift, which you most delight to use,**

b) **in the place(s) or setting(s) which God has caused to appeal to you the most,**

c) **and for those purposes which God most needs to have done in the world.**

When fleshed out, and spelled out, I think you will find that there you have the definition of your Mission in life. Or, to put it another way, these are the three Missions which you have in life.

The Two Rhythms of the Dance of Mission:
Unlearning, Learning,
Unlearning, Learning

The distinctive characteristic of these three stages is that in each we are forced to *let go* of some fundamental assumptions which the world has *falsely* taught us, about the nature of our Mission. In other words, throughout this quest and at each stage we find ourselves engaged not merely in a process of *Learning.* We are also engaged in a process of *Un*learning. Thus, we can restate the above three Learnings, in terms of what we also need to *un*learn at each stage:

• We need in the first Stage to *un*learn the idea that our Mission is primarily to keep busy *doing* something (here on Earth), and learn instead that our Mission is first of all to keep busy *being* something (here on Earth). In Christian language (and others as well), we might say that we were sent here to learn how *to be* sons of God, and daughters of God, before anything else. *"Our Father, who art in heaven . . ."*

• In the second stage, "Being" issues into "Doing." At this stage, we need to *un*learn the idea that everything about our Mission must be *unique* to us, and learn instead that some parts of our Mission here on Earth are *shared* by all human beings: e.g., we were all sent here to bring more gratitude, more kindness, more forgiveness, and more love, into the world. We share this Mission because the task is too large to be accomplished by just one individual.

• We need in the third stage to *un*learn the idea that that part of our Mission which is truly unique, and most truly ours, is something Our Creator just *orders* us to do, without any agreement from our spirit, mind, and heart. (On the other hand, neither is it something that each of us chooses and then merely asks God to bless.) We need to learn that God so honors our free will, that He has ordained our unique Mission be something which we have some part in choosing.

• In this third stage we need also to *un*learn the idea that our unique Mission must consist of some achievement which all the world will see, -- and learn instead that as the stone does not always know what ripples it has caused in the pond whose surface it impacts, so neither we nor those who watch our life will always know *what we have achieved* by our life and by our Mission. *It may be* that by the grace of God we helped bring about a profound change for the better in the lives of other souls around us, but it also may be that this takes place beyond our sight, or after we have gone on. And we may never know what we have accomplished, until we see Him face-to-face after this life is past.

• Most finally, we need to *un*learn the idea that what we have accomplished is our doing, and ours alone. It is God's Spirit breathing in us and through us which helps us to do whatever we do, and so the singular first person pronoun is never appropriate, but only the plural. Not *"I* accomplished this" but *"We* accomplished this, God and I, working together . . ."

That should give you a general overview. But I would like to add some random comments on my part about each of these three Missions of ours here on Earth.

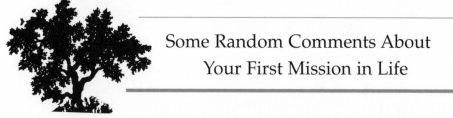

Some Random Comments About Your First Mission in Life

Your first Mission here on Earth is one which you share with the rest of the human race, but it is no less your individual Mission for the fact that it is shared: and that is, **to seek to stand hour by hour in the conscious presence of God, the One from whom your Mission is derived**. The Missioner before the Mission, is the rule. In religious language, your Mission is: to know God, and enjoy Him forever, and to see His hand in all His works.

Comment 1: How We Might Think of God

Each of us has to go about this primary Mission according to the tenets of his or her own particular religion. But I will speak what I know out of the context of my own particular faith, and you may perhaps translate and apply it to yours. I will speak as a Christian, who believes (passionately) that Christ is the Way and the Truth and the Life. But I also believe, with St. Peter, "that God shows no partiality, but in every nation any one who fears him and does what is right is acceptable to him." (Acts 10:34-35)

Now, Jesus claimed many unique things about Himself and His Mission; but He also spoke of Himself as the great prototype for us all. He called himself "the Son of Man," and He said, "I assure you that the man who believes in me will do the same things that I have done, yes, and he will do even greater things than these . . ." (John 14:12)

Emboldened by His identification of us with His life and His Mission, we might want to remember how He spoke about His Life here on Earth. He put it in this context: **"I came from the Father and have come into the world; again, I am leaving the world and going to the Father."** (John 16:28)

If there is a sense in which this is, in even the faintest way, true also of our lives (and I shall say in a moment in what sense I think it is true), then instead of calling our great Creator "God" or "Father" right off, we might begin our approach to the subject of religion by referring to the One Who gave us our Mission and sent us to this planet not as "God" or "Father" but -- *just to help our thinking* -- as: **"The One From Whom We Came and The One To Whom We Shall Return,"** when this life is done.

If our life here on Earth be at all like Christ's, then this is a true way to think about the One Who gave us our Mission. We are not some kind of eternal, pre-existent *being*. We are **creatures**, who once did not exist, and then came into Being, and continue to have our Being, only at the will of our great Creator. But as creatures we are both body and soul; and although we know our body was created in our mother's womb, our soul's origin is a great mystery. Where it came from, at what moment the Lord created it, is something we cannot know. It is not unreasonable to suppose, however, that the great God created our *soul* before it entered our body, and in that sense we did indeed stand before God before we were born; and He is indeed **"The One From Whom We Came and The One To Whom We Shall Return."**

Therefore, before we go searching for "what work was I sent here to do?" we need to establish or in a truer sense *reestablish* -- contact with this **"One From Whom We Came and The One To Whom We Shall Return."** Without this reaching out of the creature to the great Creator, without this reaching out of *the creature with a Mission* to *the One Who Gave Us That Mission*, the question *what* is my Mission in life? is void and null. The *what* is rooted in the *Who*; absent the Personal, one cannot meaningfully discuss The Thing. It is like the adult who cries, "I want to get married," without giving any consideration to *who* it is they want to marry.

Comment 2: How We Might Think of Religion or Faith

In light of this larger view of our creatureliness, we can see that *religion or faith* is not a question of whether or not we choose to (*as it is so commonly put*) "have a relationship with God." Looking at our life in a larger context than just our life here on Earth, it becomes apparent that some sort of relationship with God is a given for us, about which we have absolutely no choice. God and we **were and are** related, during the time of our soul's existence before our birth and in the time of our soul's continued existence after our death. The only choice we have is what to do about **The Time In Between**, i.e., what we want the nature of our relationship with God to be during our time here on Earth and how that will affect the *nature* of the relationship, then, after death.

One of the corollaries of all this is that by the very act of being born into a human body, it is an inevitable that we undergo a kind of *amnesia* -- an amnesia which typically embraces not only our nine months in the womb, our baby years, and almost one-third of each day (sleeping), but more importantly any memory of our origin or our destiny. We wander on Earth as an amnesia victim. To seek after Faith, therefore, is to seek to climb back out of that amnesia. Religion or faith is **the hard reclaiming of knowledge we once knew as a certainty**.

Comment 3: The First Obstacle to Executing This Mission

This first Mission of ours here on Earth is not the easiest of Missions, simply because it is the first. Indeed, in many ways, it is the most difficult. All can see that our life here on Earth is a very physical life. We eat, we drink, we sleep, we long to be held, and to hold. We inherit a physical body, with very physical appetites, we walk on the physical earth, and we acquire physical possessions. It is the most alluring of temptations, *in our amnesia*, to come up with just a *Physical* interpretation of this life: to think that the Universe is merely interested in the survival of species. Given this interpretation, the story of our individual life could be simply told: we are born, grow up, procreate, and die.

But we are ever recalled to do what we came here to do: that without rejecting the joy of the Physicalness of this life, such as the love of the blue sky and the green grass, we are to reach out beyond all this to **recall** and recover a *Spiritual* interpretation of our life. *Beyond* the physical and *within* the physicalness of this life, to detect a Spirit and a Person from beyond this Earth who is with us and in us -- the very real and loving and awesome Presence of the great Creator from whom we came -- and the One to whom we once again shall go.

Comment 4: The Second Obstacle to Executing This Mission

It is one of the conditions of our earthly amnesia and our creatureliness that, sadly enough, some very *human* and very *rebellious* part of us *likes* the idea of living in a world where we can be our own god -- and therefore loves the purely Physical interpretation of life, and finds it *anguish* to relinquish it. Traditional Christian vocabulary calls this "**sin**" and has a lot to say about the difficulty it poses for this first part of our Mission. All who live a thoughtful life know that it is true: our greatest enemy in carrying out this first Mission of ours is indeed *our own* heart and our own rebellion.

Comment 5: Further Thoughts About What Makes Us Special and Unique

As I said earlier, many of us come to this issue of our Mission in life, because we want to feel that we are unique. And what we mean by that, is that we hope to discover some "specialness" intrinsic to us, which is our birthright, and which no one can take from us. What we, however, discover from a thorough exploration of this topic, is that we are indeed special -- but only because God thinks us so. Our specialness and uniqueness reside in Him, and His love, rather than in anything intrinsic to our own *being*. The proper appreciation of this distinction causes our feet to carry us in the end not to the City called Pride, but to the Temple called Gratitude.

> What is religion? Religion is the service of God
> out of grateful love for what God has done for
> us. The Christian religion, more particularly, is
> the service of God out of grateful love for what
> God has done for us in Christ.
>
> Phillips Brooks, author of
> *O Little Town of Bethlehem*

Comment 6: The Unconscious Doing of The Work We Came To Do

You may have *already* wrestled with this first part of your Mission here on Earth. You may not have called it that. You may have called it simply "learning to believe in God." But if you ask what your Mission is in life, this one was and is the precondition of all else that you came here to do. Absent this Mission, and it is folly to talk about the rest. So, if you have been seeking faith, or seeking to strengthen your faith, you have -- willy nilly -- already been about *the doing of the Mission you were given*. Born into **This Time In Between**, you have found His hand again, and reclasped it. You are therefore ready to go on with His Spirit to tackle together what you came here to do -- the other parts of your Mission.

Some Random Comments About Your Second Mission in Life

Your second Mission here on Earth is also one which you share with the rest of the human race, but it is no less your individual mission for the fact that it is shared: and that is, **to do what you can moment by moment, day by day, step by step, to make this world a better place -- following the leading and guidance of God's Spirit within you and around you**.

Comment 1: The Uncomfortableness of One Step at a Time

Imagine yourself out walking in your neighborhood one night, and suddenly you find yourself surrounded by such a dense fog, that you have lost your bearings and cannot find your way. Suddenly, a friend appears out of the fog, and asks you to put your hand in theirs, and they will lead you home. And you, not being able to tell where you are going, trustingly follow them, even though you can only see one step at a time. Eventually you arrive safely home, filled with gratitude. But as you reflect upon the experience the next day, you realize how unsettling it was to have to keep walking when you could see only one step at a time, even though you had guidance in which you knew you could trust.

Now I have asked you to imagine all of this, because this is the essence of the second Mission to which *you* are called -- and *I* am called -- in this life. It is all very different than we had imagined. When the question, *"What is your Mission in life?"* is first broached, and we have put our hand in God's, as it were, we imagine that we will be taken up to *some mountaintop*, from which we can see far into the distance. And that we will hear a voice in our ear, saying, "Look, look, see that distant city? That is the goal of your Mission; that is where everything is leading, every step of your way."

But instead of the mountaintop, we find ourself in *the valley* -- wandering often in a fog. And the voice in our ear says something quite different from what we thought we would hear. It says, "**Your Mission is to take one step at a time, even when you don't yet see where it all is leading, or what the Grand Plan is, or what your overall Mission in life is. Trust Me; I will lead you.**"

Comment 2: The Nature of This Step-by-Step Mission

As I said, in every situation you find yourself, you have been sent here to do whatever you can -- moment by moment -- that will bring more gratitude, more kindness, more forgiveness, more honesty, and more love into this world.

There are dozens of such moments every day. Moments when you stand -- as it were -- at a spiritual crossroads, with two ways lying before you. Such moments are typically called "**moments of decision.**" It does not matter what the frame or content of each particular decision is. It all devolves, in the end, into just two roads before you, *every time*. **The one** will lead to *less* gratitude, *less* kindness, *less* forgiveness, *less* honesty, or *less* love in the world. **The other** will lead to *more* gratitude, *more* kindness, *more* forgiveness, *more* honesty, or *more* love in the world. Your Mission, each moment, is to seek to choose the latter spiritual road, rather than the former, *every time*.

Comment 3: Some Examples of This Step-by-Step Mission

I will give a few examples, so that the nature of this part of your Mission may be unmistakably clear.

You are out on the freeway, in your car. Someone has gotten into the wrong lane, to the right of *your* lane, and needs to move over into the lane you are in. You *see* their need to cut in, ahead of you. **Decision time.** In your mind's eye you see two spiritual roads lying before you: the one leading to less kindness in the world (you speed up, to shut this driver out, and don't let them move over), the other leading to more kindness in the world (you let the driver cut in). **Since you know this is part of your Mission, part of the reason why you came to Earth, your calling is clear. You know which road to take, which decision to make.**

You are hard at work at your desk, when suddenly an interruption comes. The phone rings, or someone is at the door. They need something from you, a question of some of your time and attention. **Decision time.** In your mind's eye you see two spiritual roads lying before you: the one leading to less love in the world (you tell them you're just too busy to be bothered), the other leading to more love in the world (you put aside your work, decide that God may have sent this person to you, and say, "Yes, what can I do to help you?"). **Since you know this is part of your Mission, part of the reason why you came to Earth, your calling is clear. You know which road to take, which decision to make.**

Your mate does something that hurts your feelings. **Decision time.** In your mind's eye you see two spiritual roads lying before you: the one leading to less forgiveness in the world (you institute an icy silence between the two of you, and think of how you can punish them or otherwise get even), the other leading to more forgiveness in the

world (you go over and take them in your arms, speak the truth about your hurt feelings, and assure them of your love). **Since you know this is part of your Mission, part of the reason why you came to Earth, your calling is clear. You know which road to take, which decision to make.**

You have not behaved at your most noble, recently. And now you are face-to-face with someone who asks you a question about what happened. **Decision time.** In your mind's eye you see two spiritual roads lying before you: the one leading to less honesty in the world (you lie about what happened, or what you were feeling, because you fear losing their respect or their love), the other leading to more honesty in the world (you tell the truth, together with how you feel about it, in retrospect). **Since you know this is part of your Mission, part of the reason why you came to Earth, your calling is clear. You know which road to take, which decision to make.**

Comment 4: The Spectacle Which Makes the Angels Laugh

It is necessary to explain this part of our Mission in some detail, because so many times you will see people wringing their hands, and saying, "*I want to know what my Mission in life is*," all the while they are cutting people off on the highway, refusing to give time to people, punishing their mate for having hurt their feelings, and lying about what they did. And it will seem to you that the angels must laugh to see this spectacle. *For these people wringing their hands*, their Mission was right there, on the freeway, in the interruption, in the hurt, and at the confrontation.

Comment 5: The Valley vs. The Mountaintop

At some point in your life your Mission may involve some grand *mountaintop experience*, where you say to yourself, "This, this, is why I came into the world. I know it. I know it." *But until then*, your Mission is here in *the valley*, and the fog, and the little callings moment by moment, day by day. More to the point, it is likely you cannot ever get to your mountaintop Mission unless you have first exercised your stewardship faithfully in the valley.

It is an ancient principle, to which Jesus alluded often, that if you don't use the information the Universe has already given you, you cannot expect it will give you any more. If you aren't being faithful in small things, how can you expect to be given charge over larger things? (Luke 16:10,11,12; 19:11–24) If you aren't trying to bring more gratitude, kindness, forgiveness, honesty, and love into the world each day, you can hardly expect that you will be entrusted with the Mission to help bring peace into the world or anything else large and important. If we do not live out our day-by-day Mission in the valley, we cannot expect we are yet ready for a larger *mountaintop* Mission.

Comment 6: The Importance of Not Thinking of This Mission As 'Just A Training Camp'

The valley is not just a kind of "training camp." There is in your imagination even now an invisible *spiritual* mountaintop to which you may go, if you wish to see where all this is leading. And what will you see there, in the imagination of your heart, but the goal toward which all this is pointed: **that Earth might be more like heaven. That human's life might be more like God's**. That is the large achievement toward which all our day-by-day Missions *in the valley* are moving. This is a *large* order, but it is accomplished by faithful attention to the doing of our great Creator's **will** in little things as well as in large. It is much like the building of the pyramids in Egypt, which was accomplished by the dragging of a lot of individual pieces of stone by a lot of individual men.

The valley, the fog, the going step-by-step, is no mere training camp. The goal is real, however large. "**Thy Kingdom come, Thy will be done, on Earth, as it is in heaven.**"

Some Random Comments About Your Third Mission in Life

Your third Mission here on Earth is one which is uniquely yours, and that is:

a) **to exercise that Talent which you particularly came to Earth to use -- your greatest gift which you most delight to use**

b) **in those place(s) or setting(s) which God has caused to appeal to you the most,**

c) **and for those purposes which God most needs to have done in the world.**

Comment 1: Our Mission Is Already Written, "in Our Members"

It is customary in trying to identify this part of our Mission, to advise that we should ask God, in prayer, to speak to us -- and **tell us** plainly what our Mission is. We look for a voice in the air, a thought in our head, a dream in the night, a sign in the events of the day, to reveal this thing which is otherwise *(it is said)* completely hidden. Sometimes, from just such answered prayer, people do indeed discover what their Mission is, beyond all doubt and uncertainty.

But having to wait for the voice of God to reveal what our Mission is, is not the truest picture of our situation. St. Paul, in Romans, speaks of a law "written in our members," -- and this phrase has a telling application to the question of **how** God reveals to each of us our unique Mission in life. Read again the definition of our third Mission (above) and you will see: the clear implication of the definition is that God has **already** revealed His will to us concerning our vocation and Mission, by causing it to be "**written in our members.**" We are to begin deciphering our unique Mission by studying our talents and skills, and more particularly which ones (or One) we most rejoice to use.

God actually has written His will *twice* in our members: *first in the talents* which He lodged there, and secondly *in His guidance of our heart*, as to which talent gives us the greatest pleasure from its exercise (**it is usually the one which, when we use it, causes us to lose all sense of time**).

Even as the anthropologist can examine ancient inscriptions, and divine from them the daily life of a long lost people, so we by examining **our talents** and **our heart** can *more often than we dream* divine the Will of the Living God. For true it is, our Mission is not something He **will** reveal; it is something He **has already** revealed. It is not to be found written in the sky; it is to be found written in our members.

Comment 2: Career Counseling: We Need You

Arguably, our first two Missions in life could be learned from religion alone -- without any reference whatsoever to career counseling, the subject of this book. Why then should career counseling claim that this question about our Mission in life is its proper concern, *in any way?*

It is when we come to this third Mission, which hinges so crucially on the question of our Talents, skills, and gifts, that we see the answer. If you've read the body of this book, before turning to this Epilogue, you know without my even saying it, how much the identification of Talents, gifts, or skills is the province of career counseling. Its expertise, indeed its *raison d'etre*, lies precisely in the identification, classification, and (forgive me) "prioritization" of Talents, skills, and gifts. To put the matter quite simply, career counseling knows how to do this better than any other discipline -- **including** traditional religion. This is not a defect of religion, but the fulfillment of something Jesus promised: "When the Spirit of truth comes, He will guide you into all truth." (John 16:12) Career counseling is part (we may hope) of that promised late-coming truth. It can therefore be of inestimable help to the pilgrim who is trying to figure out what their greatest, and most enjoyable, talent is, as a step toward identifying their unique Mission in life.

If career counseling needs religion as its helpmate in the first two stages of identifying our Mission in life, religion repays the compliment by clearly needing career counseling as **its** helpmate here in the third stage.

And this place where you are in your life right now -- facing the job-hunt and all its anxiety -- is the perfect time to seek the union within your own mind and heart of both career counseling (as in the pages of this book) and your faith in God.

Comment 3: How Our Mission Got Chosen: A Scenario for the Romantic

It is a mystery which we cannot fathom, in this life at least, as to why one of us has this talent, and the other one has that; why God chose to give one gift -- and Mission -- to one person, and a different gift -- and Mission -- to another. Since we do not know, and in some degree cannot know, we are certainly left free to speculate, and imagine.

We may imagine that before we came to Earth, our souls, *our Breath, our Light*, stood before the great Creator and volunteered for this Mission. And God and we, together, chose what that Mission would be and what particular gifts would be needed, which He then agreed to give us, after our birth. Thus, our Mission was not a command given preemptorily by an unloving Creator to a reluctant slave without a vote, but was a task jointly designed by us both, in which as fast as the great Creator said, "**I wish**" our hearts responded, "**Oh, yes.**" As mentioned in an earlier Comment, it may be helpful to think of the condition of our becoming human as that we became amnesiac about any consciousness our soul had before birth -- and therefore amnesiac about the nature or manner in which our Mission was designed.

Our searching for our Mission now is therefore a searching to recover the memory of something we ourselves had a part in designing.

I am admittedly a hopeless romantic, so of course I like this picture. If you also are a hopeless romantic, you may like it too. There's also the chance that it just may be true. We will not know until we see Him face-to-face.

Comment 4: Mission As Intersection

There are all different kinds of voices calling you to all different kinds of work, and the problem is to find out which is the voice of God rather than that of society, say, or the superego, or self-interest. By and large a good rule for finding out is this: the kind of work God usually calls you to is the kind of work (a) that you need most to do and (b) the world most needs to have done. If you really get a kick out of your work, you've presumably met requirement (a), but if your work is writing TV deodorant commercials, the chances are you've missed requirement (b). On the other hand, if your work is being a doctor in a leper colony, you have probably met (b), but if most of the time you're bored and depressed by it, the chances are you haven't only bypassed (a) but probably aren't helping your patients much either. Neither the hair shirt nor the soft birth will do. **The place God calls you to is the place where your deep gladness and the world's deep hunger meet.**

Fred Buechner
Wishful Thinking -- A Theological ABC

Excerpted from *Wishful Thinking – A Theological ABC* by Frederick Buechner. Copyright ©1973 by Frederick Buechner. Reprinted with permission of HarperCollins, Inc.

Comment 5: Examples of Mission As Intersection

Your unique and individual mission will most likely turn out to be a mission of Love, acted out in one or all of three arenas: either in the Kingdom of the Mind, whose goal is to bring more Truth into the world; or in the Kingdom of the Heart, whose goal is to bring more Beauty into the world; or in the Kingdom of the Will, whose goal is to bring more Perfection into the world, through Service.

Here are some examples:

"My mission is, out of the rich reservoir of love which God seems to have given me, to nurture and show love to others -- most particularly to those who are suffering from incurable diseases."

"My mission is to draw maps for people to show them how to get to God."

"My mission is to create the purest foods I can, to help people's bodies not get in the way of their spiritual growth."

"My mission is to make the finest harps I can so that people can hear the voice of God in the wind."

"My mission is to make people laugh, so that the travail of this earthly life doesn't seem quite so hard to them."

"My mission is to help people know the truth, in love, about what is happening out in the world, so that there will be more honesty in the world."

"My mission is to weep with those who weep, so that in my arms they may feel themselves in the arms of that Eternal Love which sent me and which created them."

"My mission is to create beautiful gardens, so that in the lilies of the field people may behold the Beauty of God and be reminded of the Beauty of Holiness."

Comment 6: Life As Long As Your Mission Requires

Knowing that you came to Earth for a reason, and knowing what that Mission is, throws an entirely different light upon your life from now on. You are, generally speaking, delivered from any further fear about how long you have to live. You may settle it in your heart that you are here until God chooses to think that you have accomplished your Mission, or until God has a greater Mission for you in another Realm. You need to be a good steward of what He has given you, while you are here; but you do not need to be an anxious steward or stewardess.

You need to attend to your health, *but you do not need to constantly worry about it*. You need to meditate on your death, *but you do not need to be constantly preoccupied with it*. To paraphrase the glorious words of G. K. Chesterton: **"We now have a strong desire for living combined with a strange carelessness about dying. We desire life like water and yet are ready to drink death like wine."** We know that we are here to do what we came to do, and we need not worry about anything else.

Final Comment: A Job-Hunt Done Well

If you approach your job-hunt as an opportunity to work on this issue as well as the issue of how you will keep body and soul together, then hopefully your job-hunt will end with your being able to say: "Life has deep meaning to me, now. I have discovered more than my ideal job; I have found my Mission, and the reason why I am here on Earth."

Appendix A

EXERCISES

The Flower

A PICTURE OF THE JOB OF YOUR DREAMS

*T*HESE EXERCISES present a simple version
of "The Flower" diagram, which has been
used by thousands and thousands of job-
hunters.

If you wish a more detailed Flower, and more
detailed exercises, you will find them in
The What Color Is Your Parachute Workbook,
available in your local bookstore, or from
Ten Speed Press, at 1-800-841-BOOK.
That more detailed Flower is also available
on a CD-ROM, with my voice to guide you
through the process. The CD-ROM is available
in computer stores *(for IBM-compatibles
only)* or from Bumblebee Technologies at
1-888-548-4437 or `http://www.parachute.net/`
should you wish to order over the
Internet.
For any further information, call
1-800-841-BOOK.

YOUR FLOWER

IN ORDER TO HUNT FOR YOUR IDEAL JOB, or even something close to your ideal job, you must have a picture of it, in your head. The clearer the picture, the easier it will be to hunt for it. The purpose of this booklet is to guide you as you draw that picture.

We have chosen a "Flower" as the model for that picture. While such expressions as "plugging in," "turning on," and other common phrases portray you (implicitly) as a machine, you are actually much more like a Flower than a machine. That is to say, you flourish in some job-environments, but wither in others. Therefore, the purpose of putting together this Flower Picture of yourself is to help you identify what kind of a work climate you will flourish in, and thus do your very best work. Your twin goals should be to be as happy as you can be at your job, while at the same time you do your most effective work.

There is a picture of the Flower on pages 264–265, that you can use as your worksheet.

As you can see, skills are at the center of the Flower, even as they are at the center of your mission, career, or job. They are listed in order of priority.

Surrounding them are six petals. Listed in the order in which you will work on them, they are:

1. Geography
2. Interests (Special Knowledges)
3. People Environments
4. Values, Purposes, and Goals
5. Working Conditions
6. Salary & Responsibility

When you are done filling in these skills and petals, you will have the complete Flower picture of your Ideal Job. Okay? Then, get out your pen or pencil and let's get started.

The Flower

A Picture of The Job of Your Dreams

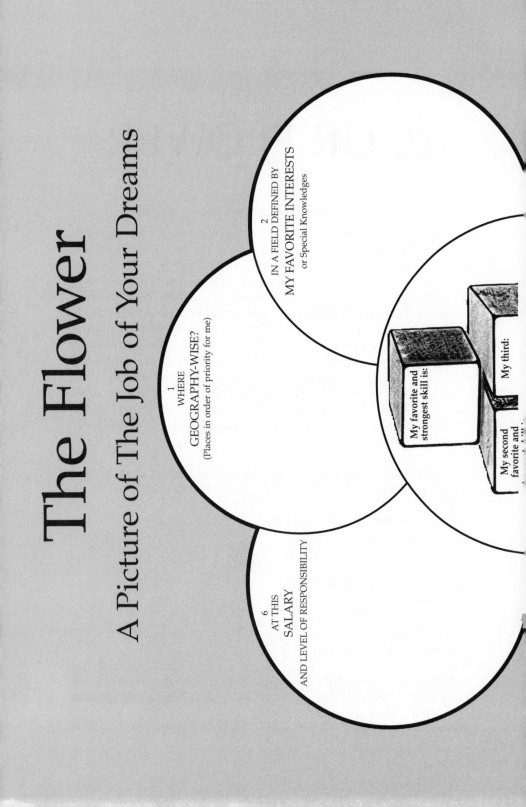

1
WHERE
GEOGRAPHY-WISE?
(Places in order of priority for me)

2
IN A FIELD DEFINED BY
MY FAVORITE INTERESTS
or Special Knowledges

6
AT THIS
SALARY
AND LEVEL OF RESPONSIBILITY

My favorite and strongest skill is:

My second favorite and

My third:

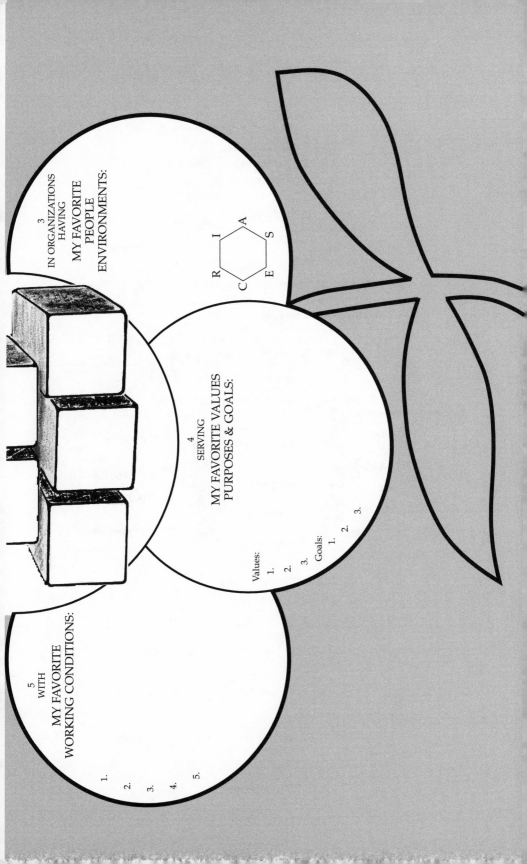

3
IN ORGANIZATIONS
HAVING
MY FAVORITE
PEOPLE
ENVIRONMENTS:

R   I
A
C   S
E

4
SERVING
MY FAVORITE VALUES
PURPOSES & GOALS:

Values:
1.
2.
3.
Goals:
1.
2.
3.

5
WITH
MY FAVORITE
WORKING CONDITIONS:

1.
2.
3.
4.
5.

Example

Your Favorite
Transferable Skills

We begin with skills. You must, first of all, identify your favorite (transferable) skills that you most enjoy using, *in order of priority or importance to you.* Here are the five steps to accomplishing that.

1. Write Your First Story

To do this, you will need to write **seven stories** about things you did just because they were fun, or because they gave you a sense of adventure, or gave you a sense of accomplishment. It does not matter whether anyone else ever knew about this accomplishment, or not. Each story can be about something you did at work, or in school, or at play -- and can be from any time period of your life. It should not be more than two or three paragraphs, in length.

> Below is a form to help you write each of your Seven Stories. *(You will obviously want to go down to Kinko's or your local copy shop and make seven copies of this form* before *you begin filling it out, for the first time. The copies work best if you make them on seven pieces of $8\frac{1}{2}$" × 11" paper,* turned sideways.)

If you need an example of what to put in each of the five columns, turn back to page 80ff here in *Parachute*. After you have written your first story, we will show you how to analyze it for the transferable skills that you used therein.

My Seven Life Stories

Column 1 Your Goal: What You Want to Accomplish	Column 2 Some Kind of Obstacle (or limit, hurdle or restraint you had to overcome before it could be accomplished)	Column 3 What You Did Step-by-Step (It may help if you pretend you are telling this story to a whining 4-year-old child, who keeps asking, after each of your sentences, "An' then whadja do? An' then whadja do?")	Column 4 Description of the Result (What you accomplished)	Column 5 Any Measure or Quantities To Prove Your Achievement

2. Analyze The Story for Transferable Skills

Once you have written Story #1 (and before you write the other six), you will want to analyze it for the transferable skills you *used*. (You can decide later if you loved those skills or not. For now, just do an inventory.)

To do this inventory, go to the list of Skills Keys found on pages 270–275, which resemble a series of typewriter keys. Transferable skills divide into:

1. <u>Physical Skills</u>: the transferable skills you enjoy, using primarily *your hands or body* -- with things, or nature;

2. <u>Mental Skills</u>: the transferable skills you enjoy, using primarily *your mind* -- with data/information, ideas, or subjects;

3. Your <u>Interpersonal Skills</u>: the transferable skills you enjoy, involving primarily *personal relationships* -- as you serve or help people or animals, and their needs or problems.[1]

Therefore you will find three sets of Skills Keys, labeled accordingly.

As you look at each key in the three sets, the question you need to ask yourself, is: "Did I use this transferable skill *in this Story* (#1)?"

That is the *only* question you ask yourself (at the moment). Then you go to the little box named #1 (under each Skill Key), and this is what you do:

If the answer is "Yes", fill in the little box, as shown below:

> Taking
> Instructions,
> Serving,
> Or Helping

Did I Use This Skill in Story

Yes █ | #2? | #3? | #4? | #5? | #6? | #7?

Ignore the other little boxes for the time being; they belong to your other stories (all the little boxes named #2 belong to Story #2, all the little boxes named #3 belong to Story #3, etc.)

My Physical Skills

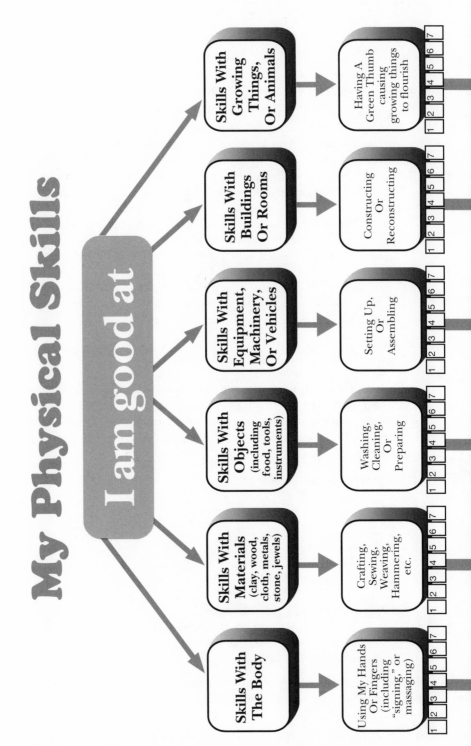

I am good at

Skills With The Body
→ Using My Hands Or Fingers (including "signing," or massaging)
1 2 3 4 5 6 7

Skills With Materials (clay, wood, cloth, metals, stone, jewels)
→ Crafting, Sewing, Weaving, Hammering, etc.
1 2 3 4 5 6 7

Skills With Objects (including food, tools, instruments)
→ Washing, Cleaning, Or Preparing
1 2 3 4 5 6 7

Skills With Equipment, Machinery, Or Vehicles
→ Setting Up, Or Assembling
1 2 3 4 5 6 7

Skills With Buildings Or Rooms
→ Constructing Or Reconstructing
1 2 3 4 5 6 7

Skills With Growing Things, Or Animals
→ Having A Green Thumb causing growing things to flourish
1 2 3 4 5 6 7

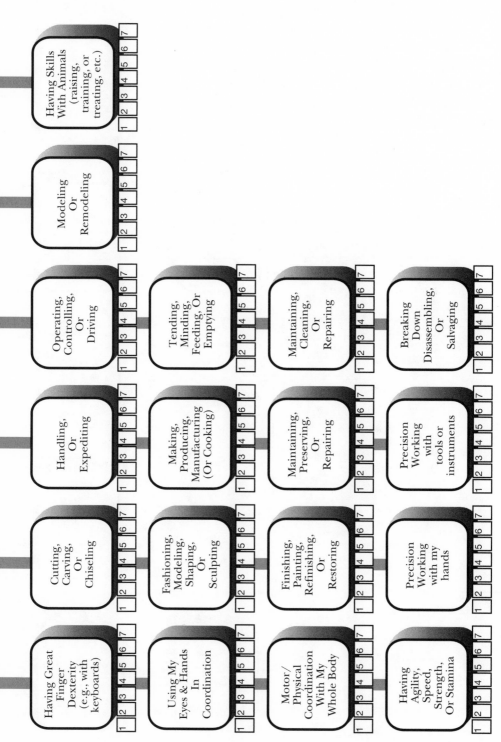

My Mental Skills

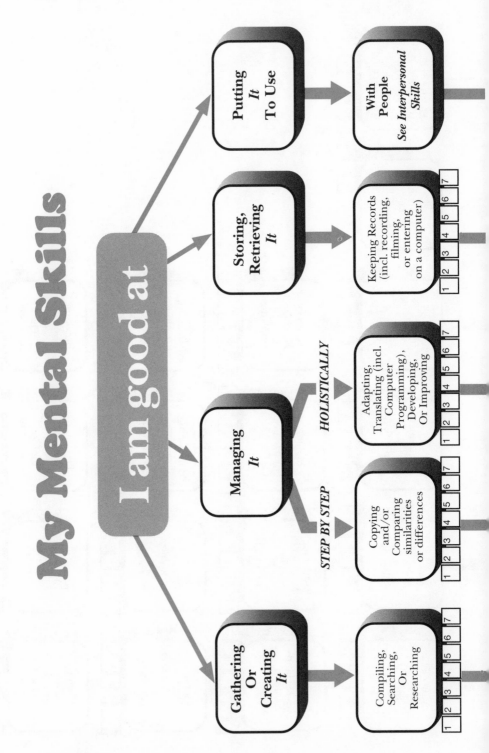

I am good at

Gathering Or Creating It

Compiling, Searching, Or Researching

| 1 | 2 | 3 | 4 | 5 | 6 | 7 |

Managing It

STEP BY STEP

Copying and/or Comparing similarities or differences

| 1 | 2 | 3 | 4 | 5 | 6 | 7 |

HOLISTICALLY

Adapting, Translating (incl. Computer Programming), Developing, Or Improving

| 1 | 2 | 3 | 4 | 5 | 6 | 7 |

Storing, Retrieving It

Keeping Records (incl. recording, filming, or entering on a computer)

| 1 | 2 | 3 | 4 | 5 | 6 | 7 |

Putting It To Use

With People *See Interpersonal Skills*

With Things
See Physical Skills

| | | | | | | |
|1|2|3|4|5|6|7|

Storing Or Filing, (in file cabinets, microfiche, video, audio, or computer)

| | | | | | | |
|1|2|3|4|5|6|7|

Retrieving Information, Ideas, Data

| | | | | | | |
|1|2|3|4|5|6|7|

Enabling Other People To Find Or Retrieve Information

| | | | | | | |
|1|2|3|4|5|6|7|

Having A Superior Memory, keeping track of details

| | | | | | | |
|1|2|3|4|5|6|7|

Visualizing, Drawing, Painting, Dramatizing, Creating Videos, Or Software

| | | | | | | |
|1|2|3|4|5|6|7|

Synthesizing, combining parts into a whole

| | | | | | | |
|1|2|3|4|5|6|7|

Problem Solving or seeing patterns among a mass of data

| | | | | | | |
|1|2|3|4|5|6|7|

Deciding, Evaluating, Appraising, Or Making Recommendations

| | | | | | | |
|1|2|3|4|5|6|7|

Computing, Working with Numbers, Doing Accounting

| | | | | | | |
|1|2|3|4|5|6|7|

Analyzing, breaking down into its parts

| | | | | | | |
|1|2|3|4|5|6|7|

Organizing, Classifying, Systematizing, and/or Prioritizing

| | | | | | | |
|1|2|3|4|5|6|7|

Planning, laying out a step-by-step process for achieving a goal

| | | | | | | |
|1|2|3|4|5|6|7|

Gathering Information By Interviewing Or Observing People

| | | | | | | |
|1|2|3|4|5|6|7|

Gathering Information By Studying Or Observing Things

| | | | | | | |
|1|2|3|4|5|6|7|

Having An Acute Sense Of Hearing, Smell, Taste, Or Sight

| | | | | | | |
|1|2|3|4|5|6|7|

Imagining, Inventing, Creating, Or Designing new ideas

| | | | | | | |
|1|2|3|4|5|6|7|

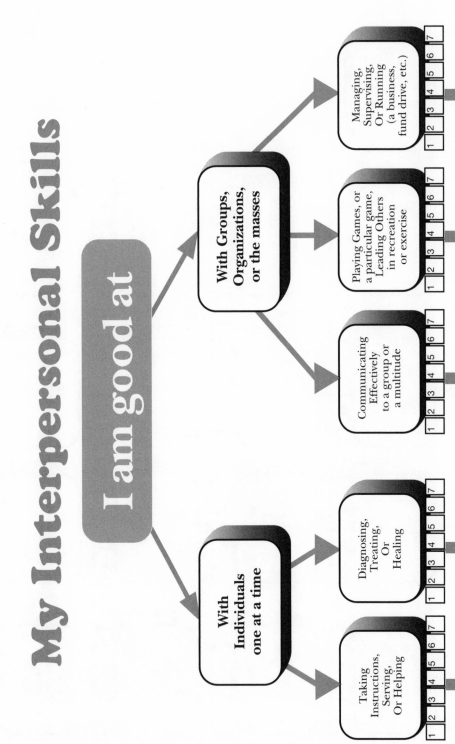

Following Through, Getting Things Done, Producing
1 2 3 4 5 6 7

Leading, Taking The Lead, Being A Pioneer
1 2 3 4 5 6 7

Initiating, Starting Up, Founding, Or Establishing
1 2 3 4 5 6 7

Negotiating between two parties, or Resolving Conflicts
1 2 3 4 5 6 7

Teaching, Training, or designing educational events
1 2 3 4 5 6 7

Guiding A Group Discussion, conveying warmth
1 2 3 4 5 6 7

Persuading A Group, Debating, Motivating, Or Selling
1 2 3 4 5 6 7

Consulting, Giving Advice to groups in your area of expertise
1 2 3 4 5 6 7

By Using Words Expressively in speaking or writing
1 2 3 4 5 6 7

By Making Presentations in person, or on TV or film
1 2 3 4 5 6 7

By Performing, Entertaining, Amusing, or Inspiring
1 2 3 4 5 6 7

"Signing," Miming, Acting, Singing, Or Playing an Instrument
1 2 3 4 5 6 7

Referring People, or helping two people to link up
1 2 3 4 5 6 7

Assessing, Evaluating, Screening, Or Selecting Individuals
1 2 3 4 5 6 7

Persuading, Motivating, Recruiting, Or Selling To Individuals
1 2 3 4 5 6 7

Representing Others, Interpreting Others' Ideas or Language
1 2 3 4 5 6 7

Communicating Well in conversation, in person, or on the phone
1 2 3 4 5 6 7

Communicating Well in writing (e.g., excellent letters)
1 2 3 4 5 6 7

Instructing, Teaching, Tutoring, Or Training Individuals
1 2 3 4 5 6 7

Advising, Coaching, Counseling, Mentoring, Empowering
1 2 3 4 5 6 7

If the answer is "No", leave the box labeled #1 blank, as shown below:

Did I Use This Skill in Story

No   #1? #2? #3? #4? #5? #6? #7?

3. Write Six Other Stories, and Analyze Them for Transferable Skills

Voila! You are done with Story #1. However, 'one swallow doth not a summer make,' so the fact that you used certain skills in this first Story doesn't tell you much. What you are looking for is **patterns** -- transferable skills that keep re-appearing in story after story. They keep reappearing because they are your favorites (assuming you chose stories where you were *really* enjoying yourself).

So, now, write Story #2, from any period in your life, analyze it using the keys, etc., etc. And keep this process up, until you have written, and analyzed, seven stories.

4. Decide Which Skills Are Your Favorites, and Prioritize Them

When you're done writing and analyzing all Seven Stories, you should now go back and look over the six pages of "Skills Keys" to see which skills got used the most often. Make a list.

Cross out any that you don't enjoy using.

Prioritize the remainder, using the Prioritizing Grids on the next two pages.

1	1	1	1	1	1	1	1	1	1	1	1	1	1	1	1	1	1	1	1	1	1	1
2	3	4	5	6	7	8	9	10	11	12	13	14	15	16	17	18	19	20	21	22	23	24

| 2 | 2 | 2 | 2 | 2 | 2 | 2 | 2 | 2 | 2 | 2 | 2 | 2 | 2 | 2 | 2 | 2 | 2 | 2 | 2 | 2 | 2 |
| 3 | 4 | 5 | 6 | 7 | 8 | 9 | 10 | 11 | 12 | 13 | 14 | 15 | 16 | 17 | 18 | 19 | 20 | 21 | 22 | 23 | 24 |

| 3 | 3 | 3 | 3 | 3 | 3 | 3 | 3 | 3 | 3 | 3 | 3 | 3 | 3 | 3 | 3 | 3 | 3 | 3 | 3 | 3 |
| 4 | 5 | 6 | 7 | 8 | 9 | 10 | 11 | 12 | 13 | 14 | 15 | 16 | 17 | 18 | 19 | 20 | 21 | 22 | 23 | 24 |

| 4 | 4 | 4 | 4 | 4 | 4 | 4 | 4 | 4 | 4 | 4 | 4 | 4 | 4 | 4 | 4 | 4 | 4 | 4 | 4 |
| 5 | 6 | 7 | 8 | 9 | 10 | 11 | 12 | 13 | 14 | 15 | 16 | 17 | 18 | 19 | 20 | 21 | 22 | 23 | 24 |

| 5 | 5 | 5 | 5 | 5 | 5 | 5 | 5 | 5 | 5 | 5 | 5 | 5 | 5 | 5 | 5 | 5 | 5 | 5 |
| 6 | 7 | 8 | 9 | 10 | 11 | 12 | 13 | 14 | 15 | 16 | 17 | 18 | 19 | 20 | 21 | 22 | 23 | 24 |

| 6 | 6 | 6 | 6 | 6 | 6 | 6 | 6 | 6 | 6 | 6 | 6 | 6 | 6 | 6 | 6 | 6 | 6 |
| 7 | 8 | 9 | 10 | 11 | 12 | 13 | 14 | 15 | 16 | 17 | 18 | 19 | 20 | 21 | 22 | 23 | 24 |

| 7 | 7 | 7 | 7 | 7 | 7 | 7 | 7 | 7 | 7 | 7 | 7 | 7 | 7 | 7 | 7 | 7 |
| 8 | 9 | 10 | 11 | 12 | 13 | 14 | 15 | 16 | 17 | 18 | 19 | 20 | 21 | 22 | 23 | 24 |

| 8 | 8 | 8 | 8 | 8 | 8 | 8 | 8 | 8 | 8 | 8 | 8 | 8 | 8 | 8 | 8 |
| 9 | 10 | 11 | 12 | 13 | 14 | 15 | 16 | 17 | 18 | 19 | 20 | 21 | 22 | 23 | 24 |

| 9 | 9 | 9 | 9 | 9 | 9 | 9 | 9 | 9 | 9 | 9 | 9 | 9 | 9 | 9 |
| 10 | 11 | 12 | 13 | 14 | 15 | 16 | 17 | 18 | 19 | 20 | 21 | 22 | 23 | 24 |

| 10 | 10 | 10 | 10 | 10 | 10 | 10 | 10 | 10 | 10 | 10 | 10 | 10 | 10 |
| 11 | 12 | 13 | 14 | 15 | 16 | 17 | 18 | 19 | 20 | 21 | 22 | 23 | 24 |

| 11 | 11 | 11 | 11 | 11 | 11 | 11 | 11 | 11 | 11 | 11 | 11 | 11 |
| 12 | 13 | 14 | 15 | 16 | 17 | 18 | 19 | 20 | 21 | 22 | 23 | 24 |

| 12 | 12 | 12 | 12 | 12 | 12 | 12 | 12 | 12 | 12 | 12 | 12 |
| 13 | 14 | 15 | 16 | 17 | 18 | 19 | 20 | 21 | 22 | 23 | 24 |

| 13 | 13 | 13 | 13 | 13 | 13 | 13 | 13 | 13 | 13 | 13 |
| 14 | 15 | 16 | 17 | 18 | 19 | 20 | 21 | 22 | 23 | 24 |

| 14 | 14 | 14 | 14 | 14 | 14 | 14 | 14 | 14 | 14 |
| 15 | 16 | 17 | 18 | 19 | 20 | 21 | 22 | 23 | 24 |

| 15 | 15 | 15 | 15 | 15 | 15 | 15 | 15 | 15 |
| 16 | 17 | 18 | 19 | 20 | 21 | 22 | 23 | 24 |

| 16 | 16 | 16 | 16 | 16 | 16 | 16 | 16 |
| 17 | 18 | 19 | 20 | 21 | 22 | 23 | 24 |

| 17 | 17 | 17 | 17 | 17 | 17 | 17 |
| 18 | 19 | 20 | 21 | 22 | 23 | 24 |

| 18 | 18 | 18 | 18 | 18 | 18 |
| 19 | 20 | 21 | 22 | 23 | 24 |

| 19 | 19 | 19 | 19 | 19 |
| 20 | 21 | 22 | 23 | 24 |

| 20 | 20 | 20 | 20 |
| 21 | 22 | 23 | 24 |

| 21 | 21 | 21 |
| 22 | 23 | 24 |

| 22 | 22 |
| 23 | 24 |

| 23 |
| 24 |

Total times each number got circled

1	2	3	4	5	6
7	8	9	10	11	12
13	14	15	16	17	18
19	20	21	22	23	24

Prioritizing Grid
for 24 Items

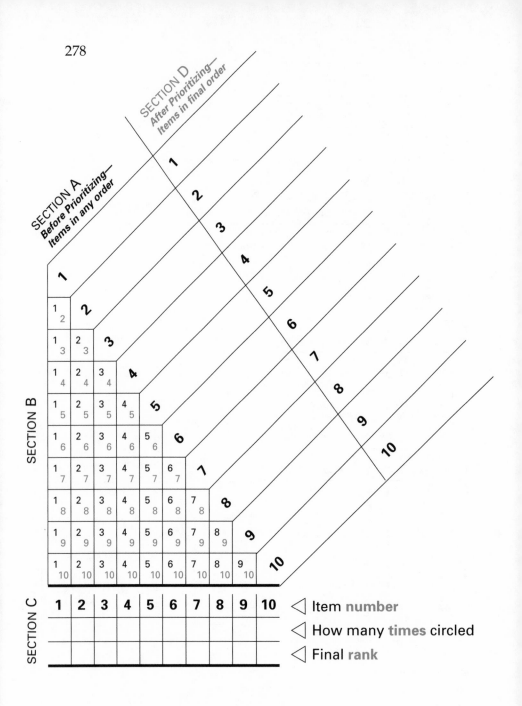

Prioritzing Grid
for 10 Items

The Prioritizing Grid

How to Prioritize Your Lists of Anything

Here is a method for taking (say) ten items, and figuring out which one is most important to you, which is next most important, etc.

• Insert the items to be prioritized, in any order, in Section A. Then compare two items at a time, circling the one you prefer -- between the two -- in Section B. Which one is more important to you? State the question any way you want to: In the case of geographical factors, you might ask. "If I were being offered two jobs, one in an area that had factor #1, but not factor #2; the other in an area that had factor #2, but not factor #1, all other things being equal, which job would I take? Circle it. Then go on to the next pair, etc.

• When you are all done, count up the number of times each number got circled, all told. Enter these totals on the TIMES line in Section C. Then notice the number of times each item was circled ("Times" = "Times Circled"). This determines the item's ranking. Most circled = #1, next most circled = #2, etc. Enter this ranking on the RANK line in Section C. If two items are circled the same number of times, look back in Section B to see -- when those two were compared there -- which one you preferred. Give that one an extra half point. List the items, now in their proper rank, in Section D.

Since you will be using this Prioritizing Grid more than once in these exercises you will want to go down to Kinko's or your local copy shop and make a number of copies of this form before you begin filling it in, for the first time.

The question to ask yourself, on the Grid, as you confront each 'pair' is: "If I were offered two jobs, and in one job I could use the first skill, but not the second; while in the other job, I could use the second skill, but not the first, which job would I choose?" When you've got your ten favorite transferable skills, in order, copy the top six onto the Flower diagram on page 264.

5. 'Flesh Out' Your Favorite Transferable Skills With Your Traits (see page 84)

In general, traits describe:
How you deal with time, and promptness.
How you deal with people and emotions.
How you deal with authority, and being told <u>what</u> to do at your job.
How you deal with supervision, and being told <u>how</u> to do your job.
How you deal with impulse vs. self-discipline, within yourself.
How you deal with initiative vs. response, within yourself.
How you deal with crises or problems.

A Check-List
of My Strongest Traits

I am very. . .

❏ Accurate
❏ Achievement-
  oriented
❏ Adaptable
❏ Adept
❏ Adept at having fun
❏ Adventuresome
❏ Alert
❏ Appreciative
❏ Assertive
❏ Astute
❏ Authoritative
❏ Calm
❏ Cautious
❏ Charismatic
❏ Competent
❏ Consistent
❏ Contagious in my
  enthusiasm
❏ Cooperative
❏ Courageous
❏ Creative
❏ Decisive
❏ Deliberate
❏ Dependable/have
  dependability
❏ Diligent
❏ Diplomatic

❏ Discreet
❏ Driving
❏ Dynamic
❏ Extremely
  economical
❏ Effective
❏ Energetic
❏ Enthusiastic
❏ Exceptional
❏ Exhaustive
❏ Experienced
❏ Expert
❏ Firm
❏ Flexible
❏ Humanly oriented
❏ Impulsive
❏ Independent
❏ Innovative
❏ Knowledgeable
❏ Loyal
❏ Methodical
❏ Objective
❏ Open-minded
❏ Outgoing
❏ Outstanding
❏ Patient
❏ Penetrating
❏ Perceptive

❏ Persevering
❏ Persistent
❏ Pioneering
❏ Practical
❏ Professional
❏ Protective
❏ Punctual
❏ Quick/work quickly
❏ Rational
❏ Realistic
❏ Reliable
❏ Resourceful
❏ Responsible
❏ Responsive
❏ Safeguarding
❏ Self-motivated
❏ Self-reliant
❏ Sensitive
❏ Sophisticated, very
  sophisticated
❏ Strong
❏ Supportive
❏ Tactful
❏ Thorough
❏ Unique
❏ Unusual
❏ Versatile
❏ Vigorous

Once you've checked off your favorites, prioritize them (using another copy of the Prioritizing Grid if necessary), and then integrate your favorites into the building blocks of transferable skills, as described on page 84.

SOME PROBLEMS YOU MAY RUN INTO, WHILE DOING YOUR SKILL-IDENTIFICATION

In trying to identify your skills, it will not be surprising if you run into some problems. Let us look at the five most common ones that have arisen for job-hunters in the past:

1. *"When I write my skill stories, I don't know exactly what is an achievement."*

When you're looking for a story/achievement to illustrate one of your skills, you're *not* looking for something that only you have done, in the history of the world. What you're looking for is a lot simpler than that. You're looking for *any* time in your life when you did something that was, at that time of your life, a source of pride and accomplishment *for you*. It might have been learning to ride a bike. It might be achieving your first quota, at work. It might be a particularly significant project that you designed, in mid-life. It doesn't matter whether or not it pleased anybody else; it only matters that it pleased you.

I like Bernard Haldane's definition of an achievement. He says it is: something you yourself feel you have done well, that you also enjoyed doing and felt proud of. In other words you are looking for an accomplishment which gave you two pleasures: enjoyment while doing it, and satisfaction from the outcome. That doesn't mean you may not have sweated as you did it, or hated *some parts* of the process, but it does mean that basically you enjoyed *most of* the process. The pleasure was not simply in the outcome, but along the way as well. Generally speaking, an achievement will have all the parts outlined on page 81f.

2. *"I don't see why I should look for skills I enjoy; it seems to me that employers will only want to know what skills I do well. They will not care whether I enjoy using the skill or not."*

Well, sure, it is important for you to find the skills you do well, above all else. But, generally speaking, that is hard for you to evaluate about yourself. *Do I do this well, or not? Compared to whom?* Even aptitude tests can't resolve this dilemma for you. So it's better to take the following circular equation, which experience has shown to be true:

If it is a skill you do well, you will generally enjoy it.

If it is a skill you enjoy, it is generally because you do it well.

With these equations in hand, you will see that -- since they are equal anyway -- it is much more useful to ask yourself, "Do I enjoy doing it?" instead of hunting for the elusive "Do I do it well?" I repeat: listing the skills you most *enjoy* is -- in most cases -- just another way of listing the skills you do *best*.

The reason why this idea -- of making *enjoyment* the key -- causes such feelings of uncomfortableness in so many of us is that we have an old historical tradition in this country which insinuates you shouldn't really enjoy yourself in life. To suffer is virtuous.

Sample: Two girls do babysitting. One hates it. One enjoys it thoroughly. Which is more virtuous in God's sight? According to that old tradition, the one who hates it is more virtuous. Some of us feel this instinctively, even if more logical thought says, Whoa!

We have this subconscious fear that if we are caught enjoying life, punishment looms. Thus, the story of two Scotsmen who met on the street one day: "Isn't this a beautiful day?" said one. "Aye," said the other, "but we'll pay for it."

We feel it is okay to talk about our failures, but not about our successes. To talk about our successes appears to be boasting, and that is manifestly a sin. Or so we think. We shouldn't be enjoying so much about ourselves.

But look at the birds of the air, or watch your pets at play. You will notice one distinctive fact about that part of God's creation: when a bird or a pet does what it is meant to do, by God and nature, it manifests true joy.

Joy is so clearly a part of God's plan for us. God wants us to eat; therefore He made eating enjoyable. God wants us to sleep; therefore He made sleeping enjoyable. God wants us to procreate, love, and make love; therefore He made sex enjoyable, and love even more so.

Likewise, God gives to each of us unique combinations of skills and talents which He wants us to contribute to His general plan -- to the symphony of the world, and the music of the spheres. Therefore, **when we use the talents He most wants each of us to use, He attends it with a feeling of great joy.** Everywhere in God's plan for His creation, joy rewards right action.

Bad employers will not care whether you enjoy a particular task, or not. But good employers will care greatly. They know that unless a would-be employee has **enthusiasm** for his or her work, the quality of that work will always suffer.

3. *"I have no difficulty finding stories to write up, from my life, that I consider to be enjoyable achievements; but once these are written, I have great difficulty in seeing what the skills are -- even if I stare at the skills keys in the Exercises for hours. I need somebody else's insight."*

You may want to consider getting two friends or two other members of your family to sit down with you, and do skill identification through the practice of 'Trioing' which I invented some twenty years ago to help with this very problem. This practice is fully described in my book, *Where Do I Go From Here With My Life?* But to save you the trouble of reading it, here is -- in general -- how it goes:

a. Each of the three of you quietly writes up some story of an accomplishment in their life that was enjoyable.

b. Each of the three of you quietly analyzes just your own story to see what skills you see there; you jot these down.

c. One of you then volunteers to go first. You read your story aloud. The other two jot down on a piece of paper whatever skills they hear you using. They ask you to pause if they're having trouble keeping up. You finish your story. You read aloud the skills *you* picked out in that story.

d. Then the second person tells you what's on their list: what skills *they* heard you use in your story. You copy them down, below your own list, even if you don't agree with every one of them.

e. Then the third person tells you what's on their list; what skills *they* heard you use in your story. You copy them down, below your own list, even if you don't agree with every one of them.

f. When they're both done, you ask them any questions for further elaboration that you may have. *"What did you mean by this skill? Where did you think you heard me using it?"*

g. Now it is the next person's turn, and you repeat steps 'c' through 'f' with them. Then it is the third person's turn, and you repeat steps 'c' through 'f' with them.

h. Now it is time to move on to a second story for each of you, so you begin with steps 'a' through 'g' all over again, except that each of you writes a new story. And so on, through seven stories.

4. *"I don't like the skill words you offer in the Exercises. Can't I use my own words, the ones I'm familiar with from my past profession?"*

It's okay to invent your own words for your skills, but it is not useful to state your transferable skills in the jargon of your old profession, such as (in the case of ex-clergy), *"I am good at preaching."* If you are going to choose a new career, out there in what people call the secular world, you must not use language that locks you into the past -- or suggests that you were good in one profession but in one profession only. Therefore, it is important to take jargon words such as *preaching* and ask yourself what is its larger form? *"Teaching?"* Perhaps. *"Motivating people?"* Perhaps. *"Inspiring people to the depths of their being?"* Perhaps. Only you can say what is true, for you. But in one way or another be sure to get your skills out of any jargon that locks you into your past career.

5. *"Once I've listed my favorite transferable skills, I see immediately a job-title that they point to. Is that okay?"*

Nope. Once you've finished your skill-identification, steer clear of prematurely putting a job-title on the skills you see. Skills can point to *many* different jobs, which have a multitude of titles. Therefore, don't lock yourself in, prematurely. *"I'm looking for a job where I can use the following skills,"* is fine. But, *"I'm looking for a job where I can be a (job-title)"* is a no-no, at this point in your job-hunt. Always define WHAT you want to do with your life and WHAT you have, to offer to the world, in terms of your favorite talents/gifts/skills -- not in terms of a job-title. That way, you can stay mobile in the midst of this constantly-changing economy, where you never know what's going to happen next.

Petal #1
Geography

Even if you *love* where you are now, or even if you're *stuck* where you are now, you never know when an opportunity may suddenly open up for you, down the road. You want to be ready. Don't wait until then to do this exercise; do it now!

The question you need to answer is: Where would you most like to live and work, if you had a choice (besides where you are now)? In answering this question, it is important -- before you come to names -- to list the geographical *factors* that are important to you.

To help you do this, fill out the accompanying chart. *(You may copy it on to a larger piece of paper if you wish, before you begin working on it. And, if you are doing this exercise with a partner, make a copy of the chart, for them also, before you start filling it out, so that each of you may have a 'clean' copy of your own.)*

My Geographical Preferences
Decision Making for Just You

Column 1 Names of Places I Have Lived	*Column 2* From the Past: Negatives	*Column 3* Translating the Negatives into Positives	*Column 4* Ranking of My Positives
	Factors I Disliked and Still Dislike about That Place		1. 2. 3. 4. 5. 6. 7. 8. 9. 10. 11. 12. 13. 14. 15.
		Factors I Liked and Still Like about That Place	

Our Geographical Preferences
Decision Making for You and A Partner

| Column 5
Places Which Fit
These Criteria | Column 6
Ranking of His/Her
Preferences | Column 7
Combining Our Two
Lists (Column 4 & 6) | Column 8
Places Which Fit
These Criteria |
|---|---|---|---|
| | a. | a.
1. | |
| | b. | b.
2. | |
| | c. | c.
3. | |
| | d. | d.
4. | |
| | e. | e.
5. | |
| | f. | f.
6. | |
| | g. | g.
7. | |
| | h. | h.
8. | |
| | i. | i.
9. | |
| | j. | j.
10. | |
| | k. | k.
11. | |
| | l. | l.
12. | |
| | m. | m.
13. | |
| | n. | n.
14. | |
| | o. | o.
15. | |

Then, this is how you use the chart. There are seven easy steps:

1. **List all the places (towns, cities, etc.) where you have ever lived.**
These go in Column 1.

2. **List the factors you *disliked* and still dislike about each place.**
Naturally, there will be some repetition. In which case, just put an extra check mark in front of any factor you already have written down, when it comes up again. All of these negative factors go in Column 2.

3. **Then take each of those negative factors and translate the negatives into positives.**
This will not *necessarily* be the opposite. For example, "rains all the time" does not necessarily translate into "sunny all the time." It might be more like: "sunny at least 200 days a year." *It's your call.* All these positive factors go in Column 3. Feel free to add at the bottom of the column here, any positive factors you remember, off the top of your head, about the places in Column 1.

4. **Now, rank your positive factors list (Column 3) in their order of importance, to you.**
They will be things like: "has cultural opportunities," "skiing in the winter," "good newspaper," etc. List your top 10 positive factors, in exact order, in Column 4.

If you are baffled as to how to prioritize these factors in exact order, use the Prioritizing Grid on page 278. In using that grid, the question to ask yourself as you confront each 'pair' is: "If I could live in a place that had this first 'factor', but not the second; or if I could live in another place that had the second 'factor,' but not the first, in which place would I choose to live?"

5. **When you are done, show this list of ten prioritized, positive factors to everyone you know, and ask them what cities, towns, or places they know of that have all or most of these factors.**
You want to particularly emphasize the top factors, the ones that are the most important to you. If there is only a partial overlap between your factors and the places your friends suggest, be sure the overlap is in the factors you placed first on your list.

6. From all the names your friends suggest to you, choose the three that look most intriguing to you, in order of your personal preference, based on what you now know.

This goes in Column 5. These are the places you will want to find out more about, until you are sure which is your absolute first preference, second, and third.

N.B. If you are doing this with a partner, you will not use Column 5. Instead, copy *their* Column 4 into your Column 6. Then alternately combine *their* first five factors and *your* first five factors, until you wind up with a list of ten altogether. (First you list their top one, then your top one, then their second preference, then your second preference, etc.) *This goes in Column 7.* It is *this* list of ten positive factors which you both then show to *everyone* you know, to ask them what cities, towns, or places they know of that have all or most of these factors, *beginning with the top ones.* From all the names those friends suggest to you, you then choose the three places that look the most intriguing to both of you, and rank them in order. This goes in Column 8.

7. Now, go back to the Flower diagram on page 264, and copy Column 5 (or 8) onto the Geography petal.

You may also, if you wish, copy the first three to five Positives, from column 4 or 7. Voila! You are done with Geography. You now know the place(s) to find out more about, through their Chamber of Commerce, the Internet, a summer visit, etc.

Petal #2
Your Favorite Interests

You will find the instructions for inventorying these in chapter 5, on pages 96–101. You may have already done the exercises there.

When you have, come back to the Flower diagram on page 264, and copy the Field(s) you selected, plus your strongest interests (favorite knowledges) on to the Interests petal, in order of priority for you.

Petal #3
Your Favorite People

With the great emphasis upon the importance of the environment, in recent years, it has become increasingly realized that jobs are environments too. The most important environmental factor always turns out to be people, since every job, except possibly that of a full-fledged hermit, surrounds us with people to one degree or another.

Indeed, many a good job has been ruined by the people one is surrounded by. Many a mundane job has been made delightful, by the people one is surrounded by. Therefore, it is important to think out what kinds of people you want to be surrounded by.

Dr. John L. Holland offers the best description of people environments. He says there are six principal ones:

1. The **Realistic** People-Environment: filled with people who prefer activities involving "the explicit, ordered, or systematic manipulation of objects, tools, machines, and animals." 'Realistic,' incidentally, refers to Plato's conception of "the real" as that which one can apprehend through the senses.

I summarize this as: R = people who like nature, or athletics, or tools & machinery.

2. The **Investigative** People-Environment: filled with people who prefer activities involving "the observation and symbolic, systematic, creative investigation of physical, biological or cultural phenomena."

I summarize this as: I = people who are very curious, liking to investigate or analyze things.

3. The **Artistic** People-Environment: filled with people who prefer activities involving "ambiguous, free, unsystematized activities and competencies to create art forms or products."

I summarize this as: A = people who are very artistic, imaginative and innovative.

4. The **Social** People-Environment: filled with people who prefer activities involving "the manipulation of others to inform, train, develop, cure or enlighten."

I summarize this as: S = people who are bent on trying to help, teach, or serve people.

5. The **Enterprising** People-Environment: filled with people who prefer activities involving "the manipulation of others to attain organizational or self-interest goals."

I summarize this as: E = people who like to start up projects or organizations, and/or influence or persuade people.

6. The **Conventional** People-Environment: filled with people who prefer activities involving "the explicit, ordered, systematic manipulation of data, such as keeping records, filing materials, reproducing materials, organizing written and numerical data according to a prescribed plan, operating business and data processing machines." 'Conventional,' incidentally, refers to the "values" which people in this environment usually hold -- representing the broad mainstream of the culture.

I summarize this as: C = people who like detailed work, and like to complete tasks or projects.

According to John's theory and findings everyone has three preferred people-environments, from among these six. The letters for your three preferred people-environments gives you what is called "your Holland Code."

> There is, incidentally, a relationship between the people you like to be surrounded by *and* your skills *and* your values. See John Holland's book, *Making Vocational Choices (3rd. ed., 1997).* You can procure it by writing to Psychological Assessment Resources, Inc., Box 998, Odessa, FL 33556. Phone: 1-800-331-8378. *The book is $29.95 at this writing.* PAR also has John Holland's instrument, called *The Self-Directed Search* (or SDS, for short) for discovering what your Holland code is. PAR says you can take the test online for a small fee (if you have Internet access) at `http://www.self-directed-search.com`

For those who don't have Internet access (or are in a hurry) I invented (many years ago) a quick and easy way to get an *approximation* of your 'Holland Code,' as it's called. I call it "The Party Exercise." Here is how the exercise goes (do it!):

On the next page is an aerial view of a room in which a two-day (!) party is taking place. At this party, people with the same or similar interests have (for some reason) all gathered in the same corner of the room.

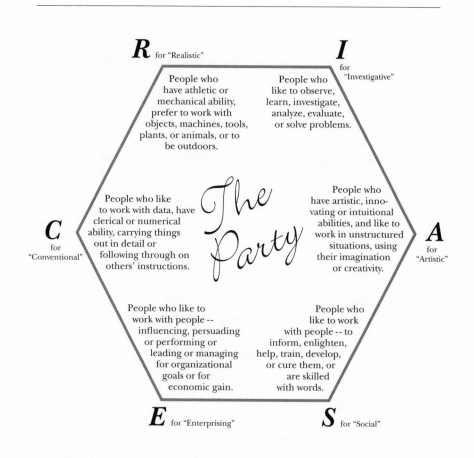

R for "Realistic"

I for "Investigative"

People who have athletic or mechanical ability, prefer to work with objects, machines, tools, plants, or animals, or to be outdoors.

People who like to observe, learn, investigate, analyze, evaluate, or solve problems.

The Party

People who like to work with data, have clerical or numerical ability, carrying things out in detail or following through on others' instructions.

People who have artistic, inno-vating or intuitional abilities, and like to work in unstructured situations, using their imagination or creativity.

C for "Conventional"

A for "Artistic"

People who like to work with people -- influencing, persuading or performing or leading or managing for organizational goals or for economic gain.

People who like to work with people -- to inform, enlighten, help, train, develop, or cure them, or are skilled with words.

E for "Enterprising"

S for "Social"

(1) Which corner of the room would you instinctively be drawn to, as the group of people you would most enjoy being with for the longest time? (Leave aside any question of shyness, or whether you would have to talk to them.) Write the letter for that corner here:

(2) After fifteen minutes, everyone in the corner you have chosen leaves for another party crosstown, except you. Of the groups that still remain now, which corner or group would you be drawn to the most, as the people you would most enjoy being with for the longest time? Write the letter for that corner here:

(3) After fifteen minutes, this group too leaves for another party, except you. Of the corners, and groups, which remain now, which one would you most enjoy being with for the longest time? Write the letter for that corner here:

The three letters you just chose, in the three steps, are called your "Holland Code." Here is what you should now do:

1. Circle them on the People petal, on page 265.

Put three circles around your favorite corner; two circles around your next favorite; and one circle around your third favorite.

2. Once the corners are circled, you may wish to write up (for yourself and your eyes only) a temporary statement about your future job or career, using the descriptors above.

If your "Code" turned out to be IAS, for example, you might write: *"I would like a job or career best if I was surrounded by people who are very curious, and like to investigate or analyze things (I); who are also very innovative (A); and who are bent on trying to help or serve people (S)."*

3. Finally, here, look over the skills you have just described *in others*, and see how much of this is also true of *you*.

What I call "The Mirror Theory" holds that we often see *ourselves* best by looking into the faces of others. Hence, once we have described the people we would most like to be surrounded by, in many cases we have also described ourselves. ("Birds of a feather flock together.") So, look over the circled items on your People petal. Are these, perchance, *your* favorite proclivities, skills, tasks, etc.? Or not?

Petal #4
Your Favorite Values & Goals

1. Values are a matter of what guides you through every day, every task, every encounter with another human being. Yet, we are often unaware of what our values are.

One way to bring values to your consciousness is to imagine that shortly before the end of your life you are invited to dinner -- and to your great surprise people have secretly come in from all over the country and all over the world, to attend a surprise testimonial dinner for You.

At the dinner, to your great embarrassment, there is one testimonial after another about the good things you did, or the good person that you were, in your lifetime. No mention of any parts of your life that you don't want to have remembered. Just the good stuff.

So, this brings us to some questions. If you get the life you really want between now and then, what would you hope you would hear at that dinner, as they looked back on your life?

If you do achieve what you want with your life, what about you would you like to have remembered, after you are gone from this earth? Here is a checklist to help you[2]:

It would be a good life, if at its end here, people remembered me as one who: (check as many items as are important to you)

❏ Served or helped those who were in need.
❏ Impressed people with my going the second mile, in meeting their needs.
❏ Was always a great listener.
❏ Was always good at carrying out orders, or bringing projects to a successful conclusion.
❏ Mastered some technique, or field.
❏ Did something that everyone said couldn't be done.
❏ Did something that no one had ever done before.
❏ Excelled and was the best at whatever it is I did.
❏ Pioneered or explored some new technology.
❏ Fixed something that was broken.

❑ Made something work, when everyone else had failed or given up.

❑ Improved something, made it better, or perfected it.

❑ Combatted some bad idea/philosophy/ force/influence/ pervasive trend -- and I persevered and/or prevailed.

❑ Influenced people and gained a tremendous response from them.

❑ Had an impact, and caused change.

❑ Did work which brought more information/truth into the world.

❑ Did work which brought more beauty into the world, through gardens, or painting, or decorating, or designing, or whatever.

❑ Did work which brought more justice, truth, and ethical behavior into the world.

❑ Brought people closer to God.

❑ Growing in wisdom and compassion was my great goal all my life.

❑ Had a vision of what something could be, and helped that vision to come true.

❑ Developed or built something, where there was nothing.

❑ Began a new business, or did some project from start to finish.

❑ Exploited, shaped and influenced some situation, market, before others saw the potential.

❑ Put together a great team, which made a huge difference in its field, industry, or community.

❑ Was a good decision-maker.

❑ Was acknowledged by everyone as a leader, and was in charge of whatever it was that I was doing.

❑ Had status in my field, industry, or community.

❑ Was in the spotlight, gained recognition, and was well-known.

❑ Made it into a higher echelon than I was, in terms of reputation, and/or prestige, and/or membership, and/or salary.

❑ Was able to acquire possessions, things or money.

❑ Other goals which occur to me:_____

When you're done checking off all the values that are important to you, go back, and pick out the ten that you care the most about, and then prioritize them in exact order of importance to you. As always, if you just can't prioritize them by guess and by gosh, then use the Prioritizing Grid on page 278.

The question to ask yourself, there, as you confront each 'pair' on the Grid is: "If I could only have this true about me, at the end of my life, but not the other, which would I prefer?" *Try not to pay attention to what others might or might not think of you, if they knew this was your heart's desire. This is just between you and God.*

Put your top three values on the Values & Goals petal, in the Flower diagram on page 265.

We turn, now from values to goals.

2. Goals are a matter of what you hope to accomplish before you die. Figuring out now, what we'd like to achieve before our life is over, gives us greater direction in our present career choices. Here are some questions, in the form of a check-list, that may prove helpful in surfacing what your goals in life are:

My goal, before I die, is to be able to help people with their need for:

❑ **Clothing** (people's need to find and choose appropriate and affordable clothing); *and in my case what interests me particularly is*_____.

❑ **Food** (people's need to be fed, to be saved from starvation or poor nutrition) *and in my case what interests me particularly is*_____.

❑ **Housing** and **Real estate** (people's need to find appropriate and affordable housing, office or land); *and in my case what interests me particularly is*_____.

❑ **Language** (people's need for literacy, to be able to read, or to learn a new language); *and in my case what interests me particularly is*_____.

❑ **Personal services** (people's need to have someone do tasks they can't do, or haven't time to do, or don't want to do, for themselves -- ranging from childcare to helping run a farm); *and in my case what interests me particularly is*_____.

❑ **Finances** (people's need to have help with budgeting, taxes, financial planning, money management, etc.); *and in my case what interests me particularly is*_____.

❑ **Acquisition** (people's need for help in buying something); *and in my case what interests me particularly is*_____.

❑ **Transportation** (people's need for travel locally or elsewise); *and in my case what interests me particularly is*_____.

❑ **Legal services** (people's need for expert counseling concerning the legal implications of things they are doing, or things that have been done to them); *and in my case what interests me particularly is_____.*

❑ **Child development** (people's need for help with various problems as their children are moving from infancy through childhood, including behavioral disabilities); *and in my case what interests me particularly is_____.*

❑ **Physical fitness** (people's need to get their body in tune through physical or occupational therapy, 'body-work,' exercise or diet); *and in my case what interests me particularly is_____.*

❑ **Health services** (people's need to have preventative medicine or help with ailments, allergies and disease); *and in my case what interests me particularly is_____ .*

❑ **Healing** including **Alternative medicine** and **Holistic health** (people's need to have various injuries, ailments, maladies or diseases healed); *and in my case what interests me particularly is_____.*

❑ **Medicine** (people's need to have help with diagnosing, treating various diseases, or removing diseased or badly-injured parts of their body, etc.); *and in my case what interests me particularly is_____.*

❑ **Mental health** (people's need for help with stress, depression, insomnia or other forms of emotional or mental disturbance); *and in my case what interests me particularly is_____.*

❑ **Personal counseling and guidance**, (people's need for help with family relations, with dysfunctions, or with various crises in their life, including a lack of balance in their use of time); *and in my case what interests me particularly is_____.*

❑ **Job-hunting, job-placement or vocational rehabilitation** (people's need to have help in finding the work they have chosen, particularly when handicapped, or unemployed, or enrolling for welfare under the new regulations); *and in my case what interests me particularly is_____.*

❑ **Life/work planning** (people's need for help in choosing a career or planning a holistic life); *and in my case what interests me particularly is_____.*

❑ **Learning or training** (people's need to learn more about something, at work or outside of work); *and in my case what interests me particularly is_____.*

❑ **Entertainment** (people's need to be entertained, by laughter, wit, intelligence, or beauty); *and in my case what interests me particularly is_____.*

❑ **Spirituality** or **religion** (people's need to learn as much as they can about God, character, and their own soul, including their values and principles); *and in my case what interests me particularly is*_____.

❑ **The needs of animals or plants** (their need for nurturing, growth, health and other life cycles which require the kinds of sensitivities often referred to as 'interpersonal skills'); *and in my case what interests me particularly is*_____.

❑ **The creating, making, marketing, handling of things**, such as: airplanes, antiques, bicycles, blueprints, books, bridges, buildings, bushes, cameras, campers, cars, catalogs, chemicals, cooking utensils, clothing, computers, crops, diagrams, electricity, electronics, drugs, farms, farm machinery, fish, flowers, gardens, groceries, guidebooks, houses, kitchens appliances, lawns, machines, magazines, makeup, manuals, medicines, minerals, money, music, musical instruments, newspapers, office machines, paints, paper, plants, radios, rivers, rooms, sailboats, security systems, sewing machines, skiing equipment, soil, telephones, toiletries, tools, toys, trains, trees, valuable objects, videotapes, wine, wood, etc.; *and in my case what interests me particularly is*_____.

❑ **Other goals** not listed above, that fascinate me are:_____.

When you're done checking off all the goals that are important to you, go back, and pick out the ten that you care the most about, and then prioritize them in exact order of importance to you. As always, if you just can't prioritize them by guess and by gosh, then use the Prioritizing Grid on page 278.

Put your top three Goals on the Values & Goals petal, in the Flower diagram on page 265.

Petal #5

Your Favorite Working Conditions

Plants that grow beautifully at sea level, often perish if they're taken ten thousand feet up the mountain. Likewise, we do our best work under certain conditions, but not under others. Thus, the question: What are your favorite 'working conditions'? actually is a question about "Under what circumstances do you do your most effective work?"

The best way to approach this is by starting with the things you *disliked* about all your previous jobs, using the following chart to list these. The chart, as you can see, has three columns, and you fill them out in the same order, and manner, that you filled out the geography chart earlier. Here too, you may copy this chart on to a larger piece of paper if you wish, before you begin filling it out. *Column A may begin with such factors as: "too noisy," "too much supervision," "no windows in my workplace," "having to be at work by 6 a.m.," etc.*

Of course, when you get to Column B, you must rank these factors that are in Column A, in their exact order of importance, to you.

As always, if you are baffled as to how to prioritize these factors in exact order, use the Prioritizing Grid on page 277 or 278.

The question to ask yourself, there, as you confront each 'pair' is: "If I were offered two jobs, and in the first job I would be rid of this first distasteful working condition, but not the second; while in the second job, I would be rid of the second distasteful working condition, but not the first, which distasteful working condition would I choose to get rid of?"

Note that when you later come to Column C, the factors will be already prioritized. Your only job, there, is to think of the "positive" form of that factor that you hated so much (in Column B). (It is not always "the exact opposite." For example, *too much supervision* (listed in Column B) does not always mean *no supervision* (in Column C). It *might* mean: *a moderate amount of supervision, once or twice a day*.)

Once you've finished Column C, enter the top five factors from there on the Working Conditions petal of the Flower diagram, on page 265.

DISTASTEFUL WORKING CONDITIONS

	Column A − Distasteful Working Conditions	*Column B* − Distasteful Working Conditions Ranked	*Column C* + The Keys to My Effectiveness At Work
Places I Have Worked Thus Far In My Life	*I Have Learned From the Past that My Effectiveness at Work is Decreased When I Have To Work Under These Conditions:*	*Among the Factors or Qualities Listed in Column A, These Are The Ones I Dislike Absolutely The Most (in order of Decreasing Dislike):*	*The Opposite of These Qualities, in order:* *"I Believe My Effectiveness Would Be At An Absolute Maximum, If I Could Work Under These Conditions:"*

Petal #6
Level & Salary

As you saw in chapter 6, on page 220, salary is something you must think out ahead of time, when you're contemplating your ideal job or career. Level goes hand-in-hand with salary, of course.

1. The first question here is at what level would you like to work, in your ideal job?

Level is a matter of how much responsibility you want, in an organization:

❑ Boss or CEO (this may mean you'll have to form your own business)

❑ Manager or someone under the boss who carries out orders, but also gives them

❑ The head of a team

❑ A member of a team of equals

❑ One who works in tandem with one other partner

❑ One who works alone, either as an employee or as a consultant to an organization, or as a one-person business.

Enter a two- or three-word summary of your answer, on the Salary and Level petal of your Flower diagram, on page 264.

2. The second question here is what salary would you like to be aiming at?

Here you have to think in terms of minimum or maximum. Minimum is what you would need to make, if you were just barely 'getting by.' And you need to know this *before* you go in for a job interview with anyone *(or before you form your own business, and need to know how much profit you must make, just to survive).*

Maximum could be any astronomical figure you can think of, but it is more useful here to put down the salary you realistically think you could make, with your present competency and experience, were you working for a real, *but generous*, boss. (If this maximum figure is still depressingly low, then put down the salary you would like to be making five years from now.)

Make out a detailed outline of your estimated expenses *now*, listing what you need *monthly* in the following categories:[3]

Housing

 Rent or mortgage payments. . . . . $ _____

 Electricity/gas. . . . . $ _____

 Water. . . . . $ _____

 Telephone . . . . $ _____

 Garbage removal . . . . $ _____

 Cleaning, maintenance, repairs[4] . . . . $ _____

Food

 What you spend at the supermarket

 and/or meat market, etc. . . . . $ _____

 Eating out . . . . $ _____

Clothing

 Purchase of new or used clothing . . . . $ _____

 Cleaning, dry cleaning, laundry . . . . $ _____

Automobile/transportation[5]

 Car payments . . . . $ _____

 Gas . . . . $ _____

 Repairs. . . . . $ _____

 Public transportation (*bus, train, plane*). . . . . $ _____

Insurance

 Car . . . . $ _____

 Medical or health-care . . . . $ _____

 House and personal possessions . . . . $ _____

 Life. . . . . $ _____

Medical expenses

 Doctors' visits. . . . . $ _____

 Prescriptions. . . . . $ _____

 Fitness costs . . . . $ _____

Support for Other Family Members

 Child-care costs (*if you have children*) . . . . $ _____

 Child-support (*if you're paying that*) . . . . $ _____

 Support for your parents (*if you're helping out*) . . . . $ _____

Charity giving/tithe (*to help others*) . . . . $ _____

School/learning

 Children's costs (*if you have children in school*) . . . . . $ _____

 Your learning costs (*adult education,*

 job-hunting classes, etc.) . . . . $ _____

Pet care (*if you have pets*). . . . . $ _____

Bills and debts *(Usual monthly payments)*
    Credit cards . . . . $ _____
    Local stores . . . . $ _____
    Other obligations you pay off monthly . . . . $ _____
Taxes
    Federal[6] *(next April's due, divided by*
    months remaining until then) . . . . $ _____
    State *(likewise)* . . . . $ _____
    Local/property *(next amount due, divided by*
    months remaining until then) . . . . $ _____
    Tax-help *(if you ever use an accountant,*
    pay a friend to help you with taxes, etc.). . . . . $ _____
Savings
Retirement (Keogh, IRA, Sep, etc.)
Amusement/discretionary spending
    Movies, video rentals, etc. . . . . $ _____
    Other kinds of entertainment . . . . $ _____
    Reading, newspapers, magazines, books . . . . $ _____
    Gifts *(birthday, Christmas, etc.)* . . . . $ _____
Total Amount You Need Each Month . . . . $ _____

Multiply the total amount you need each month by 12, to get the yearly figure. Divide the yearly figure by 2000, and you will be reasonably near the *minimum* hourly wage that you need. Thus, if you need $3333 per month, multiplied by 12 that's $40,000 a year, and then divided by 2,000, that's $20 an hour.

Parenthetically, you may want to prepare two different versions of the above budget: one with the expenses you'd ideally *like* to make, and the other a minimum budget, which will give you what you are looking for, here: the floor, below which you simply cannot afford to go.

Enter the maximum, and minimum, on your Salary & Level petal on the Flower diagram on page 264.

Optional Exercise: You may wish to put down other rewards, besides money, that you would hope for, from your next job or career. These might be:
❑ Adventure
❑ Challenge
❑ Respect
❑ Influence
❑ Popularity
❑ Fame
❑ Power
❑ Intellectual stimulation from the other workers there
❑ A chance to exercise leadership
❑ A chance to be creative
❑ A chance to make decisions
❑ A chance to use my expertise
❑ A chance to help others
❑ A chance to bring others closer to God
❑ Other:

If you do check off things on this list, arrange your answers in order of importance to you, and then add them to the Salary & Level petal on page 264.

Done!

Voila! Your flower should now be complete. At this point, go to chapter 5, on page 134f, and see how this new knowledge of yourself and your ideal job helps you to narrow down what it is you are looking for.

Footnotes

1. For the curious, "animals" are placed in this category with "people," because **the skills** required to deal with animals are more like those used with people, than like those used with "things."

2. I am indebted to Arthur Miller, of People Management, Inc., for many of these ideas.

3. If this kind of financial figuring is not your cup of tea, find a buddy, friend, relative, family member, or *anyone*, who can help you do this. If you don't know anyone who could do this, go to your local church, synagogue, religious centre, social club, gym, or wherever you hang out, and ask the leader or manager there, to help you find someone. If there's a bulletin board, put up a notice on the bulletin board.

4. If you have extra household expenses, such as a security system for example, be sure and include the quarterly (or whatever) expenses here, divided by three.

5. Your checkbook stubs will tell you a lot of this stuff. But you may be vague about your cash or credit card expenditures. For example, you may not know how much you spend at the supermarket, or how much you spend on gas, etc. But there is a simple way to find out. Just carry a little notepad and pen around with you for two weeks or more, and jot down *everything* you pay cash *(or use credit cards)* for -- *on the spot, right after you pay it.* At the end of those two weeks, you'll be able to take that notepad and make a realistic guess of what should be put down in these categories that now puzzle you. *(Multiply the two-weeks figure by two, and you'll have the monthly figure.)*

6. Incidentally, looking ahead to next April 15th, be sure and check with your local IRS office or a reputable accountant to find out if you can deduct the expenses of your job-hunt on your Federal (and State) income tax returns. At this writing, some job-hunters can, if -- big IF -- this is not your first job that you're looking for, if you haven't been unemployed too long, and if you aren't making a career-change. Do go find out what the latest "ifs" are. If IRS tells you you are eligible, keep careful receipts of everything related to your job-hunt, as you go along: telephone calls, stationery, printing, postage, travel, etc.

Two are better than one;
  for if they fall,
  the one will lift up his fellow;

  but woe to him that is alone when he falleth,
  and hath not another to lift him up.

Ecclesiastes

Appendix B

How to Choose A Career Counselor, If You Decide You Need One

YES, THERE'S A CERTAIN AMOUNT OF PRIDE IN BEING A SELF-MADE MAN, BUT TO TELL THE TRUTH, IF I HAD IT ALL TO DO OVER AGAIN I WOULD GET A LITTLE HELP.

THAVES

HOW TO CHOOSE A CAREER COUNSELOR, IF YOU DECIDE YOU NEED ONE

I wish I could say that everyone who hangs out a sign saying they are now a career counselor could be completely trusted. Nope, they can't all be. As is the case in many professions, they divide into: a) those who are honest and know what they're doing; b) those who are honest but inept; and c) those who are dishonest, and merely want your money -- in lump sums, up front.

You, of course, want a list of those who are honest and know what they're doing. Well, unfortunately, no one (including me) has such a list. You've got to do your own homework, or research, here, and your own interviewing, in your own geographical area, or you will deserve what you get.

Why do *you* have to do it? You, you, and nobody else but you? Well, let's say a friend tells you to go see so-and-so. He's a wonderful counselor, but unhappily he reminds you of your Uncle Harry. No one but you knows that you've always **hated** your Uncle Harry. That's why no one else can do this research for you -- because the real question is not "Who is best?" but "Who is best **for you**?" Those last two words demand that it be you who 'makes the call,' that it is you who does the research.

Of course, you're tempted to skip over this research, aren't you? *"Well, I'll just call up one place, and if I like the sound of them, I'll sign up.*

I'm a pretty good judge of character." Right. I hear many a sad tale from people who had this overconfidence in their ability to detect a phony, and then found out too late that they had been *taken*, by slicker sales-people than they had ever run into before. As they tell me their stories, they *cry* over the telephone. My reply usually is, "I'm sorry indeed to hear that you had a very disappointing experience; that is very unfortunate, but -- as the Scots would say -- "Ya dinna do your homework." Often you could easily have discovered whether a particular counselor was competent or not, before you ever gave them any of your money, simply by asking the right questions during your preliminary research."[1]

Another way people try to avoid this research is by saying, "Well, I'll just see who Bolles recommends." That's a stretch, because I never ever recommend anyone. Some try to claim I do, because they're in the book here. Nice try! Inclusion in this book does *not* constitute an endorsement or recommendation by me -- as I have been at great pains to make clear for the past twenty-five years. Never has. Never will.

You must do your own homework. You must do your own research.

So, how do you go about finding a good counselor? Well, you start by collecting three names of career counselors in your geographical area.

How do you find those names? Several ways:

First, you can get names from your friends: ask if any of them have ever used a career counselor. And if so, did they like 'em? And if so, what is that counselor's name?

Secondly, you can get names from the *Sampler* that begins on page 316. See if there are any career counselors who are near you. They may know how you can find still other names in your community. But I repeat what I said above: just because they're listed in the Sampler *doesn't* mean I recommend them. It only means they asked to be listed, and professed familiarity with the contents of this book (current edition).

---

1. If you are reading this too late, did pay some firm's fee all in advance, and feel you were ripped off, you will want to know about Mr. Stuart Alan Rado. Mr. Rado is a former victim of one of the career counseling agencies, and ever since he has been waging a sort of "one-man crusade" against career counseling firms which take advantage of the job-hunter. Send Mr. Rado your story, together with a self-addressed stamped envelope, and he will send you a one-page sheet of some actions you can take. It may not get your money back, but at least you'll feel better for having done *something*. His address is: 1500 23rd St., Sunset Island #3, Miami Beach, FL 33140. 305-532-2607.

Still haven't got three names? Then try your telephone book's Yellow Pages, under such headings as: *Aptitude and Employment Testing, Career and Vocational Counseling, Personnel Consultants* and (if you are a woman) *Women's Organizations and Services.*

You will discover that even the Yellow Pages can't keep up with the additional groups that spring up daily, weekly, and monthly -- including job clubs and other group activities. The most comprehensive list of *these,* in the U.S., is to be found in the *National Business Employment Weekly,* on its pages called "Calendar of Career Events." It is an extensive listing. It's available on many newsstands, $3.95 an issue, or you can order six issues for $19 directly from: National Business Employment Weekly, P.O. Box 435, Chicopee, MA 01021-0435. Their phone is: 800-JOB-HUNT (that's 562-4868) ext. 193.

Once you have three names, you need to go do some comparison shopping. You want to go talk with all three of them, and decide which of the three (if any) you want to hook up with.

Don't try to do this over the telephone, *please!* There is so much more you can tell, when you're looking the person straight in the eyes.

Cost: if this is a firm, trying to sell you a package, they will almost certainly give you the initial interview for free. On the other hand, if it's an individual counselor, who charges by the hour, you *are* going to have to pay them for this exploratory hour, or part of an hour -- even if it's only five or ten minutes. Do not expect that individual counselors can afford to give you this exploratory interview for nothing! If they did that, and got a lot of requests like yours, they would never be able to make a living. You do have the right, however, to inquire *ahead of time* how much they are going to have to charge you for the exploratory interview.

When you are face-to-face with the firm or with the individual counselor, you ask each of them the same questions, listed on the form below. (Keep a little pad or notebook with you, so you can write their answers down.)

MY SEARCH FOR A GOOD CAREER COUNSELOR

Questions I Will Ask Them	Answer from counselor #1	Answer from counselor #2	Answer from counselor #3
1. What is your program?			
2. Who will be doing it? And how long have you been doing it?			
3. What is your success rate?			
4. What is the cost of your services?			
5. Is there a contract?			

After visiting the three places you chose for your comparison shopping, you have to go home, sit down, put your feet up, look over your notes, and compare those places. You need to decide a) whether you want none of the three, or b) one of the three (and if so, which one). Remember, you don't have to choose any of the three counselors, if you didn't really care for any of them. If that is the case, then choose three new counselors, dust off the notebook, and go out again. It may take a few more hours to find what you want. But the wallet, the purse, the job-hunt, the life, you save will be your own.

As you look over your notes, you will realize there is no definitive way for you to determine a career counselor's expertise. It's something you'll have to smell out, as you go along. But here are some clues:

BAD ANSWERS

If they give you the feeling that everything will be done for you, by them (including interpretation of tests, and decision making about what this means you should do, or where you should do it) - - rather than you having to do all the work, with their basically assuming the role of coach,

(15 bad points)

You want to learn how to do this for yourself; you're going to be job-hunting again, you know.

If they say they are not the person who will be doing the program with you, but deny you any chance to meet the counselor you would be working with,

(75 bad points)

You're talking to a salesperson. Avoid any firm that has a salesperson.

If you do get a chance to meet the counselor, but you don't like the counselor as a person,

(150 bad points)

I don't care what their expertise is, if you don't like them, you're going to have a rough time getting what you want. I guarantee it. Rapport is everything.

If you ask how long the counselor has been doing this, and they get huffy or give a double-barreled answer, such as: "I've had eighteen years' experience in the business and career counseling world,"

(20 bad points)

What that may mean is: seventeen and a half years as a fertilizer salesman, and one half year doing career counseling. Persist. "How long have you been with this firm, and how long have you been doing formal career counseling, as you are here?" You might be interested to know that some executive or career counseling firms hire yesterday's clients as today's new staff. Such new staff are sometimes given training only after they're "on-the-job." They are practicing on you.

If they try to answer the question of their experience by pointing to their degrees or credentials,

(3 bad points)

Degrees or credentials tell you they've passed certain tests of their qualifications, but often these tests bear more on their expertise at career assessment than on their knowledge of creative job-hunting.

If, when you ask about their success rate, they say they have never had a client that failed to find a job, no matter what,

(15 bad points)

They're lying. I have studied career counseling programs for over twenty years, have attended many, have studied records at State and Federal offices, and I have hardly ever seen a program that placed more than 86% of their clients, tops, in their best years. And it goes downhill from there. A prominent executive counseling firm was reported by the Attorney General's Office of New York State to have placed only 38 out of 550 clients (a 93% failure rate).[2] If they make it clear that they have had a good success rate, but if you fail to work hard at the whole process, then there is no guarantee you are going to find a job, give them three stars.

If they show you letters from ecstatically-happy former clients, but when you ask to talk to some of those clients, you get stone-walled.

(45 bad points)

I quote from one job-hunter's letter to me: "I asked to speak to a former client or clients. You would of thought I asked to speak to Elvis. The Counselor stammered and stuttered and gave me a million excuses why I couldn't talk to some of these 'satisfied' former clients. None of the excuses sounded legitimate to me. We went back and forth for about thirty minutes. Finally, he excused himself and went to speak to his boss, the owner. The next thing I knew I was called into the owner's office for a more 'personal' sales pitch. We spoke for about 45 minutes as he tried to convince me to use his service. When I told him I was not ready to sign up, he became angry and asked my Counselor why I had been put before 'the committee' if I wasn't ready to commit? The Counselor claimed I had given a verbal commitment at our last meeting. The owner then turned to me and said I seemed to have a problem

---

2. For further details, go to your local library and look up "Career Counselors: Will They Lead You Down The Primrose Path?" by Lee Guthrie, in the December 1981 issue of *Savvy Magazine*, pp. 60ff.

making a decision and that he did not want to do business with me. I was shocked. They had turned the whole story around to make it look like it was my fault. I felt humiliated. In retrospect, the whole process felt like dealing with a used car salesman. They used pressure tactics and intimidation to try to get what they wanted. As you have probably gathered, more than anything else this experience made me angry."

If they claim they only accept 5 clients out of every hundred who apply, and your name will have to be put before 'The Committee' before you can be accepted.

(1000 bad points)

This is one of the oldest tricks in the book. You're supposed to feel 'special' before they lift those thousands of dollars out of your wallet. Personally, the minute I heard this at a particular agency or service, I would run for the door and never look back.

If you ask what is the cost of their services, and they reply that it is a lump sum that must all be paid "up front" before you start or shortly after you start, either all at once or in installments,

(100 bad points)

For twenty-five years I've tried to avoid saying this, but I have grown weary of the tears of job-hunters who 'got taken.' So now I say it without reservation: if the firm charges a lump sum for their services, rather than allowing you to simply pay for each hour as you go, go elsewhere. Every insincere and inept counselor or firm charges a lump sum. So, of course, do a few sincere and good counselors and firms. Trouble is: you won't know which kind you've signed up with, until they've got all your money. The risk is too great, the cost is too high. If you really like to gamble that much, go to Las Vegas. They give better odds.

If they asked you to bring in your partner or spouse with you,

(45 bad points)

This is a well-known tactic of some of the slickest salespeople in the world, who want your spouse or partner there so they can manipulate one or the other or both of you to reach a decision on the spot, while they have you in their 'grasp.'

If they ask you to sign a contract,

(1000 bad points)

With insincere and inept firms or counselors, there is always a written contract. And you must sign it, before they will help you. (Often, your partner or spouse will be asked to sign it, too.) The fee normally ranges from $1000 on up to $10,000 or more.

You may think the purpose of that firm's contract is that they are promis-

ing you something, that they can be held to. Uh-uh! *More often, the main purpose of the contract is to get you to promise them something. Like, your money. Don't . . . . . . do . . . . . it.*

You will sometimes be told that, *"Of course, you can get your money back, or a portion of it, at any time, should you be dissatisfied with the career counselor's services." Nine times out of ten, however, you are told this verbally, and it is not in the written contract. Verbal promises, without witnesses, are difficult if not impossible for you to later try to enforce. The written contract is* binding.

Sometimes the written contract will claim to provide for a partial refund, at any time, until you reach a cut-off date in the program, which the contract specifies. Unfortunately, many crafty fraudulent firms bend over backwards to be extra nice, extra available, and extra helpful to you until that cut-off point is reached. So, when the cut-off point for getting a refund has been reached, you let it pass because you are very satisfied with their past services, and believe there will be many more weeks of the same. Only, there aren't. At fraudulent firms, once the cut-off point is passed, the career counselor becomes virtually impossible for you to get ahold of. Call after call will not be returned. You will say to yourself "What happened?" Well, what happened, my friend, is that you paid up in full, they have all the money they're ever going to get out of you, and now they don't want to give you any more time.

You may think I am exaggerating: I mean, can there possibly be such mean men and women, who would prey on job-hunters, when they're down and out. Yes, ma'am, and yes, sir, there are. That's why you have to do this preliminary research so thoroughly.

I quote from the late Robert Wegmann, former director of the UHCL Center for Labor Market Studies: "One high-charging career counseling firm went bankrupt a few years ago. They left many of their materials behind in their former office. A box of what they abandoned has come into my possession. Going through the contents of the box has been fascinating.

"Particularly interesting are several scripts used to train their salespeople. The goal of the sales pitch is to convince the unemployed (or unhappily employed) person that he or she can't find a good job alone, but can do it with professional help. Hiring us, they argue, is just like hiring a lawyer . . .

"Then, at the end of the pitch, comes the 'takeaway.' The firm may not accept your money, you are warned! There will have to be a review board meeting at which your application is considered. Only a minority of applicants are accepted. The firm only wants the right kind of clients.

"That's the pitch. But the rest of the documents tell a very different story. In fact, the firm is running a series of sales contests with all the 'professionalism' of a used car lot . . .

"These salespeoeple were paid on commission. The higher the sales the higher the percentage of the customer's fee they got to keep.

"There are sales contests. The winner receives a handsome green Master's jacket. Each monthly winner qualifies for a Grand Master's Tournament, with large prizes . . .

"So take this one piece of advice . . . If someone offers to help you find a great job as long as you'll pay several thousand dollars in advance, do as follows:

"A. Find door

"B. Walk out same

"C. Do not return."

Over the last twenty years, I have had to listen to grown men and women cry over the telephone, all because they signed a contract. Most often they were executives, or senior managers, who never had to go job-hunting before, and unknowingly signed up with some executive counseling firm that was fraudulent, or at least on the edge of legality.

If you want to avoid their tears in your own job-search, don't sign anything -- ever.[3]

My advice -- for what it's worth: don't sign up with *anyone* who offers you a contract, or charges other than by the hour.

---

3. If you are **dying** to know more, and your local library has back files of magazines and newspapers (on microfiche, or otherwise) there was a period when bad firms and counselors came under heavy fire (1978-1982) and you can look up some of the articles of that period, as well as those articles which have appeared more recently, to wit:

"A Consumer's Guide to Retail Job-Hunting Services," Special Report, reprinted from the *National Business Employment Weekly*; available from National Business Employment Weekly Reprint Service, P.O. Box 300, Princeton, NJ 08543-0300. 1-800-730-1111. $8 by mail; $12.95 by fax. A *very* thorough series of articles on the industry, and its frauds, which names *names,* and gives the addresses of Consumer protection agencies in each state, to whom you may complain. **Required reading** for anyone who wants to avoid getting 'burned.'

" 'Employment counselors' costly, target of gripes," *The Arizona Republic,* 10/8/89.

"Career-Counseling Industry Accused of Misrepresentation," *New York Times,* 9/30/82.

"Consumer Law: Career Counselors and Employment Agencies" by Reed Brody, *New York Law Journal,* Feb. 26, 1982, p. 1. Reed was Assistant Attorney General of the State of New York, and more recently Deputy Chief of the Labor Bureau within that State's Department of Law; in this capacity he became the leading legal expert in the country, on career counseling malpractices, though unfortunately (for us) he now works overseas in Europe, in another profession.

"Career Counselors: Will They Lead You Down the Primrose Path?" by Lee Guthrie, *Savvy Magazine,* 12/81, p. 60ff.

"Franklin Career Search Is Accused of Fraud In New York State Suit," *Wall Street Journal,* 1/29/81, p. 50.

"Job Counseling Firms Under Fire For Promising Much, Giving Little," *Wall Street Journal,* 1/27/81, p. 33.

GOOD ANSWERS

Well, those are the bad answers. How about the good ones? Yes, there are such things: career counselors who charge by the hour. With them, there is no written contract. You sign nothing. You pay only for each hour as you use it, according to their set rate. Each time you keep an appointment, you pay them at the end of that hour for their help, according to that rate. Period. Finis. You never owe them any money. You can stop seeing them at any time, if you feel you are not getting the help you wish.

What will they charge? You will find, these days, that the best career counselors (and some of the worst, too) will charge you whatever a really good therapist or marriage counselor charges per hour, in your geographical area. Currently, in large metropolitan areas, that runs around $100 an hour, sometimes more. In suburbia or rural areas, it may be much less -- $40 an hour, or so.

That fee is for individual time with the career counselor. If you can't afford that fee, ask whether they also run groups. If they do, the fee will be much less. And, in one of those delightful ironies of life, since you get a chance to listen to problems which other job-hunters in your group are having, the group will often give you more help than an individual session would. Not always; but often. It's always ironic when *cheaper* and *more helpful* go hand in hand.

If the career counselor in question does offer groups, there should (again) never be a contract. The charge should be payable at the end of each session, and you should be able to drop out at any time, without further cost, if you decide you are not getting the help you want.

There are, incidentally, some career counselors who run free (or almost free) job-hunting workshops through local churches, synagogues, chambers of commerce, community colleges, adult education programs, and the like, as their community service, or pro bonum work (as it is technically called). I have had reports of such workshops from a number of places in the U.S. and Canada. They surely exist in other parts of the world as well. If money is a big problem for you, in getting help with your job-hunt, ask around to see if such workshops as these exist in your community. Your chamber of commerce will likely know, or your church or synagogue.

A Sampler

This is not a complete directory of anything. It is exactly what its name implies: a **Sampler.** Were I to list all the career counselors *out there*, we would end up with an encyclopedia. Some states, in fact, have *encyclopedic* lists of counselors and businesses, in various books or directories, and your local bookstore or library should have these, in their *Job-Hunting Section,* under such titles as "How to Get A Job in......" or "Job-Hunting in . . ."

The places listed in this **Sampler** are listed at their own request, and I offer them to you simply as places for you to begin your investigation with - - nothing more.

Many truly *helpful* places are *not* listed here. If you discover such a place, which is very good at helping people with *Parachute* and creative job-hunting or career-change, do send us the pertinent information. We will ask them, as we do all the listings here, a few intelligent questions and if they sound okay, we will add that place to next year's edition.

We do ask a few questions because our readers want counselors and places which claim some expertise in helping them finish their job-hunt, *using this book.* So, if they've never even heard of *Parachute,* we don't list them. On the other hand, we can't measure a place's expertise at this long distance, no matter how many questions we ask.

Even if listed here, you must do your own sharp questioning before you decide to go with anyone. If you don't take time to research two or three places, before choosing a counselor, you will deserve whatever you get (or, more to the point, *don't* get). So, please, *do your research.* The purse or wallet you save, will be your own.

Yearly readers of this book will notice that we do remove people from this Sampler, without warning. Specifically, we remove (without further notice or comment): Places we didn't mean to remove, but a typographical error was made, somehow (it happens). We also remove: Places which have moved, and don't bother to send us their new address. If you are listed here, we expect you to be a professional at *communication*. When you move, your first priority should be to let us know, *immediately*. As one exemplary counselor just wrote: "You are the first person I am contacting on my updated letterhead . . . hot off the press just today!" So it should always be. A number of places get removed every year, precisely because of their poor communication skills, and their sloppiness in letting us know where they've gone to. *Other causes for removal:*

Places which have disconnected their telephone, or otherwise suggest that they have gone out of business.

Places which our readers lodge complaints against, with us, as being either unhelpful or obnoxious. The complaints may be falsified, but we can't take that chance.

Places which change their personnel, and the new person has never even heard of *Parachute*, or creative job-search techniques.

Places which misuse their listing here, claiming in their brochures, ads or interviews, that they have some kind of 'Parachute Seal of Approval,' -- that we feature them in Parachute, or recommend them or endorse them. This is a big 'no-no.' A listing here is no more of a recommendation than is a listing in the phone book.

College services that we discover (belatedly) serve only *'Their Own."*

Counseling firms which employ salespeople as the initial 'in-take' person that a job-hunter meets.

If you discover that any of the places listed in this Sampler falls into any of the above categories, you would be doing a great service to our other readers by dropping us a line and telling us so. (P.O. Box 379, Walnut Creek, CA 94597.)

THE LISTINGS which follow are alphabetical within each state, except that counselors listed by their name are in alphabetical order according to their *last* name. To make this clear, only their last name is in **bold** type.

What do the letters after their name mean? Well, B.A., M.A. and Ph.D. you know. However, don't assume the degree is in career counseling. Ask. NCC means "Nationally certified counselor." There are about 20,000 such in the U.S. This can mean *general counseling expertise*, not necessarily career counseling. On the other hand, NCCC does mean "Nationally certified career counselor." There are currently about 850 in the U.S. Other initials, such as LPC -- "Licensed professional counselor" -- and the like, often refer to State licensing. There are a number of States, now, that have some sort of regulation of career counselors. In some States it is mandatory, in others it is optional. But, *mostly*, this field is unregulated.

Some offer group career counseling, some offer testing, some offer access to job-banks, etc.

One final note: generally speaking, the places counsel *anybody*. A few, however, may turn out to have restrictions unknown to us (*"we counsel only women,"* etc.). If that's the case, your time isn't wasted. They may be able to help you with a referral. So, don't be afraid to ask them *"who else in the area can you tell me about, who helps with job-searches, and are there any (among them) that you think are particularly effective?"*

Area Codes

Throughout the U.S. now, area codes are sub-dividing constantly, sometimes more than once during a short time-span. If you're calling a local counselor, you probably don't need the area code anyway. But if you call a phone number below that is any distance away from you, and they tell you "this number cannot be completed as dialed," the most likely explanation is that the area code got changed -- maybe some time ago. (We ask counselors listed here to notify us when the area code changes, but some do and some don't.) Anyway, call Information and check.

---

* Throughout this Sampler, an asterisk before their name, in red, means they offer not only regular job-search help, but also (when you wish) counseling from a spiritual point of view; i.e., they're not afraid to talk about God if you're looking for some help, in finding your mission in life.

ALABAMA

*Career Decisions, 638 Winwood Dr., Birmingham, AL 35226. phone 205-822-8662 or 205-870-2639. Carrie Pearce Hild, M.S.Ed., Career Counselor and Consultant.

Maureen J. Chemsak, NCC, NCCC, LPC, Director of Counseling and Career Services, Athens State University, 300 North Beaty St., Athens, AL 35611. phone 256-233-8285 or 256-830-4610.

Vantage Associates, 2100-A Southbridge Pkwy., Suite 480, Birminham, AL 35209. Phone 205-879-0501 or 205-631-5544. Michael A. Tate

Work Matters, Career Coaching, 104 Peachtree Road, Birmingham, AL 35213. phone 205-879-8494. Gayle H. Lantz

ALASKA

Career Transitions, 2600 Denali St., Suite 430, Anchorage, AK 99503. phone 907-274-4500. Deeta Lonergan, Director.

ARIZONA

The Orion Institute, Debra B. Danvenport, M.A., L.C.C., Ph.D.(c) Director, 6945 E. Cochise Road, Suite 138, Scottsdale, AZ 85253-1485. Phone 480-348-1163

Southwest Institute of Life Management, 11122 E. Gunshot Circle, Tucson, AZ 85749. phone 520-749-2290. Theodore Donald Risch, Director. M.S., CRC.

West Valley Career Services, 10720 W. Indian School, #19-141, Phoenix, AZ 85037. Phone 623-872-7303. Shell Mendelson Herman, M.S., CRC.

ARKANSAS

Donald McKinney, Ed.D., Career Counselor, Rt. 1, Box 351-A, DeQueen, AR 71832. phone 870-642-5628.

CALIFORNIA

Alumnae Resources, 120 Montgomery St., Suite 600, San Francisco, CA 94104. phone 415-274-4700.

Dwayne Berrett, M.A., RPCC, Berrett & Associates, 1551 E. Shaw, Suite 103, Fresno, CA 93710. phone 559-221-6543.

Beverly Brown, M.A., NCCC, NCC 809 So. Bundy Dr., #105, Los Angeles, CA 90049. phone 310-447-7093.

California Career Services, 6024 Wilshire Blvd., Los Angeles CA 90036-3616. phone 323-933-2900. Susan W. Miller, M.A.

Career Action Center, 10420 Bubb Rd., Suite 100, Cupertino, CA 95014-4150. phone 408-253-3200. Betsy Collard, Director, Linda Surrell, Manager, Counseling Services. *A tremendously impressive career center, one of the most comprehensive in the U.S., with a large number of job listings (81,000) and other resources, including individual counseling, workshops, books, videos, etc.*

Career and Personal Development Institute, 690 Market St., Suite 402, San Francisco, CA 94104. phone 415-982-2636. Bob Chope.

Career Balance, 215 Witham Road, Encinitas CA 92024. phone 760-436-3994. Virginia Byrd, M.Ed., Work/Life Specialist, Career Management.

Career Choices, 15360 Mendocino St., San Leandro, CA 94579. phone 510-357-3262 (DANA). Dana E. Ogden, M.S.Ed., CCDV, Counselor and Trainer.

Career Counseling and Assessment Associates, 9229 West Sunset Blvd., Suite 502, Los Angeles, CA 90069. phone 310-274-3423. Dianne Y. Sundby, Ph.D., Director and Psychologist.

*Career Development and Vocational Testing Services, 2515 Park Marina, Suite 203-B, Redding, CA 96001. phone 916-246-2871.

Career Development Center, John F. Kennedy University, 1250 Arroyo Way, Walnut Creek, CA 94596. phone 925-295-0610. Susan Geifman, Director. *Open to the public. Membership or fee.*

Career Development Life Planning, 3585 Maple St., Suite 237, Ventura, CA 93003. phone 805-656-6220. Norma Zuber, NCCC, M.S.C., & Associates.

Career Dimensions, Box 7402, Stockton, CA 95267. phone 209-957-6465. Fran Abbott.

Career Planning Center/Business Action Center, 1623 S. La Cienega Blvd., Los Angeles, CA 90035. phone 310-273-6633.

Career Strategy Associates, 1100 Quail St., Suite 201, Newport Beach, CA 92660. phone 949-252-0515. Betty Fisher.

Center for Career Growth and Development, P.O. Box 283, Los Gatos, CA 95031. phone 408-354-7150. Steven E. Beasley.

Center for Creative Change, 3130 West Fox Run Way, San Diego, CA 92111.phone 619-268-9340. Nancy Helgeson, M.A., MFCC

The Center for Life and Work Planning, 1133 Second St., Encinitas, CA 92024. phone 760-943-0747. Mary C. McIsaac, Executive Director.

*The Center for Ministry (An Interdenominational Church Career Development Center) 8393 Capwell Dr., Suite 220 Oakland, CA 94621-2123. phone 510-635-4246. Robert L. Charpentier, Director.

Stephen Cheney-Rice, M.S., 2113 Westboro Ave., Alhambra, CA 91803-3720. phone 818-281-6066, or 213-740-9112.

The **Clarity** Group Inc. 388 Market Street, Suite 500 San Francisco CA 94111. phone 415-292-4814. George Schofield, PhD (specializes in helping people who are 'stuck').

Cricket Consultants, 502 Natoma St., P.O. Box 6191, Folsom, CA 95763-6191. phone 916-985-3211. Bruce Parrish, M.S., CDMS.

Cypress College, Career Planning Center, 9200 Valley View St., Cypress, CA 90630. phone 714-484-7000

Margaret L. **Eadie,** M.A., A.M.Ed. Career Consultant, 1000 Sage Pl., Pacific Grove, CA 93950. phone 831-373-7400.

Experience Unlimited Job Club. There are 35 Experience Unlimited Clubs in California, found at the Employment Development Department in the following locations: Anaheim, Corona, El Cajon, Escondido, Fremont, Fresno, Hemet, Hollywood, Lancaster, Monterey, North Hollywood, Oakland, Ontario, Pasadena, Pleasant Hill, Redlands, Ridgecrest, Riverside, Sacramento (Midtown and South), San Bernardino, San Diego (also East and South), San Francisco, San Mateo, San Rafael, Santa Ana, Santa Cruz, Santa Maria, Simi Valley, Sunnyvale, Torrance, Victorville, and West Covina. Contact the club nearest to you through your local Employment Development Department (E.D.D.).

Mary Alice **Floyd,** M.A., NCC, Career Counselor/Consultant, Career Life Transitions. 3233 Lucinda Lane, Santa Barbara, CA 93105. phone 805-687-5462.

Jan **Fritsen,** Career Counseling and Coaching, 23181 La Cadena Drive, Suite 103, Laguna Hills, CA 92653. phone 949-786-5431

Futures . . . , 103 Calvin Place, Santa Cruz, CA 95060. phone 831-425-0332. Joseph Reimuller.

Marvin F. **Galper,** Ph.D., Third Ave., San Diego, CA 92103. phone 619-295-4450.

Jack **Geary,** MA, CRC, Geary & Associates, 1100-A Coddingtown Ctr., P.O. Box 3774, Santa Rosa, CA 95402. phone 707-525-8085.

Judith **Grutter,** M.S., NCCC, G/S Consultants, P.O. Box 7855, South Lake Tahoe, CA 96158. phone 530-541-8587.

The **Guidance Center,** 1150 Yale St., Suite One, Santa Monica, CA 90403. phone 310-829-4429. Anne Salzman, Career Counselor and Psychologist.

H.R. Solutions, Human Resources Consulting, 390 South Sepulveda Blvd., Suite 104, Los Angeles, CA 90049. phone 310-471-2536. Nancy Mann, M.B.A, President/Career Consultant.

Jewish Vocational Service, 5700 Wilshire Blvd., 2nd Floor, Suite 2303, Los Angeles, CA 90036. phone 323-761-8888.

Judy Kaplan Baron Associates, 6046 Cornerstone Ct. West, Suite 208, San Diego, CA 92121. phone 619-558-7400. Judy Kaplan Baron, Director.

Patrick **Kerwin,** MBA, NCCC, Kerwin & Associates , 926 W. Kenneth Road, Glendale, CA 91202. phone 808-246-5621

*Lifework Design,** 448 S. Marengo Ave., Pasadena, CA 91101. phone 626-577-2705. Kevin Brennfleck, M.A., NCCC, and Kay Marie Brennfleck, M.A., NCCC, Directors.

Peller **Marion,** 388 Market St., Suite 500, San Francisco, CA 94111. phone 415-296-2559.

*Lizbeth **Miller,** M.S., 3880 S. Bascom Ave., Suite 202, San Jose, CA 95124. phone 408-559-1115. Affiliated with the Christian Counseling Center.

Montgomery & Associates, Career Development Services, 2515 Park Marina Dr., Suite 203B, Redding, CA 96001-2831. phone 530-246-2871. Gale Montgomery, Director.

Olivia Keith **Slaughter,** LEP, Sunshine Plaza, 71 301 Highway 111, Suite 1, Rancho Mirage, CA 92270. phone 760-568-1544.

Transitions Counseling Center, 171 N. Van Ness, Fresno, CA 93701. phone 559-233-7250. Margot E. Tepperman, L.C.S.W.

Turning Point Career Center, University YWCA, 2600 Bancroft Way, Berkeley, CA 94704. phone 510-848-6370. Winnie Froehlich, M.S., Director.

Patti **Wilson,** P.O. Box 35633, Los Gatos, CA 95030. phone 408-354-1964.

COLORADO

Accelerated Job Search, 4490 Squires Circle, Boulder, CO 80303. phone 303-494-2467. Leigh Olsen, Counselor.

CRS Consulting, 425 W. Mulberry, Suite 205, Fort Collins, CO 80521. phone 970-484-9810. Marilyn Pultz.

Sherry **Helmstaedter,** 5040 South El Camino, Englewood, CO 80111-1122. phone 303-794-5122.

Life Work Planning, P.O.Box 1738, Berthoud, CO 80513. phone 970-532-5351. Lauren T. Murphy, Career Development Counselor.

Betsy C. **McGee,** The McGee Group, 2485 W. Main, Suite 202, Old Littleton, CO 80120. phone 303-794-4749.

Patricia **O'Keefe,** M.A., 1550 S. Monroe St., Denver, CO 80210. phone 303-759-9325.

Resource Center, Arapahoe Community College, 2500 West College Dr., P.O. Box 9002, Littleton, CO 80160-9002. phone 303-797-5805.

Women's Resource Agency, 31 N. Farragut, Colorado Springs, CO 80909. phone 719-471-3170.

YWCA of Boulder County Career Center, 2222 14th St., Boulder, CO 80302. phone 303-443-0419. A full-service career center, fees on a sliding scale. Counseling, testing, support groups, workshops, April Peterson, NCCC, Career Services Manager.

CONNECTICUT

Accord Career Services, The Exchange, Suite 305, 270 Farmington Ave., Farmington, CT 06032. phone 800-022-1480, or 860-674-9654. Tod Gerardo, M.S., Director.

Career Choices/RFP Associates, 141 Durham Rd., Suite 24, Madison, CT 06443. phone 203-245-4123.

Career Transformations, 761 Valley Road, Fairfield, CT 06432. Phone 203-374-7649. Robert N. Olsen, M.A., NCC.

James S. **Cohen**, Ph.D., Career Services, Vocational Rehabilitation Services for Injured/Disabled Workers, 205 Vernon Avenue, #211, Vernon, CT 06066. Phone 860-871-7832.

Fairfield Academic and Career Center, Fairfield University, Dolan House, Fairfield, CT 06430. phone 203-254-4220.

Jamieson Associates, 61 South Main St., Suite 101, West Hartford, CT 06107-2403. phone 860-521-2373. Lee Jamieson, Principal.

The **Offerjost-Westcott Group,** 263 Main St., Old Saybrook, CT 06475. phone 203-388-6094. Russ Westcott.

Bob **Pannone**, M.A., NCCC, Career Specialist, 768 Saw Mill Road, West Haven, CT 06516. phone 203-933-6383.

People Management International Ltd., Ltd., 8B North Shore Rd., New Preston CT 06777. phone 203-868-0317. Arthur Miller, founder and principal.

Releasing Your Original Genius™, 998 Farmington Ave., Suite 207, West Hartford, CT 06107. phone 860-561-2142. Lorraine P. Holden, M.S.W., Career/Life Planning Consultant.

Vocational and Academic Counseling for Adults (VOCA), 115 Berrian Rd., Stamford, CT 06905. phone 203-322-8353. Ruth A. Polster.

J. Whitney Associates, 11092 Elm St., Rocky Hill, CT 06067. phone 860-721-0842. Jean Whitney, Career Manager.

DELAWARE

The Brandywine Center, 2500 Grubb Road, Suite 240, Wilmington, DE 19810. phone 302-475-1880. Also at 3302 Polly Drummond Office Park, Newark, DE 19711. phone 302-454-7650. Kris Bronson, Ph.D.

YWCA of New Castle County, Women's Center for Economic Options, 233 King St., Wilmington, DE 19801. phone 302-658-7161.

DISTRICT OF COLUMBIA

Community Vocational Counseling Service, The George Washington University Counseling Center, 718 21st St. NW, Washington, DC 20052. phone 202-994-4860. Robert J. Wilson, M.S., Asst. Director for Educational Services.

George Washington University, Center for Career Education, 2020 K St., Washington, DC 20052. phone 202-994-5299. Abigail Pereira, Director.

FLORIDA

Barbara **Adler**, Ed.D., Career Consulting, 203 North Shadow Bay Dr., Orlando, FL 32825-3766. phone 407-249-2189.

Career Moves, Inc., 5300 North Federal Highway, Fort Lauderdale, FL 33308. phone 305-772-6857. Mary Jane Ward, M.Ed., NCC, NCCC.

Center for Career Decisions, 6100 Glades Rd., #210, Boca Raton, FL 33434. phone 561-470-9333. Linda Friedman, M.A., NCC, NCCC, Director.

The Centre for Women, 305 S. Hyde Park Ave., Tampa FL 33606. phone 813-251-8437. Dae C. Sheridan, M.A., CRC, Employment Counselor.

Chabon & Associates, 1665 Palm Beach Lakes Blvd., Suite 402, West Palm Beach, FL 33401. phone 407-640-8443. Toby G. Chabon, M.Ed., NCC, President.

The **Challenge: Program for Displaced Homemakers,** Florida Community College at Jacksonville, 101 W. State St., Jacksonville, FL 32202. phone 904-633-8316. Rita Patrick, Project Coordinator.

Crossroads, Palm Beach Community College, 4200 Congress Ave., Lake Worth, FL 33461-4796. phone 407-433-5995. Pat Jablonski, Program Manager.

Focus on the Future: Displaced Homemaker Program, Santa Fe Community College, 3000 N.W. 83rd St., Gainesville, FL 32606. phone 904-395-5047. Nancy Griffin, Program Coordinator. Classes are free.

Larry **Harmon**, Ph.D., Career Counseling Center, Inc., 2000 South Dixie Highway, Suite 103, Miami, FL 33133. phone 305-858-8557.

Ellen O. **Jonassen**, Ph.D., 10785 Ulmerton Rd., Largo, FL 34648. phone 813-581-8526.

Life Designs, Inc., 19526 East Lake Drive, Miami, FL 33015. phone 305-829-9008 (Sept.–May). Dulce Muccio Weisenborn.

New Beginnings, Polk Community College, Station 71, 999 Avenue H, NE, Winter Haven, FL 33881-4299 (Lakeland Campus). phone 813-297-1029.

The Women's Center, Valencia Community College, 1010 N. Orlando Ave., Winter Park, FL 32789. phone 407-628-1976.

WINGS Program, Broward Community College, 1000 Coconut Creek Blvd., Coconut Creek, FL 33066. phone 305-973-2398.

GEORGIA

Emmette H. **Albea,** Jr., M.S., LPC, NCCC, 2706 Melrose Dr., Valdosta, GA 31602. phone 912-241-0908.

Atlanta Outplacement and Career Consulting, 1150 Lake Hearn Dr., N.E., Suite 200, Atlanta, GA 30342. phone 404-250-3232. Harvey Brickley, Consultant.

* **Career Development Center of the Southeast** (An Interdenominational Church Career Development Center), 531 Kirk Rd., Decatur, GA 30030. phone 404-371-0336. Earl B. Stewart, D.Min., Director.

***Career Pathways,** 601 Broad St., Gainesville, GA 30501 phone 800-722-1976. Lee Ellis, Director. *Offers career-guidance from a Christian point of view, through the mails -- based on questionnaires and various instruments or inventories which they send you.*

Career Quest/Job Search Workshop, St. Ann, 4905 Roswell Rd., N.E., Marietta, GA 30062-6240. phone 770-552-6402. Tom Chernetsky. *Features instruction on Internet job-hunting.*

* **Center for Growth & Change, Inc.,** 6991 Peachtree Ind. Blvd., Suite 310, Norcross, GA 30092. phone 404-441-9580. James P. Hicks, Ph.D., LPC, Director.

D & B Consulting, 3390 Peachtree Road N.E., Suite 900, Atlanta, GA 30326. phone 404-240-8063. Deborah R. Brown, MSM, MSW, Career Consultant.

Jewish Vocational Service, Inc., 4549 Chamblee Dunwoody Road, Dunwoody GA 30338-6120. phone 770-677-9440. Anna Blau, Director.

St. Jude's Job Network, St. Jude's Catholic Church, 7171 Glenridge Dr., Sandy Springs, GA 30328. phone 404-393-4578.

Mark **Satterfield,** 720 Rio Grand Dr., Alpharetta, GA 30202. phone 770-640-8393.

HAWAII

Career Discovery, 4999 Kahala Ave., #408, Honolulu, HI 96816-5421. phone 808-739-9494. Nancy Hanson, M.A., NCCC.

IDAHO

* **The Job Search Advisor,** 915 W. Iowa Ave., Boise, ID 83686. phone 208-463-2375. Christopher G. Gilliam, PHR, Job Search Advisor.

Transitions, 1970 Parkside Dr., Boise, ID 83712. phone 208-368-0499. Elaine Simmons, M.Ed.

ILLINOIS

Alumni Career Center, University of Illinois Alumni Association, 200 South Wacker Dr., Chicago, IL 60606. phone 312-996-6350. Barbara S. Hundley, Director; Claudia M. Delestowicz, Associate Director, Julie L. Hays, Staff. Full Service Career Center open to the community.

Career Path, 1240 Iroquois Ave., Suite 510, Naperville, IL 60563. phone 630-369-3390. Donna Sandberg, M.S., NCC, Owner/Counselor.

Career Workshops, 5431 W. Roscoe St., Chicago, IL 60641. phone 312-282-6859. Patricia Dietze.

Jean **Davis,** Adult Career Transitions, 1405 Elmwood Ave., Evanston, IL 60201. phone 847-492-1002.

The **Dolan Agency,** 2745 East Broadway, Suite 102, Alton, IL 62002. phone 618-474-5328. J. Stephen Dolan, M.A., C.R.C., Rehabilitation and Career Consultant.

Barbara Kabcenell **Grauer,** M.A., NCC, 1370 Sheridan Road, Highland Park, IL 60035. phone 708-432-4479.

Grimard Wilson Consulting, 111 N. Wabash Ave., Suite 1006, Chicago, IL 60602. phone 312-201-1142. Diane Grimard Wilson, M.A.

Harper College Career Transition Center, Building A, Room 124, Palatine, IL 60067. phone 708-459-8233. Mary Ann Jirak, Coordinator.

David P. **Helfand,** Ed.D., NCCC, 250 Ridge, Evanston, IL 60202. phone 847-328-2787.

Barbara **Hill,** Career Management Consultant, 1512 Central St., AA3, Evanston, IL 60201. phone 847-733-1805.

Lansky Career Consultants, 330 N. Wabash #2905, Chicago, IL 60611. phone 312-494-0022. Judith Lansky, President. Julie Benesh, Adjunct Consultant.

* **Life/Career Planning Center for Religious,** 10526 W. Cermak Rd., Suite 111, Westchester, IL 60153. phone 708-531-9228. Dolores Linhart, Director. *Doing work with Roman Catholics.*

Living by Design, 106 S. Oak Park Ave., Suite 203, Oak Park, IL 60302. phone 708-386-2505. Barbara Upton, LCSW,Life/Work Planning.

* **Midwest Career Development Service** (An Interdenominational Church Career Development Center), 1840 Westchester Blvd., Westchester, IL 60154. phone 708-343-6268.

Midwest Women's Center, 828 S. Wabash, Suite 200, Chicago, IL 60605. phone 312-922-8530.

Moraine Valley Community College, Job Placement Center, 10900 S. 88th Ave., Palos Hills, IL 60465. phone 708-974-5737.

Right Livelyhood$, 23 W. 402 Green Briar Dr., Naperville, IL 60540. phone 708-369-9066. Marti Beddoe, Career/Life Counselor; or 312-281-7274, Peter LeBrun.

The Summit Group, P.O. Box 3794, Peoria, IL 61612-3794. phone 309-681-1118. John R. Throop, D. Min., President.

Widmer & Associates, 1510 W. Sunnyview Dr., Peoria, IL 61614. phone 309-691-3312. Mary F. Widmer, President.

INDIANA

Career Consultants, 107 N. Pennsylvania St., Suite 400, Indianapolis, IN 46204. phone 317-639-5601. Al Milburn, Career Management Consultant.

Sally **Jones,** Program Coordinator/Developer, Indiana University, School of Continuing Studies, Owen Hall, Room 202, Bloomington IN 47405. phone 812-855-4991.

KCDM Associates, 10401 N. Meridian St., Suite 300, Indianapolis, IN 46290. phone 317-581-6230. Mike Kenney.

William R. **Lesch,** M.S., Career & Life Transitions, Inc., 8121 Brent Ave, Indianapolis, IN 46240. phone 317-255-4840.

Performance Development Systems, Inc., 312 Iroquois Trail, Burns Harbor, IN 46304. phone 219-787-9216. William P. Henning, Counselor.

IOWA

Rosanne **Beers,** Beers Consulting, 5505 Boulder Dr., West Des Moines, Iowa 50266. phone 515-225-1245.

Jill **Sudak-Allison,** 3219 SE 19th Court, Des Moines, IA 50320. phone 515-282-5040.

University of Iowa, Center for Career Development and Cooperative Education, 315 Calvin Hall, Iowa City, IA 52242. phone 319-335-3201.

Gloria **Wendroff,** Secrets to Successful Job Search, 703 E. Burlington Ave., Fairfield, IA 52556. phone 515-472-4529.

Suzanne **Zilber,** 801 Crystal St., Ames, IA 50010. phone 515-232-9379.

KENTUCKY

The Epoch Group, 6500 Glenridge Park Place, Suite 12, Louisville, KY 40222. phone 502-326-9122. Phillip A. Ronniger.

LOUISIANA

Career Planning and Assessment Center, Metropolitan College, University of New Orleans, New Orleans, LA 70148. phone 504-286-7100.

MAINE

Susan L. **Arledge,** Life-Planning /Career Consultant, 50 Exeter St., Portland, ME 04102. phone 207-761-7755.

Career Perspectives, 75 Pearl St., Suite 204, Portland, ME 04101. phone 207-775-4487. Deborah L. Gallant.

Heart at Work, 78 Main St., Yarmouth, ME 04096. phone 207-846-0644. Barbara Sirois Babkirk, M.Ed., NCC, L.C.P.C., Licensed Counselor and Consultant.

Johnson Career Services, 34 Congress St., Portland ME 04101. phone 207-773-3921. R. Ernest Johnson.

Suit Yourself International Inc, 120 Pendleton Point, Islesboro, ME 04848. Phone 207-734-8206. Debra Spencer, president

Women's Worth Career Counseling, 18 Woodland Rd., Gorham, ME 04038. phone 207-892-0000. Jacqueline Murphy, Counselor.

MARYLAND

*Call to Career, 8720 Georgia Ave., Suite 802, Silver Spring, MD 20910. phone 301-961-1017. Cheryl Palmer, M.Ed., NCC, NCCC, President.

Career Perspectives, 510 Sixth St., Annapolis, MD 21403. phone 410-280-2299. Jeanne H. Slawson, Career Consultant.

Careerscope, Inc., One Mall North, Suite 216, 1025 Governor Warfield Pkwy., Columbia, MD 21044. phone 410-992-5042 or 301-596-1866. Constantine Bitsas, Executive Director.

Career Transition Services, 3126 Berkshire Rd., Baltimore MD 21214-3404. phone 410-444-5857. Michael Bryant.

College of Notre Dame of Maryland, Continuing Education Center, 4701 N. Charles St., Baltimore, MD 21210. phone 410-532-5303.

Goucher College, Goucher Center for Continuing Studies, 1021 Dulaney Valley Rd., Baltimore, MD 21204. phone 410-337-6200. Carole B. Ellin, Career/Job-Search Counselor.

Anne S. **Headley,** M.A., 7100 Baltimore Ave., Suite 208, College Park, MD 20740. phone 301-779-1917.

Kensington Consulting, 8701 Georgia Ave., Suite 406, Silver Spring, MD 20910. phone 301-587-1234. David M. Reile, Ph.D., NCCC, Barbara H. Suddarth, Ph.D., NCCC.

Maryland New Directions, Inc., 2220 N. Charles St., Baltimore, MD 21218. phone 410-235-8800. Rose Marie Coughlin, Director.

Irene N. **Mendelson,** NCCC, BEMW, Inc., Counseling and Training for the Workplace, 7984 D Old Georgetown Rd., Bethesda, MD 20814-2440. phone 301-657-8922.

Prince George's Community College, Career Assessment and Planning Center, 301 Largo Rd., Largo, MD 20772. phone 301-322-0886. Margaret Taibi, Ph.D., Director.

TransitionWorks, 10964 Bloomingdale Dr., Rockville, MD 20852-5550. phone 301-770-4277. Stephanie Kay, M.A., A.G.S., Principal. Nancy K. Schlossberg, Ed.D., Principal.

MASSACHUSETTS

Boston Career Link, 281 Huntington Ave., Boston, MA 02115. phone 617-536-1888.

Changes, 29 Leicester St., P.O. Box 35697, Brighton, MA 02135. phone 617-783-1717. Carl Schneider. Career counseling and job hunt training. Individual or group therapy for job hunters. Carl is one of the most giving-service-to-people counselors that we have in this Sampler. He's been listed here for 20 years (and counting).

Career Link, Career Information Center, Kingston Public Library, 6 Green St., Kingston, MA 02364. phone 781-585-0517. Free videos, audiocassettes, and books on job search, plus computerized career guidance (SIGI), public access computer, and workshops. Sia Stewart, Director of the Library.

*Career Management Consultants, Thirty Park Ave., Worcester, MA 01605. phone 508-853-8669. Patricia Stepanski Plouffe, President.

Career Resource Center, Worcester YWCA, 1 Salem Square, Worcester, MA 01608. phone 508-791-3181.

Career Source, 185 Alewife Brook Pkwy., Cambridge, MA 02138. phone 617-661-7867. *This place inherited the Radcliffe Career Services Office's library, after that Office closed permanently.* Also offers career counseling.

*Center for Career Development & Ministry, 70 Chase St., Newton Center, MA 02159. phone 617-969-7750. Stephen Ott, Director.

Center for Careers, Jewish Vocational Service, 105 Chauncy St., 6th Fl., Boston, MA 02111. phone 617-451-8147. Lee Ann Bennett, Coordinator, Core Services.

Jewish Vocational Service, Mature Worker Programs, 333 Nahanton St., Newton, MA 02159. phone 617-965-7940.

Linkage, Inc., 110 Hartwell Ave., Lexington MA 02173. phone 781-862-4030. David J. Giber, Ph.D.

Wynne W. **Miller,** Coaching & Career Development, 15 Cypress St., Suite 200, Newton Center, MA 02459-2242. phone 617-527-4848. Practical career counseling oriented toward finding meaning and mission.

Murray Associates, P.O. Box 312, Westwood, MA 02090. phone 617-329-1287. Robert Murray, Ed.D., Licensed Psychologist.

Neville Associates, Inc., 10 Tower Office Park, Suite 416, Woburn, MA 01801. phone 781-938-7870. Dr. Joseph Neville, Career Development Consultant.

Smith College Career Development Office, Drew Hall, 84 Elm St., Northampton, MA 01063. phone 413-585-2570. Career counseling services to the community. Jane Sommer, Associate Director.

Phyllis R. **Stein,** 59 Parker St., Cambridge, MA 02138. phone 617-354-7948. *Phyllis was the Director of Radcliffe Career Services for two decades, until its close. She is now doing private career counseling and workshops at the address above.*

Wellness Center, 51 Mill St., Unit 8, Hanover, MA 02339. phone 781-829-4300. Janet Barr.

MICHIGAN

Careerdesigns, 22 Cherry St., Holland MI 49423. phone 616-396-1517. Mark de Roo.

Jewish Vocational Service, 29699 Southfield Road, Southfield, MI 48076-2063. phone 248-559-5000.

Lansing Community College, 2020 Career and Employment Development Services, PO Box 40010, Lansing, MI 48901-7210. phone 517-483-1221 or 483-1172. James C. Osborn, Ph.D., LPC, Director, Career and Employment Services.

*Life Stewardship Associates, 6918 Glen Creek Dr., SE, Dutton, MI 49316. phone 616-698-3125. Ken Soper, M.Div., M.A., Director.

New Options: Counseling for Women in Transition, 2311 E. Stadium, Suite B-2, Ann Arbor, MI 48104. phone 313-973-0003. Phyllis Perry, M.S.W.

Oakland University, Continuum Center for Adult Counseling and Leadership Training, Rochester, MI 48309. phone 313-370-3033.

University of Michigan, Center for the Education of Women, 330 East Liberty, Ann Arbor, MI 48104. phone 313-998-7080.

Women's Resource Center, 252 State St. SE, Grand Rapids, MI 49503. phone 616-458-5443.

MINNESOTA

Richard E. **Andrea,** Ph.D., 1014 Bartelmy Lane, Maplewood MN 55119-3637. phone 612-730-9892.

Associated Career Services, 3550 Lexington Ave. N., Suite 120, Shoreview, MN 55126. phone 612-787-0501.

Career Dynamics, Inc., 8400 Normandale Lake Blvd., Suite 1220, Bloomington, MN 55437. phone 612-921-2378. Joan Strewler, Psychologist.

Human Dynamics, 3036 Ontario Rd., Little Canada, MN 55117. phone 612-484-8299. Greg J. Cylkowski, M.A., founder.

*North Central Career Development Center (An Interdenominational Church Career Development Center), 516 Mission House Lane, New Brighton, MN 55112. phone 612-636-5120. Kenneth J. McFayden, Ph.D., Director.

Prototype Career Services, 626 Armstrong Ave., St. Paul, MN 55102. phone 800-368-3197. Amy Lindgren, and Julie Remington, Counseling psychologists.

Stanley J. Sizen, Vocational Services, P.O.Box 363, Anoka, MN 55303. phone 612-441-8053.

Southwest Family Services, 10267 University Ave. North, Blaine, MN 55434. phone 612-825-4407. Kathy Bergman, M.A., LP. Career planning services.

Working Opportunities for Women, 2700 University Ave., #120, St. Paul, MN 55114. phone 612-647-9961.

MISSISSIPPI

Mississippi Gulf Coast Community College, Jackson County Campus, Career Development Center, P.O. Box 100, Gautier, MS 39553. phone 601-497-9602. Rebecca Williams, Manager.

Mississippi State University, Career Services Center, P.O. Box P, Colvard Union, Suite 316, Mississippi State, MS 39762-5515. phone 601-325-3344.

MISSOURI

Rod C. Cannedy, Ph.D., Forest Institute of Professional Psychology, 2885 West Battlefield Rd., Springfield, MO 65807. Phone 417-823-3477.

Career Center, Community Career Services, 110 Noyes Hall, University of Missouri, Columbia, MO 65211. phone 573-882-6803.

Career Management Center, 8301 State Line Rd., Suite 202, Kansas City, MO 64114. phone 816-363-1500. Janice Y. Benjamin, President.

*Midwest Career Development Service (An Interdenominational Church Career Development Center), 754 N. 31st St., Kansas City, KS 66110-0816. Ronald Brushwyler, Director.

Women's Center, University of Missouri-Kansas City, 5100 Rockhill Rd., 104 Scofield Hall, Kansas City, MO 64110. phone 816-235-1638.

MONTANA

Career Transitions, 321 E. Main, Suite 215, Bozeman, MT 59715. 406-587-1721. Estella Villasenor, Executive Director. Darla Joyner, Assistant Director.

NEBRASKA

Career Management Services, 5000 Central Park Dr., Suite 204, Lincoln, NE 68504. phone 402-466-8427. Vaughn L. Carter, President.

*Olson Counseling Services, 8720 Frederick, Suite 105, Omaha, NE 68128. phone 402-390-2342. Gail A. Olson, P.A.C.

Student Success Center, Central Community College, Hastings Campus, Hastings, NE 68902. phone 402-461-2424.

NEVADA

Career/Lifestyles, Alamo Plaza, 4550 W. Oakey Blvd., Suite #111, Las Vegas, NV 89102. phone 702-258-3353. Carol J. Cravens, M.A., NCC.

Greener Pastures Institute, 6301 S. Squaw Valley Rd., Suite 1383, Pahrump, NV 89048-7949. phone 800-688-6352. Bill Seavey.

NEW HAMPSHIRE

Individual Employment Services, 90-A Sixth St., P.O. 917, Dover, NH 03820. phone 603-742-5616. James Otis, Employment Counselor.

NEW JERSEY

Adult Advisory Service, Kean College of New Jersey. Administration Bldg., Union, NJ 07083. phone 908-527-2210.

Adult Resource Center, 100 Horseneck Road, Montville, NJ 07045. phone 201-335-6910.

Arista Concepts Career Development Service, P.O. Box 2436, Princeton, NJ 08540. phone 609-921-0308. Kera Greene, M.Ed.

Beverly Baskin, M.A., Baskin Business & Career Services, 6 Alberta Dr., Marlboro, NJ 07746-1202. phone 800-300-4079. Offices also in Woodbridge, and Princeton.

Behavior Dynamics Associates, Inc., 34 Cambridge Terrace, Springfield, NJ 07081. phone 201-912-0136. Roy Hirschfeld.

Career Options Center, YWCA Tribute to Women and Industry (TWIN) Program, 232 E. Front St., Plainfield, NJ 07060. phone 908-756-3836, or 908-273-4242. Janet M. Korba, Program Director.

Center for Life Enhancement, 1156 E. Ridgewood Ave., Ridgewood, NJ 07450. phone 201-670-8443. David R. Johnson, Director of Career Programs.

Jerry Cohen, M.A., NCC, NCCC, Chester Professional Bldg., P.O. Box 235, Chester, NJ 07930. phone 908-789-4404.

Loree **Collins,** 3 Beechwood Rd., Summit, NJ 07901. phone 908-273-9219.

Douglass College, Douglass Advisory Services for Women, Rutgers Women's Center, 132 George St., New Brunswick, NJ 08903. phone 908-932-9603.

Juditha **Dowd,** 3640 Valley Rd., Liberty Corner, NJ 07938. phone 908-439-2091.

Sandra **Grundfest,** Ed.D., Princeton Professional Park, 601 Ewing St., Suite C-1, Princeton, NJ 08540. phone 609-921-8401. Also at 11 Clyde Rd., Suite 103, Somerset, NJ 08873. phone 908-873-1212.

Susan Guarneri Associates, 1101 Lawrence Rd., Lawrenceville, NJ 08648. phone 609-771-1669. Susan Guarneri, M.S., NCC, NCCC, and Jack Guarneri, M.S., NCC, NCCC. Career and job-search counseling.

The **Job Club,** Princeton Unitarian Church, Cherry Hill Rd., Princeton, NJ 08540. phone 609-924-1604. Free service, open to the community.

JobSeekers in Princeton NJ. Trinity Church, 33 Mercer Street, Princeton, NJ 08542. phone 609-924-2277. Meets Tuesdays, 7:30 - 9:30 p.m. *The oldest continuing job club, run by volunteers, in the country.*

Job Seekers of Montclair, St. Luke's Episcopal Church, 73 S. Fullerton Ave, Montclair NJ 07042. phone 201-783-3442. Meets Thursdays 7:30-9:30 p.m.

Mercer County Community College, Career Services, 1200 Old Trenton Rd., Trenton, NJ 08690. phone 609-586-4800, ext. 304. Career and job-search counseling. Open to non-students (though with a fee).

Metro Career Services, 784 Morris Turnpike, Suite 203, Short Hills, NJ 07078. Phone 973-912-0106. Contact: Judy Scherer, M.A.

Lester Minsuk & Associates, 29 Exeter Rd., East Windsor, NJ 08520. phone 609-448-4600.

*****Northeast Career Center** (An Interdenominational Church Career Development Center), 407 Nassau Street, Princeton, NJ 08540. phone 609-924-9408. Roy Lewis, Director.

Princeton Management Consultants, Inc., 99 Moore St., Princeton, NJ 08540. phone 609-924-2411. Niels H. Nielsen, M.A., job and career counselor.

Resource Center for Women, 31 Woodland Ave., Summit, NJ 07901. phone 908-273-7253. Juditha Dowd, Coordinator of the Career Division.

NEW MEXICO

Young Women's Christian Association, YWCA Career Services Center, 7201 Paseo Del Norte NE, Albuquerque, NM 87113. phone 505-822-9922.

NEW YORK

Carol **Allen,** Consultant, 560 West 43rd St., Suite 5G, New York, NY 10036. phone 212-268-5182. Career Management/Spirited Worker Seminars.

Alan B. **Bernstein** CSW, PC, 122 East 82nd St., N.Y., NY 10028. phone 212-288-4881.

Career Development Center, Long Island University, C.W. Post Campus, Brookville, NY 11548. phone 516-299-2251. Pamela Lennox, Ph.D., Director.

Career Resource Center, Bethlehem Public Library, 451 Delaware Ave., Delmar, NY 12054. phone 518-439-9314. Denise L. Coblish, Career Resources Librarian.

Career Strategies, Inc., 350 West 24th St., New York, NY 10011. phone 212-807-1340. "CB" Bowman, President.

Career 101 Associates, 230 West 55th St., Suite 17F, New York, NY 10019. L. Michelle Tullier, Ph.D., Director. phone 212-333-4013.

The John C. **Crystal Center,** 152 Madison Ave., 23rd fl., New York, NY 10016. phone 212-889-8500, or 1-800-333-9003. Nella G. Barkley, President. *(John, the original founder of this center, died ten years ago; Nella, his business partner for many years, now directs the center's work.)*

*****Judith Gerberg Associates,** 250 West 57th St., New York, NY 10107, 212-315-2322. Judith Gerberg.

Hofstra University, Career Counseling Center, Room 120, Saltzman Community Center, 131 Hofstra, Hempstead, NY 11550. phone 516-463-6788.

Kingsborough Community College, Office of Career Counseling and Placement, 2001 Oriental Blvd., Rm. C102, Brooklyn, NY 11235. phone 718-368-5115.

Janice **La Rouche** Assoc., 333 Central Park W., New York, NY 10025. phone 212-663-0970.

Livelyhood Job Search Center, 301 Madison Ave., 3rd Floor, New York, NY 10017. phone 212-687-2411. John Aigner, Director.

James E. **McPherson,** 101 Ives Hall, Cornell University, Ithaca, NY 14853-3901.

New Options, 960 Park Ave., New York, NY 10028. phone 212-535-1444.

Onondaga County Public Library, The Galleries of Syracuse, 447 South Salina St., Syracuse, NY 13202-2494. phone 315-435-1900. Karen A. Pitoniak, Librarian, Information Services. Has InfoTrac, a computerized index and directory of over 100,000 companies, plus other job-hunting resources.

Orange County Community College, Counseling Center, 115 South St., Middletown, NY 10940. phone 914-341-4070.

Celia **Paul Associates,** 1776 Broadway, Suite 1806, New York, NY 10019. phone 212-397-1020.

Personnel Sciences Center, Inc. 276 Fifth Ave., Suite 704, New York, NY 10001. phone 212-683-3008. Dr. Jeffrey A. Goldberg.

Leslie B. **Prager,** M.A., The Prager-Bernstein Group, 441 Lexington Ave., Suite 1404, New York, NY 10017. phone 212-697-0645.

Psychological Services Center, Career Services Unit, University at Albany, SUNY, Husted 167, 135 Western Ave., Albany, NY 12222. phone 518-442-4900. George B. Litchford, Ph.D., Director. Individual and group career counseling.

RLS Career Center, 3049 East Genesee St., Suite 211, Syracuse, NY 13224. phone 315-446-0500. Rebecca A. Livengood, Executive Director.

Allie **Roth,** 160 East 38th St., New York, NY 10016. phone 212-490-9158.

Schenectady Public Library, Job Information Center, 99 Clinton St., Schenectady, NY. Has weekly listings, including job search listings of companies nationwide.

Scientific Career Transitions, Stephen Rosen, Science & Technology Advisory Board, 575 Madison Ave., 22nd Fl., New York, NY 10022-2585. phone 212-891-7609. Works with unemployed and underemployed scientists, specializing in émigrés from the Soviet Union.

VEHICLES, INC., Life Skills and Career Training, 1832 Madison Ave., Room 202, New York, NY 10035-2707. phone 212-722-1111. Janet Avery.

Volunteer Consulting Group, Inc., 6 East 39th St., 6th Floor, New York, NY 10016. Phone: 212-447-1236

WIN Workshops (Women in Networking), Emily Koltnow, 1120 Avenue of the Americas, Fourth Floor, New York, NY 10036. phone 212-333-8788.

NORTH CAROLINA

*****The Career and Personal Counseling Service** (An Official Interdenominational Church Career Development Center) St. Andrew's Presbyterian College, Laurinburg, NC 28352. phone 919-276-3162 Also at: 4108 Park Rd., Suite 200, Charlotte, NC 28209. phone 704-523-7751 Elbert R. Patton, Director

Career Consulting Associates of Raleigh, P.O. Box 17653, Raleigh, NC 27619. phone 919-782-3252. Susan W. Simonds, President.

Career, Educational, Psychological Evaluations, 2915 Providence Rd., Suite 300, Charlotte, NC 28211. phone 704-362-1942.

Career Focus Workshops, P.O. Box 35424, Greensboro, NC 27425. phone 336-643-1025. Glenn Wise, President.

Career Management Center, 3203 Woman's Club Dr., Suite 100, Raleigh, NC 27612. phone 919-787-1222, ext. 109. Temple G. Porter, Director.

Sally **Kochendofer,** Ph.D., Northcross Professional Park, I-77 Exit 25, 9718-A Sam Furr Rd., Huntersville, NC 28078. phone 704-362-1514. Career-change counselor.

Diane E. **Lambeth,** M.S.W., Career Consultant. P.O. Box 18945, Raleigh, NC 27619. phone 919-571-7423.

Life Management Services, LC, 301 Gregson Dr., Cary, NC 27511. 919-481-4707. Marilyn and Hal Shook. *The Shooks originally trained with John Crystal, though they have evolved their own program since then.*

Joyce **Richman & Associates, Ltd.,** 2911 Shady Lawn Dr., Greensboro, NC 27408. phone 910-288-1799.

Bonnie M. **Truax,** Ed.D., NCCC, Career/Life Planning and Relocation Services, 2102 N. Elm St., Suite K1, Greensboro, NC 27408. phone 910-271-2050. Free support group.

Women's Center of Raleigh, 128 E. Hargett St., Suite 10, Raleigh, NC 27601. phone 919-829-3711.

NORTH DAKOTA

Business & Life Resources Career Development Center, 112 North University Dr., Suite 3300, Fargo, N.D. 58103. phone 800-950-0848. Gail Reierson.

OHIO

Adult Resource Center, The University of Akron, Buckingham Center for Continuing Education, Room 55, Akron, OH 44325-3102. phone 216-972-7448. Sandra B. Edwards, Director.

Career Initiatives Center, 1557 E. 27th St., Cleveland, OH 44114. phone 216-574-8998. Richard Hanscom, Director.

Career Point, Belden-Whipple Building, 4150 Belden Village St., N.W., Suite 101, Canton, OH 44718. phone 216-492-1920. Victor W. Valli, Career Consultant.

Cuyahoga County Public Library InfoPLACE Service, Career, Education & Community Information Service, 5225 Library Lane, Maple Heights, OH 44137-1291. phone 216-475-2225.

*****Diversified Career Services, Inc.,** 2490 Edington Rd., Columbus, OH 43221. phone 614-481-0508. Laura Armstrong, LPC, NBCC, Owner/President. Bob Armstrong, M.Div., Ph.D., LPC.

The **Human Touch,** 260 Northland Blvd., Suite 234, Cincinnati, OH 45246. phone 513-772-5839. Judy R. Kroger, LPC, Career and Human Resources Counselor.

J&K Associates and Success Skills Seminars, Inc., 607 Otterbein Ave., Dayton, OH 45406-4507. phone 937-274-3630, or 937-274-4375. Pat Kenney, Ph.D., President.

*KSM Careers & Consulting. 1655 W. Market St., Suite 506, Akron, OH 44313. phone 330-867-0242. Kathryn Musholt, President.

*Midwest Career Development Service (An Interdenominational Church Career Development Center), 1520 Old Henderson Rd., Suite 102B, Columbus, OH 43221-3616. phone 614-442-8822.

New Career, 328 Race St., Dover, OH 44622. phone 216-364-5557. Marshall Karp, M.A., NCC, LPC, Owner.

*Professional Pastoral Counseling Institute, Inc., 8035 Hosbrook Rd., Suite 300, Cincinnati, OH 45236. phone 513-771-5990. Judy Kroger, Counselor.

Pyramid Career Services, Inc., 2400 Cleveland Ave., NW, Canton, OH 44709. phone 330-453-3767. Maryellen R. Hess, Executive Director.

Anne Woods, 8225 Markhaven Ct., W. Worthington, OH 43235. phone 614-888-7941.

OKLAHOMA

Martha Stoodley, Rt. #1, Box 575, Checotah, OK 74426-9742.

Transitions Counseling Center, 6216 S. Lewis Ave., Suite 148 Tulsa, OK 74136. phone 918-742-4877. Michelle Jones, M.S., Owner/Career Counselor.

OREGON

Career Development, PO Box 850, Forest Grove, OR 97116. phone 503-357-9233. Edward H. Hosley, Ph.D., Director.

Career Pathways, P.O. Box 271, Corvallis, OR 97339-0271. Phone 541-754-1958, Peggy Carrick, M.A.,LPC,NCC, Founder

Joseph A. **Dubay,** 425 NW 18th Ave., Portland, OR 97209. phone 503-226-2656.

Lansky Career Consultants, 9335 S.W. Capitol Highway, Portland OR 97219. phone 503-293-0245. Judith Lansky, M.A., President.

Verk Consultants, Inc., 1190 Olive St., PO Box 11277, Eugene, OR 97440. phone 541-687-9170. Larry H. Malmgren, M.S., President.

PENNSYLVANIA

Career by Design, 1011 Cathill Rd., Sellersville, PA 18960. phone 215-723-8413. Henry D. Landes, Career Consultant.

Career Development Center, Jewish Family & Children's Center, 5737 Darlington Road, Pittsburgh, PA 15217. phone 412-422-5627. Linda Ehrenreich, Director.

Center for Adults in Transition, Bucks County Community College, Newtown, PA 18940. phone 215-968-8188.

Center for Career Services (CCS), 1845 Walnut St., 7th floor, Philadelphia, PA 19103-4707. phone 215-854-1800. William A. Hyman, Director. Lucy Borosh, Aviva Gal, Tracey Tanenbaum, Career Counselors.

Carol **Eikleberry,** Ph.D., 1376 Freeport Rd., Suite 3A, Pittsburgh, PA 15238. phone 412-963-9008.

Lathe **Haynes,** Ph.D., 401 Shady Ave., Suite C107, Pittsburgh, PA 15238. phone 412-361-6336.

Jack **Kelly,** Career Counselor. Career Pro Resume Services, 251 DeKalb Pike, Suite E608, King of Prussia, PA 19406. phone 610-337-7187.

Jane E. **Kessler,** M.A., Licensed Psychologist, 252 W. Swamp Rd., Suite 56, Doylestown, PA 18901. Phone: 215 348 8212.

*Lancaster Career Development Center (An Interdenominational Church Career Development Center), 561 College Ave., Lancaster, PA 17603. phone 717-397-7451. L. Guy Mehl, Director.

Options, Inc., 225 S. 15th St., Philadelphia, PA 19102. phone 215-735-2202. Marcia P. Kleiman, Director.

Priority Two, P.O. Box 343, Sewickley, PA 15143. phone 412-935-0252. *Five locations in the Pittsburgh area; call for addresses.* Pat Gottschalk, Administrative Assistant. No one is turned away for lack of funds.

RHODE ISLAND

Career Designs, 104 Rankin Ave., Providence, RI 02908-4216. phone 401-521-2323. Terence Duniho, Career Consultant.

SOUTH CAROLINA

Career Counselor Services, Inc., 138 Ingleoak Lane, Greenville, SC 29615. phone 864-242-4474. Al A. Hafer, Ed.D., NCCC, NCC, LPC.

Greenville Technical College, Career Advancement Center, P.O. Box 5616, Greenville, SC 29606. phone 864-250-8281. F.M. Rogers, Director.

SOUTH DAKOTA

Career Concepts Planning Center, Inc., 1602 Mountain View Rd., Suite 102, Rapid City, SD 57702. phone 605-342-5177, toll free phone 1-800-456-0832. Melvin M. Tuggle, Jr., President.

University of Sioux Falls, The Center for Women, 1101 W. 22nd St., Sioux Falls, SD 57105. phone 605-331-6697. Tami Haug-Davis, Director.

TENNESSEE

*Career Achievement, NiS International Services, 1321 Murfreesboro Road., Suite 610, Nashville, TN 37217. phone 615-367-5000. William L. (Bill) Karlson, Harry McClure, Manager.

*Career Resources, 2323 Hillsboro Rd., Suite 508, Nashville TN 37212. phone 615-297-0404. Jane C. Hardy, Principal.

*Dan Miller, The Business Source, 7100 Executive Center Dr., Suite 110, Brentwood, TN 37027. phone 615-373-7771.

*RHM Group, P.O.Box 271135, Nashville, TN 37227. phone 615-391-5000. Robert H. McKown.

World Career Transition, P.O. Box 1423, Brentwood, TN 37027-1423. phone 800-366-0945. Bill Karlson, Executive Vice-President.

YWCA of Nashville and Middle Tennessee, Career/Life Planning Program, 1608 Woodmont Blvd., Nashville, TN 37215. Phone 615-269-9922.

TEXAS

Austin Career Associates, 901 Rio Grande, Austin, TX 78701. Phone 512-474-1185, Maydelle Fason, Licensed Career Counselor.

Career Action Associates, 12655 N. Central Expressway, Suite 821, Dallas, TX 75243. phone 214-392-7337. Joyce Shoop, LPC. Office also at 1325 8th Ave., Ft. Worth, TX 76112. phone 817-926-9941. Rebecca Hayes, LPC.

Career and Recovery Resources, Inc., 2525 San Jacinto, Houston, TX 77002. phone 713-754-7000. Beverley Marks, Director.

Career Management Resources, 1425 Greenway, Suite 203, Irving, TX 75038. phone 972-518-0101. Mary Holdcroft, M.Ed., LPC, NCC, NCCC.

Richard S. Citrin, Ph.D., Psychologist, Iatreia Institute, 1152 Country Club Ln., Ft. Worth, TX 76112. phone 817-654-9600.

Counseling Services of Houston, 1964 W. Gray, Suite 204, Houston, TX 77019. phone 713-521-9391. Rosemary C. Vienot, M.S., Licensed Professional Counselor, Director.

Employment/Career Information Resource Center, Corpus Christi Public Library, 805 Comanche, Corpus Christi, TX 78401. phone 512-880-7004. Lynda F. Whitton-Henley, Career Information Specialist.

Maydelle Fason, Employment Consultant, 1607 Poquonock Road, Austin, TX 78703. phone 512-474-1185.

New Directions Counseling Center, 8140 North Mopac, Bldg. II, Suite 230, Austin, TX 78759. phone 512-343-9496. Jeanne Quereau, M.A., LPC.

*New Life Institute, 1203 Lavaca St., Austin, TX 78701-1831. phone 512-469-9447. Bob Breihan, Director.

Chuck Ragland, Transformational Consultancy, 2504 Briargrove Dr., Austin, TX 78704-2704. phone 512-440-1200.

San Antonio Psychological Services, 6800 Park Ten Blvd., Suite 208 North, San Antonio, TX 78213. phone 210-737-2039.

*Southwest Career Development Center (An Interdenominational Church Career Development Center), Box 5923, Arlington, TX 76005. phone 817-640-5181. Jerry D. Overton, Director-Counselor .

*Mary Stedham, Counseling/Consulting Services, 2434 S. 10th, Abilene, TX 79605. phone 915-672-4044.

VGS, Inc. (Vocational Guidance Service), 2600 S.W. Freeway, Suite 800, Houston, TX 77098. phone 713-535-7104. Beverley K. Finn, Director.

*Worklife Institute Consulting, 7100 Regency Square, Suite 210, Houston, TX 77036. phone 713-266-2456. Diana C. Dale, Director.

UTAH

University of Utah, Center for Adult Development, 1195 Annex Bldg., Salt Lake City, UT 84112. phone 801-581-3228.

VERMONT

Career Networks, 7 Kilburn St., Burlington, VT 05401. phone 800-918-WORK. Tim King, President.

VIRGINIA

The BrownMiller Group, 122 Granite Ave., Richmond, VA 23226. phone 804-288-2157. Sally Brown, Bonnie Miller.

*Career and Personal Counseling Center, 1904 Mt. Vernon St., Waynesboro, VA 22980. phone 703-943-9997. Lillian Pennell, Director.

Change & Growth Consulting, 1334 G St., Woodbridge, VA 22191. phone 703-494-8271; also: 2136-A Gallows Road, Dunn Loring (Tyson's Corner area), VA 22027. phone 703-569-2029. Barbara S. Woods, M.Ed., NCC, LPC, Counselor.

Educational Opportunity Center, 7010-M Auburn Ave., Norfolk, VA 23513. phone 804-855-7468. Agatha A. Peterson, Director.

Fairfax County Office for Women, The Government Center, 12000 Government Center Pkwy., Suite 38, Fairfax, VA 22035. phone 703-324-5735. Elizabeth Lee McManus, Program Manager.

Golden Handshakes, Church of the Epiphany, 11000 Smoketree Dr., Richmond, VA 23236. phone 804-794-0222. Jim Dunn, Chairperson;

also at Winfree Memorial Baptist Church, 13617 Midlothian Turnpike, Midlothian, VA 23113. phone 804-794-5031. Phil Tibbs, Volunteer Coordinator.

Hollins College, Women's Center, P.O. Box 9628, Roanoke, VA 24020. phone 703-362-6269. Tina Rolen, Career Counselor.

Mary Baldwin College, Rosemarie Sena Center for Career and Life Planning, Kable House, Staunton, VA 24401. phone 703-887-7221.

McCarthy & Company, Career Transition Management, 4201 South 32nd Rd., Arlington, VA 22206. phone 703-761-4300. Peter McCarthy, President.

Office for Women, The Government Center, 12000 Government Center Parkway, Suite 318, Fairfax, VA 22035. phone 703-324-5730. Betty McManus, Director.

Psychological Consultants, Inc., 6724 Patterson Ave., Richmond, VA 23226. phone 804-288-4125.

Virginia Commonwealth University, University Career Center, 907 Floyd Ave., Room 2007, Richmond, VA 23284-2007. phone 804-367-1645.

The Women's Center, 133 Park St., NE, Vienna, VA 22180. phone 703-281-2657. Conda Blackmon.

Working From The Heart, 1309 Merchant Lane, McLean, VA 22101. Jacqueline McMakin and Susan Gardiner, Co-Directors.

WASHINGTON

Career Management Institute, 8404 27th St. West, Tacoma, WA 98466. phone 253-565-8818. Ruthann Reim, M.A., NCC,CMHC, President.

*****Center for Career Decisions,** 3121 East Madison St., Suite 209, Seattle, WA 98112. phone 206-325-9093. Larry Gaffin, Career counseling and consulting.

Centerpoint Institute for Life and Career Renewal, Career Consultants, 624 Skinner Bldg., 1326 Fifth Ave., Seattle, WA 98101. phone 206-622-8070. Carol Vecchio, Career Counselor. *A multifaceted center, with various workshops, lectures, retreats, as well as individual counseling.*

Diane **Churchill,** 508 W. Sixth, Suite 202, Spokane, WA 99204. phone 509-458-0962.

*****Bernard Haldane,** 900 University Street, #17-E, Seattle, WA 98101. phone 206-382-3658. A pioneer in the clergy career management and assessment field, Bernard teaches seminars and trains volunteers to do job-search counseling. *This individual service is not to be confused with the agency that bears his name, of which he gave up ownership long ago.*

The Individual Development Center, Inc. (I.D. Center), 1020 E. John, Seattle, WA 98102. phone 206-329-0600. Mary Lou Hunt, NCC, M.A., President.

*****People Management Group International,** 924 First St., Suite A, Snohomish, WA 98290. phone 206-563-0105. Arthur F. Miller, Jr., Chairman.

WEST VIRGINIA

Ed **Jepson,** 2 Hazlett Court, Wheeling, WV 26003. phone 304-232-2375.

Frank **Ticich,** MS, LPC, Career Consultant, 153 Tartan Drive, Follansbee, WV 26037

WISCONSIN

Making Alternative Plans, Career Development Center, Alverno College, 3401 S. 39th St., P.O. Box 343922, Milwaukee, WI 53234-3922. phone 414-382-6010.

David **Swanson,** Career Seminars and Workshops, 7235 West Wells St., Wauwatosa, WI 53213-3607. phone 414-774-4755. *David was on staff at my two-week workshop twenty times.*

WYOMING

Barbara W. **Gray,** Career Consultant, P.O. Box 9490, Jackson, WY 83002. phone 307-733-6544.

University of Wyoming, Career Planning and Placement Center, PO Box 3195/Knight Hall 228, Laramie, WY 82071-3195. phone 307-766-2398.

U.S.A. - - NATIONWIDE

Forty Plus Clubs. A nationwide network of voluntary, autonomous nonprofit clubs, manned by its unemployed members (who must give a certain number of hours of service per week on assigned committees), paying no salaries, supported by initiation fees *(often around $500)* and monthly dues *(often around $60 per month)*. Varying reports, as to their helpfulness. However, one reader gave a very good report on them recently: *"I would just like to let you know that 40+, for me, has been a really big help. They provide good job search training. . . But even more importantly, for me, is the professional office environment they provide to work out of, and the fellowship of others who are also looking for work . . . As they say at 40+, 'It's hell to job search alone.'"*

If you have Internet access, a list of the North American 40+ chapters is to be found at:

http://www.fp.org/chapters/htm

Eleven of these chapters have their own Web site; in my opinion the best and most up-to-date one belongs to the Greater Washington chapter:

http://www.fp.org/

For those who lack Web access, at this writing there are clubs in the following cities (listed alphabetically by States): <u>California:</u> San Diego, Orange, Los Angeles, Oakland; <u>Colorado:</u> Lakewood, Ft. Collins, Colorado Springs; <u>District of Columbia:</u> Greater Washington; <u>Hawaii:</u> Honolulu; <u>Illinois:</u> Chicago; <u>Minnesota:</u> St. Paul;

New York: New York, Buffalo; Ohio: Columbus; Oregon: Beaverton; Pennsylvania: Philadelphia; Texas: Houston, Dallas; Utah: Salt Lake City; Washington: Bellevue; Wisconsin: Brookfield; and in Canada: Toronto.

If you live in or near any of these cities, you can check the *white* pages of your Phone Book (under "Forty Plus") for their address and phone number.

CANADA

(These are listed by Provinces, from East Coast to West Coast, rather than in alphabetical order)

Sue **Landry,** Enhancing Your Horizons Consulting, 25 Birchwood Terr., Dartmouth, Nova Scotia B3A 3W2. phone 902-464-9110.

careerguide, Ryan Bldg., 3rd Floor, 57 Carleton St., Fredericton, New Brunswick. phone 506-459-4185. Elspeth (Beth) Leroux, B.A., B.Ed., M.Ed.

Jewish Vocational Service, Centre Juif D'Orientation et de L'Emploi, 5151, ch. de la Côte Ste-Catherine, Montréal, Québec, H3W 1M6. phone 514-345-2625. Alta Abramowitz, Director, Employment Development Services. *Uses both French and English versions of Parachute.*

Kenneth **Des Roches,** André Filion & Associates, Inc., 151 Slater Street, Suite 500, Ottawa, Ontario K1P 5H3, Canada. Phone 613-230-7023

After Graduation Career Counseling, 73 Roxborough St. West, Toronto, Ontario M5R 1T9. phone 416-923-8319. Teresa Snelgrove, Ph.D., Director.

Donner & Wheeler and Associates, Career Development Consultants, Health and Social Services Sector, 1055 Bloor St. East, Mississauga, Ontario L4Y 2N5. phone 905-949-5954. Offers workshops particularly for those in the health and social services sector. Mary M. Wheeler.

Hazell & Associates, 60 St. Clair Avenue East, Seventh Floor, Toronto, Ontario M4T 1N5. phone 416-961-3700.

Mid-Life Transitions, 2 Slade Ave., Toronto, Canada M6G 3A1. phone 416-653-0563. Marilyn Melville.

YMCA Career Planning & Development, 42 Charles Street East, Toronto, Canada M4Y 1T4. phone 416-928-9622.

Changes by Choice, 190 Burndale Ave., North York, Ontario M2N 1T2. phone 416-590-9939. Patti Davie.

Susan **Steinberg,** M.Ed., 74 Denlow Blvd., Don Mills, Ontario M3B 1P9. phone 416-449-6936.

Judith **Puttock,** B.B.A., C.H.R.P., Career Management Consultant, Strategic Career Options, Planning & Education (SCOPE), 913 Southwind Court, Newmarket, Ontario. phone 905 898-0180.

Harold **Harder,** B.Sc.,B.Admin.St. The Precision Group, 400 Matheson Blvd. East, Unit 18, Mississauga, Ontario L4Z 1N8. phone 905-507-8696.

Human Achievement Associates, 22 Cottonwood Crescent, London, Ontario N6G 2Y8. phone 519-657-3000. Mr. Kerry A. Hill.

David H. **Wenn,** B.A., M.Ed. Career Counseling. 9 Lindbrook Court, London, Ontario N5X 2L4. phone 519-660-0622.

Job-Finding Club, 516-294 Portage Ave., Winnipeg, Manitoba R3C 0B9. phone 204-947-1948.

People Focus, 712 10th St. East, Saskatoon, Saskatchewan S7H OH1. phone 306-933-4956. Carol Stevenson Seller.

Work from the Heart, 8708 136 St., Edmonton, Alberta T5R 0B9. phone 403-484-8387. Marguerite Todd.

Susan **Curtis,** M.Ed., 4513 West 13th Ave., Vancouver, British Columbia V6R 2V5. phone 604-228-9618.

Alice **Caldwell,** P.B. #19009, 4th Avenue Postal Outlet, Vancouver, British Columbia V6K 4R8. phone 604-737-7842.

Conscious Career Choices, 2678 W. Broadway, Suite 203B, Vancouver, B.C. V6K 2G3. phone 604-737-3955. Marlene Haley, B.A., M.Ed., Career counselor.

OVERSEAS

(Listed by country and city, which are in bold type.)

Cabinet Daniel Porot, 1, rue Verdaine, CH-1204 **Geneve, Switzerland.** phone 41 22 311 04 38. Daniel Porot, Founder. *Daniel was co-leader with me each summer at my international Two-Week Workshop for twenty years.*

Kessler-Laufbahnberatung, Alpenblickstr. 33, CH-8645, **Jona B. Rapperswil, Switzerland.** phone 055 210 09 77. Peter Kessler, Counselor.

•Lernen•Beraten•Begleiten•, Maria Bamert-Widmer, Churerstrasse 26, CH-8852, **Altendorf, Switzerland.** Phone 055 442 55 76

Han-U. Sauser, Beratung und Ausbildung, Rosenauweg 27, CH-5430 **Wettingen, Switzerland.** phone 056 426 64 09.

Peter Baumgartner, Lowen Pfaffikon, Postfach 10, 8808 **Pfaffikon, Switzerland.** phone 055 415 66 22.

Madeleine Leitner, Dipl. Psych. Ohmstrasse 8, 80802, **Munchen, Germany.** phone 089 33 04 02 03.

Career Development Seminars, offered at Westfalische Wilhelms-Universitat Muenster, Dez. 1.4 Wissenschafliche Weiterbildung, Schlossplatz 2, 48149, **Munster, Germany.** phone 0251 832 4762; and at Universitat Bremen, Zentrum fur Weiterbildung, 28359 **Bremen, Germany.**

phone 0421 218 3409. Both taught by John Carl Webb, Brunnenweg 10, 48153 **Muenster, Germany.**

Bridgeway Associates Ltd., Career Consultants, Bradford Ct., Bradford St., **Birmingham, England** B12 0NS. phone 0121 773 8770. Also at: Museum House, 25 Museum St., **London, England** WC1A 1JT. phone 0171 323 1587. Jane Bartlett.

Anne Radford, 303 Bankside Lofts, 65 Hopton Street, **London England** SE1 9JL. phone 7000 077 011.

The Chaney Partnership, Hillier House, 509 Upper Richmond Rd. West, **London, England** SW14 7EE. phone 081 878 3227. Isabel Chaney, B.A.

Career Development. 10 York Pl., Brandon Hill, **Bristol, England** BS1 5UT. phone 0117 9254363. Philip Houghton.

Castle Consultants International, 140 Battersea Park Road, **London England** SW11 4NB. phone 44 171 798 5688. Also: 9 Drummond Park, Crook of Devon, **Kinross, KY13 7UX, Scotland.** phone 0171 798 8804. Walt Hopkins, Founder and Director.

Brian McIvor & Associates, Newgrange Mall, **Slane, County Mead, Ireland.** phone 00 353 41 988 4035. *Brian has been on staff at my international two-week workshop for three years.*

Adigo Consultores, Av. Doria 164, **Sao Paulo SP, 04635-070 Brazil.** phone 55 11 530 0330. Alberto M. Barros, Director.

Centre for WorkLife Counselling, Suite 3, 5 Earl St., Mosman, P.O. Box 407, **Spit Junction NSW 2088, Australia** phone 61 2 9968 1588, fax 61 2 9968 1655. Paul Stevens, Director. (Paul has been the dean of career counseling in Australia for many years.)

The Growth Connection, Suite 402, 4th Floor, 56 Berry St., **North Sydney, NSW 2060 Australia.** phone 61 2 9954 3322. Imogen Wareing, Director.

Life by Design, Suite 19, 88 Helen St., **Lane Cove 2066 NSW, Australia.** phone 61 2 9420 8280. Ian Hutchinson.

Narelle Milligan, Career Consultant, 4 McLeod

Place, **Kambah ACT 2902, Australia.** Phone 61 2 6296 4398

Designing Your Life, 10 Nepean Pl., **Macquarie, Australia,** ACT 2614. phone 61 6 253 2231. Judith Bailey.

New Zealand Creative Career Centre, Ltd., 4th Floor, Braemar House, 32 The Terrace, P.O. Box 3058, **Wellington, New Zealand.** phone 64 4 499 8414. Felicity McLennan.

Life Work Career Counselling, P.O. Box 2223, **Christchurch, New Zealand.** phone 64 03 379 2781. Max Palmer.

Career Makers, PO Box 277-95, Mt. Roskill, **Auckland, New Zealand.** phone 649 817 5189. Liz Constable.

Find A Job You Can Love, 2/8 Hatton St., Karori, **Wellington, New Zealand.** phone 64 4 476 2554. Tim Martin.

Transformation Technologies Pte Ltd. 122 Thomson Green, **Singapore** 574986. phone 65 456 6358. Anthony Tan, Director.

*Readers often write to ask us which of these overseas counselors are familiar with my approach to job-hunting and career-changing. The answer is: **every one of the counselors listed above,** have attended my two-week workshop, and therefore know my approach well.*

Other overseas counselors not trained by me, but who may still be quite helpful to you, since they are experienced counselors, and are familiar with Para-chute, are:

Judy Feierstein, M.A., 46/2 Derech Bet Lechem, **Jerusalem 93504, Israel,** phone (02) 71 06 73.

Lori Mendel, 14/3 Zui Bruk, **Tel Aviv 63423, Israel,** phone (03) 29 28 30.

Johan Veeninga, Careers by Design, Business Park "De Molenzoom," P.O. Box 143, NL-3990 DC, **Houten/Utrecht, The Netherlands.** phone 31 (0) 3403 75153.

Employment agencies for Overseas jobs:
Safe Jobs in **Japan,** 56 Northwood Ave., Bridgewater, NJ 08807. (`http://www.safejobsin-japan.com`) phone 908 231 0994. Located in Japan, they place college graduates who wish to teach conversational English in Japan. Above is their U.S. administrative support office.

Richard Bolles, What Color Is Your Parachute?
International Workshop held in the U.S.A.

When the subject of counseling comes up, I am asked endlessly whether or not I do any counseling or teaching.

The answer is: I do group teaching once a year, in the summer, in Bend, Oregon, at an International workshop I put on, there.

We receive many letters and phone calls inquiring about this, so I hope you won't mind if I give you the details right here, in order to cut down on our mail and phone calls.

It is called:

The International Two-Week Workshop
on LIFE/Work Planning
at Mount Bachelor Village, Bend, Oregon

This workshop *(as its name indicates)* is international in scope. Past participants have come from all parts of the world -- in addition to the U.S., we have had participants from Canada, England, Wales, The Netherlands, France, Switzerland, Italy, Germany, Scandinavia, Gabon, Zimbabwe, South Africa, Panama, Costa Rica, Venezuela, Brazil, New Zealand, Australia, Singapore, Hong Kong, China, and Japan. As to vocational background, half of those attending are usually career-counselors or those who want to be; the other half are: job-hunters of all ages, career-changers, homemakers, union organizers, CEOs, teachers, people facing a move, people facing retirement, the recently

divorced, college students, clergy and those who are currently unemployed. They have ranged from 16–74, in age.

The workshop is held in late July or early August. The dates in 2000 are scheduled to be: **July 28th–August 11th, 2000 A.D.** And in the year 2001 the dates are scheduled to be August 3–17, 2001 A.D.

Mount Bachelor Village is a beautiful and popular resort on the outskirts of **Bend, Oregon,** *which -- as everyone knows -- is the center of the United States (Honolulu is 3,000 miles to the West, New York City is 3,000 to the East).*

It is warm and sunny there and many of our meetings are outdoors. Most of our meals are outdoors as well.

I lead the workshop the entire two weeks. The exercises are done in various ways: in the large group, in groups of sixes, in groups of three, and individually.

The total teaching time at this workshop exceeds 100 hours.

The cost for the 100 hours is $2000 (i.e. $20/hr.) -- which we believe to be a very reasonable tuition, these days.

> *For those who get their registration in prior to midnight on December 31, 1999, there is a special "Early Bird Registration" price of $1,000 tuition, instead of the $2,000. (If you miss that date, you have to wait until Early Bird Registration next year to get this discount. There are no exceptions.)*

At any time of the year, if you live outside the U.S., and your exchange rates are unfavorable or the cost of airfare high, you can inquire about 'our International Rate.'

Room and board *is in addition to the tuition.* For double occupancy (we pair you with a roommate of the same sex), the cost is approxi-

mately $145/day for your room, lunch and dinner; or $2000 for the two weeks. For single occupancy (a room to yourself) the cost is $179/day for your room, lunch and dinner; or $2500 for the two weeks. You're on your own for breakfast, though we do have a Continental break-fast -- coffee/tea and pastries -- available without charge, at the be-ginning of each morning's first session.

The workshop is filled on a strictly first come, first served, basis, and is limited to the first 48 people who apply. However, there are usually some last-minute cancellations, so always phone or fax us to inquire, rather than simply concluding that it is already filled.

If you wish additional information, or wish to request a brochure and registration blank, contact:

> Norma Wong, Workshop Registrar
> What Color Is Your Parachute?
> P.O. Box 379
> Walnut Creek, CA 94597-0379

Fax No.: 1-925-837-5120 (twenty-four hours a day)
Phone No.: 1-925-837-3002 (9 a.m.–5 p.m. Monday thru Friday, Pacific Coast Time)

Index

Update 2001

TO: PARACHUTE
P.O. Box 379
Walnut Creek, CA 94597

I think that the information in the 2000 edition needs to be changed, in your next revision, regarding (or, the following resource should be added):

_____

_____

_____

_____

_____

_____

I cannot find the following resource, listed on page _____:

_____

_____

_____

_____

_____

_____

Name _____

Address _____

Please make a copy.

Submit this so as to reach us by February 1, 2000. Thank you.

Other Resources

Additional materials by Richard N. Bolles
to help you with your job-hunt:

The What Color Is Your Parachute? Workbook
This handy workbook leads the job-seeker
through the process of determining exactly
what sort of job or career they are most
suited for, easily streamlining this potentially stressful and confusing task. $9.95

Job-Hunting on the Internet,
1999 Edition, revised and expanded.
This handy guide has quickly established
itself as the ideal resource for anyone who's
taking the logical step of job-hunting on
the Internet. $8.95

The Three Boxes of Life,
And How to Get Out of Them
An introduction to life/work planning. $18.95

How to Find Your Mission in Life
Originally created as an appendix to *What
Color Is Your Parachute?*, this book was written
to answer one of the questions most often
asked by job-hunters. $5.95

Job-Hunting Tips for the So-Called Handicapped
A unique perspective on job-hunting and career-
changing, addressing the experiences of the
disabled in performing these tasks. $4.95

The Career Counselor's Handbook
(with Howard Figler)
A complete guide for practicing or aspiring
career counselors. $14.95

For additional copies of *What Color Is Your Parachute?*
or other fine books and posters from Ten Speed Press,
please visit our Web site at www.tenspeed.com,
or call us at 1-800-841-2665.

For additional insight and advice from Richard N. Bolles,
please visit the companion site to *What Color Is Your
Parachute?* at www.JobHuntersBible.com.

BACKPACKINGLIGHT®

LIGHTWEIGHT
Backpacking and Camping

BY

George Cole

Carol Crooker

Alan Dixon

Rick Dreher

Lee Van Horn

Ryan Jordan

David Schultz

Stephanie Jordan

Alison Simon

Bill Thorneloe

Ellen Zaslaw

EDITOR

Ryan Jordan

MANAGING EDITORS

Alan Dixon and Vic Lipsey

Mission

evangelism

To establish a worldwide community network of interconnected core users where backcountry wilderness adventure is not just a passive interest, it's a passionate tenet of their lifestyle.

discipleship

To provide advanced backcountry skills to a core-user group that drives trends through acute industry awareness, expectations of exceptional gear performance, and zero tolerance for mediocrity. **BACKPACKING**LIGHT® will accomplish this mission with publications that are

challenging

insightful

authoritative

SUBSCRIBE

BACKPACKINGLIGHT®

Pack less. Be more.

1   ## Subscribe to Backpacking Light Magazine
4 quarterly issues to your door
Premium content beyond the website

2   ## Add an online membership
Save 20%

3   ## Go now
BackpackingLight.com/subscribe

WANT BOTH SUBSCRIPTIONS? **Good news:** When you purchase a
one-year subscription to our magazine and to the website, you'll receive
20% off the magazine price.

ALREADY A WEBSITE SUBSCRIBER? Log in under your existing
membership account. When you add the print subscription to your
shopping cart, you'll receive the 20% discount at checkout.

POSTAGE: Domestic (U.S.) postage is included in the cost of subscription.
For International orders, USD$16 surcharge will be added per year.

Beartooth Mountain Press
1627 West Main Street, Suite No. 310
Bozeman, MT 59715-4011
http://www.beartoothmountainpress.com
Email: info@beartoothmountainpress.com

editor: Ryan Jordan
managing editors: Alan Dixon and Vic Lipsey
contributing authors: George Cole, Carol Crooker, Alan Dixon, Rick Dreher, Lee
    Van Horn, Ryan Jordan, David Schultz, Stephanie Jordan, Alison Simon, Bill
    Thorneloe, Ellen Zaslaw
cover photo: Ryan Jordan carrying 9 pounds of gear, food, and water through
    Montana's Spanish Peaks Wilderness
cover design: Beartooth Mountain Press
layout and manufacturing: Venture Arts (www.venturearts.com)

ISBN 0-9748188-2-8

Acknowledgments

So many hands touched this book that it's no easy task to comprehend how it came together, let alone acknowledge them all in writing. Putting a project of this magnitude together and considering the various perspectives of multiple enthusiastic authors in the process is somewhat like dropping a bag of marbles off the tip of the Matterhorn and seeing where they land: You just never know. But land they do (and did), and each landing zone featured something very special that you can never grasp when you're writing a book by yourself: the value of unique and different perspectives.

The last time I read the entire manuscript, this epiphany exploded right in front of me, so the obvious place to start is with the founding authors of the volume: George Cole, Lee Van Horn, Alan Dixon, Rick Dreher, and Dave Schultz—all who joined me in writing this book's precursor, *Lightweight Backpacking 101* (Beartooth Mountain Press, 2003), and who spent countless hours in the planning stages of *Lightweight Backpacking and Camping* to define its vision and purpose. Also, to the other contributing authors that were either invited to submit content to the volume or who appear in the encore section (part 5) or appendices as authors of some of the outstanding articles and gear lists that have appeared in BackpackingLight.com through the years: Carol Crooker, Bill Thorneloe, Ellen Zaslaw, Alison Simon, and Stephanie Jordan.

This book would not have been possible without the creative energy of Vic Lipsey and company at V Major Creative in Seattle. Their editorial expertise, design prowess, and enthusiasm for the subject are worth more than the lightest gear money can buy. Well, OK, almost.

In addition, Alan Dixon deserves much of the credit for how this project has evolved. *Lightweight Backpacking 101* was largely organized, edited, and managed by Alan. His investment in putting that volume together, and in helping guide the initial vision of this one, are greatly appreciated. Alan's been instrumental in contributing to the lightweight backpacking movement as we know it today with tremendous enthusiasm, willing to experiment off the grid du normale, and an analytical approach to solving various ultralight dilemmas. Alan and I first met on an unnamed ridge in the Tetons in 2001 after exchanging GPS coordinates by email. I've enjoyed every moment together, be it scrambling across the Wind River Crest, finding big trout in the Uintas, or rappelling all through the night in defeat off of the Middle Teton.

My family deserves as much kudos for the completion of this book as anyone listed here. My wife, Stephanie, and son, Chase, had to undergo sacrifices that no one in their right minds should have to endure. Remarkably, saying no to them with "I can't, I have to work on the book" never once invited anything but a supportive "OK, go for it." I can't thank them enough. This is as much their book as it is ours, but not by entitlement: by love.

Finally, none of the enthusiasm about lightweight backpacking that was channeled into these pages would have been possible without the unquenchable lust for lightweight gear and knowledge that occupies the minds and hearts of backpackers everywhere. These are the folks for which these books, and Backpacking Light, were written. And so, a tremendous thanks to both the readership and the staff of Backpacking Light for fueling the fire that makes this so much fun.

DISCLAIMER

We didn't really want to waste a whole page on this, but our attorney said we sort of had to. If it was up to us, we'd keep it brutally simple:

> Your mama ain't watching out for you.
> Don't be an idiot.

But despite the fact that this one line should be sufficient, the legal guys tell us that it wouldn't be enforceable in a court of law. So here's the rest. This book is a compilation of information, perspectives, and opinions and is provided to the reader with no warranty whatsoever. This is not a safety manual. In contrast, it provides information about taking more risks when you enter the backcountry. Consequently, it is not intended for beginning backpackers or those that otherwise do not already know how to stay dry and warm in inclement weather, possess wilderness survival skills, and know how to recognize and avoid dangerous situations. Therefore, be warned that you must exercise your own judgment in evaluating the accuracy, applicability, and utility of the information provided herein.

THERE ARE NO WARRANTIES, WHETHER EXPRESS OR IMPLIED, THAT INFORMATION PROVIDED IN THIS BOOK IS ACCURATE OR RELIABLE. THERE ARE NO WARRANTIES OF FITNESS OR TIMELINESS FOR A PARTICULAR PURPOSE OR THAT THIS BOOK IS MERCHANTABLE. YOUR USE OF THIS BOOK INDICATES YOUR ASSUMPTION OF THE RISK THAT IT MAY CONTAIN ERRORS AND IS AN ACKNOWLEDGEMENT OF YOUR OWN SOLE RESPONSIBILITY FOR YOUR HIKING, BACKPACKING, AND MOUNTAINEERING SAFETY.

Table of **Contents**

Preface:
The Benefits of Going Light

Some hikers, upon converting to the ultralight style of backpacking, become rabid proselytizers for the cause, convinced that everyone needs to get their base pack weight below 10 pounds to avoid the eternal damnation of 65-pound packs. Though it may border on blasphemy—since a good chunk of my recent life has been devoted to creating ultralight gear and getting it into the hands of like-minded enthusiasts—I'm not convinced that everyone needs a small base pack weight. If you are young, in great physical shape, your trips consist entirely of relatively short distances into the backcountry to establish base camps for day trips, and you already own a bunch of traditional backpacking gear, you can probably save yourself the trouble of reading this book.

Good for the Body

For the rest of you, there are many benefits to going light. The most obvious is perhaps the physical benefit. For anyone who is older than 25 (or younger than 16!), whose career and rest of life doesn't leave as much time as they would like to work out, who has an old sports/war injury, who has some kind of disability (any part of the body that doesn't work as well as the norm), who has limited vacation time in which to recreate, lightening your pack weight will be a blessing. Your body will thank you for carrying a lighter pack. A lighter pack will

- Be easier on your joints and muscles
- Help prevent aggravating old injuries
- Allow you to maintain your outdoor activities to a ripe old age

I have received many excited letters from graying outdoor enthusiasts who had resigned themselves to giving up backpacking for good, only to find out that with ultralight gear and techniques they were once again able to spend time in the backcountry that they loved.

A lighter pack allows longer daily travel distances, putting more of the backcountry within reach. Now with a three-day weekend you can see countryside that would have required a week off of work using traditional backpacking techniques. As you get further into the backcountry, you get to enjoy less crowded trails and more solitude. The ability to travel further can extend your backpacking into the shoulder seasons of early spring and late fall, where previously the shorter days were an impediment to any serious trip.

Good for the Environment

Besides having less impact on your limbs and ligaments, a lighter load can result in a reduced impact on the backcountry. Many ultralighters, freed from the slavish adherence to short grinds between established campsites, use their ability for enhanced distances and greater flexibility to practice stealth camping. Adopting proper "Leave No Trace" ethics, the ultralighter can reduce their impact on the backcountry. They don't need to camp near water like everyone else. Their lighter loads allow them to enjoy dinner near the water and hike on a few miles, avoiding overuse of the waterside sites and opening up some new pristine vistas from their stealth site.

To the extent that ultralight techniques allow more people to enjoy the backcountry, this can foster a greater base of ownership and involvement in preserving that backcountry, donating time and resources to protect it.

Good for the Mind

Besides keeping your body active later in life, going light helps keep your mind active and healthy. Techniques and knowledge are a big part of lightening your pack weight. Often you rely on your experience to reduce the amount of gear you carry. Some ultralight gear requires a little more thought to use than the standard issue stuff.

For instance, a nice 4-pound tent is fairly easy to set up just about anywhere. But if you are carrying an 8-ounce tarp, you will need to be more clever about where you camp and you will need to know some techniques to fashion the tarp into a worthy shelter. Lightening your load engages your mind in your backcountry adventure. This engagement starts before the trip, as you gather information, analyze options, and refine gear lists. As you educate yourself online and through books such as this, you help to keep the brain cells active. Studies have shown that is integral to a long and healthy life.

Good for Simplicity

Going light helps to simplify your life. Through the tenets of multiple-use items and taking less gear, the number of items in your pack drops with the overall weight. Less gear to pack means it's easier to get out. In this day and age of busy careers, multiple kid activities, and overlapping commitments, having a simple kit may make the difference of you getting out on a trip or not. Even if you haven't planned anything, when you're prepared and flexible there will be times you can jump into a trip when an original participant cancels at the last minute.

Besides the obvious benefit of less weight, having less gear is a freeing experience in that you have less stuff to keep track of on the trail. (On the flip side, with your gear honed down to a minimum, if you lose something, it was probably something that you really needed.)

Good for Relationships

One of the more esoteric benefits of going light is the ability to build relationships with the people who design and make your gear. It is unlikely that the average hiker will be able to pick up the phone and easily get hold of a major manufacturer's designer for a gear discussion. But since much of the cutting-edge ultralight gear being produced is coming out of cottage manufacturers, you get the opportunity to ask detailed questions of the people making the equipment. In many cases, you have real input into the design of the next generation of ultralight backpacking gear. Many ultralight products on the market today bear the mark of individual enthusiasts who asked for tweaks to suit their own needs. If you value the diversity of small business, going lighter provides you ample opportunity to support smaller shops.

Good for More

Sometimes the benefits of going light aren't so much that you get that light, but that you make room for your passion. I have photographer friends that will leave home a stove and subsist on cold mashed potatoes so that they can make room for 10 pounds of camera gear. Similarly, climbers who carry ample racks of hardware to ply their craft benefit from going light on everything else.

Since the journey to lightness is largely a cerebral one, where does one start? Self-education is critical to avoid getting in a situation where you didn't bring enough gear to be safe for your experience level. Your journey should be one of baby steps, learning and trying a couple of new things on each trip, finding what works for you and what doesn't. There are many online email lists that are a great resource. Basically, any list having to do with long hikes—such as the Pacific Crest Trail, Continental Divide Trail, or Appalachian

Trail—will have a following of experienced ultralighters. There are beginning to be significant books with the latest in-

formation on ultralight backpacking, like the book you are holding now. If you have not already read it, I highly recommend the book *Lightweight Backpacking 101*, also published by Beartooth Mountain Press. So dive in and start your own journey to lightness!

GLEN "HOMEMADE" VAN PESKI
Founder, Gossamer Gear

Introduction

Lightweight backpacking is not about sacrificing comfort, safety, or a good time. It's not some insane practice of walking in marathon racing shorts, foraging for roots, and shivering the nights away under a tarp the size of a handkerchief. Nor is lightweight backpacking about carrying gear with seams that explode when you sneeze. And it's certainly not about having the best, most expensive gear money can buy. In fact, lightweight backpacking is often quite the opposite of that.

Lightweight backpacking is about doing more with less. On the surface, doing more with less implies that you can go farther, faster, and longer in more safety and comfort with a light pack than with a heavy pack. However, it's a lot deeper than that. A light pack isn't enough.

If you put a light pack full of the latest and greatest lightweight gear on an inexperienced hiker and bid him bon voyage into the wilderness, he may very well enjoy the experience. However, if he does not understand the limitations, utility, and function of lightweight gear, he could come back thoroughly frustrated and never set foot into the wilderness again with a pack that weighs less than 40 pounds. Worse, he may never return to backpacking. Even worse yet, he could get injured

(L to R) Alan Dixon, Glen Van Peski, and Ryan Jordan at a high pass near the northern terminus of the Wind River High Route. They left the trailhead with 42 pounds of gear and food — combined — in September 2003 and arrived four a half days later at the southern end, 70 miles, two snowstorms, and temperatures down to 14 °F under their belts.

or die because of his lack of knowledge and experience using lightweight gear in hostile environmental conditions.

So lightweight backpacking is about technique as much as it's about the gear. In fact, proper technique is so important for increasing your safety with a lightweight kit that the two must go hand in hand. Solid backcountry skills allow you to take lighter gear. Virtually anyone can carry a four-season tent, heavy synthetic sleeping bag, plenty of extra food and clothing, a GPS, and satellite or cellular communications devices to survive a mainstream wilderness experience. But if you are going light, you must do so with competency. Lightweight gear does not replace a lack of experience or skill.

The goals of this book are simple:

1. To justify the benefits of lightweight backpacking
2. To present the reader with several options in technique and gear
3. To empower the reader with knowledge to go out on her own

Part 1

Part 1 of this volume builds the foundation to justify the benefits of lightweight backpacking by discussing concepts that present the art and science of walking. It begins appropriately with the category of equipment that is arguably more important that any piece of gear or apparel a lightweight backpacker will use: footwear.

Lee Van Horn's treatise on footwear (chapter 1) includes a comprehensive discussion of lightweight backpacking shoes. Simply put, shoes have such a profound impact on the lightweight backpacking experience because (1) the type of footwear you are able to wear depends in large part on the weight of the pack, and (2) the type of footwear you choose governs the transfer of energy and shock to the rest of your lower torso and spinal joints. Since this book's manuscript was finalized, I've been diving into research about ultralight footwear and experimenting with shoes lighter than anything the market has previously seen. I've been strengthening my feet, hiking in shoes with less support — more akin to slippers than hiking shoes — and have been making some dramatic discoveries. In particular, that with proper conditioning the natural features of the feet (as long as the arch is supported and the heel pad retains its shape for shock absorption) are ideally suited for transferring energy to the rest of your body. I'm finding that I can walk longer distances in less supportive footwear — with a light pack — than I've ever been able to do before. Ten years ago, a 30-mile day of backpacking was relatively uncommon except among the elite. Now those kinds of distances are accessible to those carrying lightweight backpacks and wearing the proper footwear.

In chapter 2 I discuss what may be the most sought after piece of equipment by gear junkies: the backpack. However, rather than be a survey of lightweight backpacks, this chapter addresses how a backpack impacts the biomechanics of the body and how the lightweight backpacker can capitalize on certain features of backpack design and packing to get the most out of their packing system. Types of backpacks are discussed, including a regurgitation of the age old "ultralight" debate of frame versus frameless backpacks. The justification is based on load stability and moment-concept physics, indicating why an internal frame pack will—in theory at least—almost always outperform a frameless pack, in spite of the extra weight of the frame.

In chapter 3, George Cole integrates the concepts presented in chapters 1 and 2 to present the definitive conclusions that justify the benefits of lightweight backpacking from the physical, biomechanical, and physiological standpoint of walking long distances over uneven terrain. Nowhere else has this subject been treated in the ways that we've presented in chapters 1–3 of this book. Although the reading can be difficult at times (it may actually require you to think about and study the concepts, so don't expect a lazy read, especially in chapters 2 and 3), it will empower you with the foundational principles that show why lightweight backpacking feels good!

Appropriately, this section on walking closes with a discussion of navigation. Lighter in concept and requiring less studiousness than the three previous, chapter 4 discusses the core tools that make for efficient navigation and why and how lightweight backpackers can both choose and use those tools to the best advantage. George's navigation presentation is not meant to be a comprehensive primer on navigation tools and techniques. With the advancement of GPS technology and computerized custom mapmaking tools, we'll undoubtedly see some incredible progress in this field in the coming years. For the lightweight backpacker, I hope that you take home these messages: (1) that navigation is an essential skill to improving your speed and accuracy in wilderness travel, and (2) that an understanding of map reading will allow you

Ultralight, Utah-style. The relatively benign summer weather of the Uinta Wilderness in NE Utah provides an excellent proving ground for ultralight backpacking. **(L to R) Ryan Jordan, Alan Dixon, and Carol Crooker** carrying packs that weigh 6 to 8 pounds each, minus food and water.

to plan trips more effectively so you take less gear. Many a time I've sat down and meditated over a planned wilderness route on a detailed topographical map and identified the best potential campsites, cross country routes, and bailout options that allow me to lighten my pack.

Part 2

In this section titled "Protection from the Elements," we present a detailed discussion of how to deal with adverse environmental conditions, specifically: cold, heat, wind, rain, snow, and insects. To understand how stuff works and why you might select specific components of clothing, sleep, and shelter systems. This section opens up with a basic and simple discussion of thermoregulation, custom tailored for the needs of an ultralight backpacker (chapter 5).

In chapter 6, BackpackingLight.com's product review director, Alan Dixon, discusses lightweight clothing systems, with specific attention to base layers, wind shirts, high-loft insulating garments, and rainwear. The beginning lightweight backpacker will really appreciate Alan's presentation of different system weights. There are magnificent advantages to be gained by reducing both the weight and volume of your clothing systems. Intelligent decisions can be made so that you don't sacrifice warmth or protection when the storm does come.

In chapter 7, Lee Van Horn presents an overview of sleep systems (sleeping bags, mattresses, and bivy sacks) from the most basic fundamentals of design, so the lightweight backpacker understands the limitations of today's cutting-edge sleep systems (including so-called variable girth and top bags) and how best to integrate them into their own gear kits.

Chapter 8 introduces BackpackingLight.com's section editor, Rick Dreher, with a lighthearted discussion of shelter systems. This chapter is unique from those in other books, which plagiarize the same section headings from each other: "Tents," "Tarps," and "Other Types of Shelters." Rick takes a different approach, building a foundation of shelter system principles, from design considerations and environmental context (warm and dry versus cold and wet), to moisture control issues, and shelter choices. And unlike other books, tarps are smack dab in the forefront of other choices, rather than as a casual afterthought. We provide you with sound information on tarp selection, pitching, and considerations for selecting tarps versus other types of shelters (see also chapter 14: "Advanced Tarp Camping Techniques").

Lighweight is **not** just for summer backpacking. **(L to R) Dave Schultz, Don Johnston, and Alan Dixon** make their way with light packs on snowshoes and skis through Montana's Beartooth Wilderness in the winter.

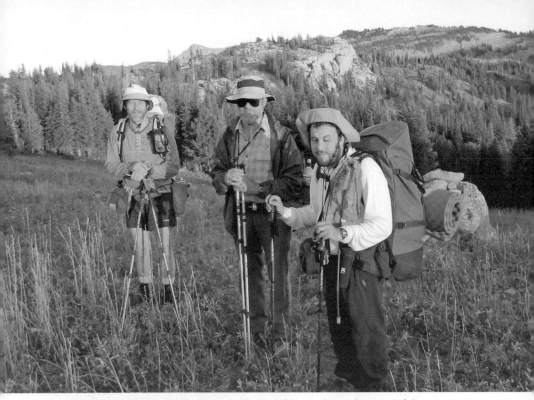

Don Johnston, Don Ladigin, and Ken Knight near the northern end of the
Teton High Route, which spans 70 miles along the true crest of Wyoming's Teton
Range. Most people hike the High Route in 10 days with a resupply. With lightweight
gear and good weather, we finished with sub-20 pound packs in four a half days.

Part 3

If you know why you need to go light and how to do it in
the face of inclement conditions, you are most of the way to
becoming a lightweight backpacker. And instead of comprehensive discussions of the neat little gadgetry that makes this
business so much fun, we dive into the third most important
aspect of maximizing your performance on the trail: hydration and nutrition.

   In chapter 9, George returns with a great introduction
to lightweight hydration options, where we've simply done
away with the de facto standard of water treatment: the unfortunately ubiquitous pump-style water filter. I will grant
that there may still be situations where such filters may be
warranted, but most of the authors of this volume have
enjoyed wilderness waters from every corner of the world.

Pump style water filters have long since been relegated to our gear museums (our spouses call these closets, basements, or attics). Not only does George discuss water treatment gear and supplies, but presents considerations for creating effective and efficient hydration strategies while on the trail (see also chapter 16: "Hiking Efficiency").

Chapter 10 synthesizes the thoughts of Lee, myself, and Dave Schultz in "Trail Food, Backcountry Cooking, and Nutrition." It is in this chapter that we not only discuss concepts like caloric efficiency and menu planning, but also more practical considerations of lightweight hikers, including packing food for minimum volume and creating meals that are utterly simple to prepare while remaining tasty and nutritious. Finally, and appropriately, we close the chapter with a discussion of both lightweight and ultralight cooking systems, as well as bear bagging techniques. In this chapter, more than any other perhaps, we wholeheartedly denounce the 1960's NOLS-esque nutrition theology that has become like religion to some and has infectiously permeated backpacking literature for four decades. I expect more advances in backpacking food, nutrition, meal preparation, and stove performance to come down the pike in the coming years. Combine all of this with light packs and an understanding of how to hike efficiently (using less calories to travel farther distances), and we have a recipe for plenty of new concepts in wilderness travel that are more consistent with the lightweight philosophy.

Taking care of your body is not just about keeping it well fed and hydrated. Particularly on long-distance hikes, hygiene is an important consideration as well. This is presented in chapter 11 by George and myself, with some womanly interjection for those subjects in which we're less . . . experienced . . . by Ellen Zaslaw. Skin, feet, teeth, toilet, low-impact camping, and insect protection—it's all here, and in the right amount of depth to allow the Linuses among you to plow through it quickly while still picking up some nuggets of knowledge that we'll all appreciate when we meet you on the trail.

Part 4

By now, you will have understood the basic foundation systems of lightweight backpacking: walking/navigation/ packing systems, clothing/sleep/shelter systems, and hydration/nutrition systems. An in-depth survey of the lightweight backpacking gear market will help you reduce your pack weight to remarkable levels. Many today are now practicing a superultralight style of backpacking, whereby their base pack weights without food and water are less than five pounds. The lunatic fringe? Perhaps, but the perceived reality for the uninformed public and mass media is that people carrying light packs are fools, walking time bombs waiting for a search and rescue crew to come bail them out when the weather turns south. Of course, all of this is utter hogwash. In my lightweight backpacking seminars to search and rescue agencies all over the country, an overwhelming majority of them indicated that most calls for rescues to hikers and backpackers were to those who were either inexperienced or were in trouble because they had overly heavy packs, or both.

However, that does not mean that we lightweight backpackers must ignore the real risks that come with leaving that extra change of clothing at home or electing to use a tarp rather than a tent when traveling to the mountains.

Consequently, part 4 deals very purposefully with two important subjects that must not be ignored by any wilderness traveler, but especially, must remain in the forefronts of minds of lightweight backpackers: first aid and emergency preparedness.

In chapter 12, George presents a basic plan of risk management. I encourage you to read this chapter over and over until risk management becomes a core ethic for pre-trip planning. You must always understand the change in risk associated with leaving, or taking, any piece of gear, altering your route, going solo versus with companions. As important but perhaps the least understood aspect of risk management among lightweight backpackers is to design and know your bailout options, and use them if you have to. Heroes don't die trying to be heroes while solo backpacking.

Dave and I address first aid in chapter 13. Instead of discussing those first-aid situations that could happen to you, we present those that normally do, with lightweight solutions for dealing with them. Dave and I have a long history of bantering back and forth about first-aid gear (see also chapter 19: "Face-Off, First Aid, and Emergency Gear"), but we agree on the same core principles: Take the gear you need for the emergencies you expect to encounter, and capitalize on your skill, knowledge, and ability to innovate when unexpected situations arise.

By the end of Part 4, you will be ready to hit the trail, rejuvenated and energized with a serious foundation of lightweight backpacking principles! Now grab your gear and do it. No book, magazine, or website can ever hope to replace actual experience. And don't be afraid to try new things and gain new experiences in low-risk environments. Camp in the backyard when a winter storm warning is issued so you know how your lightweight shelter can handle the wind. Take a walk in shorts, T-shirt, wind shirt, and running shoes on a local trail at night when it's pouring down rain so you know how your body will react to your clothing system. (Just keep the keys to the car handy.) And, don't ignore the benefit of practicing lightweight backpacking on overnight trips close to home. Make it easy on your family and job. Leave after dinner, and be back home or to work by lunch the next day. "Just do it" as the slogan says, and become your own expert at lightweight backpacking.

Part 5

Part 5 closes the book with some of the classic articles originally published on the BackpackingLight.com website. We've selected those that will withstand the test of time, and thus warrant inclusion in a book format to be enjoyed for years to come. In addition, we've tried to select those that will get your thought processes going and possibly invoke some controversy. These cater to more advanced lightweight backpackers (see chapter 14: "Advanced Tarp Camping Techniques for Inclement Conditions," chapter 15: "Superultralight: Breaking the 5-Pound Barrier," Chapter 16: "Hiking Efficiency: A Day in the Life of an Ultralight Hiker," and chapter 19: "Face-Off: First Aid and Emergency Gear).

In addition, I've included two chapters that get to the core of what any activity is about: relationships. I love solo hiking and its benefits: Remote solitude provides an avenue for intro-spection and relationship with God that is extremely difficult to procure in today's hectic society. But a solo life is a lonely life, and lightweight backpacking opens up new avenues for sharing the wilderness with your family. To that end, please enjoy chapters 17 ("Lightweight Backpacking with Young Children") and 19 ("Lightweight Backpacking for Couples") and show others the fruits and fun of going light.

Finally, it's no great surprise that lightweight backpacking is appealing to those who don't have the strength of an elite mountaineer — which of course, includes most of us — but espe-cially caters to youth, seniors, and women. To that end, we've included a fantastic discussion of lightweight backpacking in the context of women's issues (chapter 20) by Ellen Zaslaw. Read it and find out how a water pistol or crushed aspirin might find their way onto a woman's gear list.

Conclusion

My own passion for lightweight backpacking was fueled by seeing how far a thirteen-year-old Boy Scout could walk if I cut his pack weight in half — from more than 40 to less than 20 pounds. I figured he could walk twice as far. I was wrong. He could walk three times the distance. In 1991, I validated the lightweight approach with a group of six High Adven-ture Boy Scouts ages thirteen to seventeen. When I told them we were going ultralight, they balked. When I told them I wanted us all to walk 100 miles in 4.5 days, and that nobody in the Scouting community has ever done this before, they were turbocharged. We walked out of Camp Parsons with five days of food and no Scout was carrying more than 17 pounds of gear and food. Five days later, we arrived back in Camp after a 112-mile trek, and the boys had become young men — not mules. They experienced a sense of adventure and exploration that no one carrying a heavy pack could have ever appreciated.

Daily I am awed and pleased by the fire that lights up in the heart of someone when they realize they can cut their pack weight in half simply by thinking a little differently about what they want from a wilderness experience. To see light packs, smiling faces, and warm hearts on seventy-year-old hikers in the Tetons and seven-year-old first graders on the Appalachian Trail — those are the real rewards for me!

Godspeed and go light,

RYAN JORDAN
Publisher, Backpacking Light Magazine
Bozeman, Montana

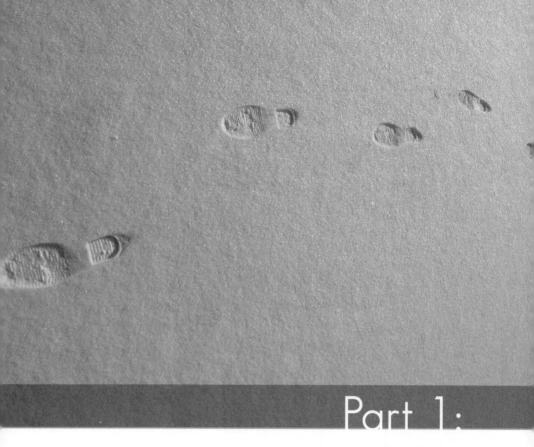

Part 1:

The Art and Science of **Walking**

Chapter 1: **Footwear**

By Lee Van Horn

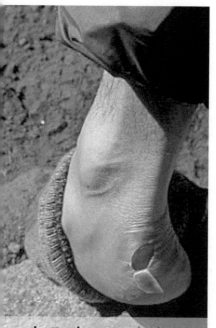

Inattention to properly selecting and using your footwear, combined with excessive pack weight, can lead to blisters.

Backpackers can attest to the detrimental effects that the inattention to foot care can have on an otherwise pleasant trip. A tiny blister on your little toe can make it difficult for you to even focus on the wildflowers in the field you might be walking through. Maintaining healthy feet is a primary concern in the wilderness, not only to increase the pleasure of your outdoor experience, but also to preserve the working condition of your only mode of transportation. Using shoes and socks to protect, support, and warm your feet is the primary means to this end. Other prevention and treatment efforts are also sometimes called for to reduce the likelihood of blisters and other foot problems. This chapter primarily discusses aspects of foot care unique to lightweight backpacking.

Why Lightweight Footwear?

"Weight is even more important on the feet than the back." In his 1906 book, *Camping and Woodcraft*, Horace Kephart calculated the results of wearing boots just one pound too heavy.

> ". . . in ten miles there are 21,120 average paces. At one extra pound to the pace, the boots make you lift in a ten mile tramp, over ten tons more footgear." In 1953 the successful Mount Everest expedition came to the conclusion that in terms of physical effort one pound on the feet is equivalent to five pound on the back. A consensus of informed opinion now seems to support that assessment. (*The Complete Walker III*, Colin Fletcher, 1984, pp 53–54)

Those going back to heavyweight boots after many trips with lightweight alternatives can verify that the difference in comfort over long distances is significant. On one recent trip with only 14 miles and 2,000 feet elevation gain over two days, I wore my old mountaineering boots in response to paranoia over the possibility of encountering mud and snow while visiting a new area. My legs felt worse after that trip than coming back from any of my other overnight backpacking trips with trail-running shoes, which typically included 30 miles of trail and 6,000 feet of elevation gain in two days. Because of its impact on the hiking experience, light footwear is a foremost consideration when outfitting for backpacking.

The Anatomy of a Boot

To understand the differences in backpacking footwear, let's take a few minutes to dissect a walking boot/shoe. It consists of an *upper* section that encloses your foot and secures your foot to the rest of the shoe. The upper is then attached to a *sole* that includes a *shank* to provide stiffness, a *midsole* that acts as a shock absorber, and an *outer sole* that provides traction. In most shoes and boots there is also a removable *insole* directly inside that provides additional cushioning, arch support, and lateral stability. Together, these components allow the shoe to perform its primary functions: protecting the foot, stabilizing the foot (especially the ankle and arch), absorbing impact, and optimizing propulsion.

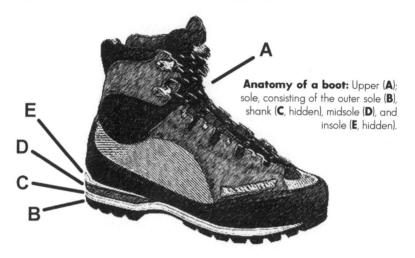

Anatomy of a boot: Upper (**A**); sole, consisting of the outer sole (**B**), shank (**C**, hidden), midsole (**D**), and insole (**E**, hidden).

The Myth of Dry Feet

The most common myth drilled into our minds by backpacking experts is that you need to keep your feet dry. The necessity of maintaining dry feet is a matter of debate, especially among the lightweight backpacking community. The reasons for questioning this edict are related to the performance costs of using footwear with waterproofing technologies. Typically, a waterproof shoe is obtained by constructing an upper that covers the whole foot with a waterproof barrier. Two technologies are the most common.

- Constructing an upper with treated (e.g., silicone impregnation) full-grain or split-grain leather
- Adding a waterproof-breathable membrane to the material used to construct the upper

Full-grain leather boots, when treated, will repel water at the surface, thus keeping the entire upper dry. However, the treatment tends to wear off quickly in the field. In truly wet conditions, where feet are often immersed in mud, slush, snow, or heavy rain, even the best waterproofing treatments wash out quickly. Further, 100 percent full-grain or split-grain leather constructions are generally only available in boot styles — typically, very heavy and rugged boots.

Waterproof-breathable membranes (commonly, Gore-Tex) that are typically laminated or sewn between the upper's outer and inner materials are designed to prevent water entry while at the same time allowing moisture vapor and perspiration to escape, keeping your feet dry. Such membranes are prone to tremendous stresses over long-distance walking and commonly fail in their ability to repel water. In addition, because there is no ventilation for the foot, there is a higher likelihood of sweat wicking into the region at the interior surface of the membrane and preventing it from expelling moisture vapor.

In comparing these two technologies we've generally found few differences in their ability to keep your feet dry from accumulated perspiration. In other words, they are poorly breathable solutions. In addition, because of the poor drainage of water from the interior of the boot combined with

Brasher Boots GTX: Lightweight, full-grain leather boots with a waterproof-breathable (Gore-Tex) membrane. 32 oz/pr, size Men's 8.

its limited breathability, drying times are generally very long. Most experienced lightweight backpackers consider shoes and boots using such technologies to be suitable only for cold weather and winter conditions, where the risk of cold feet from outside moisture outweighs the risk of wet feet from interior perspiration. Generally, waterproof shoes and boots, regardless of the type of waterproofing technology used, are more expensive than their non-waterproof counterparts.

The extreme alternative to a waterproof shoe is one constructed with an upper made with permeable fabrics that breathe, are well-ventilated, and drain water readily from the interior of the shoe. Such construction allows your foot and sock to dry relatively quickly after the shoe has been immersed and is less likely to accumulate moisture in the sock and shoe interior in response to perspiration. The uppers of such shoes are made with hydrophobic materials that will not absorb water and often include synthetic mesh panels built in the uppers to enhance breathability, ventilation, and drainage. Shoes made with uppers containing a lot of mesh are less appropriate for cold-weather hiking — the mesh does not retain heat as well as non-mesh fabrics. However, for most summer hiking and quite a lot of three-season hiking,

Salomon Tech Amhibian: Trail shoes that keep your feet cool and dry fast: mesh uppers provide breathability, ventilation, and water drainage. 26 oz/pr, size Men's 8.

Keeping your feet dry is important in cooler weather. Here, Alan Dixon leaps a creek in Wyoming's Wind River Mountains on a 45 degree day. In warmer conditions, wet feet are sometimes a blessing, providing cool and refreshing comfort.

these kinds of shoes work very well. Your ability to walk for a while with wet feet — after walking through a stream, thunder shower, or dew-saturated meadow — opens your footwear options to a wide variety of comfortable and very light choices.

For wetter walking conditions — sustained rain, snow-melt periods, or river canyon travel — using mesh-paneled footwear may result in wet feet for days at a time. This may not be as bad as it sounds. Experience will dictate sock and shoe combinations that prevent walking in sponges while providing the right balance of warmth and fast drying times. For many lightweight hikers, the tradeoffs of using footwear with mesh uppers far outweigh the perceived discomfort of walking in wet feet, (a perception that often decreases with experience).

For both physiological and emotional reasons walking with wet feet is simply not an option for some people. Emotional perceptions aside ("I don't like the way it feels"), some feet are physiologically sensitive to excessive moisture. If I walk long distances in warm, wet socks the skin on my soles crinkles up, like your hands do if you take a long hot bath. After a few hours, walking on the skin folds causes considerable pain. Others are able to walk for days on end with wet feet and never experience this. Conditioning may play a role in this physiological predisposition to skin-fold development. This problem is not as common for long-distance hikers as for the casual weekend enthusiast.

Selecting waterproof versus mesh-vented shoes is a personal choice. Before discounting the notion of using mesh-vented footwear, try it first. In general, lightweight backpackers perceive comfort to be higher while walking in wet feet in a 12-ounce trail-running shoe versus having dry feet in a 32-ounce leather or Gore-Tex boot.

The lightest styles of trail-running shoes suitable for lightweight backpacking (less than 13 ounces per shoe with good lateral stability and midsole cushioning) are made by Montrail, Merrill, Salomon, and New Balance. After using several other types of non-waterproof trail-running shoes, my own shoe of choice is the Montrail Vitesse. They weigh about 12 ounces per shoe (men's size 9); are constructed with a synthetic and hydrophobic upper with mesh panels; and offer excellent lateral stability, traction, and cushioning. Typically, a pair lasts about 500 trail miles. Although the Vitesse works for me, it may not work for you. Shoe choice must always be dictated by fit, and we all have different shaped feet. Some trial and error will be required before you are able to settle into a model of shoe that works consistently for you.

Winter Considerations

During the winter it is more important to keep your feet dry, not only for comfort, but also for safety when there is a higher risk of frostbite and trench foot. Further, continuous exposure to snow, especially at temperatures near or above freezing, will put the best waterproofing technologies to the test. Using trail-running shoes or lightweight hiking boots with a fabric upper and a waterproof-breathable membrane is one option. While reasonably effective at preventing the intrusion of outside moisture, perspiration accumulates rapidly in the shoe. Your biggest challenge will be keeping your feet warm at the end of the day. After you stop moving, accumulated perspiration in the shoe facilitates conductive heat loss. Cold feet are common. And unless you sleep with your shoes inside your sleeping bag at night, you may have to deal with the prospect of frozen shoes in the morning.

Winter backpacking requires a different footwear mentality if you are snowshoeing in very cold conditions. Some backpackers who insist on lightweight footwear for winter conditions pair them with insulated overboots (e.g., Neos, Forty Below, or Outdoor Research), separate camp booties with down or high-loft synthetic insulations (Sierra Designs or Nunatak USA), or vapor-barrier socks (RBH Designs, GoLite, Integral Designs). For winter snowshoe expeditions Ryan Jordan, BackpackingLight.com's publisher, uses a light, flexible, and warm system that stays dry for long periods of time in the worst conditions. He wears Brasher Supalite boots, which have 2-millimeter leather uppers, a Gore-Tex membrane, and weigh only 2 pounds. For socks, he wears a thin merino wool liner sock (Smartwool) under a fleece vapor-barrier sock (RBH Designs). Instead of using gaiters, Ryan wears a pair of neoprene overboots (Forty Below). The waterproof neoprene keeps moisture from entering, the overboot's high gaiter is suitable for deep snow, and the vapor-barrier sock prevents the accumulation of moisture in the sock's insulation or the boot lining. Insulation is provided by the neoprene of the overboot, the leather of the boot, and the fleece of the sock. The entire system weigh only 27 ounces per foot, which is lighter than the weight of most leather boots alone and far lighter than conventional gaiter-insulated-boot-winter-sock combinations.

For less aggressive terrain, a trail shoe combined with a lightweight overboot may prove useful for snowy, cold conditions. Carol Crooker, editor-in-chief of BackpackingLight. com, snowshoes in lightweight trail-running shoes tucked warmly inside the protection of an Outdoor Research low overboot—less than 1.5 pounds per foot.

Do you need boots?

The second issue that differentiates many lightweight backpackers is their tendency to dogmatically reject leather boots. Traditional backpacking boots are, for the most part, unwieldy 2–3 pound (each) affairs with thick leather uppers, steel shanks, and aggressively lugged outer soles. Leather uppers provide good protection from bashing your ankle bone, are reasonably waterproof if treated properly, and the steel shank provides a protective barrier between your foot and sharp rocks on the ground. In addition, the steel shank provides longitudinal stiffness that can minimize arch fatigue and tendonitis for long distances while carrying a heavy pack. Backpacking boot midsoles tend to be rather firm, and the outer sole has a deep tread, which provides more traction in mud and snow.

But backpacking boots are not without their disadvantages, many of which have been discussed. Boots have their advantages and are indeed recommended for backpacking with heavy loads or when traction for snow and mud is needed.

La Sportiva Trango S: Even "mountain boots" are getting lighter. 48 oz/pr, size Men's 8.

Boot designs continue to evolve. Even leather boots with lug soles are getting lighter. Climbing boots with synthetic uppers, such as the La Sportiva Trango S, can weigh as little as 48 ounces per pair (men's size 8). However, for most three-season hiking (spring, summer, and fall), carrying a lightweight backpack while wearing running shoes will be preferred by most — an experience akin to driving a sport car with the top retracted as opposed to a diesel bus.

Other Footwear Options

In addition to boots and shoes, there are a few other options for those carrying a light pack: going barefoot or wearing moccasins or sandals. Hiking barefoot provides your feet with no protection or support. To be successful, this option requires very tough feet that are well conditioned in order to avoid injury. Barefoot aficionados have walked the entire length of the Appalachian Trail and have climbed the Owen-Spalding Route on Wyoming's Grand Teton — a technical climb typically not attempted by those without specialized rock-climbing footwear. However, if you are unconditioned, barefoot hiking for appreciable distances can cause serious foot problems, including arch collapse leading to tearing of the plantar fascia tendon, dermal separation of skin layers in the foot sole, and excessive skin cracking from dehydration of the skin.

Similarly, moccasins provide only the function of an upper and none of the supportive benefits of a shoe's sole construction. Since the primary function of a shoe is to give the foot support, stability, shock absorption, and protection, moccasins offer few advantages over barefoot hiking.

Behind boots and shoes, sandals are the third most popular type of footwear. However, they are found on only a twinkling minority of backpackers. With advances in sandal technologies for both supportive strapping and protective and cushioning soles, sandals are gaining popularity among the lightweight backpacking community. Somewhat surprisingly, sandals tend to weigh more than trail-running shoes. Further, they generally lack most of the shock-absorbing qualities of these shoes, owing to their single-density and/or single-material sole construction. And it is difficult to use aftermarket insoles with them. Sandals are occasionally useful as a second pair of shoes carried by backpackers, for camp footwear or stream crossings. And, we are told by traditional backpackers lugging forty or fifty pound packs, that they are useful for hiking when your feet hurt from walking in heavy boots all morning! Backpackers that wear trail-running shoes find sandals to be less useful than those wearing boots, since a trail-running shoe is typically quite comfortable when worn in camp—just loosen the laces a bit. Plus, sandals dry relatively quickly after a stream crossing.

Finally, very light (4–8 ounces each) flip flops or sandals can be purchased at discount stores for only a few dollars. Shoe-clad backpackers wanting to keep their feet dry when crossing streams or wanting a little more air while in camp sometimes carry these.

A word of caution is in order here. Lightweight shoes are best seen as part of a lightweight backpacking system. Wearing trail-running shoes with a 45-pound pack may be possible but requires a level of ankle strength that most weekend adventurers have not developed in their 9 to 5 desk jobs. The change to low-cut backpacking shoes should take place simultaneously with or following the process of reducing your pack weight. Further, it is critical that backpackers remain self-conscious of their foot health. While on the trail you should be attentive of the condition of your feet and ankles. Blisters are most effectively treated in their earliest stages of formation (e.g., before a hot spot evolves to a liquid-filled blister). Likewise, ankle pain is an indicator that the biomechanics of your lower leg are not functioning optimally and should signal the need to diagnose and address the root problem. If your ankles are hurting badly or if they are collapsing—"turning over"—more often than usual, you should consider halting your progress, resting the injury, and trying a different pair of boots or shoes.

Some experienced backpackers consider the use of trail-running shoes to be optimized with a pair of trekking poles.

Trekking poles increase stability and balance, and take weight and strain off of ankles and knees. If you don't currently use them, consider getting a pair before making the switch to trail-running shoes.

Fitting your Footwear

We expect a lot out of a shoe: stability, cushioning, traction. The many functions that a shoe is expected to perform are made more difficult by the fact that every foot is different in size and shape. Unfortunately, a single model offering different sizes or widths does not guarantee a proper fit. Variability in foot volume, instep height, arch shape, foot taper, and toe configuration leads to a simple but not always obvious conclusion: There is no ideal shoe. Finding a shoe that works optimally for you over long distances in the backcountry will require that you invest the time to try a variety of different shoes. Simply put, getting a shoe to "fit" at your local outdoor retailer doesn't guarantee that it will perform to demanding use while hiking long distances. Because of the trial-and-error process that governs anybody's quest to find their perfect shoe, footwear may turn out to be one of your more expensive purchases when outfitting yourself. And, when you finally find the shoe that works for you — don't start over — buy a few extra pair. The style may be gone next season.

Insoles

An insole, also called a *footbed*, lies immediately under your foot inside the shoe. Insoles are typically removable (thank goodness) because those included with most shoes are cheap afterthoughts. A high-quality insole has a heel cup that provides additional support for your arch and shock absorption, holds your heel in place, and keeps your foot from slipping around in the shoe. Another advantage of the heel cup is that it prevents flattening of the heel pad, a process that subjects your talus bone to unnecessary stress.

Several companies make off-the-shelf insoles specifically designed for outdoor sports. Other companies will custom make insoles for your particular feet. The lightweight back-packer should pay attention to insole weight in order to minimize the shoe weight. Generally, gel and neoprene-based insoles are heavier that those made with closed-cell foams.

Socks

Now that you have a pair of trail-running shoes, it is time to get socks. Differences in sock weight relate largely to thickness and yarn material. If you need to keep your feet warmer in cooler conditions, then you might consider thicker socks. If you are hiking in the summer, your feet will stay cooler with thinner socks. The system of using a thin silk or polypropylene sock under a more traditional wool or nylon/polyester sock has been a popular approach for years but is less so among the lightweight backpacking community. Sock manufacturers continue to improve next-to-skin knitting patterns for better moisture movement and comfort. In any case, there seems to be little need to use a liner sock, which saves a couple ounces on your feet or in your pack. However, an extra pair of liner socks may provide just enough warmth to keep your feet comfortable in cold conditions. And two thin pairs of socks typically dry faster than a single thick pair.

What about the material? It is almost universally accepted that cotton is inappropriate for outdoor performance socks. When cotton gets wet, its fibers lose their resiliency and mat together. Any insulating value and ventilation are lost. Because of this, cotton takes an extremely long time to dry and can thus prove to be dangerous in cold conditions.

This leaves two material categories remaining: synthetic and wool. Synthetics wick water poorly, but they do resist water absorption. This can be a desirable property, especially if you are using a non-waterproof system where you expect your feet to get wet and then want them to dry out quickly. Thinner synthetic socks, such as those made with polyester (e.g., Coolmax), tend to dry very quickly. Synthetics are somewhat effective insulators and lose little of their insulating properties when wet.

Wool socks are warmer than synthetic socks and do a much better job wicking water away from your feet. Wool does take a while to dry when wet, but wool socks generally feel drier to the touch and less clammy than synthetics. In addition, the reaction of water molecules during their adsorption to wool fibers results in heat storage — and release upon evaporation — that makes thin wool socks quite comfortable in warmer temperatures. Most of the wool hiking socks available are actually a blend that includes synthetic yarns as well. When buying wool socks, select those with merino wool fibers. Merino wool fibers are finer, itch far less than traditional "ragg" wools, and wick moisture better.

Trekking poles

Trekking poles have become increasingly popular for backpackers in the last decade. The use of poles is important to lightweight backpackers because they are effective mechanisms for transferring weight and impact stresses from your legs and feet to your arms. Thus, while the use of poles increases the total weight that you are carrying on the trail, distributing the load from your legs to your arms can reduce the amount of work done, achieving benefits similar to those realized when reducing pack weight. In general, lightweight backpackers tend to use poles, but there is a large degree of individual variation due to personal preference. See what works for you.

Poles come in several varieties. The cheapest are homemade walking sticks. To make one, cut down a tree (hardwood) between 1 and 1.5 inches in diameter. Dry out a 4–6 foot section and scrape away the bark for a handle. Lighter poles can be purchased from a variety of manufacturers. They are typically offered in two or three collapsible sections, which add weight and cost but is an essential feature if you are taking them while traveling. There also exists a variety of lightweight poles made with ultralight aluminum alloys and carbon fiber. These weigh as little as 13 ounces per set. A few cottage manufacturers (including Gossamer Gear and Bozeman Mountain Works) have single-piece, carbon-fiber designs that weigh 4–7 ounces a pair.

Snowshoe Backpacking in the Montana Beartooths. Dave Schultz, in the back, is snowshoeing on Northern Lites snowshoes and pulling a pulk instead of carrying a backpack.

Winter Footwear

Winter backpacking presents an array of challenges, not the least of which is selecting footwear. Footwear must change in the winter because they must meet the additional requirement of being warm. Cold feet can be dangerous, quickly leading to frostbite. Keeping feet warm during the day is easy enough so long as you keep moving and wear warm socks. But, once you have stopped for the night, how do you keep your feet warm? If there is no snow, the answer may simply be to add more socks. In cold weather with no snow feet will generally stay dry.

In snow, staying warm requires staying dry and providing insulation. Even when wearing gaiters and waterproof trail-running shoes, my feet are wet by the end of a day of snow hiking. This generally leads to an uncomfortable night with cold feet. Full-grain leather boots tend to fare better in the snow, being both warmer and more likely to keep the water out. Although for multiple days you can still expect them to get soaked. And they have the added inconvenience

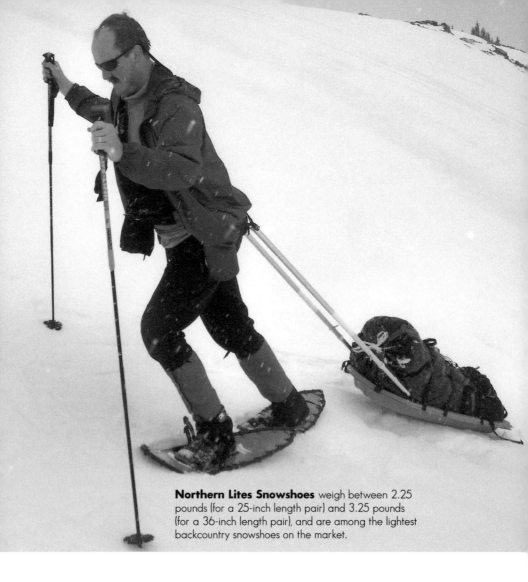

Northern Lites Snowshoes weigh between 2.25 pounds (for a 25-inch length pair) and 3.25 pounds (for a 36-inch length pair), and are among the lightest backcountry snowshoes on the market.

of being very difficult to put on when frozen. Trail-running shoes can be softened by squeezing them to crack up the ice so they will go on your foot.

Several options are available for warming feet in cold weather. The first is the use of vapor-barrier socks. These socks add some warmth, but their real benefit is that they minimize the effects of perspiration on hiking socks and shoe or boot insulation.

A second option involves using insulating footwear for sleeping (e.g., booties with a foam sole and down or high-loft synthetic insulation). Some hikers also keep a dedicated pair of dry wool or fleece socks available for sleeping.

Finding a system that works for you is important and must be done with care. Just because something should work in theory does not mean that it will work on the trail. Try it out in controlled conditions or bring backups along while you are tuning a system.

Finally, in the deep snow of mid winter, backpacking involves the use of some sort of mechanism to keep you on top of the snow (flotation). The option that is the lightest, simplest, and easiest to learn is snowshoeing. Snowshoes are devices that give your foot more surface area, distributing your weight across a larger amount of snow. In theory this enables your foot to stay on top of the snow, rather than sinking. In practice, the efficacy of snowshoes depends very much on the quality of the snow. In powder, you will still sink, but not nearly so deeply. On a hard crust during a spring morning, you may not sink at all. The difference in effort needed to hike in powder versus consolidated snow is immense and needs to be factored into every trip. In any case, snowshoeing is a sport that makes it relatively easy to backpack in the winter, an incredibly rewarding endeavor, although certainly requiring more effort.

The application of lightweight techniques to snowshoeing basically involves finding lightweight snowshoes and a light-and-warm footwear system. There is currently only one company that makes a truly ultralight snowshoe: Northern Lites. Northern Lites offers several models of snowshoes over a wide range of prices and sizes. Mountain Safety Research (MSR) is well known for relatively light snowshoes more suitable for aggressive travel in a mountaineering context. More information on snowshoeing techniques, snowshoe selection criteria, and snowshoe reviews can be found at BackpackingLight.com.

Snowshoeing is greatly facilitated by using either ski or trekking poles with snow baskets. The issues addressed above concerning trekking poles apply even more strongly in the snow. The added balance and ability to get out of holes makes them nearly indispensable. Serious snow hikers, climbers, and skiers tend to favor stiffer, one-piece carbon poles over the three-section aluminum alloy poles favored by trail hikers. One example of such poles are the Bozeman Mountain Works Stix, available as a custom-length pole with EVA foam grips. They have more lateral stiffness than any aluminum pole on the market and weigh less than 6 ounces per pair.

Conclusion

In conclusion, your footwear system is an indispensable part of your lightweight backpacking experience, with weight reductions in footwear having as much or more impact than those in your pack. Perhaps more so than other areas, your final choice of a footwear system will be a personal decision that may change over time. If you approach the selection of footwear as an informed consumer and try the different available options, you will probably have a much better end result than the average backpacker who finds the boot that fits best at the local outfitter and then lives, or suffers, with it until it wears out.

Chapter 2: **Backpacks**

By Ryan Jordan

State of the Market

In a recent survey of 2000–5000 cubic inch internal frame backpacks distributed in the US, the most popular genre among lightweight backpackers, we learned the following with 48 different models from nine major manufacturers.

Average retail price: $207 ± $75
    Low: $85.00
    High: $425.00
Average volume: 3,450 ci ± 900 ci
    Low: 2,080 ci
    High 5,000 ci
Average weight: 4.7 lbs ± 1.4 lbs
    Low: 2.4 lbs
    High: 7.4 lbs
Average volume/weight ratio: 47 ci/oz ± 10 ci/oz
    Low: 32 ci/oz
    High: 91 ci/oz
Average volume/price ratio: 18 ci/$ ± 6 ci/$
    Low: 10 ci/$
    High: 41 ci/$

The ± range indicates one standard deviation. Thus, statistically speaking, approximately two-thirds of the packs surveyed fall into the range of one standard deviation (lower or higher) from the average, leaving the remaining one-third of the packs as higher (one-sixth) or lower (one-sixth) than this range. From this data, we can deduce, quite arbitrarily, that lightweight backpacks are those in the lower one-sixth of the weight class and in the upper one-sixth of the volume/weight class. This implies that unless you are shopping around for a pack that is less than 3.3 pounds and/or has a volume/weight ratio of 57 cubic inches/ounce or higher, then by industry standards you probably aren't looking at a lightweight pack.

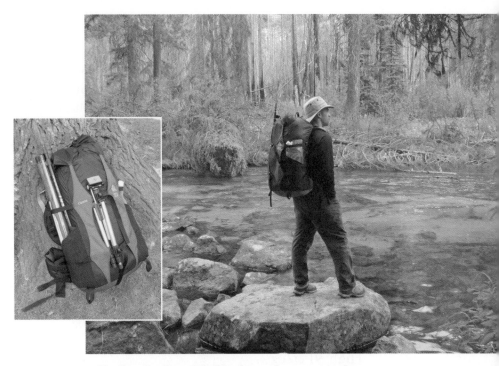

The **Granite Gear Nimbus Ozone** focuses on simplicity combined with a comfortable harness and internal frame, and provides a load carrying capacity of more than 40 pounds for a pack weight of less than 3 pounds.

Not addressed in this analysis is an understanding of the pack's carrying capacity. All packs surveyed feature an internal frame with at least one vertical frame stay. Most, if not all, of these types of packs are capable of carrying 25 or more pounds, which is a typical weight for the lightweight backpacker venturing out for a two- to five-day backpacking trip. However, if your particular lightweight backpacking application requires a higher weight (e.g., to carry a substantial amount of food for a few weeks without resupply), then you might also consider packs with a slightly lower volume/weight ratio. Those can be indicative of more substantial frames designed for heavier loads.

The ideal parameter that addresses carrying capacity is the ratio of carrying capacity (in pounds) to the weight of the empty pack. However, since carrying capacity is such a subjective parameter that depends on many factors, not the least of which is an individual's tolerance for discomfort, then trying to identify such a parameter would be a futile exercise. Further, it highlights the inappropriateness of including in our survey frameless packs, which tend to have higher volume/weight ratios than packs with internal frames.

Such a standard (volume/weight ratio) provides a useful baseline for evaluating packs for lightweight backpacking and for comparing different products. However, it should only serve as a baseline. You should recognize several important factors that contribute to a pack-buying decision, including design basics, such as frame and packbag construction. In addition, in order get the most out of a lightweight pack, you must have a fundamental understanding of how to use it—e.g., pack it and carry it. The focus of this chapter is to offer you a foundation of knowledge that will allow you to properly select, and use to its maximum efficiency, a lightweight pack.

Biomechanics of Backpacking

We begin with a discussion of biomechanics, the study of the forces of muscles and gravity on the skeletal structure.

Wilderness walking is a process that can be broken down into three primary directions of movement:

- Forward — and, God forbid, backward
- Upward — and downward
- To one side — and back again

Forward progress is usually the primary long-term goal of any backpacker and is the direction with which we concern ourselves most when hiking on a flat, easy trail. When forward direction dominates our walking movements (requiring little upward thrust beyond that of lifting our feet), we are using primarily our lower back and leg muscles for propulsion and our hip and leg joint systems to absorb the shock of impact with each step, which is quite minor. Consequently, while the advantages of a light load are significant over long distances, the short-term effects induced by carrying a heavy load on flat terrain are not particularly troublesome.

In contrast to forward movement, upward movement (hill climbing) places a tremendous demand on the body's musculature — in particular, the muscles of the lower back, quadriceps, and calves. The motion of step climbing causes the body's center of gravity to shift forward. Consequently, climbing with a pack that is loaded such that its center of gravity is high in the packbag will induce a *moment arm* (the perpendicular distance between the body's center of gravity and that of the pack) that will tend to pull a hiker backward while climbing. Even minor imbalances, while not being particularly noticeable initially, will eventually exact their toll on the body. The classic symptom is mild to severe lower back pain while hiking, resulting from the inability of weak back muscles to stabilize abdominal muscles that are working overtime to keep the body in balance. Minor load imbalances can result in major discomfort after hiking a fifteen- or twenty-mile day.

Downhill hiking deemphasizes the musculature and places extreme stress on the body's bones, joints, and cartilage structures, which serve to dampen the impact of downward forces resulting from gravity. Pack weight can have a significant impact on comfort when hiking downhill. Heavy loads induce massive impact forces on relatively small shock absorption areas—including the spine, hip, knee, and ankle.

Perhaps the least understood of the biomechanical movements during backpacking is that of *lateral* (sideways) motion that occurs when hiking on uneven terrain—e.g., cross country travel or very rocky trails. In short, significant lateral motion occurs when one foot placement is lower, or higher, than the other in a motion that might be analogous to climbing a hill with sideways shuffling steps. For a foot placement that occurs lower than the other, the same principles that apply to downhill load carrying and balance apply—the bones and joints bear the brunt of the load. However, the ligaments and tendons now play a much more significant role than in downhill-forward hiking because of the unusual requirements for lateral stabilization of the joints in response to torque on these joints exerted by a momentarily imbalanced load. For a foot placement that occurs higher than the other, the same principles for uphill load carrying and balance apply: The musculature is employed for progress. Again, the ligaments and tendons of the hips, knees, and ankles are taxed in order to stabilize the bone structure as lateral movement occurs, though not as seriously as in a downward foot placement.

Biomechanical Basis for Lightweight Backpacking

In summary, this discussion highlights the important biomechanical processes involved in backpacking:

- IMPACT FORCES absorbed by bones, joints, and cartilage during downward movement—a function of the pack's weight
- JOINT STABILIZATION forces borne by tendons and ligaments during upward, downward, and lateral movement—a function of torque exerted by the pack
- GRAVITY FORCES counteracted by muscle contraction for upward movement—a function of the pack's weight

The force due to gravity, that is, the force that must be overcome by muscles for hill climbing, or the force that must be absorbed by bone and joint shock while downhill hiking, is defined by the mathematical relationship

$F = mg$, where . . .
   m = the mass of the object — the sum total of a person's weight plus their pack weight in kilograms
   g = acceleration due to gravity (e.g., 9.8 m/s2)

Thus, the benefits of a light pack are readily apparent. For hiking on a treadmill with no incline, a 75-kilogram person that typically carries a 25-kilogram pack (100 kilogram total) might expend 10 percent less energy (energy is proportional to work = force · distance walked) if they carried a 15-kilogram pack (90 kilogram total). For a 40 percent reduction in pack weight (25–15 kilograms), this difference does not seem large. However, backpacking is not appropriately characterized by perfectly flat terrain. The inappropriate assumption here is that the center of gravity of the body is not changed by the presence of a loaded pack that causes a torque that must be countered by the body. Finally, this 10 percent savings in work assumes that the relationship between pack weight reduction and effort expended is linear. And as the world's elite adventure racers, alpinists, and ultrarunners will tell you, that relationship is simply not true.

Consider this simple test. Before going to bed, do as many pushups in a row as you can. On the next night, add a pack with 10 pounds of weight and do the same exercise. On each subsequent night, add 5 pounds of weight to the pack and repeat the exercise until you can no longer complete more than 5 pushups.

The results will show that the number of pushups (and energy expenditure on a trek) is not a linear function of pack weight, or even pack weight plus body weight. In fact, it will be clear that at loads greater than X percent of your body weight performance decreases dramatically. Hopefully, this exercise illustrates the importance of reducing pack weight in order to

1. Expend less energy
2. Meet more physically demanding challenges, such as longer distances and steeper trails

This exercise emphasizes the downward force of gravity that exerts itself at the center of gravity of both the pack and the body. The horizontal distance between these two distances is called the *moment arm*. In turn, the force exerted on the body's musculature to remain stable by that moment arm, which I refer to as *pack torque* (T), is defined as the rotational force exerted by the pack on the body

$T = Fr$, where . . .
  r = the moment arm length

Thus, when you recognize that torque is a function of pack weight and not of body weight, the benefits of carrying a light pack are directly proportional to the pack weight. This is in contrast to pure gravity, which is a function of body weight plus pack weight. Thus, the benefits of lightweight backpacking increase in importance as the difficulty of terrain increases.

For example, consider a pack weighing 25 kilograms with its center of gravity located approximately 25 centimeters behind that of the body. The resulting pack torque in the downward direction (gravity) is 625 kilogram-centimeters, counteracted primarily by the musculature of the back and shoulders while walking. Now, consider the pack torque of a 15-kilogram pack with the same center of gravity: 375 kilogram-centimeters, which results in a full 40 percent decrease in strain on the musculature responsible for counteracting this torque. If you allow the lighter load to occupy a lower pack volume (thinner pack) with a center of gravity located only 15 centimeters from that of the body, it results in a pack torque of 225 kilogram-centimeters. A 64 percent reduction in muscle stress (torque) for only a 40 percent reduction in pack weight!

The discussion of pack torque also highlights the importance of proper packing techniques, which will be addressed later in the chapter.

Suspension Anatomy

One of the most contested debates among lightweight backpackers is whether or not the backpack should have a frame, either external or internal. Obviously, for heavier loads greater than 30 pounds, a frame facilitates load carrying. However, does a frame offer benefits for lighter loads? We'll start by providing a basic understanding of the anatomy of a typical suspension system.

Pack torque described. A 25 kg pack with its center of gravity located approximately 25 cm behind the body's center of gravity **(left image)** exerts a downward pack torque of 625 kg-cm. Reduce the packweight by 40% to 15 kg and simultaneously bringing the center of gravity of the pack closer to the body by 10 cm **(right image)** and a pack torque of 225 kg-cm results—a 64% reduction in torque on the body's musculature!

SHOULDER STRAPS

The most fundamental component of the suspension system is the shoulder strap assembly. Shoulder straps should serve one primary purpose only: to keep the center of gravity of the pack as close as possible to that of the body. The shoulder straps do have some load-carrying ability, but 10–15 pounds is usually the maximum comfort range. The body's collarbone structure does not provide a particularly effective load-bearing surface, due to its small surface area for weight distribution. Consequently, packs lacking a hip belt are usually insufficient for carrying loads of more than about 15 pounds. Although, some ultralight backpackers believe that such simple systems are adequate for carrying 20 pounds of weight over a short distance (e.g., at the beginning of a hike lasting several days).

HIP BELT

Because the pelvis offers a larger surface area and bone structure for distributing a load than the collarbone, the hips are much more capable than the shoulders for load bearing. Consequently, the hip belt's key design feature should be a large surface area for weight distribution when in contact with the pelvic bone structure. However, most commercial hip belts are too narrow for effective weight distribution. Further, these hip belts are manufactured with technologies that actually reduce their load distribution effectiveness, including relatively inflexible molded polyethylene sheets that are unable to adapt to the wide range of hip shapes and sizes of prospective buyers. Manufacturers will argue that carrying massive loads of 50–70 pounds require stiff belts to prevent their collapse under the load. If you believe this false claim, I suggest that you review packs manufactured by Dan McHale in Seattle, Washington. Dan builds expedition backpacks suitable for loads up to 100 or more pounds with a nice, wide belt that uses no stiffeners in its construction. Manufacturers of products targeting lightweight backpackers would do well to design hip belts with less padding, more width, and more flexibility, so that the surface area in contact between the hips and the belt is maximized.

FRAME: LOAD TRANSFER

Most hikers (and manufacturers) believe that the purpose of a frame is to transfer the weight of the load in part or whole from the shoulders to the body's iliac crest via the pack's hip belt. For light loads, such weight transfer can be accomplished simply by effectively packing a tight load into the packbag, resulting in some inherent stiffness that does not collapse when weight is transferred to the hip belt.

For most soft backpacking loads packed reasonably tight in a frameless pack, one can achieve sufficient load transfer capability with loads of up to about 20 pounds. The looser the load is packed, the less weight can be effectively transferred. The addition of foam stiffeners, including foam back pads, or "bivy pads" commonly found in climbing backpacks, can increase load transfer capability by a few pounds. To achieve further load transfer ability in a frameless pack, one can fold a sleeping pad (e.g., in quarters) and lay it inside the pack against the back, so that its total thickness is an inch or more. This trick can also be used with self-inflating air/foam-core pads by inflating the pad after the pack has been loaded. To achieve even more load transfer ability with a sleeping pad, lightweight backpackers commonly roll the pad into a cylinder and then pack the gear inside the core of the cylinder. It is usually accepted that such techniques are sufficient for loads in the 20–25 pound range. Many find comfort at loads up to 30, and less commonly, up to 35 pounds.

FRAME: LOAD STABILIZATION

So if a frameless pack, using creative packing techniques and the judicious application of a sleeping pad, can effectively carry 25–35 pounds in comfort, then should a pack with a frame be considered at all?

It can be argued that the addition of a very light internal frame with enough stiffness to allow complete load transfer between shoulders and hips aids tremendously in load stabilization, where load stabilization is defined as the ability of the frame to prevent the load from shifting in any direction in response to rapid movements.

A good illustration of a frame's ability to stabilize a load can be made using any internal frame pack by comparing the pack's load stability with and without its frame stays. Load it to three-fourths capacity with 25–35 pounds, the volume that might occur toward the middle and end of a long backpacking trip and after much of the food has been consumed. Then quickly climb a flight of stairs with a shuffling side step, accentuating the unbalanced movements encountered during hiking on rough terrain, and notice how the presence of the frame maintains the packbag shape and prevents it from working against you by keeping its center of gravity close to the same location.

The biggest disadvantage to a frameless pack packed with a significant amount of weight and below its volume capacity is that the contents shift while hiking

Ptarmigan showing pad for frame support: The 32-ounce Bozeman Mountain Works Ptarmigan ultralight alpine climbing pack uses a folded bivy pad encased in a mesh sleeve on the outside of the pack's back panel to provide longitudinal stiffness, frame support, padding, and insulation.

rough terrain. Consequently, the location of the pack's center of gravity shifts with each step and the process of load stabilization requires effort (energy) from your body to correct the imbalance. Viewed from the context of a single step, this effect is undoubtedly quite minor. But considering that the average hiker takes around 2,000 steps per mile of trail, and as much as 20,000 (10 miles) or even 60,000 steps (30 miles) in a single day, such miniscule effects can exact their toll on the body by the end of a good day's walk. The addition of a frame that can potentially prevent movement of a 15-kilogram pack's center of gravity by only one centimeter can save up to 15 kilogram-centimeters of pack torque with each step. If one were to take 40,000 steps over the course of the day, the cumulative force saved by the body's musculature, bone, and joint system would be 6000 kilogram-meters, the same amount of force required to stabilize a 6000-kilogram weight (medium duty semi truck) concentrated on a plank held out 1 meter from the body.

FRAME-STAY CHARACTERISTICS

The stiffness of the frame is an important consideration. A stiff frame-stay material (e.g., a carbon fiber tube) provides plenty of support for both load transfer and load stabilization but lacks shock absorption. That transmits greater impact forces to your hips from a bouncing load, and is accentuated when descending a steep hill. On the other hand, a frame stay resembling a limp noodle (e.g., Delrin) fails to provide enough support for load transfer, and provides so much shock absorption that the frame collapses with each step. Your pack loses the ability to stabilize the load, thus requiring extra effort from your body to counteract a shifting center of gravity.

Aluminum is the most popular type of frame stay material, with the 7075-T6 grade considered to be of the highest quality due to its "springiness" and resistance to permanent deformation under load. Both characteristics contribute to load stabilization and maintaining a fixed location for the pack's center of gravity. Frames that are less stiff than aluminum do not afford any particular advantages. A carbon fiber frame stay (e.g., usually tubing approximately 3/16" in diameter), although very stiff, affords a unique advantage. A set of carbon fiber frame stays with the same load transfer ability as 7075-T6 aluminum can be as much as 600 percent lighter. It is not uncommon to have a set of carbon fiber rods weighing near 1 ounce. However, because of the stiffness of carbon fiber, they are best used in packs that won't be housing loads greater than about 15–20 percent of one's body weight.

Factors other than frame material that affect the stiffness of the frame stay include both its cross-sectional shape (tubing cylinders are more stiff than rods or bars) and its dimensions (shorter = more stiff; thicker = more stiff; wider = more stiff).

Suspension Gimmicks

A well-integrated shoulder strap, hip belt, and frame-stay system are the only requirements for a backpack suitable for lightweight backpacking with loads less than 40 pounds. Unfortunately, too many pack manufacturers have added complexity (and weight) to suspension systems, including "load lifter" straps, adjustable straps that attach the top of the frame to the shoulder strap crest. And "hip stabilizer" straps, adjustable straps that attach to the bottom of the frame or bottom corner of the pack to the location on the iliac crest of the hip belt. Both of these features are included by mass market manufacturers primarily to expand the range of fit for a given harness. But they also sell the consumer false claims that they will provide increased stabilization or comfort. The ideal pack should have a harness (shoulder strap and hip belt) that fits the consumer's body dimensions perfectly. In reality, however, such precise fitting is seldom available in mass market packs and requires that the consumer seek a custom-built back.

In a recent series of suspension performance research studies conducted by BackpackingLight.com, the product review staff discovered that the most important characteristics that contributed to load stabilization were the width of the hip belt and extent to which the hip belt, shoulder straps, and frame were integrated. Load-lifter straps and hip-stabilizer straps played little role in load stability and served only to fine tune sizing. More recently, we've discovered that cinching down hip-stabilizer straps to secure the load into the lumbar region inhibits your body's natural range of motion and increases spinal fatigue over the course of a long day of walking

Ultralight Frameless Backpacks

Although the preceding discussion focuses on justifying the use of a load-control system for even lightweight pack loads, there are situations when frameless, ultralight packs are useful. They offer several advantages.

1. They conform softly to the contours of your back, and thus, may be more appropriate for those with bone structure defects or spinal problems.

2. They are compressible and make a great companion for traveling or to use as a summit/day hiking pack in the context of spending several days at a base camp.

3. For less strenuous hiking, the loss in load transfer efficiency may be acceptable to those who simply want to carry gear that is as light and as simple as possible.

Dealing with Variable Volume Loads

During a multi-day backpacking trek, the volume of the pack contents changes considerably, due primarily to food consumption. There are two approaches to dealing with this. The first relies on the use of an extension collar to the main packbag that allows for extra volume to ride well above the crests of the shoulders during the beginning of a trek. Unfortunately, a full extension collar's height can cause serious instability on rough terrain.

The alternative approach is the use of a compression system (straps, cord, etc.), used toward the end of a trek for stabilizing under-capacity loads by compressing the pack's volume and center of gravity toward the back.

The McHale Subpop cord compression system (shown here on a McHale Summit Pack) uses a different means of stabilizing an under-volume load: non-stretch cord laced around the packbag. This is the lightest and most effective load compression system we've tried, with the potential to evenly compress the load rather than force a misshaped pack with point compression straps. The weight of the cordage on this pack is less than one ounce.

Packbag Size

Choosing the size of a pack seems to be one of the most personal issues in pack selection. The argument for large-volume packs is that insulating clothing and sleeping bags have plenty of room to loft, since those can be damaged by compression. And there is enough volume to accommodate all of one's gear without strapping it to the outside of the packbag. The primary disadvantage to large packs is that for under-capacity loads, they can make it difficult to stabilize the center of gravity without an effective compression system. Further, a large load by its very nature results in a center of gravity that is farther from the body's center of gravity. The result is a pack that requires more energy for the body to stabilize—and more strain on the body's musculature. Contrary to popular belief, larger packs are not significantly heavier than their smaller counterparts. Much of the weight is found in the suspension system and harness, which is not necessarily dependent on pack volume.

The main disadvantage of a small pack may be the inability to accommodate all of one's equipment for a particular trek, requiring the use of extension collars and external attachment points. In turn, these destabilize the load and can make for obstructive travel in brushy or mountainous terrain.

Thus, a good rule of thumb for pack sizing is this: Use a pack that is just large enough to accommodate all of your equipment and supplies for a trek, and make sure it has an effective compression system for stabilizing the load as food and other supplies are consumed during the trek. Although some accomplished ultralight backpackers have found a 30-liter pack suitable for weekend trips, the most popular packs for lightweight backpacking seem to fall in the 40–45 liter range for weekend hikes and 55–65 liters for multi-day trekking.

Packbag Fabric

The lighter packbag fabrics range from ultralight spinnaker cloth 0.8 ounce/yard^2 (e.g., Gossamer Gear G5, a 7-oz pack with 65L of volume) to 8-ounces/yard^2 ballistic nylon that typically results in an internal frame pack weight of about 4–5 pounds for a 65-liter pack. The tradeoff with weight is fabric durability (primarily abrasion resistance). When selecting a pack fabric, consideration should be given to the type of terrain you expect and how many miles you want the pack to serve you. More durable fabrics are more appropriate for bushwhacking and rock climbing. Greater durability equals longer pack life. Longer pack life equals greater return on investment.

Other Features

A single, one-compartment packbag with a harness provides the basis for any pack. Compression systems and extension collars allow you to adjust pack volume in response to changing load volumes. External pockets, especially top and side pockets, disrupt the load stabilization and pack profile during climbing or bushwhacking. However, the external pockets may be worth their weight for the ability to help you remain organized and allow quick and easy access to some supplies without opening the main packbag, particularly in inclement weather. The addition of any other features should be examined carefully, especially the presence of zippers. They are heavy, prone to failure, and allow points of entry for rainwater.

Loading the Pack

Ideally, a pack should be loaded so that its center of gravity relative to the body's center of gravity is in a location appropriate to the terrain. For example, the pack's center of gravity for downhill hiking should be in the upper back to improve the ability for the bones and joints to absorb the impact from gravity forces on the pack. For uphill hiking, the pack's center of gravity should be as close as possible to the body's center of gravity (usually the lower back) to minimize rotational motion due to pack torque and, thus, decrease stress on back and shoulder muscles.

However, the backpacker usually encounters many different types of terrain and grades of steepness throughout the day. It would be impractical to repack the pack when the terrain or grade changes. A realistic compromise is to pack gear in the packbag such that the pack's center of gravity is located a little higher than that of the body's but as close to the back as possible.

A good approach is to pack the sleeping bag (low-density and provides lumbar cushioning) in the bottom of the pack, the food on top of it (high-density and usually controls the pack's center of gravity), followed

The ideal location for the center of gravity for a pack **(square)** is a little higher than that of the body's **(circle)** but as close to the back as possible.

by the rest of the gear, with heavier items close to your back and lighter items away from your back.

As one decreases the total weight of the load, less emphasis needs to be placed on packing with the center of gravity location in mind. Greater emphasis can be placed on packing with convenience in mind. In such a case, one can pack contents in the order that they are needed throughout the day, rather than worry at all about their relative densities. Such is a significant freedom associated with lightweight backpacking.

Rain Protection

There is no such thing as an ultralight backpack that is also waterproof. A truly waterproof pack is made with heavier materials, such as polyurethane-coated vinyl or PVC cloth with welded seams and a dry bag closure. Those features also result in a pack that is a far cry from ultralight.

There are two approaches to protecting your pack from the rain: pack cover or pack liner. Waterproof pack covers offer few advantages over pack liners. In particular, they are subject to failure because they are exposed to abrasion, tearing, and puncture from brush and rocks. They also limit access to pack contents housed in either external pockets or the main packbag. Finally, they fail to protect the pack contents at the location where the packbag is often the wettest: down your back.

Pack liners, on the other hand, afford many advantages. They are protected from external abrasion. They do not interfere with access to pack contents. And they completely enclose the contents within the packbag. Pack liners can be made with waterproof-coated nylon cloth. Fully sealed seams, either factory-taped or sealed by hand with a polyurethane or silicone-based compound, provide additional moisture protection. Sewn waterproof nylon liners are the most durable and elegant type, with silicone-coated nylon (1.4 oz/yd^2) liners providing adequate protection for a 65-liter pack at a scant 4 ounces in weight. There is an alternative solution that is cheaper, lighter, and disposable. A trash compactor bag typically weighs less than 3–4 ounces.

The small fraction of the ultralight hiking community who wear ponchos as opposed to jackets claim that system works the best for keeping a pack dry. Having used a poncho as my primary raingear and shelter for several hundred nights of backpacking in recent years, I find it hard to argue. A poncho, unlike a pack cover, effectively covers the entire pack and body, offering no chance for water to find its way into or onto the packbag.

The Pack as Insulation

When selecting both the clothing and sleep system, the lightweight backpacker should not forget the value of a backpack. Because a pack provides tremendous insulation for the back, one should factor it into their clothing system as insulation while hiking in cold weather.

In addition, the pack can be used as ground insulation for the lightweight backpacker's bed, especially if it has a built-in foam pad as its back pad. Lightweight backpackers commonly use two-thirds- or even half-length sleeping pads for torso insulation, using the pack as insulation for the lower legs and feet.

Conclusion

The pack can be one of the most expensive purchases by a lightweight backpacker. It's not uncommon for a 50-liter pack weighing less than 3 pounds to retail for more than $300. Such packs, of a suitable design, are probably the most appropriate for pushing the limits of lightweight backpacking with heavier loads over longer distances.

Has the ultralight backpacker really "arrived" when his pack has become his simplest piece of equipment — e.g., a homemade bag with shoulder straps sewn using $25 worth of materials on a winter weekend? Or is the more experienced ultralighter one who can take a three-pound internal frame pack and carry a load for 500 continuous miles?

Consider that Grandma Gatewood hiked the 2,100 mile Appalachian Trail using a natural fiber cloth gunny sack slung over her shoulder. John Muir often traveled for days in the Sierras with nothing more than a small leather satchel. Even today, wilderness survival enthusiasts travel uncanny distances without packs at all, relying solely on their ability to get by with minimal supplies carried only in a tiny fanny pack or their pockets.

Chapter 3: **Pack Weight**

By George Cole

Backpackers walk. Some backpackers walk a lot. Along with carrying our houses on our backs, walking is what defines us. Most of us do it without thinking about it, at least until sore knees or blisters draw our attention.

However, walking is not a simple activity. It requires a complex series of interactions between most of the bones, muscles, tendons, and joints of the trunk and lower limbs. These interactions result in relocations of body mass that sequentially and repetitively destabilize and restabilize the body's axial balance while realigning its structural support. Properly coordinated by the nervous system, the net effect of these interactions is to maintain the body's upright posture while moving it forward in space.

Interactions are both *interdependent* — each interaction is dependent on others — and *extradependent* — each interaction varies in response to the external conditions that exist at the moment the interaction occurs. For backpackers, important external conditions are the slope of the walking surface, surface traction and regularity, wind speed, pack weight, and the relationship of these conditions to each other and to the direction of travel. While we can accommodate various combinations of moderate conditions, an extreme of any one condition can make it impossible to successfully complete a crucial interaction. At that point, we either stop walking or we fall.

As backpackers we prepare for extremes of terrain, weather, and surface, and we plan our routes in order to reduce the probability of encountering those extremes. However, we have no direct control over them. On the other hand, we can control how much weight we carry in our backpacks.

The Importance of the Body's Center of Gravity

The body's center of gravity is located at the point where the body's *mass* (weight) is balanced in three dimensions. In other words, the center of gravity is located at the point where the mass above the point is equal to the mass below the point, the mass in front of the point is equal to the mass behind the point, and the mass to one side of the point is equal to the mass on its opposite side. When standing still, unclothed, and without a pack, that point is on the *axis* (mid-line) of the trunk and is roughly in line with the hip joints.

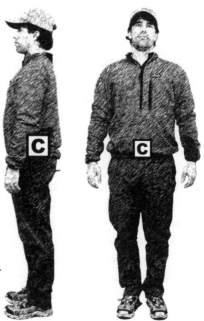

Location of the center of gravity of a hiker not wearing a pack.

In the context of backpacking, walking can be thought of as controlled falling. To begin walking we push off with one foot while slightly leaning forward, moving our center of gravity forward of its original base of support. Then, in order to avoid falling, we lift the other foot and swing it forward, seeking a new base of support. If we can plant the leading foot and successfully establish a new base of support, we then pivot the leg above it under a now moving center of gravity. At the same time we swing the other foot forward into a position where it, in turn, can provide a new base of support.

To continue walking we repeatedly stride underneath a moving center of gravity, first with one leg and then the other. Throughout a *stride* (gait cycle), the center of gravity does not travel far from the horizontal plane of the hip joints, although it does move side to side—first over one leg and then the other—as each leg becomes the body's primary supporting member. It also rises about two inches above the walking surface as each leg pivots underneath it.

The speed with which the center of gravity moves forward in space also varies during the gait cycle. When pushing off at the beginning of a stride we force the center of gravity to speed up, and when planting the other foot we force it to slow down. The center of gravity attains its greatest speed immediately before we plant the leading foot.

Weight carried in a backpack has two major effects on the center of gravity. First, assuming that the pack is firmly affixed to the back and that the pack load is balanced from side to side, the center of gravity will move upward and to the rear relative to its "unloaded" position. How much the center of gravity moves upward and to the rear will depend upon the weight of the load and its top-to-bottom and front-to-back distribution in the pack.

Comparison of the location of the center of gravity in a hiker without **(square)** and with **(circle)** a backpack. Wearing a pack shifts the center of gravity upward and backward, the extent of which depends on the weight of the pack and how it is loaded.

Second, because pack weight increases the total weight of the body and all that the body is carrying (e.g., the *system weight*, commonly known as the "full skin-out weight") it also increases the momentum of the body mass, expressed through the center of gravity. The increase in momentum is directly proportional to the increase in system weight. An increase in pack weight—and momentum—has profound implications on backpacking because it is directly proportional to the forces required to be exerted by your joints, bone, and musculature to decelerate your body's movements as you hike.[1] Important decelerations that every hiker is familiar with include catching a fall if one foot slides off the trail, or the constant pounding that occurs while hiking down a steep incline.

As indicated above, walking is the act of propelling our center of gravity forward. So in order to walk, backpackers must compensate for the *rearward* shift in the center of gravity caused by the weight of the pack. We do so simply by leaning forward from the waist. When leaning forward we pivot the trunk around our hip joints so that the shift in the location of the center of gravity associated with a slight to moderate forward lean (e.g., 0–45 degrees) is horizontal. Since "normal" walking without a pack requires a small amount of forward lean at the beginning of each stride, this act of adjustment is familiar and easily accommodated.

A moderate forward lean induces a horizontal shift in the center of gravity, which increases stability. The center of gravity shifts from an upright position (**square**) to a leaning position (**circle**) by moving down and forward in response to leaning.

However, backpackers are unable to make adjustments that accommodate the *upward* shift in the center of gravity. While leaning far enough forward eventually lowers the center of gravity (e.g., when the angle of the trunk is between 45–90 degrees), the usefulness of that adjustment is limited by how far we can lean without doing a face plant or making forward progress impossible. Thus, conventional thinking has taught us that the best way to make adjustments for our system center of gravity in the vertical dimension is by redistributing the load in our pack.

Redistributing the pack load is not a complete solution. While it is more energy efficient to carry heavier items close to the body, making changes in vertical load distribution offers mixed results.

If heavy items are carried high in the pack, then we won't need to lean forward as much to adjust for the rearward shift in the center of gravity (better posture for walking). However, the upward shift in the system center of gravity will be greater, resulting in more energy expended in order to maintain balance. Conversely, if heavy items are carried low in the pack, then the upward shift in the center of gravity will be less (better balance), but more lean will be required to adjust for its rearward shift (poorer posture for walking).

Because of these contradictory effects, there is always a sacrifice — optimize walking posture (high center of gravity) or improve load balance (low center of gravity). Thus, perhaps the best way to minimize the effects of both excessive forward lean and poor balance is to minimize the effects of gravity on the system. In other words, reduce pack weight.

That is not to say that individuals cannot accommodate the combined effects of a "heavier" center of gravity to an amazing extent. Foot soldiers and Sherpa porters regularly carry as much as 100 percent of their body weight in their packs. In many cultures, men and women alike walk with staggering loads balanced on their heads. Even inexperienced backpackers can make instantaneous changes in their posture and gait and set out with sixty pound packs. And, we've all encountered that hearty mountaineer laboring up the side of a peak with as much as eighty pounds on his or her back.

These feats are made possible by the fact that human beings are not born with walking skill. We don't even try for the first nine months or so. Then we spend the next six to eight years learning and practicing the basics while accommodating our particular physiological limitations and the constraints of our environments. Consequently, we are quite used to learning to accommodate (terrain, physiology, loads) in the act of walking.

However, learning is not the only issue in carrying heavy loads. For porters and foot soldiers it is a job requirement. For those amazing individuals who can carry forty pounds or more of food and water on their heads, it is a matter of survival. As a result, all of those individuals spend a good deal of time doing it. Over time they condition their bodies to its demands. Their muscles and bones adapt to the movements, they get stronger, and their coordination and dynamic sense of balance improves.

On the other hand, recreational backpackers carry weight on their backs for fun. Most do it too infrequently to benefit from any sort of meaningful, long-term conditioning effects. Therefore, backpackers who carry heavy loads are more likely to suffer from a variety of immediate and long-term problems.

Problems Carrying Heavy Packs

As any veteran of carrying a heavy pack can attest, maintaining balance (resisting falling) is the most immediate problem. A higher center of gravity makes balancing more difficult. When standing still, we can compensate for a higher center of gravity by moving our feet apart for a broader base of support. But walking requires a constantly changing and limited base of support. We tend to stand and walk with our feet closer together. In a "single-stance phase," or at the point at which one foot bears 100 percent of the system weight and the other foot moves forward, the base of support can be as small as the ball and toes of a single foot.

The single-stance phase of the gait cycle is that point where 100% of the weight of the hiker + pack is supported by a single foot (and sometimes, only the ball or heel of that foot). This is the point in the gait cycle where the center of gravity is the most difficult to control because it is at a point of maximum acceleration or deceleration.

Not only is more force needed to get a heavier center of gravity moving, more force is needed to slow it down. While walking, we can either

- Walk in a controlled fashion so that we can easily decelerate the forward motion of the center of gravity with each foot plant (e.g., hiking down a steep incline)
- Walk too fast, such that the center of gravity moves outside of its base of support and we fall

In addition to accelerating and decelerating the forward motion of the center of gravity, we must also accelerate and decelerate the side-to-side motion of the center of gravity as it moves over the supporting leg during each stride — or outside of the base of support, as is common on uneven terrain. Otherwise, it moves beyond its base of support far enough that we are unable to decelerate it. Again, we fall.

Forcing muscles to repeatedly overcome the momentum of the center of gravity results in muscle fatigue. Muscle fatigue results in a loss of muscle strength. And a loss of muscle strength results in a loss of control over a moving center of gravity. That is why we are more likely to fall at the end of a long day. And despite how well conditioned we are, a heavier center of gravity results in greater muscle fatigue.

Finally, when walking on level ground we have only a fraction of a second in the course of each stride to change our minds about where we want to plant our leading foot. Our ability to do so depends largely on being able to alter the trajectory of the center of gravity as it descends from its peak in the gait cycle. The heavier a pack weighs, the greater the momentum that its center of gravity exerts, and greater is both the force and the time required to alter its trajectory. Since backpackers regularly seek out places where the surface is irregular and the traction poor, even a tiny delay in response time can result in an insecure foot plant. Down we go. This particular problem is complicated by the fact that backpackers who carry heavy loads often wear heavy boots.

A heavy boot greatly increases the momentum of the leading foot and, therefore, increases the time it takes to change either its trajectory or its orientation.

On an ascending slope, the descent of the center of gravity from its peak in the gait cycle is shortened. Therefore, if we're maintaining our pace, we have marginally less time to change our minds about where our heel should strike the ground. However, because the center of gravity has had less time to gather speed as it falls from its peak in the gait cycle, and because we usually walk slower when going uphill, planting the leading foot is usually less problematic while walking uphill than when on level ground.

A downhill slope lengthens the descent of the center of gravity from its peak in the gait cycle. While this does give us marginally more time to change where and how we plant the leading foot, it also gives the center of gravity time to gather speed. Because most backpackers are not accustomed to slowing a heavier center of gravity as it falls, it is likely that it will be moving faster when the leading foot strikes the ground. High-school physics teaches us that force equals weight multiplied by acceleration. So the force with which the leading foot strikes the ground will be greater than if only the "weight" of the center of gravity increases. In fact, when stepping off a log or a rock, this force may be equal to six or seven times the weight of you and your pack. Therefore, an insecure foot plant, one that allows the ground reaction force to be translated into a sliding motion, is much more likely to result in a fall, especially on an irregular or slippery surface.

Carrying heavy loads can have other immediate and long-term implications: joint or musculature failure. A muscle that is not strong enough to overcome the momentum of the center of gravity can tear. As indicated above, a fatigued muscle loses strength. More seriously, an overstretched tendon will pull loose from its attachment point on a bone. A bone forced beyond its elastic bending point will break. And a misaligned joint subjected to too much pressure will shear. Even an aligned joint subjected to excessive pressure will fail from a compression fracture or rupture of its shock-absorbing pad of cartilage.

It would be bad enough if an increase in pack weight increased the probability that these problems would occur in a simple linear fashion, but the stress on muscles, tendons, bones, and joints increases at an escalating rate as the angle of a joint gets more acute. In order to better absorb the shock of impact when the leading foot strikes the ground, it is natural to have the knee slightly bent at impact, letting the thigh muscles act as shock absorbers. When walking on level ground without a pack a normal knee joint is bent about two degrees at the moment of impact. A knee joint bent at two degrees is subjected to a compressive force that is equal to about half the weight of the body.[2] Following impact, the joint continues to bend another 13 degrees while slowing the descent of the center of gravity to its lowest point in the gait cycle. A knee joint bent at 15 degrees is subjected to a compressive force that is equal to about 1.5 times the weight of the body.

Now add the weight of the pack. It will take longer to slow the momentum of the center of gravity as it descends to its lowest point in the gait cycle. The knee will be forced to bend more after impact. The heavier the pack, the more the knee will be forced to bend. If the angle of the knee reaches 20 degrees, it will be subjected to a compressive force of about twice the system weight (body + pack). And that's just while walking on level ground.

Step up on a rock or log or step down off a ledge. It is not unusual to bend the knee 90 degrees or more. A knee bent at 90 degrees will be subjected to a compressive force equal to three to four times the system weight. A knee bent at more than 90 degrees will result in a force that can reach six to eight times the system weight. Multiply that by the weight of you, your clothing, and your fully loaded pack and think about descending a steep and rocky trail. Even just a few extra pounds of pack weight can have a dramatic effect on the force that is translated to your joints.

Fortunately, however, the most common weight-induced injury is neither severe nor life threatening, just painful and tedious to remedy: blisters. Unconditioned skin that is forced to move against a surface while under pressure will eventually blister, especially when moist. All backpackers subject the skin on the foot sole, edge, and between their toes to greater pressure than normal. The heavier the pack, the greater the pressure. Since most backpackers who carry heavy loads also wear hot, heavy boots that aren't properly fitted or broken in, the risk of getting a blister is high. And how about those black toenails that result from the constant pounding of your toes in the footbox of your boot? What a relief when they finally fall off!

Choice of Footwear

While every backpacker has his or her particular reasons for carrying weight in their pack, at least one of the following applies when someone chooses to wear heavy boots.

- The first reason is probably unconscious. Wearing heavy boots at the extent of the lowest limbs lowers the body's center of gravity and compensates somewhat for the raised center of gravity of a heavy pack. Mathematically, the theory has no substance, and the beneficial effect is negligible.
- Wearing boots is traditional and universally accepted. "If you're going backpacking, you should wear boots," the retailers tell us. In fact, boots have become as commercially symbolic of the backpacking experience as the backpack itself.
- There are related issues of traction and cushioning, and the perception that boots are superior in both regards.
- Many backpackers indicate that their ankles need support when carrying a heavy pack.
- A boot offers protection from the intrusion of sharp or hard objects.

We'll address the last two issues: perception of ankle support, and protection of sharp/hard objects.

Pack weight magnifies shear forces in the ankle joint. Those forces can cause a misaligned ankle to deform to one side or the other, resulting in a strain, sprain, cartilage rupture, or break. A boot with a high collar that surrounds the ankle can provide it with some support to resist ankle deforming. However, unless a boot provides absolutely rigid side-to-side support (e.g., a plastic ski boot) only compression of the ankle collar, via the lacing system, supports the ankle. If the collar is laced tightly enough to compress the ankle and stop it from deforming, it will also decrease the movement of other joints (e.g., knees). This results in substantial deterioration in the function of the joint and the inability to transfer impact forces throughout the entire leg and back.

The ankle, despite the fact that its range of motion is small relative to that of the knee, serves a number of important functions in helping us get from here to there. First, the ankle helps absorb the force with which the heel strikes the ground, smoothing the transition of the leg from its swing-through phase to its weight-bearing phase in the gait cycle. Second, the ankle allows us to pivot the leg while keeping the foot flat on the ground, making full use of the foot as a base of support. Third, the ankle allows us to use our calf muscles in toeing-off. Fourth, the ankle allows us to lift the toe of the foot so that it clears the ground during the leg's swing-through phase. Finally, it allows us to adjust rapidly to changes in the front-to-back and side-to-side slope of the walking surface, helping to maintain balance.

In tribute to the Designer of the leg, it is indeed possible to walk with both ankles completely immobilized, although there are costs for doing so. It is generally accepted among the physiological research community that such a motion requires about 4–5 percent more energy per step (8–10 percent for a completed gait cycle). And it makes losing our balance more likely. Certainly, most of us have walked behind a boot-clad hiker and noticed how often a fall was initiated when he or she stubbed the toe of one boot on the ground as it swung forward. And, we also remember how many times we've fallen when we could not get the sole of our boot flat on a slippery inclined surface because of the inability to flex our ankle enough due to immobilization of the ankle by the boot collar.

While compression of an ankle collar can protect the ankle from a sudden side-to-side force, that force will have to be absorbed further up the leg. In a slip or fall, a booted hiker is more likely to initiate a strain or sprain in the knee, hip, or back. Worse results can occur. The knee or hip can dislocate. And there is always the dreaded top-of-boot break — a totally immobilizing injury that nearly always requires assisted evacuation.

Although you may live long enough to get rescued, and while you will usually recover well enough from breaks and sprains to be able to continue backpacking, such injuries can really take the fun out of a hike! And they don't happen often, but they usually happen in a setting where medical help is not immediately available. If they also result in a fall where other injuries occur, they can indeed be life threatening. In preparation for them, many backpackers carry extensive first-aid kits and supplies, often including ankle injury management items, such as inflatable splints and compression bandages. Those make a heavy pack even heavier.

In reference to the less serious collisions between the ankle and hard or sharp objects, we've already discussed how a heavy pack and boots limit your ability to precisely target the ground to plant your leading foot. How many side and top-of-foot collisions result from poor foot targeting? Frankly, we don't know. It is our experience that wearing lighter boots, or better yet, lightweight trail shoes, while carrying less than a total of 25 pounds has resulted in far fewer side and top-of-foot collisions than when we wore boots and carried 50 pounds.[3]

Due to the force required to accelerate and decelerate the weight of your boot or shoe at the end of a swinging leg — since this location is farther from the center of gravity than any other place in your body or pack — a shoe or a boot takes a far greater toll on energy expenditure than an equal amount of weight carried in a pack. In fact, walking in a shoe or boot takes about 4–9 times the energy it takes to carry the same shoe or boot. This is calculated by considering the differences of the length of the moment arms — the perpendicular distance between the body's center of gravity and that of the pack — around the center of gravity for a shoe on the foot versus a shoe in the pack. Add this to the extra energy and joint stress resulting from walking with both ankles immobilized by compressed boot collars and the penalties are even more severe.

Consider that even a desert backpacker walking along mudflats in moderate temperatures while wearing heavy boots will expend more energy than if he or she is wearing lighter footwear. Now, factor in cooler temperatures that require more energy to stay warm, mountain terrain and more energy to go up and down hills, and higher altitudes that require more energy to maintain physiological function. The impact of footwear weight becomes even more important. It's no wonder that the manufacturer of the 9-pound expedition backpack was overheard saying to his banker, "The more you carry, the more you need to carry."

Energy Expenditure

The physical work performed by a backpacker while carrying a pack results primarily by counteracting the force of gravity. We do work when we lift weight off the ground. When we walk we do two types of lifting.

We've already discussed the first type of lifting. The average unloaded walker lifts his or her center of gravity off the ground a few inches with every step. If he or she moves forward 24 inches with every step, a typical trail stride, then in a surface mile he or she will take 2,640 steps. If the walker also weighs 100 pounds, then he or she will do 100 foot-pounds of work with every six steps, or 44,000 foot-pounds of work every mile.[4] Strap a 20-pound pack on that walker and he or she will do 52,800 foot-pounds of work covering the same mile. Increase the load by 20 pounds and the work required will be 61,600 foot-pounds.

The second type of lifting performed by backpackers occurs when ascending a slope. Let's say our 100-pound backpacker carries a 40-pound pack up a continuous mile-long slope that gains one hundred feet in elevation. The increased work imposed by lifting 140 pounds one hundred feet will be 14,000 foot-pounds. Therefore, the total work required of our backpacker will be something less than 75,600 foot-pounds. We say less because the slope's incline will account for some of the distance that the backpacker has to lift his or her center of gravity with each step.[5]

More realistically, let's say that our backpacker climbs a total of three-thousand feet during the course of a ten-mile day in mountainous terrain. Carrying a 40-pound pack he or she will have performed about 1,000,000 foot-pounds of work by the end of the day (e.g., walking ten miles with 40 pounds plus lifting 140 pounds three-thousand feet). However, had our backpacker been carrying a 20-pound pack he or she would have performed only about 900,000 foot-pounds of work. That's a difference of 100,000 foot-pounds, or the work it would take to lift a fully loaded tractor trailer one foot off the ground.

What about descending? After all, gravity is now doing the work for you, right? And shouldn't a heavy pack afford some benefit on downhill slopes?

The short answer is no. Of course, descending any slope is easier than going up it. Less work is required because we're not actually lifting any weight. However, it's not as easy as walking on level ground, because whatever amount of weight we're carrying is trying to fall down the slope. We have to stop it from falling (decelerate it) with each step. The braking that we do with the leg muscles takes energy. The heavier the pack, the greater the energy required to decelerate it. In fact, when a downhill slope exceeds a pitch of about 6 degrees, then progressively more energy is required to descend the slope with each additional degree of downward incline.

So don't think that descending three thousand feet with a heavy pack negates any of the energy cost of ascending three thousand feet with the same pack! The descent actually requires more energy than if we had climbed three thousand feet then walked the rest of the distance on level ground. That's why we didn't correct our estimate above for slope efficiency. It's also the reason why we believe it's misleading when planning a route to only consider net elevation gain.

Length of Stride, Pace, and Mileage

Please recall that even an inexperienced backpacker can instantaneously adapt his or her posture and gait and set off with a 60-pound pack by leaning forward to compensate for the effects of pack weight on the center of gravity. So what other adaptations should be considered?

When walking, a backpacker's neuromuscular system automatically attempts to find the combination of stride length and frequency that requires the least amount of energy to continue moving forward. Given the combined effects of slope, surface traction and regularity, wind speed, and pack weight, that's why we shorten our stride and slow our speed when we're going uphill: It minimizes the energy required to take a step. Less obvious is why we shorten our stride and slow our speed when walking on a sandy or slippery surface. Not only does a shorter stride and slower speed give us more control over our balance, it allows us to minimize the amount of energy that is expended with each small slip of the foot.

We respond similarly with weight on our back. When we shorten our stride, we decrease the distance that we must lift the center of gravity with each step. To prove this to yourself, stand next to a wall. Step forward three feet in a single stride and hold still as soon as you plant your leading foot. Have a buddy make a pencil mark at eye level. Then return to your standing position. Now step forward two feet in a single stride and make another eye-level mark. The vertical distance between the two-foot mark and the three-foot mark is the amount of lifting you will avoid by shortening your stride length from three feet to two feet. Of course, in the field you won't shorten your stride that much. The amount will vary according to other conditions. However, the energy savings per step will be proportional to the amount you shorten it.

"Wait a minute. If I shorten my stride, I'm going to have to take more steps to cover the same distance and I'll end up expending the same amount of energy." There is some truth to that presumption, but the automatic mechanism that controls stride length doesn't factor in how far we're going to walk, only how much energy will be required for us to take the next few steps. If we concentrate, we can override the automatic mechanism for a while. But sooner or later it will again be subconsciously controlled. Fighting this system of neuromuscular regulation will ultimately result in excess energy expenditure because of the physiological inefficiency that results in taking strides that are too short or too long.

Because stride length (distance per step) and pace (distance in a given time) are strongly related, the net result is that we slow down when carrying weight. The more weight we carry the slower we walk and the less distance we can cover in a day. If we're planning just three miles on Friday and then camp for the rest of the weekend, this doesn't matter. However, carrying more weight will appreciably shorten the distance we can expect to cover in a day if we plan to walk from dawn to dusk.

Conclusion

Is backpacking simply walking? While it does seem a simple activity, it is far more complex than most have given though to, especially when you encounter extremes of terrain, weather, and surface. Add to this pack weight and you have a body constantly seeking to restabilize and keep from falling. While earth and weather are still uncontrollable, what you wear and what you carry is fully within your power. Pack weight, clothing weight, and distribution play an immense role in just how far you can travel in a day.

End Notes

[1] If the load is not balanced from side to side, the center of gravity will move upward, to the rear, and to one side of its unloaded location, depending on which side of the pack is heavier. If the load can shift inside the pack or the pack is not firmly affixed to the back, each stride will result in the center of gravity moving up and down, backward and forward, and from side to side relative to its loaded and unmoving position. All of these conditions will make the act of walking more energy consuming.

[2] The compressive force on a bent knee is the force exerted by the kneecap trying to keep the joint from rupturing. This force is supplied by muscles contracting against the resistance of bones and is directed over the kneecap through tendons.

[3] OK, so you've been listening and you get your pack weight down to 25 pounds. You are now considering giving up your 6-pound mountaineering boots for 2-pound trail runners. Still worried about that protruding ankle and all those nasty rocks? Wear a crew type sock and roll it down to form a partial cushion around the ankle joint. If the sock has a high percentage of moisture transporting fibers (e.g., merino wool), it will also make a reasonably effective sweat sump.

[4] A *foot-pound* is a standard measure of work. One foot-pound of work is the amount of work it takes to lift a 1-pound weight one foot off the ground.

[5] A hiker most efficiently ascends slopes with an incline that eliminates most of the two-inch descent of the center of gravity during each step. For the average backpacker, that incline will be approximately 8 percent slope (e.g., one that rises about two inches for every twenty-four inches traveled). Over a surface mile a continuous 8 percent slope amounts to an elevation gain of about 440 feet.

Chapter 4: **Navigation**
Lightweight Principles and Equipment

By George Cole

Perhaps nothing settles the issue of one's relationship to the wilderness as clearly as getting lost in it. We may emerge from the experience unscathed, but no one comes back unchanged. And from that time forward we will either look toward the backcountry or away from it when seeking refuge. Of course, luck notwithstanding, the quality of the experience will depend in large part on our mental and physical preparation for it. The wise backcountry traveler will prepare him or herself accordingly.

However, unless we want to, there's no need to ever come to the realization that we have absolutely no idea where we are. Several hundred dollars will buy a half pound of high-tech hardware that will allow us to walk almost anywhere on earth without getting lost. While there are veteran backpackers who swear by navigation arts that predate Western civilization, at this point in history we can choose whether to rely more on science and technology than art in finding our way. High-tech backcountry navigation will require a level of artistry on our part, but we'll only have to learn to read the sun and stars if we have a mind to.

As you might expect, we're defining navigation as the art and science of knowing where we are in relation to where we want to be. The science part has to do with choosing the right tools for the conditions we expect to encounter. The art comes in learning to use the tools in a variety of situations, and using our wits.

The Science: Choosing the Right Tools

There are two principles that guide our selection of navigational gear. The first is a basic, ultralight gear-selection principle: Carry only what you are likely to need. The second relates to the necessity of backing up high-tech and potentially fragile gadgets with more robust, low-tech ones. However, whatever level of technology we choose, we can still put together a system that qualifies as ultralight. There's at least one top-of-the-line, ready-for-all-contingencies, fully redundant, high-tech system that is not much heavier than a basic low-tech system.

Start with a pre-trip analysis. First, note how familiar you are with the area you'll be traveling in. Then, decide whether you'll be traveling on or off trail. If going on trail, do a bit of research to find out if the trail is maintained and marked; and if marked, how well marked. Also, determine what the terrain will be like, the maximum elevation, and whether you'll be doing lots of ups and downs. Knowing the region, season, and elevation, do more research to find out if you can expect fog, rain, snow, or sunlight, and if you'll be spending a lot of time under dense tree cover or deep in canyons or gorges. Then determine whether water is within a day's walk of any point in the area. Finally, decide how much night travel you'll be doing.

Having assembled the above information, answer the following questions:

1. How likely is it that I will become lost?
2. What are the likely consequences of becoming lost?

Then you can decide what navigation gear to take.

There are two categories of gear that we consider. The first is gear for finding your location:

- Compass
- Altimeter
- GPS receiver
- Maps
- Mapping software
- Telescope
- Trail-tracking supplies (e.g., paper and writing implements)
- Trail, route, or area guides

The second is gear that controls the amount of light we'll have for navigation:

- Lighting devices
- Sunglasses
- Sunshades

For example, if we're going on the Appalachian Trail (AT) in summer, we know the trail will be well marked, well maintained, frequently used, and easy to follow, even in the heaviest fog or rain. If we stay on the trail, it is not likely that we will become lost. And if we do become lost, we'll have ready access to water and shelter, should not be in constant danger of hypothermia, and will probably quickly encounter someone who can tell us where we are. Therefore, if we're familiar with the section of trail we'll be walking, we may take no navigation aids at all. If we don't know the area, we'll take a current map or trail guide and a wristband compass to keep us headed either southwest or northeast. We'll also take sunglasses or a brimmed hat. If we're going to walk only during the day, we'll carry one or two single-bulb LED lights.

On the other hand, if we're going into an unknown alpine wilderness area in winter, we'll know that we may need almost constant help in finding our way, as there will be no trails to follow. We'll also know that blizzard conditions could render us virtually blind, and the consequences of becoming lost could be irrevocably severe. Therefore, we'll take the best waterproof, GPS-compatible, topographical maps we can find; waterproof writing paper and implements; and the highest quality barometric altimeter, magnetic compass, and GPS receiver we can afford. We will have prepared our maps with route and GPS waypoint markings, will have uploaded route and waypoint markings to the GPS receiver, and will have spare batteries on hand. We'll also take snow-tested sunglasses or goggles and a headlamp that will allow us to navigate hands-free at night or in whiteout conditions. We may even pack a telescope for good measure.

As indicated previously, however, this full-bore system doesn't need to weigh all that much more than a basic AT system. A Suunto wristband compass and a good AT map or trail guide will weigh 2–4 ounces, and a couple of Photon Freedom LED lights will add another ounce.

Alternatively, a Garmin eTrex Vista GPS receiver weighs 5.5 ounces with lithium batteries, can be preloaded with Garmin MapSource topographical maps, and includes an electronic compass and barometric altimeter. A backup Brunton Eclipse GPS-compatible magnetic compass weighs 2 ounces, a Rite-in-the-Rain all-weather mini-notebook weighs 0.6 ounces, a Fisher Space pen weighs 0.5 ounces, and a belt pouch to carry it all weighs 1.5 ounces. A good winter-capable headlamp, such as the Princeton Tec EOS, may add another 4 ounces or so. And a Zeiss Mini-Quick monocular weighs less than 1 ounce. That's a grand total of about 16 ounces, including spare lithium batteries for the Vista and a handful of waterproof Teslin synthetic maps custom-prepared and printed by National Geopgraphic's TOPO! mapping software.

Even lighter alternatives are available. You can bring a smaller GPS unit (e.g., Garmin Gekko 301), altimeter watch/compass (e.g., Suunto X6), and maps that all weigh less than 6 ounces. By using an integrated GPS altimeter/compass watch (e.g., Suunto X9) and a lightweight map with an Photon Freedom LED light, the total weight of your navigation gear can weigh less than 4 ounces.

The Art: Using the Tools

Learning to use the navigation gear is not something you leave until the night before the trip. Otherwise, as with first-aid gear you're not familiar with, you're better off leaving it at home. sing it incorrectly—or not at all—can get you into trouble. We've found it best to develop the art of backcountry navigation when you don't need it, such as on walks around the neighborhood or weekend trips to well-known backpacking areas. Further, use your navigation gear as often as you can and in every situation you can. Some of the higher tech gadgets may take awhile to master and may have quirks that only become apparent in certain situations.

There is a wealth of information available on how to use any piece of gear you choose to carry. Whole books have been devoted to the subject of backcountry navigation, and there are now numerous websites that address virtually every aspect of navigating with any combination of tools. However, none of this information will be of much use until you make it work. So, set out to become a practical student of modern backcountry navigation—before you need to be. Here's a plan for doing so, starting with the lowest tech arts you'll need to master.

LEARN TO USE A TOPOGRAPHICAL MAP

Get a topographical map of an area you know well. If you can obtain a map of your neighborhood, start with that. Spend fifteen minutes looking carefully at the map and its associated legends, scales, and indicators. Refer to a reference on topographical maps if you encounter things that are not intuitively clear.

Then walk about the area with the map in hand, stopping every hundred yards or so to look around you. If you don't have good sightlines where you stop, move to where you do. Locate where you think you are on the map, and orient the map so that it conforms to what you're seeing. Then turn to each of the four major compass headings and, while keeping the map correctly oriented, note which features of the terrain correspond to which markings on the map. Try to acquire a sense of what the map really represents, especially as it relates to elevation and the contours of the terrain.

LEARN TO USE A MAGNETIC COMPASS

Purchase or borrow a magnetic compass. If you choose to purchase a compass, we'd recommend that you purchase a GPS-compatible one, as you'll probably need the compatibility later. Refer to a reference on using a compass. It's not rocket science, so almost any reference that's intelligibly written will do.

After you have a basic understanding of how a compass works, take the compass with you on a walk around your neighborhood. Stop every hundred yards or so and determine what your *heading* is—the direction you're facing relative to either magnetic or true north). Then pick a feature of the terrain and determine its *bearing*—what direction the feature is from the spot where you're standing relative to magnetic or true north). Pay particular attention to how the compass behaves when you're close to a magnetic object, such as a manhole cover.

Once you're bored with walking around the neighborhood, go to a large open space. Put a quarter on the ground. Walk several hundred yards away from the quarter, making at least four turns on the way. Note on a piece of paper the exact direction you're heading on each leg of your route and the number of steps you take in each leg. At the end of the route, reverse your direction. Use your notes and your compass to find your way back to the quarter. Practice in different spaces until you can find the quarter every time.

Then move to a wooded area. Up the ante by trying to find a dollar bill left under a stone. Use objects as landmarks to help you move in straight lines.

USE YOUR COMPASS AND TOPOGRAPHIC MAP IN ROUTE TRACKING

Obtain a topographical map of a nearby, contained wild area (10 to 25 square miles) that you don't know well. If you can obtain a map of a nearby state park, start with that. Spend half an hour studying the map carefully. Knowing what season it is, imagine what the terrain will actually look like, and note features that you'd like to find. Pencil in a bushwhacking route on the map, being careful not to route yourself off a cliff.

Make a copy of the marked map. Indicate on the copy when you intend to return home, and leave it with someone you trust. Then, starting early in the day, go to the wild area with the map, a compass, water, and snacks. Make sure that the compass is corrected for declination. Starting in the parking lot, take bearings on all the major terrain features you can identify. Identify those features on the correctly oriented map, and do a rough estimate of your position. Using the map and the compass, determine where you are in relation to the beginning of your route and guide yourself to it.

Using the map and compass, follow your intended route. Take headings frequently. If you can see terrain features well enough to identify them, do the following exercises sequentially every hundred yards or so:

1. Take bearings on at least two terrain features you can see from your position, identify them on the map, and calculate where you are on your route (or off your route, as the case may be)
2. Get bearings on terrain features from the map (relative to your suspected position on the route), and try to locate them on the landscape. Correct your estimate of your actual position, and return to your route if necessary.

If you can't see terrain features clearly, use your route-tracking skills in order to get to and from a position where you can see clearly. In addition to tracking the route, use the *contour* (elevation) lines on your map to establish if you should be going up, down, or traversing a slope.

ADD A BAROMETRIC ALTIMETER FOR ROUTE TRACKING

After you've survived and/or sufficiently recovered from the experience, go back out and do it again. However, this time, take a calibrated barometric altimeter. Use the altimeter and the contour lines on the map to add a third dimension to the two-dimensional information supplied by the compass.

USE YOUR GPS RECEIVER, BAROMETRIC ALTIMETER, AND TOPOGRAPHIC MAP

The lightest backcountry GPS receivers that we've tested so far are the eTrex and Gekko models made by Garmin and the wrist-mounted X9 by Suunto. In particular, the Garmin eTrex Vista, eTrex Summit, Gekko 301, and the Suunto X9 are

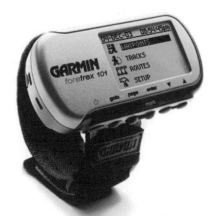

Two of the most popular - and effective - ultralight GPS units on the market. The **Garmin Geko 301 (left)** provides full GPS and environmental sensor functionality into a tiny package that weighs 3 oz with lithium batteries, while the **Garmin Foretrex 101 (above)** offers wrist-wearable convenience at less than 3 oz with lithium batteries when ready access to the GPS has the ability to increase your hiking efficiency.

attractive because they incorporate a barometric altimeter and therefore satisfy another axiom of the ultralight creed: multi-functionality.

Take plenty of time to learn about the UTM grid system and how your new receiver works. You probably won't wait more than ten seconds to use it after you first take it out of the box, but if you spend some time with the user manual, you'll discover it can do all sorts of interesting things.

If you can afford it, buy one of the major mapping software programs. Spend plenty of time learning how to use it by uploading routes and waypoints to the receiver and printing your own custom maps with it. Some programs allow you to duplicate the route and waypoint markings on the GPS with similarly marked paper maps. For the ultimate in weatherproof maps, use one of the synthetic map sheets as a substrate, most of which are ink-jet printer compatible.

Finally, get outside and use the receiver in conjunction with an altimeter, your custom maps, and your GPS-compatible compass. Based upon your experiences with map and compass alone, you'll be amazed at how easy it is to find your way. In fact, it's too easy. So never rely on a GPS by itself. Always take your compass. After all, you will have invested a lot of time in learning how to navigate with just a compass, and knowing how may save your life when you discover you forgot to pack extra batteries.

Conclusion

Navigation is the art and science of knowing where you are in relation to where you want to be. For the ultralighter, there are two principles to guide you: Choose the right tools for the conditions you expect to encounter, and only carry what you need. High-tech navigation may require a certain level of artistry, but remember to always back up high-tech, and potentially fragile, gadgets with your wits and reliable low-tech, tried-and-true systems.

Part 2:

Protection from the Elements

Chapter 5: **Thermoregulation**

By Ryan Jordan

The term *thermoregulation* refers to the regulation of body temperature. The literature on physiological thermoregulation and how clothing can affect it is already vast. If you're interested in a comprehensive review of thermoregulation in an outdoor context, refer to the excellent *Secrets of Warmth* by Hal Weiss (The Mountaineers, 1992).

This article focuses primarily on specific classes of apparel, shelter, and sleep systems for cold, wet conditions. We'll cover clothing systems for hot and dry weather elsewhere. Specifically, this chapter covers three major topics:

- Mechanisms of heat generation
- Mechanisms of heat loss
- The design of equipment to minimize heat loss

Mechanisms of Heat Generation

Even in cold conditions, heat generation can be a problem. Excess heat generation from vigorous activity can result in sweating that leads to rapid evaporative cooling and the eventual breakdown of the body's thermoregulatory capacity. We'll consider this problem later. For now, let's assume that conservation of every bit of the body's heat is a desirable condition and address the primary means by which the body gains heat in cold conditions.

METABOLISM

Your best source of heat is generated internally by your body's metabolic engine. It is fueled by calories gained from the metabolism of food. When you reduce caloric intake, you can reduce your body's ability to produce heat. In a recent alpine climb in Wyoming's Teton Range, Alan Dixon and I spent 38 hours without sleep and with only enough calories for a 12-hour climb as we engaged in a difficult descent out of a summit snow-and-ice storm. By the end of the route, as we approached our car on a sun-warmed trail in 60-degree temperatures at the valley floor, we were still shivering — while wearing our PolarGuard 3D-insulated belay parkas. Our metabolic engines, which had been fueled by more than 300 calories per hour for the first twelve hours of the climb, had slowed to a crawl.

It's a futile exercise to calculate the proper number of calories needed for a given level of exertion while simultaneously trying to account for environmental factors — such as temperature, wind, and precipitation. The National Outdoor Leadership School (NOLS) has devised elegant predictive models for caloric consumption that significantly overestimate the amount of food required for most individuals. This results in extra comfort but not necessarily extra safety. Consider that the 2–5 pounds of extra food recommended by NOLS could be better spent on warmer insulation or dropped from a pack altogether to reduce the energy expended to carry the extra weight. Such conservative predictions do not necessarily make sense from a safety standpoint.

It is well known via any of a variety of textbook formulas that the *basal metabolism* (minimum calories a body needs each day) of an average male of 150 pounds, 5´8″ in height, and 30 years of age is approximately 1,600 to 1,800 calories — with an average level of active metabolism adding 400 to 800 additional calories. It can be assumed that a hiker carrying a light pack and who understands the processes of walking efficiently, regulating both their metabolism and activity level, should be able to hike several miles a day across moderate terrain and expend as little as 2500 to 3000 calories per day. One must keep in mind that caloric needs will increase in response to colder temperatures, higher altitudes, a faster hiking pace, more body mass, or a change in body mass to a higher muscle/fat ratio that occurs on a long-distance hike. However, most people make the mistake of overestimating these needs, especially on hikes of less than two weeks in length.

Lightweight backpackers wishing to reduce their food weight must learn to hike efficiently, carefully monitor their exertion rate, and maintain its constancy. Thus, they will be able to expend energy that takes maximum advantage of the body's walking momentum, rather than expend excess energy to fuel rapid changes in momentum resulting from accelerating and decelerating the body.

Another approach is to design a balanced diet with a high caloric density, a subject that is addressed adequately in many other texts.

RADIATIVE HEAT ABSORPTION

Sunlight provides some ability to add heat to your body. You can easily notice this if you are wearing dark exterior clothing on a cold, sunny day. Due to weather variability, however, you can't rely on the sun as a heat source in the backcountry.

ACTIVITY

Exercise creates heat. Increased use of muscles leads to increased metabolism. While some of the caloric burn is used to fuel muscles, much of it is wasted as excess heat, which is then lost through conduction, convection, radiation, respiration, or evaporation.

EXTERNAL HEAT

In the winter, you may want to consider artificial heat sources. Chemical hand and toe warmers are among the most popular gear items in the overnight kit of a backcountry skier, snowshoer, or mountaineer. Firebuilding, of course, is the classic example of external heat and remains a skill that has probably saved more individuals from hypothermic death than we care to acknowledge, especially in an outdoor culture that increasingly eschews the skill, art, and joy of firebuilding as part of a utopian no-trace ethic. Finally, it is well known that core treatments of hypothermia include warm drinks and shared body heat with another person.

Mechanisms of Heat Loss

In order to design appropriate clothing and sleep systems, we must first understand the primary mechanisms of heat loss.

CONDUCTION

Conduction is defined as the transfer of heat from a warmer object to a cooler object when the two objects are in direct contact with each other. Backpackers experience conductive heat loss anytime the body is in direct contact with cold ground. While hiking, the primary source of conductive heat loss is out of the feet via the soles of your footwear. While at rest, conductive heat loss occurs while sitting or lying on the cold ground. Conduction is also a major source of heat loss in wet clothing, due to water's excellent conductive properties.

CONVECTION

Convective heat loss occurs in response to the movement of a fluid or gas. In outdoor clothing systems, convective heat loss occurs when warm air next to the body and in the clothing is displaced by cool air from the outside. The biggest factor contributing to convective heat loss, of course, is wind.

In addition to wind-induced, "forced" convection, "passive" convection occurs via the chimney effect: when cool, dense air moves into our clothing at pant cuffs and waist hems and replaces the warm, light air exiting out of our neck hems and other vents.

RADIATION

Radiative heat loss from the human body occurs primarily as a result of infrared emission. Often it occurs on cold, clear nights and is readily noticeable after sunset. Cloud cover dampens the effect of radiative heat loss by reflecting a significant portion of radiant heat back to the earth's surface. A backpacker carrying a properly designed cold-weather clothing system will not experience a significant amount of radiative heat loss.

EVAPORATION

Evaporative heat loss is a desert hiker's best friend and a winter traveler's worst enemy. Evaporation occurs when a liquid (e.g., sweat) changes phase to a vapor. This phase change requires heat. Unfortunately, your body heat drives this phase change. Evaporative heat loss may be most noticeable in context of the "flash-off" effect, which occurs after a period of intense physical activity and sweating in cold conditions, followed by rapid evaporation and chill after stopping to rest.

Evaporative heat loss from perspiration can occur in one of two ways. *Sensible* perspiration is caused by the formation of liquid sweat droplets at the skin surface in response to excessive heat. This heat is usually the result of being dressed too warmly for a given activity level. *Insensible* perspiration is the direct emission of sweat vapor from the skin in response to a humidity gradient (e.g., your skin is drying out). Insensible perspiration is most significant while at rest or sleeping, while sensible perspiration is most significant during periods of activity.

RESPIRATION

Technically, respiration combines the processes of evaporation (moisture in the lungs) and convection (displacement of warm air in the lungs by cold air from the outside environment). Because humidity in the lungs is at 100 percent, respiration is an important heat sink in cold, dry conditions.

Significant moisture, and thus, body heat, can be lost when that moist air is exchanged with drier outside air. In addition, some body heat is lost to the process of warming the cold air entering your lungs.

Minimizing Heat Loss with Apparel and Equipment

By now you should have already thought of obvious ways to use your clothing and other equipment to minimize the various mechanisms of heat loss. We'll explore some of the principles for preserving your body heat below.

MINIMIZING CONDUCTIVE HEAT LOSS

Recall that conductive heat loss occurs when your body is in contact with the ground surface or other cold objects. These can include shoes, sleeping pads, ice axes or trekking poles, sunglasses or goggles, and even metal zippers, which have been known to induce frostbite on the chin of more than one winter mountaineer.

Minimizing conductive heat loss through the feet simply requires a barrier between your bare feet and the ground. This barrier will include socks, insoles, and the sole of your shoe or boot. Thick, minimally compressible socks made with a high-density wool, synthetic, or blend, combined with insoles made of closed-cell foam or *loden* (felted) wool provide good in-shoe protection. Shoes with thick midsoles and those with lugged soles minimize direct contact with the ground surface and provide the basis for good winter footwear. Of course, sole design to prevent conductive heat loss through the feet is only part of the story. Convective, evaporative, and to a lesser extent, radiative heat loss also occur in the feet.

To preserve heat while sleeping, an insulating ground pad is a must. Ground pads that entrap dead air by minimizing passive convection within the pad are typically the most effective. Consequently, one usually sleeps warmer but not as cushioned on a closed-cell pad, than on an inflatable pad. This is because significant passive convection can occur through

Conductive heat loss can be minimized by sitting on your sleeping pad or backpack. You will also lose less heat when sitting and sleeping on forest duff than on rock, gravel, or snow, due to the higher thermal conductivity of rock (and frozen water) than organic materials. Here, the author is sitting on a closed-cell foam sleeping pad to prevent unnecessary loss of body heat to snow, and insulating his stove system on a heat-tolerant plastic snow shovel ("Snowclaw" type).

the inflatable pad's open-cell foam insulation. To minimize pad weight while still maintaining comfort, consider combining a torso-sized, closed-cell (or inflatable) foam pad for the main part of your body with a backpack for the lower legs. Rest the head and neck on shoes or clothing to prevent conductive heat loss in those areas.

Conductive heat loss through the hands is well known among backcountry skiers and climbers. This occurs when the blood vessels in the hand constrict while gripping an already cold tool or pole. In general, the best prevention against this type of heat loss is the use of minimally compressible insulation in the palms of your gloves or mitts. Some manufacturers have recognized the need for this and are offering handwear that is insulated with easily compressible insulation for the back of the hand (to minimize weight and maximize warmth) and with minimally compressible insulation (e.g., fleece) for the palm side.

MINIMIZING CONVECTIVE HEAT LOSS

Convective heat loss occurs in response to wind (active convection) and the chimney effect of air movement in clothing (passive convection). Windproof clothing worn over insulating clothing capable of trapping dead air in its thickness provides reasonable insurance against convective heat loss. The value of a very thin windshirt for outdoor activities cannot be emphasized enough. The windshirt should be highly breathable to minimize overheating and speed moisture vapor movement out of the clothing system, and very thin

Convective heat loss occurs most prominently in the presence of wind. Consequently, a wind-resistant jacket is commonplace in the kits of alpine hikers. Passive convection (the "chimney" effect) can be better controlled in a garment that includes plenty of ventilation options, including adjustable wrist cuffs and hem, torso vents, a full-front zipper, pit zips, and a hood. This plethora of features can be found in lightweight garments like the Feathered Friends' EPIC Jackorak (8.6 oz, size M) or Montane Lite Speed Jacket (shown here, 5.2 oz, size L).

so as not to contribute significantly to the insulation of a clothing system. Insulation weight is most efficiently spent in other areas.

Clothing should be evaluated for its ability to control, rather than just prevent or minimize, passive convection. Clothing with adjustable cuffs and hems that can be fully opened or fully closed provides the most versatility. Tighten the cuffs and hems to preserve heat, and loosen them up to vent heat and cool down.

In a sleep system, you can minimize active convective heat loss due to wind by using a bivy sack, pitching a low tarp, or sleeping in a completely walled shelter (e.g., a pyramid shelter staked to the ground or a tent). Passive convection in a shelter is usually desirable. Many are designed with strategically placed low and high vents to promote the chimney effect, which minimizes accumulation of humid air in the shelter to reduce condensation.

MINIMIZING EVAPORATIVE HEAT LOSS

Vapor-barrier clothing is the only sure way to prevent evaporative heat loss. Vapor-barrier fabrics are not only waterproof, but completely impermeable to moisture vapor as well. Consequently, evaporative heat loss cannot occur, because the microclimate inside the vapor barrier is a closed system that approaches equilibrium between water and vapor phases. Vapor-barrier clothing requires a high level of attentiveness to your body's physiology and frequent fine-tuning of your clothing system to prevent sweating. Thus, it is not very popular among mainstream outdoorsmen. Accumulation of liquid moisture in a vapor-barrier microclimate creates a new and significant method of heat loss: conductive cooling as heat loss to water in the system. Because of this, vapor-barrier clothing tends to be wholly impractical for high-exertion activities.

MINIMIZING RADIATIVE HEAT LOSS

In inclement conditions, some assume radiative heat loss to be negligible relative to other heat-loss mechanisms (e.g.,

Radiative heat loss is most significant between sunset and sunrise, when the atmosphere loses tremendous amounts of heat that was absorbed by sunlight throughout the day. The best defense against radiative heat loss is thick insulation, like this Rab Quantum Endurance Down Jacket (22 oz, size M).

wind-induced convective heat loss and evaporative cooling). In windless conditions when the body is not active, it can be significant—especially at night. Radiative heat loss can be minimized by one of two methods. The first is by wearing a reflective barrier (such as aluminized nylon or Mylar) near the skin capable of reflecting infrared radiation back to the body. The second is by wearing thick clothing (e.g., down or high-loft synthetic fill garments). The latter strategy is effective because infrared radiation cannot travel through thick insulation, and thus, most of the infrared radiation lost by the body can remain entrapped in the clothing system rather than exiting out to the environment.

MINIMIZING RESPIRATORY HEAT LOSS

Respiratory heat loss can be significant in cold, dry conditions. And not breathing is an impractical heat conservation strategy. In theory, respiratory heat loss can be minimized by breathing air that has been pre-warmed and/or pre-humidified prior to taking it into the lungs. High-altitude climbers and Arctic travelers know that breathing through a fleece balaclava or face mask can improve respiratory comfort by increasing the humidity and warmth of air entering the lungs. Some innovative "heat exchange face masks" specifically designed to magnify this effect are now appearing on the market.

WARM WHEN WET?

This chapter would not be complete without addressing a common marketing claim prevalent among manufacturers of synthetic insulation: "warm when wet." The presence of liquid moisture in any insulating material results in

1. More rapid conduction of heat from the body than in a dry material
2. Displacement of air volume normally used to house effective insulation (dead air)
3. Evaporative cooling that results from the use of body heat to induce a phase change from liquid to vapor

In addition, the absorption of liquid moisture into a knit, woven, or high-loft insulation causes fiber structure to collapse, decreasing the insulation resiliency. This reduces the thickness of the insulation further and magnifies the effects listed above.

While there are both natural and synthetic fibers more resistant to fiber-structure collapse induced by liquid moisture, there is no fiber in existence, be it natural or manmade, that can fairly make the claim that it is warm when wet.

The Impact on Lightweight Backpacking

The most important impact of thermoregulation on lightweight backpacking is rooted in the skill of the hiker. Hikers who understand thermoregulation, the body's response to metabolic and environmental stress, and the response of apparel and sleep systems to moisture and heat resulting from physiological activity and environmental conditions, can effectively and safely reduce their clothing and sleep system weight in the backcountry. On the other hand, failure to understand the complicated relationship between thermoregulation, physiology, environmental conditions, and equipment can result in a failure of the hiker's body, the hiker's gear, or both. This can lead to hypothermia and death. You must understand that as you reduce the weight of gear that keeps you warm and dry, you must also accept some reduction in safety margin.

Chapter 6: **Clothing Systems**

By Alan Dixon and Ryan Jordan

More backpackers agonize over what clothing to take on a trip than probably any piece of gear. The agony is justified. If your clothing system works, you'll be warm, dry, happy, at peak mental and physical performance, and most importantly, safe. However, if it fails, you may be cold, wet, and miserable, reducing your physical capability and mental acuity. At worst, improper clothing decisions can leave you hypothermic and in a life-threatening situation. To stay warm and dry with light clothing requires careful attention to each piece and how all of your garments will work together and with your sleeping gear and shelter.

Saving Weight

Most backpackers take too much clothing. You don't need five, six, or seven torso layers to stay warm in the backcountry, even in the winter. Consequently, the most fundamental lightweight backpacking principle related to clothing is: Take fewer garments. Most ultralight backpackers agree that it makes little sense to carry more clothing than you can wear at any given time.

Taking fewer layers also means selecting individual pieces that offer great versatility. For example, a waterproof-breathable shell with excellent ventilation may serve well as both a rain jacket and a windshirt. Likewise, a high-loft (e.g., down or Polarguard) insulating garment not only keeps you warm in camp, but you can wear it to bed and possibly get away with a lighter sleeping bag.

The second fundamental principle of selecting lightweight backpacking clothing is: Select lighter clothing with fewer features. Do you really need handwarmer pockets and zip-up collars on every torso layer? Will an 8-ounce rain jacket serve well enough for summer backpacking, instead of the 24-ounce parka you used to climb Mount Rainier? View each piece of clothing as part of a larger system. Then step back to take a look at the functionality of the system. You'll be able to discern which features are important and which features aren't so you can start shaving weight.

Often there will be a lighter garment that performs as well or better than what you are currently carrying. There are a lot of apparel options in the specialty outdoor industry, with new entries to the market appearing every spring and fall. Research the market thoroughly, and don't necessarily rely on your local outfitter to advise you on what clothing is the lightest available for your needs. Your efforts will pay off.

HIDDEN WEIGHT IN CLOTHING SYSTEMS

Alan recently compared his gear lists from two nearly identical backpacking trips taken before and after his conversion to ultralight backpacking. Expecting the dramatic differences in the weights of the backpack, shelter, and sleeping bag, Alan was most surprised at the differences in weight of his clothing system — more than 6 pounds. On the late-season ultralight trip, which was a visit above 10,000 feet in the Sierras with subfreezing nighttime temperatures, Alan was never cold or uncomfortable using his newer, lighter clothing system. The keys to lightening his load were including fewer garments and taking the lightest in the class.

Table 6.1 illustrates how much weight can be saved by invoking these key principles to develop a lighter clothing system:

Table 6.1

WEIGHT (oz)	TRADITIONAL SYSTEM	WEIGHT (oz)	ULTRALIGHT SYSTEM
18.0	3-Layer WP/B Jacket	8.0	Ultralight 2-Layer WP/B Rain Jacket
14.0	3-Layer WP/B Pants	5.0	Ultralight 2-Layer WP/B Rain Pants
24.0	300 Wt Fleece Jacket	12.0	Synthetic Fill Pullover
10.0	200 Wt Fleece Vest	n/a	
10.0	Midweight L/S Zip-T	6.0	Lightweight Zip-T
7.0	Extra Hiking T-Shirt	n/a	
9.0	Midweight Bottoms	5.0	Lightweight Bottoms
4.0	200 Wt Fleece Balaclava	1.0	Polypropylene Balaclava
3.0	200 Wt Fleece Hat	1.0	100 Wt Fleece Hat
3.0	Windstopper Fleece Gloves	1.0	PowerStretch Gloves
4.0	Mountaineering Mitt Shells	1.0	2-Layer Waterproof Rain Mitts
28.0	Camp Shoes (Sneakers)	n/a	none (already wearing trail shoes!)
7.0	2 Pr Extra Socks (Midweight)	2.0	Spare Socks (Lightweight)
8.8 lbs	Total Clothing Weight Carried	2.6 lbs	Total Clothing Weight Carried
	Total Clothing Weight Saved	**6.2 lbs**	

Before taking the plunge and throwing out all of your clothing, exercise some caution. As you decrease the amount of clothing you bring, you need to be smarter about how and when to use it. Understand the limitations of lighter clothing (less durable, not as water resistant, etc.), and realize that you may be creating less margin for error if you aren't carrying spare dry clothing to change into when a severe storm leaves you wet and cold. The smart backpacker will test lighter clothing systems on shorter trips with backup clothing and a realistic bailout scenario before committing a new ultralight system to more serious inclement weather conditions in a remote environment.

Basics of Clothing Integration

Garments layered over each other in different combinations give a hiker the ability to adapt to a variety of environmental conditions. Clothing can be used to manage heat (from both the body and the outside environment), cold, and moisture (from both perspiration and precipitation). The ultralight backpacker understands that only a few pounds of clothing, judiciously selected, can be used to survive not only the blazing heat of the desert, but also the freak torrential downpours of a summer thunderstorm and the cold snow of early fall.

It's important to keep in mind that a May hike in the slot canyons of southern Utah requires a different clothing system than a January ski backpacking tour in the Canadian Rockies. But the system concept remains essentially the same. A versatile layering system usually includes three basic components:

- Next-to-skin base layer
- Insulating garment
- Wind/precipitation shell garment

The Base Layer

The base layer, commonly known as "long underwear," is typically worn next to your skin. Its primary function is to manage the next-to-skin temperature and moisture microclimate. It is typically the most important piece of clothing with respect to managing your body's internal temperature while active (thermoregulation).

BASE LAYER WEIGHT

Many flavors of base layers exist. Manufacturers in the outdoor industry have generally come to a consensus about base-layer nomenclature, with different *weights* of garment fabrics for different conditions. The most popular weights include silkweight (summer), lightweight (two-season), midweight (three-season), and expedition weight (winter). However, such naming conventions have done more to confuse backcountry travelers than to help them, luring them into thinking they need base layers that are heavier than necessary for a given set of conditions.

In general, we have little utility for base layers other than the absolute lightest and thinnest we can find. Midweight or expedition-weight knitted garments should *never* be worn next to skin, especially in the winter. When you sweat or get wet from precipitation, they absorb copious amounts of water and take a very long time to dry. They can sap significant quantities of body heat while evaporating that moisture. In colder conditions, two ultralight base-layer garments will typically be warmer. They trap warm air between the layers, dry faster, manage moisture better, and offer more versatility in a wider range of temperatures. It's no accident that the most respected mountaineering guides on the earth's coldest mountains encourage their clients to layer several light layers next to skin, rather than wearing expedition-weight base layers as the first layer.

BASE LAYER FABRICS

The three dominant fabrics used in base-layer garments are polypropylene (e.g., Lifa), polyester (e.g., Capilene, Coolmax), and merino wool (e.g., Smartwool).

Polypropylene is the oldest of the synthetics and is still the lightest base-layer fiber available. Polyester has replaced polypropylene as the de facto standard material because of the ease at which its surface can be modified through chemical treatment to promote varying degrees of wicking. In addition, polyester is not as heat sensitive as polypropylene, and it can be successfully laundered by careless backpackers who have better things to do than read fabric care labels.

Prior to the development of next-to-skin synthetic fabrics, wool was the standard for many years but earned a reputation for itchiness. When polypropylene was introduced in the 1970s, hordes of backcountry enthusiasts embraced the synthetic and filed their woolies into basement closets. However, advances in sheep engineering — that is, *genetic* engineering — wool fiber processing, and wool knitting have resulted in the resurgence of merino wool base-layer garments. The US manufacturer Smartwool has established its brand and reputation on this fabric.

Merino wool and superfine merino, a merino wool with a fiber diameter less than 18 microns, are now offered as base layers by most major long-underwear manufacturers. There are two distinct advantages over wool base layers from a generation ago: Its fine diameter does not induce itching (for the vast majority of the population, at least), and it manages moisture far better than its thick-fibered great uncle.

But the primary advantage of merino wool is its ability to absorb water molecules into its protein structure — a covalent chemical reaction that is capable of storing and releasing heat. Consequently, merino wool is the poster child for thermoregulation and is well known for its ability to "keep you cool when it's warm, and warm when it's cool." Manufacturers of synthetic fibers have been trying to replicate this unique property of wool for decades. They are still falling short.

Nonetheless, synthetics have some advantages over wool. They absorb less water per weight than wool, so they dry out faster. Advocates of merino wool claim that wool absorbs moisture into its fiber structure, so it leaves you "feeling" drier than the non-absorbent synthetics, well known for feeling "clammy" or "sticky" when you are sweating. In addition, synthetics are still a bit lighter than merino wool, although the gap is closing as advances in wool processing and knitting technologies move forward.

Perhaps one of the more noticeable differences between merino wool and synthetics is that synthetics are famous for their ability to stink to high heaven after a few hard trail days. Merino wool seems to manage body odor far better. It remains the base layer standard for Arctic explorers who may wear the same shirt for weeks at a time.

Silk has also been used for ultralight base layer garments. Like wool, silk is a natural fiber that offers some temperature regulating potential due to its ability to absorb water molecules into its protein structure. However, unlike wool, which retains its crimped fiber structure when wet, silk fibers collapse more easily as water absorbs into them. Water displaces air in the fabric interstices and effectively eliminates any insulating ability. Like cotton, wet silk can take a long time to dry and can rapidly conduct heat away from the body. Silk garments are most appropriate for midsummer backpacking in moderate and warm climates.

In the backpacking world, polypropylene remains the king of ultralight base layer fibers. A pair of ultralight polypropylene tights is available from the Early Winters Company, and weighs a scant 1.5 ounces in a Men's size medium.

BIDIRECTIONAL WICKING FABRICS

Bidirectional wicking is the process by which water moves through a fabric along a capillary gradient driven from large pores (low fiber density) to small pores (high fiber density). Some manufacturers make garments with bidirectional fabrics that are designed to promote moisture movement away from the skin and into the outside environment. Examples include Patagonia R0.5 and R1 fleece and Paramo Parameta S. Because less fiber ends are in contact with your skin in a bidirectional fabric, many users perceive them to be more comfortable. Their primary advantage is the ability to promote wicking of moisture off the skin and dispersion of that moisture to the outside face of the fabric, where it can more rapidly evaporate.

BICOMPONENT TEXTILE CONSTRUCTIONS

A bicomponent fabric consists of two fabric layers having different physical properties. The classic example of a bicomponent construction is the Pertex-and-pile garments on which Buffalo Clothing Systems of the UK has built its reputation. As is the case of the Buffalo O3 Shirt, an inside face of polyester fishnet is mated with Pertex Quantum, a tightly woven microfiber nylon, to create a single garment that can be worn next to skin but provides functional wind and water resistance. Similar two-layer bicomponent constructions are available from Patagonia's Zephur and Stretch Speed Ascent

Jackets, Marmot's Driclime Windshirt, and Rab Carrington's V-Trail Top. The primary benefit of these garments is their versatility in cool conditions. A single layer can be used to provide next-to-skin wicking performance, insulating ability, and wind and water resistance. The nature of their construction — open weave or knitted inner faces with tightly woven outer faces — means that these garments also possess bidirectional wicking properties.

Perseverance Mills of the UK has developed an innovative fabric that has both bidirectional and bicomponent properties woven into a single fabric layer: Pertex Equilibrium. Used in hiking clothing and wind jackets, Pertex Equilibrium is manufactured with large-diameter yarns in a more open weave on the inner face, and fine diameter yarns with a tighter weave on the outer face. We've been testing the fabric in hiking pants and wind jackets for about a year and are pleased with the results. Pertex Equilibrium has proven itself to be exceptionally comfortable next to the skin. It offers excellent breathability at high exertion levels and manages mild to moderately inclement wind, rain, and snow very well.

Hiking Clothing

Your selection of hiking clothing will be dictated primarily by personal preference and style, and secondarily by the climate at the geographical location where you are hiking. This combination will govern whether you hike in short sleeves or long sleeves and shorts or long pants. Any of these garments can be made with lightweight woven fabrics (nylon or polyester), soft shell fabrics (e.g., stretchwoven nylon), or knit fabrics (synthetic or wool). Because of the plethora of styles and fabrics that are available, we cannot hope to treat them all in this short chapter. Therefore, we will instead focus on one particular system of clothing that offers significant weight advantages when taken into consideration with your entire system of clothing, sleep, and shelter systems.

HIKING SHIRT

We like hiking in our base-layer shirt. Most commonly, this is a long-sleeve, fitted (but not tight), lightweight merino wool knitted crew.

The advantages of merino wool have already been clarified, but the most important reasons for using a merino wool crew as a hiking shirt are that

1. It plays a key role in your body's thermoregulation, so it keeps you cool when it's warm and warm when it's cool
2. You are wearing your base layer instead of carrying it, saving weight in your pack
3. It adds simplicity to your layering system. As it gets cooler, you are already wearing your base layer. There is no need to take off a hiking shirt and replace it with your base layer, which is the normal limitation of conventional summer layering systems.

The primary concerns hikers have about wearing a merino wool base layer are overheating and the lack of mosquito protection. We've found the lightest merino wool shirts on the market (e.g., Smartwool's Microweight and Lightweight series) to be remarkably comfortable in warm conditions, even as high as 80 degrees. At higher temperatures, most hikers will opt for thinner shirts that entrap less insulating air, including two-layer Supplex nylon (e.g., Railriders Eco-Mesh shirt) and silkweight polyester (e.g., Patagaonia Silkweight Capilene). Other options for very warm temperatures include open mesh, or fishnet, fabric constructions, such as those manufactured by Brynje in Norway (polypropylene). The additional advantage of fishnet fabrics is that they can be easily extended for cool weather. When worn as a base layer under other layers, the interstices of the fishnet construction entrap warm air pockets.

The concern over lack of mosquito protection afforded by knitted garments, such as a merino wool base layer, is justified and is the primary motivation for wearing tightly woven garments made from fabrics such as two-layer Supplex nylon. However, merino wool base layers can be used successfully in mosquito-rich areas simply by treating the base layer with Permithrin, a very effective insecticide appropriate for next-to-skin clothing use. In areas where mosquitoes are severe, an ultralight, highly breathable windshirt (e.g., Montane Aero Smock or Rab Quantum Top) can be used over the base layer to ward off the little buggers.

HIKING PANTS

For virtually all conditions, we recommend wearing hiking pants. The advantages of pants over shorts are numerous. Pants protect your legs from poison plants, biting insects, the harmful UV rays of direct sunlight, and abrasion from rocks and brush. Pants also offer more versatility, as they may provide enough protection from light rain, wind, and cooler temperatures, when many shorts aficionados will be scrambling to don a second layer. Finally, pants offer the appropriate modesty when you get off the trail and visit town for resupply on a long-distance walk. The exception to this general rule of thumb is on shaded trails where the exposure of bare skin to direct sunlight is not so severe and where skin contact hazards such as biting insects or poison plants is minimal.

Pacific Northwest mountaineers are famous for the "Cascade Hiking and Climbing Uniform," which consists of a pair of base-layer bottoms under light nylon shorts. Fashion consciousness aside, this system offers the advantages of being able to wear your base layer as part of your hiking apparel, saving weight in your pack. However, most base layer bottoms are knitted pieces that are not durable enough to withstand much abrasion. Consequently, many hikers are moving to more robust fabrics in their hiking pants, with Supplex nylon and various lightweight stretch woven nylon fabrics leading the charge.

Two of the most interesting new hiking pant fabrics to hit the market are Cloudveil Inertia, the lightweight stretch woven fabric used in their Rodeo (12 oz) and Prospector (10 oz) pants, and Pertex Equilibrium, licensed for use to a number of manufacturers. Inertia is a bidirectional fabric with a tightly woven outer shell and a brushed inner face for next-to-skin comfort and good wicking properties. More important, it offers some stretch, making it a supremely comfortable pant for more active hikers and climbers who need more mobility from their clothing without a baggy fit. Pertex Equilibrium, which appears in the GoLite Synergy Pant (10 oz), is a bicomponent, bidirectional fabric that also offers excellent next-to-skin comfort with slightly better weather resistance, and slightly less wicking, than Inertia.

Both fabrics offer significant performance gains over the de facto standard in hiking pant fabric: two-layer Supplex nylon used in most "cargo-style" hiking pants from Railriders, REI, Columbia, and others. Supplex pants cling to your skin uncomfortably when wet, and their lack of a textured inner surface can make them abrasive when worn next to skin. Inertia and Equilibrium are more weather resistant and more insulative than Supplex, while retaining breathability that is on par with Supplex.

For most summertime hiking in temperate climates like the Continental US, most ultralight hikers who wear pants will pack only one extra layer for their legs—either rain pants (using their hiking pants as a base layer) or a knitted base layer (using their hiking pants as a shell layer). The former strategy is most appropriate for wetter climates like the Pacific Northwest, while the latter strategy is ideally suited for drier climates, like the northern Rockies.

HEADWEAR

Hats protect you from the sun and rain, and depending on design, may provide some protection from biting insects. For general use and sun protection, select a light nylon hat with a wide brim to shade the eyes and face. Many backpacking hats also have a drop skirt to give almost complete sun protection to face and neck. A high-collared shirt combined with a hat that provides plenty of shade may eliminate the need for sunscreen for your face and neck. Lightweight nylon hats that provide plenty of shade usually don't weigh more than 3 ounces.

Even if it's not made with waterproof fabric, a nylon hat coated with a DWR finish can shed a reasonable amount of rain and snow. Some hikers like a broad-brimmed hat (e.g. Tilley or Seattle Sombrero) used with hoodless rain jacket, preferring the freedom in vision and hearing relative to wearing a jacket with a hood. For long periods of driving rain in cold weather, most hikers will find that only a good rain jacket hood will keep your head warm and dry. Unfortunately, many jacket hoods have short, flimsy brims that do not provide adequate protection for the face. This is especially true if you wear glasses. A hat with a good bill is great to wear with a deficient hood. It will keep the hood off your face and rain out of your eyes.

Some hikers think that a balaclava is one item that should never be left behind, whether for a basic day hike or a multi-day winter trip. Balaclavas perform many of the functions of a hat but also insulate your head and neck, and provide better wind protection — at the expense of overheating in the neck area.

The human body loses a disproportionate amount of heat out of the head and neck because of the close proximity of the major arteries and veins near the skin surface and because of the relatively high surface-area-to-volume ratio of the head and neck. In addition, since many hikers don't like the confining nature and inhibited breathability/ventilation caused by wearing a shell hood, a balaclava provides some wind protection for this part of the body without requiring you to don a fully windproof shell. This makes a balaclava useful for regulating your body temperature quickly and easily while hiking. You can take it off and stuff it in a pocket for hiking uphill, and pull it out while at rest or traversing a windy ridge.

Thin, base-layer balaclavas that weigh 1–2 ounces provide far more versatility than thicker fleece balaclavas. They are more breathable and can be used in a wider range of conditions. A thin balaclava provides enough temperature regulation to prevent taking it on and off as frequently as a fleece balaclava.

The standard hat (often called a "watch cap") usually weighs 1–2 ounces, is made of fleece or merino wool, and provides plenty of head insulation for mild summer conditions. Its simplicity, low pack volume, and usefulness in regulating temperature make it an essential component of most ultralight hiking kits. The primary disadvantage of thin poly and merino watch caps is their lack of loft — usually less than 0.2 inches.

A relatively new product to hit the US market, the PossumDown Beanie Hat, blends merino wool with high-loft Australian possum fibers to achieve a very warm hat that weighs only 1.4 ounces. Other high-loft watch caps are typically made of 300 weight fleece and weigh 2–3 ounces.

Combining a thin balaclava with a high-loft, low-weight watch cap offers more versatility for three-season hiking than a single, heavier "bomber cap" or fleece balaclava more sensitive to overheating. When wet, the fleece dries slower than the two lighter layers, which can be separated to dry more quickly.

For very cold weather, breathing through a face mask keeps humidity near your mouth high. That can help reduce evaporative heat loss during respiration and reduce the heat loss associated with rewarming inhaled cold air. A face mask works both by warming the air you breathe, by storing heat released during exhalation, and by increasing the moisture of the air you breathe by minimizing moisture lost during exhalation.

GLOVES

"Always carry spare gloves," goes the mantra of the mountaineer, one that has unfortunately instilled fear into anyone who picks up a backpack for any kind of journey. "Gloves are easily dropped, blown off windy ridges, mislaid in a pack, and otherwise lost."

The reality for the backpacker is quite different: If you lose your gloves, grin and bear it. Just put your hands in your pockets or withdraw them into your jacket sleeves. For colder conditions, get creative. More than one mountaineer who has lost their gloves has worn their spare socks on their hands and used stuff sacks for mitten shells.

Gloves are an incredibly useful piece of equipment. Their primary functions are to keep your hands warm and to protect them from the numbing effects of wind chill, especially in wet conditions. In the winter, gloves are absolutely essential for preventing frostbite. In the winter, or in the high mountains of Alaska, the Andes, or the Himalaya, carrying a spare pare of gloves makes perfect sense. You want to keep your digits.

But for most situations that backpackers face in temperate climates, especially during the summer months, gloves are primarily a comfort item. As the temperature approaches 45°F and lower, wearing gloves prevents your fingers from going numb and greatly improves your dexterity for performing camp chores and handling navigation equipment on the trail. Gloves are by no means required to keep your hands warm, but they do make life easier.

Perhaps the most versatile handwear you can include in your backpacking kit is a pair of lightweight, breathable fleece or wool gloves. Fleece offers more loft than merino wool, but fleece and high-loft ragg wool gloves weigh 3 ounces or more per pair. Like the unique PossumDown Beanie Hat, the PossumDown Gloves provide more loft than 100 percent merino and weigh less (1.2 oz, size M) than many base-layer, synthetic liner gloves from other manufacturers. A pair of lightweight gloves provides plenty of hand protection for most summer trips.

In windier climates, some hikers like windproof fleece gloves. However, windproof fleece at its lightest weights is not particularly warm and is typically slow to dry because of inhibited breathability through the windproof membrane. In addition, construction methods for windproof fleece include bulky interior seams that can be uncomfortable while hiking with trekking poles or ice axes. One of the more comfortable, and lighter, products on the market is the now discontinued Outdoor Research Windstopper Tech glove (2.2 oz, size M), which offers a polyurethane-patterned palm that improves durability and friction when handling tools or poles.

In general, two-layer glove systems work well enough. Many ultralight backpackers also pack a very light pair of waterproof shell mitts for rain and wind protection. A homemade pair can be made using silicone coated nylon, at a weight of less than half an ounce. For a more robust and comfortable system, the Outdoor Research Rain Mitts and Lobster Claw Rain Mitts (1.5 oz, size L) provided waterproof-breathable protection in a very compact package. They've since been replaced by a heavier, more durable mitt shell that weigh twice as much.

Gone are the days where three-season, lightweight back-packers carry the old standard of liner gloves, windproof gloves, and gauntlet style shell mitts. For the ultralight fringe, simply withdrawing your hands into your poncho or rain jacket sleeves can provide enough protection to allow you to forgo the use of rain mitts. Simply using a pair of high-loft fleece or possum-wool gloves often provides plenty of warmth while hiking, even when your gloves are very wet.

Mittens may be your only option to stay warm if the weather goes wintry or you have hands that run cold. Gloved hands provide substantial surface area for heat loss relative to mittened hands. In addition, fingers in a mitten can share (conserve) body heat, where fingers in a glove are essentially isolated and insulated from each other. It follows that a pair of 3-ounce mittens can be far warmer than a pair of 3-ounce gloves. For maximum warmth/weight ratio, a pair of lightweight fleece mittens may be all you need if you value finger warmth over dexterity.

Fingerless gloves are a way to provide warmth and dex-terity. They are great when you need to do things like tie a knot in fishing line or operate a stove. A pair of windproof fleece fingerless gloves can weigh as little as 2 ounces. Com-bined with thin liner gloves for colder conditions and/or a pair of lightweight mitt shells, fingerless gloves are the core item in many hikers' handwear systems.

Mitts and gloves insulated with high-loft insulation, such as thick fleece, goose down, Primaloft, or Polarguard, are typically useful only for winter conditions. Even so, most models are still too heavy to consider in the context of lightweight backpacking. Notable exceptions are the Integral Designs Down Mitts (4 oz, size M) and the RBH Designs Ultralight Vapor Mitts (6.5 oz, size M). The Down Mitts provide excellent insulation at rest stops or in camp, while the Ultralight Vapor Mitts (vapor barrier, fleece lined), with their leather palm, long gauntlet, and waterproof silnylon shell, are more suitable for active conditions in severely cold or inclement weather.

Wind and Rain Protection

People have strong feelings about staying warm, dry, and comfortable in inclement weather — and for good reason. The ideal shell fabric for inclement conditions has the following properties:

- Waterproof enough to withstand a Tasmanian rain
- Windproof enough for the Dakota Badlands
- Breathable enough so you didn't sweat while climbing north out of Bly Gap
- Durable enough for slide alder bushwacking
- Compressible enough to fit into a water bottle pocket — with your water bottle
- Fashionable enough to make you look like a million bucks on a gray and rainy day
- Light enough not to aggravate you because it sat in the bottom of your pack for the length of your 10-day trek during a freak drought period.

The ideal shell does not exist. Manufacturers of shell garments almost offer as much unsubstantiated marketing hype about the performance of their shell garments as the manufacturers of backpacks.

Ultimately, you'll need to select a shell that performs well in areas that are important to you and hope that it does a reasonable job in other areas. Because of the multitude of shell garments that are on the market, we can't hope to discuss even a fraction of them here. Nor can this text hope to provide information about technical fabrics that won't be out of date next season. We'll simply discuss the overall features of shell categories, provide examples of exceptional products in those categories, and arm the reader with as much information as possible to allow them to make a reasonably informed decision.

CLASSES OF SHELL FABRICS AND GARMENTS

Highly breathable, wind-resistant, microfiber windshirts

The following fabrics fall into the class of garments commonly referred to as "windshirts."

- Ultralight, 1.1-ounce ripstop nylon — used in the Wild Things Windshirt and one of the favorite fabrics of the make-your-own-gear community
- Pertex Quantum — used in the Montane Aero Smock and Rab Quantum Top
- Pertex Microlight — Montane Featherlite Smock and Montane Light Speed Jacket
- Microfiber polyesters — GoLite Bark and Marmot Chinook

Windshirts typically weigh 3.5 to 6.0 ounces, with lighter models offered as pullover styles without hoods. These windshirts are made with fabrics that weigh as little as 0.9 ounces/yd^2, and compress to a volume smaller than a typical mug of coffee. A common feature is that they offer more breathability, faster drying time, lighter weight, and more compressibility than virtually any other garment on the market. Their primary performance advantage is realized when they are worn over a single base-layer shirt. The windshirt adds surprising warmth, wind protection, light rain and snow protection, and a barrier against biting insects.

Moderately breathable, water-resistant, coated nylon "shower shells"

A new class of windshirt fabrics has emerged in the past few years. These are typically woven nylon fabrics with a light acrylic (e.g., GoLite Helios) or polyurethane (e.g., Ibex Bug Wing) coating. Such fabrics are more water resistant than microfiber, so they are marketed primarily to the running and day-hiking community. If you get caught in a squall, they offer enough rain protection to get you back to the trailhead reasonably dry.

For the backpacker, they are useful when combined with a poncho: Wear the shower shell for light to medium rain, donning the poncho only for more severe storms. Because of their limited breathability relative to fabrics like Pertex Quantum or 1.1-ounce nylon, they are less suitable for high-exertion activities, such as vertical climbing and rigorous uphill hiking, or for use in warmer conditions. Their key advantage is the added water resistance. Like their more breathable cousins, shower-shell fabrics are also very light in weight and highly compressible. Hooded, full-zip jackets typically weigh 4.0–5.5 ounces.

Low-water absorption, fiber-encapsulated fabrics

Low-water absorption fabrics were popularized by Nextec's EPIC technology, which encapsulates individual fibers with a very thin silicone-based coating that minimizes the absorption of water into the finished fabric structure. Their key benefit is not the water resistance of the fabric, but rather the rapid drying time. In fact, the water resistance of EPIC-treated fabrics breaks down rapidly as the coating fails (e.g., gets dirty from sweat, body oils, and dirt). However, because EPIC-treated fabrics hold so little moisture at the fiber surface and in the interstices of a finished fabric, they dry remarkably fast. This feature is a significant benefit when hiking in conditions of intermittent rain and snow.

One of the disadvantages of EPIC garments is their limited breathability, especially when wet. Tests performed by the US Army's Natick Lab suggest that EPIC breathability is less than many of the other similar fabrics on the market.

EPIC is used in shell jackets from Wild Things and Go-Lite. Similar encapsulation technology is used in garments by Patagonia. However, one of the more innovative designs in EPIC shells is the Jackorack from Feathered Friends in Seattle, Washington. The EPIC Jackorack weighs 8.6 ounces (size M), has huge torso vents and pit zips, a roomy hood, and a long hem. We've used the Jackorack with great success in a variety of conditions and find it to be one of the most versatile, fully-featured wind shells available.

Stretch-woven soft shells

In spite of childish arguments among outdoor specialty manufacturers regarding the definition of a soft shell, a recent survey indicates that more than 85 percent of backpackers identify the term with stretch-woven, non-waterproof fabrics. This is the foundation for the popular line of Cloudveil's soft shell apparel that uses stretch-woven textiles manufactured by Schoeller of Switzerland. Since that time, virtually every major outdoor specialty manufacturer has entered the soft shell market with lofty promises of "weather resistance and unparalleled breathability."

Although some light soft shell garments exist (e.g., Cloudveil Prospector Pullover, 8.0 ounces, size M), few of them are going to save weight in a clothing system for most three-season backpackers. Much of the time, they will simply be dead weight in the backpack, especially during the summer.

The real utility of soft shell garments is realized in fringe seasons—late fall, early spring—and winter conditions in the mountains, where a backpacker is wearing a jacket all of the time while moving. Because soft shell fabrics have a more open weave, they are more breathable than microfiber nylon and polyester fabrics used in most windshirts. In addition, because many soft shell fabrics are multilayer weaves (e.g., Schoeller Dryskin Extreme) or bicomponent constructions (e.g., Ibex ClimaWool or Polartec PowerShield), they offer some insulating loft.

Soft shell fabrics are not waterproof. They are woven so that the fabric face is tight and naturally promotes water shedding. This, combined with their excellent breathability, means that soft shell garments can often be more comfortable than windshirts during high-exertion activities in cold, inclement conditions short of a downpour. Skiers, winter climbers, and snowshoe backpackers are particular fans of soft shell garments because of their ability to regulate temperature in cold conditions and provide plenty of protection from falling snow.

Soft shell fabrics offer several disadvantages that make them impractical for most summer backpacking. They are heavier and generally warmer to hike in than windshirts — the lightest jackets range from 12–18 ounces. They absorb quite a lot of water, relative to the ultralight windshirt fabrics, and take a long time to dry if they get wet.

A range of soft shell fabrics exist, offering the consumer a variety of different weights, levels of breathability, warmth, and moisture protection. In order of decreasing breathability and increasing wind and water resistance, notable fabrics for lightweight backpackers include:

- Cloudveil Inertia — used in the Prospector Jacket, 12 oz
- Schoeller Dynamic — used on the Black Diamond Alpine Shirt, 14 oz
- ClimaWool — Ibex Icefall Jacket, 16 oz
- Schoeller Dryskin Extreme — Cloudveil Serendipity Jacket, 17 oz
- Polartec Powershield Micro — GoLite Momentum Jacket, 15 oz

Waterproof-breathable rain jackets

Waterproof-breathable fabrics typically offer less breathability than windshirt fabrics. Commonly used in what backpackers recognize as "rain jackets," they include Gore-Tex, eVENT, and others. The objective of waterproof-breathable rain jackets is simple: to provide protection that is completely impermeable to water and wind. Because of their limited breathability, these garments are intended primarily for inclement conditions and to protect the body against the chilling effects of wind and cold rain during low-to-moderate exertion activities, such as level hiking or performing camp chores.

Waterproof-breathable fabrics use a variety of technologies that most commonly include some combination of microporous polyurethane coatings and PTFE or nonwoven polypropylene membranes.

- Nonwoven polypropylene membranes — used in Rainshield, Frogg Toggs, and DriDucks garments — are among the most breathable and least expensive
- Next are PTFE-only constructions — e.g., eVENT
- PTFE-polyurethane laminates — e.g., Gore-Tex Pac-Lite III and XCR
- Polyurethane coatings — e.g., Marmot Precip, Patagonia Specter

Because the primary disadvantage is the limited breathability of the fabric, it is worthwhile to add ventilation features, such as pit zips, full-front zippers, and vented torso pockets. Also, waterproof-breathable fabrics are, as a general rule, heavier than the windshirt fabrics. Notable exceptions include the polypropylene laminates, which are used in full-zip hooded rain jackets weighing as little as 5 ounces (e.g., Rainshield O_2 Jacket) and Gore-Tex Pac-Lite Matrix (used in the Haglöfs LIM Jacket, 8.6 oz).

Generally, most waterproof-breathable, woven nylon fabrics are durable enough for trail backpacking and intermittent or occasional bushwacking or rock scrambling. Nonwoven polypropylene laminates must be used with greater care, as their tear strength is less than that of nylon.

A more comprehensive discussion of waterproof-breathable technologies, advantages, and disadvantages is available in the article, "Waterproof Breathable Fabric Technologies: A Comprehensive Primer and State of the Market Technology Review" by Alan Dixon. (February 10, 2004; www.backpackinglight.com; ISSN 1537-0364).

Waterproof-nonbreathable rain jackets

Long before waterproof-breathable nylon fabrics came on the market, rainwear was made with polyurethane-coated nylon, a nonbreathable class of fabric that was better known for its ability to retain sweat and soak you from within than for its ability to repel rain. Waterproof-breathable fabrics heralded the death of these rain jackets, at least in the outdoor specialty industry. However, recent innovations in waterproof-nonbreathable fabrics that have driven price and weight down are keeping lightweight backpackers interested in this category.

The Sierra Designs Backpackers Rainwear Jacket (12 oz) offers pit zips, torso vents, and a full-zip, hooded jacket that fits comfortably and works well for less than $70. Lighter options exist but are rare outside the cottage industry. A rain jacket made from 1.4 ounces/yd² silicone-coated nylon is manufactured by Dancing Light Gear of Georgia and weighs less than 5 ounces. Similar offerings are made by Stephenson's of New Hampshire and Equinox of Pennsylvania.

Ponchos

Ultralight backpackers have long been a fan of ponchos, and more specifically, poncho-tarps, those dual-use items that can double as both raingear and shelter. Ponchos are most commonly made with waterproof-nonbreathable fabrics, with 1.4 ounce/yd² silicone-coated nylon being the fabric of choice among the ultralight hiking community. Silicone-coated nylon poncho-tarps typically weigh 7–10 ounces and are offered by GoLite, Integral Designs, Equinox, Dancing Light Gear, Oware USA, and others. Hilleberg makes a waterproof-breathable bivy sack that doubles as a poncho, but its utility as rainwear is limited by a copious amount of fabric and relatively heavy weight (24 oz). Lighter ponchos that do not serve double duty as tarps are available from Stephenson's (silicone-coated nylon, 7 oz). And a lighter poncho-tarp made with silicone-coated sailcloth, the SpinPoncho (6.5 oz), is available from Bozeman Mountain Works.

The primary limitation of a poncho is taming its fabric in the wind. Having used ponchos in extremely windy conditions on the coast and even above treeline in the mountains, we offer some guidance in dealing with this challenge. Look for ponchos that have strategically placed side snaps or zippers and a rear hem drawcord that can be tied to the front of its wearer like a belt. These ponchos go a long way in offering you a warm, dry haven in a wild storm. In addition, because ponchos are made using nonbreathable fabrics, significant condensation can build up in the shoulder area, where the fabric is in contact with the rest of your clothing.

The benefits of ponchos are numerous:

- They can serve as a pack cover
- They are generally lighter and cheaper than a rain jacket
- They offer excellent ventilation — aiding comfort and keeping you cool during high exertion
- The poncho-tarp is probably the lightest possible combination of shelter and raingear that can be carried by the ultralight backpacker

Umbrellas

Considered by some to be the summa cum laude of breathable rain protection, the umbrella is worth considering under the following conditions:

- You are creative enough to affix it to your pack so you don't have to carry it for hours on end
- You are not trying to use it in very windy situations
- You are carrying a rain jacket as backup

Umbrellas may be considered the icon of eccentricity among the ultralight community. But used properly in mild conditions, there may be no more comfortable way to hike in the rain.

USE YOUR SHELL INTELLIGENTLY

Many backpackers unfairly blame manufacturers on poor raingear performance. Often, backpackers simply don't understand how to properly use a rain shell. Most dissatisfaction stems from overwhelming the garment's capacity to breathe, resulting in the accumulation of excessive moisture that wets the base and insulating layers. Even highly breathable windshirts and soft shells can cause excessive moisture accumulation, clamminess, and discomfort under the right conditions.

Unfortunately, you can't teach someone how to use a rain jacket through a book or magazine article. Experience is king, and only by understanding the complex relationship between your body's physiology, level of exertion, environmental conditions (wind, humidity, and temperature), and garment functionality (fabric breathability, ventilation features) can you begin to understand the limitations of raingear in terms of how it manages internal moisture. So we offer here only the basic framework for managing moisture in shell garments:

- When making adjustments to your clothing system in inclement conditions, your singular goal in terms of regulating body temperature should focus on keeping your base layer as dry as possible.
- While wearing a shell, start by layering it only over your base layer. It will provide a surprising amount of warmth. A mistake that is commonly made by backpackers is to stop when it begins to rain, perceive the potential danger of hypothermia, and add a fleece jacket *and* a waterproof-breathable rain jacket. The result is often an overdressed hiker who begins to destroy the insulating properties of his base layer and clothing by overheating and sweating.
- Take full advantage of your shell garment's ventilation features to exchange warm, moist air building up inside your shell with cooler, drier air from the environment. Pit zips, torso zips, front zips, hood openings, wrist cuffs, and hem drawcords can all be used to regulate both moisture accumulation and body temperature. Ventilation is a far more effective method for reducing moisture accumulation than garment breathability alone.

SHELL PANTS?

Most of the previous discussion applies to shell pants as much as it does to shell jackets, with one notable exception. While active, the body loses much more heat in the torso than in the legs — although while climbing, quadriceps can produce a tremendous amount of heat. Consequently, you are more prone to overheating your torso than your pants. Thus, two general lightweight backpacking philosophies exist:

1. Because the body loses less heat through the legs, shell pants are not as critical as a shell jacket while hiking in the rain. Many ultralight hikers don't even carry shell pants during the summer. Exceptions exist. In very cold, wet, and windy conditions, shell pants that provide full leg coverage are essential to prevent the upper legs from getting wet, either directly from external precipitation or indirectly from the wicking of moisture up the legs of hiking pants.
2. Because the legs are less sensitive to heat loss, they require less sophisticated temperature regulation. Consequently, for moderate backpacking adequate shell pants can be made with lighter fabrics, fewer features (e.g., ventilating side zips), cheaper materials, and/or less breathable fabrics (e.g., silicone-coated nylon, instead of waterproof-breathable Gore-Tex).

Some hikers prefer rain chaps under a long jacket or poncho. Silicone-coated nylon rain chaps, which weigh around 3 ounces for the pair, are available from Moonbow Gear in New Hampshire.

Insulating Garments

FLEECE

For many years, the standard material for insulating garments has been polyester fleece. Lightweight fleece pullovers and jackets of reasonable quality are manufactured by dozens of outdoor specialty companies that offer them at impossibly high prices considering that garments having a similar degree of functionality are now available at discount and big box stores for less than $20. The wide availability of cheap fleece remains the reason why outdoor specialty manufacturers are spending less energy developing innovative fleece products and more energy on other insulating garments.

Although fleece has the lowest dry insulating value, it still has a place. Fleece breathes well, and retains most of its insulating value (loft) when wet. Because of its breathability, it may be the best insulation for use under a shell in cold weather. In this application, its breathability and moisture transport may outweigh its inefficiency as an insulator.

Fleece is the least compressible of the insulating materials discussed here and takes up a tremendous amount of room in the smaller packs coveted by most ultralight backpackers.

Windproof fleece is offered by most major outdoor specialty manufacturers. However, due to its limited breathability, it is not a particularly comfortable garment for high-exertion backpacking. And it's heavy. Windproof fleece jackets weigh 16–32 ounces or more. If you want a windproof insulating garment, you're better off with high-loft insulation.

Chief among insulating garments are those with *high-loft* insulation.

- High-quality goose down
- Primaloft — a short-staple synthetic fiber
- Polarguard — a continuous-filament synthetic fiber

HIGH LOFT

High-loft insulating clothing offers the highest warmth/weight ratio of any clothing available. You'll use your high-loft apparel on cool evenings and mornings in camp, and probably at rest stops in cold weather. High-loft clothing provides insurance if you run into extremely inclement weather. It can supplement a lightweight sleeping bag, providing core warmth to extend the comfort range of your bag to cooler temperatures. Used alone with a bivy sack, high-loft insulating clothing can be suitable as a sleeping bag, common for alpine and adventure racing bivouac camps.

The ideal high-loft insulating garment includes the following:

- Warm enough for the coldest conditions
- Maintains its insulating loft when wet
- Manufactured with ultralight shell and lining fabrics for minimum weight
- Highly compressible
- Absorbs little water and dries quickly
- Has durable insulation that lasts forever

The ideal high-loft insulating garment does not exist.

High-loft insulating garments are distinguished primarily by their style (vest, pullover, jacket, pants) and secondarily by their insulation and shell materials.

Insulated vests are the lightest high-loft garments available. The Western Mountaineering Flight Vest (850-fill down with a full-front zipper and handwarmer pockets) weighs a scant 5 ounces in a size M. Synthetic insulated vests are available from GoLite, Patagonia, Moonstone, and others, and typically weigh 8–12 ounces.

Lightly insulated pullovers are the coveted darling of the ultralight backpacking community, typically offering the highest warmth/weight ratios of any insulating garment. These no-frills apparel pieces typically weigh between 10–16 ounces and are filled with Primaloft or Polarguard synthetic insulation. Examples include

- MEC Northern Lite — Primaloft PL1, 12 oz
- Rab Photon Smock — Primaloft PL1, 12 oz
- Patagonia Micro Puff — Polarguard Delta, 11 oz
- Berghaus Infinity Lite — Primaloft PL1, 9.7 oz
- Bozeman Mountain Works Cocoon — Polarguard Delta, 8.0 oz

The Rab Photon Smock certainly offers the most features, including handwarmer pockets, a drawstring collar and hem, and a deep 2-way zipper. The Bozeman Mountain Works Cocoon achieves its very light weight by using unscrimmed

Polarguard Delta insulation that is not subjected to the compressive destruction induced by a quilting machine, along with a Pertex Quantum shell and lining.

Lightweight synthetic jackets and hooded jackets are also available from companies such as Wild Things, GoLite, Patagonia, and others, with weights ranging from 14–18 ounces. Ultralight down jackets from 10–12 ounces are available from Western Mountaineering, Feathered Friends, and GoLite. Notable in this category are the thinly insulated MontBell Ultralight Inner Jacket (down) and Thermawrap Jacket (synthetic). Both weigh about 8 ounces. Also notable is the Western Mountaineering Flight Jacket, which offers three times the loft for only 2 additional ounces in weight.

More options exist for those looking for winter backpacking insulation. Hooded, "belay jackets" are available from Rab, Integral Designs, GoLite, Nunatak, Feathered Friends, and Wild Things, and typically weigh 22–28 ounces. At the lighter end of this spectrum is the Rab Quantum Down Jacket, which offers a Pertex Quantum lining and shell, sewn-through baffling, and 850+ fill goose down. At only 21 ounces, this may be the highest warmth/weight ratio of any insulated jacket in its class.

DOWN VERSUS SYNTHETIC

Down is hydrophilic. It absorbs moisture, resulting in consolidation of plumules that collapse the interstitial space responsible for trapping warm air for insulation. In contrast, synthetic insulations are generally hydrophobic and do not absorb moisture. Loft collapse is less sensitive to moisture.

The choice between down and synthetic depends on the climate at your destination, length of trip, and intended end use.

Generally, wet and humid conditions—such as those found in the Scottish Highlands, New Zealand Alps, or Pacific Northwest of the US—demand synthetic insulation. Drier areas—such as the desert Southwest of the US, Rocky Mountains, or during the winter—allow for the use of down garments.

Even in wet areas, the well-outfitted ultralight backpacker will have both down and synthetic insulating garments ready, making a final decision after reviewing a last-minute weather report.

Garments filled with down will nearly always be lighter than garments filled with synthetic insulation. High-grade down (800-fill or higher) is expensive, but garments and sleeping bags made with it are on the top of the wish lists of every ultralight backpacker seeking to bring pack weight down as low as possible.

PRIMALOFT VERSUS POLARGUARD

The choice between the two high-performance synthetic insulations is made more difficult by each manufacturer's marketing strategies, which claims that one is better than the other. For the purposes of this discussion, we'll focus on each manufacturer's premier product in terms of warmth/weight ratio for ultralight garments: Primaloft PL1 and Polarguard Delta, both of which are available in various weights.

Primaloft PL1 is a short-staple fiber, which means that it requires a *scrim* layer during the quilting process to stabilize the insulation and prevent it from shifting. This scrim adds about 0.5 ounce/yd² to the insulation weight. In contrast, Polarguard Delta is made with continuous filament fibers and does not require the additional weight of a scrim. In reality, both insulations are nearly always manufactured with a scrim layer. A scrim is required for machine quilting and makes the manufacturing process simpler and cheaper.

Because PL1 is a short-staple fiber, it may suffer more loft degradation than Delta. It is well known that PL1-insulated garments and sleeping bags have a shorter life expectancy than Delta-insulated garments. However, this may not be so important to ultralight backpackers, who commonly replace their insulating garments as new styles and technologies hit the market.

Also, a garment made with PL1 is softer and drapes more comfortably than a Delta-insulated garment. Because PL1 "feels more like down," it is an excellent insulation to use if your primary distribution strategy is to trigger feel-good sales in a retail floor!

Other factors aside, the primary battle between the synthetic insulation champs is fought in the area of water resistance and warmth when wet. The differences between PL1 and Delta are related primarily by their water absorption capacity, drying time, and ability to maintain loft when wet. In our tests, garments insulated with Polarguard Delta generally absorb more water per unit weight than equivalent garments insulated with Primaloft PL1. However, if soaked, Delta-insulated garments are easier to wring out to a lighter weight, take less time to dry, and are restored to a higher level of loft.

In reality, the chance that you'll completely soak your synthetic garment is slim. Garments made with either Primaloft PL1 or Polarguard Delta are likely going to serve your insulating needs equally well, with a slight advantage given to Polarguard Delta-insulated garments due to a higher loft/weight ratio and life expectancy of the loft (durability).

Other synthetic insulations do exist, but they cannot match the loft/weight ratio of PL1 or Delta and are not generally found in higher quality outdoor specialty goods.

Fortunately, insulating garments aren't as complex as shells. There are only three main types of insulation: fleece, synthetic fill, and down. For most hikers, a synthetic-fill jacket is probably the best choice. It combines the best combination of insulating performance, safety when wet, and cost.

Summary of Insulating Materials

The following table summarizes the comparison of fleece and high-loft insulating garments.

FLEECE

Pros

- Excellent breathability, wicking, and wet-weather warmth (loft retention)

- Good for use under a shell as insulation in cold weather at high exertion levels—e.g., winter mountaineering, cross country skiing
- Low cost

Cons
- Poor warmth/weight ratio
- The poorest insulator in dry conditions—by a large margin
- Not very compressible or
- Not very windproof—needs a shell to achieve full insulating performance
- Not a good choice except for high-exertion activities or limited funds

SYNTHETIC FILL
Pros
- Probably the best all-round insulation
- Generally, 3x more loft than fleece for the same weight
- Good wet-weather warmth (loft retention)
- Far more compressible than fleece
- Windproof
- Thinly insulated garments are useful layering pieces

Cons
- When dry, not nearly as good of an insulator as down
- Higher cost than fleece
- Insulation breaks down and will lose loft over time
- Much less compressible than down
- Shelled construction can inhibit breathability

DOWN
Pros
- When dry, 800+-fill down offers up to 4x the loft of an equivalent weight of synthetic fills and up to 12x the loft of fleece

- Shelled design makes it windproof
- Most compressible of the three
- Very durable insulation that retains loft for years with proper care

Cons

- High-fill down is very expensive and requires more expensive manufacturing processes.
- Down insulation is very sensitive to humidity and moisture — must be kept dry to retain insulating performance.
- Dries very slowly, if at all, in the field.
- Shelled design can inhibit breathability

A NOTE ON FILL POWER

The insulating performance of down is measured in *fill power*. A known weight of down is placed in a graduated cylinder with a lightly weighted disc resting on top of the down surface. The volume of the cylinder occupied by down is then measured and noted as its fill power. Lower quality down is usually in the range of 550–650 cubic inches per ounce. The highest quality down is rated as 850+.

Clothing Systems

As one might expect, the combination of layering pieces that can be used for a comfortable clothing system in the wide range of conditions you will encounter for three-season backpacking is overwhelming. Most ultralight backpackers keep their clothing systems relatively simple. By far, one of the lightest and simplest systems, suitable for June–August backpacking in most of the US, is comprised of:

- Thin, synthetic, long-sleeve, base-layer crewneck shirt (e.g., GoLite C-Thru, 4.5 oz)
- Synthetic insulating pullover (e.g., Bozeman Mountain Works Cocoon, 8.0 oz)
- Waterproof-breathable, nonwoven polypropylene rain jacket (e.g., Rain Shield Multi-Use Jacket, 4.5 oz)

- Bidirectional woven nylon hiking pants (e.g., GoLite Synergy, 9.0 oz)
- Waterproof-breathable, pull-on rain pants (e.g., Go-Lite Reed, 4.5 oz)
- Knit wool gloves (e.g., PossumDown Gloves, 1.2 oz)
- Knit wool beanie hat (e.g., PossumDown Beanie, 1.4 oz)

Substitutions or additions to a clothing system like this will depend on personal preference for garment styles. Some people prefer jackets to pullovers. Depending on expected weather, a 3-ounce windshirt might be added if you're venturing into a dry, windy area. Or you might replace the rain jacket and tarp/tent with a poncho-tarp. And depending on the terrain you'll be hiking, a more durable rain jacket may be preferred for a fair bit of bushwhacking.

Clothing systems for winter conditions where temperatures are always below freezing are not all that different but do demand a few notable changes. Waterproof-breathable shell jackets and pants are often replaced with water-resistant, windproof garments, or soft shell garments. Insulating garments are nearly always heavier. In more extreme conditions, such as winter Arctic snowshoeing or mountaineering, more layers may be desirable, focusing primarily on additional lightweight, fast-drying base layers and more robust hand and headwear.

For very wet conditions, lightweight rain mitts, a broad-brimmed rain hat, and waterproof gaiters might be added. The next section focuses on managing moisture in wet and cold conditions.

Moisture Management

Moisture management is a critical skill for cold weather hiking with ultralight gear. If an article of clothing gets saturated, it will likely take a long time to dry. In the meantime, the moisture works against you, sapping body heat and creating a general sense of emotional and physical discomfort.

For example, a pair of gloves can get pretty sweaty during a day of winter hiking. If you take them off at a rest stop and lay them on a stump for ten minutes while you eat a snack, they may be frozen solid when you return. A better strategy is to tuck them inside your shell against your chest, where they'll stay warm until you need them again.

One of the only ways to dry wet clothing in cold weather is to take it into your sleeping bag with you at night. But this can have serious consequences. Too much damp clothing in your sleeping bag may overwhelm the breathability of your bag, and you'll compromise the bag's insulation — dangerous in cold conditions. With ultralight down sleeping bags, taking a significant amount of wet clothing to bed when you expect outside temperatures to be less than 40°F will cause serious moisture accumulation in the down insulation. Below 40°F, the *dew point* (where moisture vapor condenses to water) can be inside the sleeping bag's insulation, although it's also dependent on humidity, wind, and other factors. If so, moisture evaporating from your wet clothing will simply reform as liquid in the sleeping bag insulation.

The best option is not to get your clothing wet in the first place, a learned skill requiring careful attention to moisture management when hiking — and sweating — in cold and wet conditions. Other more reactive measures that can be employed in wet conditions include:

1. Stop early to set up camp. It's far easier to set up camp and keep your gear and clothing dry in the daytime than after dark.
2. If you are a fan of sleeping in a bivy sack under a tarp, consider bivy sacks that are more breathable than waterproof (e.g., those made with Pertex Quantum shells or EPIC). More breathable fabrics let moisture from wet clothing pass, rather than condense on the inside of the bivy sack shell and wet your sleeping bag.
3. If you carry a poncho-tarp for both raingear and shelter, include a more water-resistant windshirt in your clothing system (e.g., GoLite Helios or Ibex

Bug Wing). It will keep you dry enough in the short time required to remove your poncho and set it up as shelter while it's raining.

4. You will always dry clothing the fastest with body heat during active periods. Often, a wet base layer will be dry after only the few minutes required to set up camp and perform basic chores. Take advantage of this period of activity to both burn and ventilate a significant amount of moisture out of your clothing system, and minimize the amount of moisture you take into your sleeping bag with you.

5. Direct sunlight is a godsend on trips characterized by constant rain. Take advantage of any break in the weather to hang and dry sleeping bags, insulating clothing, and other wet items.

VAPOR BARRIERS

Moisture accumulation in clothing caused by perspiration is more of a problem in cold weather. It is commonly believed that (waterproof-nonbreathable) vapor-barrier clothing worn next to the skin prevents sweating and thus, keeps outer clothing layers dry by blocking perspiration. Nothing could be further from the truth. Vapor-barrier clothing used while active causes overheating, increases the body's perspiration response, and results in the massive accumulation of perspiration in clothing as a result of sweat wicking out of the vapor-barrier clothing and into the other layers.

Vapor-barrier clothing is best used to block *insensitive* perspiration—the dominant form of moisture loss through the skin when you are not active (sitting in camp, sleeping, etc.). As such, cold weather adventurers and mountaineers have long known the benefits of using vapor-barrier sleeping bag liners in their sleeping bags to protect the loss of loft of their insulation on extended trips in subzero weather.

The use of vapor barriers in insulated hand and footwear has profound implications. Because heat loss through hands and feet is so significant in cold conditions due to a high surface area/volume ratio of the extremities and their distance from the warm blood of the body's core, the ability to keep hand and foot insulation as dry as possible to minimize conductive and evaporative heat loss is very important. For very cold conditions, vapor-barrier hand and footwear is extremely useful.

Vapor-barrier clothing is manufactured by Stephenson's, Wild Country, Integral Designs, and RBH Designs. Only Stephenson's makes vapor-barrier shirts, and RBH Designs makes a complete line of excellent vapor-barrier handwear. Wild Country, Integral Designs, and RBH Designs offer a variety of insulated and non-insulated vapor-barrier socks.

In the context of designing an ultralight cold weather sleeping system, vapor-barrier clothing — shirts and pants — is more appropriate than vapor-barrier liners. With vapor-barrier sleeping bag liners, one must sleep naked or wearing only a single thin base layer. This prevents the use of other pieces in your clothing system and requires a heavier, warmer sleeping bag. With a vapor-barrier shirt and pants, one can wear the vapor-barrier clothing next to skin and layer over it their remaining insulating clothing. Plus, it does double duty as in-camp wear. Ideally, this offers several advantages: Moisture emitted by the body during the night (insensitive perspiration) does not accumulate in your clothing or sleeping bag and the entire system dries itself. In practice, it doesn't quite work this way, because most currently available vapor-barrier clothing is not waterproof enough at the seams to prevent the wicking of liquid moisture from within the vapor barrier to outer layers of clothing. Also, some of the fabrics assumed to be vapor impermeable allow enough moisture to pass through them to result in condensation. Thus, the ideal vapor-barrier clothing must be waterproof, vapor impermeable, have sealed seams, and offer adequate seals at cuffs and hems to prevent the escape of moisture.

Dealing With Heat and Sun

Even in the most temperate months the desert is a harsh environment. One can see daytime highs that reach 90 degrees and nighttime lows down to freezing. The classic example of these extreme conditions is a backpacking trip from the south rim to the north rim of the Grand Canyon.

The same principles we've outlined for selecting and using a clothing system apply to desert travel, with a few important exceptions. During the day, your main goal is to stay cool and protected from the sun. At night and in the early morning, you'll want enough warm clothes to keep you comfortable while standing around in the freezing temperatures of a shady narrows or canyon rim. The desert is warm and dry for much of the day, so moisture management is not as critical as in other environments. If you get anything wet, it will usually dry on its own after a few hours of hiking.

For a hiking shirt and pants, select the lightest fabrics you can find. Some hikers will prefer shorts over pants but that choice will depend largely on the desert locale and the nature of environmental hazards (e.g., thorny desert plants, rock sliding, and intense sunshine). UV exposure from direct sunlight is a real concern in the desert. To keep things simple and avoid reapplying sunscreen to your entire body, a long-sleeve shirt with a high collar, long pants, and wide-brimmed hat comprise a clothing system beloved by many desert travelers.

Choose light-colored hiking clothing. It will certainly show dirt a bit more, but the difference in comfort over black or dark clothing is dramatic.

In a desert, precipitation is rare. If you do get rain, it will most likely be from a desert thunderstorm in the middle of the day, when temperatures are very warm and the risk of hypothermia is very low. You may be able to get by with a water-resistant shell, such as a windshirt, as your sole rain garment. A poncho is another great option. Few experienced desert ultralight backpackers take rain pants. As always, check the long-term weather forecast before making final decisions on raingear, and be smart about your choices.

Conclusion

Your clothing is one of the most important pieces of equipment you take on any hike. With proper selection you'll be warm, dry, happy, at peak mental and physical performance, and most importantly, safe. With poor selection, you may have some very cold, wet, and miserable nights, and you may face diminished performance in critical conditions. Even so, ultralight backpackers agree that it makes little sense to carry more clothing than you can wear at any given time. Therefore, they take fewer garments, making sure each one offers great versatility and functionality.

Desert and high-mountain summer headgear: a wide-brimmed hat, like the **Tilley LT (3.0 oz)**, made with microfiber nylon, offers a good balance between breathability for warm conditions and wind / water resistance when the weather turns sour. On a hot day, soaking the hat in a stream and then wearing it wet provides comfort through evaporative cooling of the head.

Chapter 7: **Sleep Systems**

By Lee Van Horn

Ultralight backpackers covet a high-quality sleeping bag more than any other piece of gear. Any item that, when stuffed, is smaller and lighter than a loaf of bread and can keep you warm in temperatures in which you would otherwise freeze to death warrants high praise!

After spending a long day hiking in inclement conditions, the comfort that a warm, dry sleeping bag provides causes many backpackers to shell out hundreds of dollars on their perfect nighttime cocoon.

In addition to a backpack and a shelter, significant savings of a hiker's total pack weight can be accomplished by simply replacing their sleeping bag. For example, many synthetic bags rated to 30°F weigh about 2.5–3.0 pounds, but a high-fill down bag with ultralight shell materials rated to an equivalent temperature can weigh 2 pounds less.

An ultralight sleeping bag can be the most expensive purchase a backpacker makes. The lightest sleeping bags available use ultralight shell materials that require a tight enough weave to be downproof and are relatively expensive. Plus, high-fill down requires extensive and expensive processing. In light of this, we'll discuss features to look for in the ideal ultralight sleeping bag, and also evaluate some alternatives that won't break your back — or your bank account.

Sleeping Bag Warmth

Sleeping bags, like insulating apparel, keep you warm by minimizing the loss of body heat. As discussed in the chapter on thermoregulation, heat that is generated by your body escapes via four processes: evaporation, conduction, radiation, and convection. Evaporation is the energy lost when liquid water (sweat) changes to vapor. Conduction is the transfer of heat to anything you touch that is colder than yourself (e.g., snow, rock, ground). Radiation is the emission of thermal energy from uncovered body surfaces. And convection is heat loss due to air movement around your body (e.g., wind).

In the construction industry, the effectiveness of insulation at retaining heat is known as its *R-value*. This describes how well a type of insulation can resist heat loss. R-values are proportional to warmth: Warmer insulations are designated with higher R-values. Since R-values are also proportional to the thickness of the insulation — thicker insulations have higher R-values — it follows that thicker sleeping bags are warmer.

The thickness of a sleeping bag's insulation is called its *loft* and is most often reported as the thickness of the entire sleeping bag. Loft can be calculated by laying a sleeping bag on the ground and measuring the thickness of the bag. In practice, the thickness of the bag varies slightly along its length. Loft is thinner at the baffle seams and thicker at the baffle midpoints. Differences in loft along the length of a sleeping bag are more pronounced in overstuffed down bags than in synthetic fill bags.

Unfortunately, total loft isn't a fair indicator of a sleeping bag's warmth. Much of the insulation on the bottom of a sleeping bag remains compressed while lying in it. So insulation in the lower layer may not contribute significantly to the overall insulating capacity of the bag. Consequently, measuring the sleeping bag's upper-layer loft is a more accurate predictor of a bag's warmth.

Although many factors contribute to how warm you will sleep — including physiology and metabolism, sleeping bag design, clothing, and weather — some general rules of thumb apply to sleeping bag thickness and warmth. Typically, experienced ultralight backpackers use sleeping bags that have an upper-layer thickness of

- One inch for camping at nights between 40°–55°F
- Two inches for the range of 25°–40°F
- Three inches for 10°–25°F

Convective heat loss results primarily when your shelter is not protected from wind, but can be minimized by the sleeping bag's shell material. Convective heat loss becomes significant in down bags that have sewn-through baffling, or in synthetic bags that have sewn-through stitching of the insulating material. This results in zero-loft areas at the stitch lines, causing dramatic losses of heat when the sleeping bag is exposed to even slight winds.

Tarp campers are well aware of convective heat losses. A sleeping bag that can keep you warm on a windless 20°F night may result in a cold and uncomfortable 35°F night in the wind. To address this, the experienced tarp camper pitches a windward tarp wall directly to the ground and/or uses a bivy sack over the sleeping bag, which reduces the impact of wind on heat loss by creating an additional still layer of insulating air between the sleeping bag's outer shell and the inner surface of the bivy sack. Even where the bivy sack comes into contact with the sleeping bag shell and eliminates any air space, the double layer adds enough wind resistance to dramatically improve the performance of the sleeping bag system in windy conditions.

Conductive heat loss also needs to be addressed by your sleeping system. That is the reason why most backpackers use insulating, closed-cell foam sleeping pads in cold conditions or when camping on snow. It only takes one night of trying to sleep on cold ground before you realize the utility and comfort provided by a sleeping pad that is *incompressible* (to preserve the thickness of the sleeping pad under body weight) and *porous* (to entrap insulating air).

Finally, heat is also lost through evaporation while you sleep. You lose moisture through perspiration and respiration. The process by which your body heat is used to change this water from liquid to vapor causes evaporative heat loss. It is easily observed in the form of condensation on the walls of your shelter in the morning. This is caused by your emitted moisture vapor condensing onto the cold wall of the shelter.

Although there are methods to minimize evaporative heat loss, they are usually add-ons to your sleeping system, rather than already incorporated into the sleeping bag. And they are rarely used. Examples include vapor-barrier clothing, sleeping bag liners, and heat-exchanging face masks.

Sleeping Bag Designs

Now that we've reviewed the basics of staying warm at night, we can discuss the major design features that allow a sleeping bag to live up to this task in combination with the rest of your clothing and sleep systems.

RECTANGULAR VERSUS MUMMY

The most obvious difference in sleeping bag types is the shape: rectangular or mummy.

A rectangular bag is just that: an insulated rectangular sack that is usually zippered on one side and the bottom. The top remains open for your head.

Mummy bags are shaped more to the contours of the human body: wide in the torso and narrow in the legs. Often they include a hood with a drawstring that allows you to close the bag around your head, leaving only a small hole from which to breathe.

The primary advantage of a rectangular bag over a mummy bag is that it provides plenty of room in the legs, a benefit for bigger folks or for those who like to roll around a bit, cross their legs, pull a leg up to their chest, etc. In addition, rectangular bags can be completely unzipped into a quilt, giving the hiker flexibility on warmer nights, or allowing one bag to be shared as a quilt between two friendly people.

Rectangular bags, however, are not terribly popular among ultralight backpackers. Their excess interior real estate means that they are less efficient than mummy bags at keeping you warm. Comparing two bags with a similar temperature range and similarity of construction (shell material and fill type), the mummy bag will be lighter than the rectangular bag by 20–40 percent. In addition, a hooded mummy bag is usually more efficient at keeping you warm than a rectangular bag, which is often hoodless.

Some backpackers will find a compromise in hybrid designs that offer an efficient mummy shape and a hood, but with a less aggressive torso-to-leg taper.

TOP BAGS AND QUILTS

At the other end of the spectrum from a mummy bag with a contoured shape is a simple, rectangular, insulated quilt that can simply drape over you at night. These designs are primarily suited to mild conditions. Few backpackers find quilts efficient enough to keep them warm at temperatures below about 50°F.

One step up from a rectangular quilt is a tapered quilt—wide in the shoulders, narrow in the footbox—with the bottom edges and part of the lower side edges sewn into a footbox for maximum efficiency. This concept addresses the need to keep the feet and legs warmer at night, an area less insulated than the torso simply by nature of the clothing systems used by most backpackers. Such quilts can be effectively used down to temperatures around freezing when combined with proper warm headwear and other clothing.

Adding a few straps to the side edges and a drawcord at the neck of the sewn-footbox-quilt design gives the hiker the ability to secure the straps under a sleeping pad. This eliminates cold spots at the pad edge, common when using quilts that are loosely draped. Such *arc cross-section* designs are capable of keeping you comfortable in temperatures well below freezing when combined with appropriate warm headwear. The adjustable straps provide variable girth control to accommodate a wide variety of clothing systems.

The variable girth, arc cross-section quilt is certainly one of the most versatile sleeping bag designs. It was originally proposed, and has since been further advanced, by Don Johnston, a lightweight backpacker from Maryland. Nunatak USA of Twisp, Washington, has commercialized the concept in their Arc Alpinist. Don has graciously offered his design concept to the public domain, so expect similar designs from other manufacturers to appear in the near future. More information and history about the design is detailed in "The Arc Bag Concept: Saving Weight with Variable Girth Sleeping Bags Having an 'Arc' Shaped Cross Section" by Ryan Jordan (BackpackingLight.com, April 29, 2001).

Hybrid designs modeled after mummy bags but eliminating bottom insulation, have been around for several years. They include designs from Macpac of New Zealand and Rab Carrington of the UK. More recently, Western Mountaineering, Big Agnes, and Si-

A variable girth sleeping bag, like this design from Nunatak USA, weighs 22 oz and has tapered loft ranging from three inches (single layer) of 800+ fill down in the torso to more than nine inches (double layer) in the footbox. This bag is used by Ryan Jordan in conjunction with normal three-season clothing for temperatures down to the single digits (Fahrenheit).

erra Designs in the USA have created similar products. Some of these replace bottom fill with a fabric sleeve into which a sleeping pad can slide, effectively creating a cohesive sleeping-bag-and-pad unit that addresses the problem of sliding off your sleeping pad while moving around at night.

**The Rab Carrington Elite
Top Bag** weighs only 14 ounces
and provides an inch and a half
of top-layer down in this fixed-girth,
hoodless design with no bottom insulation.

ADDITIONAL FEATURES

We've discussed many of the features common to typical ultralight sleeping bags. Here are a few more features to consider.

As mentioned earlier, sleeping bag typically consists of an outer shell, an insulating layer, and an inner shell. Often, there is a zipper down the side that allows for entry, ventilation, and joining of two similar bags. On bags designed for colder weather, the zipper may be backed by an insulated *draft tube* that prevents warm air from escaping through the zipper. Some cold-weather bags also have a draft collar, an insulating tube across the upper chest and neck that prevents warm air from escaping your torso and out the hood opening.

Down sleeping bags contain *baffles*, which are pockets or boxes of down insulation. Baffles prevent the down feathers from migrating around the bag, eliminating cold spots and maintaining an even layer of insulation across the body. On some bags, baffles are created by sewing the outer layer of fabric to the inside liner, called *sewn-through baffles*. Down insulation fills the pocket between the seams. The primary advantage of sewn-through baffles is their lower cost of construction and weight savings. But warm air can escape through any non-insulated seam, creating cold spots that are noticeable on very cold nights and in windy conditions. Sewn-through baffling is usually for sleeping bags designed for temperatures above freezing.

Down bags designed for cooler temperatures have interior vertical baffles commonly made with noseeum mesh fabric. The baffles hold the down between the inner and outer shells in a box, rather than a pocket. Box baffles can be continuous tubes that run completely around the girth of the bag, or be blocked at the sides with a side baffle. Continuous baffles allow down to be shifted between the top and bottom layers of the bag, which provides some versatility across a wider temperature range. Blocked baffles, however, provide better down control, eliminating the shifting of down out of the upper baffles during the night.

DOWN VERSUS SYNTHETIC FILL

The argument between down and synthetic fill insulations for sleeping bags is not unlike those discussed previously for insulating clothing in the previous chapter. Keeping sleeping bags dry in the summer is usually less challenging than keeping insulating clothing dry, even in inclement conditions. With prudence, care, and some experience, virtually anyone can enjoy the weight-saving benefits of a down sleeping bag, even in the wet climates of areas like the Cascade Mountains of British Columbia or the White Mountains of New Hampshire.

Synthetic bags have their place, even for ultralight backpackers. For extended outings in wet and humid climates where the risk of being able to dry your bag is minimal, synthetic insulation makes sense. In addition, climbers and hikers that spend several nights in a row in a waterproof-breathable bivy sack will soak a down bag in short order, if only from condensation of moisture that does not pass through the poorly breathable fabric of the bivy sack. The combination of wet weather, high humidity, lack of sunlight, and cold temperatures that increase condensation of moisture in your bag's insulation can be particularly problematic for down bags.

Synthetic insulations retain far more loft than down bags as they absorb moisture, and thus, can retain a great deal of their ability to insulate (even after wringing out the bag following immersion in water).

In spite of the extra care required to keep a down bag dry, the advantages of a down bag over a synthetic bag are significant. High-fill down is far lighter for an equivalent thickness than even the best synthetic insulations. Down compresses to a smaller size, saving space in your pack. They are also less sensitive to insulation damage after repeated packing. Thus, they have a longer lifespan. A synthetic bag will lose 50 percent or more of its loft after a hundred days of continuous use. A properly cared for down bag will retain 75 percent of its loft for ten or more years. These advantages make down bags the primary choice of most ultralight backpackers.

To protect your down bag while packed in wet conditions, don't rely on ultralight silicone-coated nylon stuff sacks. Typically, they are only waterproof to 1–5 psi. Higher pressures can be exerted against the stuff sack wall when in the pack. Perhaps the lightest option for keeping your down bag dry in the pack is to find the lightest stuff sack and line it with a Mylar turkey roasting bag or lightweight plastic garbage bag. The stuff sack will allow you to compress the down bag into a manageable size and keep it organized in your pack. The liner bag will provide water protection. An ultralight sleeping bag stuff sack, such as the Bozeman Mountain Works SpinSack (0.5 oz, size M), combined with a Mylar bag (0.2 oz) is a lighter combination than most ultralight stuff sacks that claim to be totally waterproof.

More aggressive options at keeping your sleeping bag (and your other gear) dry is to use heavy-duty trash compactor bags (2.5–3.5 oz) as pack liners, waterproof silicone-coated nylon pack covers (3–6 oz), or a poncho long enough to cover your backpack.

TEMPERATURE RATINGS AND SHELL MATERIALS

As indicated earlier, a sleeping bag's loft is a reasonable measure of how warm a sleeping bag will keep you at night, but it doesn't tell the whole story. Sleeping bag features, individual physiology and metabolism, clothing worn, and environmental conditions are the primary factors contributing to how warm you will sleep at night. Considering the complexity of these relationships, you can begin to appreciate the range of temperatures for which any individual sleeping bag might be applicable. Still, one of the first questions that an inexperienced backpacker wants answered about a sleeping bag is, "What is its temperature rating?"

Most customers assume that sleeping bags are rated by the manufacturer according to the lowest temperature at which they are expected to keep you warm. In reality, because no reliable industry standard exists, bag temperature ratings are nothing more than indicators of relative warmth within an individual manufacturer's product line. People sleep differently. Some are always cold and need more insulation, and others sleep warm and need less. The bottom line is that the bag needs to keep *you* warm, so everyone needs to buy a bag to suit his or her individual needs.

The key determinant of the bag's warmth is the thickness of the loft. Measuring loft is, therefore, a useful way of comparing the warmth of different bags. However, a comparison of bags of different manufacturers will find a large degree of variability. Plus, when designing a lightweight gear kit, most ultralight backpackers combine the temperature rating of a bag with their clothing system. Thus, a bag with a temperature rating to 30°F may provide plenty of warmth when used in conjunction with insulation clothing for a mild winter night.

As mentioned earlier, temperature ratings depend on more than just loft. Controlling drafts is important, as well. Insulating air inside your bag, warmed by your body's metabolic engine, is hard-earned. Many ultralight bags on the market today seem designed more to release this insulating air than retain it. There exists quite a debate regarding the relative warmth of a hoodless quilt versus a traditional, zipperless mummy sleeping bag of the same weight and materials—which is thinner but seal drafts better. By talking to experienced users of both systems, it appears that the effectiveness of the hoodless quilt depends on the ability to maintain an adequate seal at the sleeping pad and to maintain sufficient loft in the shoulders while keeping the neck closed to seal drafts. After surveying the market for designs that met these criteria, we found several manufacturers offering version of hoodless bags and quilts for ultralight backpacking, including Fanatic Fringe, Nunatak, GoLite (now discontinued), Rab, and Big Agnes. Imperfections in all of them leave the market wide open for innovation in this category.

Adding a windproof outer shell can have significant benefits to maintaining the insulating value of a sleeping bag in cold, windy climates, especially for tarp campers. The addition of a highly windproof shell, such as a tightly woven microfiber (e.g., Pertex 6 or EPIC) or a fabric with a microporous laminate or coating (e.g., DryLoft, Pertex Endurance, or eVENT) to a bag can decrease the temperature at which the bag is comfortable.

While such shells provide additional protection against wind and moisture, they must be breathable, or excessive perspiration will build up in the bag and condense on the inside surface of the outer shell, soaking the insulation. On long trips in cold weather, the consequence of this can be severe. There are reports of Arctic explorers with sleeping bags that accumulate five to ten times their own weight in ice over the course of several weeks.

The need for these shells for summer backpacking is debatable. Hikers that camp in traditional double-walled tents certainly don't need them — their shelter largely protects them from wind, and condensation on the inner walls in such shelters is minimal.

Tarp campers find windproof sleeping bag shells to be more useful, but usually only in mountainous areas or during colder seasons. Of greater benefit to tarp campers is the additional water resistance windproof shells provide, affording additional protection from errant rain spray and allowing for a smaller, lighter tarp. However, the current trend among tarp campers looking for more stormworthy systems is the use of ultralight sleeping bag covers and bivy sacks.

The market for wind-and-water resistant sleeping bag shells is dominated by winter camping products, where frost, spindrift, and spilled foods tends to wreak havoc on the ultralight gossamer materials of lightweight summer bags.

Fitting your Bag

Your sleeping bag must fit, and you should pay no less attention to this matter than if you were fitting a piece of tailored clothing. If a bag is too small, you will compress the insulation from the inside and the bag will lose some of its ability to insulate. If it is too big, there will be extra space to warm up, and you'll be carrying more bag than you need.

Ideally, the bag should be as tight as you can fit into comfortably — considering your normal nighttime body movements — without compressing the loft on the top or sides.

INCREASING EFFICIENCY

There are several ways that you can greatly improve the efficiency of your sleeping system. The most obvious method is to combine it with the insulating qualities of your clothing, which can be used in three distinct ways:

- Clothing can be worn normally inside the bag
- It can be draped over you inside the bag
- It can be draped over the outside of your bag

Wearing clothing inside the bag provides the best mobility, eliminating the need to shuffle layers around every time you turn over.

Layering clothing over you inside the bag provides the most efficient method of heat retention. It allows body limbs to share warmth, like fingers in a mitten, while increasing the overall loft and draft control in your sleeping bag. Effective layering techniques inside the bag include wrapping an extra shirt over and around your shoulders to help seal the hood opening, or layering a full-zip down jacket over your chest to increase loft. Be watchful of adding too much clothing inside your sleeping bag. You'll run the risk of compressing loft from the inside and reducing the warmth of your system.

Layering clothing outside the sleeping bag, on top, is simply not recommended for down bags. You're more likely to reduce the overall loft of your system than enhance it. Further, with the exception of winter-class down parkas, lightweight clothing doesn't lend itself to efficient layering over a sleeping bag. The exception to layering over a sleeping bag is the use of a waterproof-breathable rain jacket draped over the foot or head ends of a sleeping bag during a severe rainstorm — a bivy-camping trick that has been used by mountaineers for decades.

A second way to increase the effectiveness of your bag is to sleep with your spouse, child, or climbing partner. Sleeping together allows you to share heat and get away with a lighter sleeping bag. Adding a partner is sort of like putting a second furnace inside a house: Neither one has to work as hard to keep the house warm. Even mummy-shaped sleeping bags mate well. Just get one right-zip and one left-zip bag — the same type to ensure the zippers will mate.

Sleeping with a partner is not all it's cracked up to be. Spouses are notorious for sleeping comfort differences. One may sleep warm and kick off the covers, while the other may sleep cold. This can be partially addressed by having the cold partner layer on more clothing. Children, especially toddlers and preschoolers, are noted for their ability to kick, thrash, and otherwise prevent a snuggling adult from a peaceful night's rest. And climbing partners — well, let's just say you need to be awfully good friends to pull this off.

Another way to increase bag efficiency is to use a face mask. This reduces evaporative and conductive heat loss. There are several options, from a simple silk scarf wrapped around your head, to full-face balaclavas with fancy heat exchangers built in to the mouth and nose areas. Drugstore face masks that reduce the inhalation of particulate dust and allergens are very light and also quite effective at warming the air you breathe and reducing evaporative heat loss.

Mattresses

Not long ago I was on a winter trip with a friend, camping on snow. We hit the sack early, and not an hour afterward, I awoke to a terrible chattering sound. After several minutes I realized that this chattering was my friend's teeth. Torn from my blissfully warm state I really started worrying. Although his bag was at least as warm as mine (it was rated to 0°F and mine was a 25°F), the problem was in the ground insulation. He was using just one thin inflatable mattress while I slept on two closed-cell foam pads. After he put his backpack and all the other gear he could find under his bag, he was able to make it through the night in reasonable comfort. This example of heat loss through conduction was especially dramatic. The snow quickly drew the heat away from his body through the inflatable pad and the compressed loft of his sleeping bag.

Thus, the primary purpose of a ground pad is to reduce heat loss due to conduction. It's a nearly indispensable part of the sleeping system in cooler conditions. A secondary purpose of a ground pad is to provide a softer sleeping surface. The degree to which a sleeping pad is needed for comfort depends on the sleeper. When I used to camp as a child I used no sleeping pad and never had a problem sleeping right on the ground. Now, I'm happy to carry a closed-cell foam pad, as my bones tend to ache a little more.

There are three types of sleeping pads used for backpacking:

- Air mattresses
- Closed-cell foam pads
- Open-cell (self-inflating) foam pads

AIR MATTRESSES

Air mattresses are more comfortable than sleeping on the ground, but they provide little protection from conductive heat loss. The reason is that there is only one layer of air underneath you. It quickly loses any heat that you generate into the ground. However, Stephenson and Exped both offer air mattresses filled with down fibers, and Big Agnes and

Pacific Outdoor Equipment offer air mattresses filled with short-staple synthetic fibers. Both down- and synthetic-filled air mattresses dramatically improve their cold-weather insulating ability. Some can be used successfully on snow in the winter.

The gold standard for lightweight backpackers is the closed-cell foam pad, incarnations of which are manufactured by Gossamer Gear, Cascade Designs, Pacific Outdoor Equipment, and a host of other companies. Most of them are derivates of EVA foam, which provides good flexibility at low temperatures, low water absorption, and excellent insulation. Lesser quality closed-cell foams are available. They are typically distributed through big box and discount sporting goods stores. Generally, they are less durable, absorb more water, and are brittle at cold conditions.

Closed-cell foam pads provide the best insulation/weight ratio and are also the lightest type of pad available. However, many hikers find that closed-cell foam pads do not provide enough cushioning on hard ground. This discomfort spawned the invention of open-cell foam with an air mattress, thus creating the category of *self-inflating* mattresses. These have the ability to passively inflate simply by opening the valve and waiting several minutes. Self-inflating mattresses are made by Slumberjack, Cascade Designs, Pacific Outdoor Equipment, and others. Open-celled foam pads require far more weight—in foam, valve, and mattress shell—to provide the same insulating ability as closed-cell foam pads. So their advantages are primarily limited to compactibility and ground comfort. They are also more expensive. High-quality, lightweight pads cost $70 or more, compared to $10–$30 of most closed-cell foam pads.

Open-cell foam pads come in different sizes. The most common widths are 20″ (standard) and 24″ (wide) and three pad lengths: 78″ (long), 72″ (full) and 54″ (3/4). Full-length pads provide insulation from head to foot for most. The 3/4-length pad insulates from your head to your thighs, recognizing that not as much insulation or comfort is needed for the feet and lower legs. They can be propped up on a backpack or on unworn clothing.

Ultralight backpacking equipment manufacturers are beginning to recognize the demand for "shortie" pads that insulate only from shoulders to hips—torso length. Some options include the NightLight, a convoluted (egg crate), closed-cell foam pad offered by Gossamer Gear, and the TorsoLite, a self-inflating mattress from Bozeman Mountain Works. These torso pads rely on other gear to pad the head and legs.

Finally, recall that you don't always need sleeping pads in the wilderness. I went many years without any sleeping bad and slept fine—not in the winter, though. Sleeping in soft campsites atop a thick layer of forest duff can be both warm and comfortable, even on cold nights. So if you are able to sleep on the ground, and you need very little insulation, feel free to leave the ground pad behind. Going without is the cheapest and most effective way to reduce pack weight.

BIVY SACKS

Bivy sacks are typically waterproof-breathable bags that form an outer layer for your sleeping system, enclosing you, your bag, and your sleeping pad. Most bivy sacks are one-person shelters with no pole structure. They are discussed in this chapter because they add insulation to your sleeping system and are commonly used by ultralight hikers in conjunction with a tarp, poncho, or snow shelter.

Bivy sacks are generally made of windproof, woven nylon and can lessen the convective heat loss of your sleep system. In still air, a bivy sack provides little added benefit for its weight, considering that it could be better spent on additional down fill for your sleeping bag. However, in windy, wet, or snowy conditions where the shell of your sleeping bag could compromise its down insulation, the use of a bivy sack can add tremendous warmth.

Bivy sacks that have added features to improve their livability, including elaborate hooped poles and complicated zipper configurations, are essentially single-wall tents that require a very small footprint. A small footprint is one of the primary advantages of using a bivy sack as a standalone shelter. But such configurations, which typically weigh 2–3 pounds, can be as heavy as a far roomier and more comfortable solo tent.

A simple bivy sack should not be used to reduce your bag weight, but to improve your sleep system performance in stormy or wet conditions. Thus, there are lighter, breathable (but not waterproof) bivy sacks that are meant not as shelters, but as protective covers for a sleeping bag. The degree to which these are waterproof varies, but they are generally at least water and wind resistant. Breathable bivy sacks tend to be much lighter than their waterproof-breathable counterparts because they use lighter fabrics, less weatherproof zippers, etc. The primary purpose of a breathable bivy sack is to decrease convective heat loss from wind and protect against occasional exposure to water. In addition, they dramatically improve the performance of sleeping quilts and hoodless bags. Breathable bivy sacks are useful in situations with very high condensation — single-walled tents, snow caves — or where you expect to get splashed under a tarp. Breathable bivy sacks can be as simple as two sheets of fabric sewn together and can be made easily as a homemade project. Commercial versions with zippers, mosquito netting windows, hoods, and contoured footboxes are available from the likes of Bibler, Bozeman Mountain Works, Equinox, Outdoor Research, and Oware.

The biggest complaint reported by bivy users is the accumulation of condensation. Because the formation of condensation in any shelter is driven more by the interior ventilation of the shelter and outside wind, which helps the shelter pump out internal moisture, it makes sense that poorly ventilated bivy sacks are more prone to condensation than other shelter designs.

If perspiration can't escape through the bivy fabric, then insulation and down bags will lose their insulation rapidly. The worse possible combination of a sleeping bag and shelter is an ultralight down bag with a gossamer fabric shell in a waterproof-breathable (e.g., Gore-Tex) bivy sack on a night that is cold, clear, and still. Several nights of this without the ability to dry out your bag will be far more detrimental than the inability to stay dry getting in and out of the bivy sack during a rainstorm.

Bivy sack users report that if the sleeping pad is placed inside the bivy sack, rather than laying the bivy sack atop the pad, a warmer microenvironment is maintained and condensation decreases. I use a homemade breathable bivy sack for tarp camping, snow cave camping, and occasionally, in my single-wall tent. The bag is made of Activent (formerly manufactured by Gore and similar to Gore-Tex). It weighs 8 ounces. However, I find that the material is not breathable enough and does get some condensation on the inside, particularly when I sleep under the stars on a clear night. My breathable bivy sack also has a hood made of wedding veil material to control insects when sleeping under a tarp, a 0.5-ounce addition that can help solve one of the biggest problems of tarps: bug resistance.

Other materials used in breathable bivy sacks include EPIC by Nextec. It absorbs very little water, dries fast, is highly weather and wind resistant, but breathes poorer than most microfibers. EPIC is used in bivy sack designs by Bibler (Winter Bivy) and Oware (EPIC Bivy). Lightweight, uncoated nylon is poorly weather resistant but highly breathable and is used in simple and affordable designs by Equinox. Pertex Quantum, an ultralight nylon microfiber commonly used in ultralight sleeping bag shells, provides some balance of weather protection with exceptional breathability and is the lightest of the alternatives. It is used in the Bozeman Mountain Works Vapr Bivy, a 6.5-ounce bivy sack with a waterproof floor large enough for a winter sleeping bag with a full hood. It also has a two-way zipper that accommodates a netting window for buggy nights.

The Sleeping System

Now that we've discussed the theory of sleeping warm and the different components of a sleeping system, you need to decide what will work for you. Your sleep system will depend on where you hike, your awareness of your body's own physiological nuances, your level of experience, and how much money you're willing to spend. And don't forget about how your sleeping system will integrate with your clothing and shelter systems.

A good place to start is to determine the lowest temperature you are likely to encounter on the trail and use it as the starting point for how warm your sleeping system needs to be. Second, try to determine how warm you sleep while in the backcountry. Only experience can provide you with this data. Unfortunately, there are no meaningful generalizations. Backyard camping, car camping, and single overnight backpacking trips won't give you the physiological data points you need to predict your body's response to cold on longer trips. Keep in mind that your body adapts to cold conditions over time, so you should be sleeping warmer on the fifth

An ultralight sleep system by Bozeman Mountain Works, ideally suited for tarp camping in comfort and style: a self-inflating torso-sized mattress (TorsoLite, 10 oz), variable girth sleeping bag (Arc X, 16 oz), and a Pertex Quantum bivy sack with silnylon floor (Vapr Bivy, 6 oz).

night of your backpacking trip than on the first. However, long-distance hikes reduce fat and generally degrade physiological performance, so you could be sleeping cold again as the weeks and months of a hike tick by.

The basic components of any sleep system include a sleeping pad and bag. The ultralight backpacker recognizes the ability to integrate other gear and clothing for warmth and padding, so that full-length pads are generally unnecessary. Tarp campers require a ground sheet, the lightest alternative, but more are finding that the wind and rain spray resistance of a breathable bivy sack with a waterproof floor is a better option, especially in buggy or mountainous environments. A typical minimalist sleeping system for three seasons in the mountains of the Western US (Rockies, Sierras, Cascades) that integrates clothing can weigh as little as 2 pounds. And it doesn't have to give up the comfort of down insulation, a self-inflating mattress, or protection from biting insects.

Adding a few simple items can extend the basic three-season system described above to colder temperatures. A closed-cell foam pad, face mask, and warmer insulating jacket can help you sleep comfortably into subfreezing conditions without buying a new sleeping bag. But at some point a dedicated winter system may be desirable for simplicity.

Chapter 8: **Shelter**

By Rick Dreher

One of the happy challenges that hikers tackle is finding shelter for the night. Yurts and lean-tos, tarps and teepees, igloos and snowcaves, tents and hammocks — they all aim to keep you comfortable during your nights in the wilderness.

Your shelter can be more than simply a spot to sleep. In the best of times it's a place to reflect on your journey and consider the rewards of being out in the wilderness. Sometimes it's a comfy cocoon while a storm howls and rages inches away. Sometimes it's a window on a 100-mile panorama of mountaintops. Or a ringside seat to the inner workings of an elk herd. Sometimes, your shelter is a respite from clouds of shrieking bloodthirsty insects.

Not every night goes according to plan. Fierce winds rip tents and tarps from their moorings and threaten to send them to the next county. Rain insinuates itself through seams and zippers and doors and floors, making you cold, wet, and worried that morning will never arrive. Relentless mosquitoes on a hot muggy night force you to button up so much that you end up in a puddle of your own sweat. Snow piles onto walls, pressing in until you've scarcely got room to turn over. Rodents large and small cavort, chew, and tap dance in and out of your dreams—and your gear and your food.

For the lightweight backpacker, shelter is a three-part challenge—all while maintaining the minimalist approach to weight and bulk.

- Select the right shelter
- Master how to use that shelter in a wide range of conditions
- Choose the right place to set up camp

Shelter Basics

Shelter can be a roof; a roof and walls; or a roof, walls, and floor. Shelter can be a feature of your destination, something you carry with you, or something you create when you arrive. Different destinations dictate different shelter types, depending on campsite and conditions. Most commonly, campers need to get out of the weather—the cold, wind, rain, or snow. In other regions and times of year, it might mean sun, heat, and dust. Sometimes, even in the most pleasant of weather, shelter is needed to keep nature's critters at bay—including the two-legged hominid type as well.

As is emphasized throughout this book, planning is paramount to the lightweight backpacker. We have to research the conditions we'll be facing before making our shelter selection. You don't lug a full mountaineering tent to the desert, and you don't tote a tarp to Everest camp 3.

The *al fresco* approach. Many hikers prefer nothing at all, sleeping out in the open when they can. It simply requires that you predict conditions as part of your trip planning, and size up conditions in the field as you get ready to select your sleeping site for the night.

A ROOF OVER YOUR HEAD

A wilderness shelter can be tight as a 55-gallon drum or as gauzy as one of Salome's veils. When and why do you choose one over the other? Cozy/sweltering/clammy/frigid—what can happen during the night?

Our primary focus here is on fabric shelters for the backpacker. With some exceptions, these take one of five forms:

- Tents
- Tarps
- Bivy sacks
- Teepees
- Hammocks

When selecting a shelter, the lightweight hiker keeps in mind the following ratio: *pounds per sleeper* (PPS), as in, pounds of shelter carried per person who will be sleeping in it. Summertime conditions can often accommodate a PPS of less than 2 and even less than 1. Wintertime travel, or a trip into chronically unsettled climes, can dictate a PPS far higher. Only after you've determined what conditions you're facing can you sink your teeth into shelter selection.

The successful lightweighter looks at shelter one piece at a time. What comprises a shelter? Simply put, it's everything that combines into creating your home for the night:

- Fabric body — be it a tent, tarp, teepee, or hybrid
- Groundcloth — your floor, if not an integral part of the body
- Skeleton — generally, any support poles
- Rigging — lines and stakes

If little lightbulbs are glowing above your head as you think, *Hey, I can use something I'm already carrying for one of these parts*, you're on the right track. A poncho can serve as a tarp for one, or as a groundcloth if used carefully. Trekking poles can support tarps and certain tents, as can handy sticks. Sometimes poles are avoided completely by rigging a ridgeline between trees or dropping a topline from a handy overhead branch. Rocks, sticks, or bags filled with gravel or snow can fill in as stakes.

Nothing weighs less than . . . nothing. If sleeping under the stars appeals to you and you have confidence that conditions warrant it, carry no shelter at all. Just you, the ground below, and the sky above. What could be simpler? You can even skip the groundcloth if you carry a pad that won't be damaged foam-a-terra. It's not at all uncommon on longer trips to choose sleeping al fresco, even if shelter is at hand. But in most parts of the globe, if the trip is going to be longer than a night or two, it's not the smartest approach to leave everything to chance. Our good search-and-rescue friends would certainly encourage you to be prepared for the unexpected. This book does the same. We will show how you can carry a complete shelter system that won't weigh you down.

WARM AND DRY VERSUS COLD AND WET

Fabric shelters provide warmth by fending off moisture, protecting us from the wind, and in the case of tents, trapping some of our body heat. Even tarps may play some role in capturing heat radiated from the earth and our bodies, but not a lot. On a cold, calm night, temperature readings taken inside and out will show that the tent is several degrees warmer. Windy weather will carry tent heat off more quickly, but the protection from wind chill might be even more important. We have to be careful, though, not to let this temperature advantage be overwhelmed by moisture. Think of the worst-case scenario: an unventilated tent entirely made of impervious material. Our respired and perspired moisture would begin condensing on the walls the minute we closed the door. After a few more minutes the condensation would accumulate into drops that would gather and run down the walls in rivulets and drip on us from the ceiling. Quite soon, this water would pond on the floor.

Not a big bother, though, because we'd soon be passed out from the accumulation of carbon dioxide.

The opposite of the impermeable tent is one made entirely of netting, with a separate fly that's used in cool or wet weather. In fact, most so-called, three-season tent designs use considerable mesh in their bodies to aid airflow and carry away excess heat and moisture. The question remains, what happens to that moisture when it gets to the top of the fly? Does it accumulate there and inevitably condense, or can it disperse? A few tents have one or more vents atop the fly. Others rely on the circulation afforded by the gaps between tent body and fly and the fly and the ground. In practice, the effectiveness of these strategies depends on conditions.

Some staunch tarp advocates consider this drenching to be the inevitable fate of all tent dwellers. But there are at least as many staunch tent dwellers that have never been soaked out in this fashion. There are too many variables to declare either side as entirely right. The proof is too tangled up with all those variables — tent design and location, climate and present conditions, the occupants and how they use the tent, the position of Jupiter and the price of a cup of coffee in Duluth. Vancouver Island's soggy west coast presents an entirely different set of challenges and requirements than the high and arid Gobi Desert. Chances are good that you'll be doing most of your camping in conditions somewhere between these extremes.

MOISTURE CONTROL

Moisture is an excellent conductor of heat. Air, by contrast, is an insulator and doesn't conduct heat nearly as well. To stay warm we must stay dry, and that is shelter's most important role.

Moisture sources can be obvious. Rain and snow are the prime culprits, and much of our shelter's responsibility revolves around keeping it away. Fog is another source and, traveling quietly like a cat, can invade your sleeping quarters in spite of the roof. California's coastal redwood forest ecosystems depend on fog as their moisture for the otherwise dry summer and fall. The trees accumulate moisture in droplets that gather and literally rain from the drooping redwood branches. The lush redwood undergrowth — home to the famous banana slug! — is testament to the system's effectiveness. In this elegant model, we find there's a way to get wet without a drop of real rain. Heavy fog can wet everything in an open-walled shelter.

Even without visible fog, humid air can be wet and cold enough that our breath and insensible sweat will nudge the air to the point where condensation forms on tent ceiling and walls, on sleeping bag shells, and inside sleeping bag insulation. Tarps and well-ventilated tents are generally best at dissipating hiker-generated moisture. Tight, impervious, waterproof tents and snow shelters are the worst. Single-walled, waterproof-breathable tents are an interesting case and discussed in more detail later.

The science behind condensation is simple: The colder the air, the less moisture it can hold. Condensation forms when moist air is either chilled—fog—or contacts a cold-enough surface—surface moisture, or dew. The temperature at which condensation forms is called the *dew point*, something we're all familiar with from the local weather forecast. Greater altitudes with lower barometric pressure wring even more moisture out of the air.

The primary means of combating condensation in a shelter is to improve ventilation. To this extent, flat sheet tarps are the most condensation-resistant shelters. They do not restrict airflow by forcing it through vents, doors, or around beaks.

The other major source of moisture is the ground. Saturated soil and springtime snowpack can pump lots of water into the air and microclimate of your wilderness bedroom. Your groundcloth, bivy sack floor, or tent floor seals this moisture out.

Tarps

Nylon, twine, stakes, poles, some creativity—*voilá*, a bedroom! The humble tarp represents shelter at its most basic, yet at its lightest and most versatile. Fabric advances give us astonishingly light and strong tarps that can, for example, shelter two or three at less than a pound. If you're in an area with enough trees or brush to leave your poles at home, the addition of lines and stakes along with a groundcloth completes your shelter.

A tarp is a flat piece of fabric with grommets or loops at the corners and at intervals along the sides. Sometimes, there are one or more loops down the center as well. Some tarps are square, but most are rectangles. Sizes vary, with a generally acceptable minimum being 5´ x 8´ feet to perhaps 10´ x 12´. An 8´x 10´ tarp is a popular size that can easily shelter two and even three sleepers if need be. A typical 8´x 10´ tarp made from silicone-coated nylon weighs 1–2 ounces under a pound and costs a little under $100. Folded, it takes up a tiny portion of precious pack space — a dinner-sized burrito's worth. And what a burrito!

Other tarps, made of the more common, urethane-coated nylon are available at perhaps half the price and twice the weight of the silnylon. Even at 2 pounds, a bargain tarp is still a lightweight trail home. Don't hesitate to use one of these, especially if you aren't sure whether or not tarping is for you.

Even cheaper are tarps of plastic sheeting or even Tyvek. A sheet of 4-millimeter plastic can make an adequate shelter. The challenge is attaching your lines so that they'll hold and won't tear the plastic or pull off. There are several ways to accomplish this. One is to tie directly to the tarp with a sheetbend knot. This works pretty well on the corners, less well along the sides. The second method is to form a pocket in the plastic with a smooth pebble or small pinecone, for example, and tie it off with a piece of line. The third is to use one of the devices sold for this purpose. One such device is called the *Visklamp* and is a variation on the second method above. It's a wire "key" that fits over a small rubber ball that you place behind the sheeting. The guyline ties to the wire.

TYVEK AND THE BLUETARP

Tyvek is a brand of spun polyethylene made by Dupont. There are a myriad of Tyvek varieties, but the one that commonly interests backpackers is the HomeWrap type. Tyvek is quite tough, being both tear and puncture resistant. The problem with HomeWrap is that it's uncoated and, therefore, porous. This makes perfect sense in home construction, where its breathability prevents the damage of moisture buildup in wall cavities. It makes less sense for its potential use as rain protection. Nevertheless, Tyvek has its adherents and is suitable for shelter in all but the hardest rain.

The ubiquitous bluetarp — the grommetted, fiber-reinforced, plastic jobs sold by the millions at discount stores everywhere — are a legitimate waterproof shelter option. They are neither lightweight nor especially compact. Their stiffness makes them challenging to set up and extraordinarily bulky. Groundcloths made from bluetarp fabric wear like iron but, again, are heavy.

GROMMETS OR LOOPS

Grommets in your tarp can fail by tearing out. They're especially troublesome in silnylon, because the fabric is particularly thin and slippery. In urethane-coated nylon they're more likely to stay put under stress. Silnylon tarps are better when made with webbing loops instead of grommets.

SEAM SEALING

Fabric tarps wider than 5 feet will have a center seam running down their length. (Five feet is a typical maximum width for bulk fabric rolls.) Generally, the seam is flat-felled and does not need to be sealed for silnylon tarps, but it definitely needs to be sealed for urethane-coated nylon tarps. In the case of standard coated nylon a number of sealants are available. They come either in a bottled liquid that can be brushed or daubed, on or in a thicker form in a tube that is squeezed, brushed, or spread on using an irrigation syringe (McNett Seam Grip is a popular and effective brand).

Stealth 1 Tarp by Bozeman Mountain Works; Madison River, Beartrap Canyon, Montana.

Silicone nylon requires silicone sealant. This can either be a commercial preparation, such as McNett SilNet, or a homebrew made by thinning silicone sealant with a solvent, such as paint thinner or even white gas. A complete seam-sealing job covers the fabric joints and the stitching lines on both sides. For the common flat-felled center seam, you'll want to coat the two stitching lines and the seam itself—where the two pieces of fabric meet. Sealing the tie-out points is not necessary to prevent leakage, but it protects the seam from water absorption and increase seam strength when under stress.

An 8' x 10' tarp pitched as an **A-frame shelter with trekking poles**. A minimum of six stakes are required, but 8-12 stakes adds stability in high winds. Guylines can be used at the corners and sides (shown here) for more interior room and better ventilation, or the corners and sides can be staked directly to the ground for better wind resistance.

TARP CONFIGURATIONS

There are a lot of ways to pitch a tarp: some simple and obvious, some rather complex and elegant. Cut a sheet of typing paper to 8 x 10 inches and you have a practice tarp that is a miniature replica of a full-size 8-x-10-foot backpacking tarp. What options do you have? You can practice all of the following. An office meeting is a highly recommended place to practice.

THE A-FRAME

Think pup tent without the front and back doors and floor, and you've got the basic A-frame tarp. At a minimum, you need a ridgeline and attachment at the four corners. In practice, it's generally necessary to use more anchoring lines, especially if there's any wind or rain.

One set of end corners of a tarp pitched in **A-frame mode** can be drawn inward and staked to create a closed end for more weather resistance.

THE FLYING DIAMOND

Turn your tarp 45 degrees, making one corner the foot and the opposing corner the entrance, and you have the basics of the flying diamond. Useful in foul weather, the flying diamond

Pitched in the **Flying Diamond** configuration, an 8' x 10' tarp provides terrific headroom, shead, overhead rain protection, and wind resistance from two sides. However, if the wind shifts and weather is stormy, the massive open front leaves you exposed to the elements. Use creativity in pitching the flying diamond according to weather and the number of people under your tarp. Lower the peak for better weather resistance, increase the height of the sides with guylines for better ventilation, or add trekking pole(s) to the interior (**shown**) to improve headroom and stability.

doesn't provide the maximum living space but protects from weather on three of four sides. The opening is generally the only corner supported by a pole. The flying diamond works best with a square tarp—a 9' x 9' is ideal. But it also works with rectangles if the length and width aren't too different.

THE FLAT ROOF AND LEAN-TO

It's possible to string your tarp as a flat roof—an awning. This is a good method in fair weather, especially if sun protection is desired. If you're lucky enough to be able to do so from trees and bushes, you can have a high ceiling and no guylines to trip over. The flat roof is the worst configuration in the rain. Not only will it allow the weather in from all sides, water

A flat tarp gives you maximum creativity in creating a shelter that meets your needs, adapts to the environment, and reflects your style. Pitching a tarp elegantly is as much about art as it is about technique. Here, dual trekking poles are used to create more headroom in an 8' x 10' tarp, with two and a half sides pitched directly to the ground for weather resistance.

will pool in your awning and either bring it to the ground or gush off in multi-gallon surges.

A variation, the *lean-to*, has one side—usually a long side—guyed or staked directly to the ground and the other elevated as the opening. The lean-to, with its ground-level "foot" pitched into the wind, is simple, roomy, and offers good weather protection.

In truly foul weather, you may have neither the means, the time, nor the desire to make an elegant tarp home. It's possible to quickly make an effective shelter by loosely guying down the four corners and raising a pole in the center. Once you've claimed this space out of the rain, you can arrange your gear underneath and adjust your shelter as time allows and needs dictate. While it will protect against stormy weather from all sides, the tarp teepee isn't the simplest to get in and out of.

TARPS THAT AREN'T FLAT

The simple tarp is a noble thing, providing a myriad of shelter possibilities. But there are weaknesses inherent to that flat sheet of cloth. First, it is impossible to rig them to be perfectly flat, with no sags, folds, or wrinkles. Beyond the aesthetics of not having a picture-perfect pitch, the sags and folds reveal high and low stress points, indicating areas of weakness. Rain can collect in folds, causing further sagging, and the whole works will flap in the wind. Lots of guy points and clever rigging reduce but never completely eliminate these flaws.

In response, some tarp designs incorporate angled ends that form small downward sloping "porch" areas at the head and foot. These help strengthen and stabilize the tarp, and enable it to better shed rain and wind, increasing protection for the sleepers. Other tarps incorporate *catenary* designs that provide a natural curve along the ridgeline or sides. Think of a chain spanning two fence posts: It always is bowed in a curve described as catenary. By replicating this curve in the ridgeline, the tarp's natural tendency to sag down its center is incorporated into the design. Such wing-style tarps pitch beautifully and can be guyed drum-tight. They are probably the strongest of all tarp-style shelters. They can't, however, be pitched in the many variations of the flat tarp.

Stealth Poncho Tarp by Bozeman Mountain Works; Lost Coast, California

Stealth Poncho Tarp by Bozeman Mountain Works – Spanish Peaks, Montana – pitched in a hybrid style: A-frame at the foot end, and lean-to at the head end. This pitch provides the better protection of an A-frame pitch while still affording the views and ventilation of a lean-to pitch.

WHEN THE WEATHER TURNS FOUL

Anybody who tarps often enough will be blessed with a stretch of awful weather. You can keep wind and rain at bay by first picking a high or sloped piece of ground that won't channel or puddle water into your sleeping quarters. This can be a challenge, especially in established campsites that typically have several well-used tent sites forming perfect little ponds in the rain. If it's already raining, you can easily spot these sites and avoid them, but if rain is still only threatening, you'll need all your observation skills to find the right site.

Become a weatherman. Try to determine which way the prevailing winds are blowing, and set up your shelter with the foot end into the wind. Pitch the foot and sides as low as possible without actually contacting your sleeping bag. If your tarp has guy points on the sides and in from the edges, using them will pull the walls up and away from you, add interior space, reduce flapping, and prevent rain from pooling on the tarp itself and coming off in waves.

If it's raining while you are setting up, use your basic pitch to gain fast shelter for yourself and your gear. Once out of the rain, you can get organized, change out of your wet clothes, and watch the conditions to decide how to do the

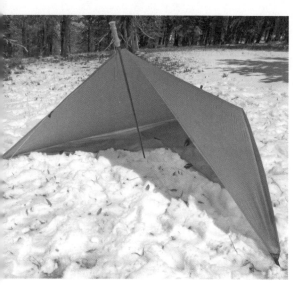

In the half-pyramid configuration, a tarp provides outstanding weather resistance when pitched with the foot of the tarp into the wind. This 8' x 10' tarp requires only four stakes (peak, two front corners, and rear center), with the rear corners tucked inward to provide a dry place for gear storage, useful when camping on snow or wet ground.

rest of your rigging. You might even cook dinner first or have a hot drink to take off the chill. Then take as much time as you need to fix your home, even if it means making the head end the foot, and vice versa. In the mountains especially, the wind can shift and swirl, channeled by the land's contours.

If your tarp is large enough, segregate your wet and dry gear. Hang wet clothing from the ridgeline (if you use one). Footwear is kept by the front door, out of the rain, and safely away from your sleeping area. It's sometimes advisable to keep wet gear on a small tarp or plastic trash bag. Don't keep anything that's dripping wet on your main groundcloth, lest water run toward your dry clothes and sleeping gear. If you have a poncho, you can extend your tarp's front entrance for a really large, protected sleeping and relaxing space. Finally, once you're battened down, enjoy the storm from the comfort of your bed and perhaps think about the less fortunate folks back home trapped in their boring houses.

BUGS

Into every tarper's life some bugs crawl. Be it resolute carpenter ants skidding audibly down your nylon sleeping bag or incessant whining clouds of mosquitoes, your missing walls, doors, and floor open you wide to the invading hordes. (Okay, you're the invader, but the better you sleep, the sooner you'll leave.) Some bug netting can stave off the invasion. There are several options.

Headnet

A netting sack large enough to cover your sleeping bag's head is the minimum to keep bugs out of your bag and off your face. You may need to sew Velcro patches to the bag and netting to keep it in place. If you're hot and need to sleep partway out of your bag, you'll defeat the netting's protection.

Netting bivy

Several framed netting shelters are available. Some cover the sleeping bag's top two-thirds, allowing you to leave your arms out. The framework keeps the netting well off your face, meaning that mosquitoes can't bite you through it. The A-16 Bivy cleverly collapses into a disk that packs away easily. The Outdoor Research (OR) Bug Bivy is full-length, with a single hoop and coated nylon floor. While heavier than some of the competition, the OR bivy gives complete protection and can replace your groundcloth. It even provides a (tight) space for changing and allows you to sleep completely out of your bag on hot nights. Most bivy manufacturers offer netted openings to keep the bivy sack ventilated in warmer, buggy conditions.

Netted tarp

Netting doors and skirts can be sewn to a tarp and give surprisingly good protection while keeping ample ventilation. An added benefit is the netting catches rain splatter and slows the wind. Long netting skirts can be tucked under gear, rocks, sticks, the groundcloth—anything to hold it in place and keep your neighbors at bay.

Suspended netting shelter

You can fashion a netting tent underneath a tarp. This can be anything from an informal length of gathered netting suspended from the ridgeline to a full-blown netting tent with doors and floor, such as those made by GoLite and Oware.

THE GROUNDCLOTH

If the tarp is your roof and walls, then your groundcloth is your floor. You'll want one large enough to accommodate your sleeping area, gear, and clothing. If two or more are sharing the space, it's best to have a single cloth big enough for all. Groundcloths are, to an extent, sacrificial. They are, after all, what's between you and the cruel earth. Depending on what, where, and how they're used, a groundcloth can last a few nights or an entire PCT thru-hike. The cautious will begin simple, light, and cheap, and move up as the need arises.

There are several types. Groundcloth can be made of plastic sheeting, Mylar, Tyvek, fiber-reinforced plastic, or coated nylon.

Plastic sheeting ranges from thin, painter's dropcloths (1–2 mm), to the heavier weights used in the construction industry (3–6 mm). The thinner dropcloths are light, cheap, and compact, but puncture easily. Heavier weight plastic is plenty strong but can be quite slippery and heavy. All plastic attracts a lot of dirt.

Mylar is strong for its thickness and very light, but crinkles underneath. The Mylar used in emergency blankets punctures easily. Stronger Mylar sheeting is used in the construction industry and can be purchased at big box home improvement stores.

Tyvek, discussed earlier, is very strong. Crinkly when new, you can run it through a washing machine to soften it before using. A gentle rinse cycle is sufficient. Remember not to rely on Tyvek if you're going to be in very wet conditions.

Fiber-reinforced plastic is heavier than most of the other options, but is nearly indestructible. The emergency blanket version, which is aluminized on one side, is often purchased on the premise that some heat will be reflected back to the sleeper. Don't count on it.

Urethane-coated nylon groundcloths are among the more expensive options but do a good job without being slippery. Silicone-coated nylon groundcloths are lighter, strong enough, exceedingly slippery, and effective dirt magnets. The slipperiness can be reduced by applying a pattern of silicone sealant in dots or stripes across the surface. The silicone might slow the sliding if the bead is large enough, but it will add weight.

Tents

The most popular of all wilderness shelters is the tent. And why not? Tents are the closest thing to a home away from home that you can carry on your back. There's something almost magical about unrolling the wad of nylon and string from its sack and in a few minutes having it become your own little fabric fort.

Tents vary from the miniscule to airy multi-room palaces. Some are single skinned and others are double walled. Tents without floors are discussed elsewhere. For our purposes, a tent, at a minimum, has a floor, door, roof, and walls.

It's the separation from the outdoors that many tent detractors dislike, preferring as they do, to sleep in the open, or at most, under a tarp. They have a point. There is perhaps more a sense of being outdoors when the view is 360 degrees from under a tarp. But when the storm is lashing, the bugs bombing, the wind ripping, or the neighbors' eyes prying, a tent can be the better place. Tent detractors also maintain that tents are fatally flawed because they drench their occupants in condensation. It's certainly possible and does happen. But proper tent design and correct use can keep this problem under control in most situations. (And lest we kid ourselves, under-tarp soakings happen too.)

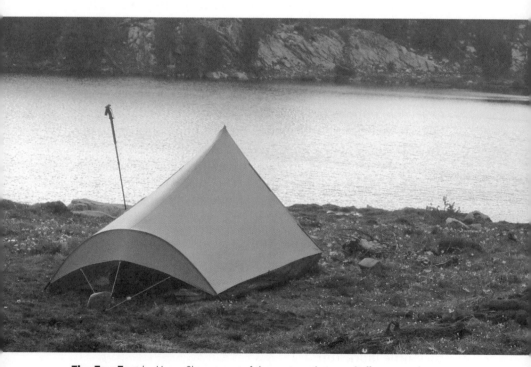

The TarpTent by Henry Shires is one of the most aesthetic and effective single-wall shelters available. The two-person Squall model, shown here in the Spanish Peaks of Montana, weighs less than 2 pounds and provides effective protection from weather and insects with excellent views and ventilation through the mesh front door.

TENT TYPES

We'll focus primarily on double versus single wall, and free-standing versus hoop tents.

Double wall

Most common of all tents, the double-wall combines a tent body (floor, walls/ceiling, and door) with a separate waterproof nylon or polyester rainfly. The floor is most commonly made of nylon waterproofed with a heavy urethane coating, and the walls, doors, and ceiling of noncoated nylon — either ripstop or taffeta. Floor seams, either across the floor or up the sides and corners, are factory taped in all but the least expensive models, making them impervious to water. Most floors extend some amount up the walls, the theory being that this "bathtub" keeps striking rain and even pooling water at bay.

All but the most serious mountaineering tents are fitted with netting-backed vents and windows. Airflow, as we shall see, is important. Schemes to keep both the air flowing and the insect world at bay are an important part of tent design. The rainfly will stretch at least over all windows, doors, and uncoated portions of the tent body. Some rainflys completely enclose the tent, extending sideways well beyond the doors to form *vestibules* — like little front porches. Rainflys must never touch the tent body. The airspace between body and fly is needed to carry away moisture and to prevent condensation from forming inside the tent. Fly edges also have to stop short of the ground to allow air to flow underneath, lest they smother the tent occupants and trap moisture.

Single wall

Simpler and generally lighter than double-wall tents are single-wall tents. These fall into two camps: breathable and ventilated impermeable.

In the first kind, breathable fabrics, similar to those used in waterproof-breathable raingear, comprise the walls, doors, and ceiling. Designed and used correctly, they keep rain out yet don't collect significant interior condensation, since interior moisture can be driven through the walls. Those made of impermeable fabrics take the other route: adding extensive and aggressive ventilation schemes to keep airflow high and limit accumulation of interior moisture and subsequent condensation. In-between are mountaineering single-wall tents of fabrics that breathe well enough in the mountains where the air is typically drier.

Single-wall tents were on their way to claiming a large portion of the backpacking market when, in the 1980s, they were hit by US federal regulations requiring fire-retardant tent fabrics. The Gore-Tex fabrics commonly in use at the time didn't meet the regulations, and the tents disappeared from the market. Today, there are a few waterproof-breathable tents available. They are mostly freestanding models, and many are aimed at the mountaineering market. They are reasonably light and are certainly worth considering. It should be noted that they also tend to be expensive.

In use, single-wall tents require some different techniques than the typical double-wall design. They sometimes have doors exposed to the elements, meaning that there is no vestibule. Ventilation is usually provided by vents, windows, or netting-backed doors. However, there's another trick that dates back to the Gore-Tex tents made by Early Winters. They recommended that, if the tent were suffering from condensation, to shut the doors and windows. This traps more heat and increases the temperature differential between indoors and out, driving the moisture through the fabric. Remarkably, given the right combination of environmental conditions, this does the trick and can be helped along considerably by a candle.

Single-wall impermeable tents make no concessions in the need for aggressive ventilation. The best scheme is to let in air at ground level and vent at or near the tent's high point (hot, moist air rises). Some are equipped with massive awning-protected windows that usually vent quite effectively.

Freestanding tents

Freestanding tents are supported by a crisscrossing set of poles that completely support the tent and fly without significant guying. These take a bewildering variety of shapes. The simplest have rectangular floors and use a pair of poles that attach at opposite corners, crossing overhead dead center. As poles are added to the tent design, complexity abounds. There are many, many three-, four-, five-, and even six-pole designs. The poles are sometimes erected inside the body, especially with single-wall tents, leaving a smooth exterior that doesn't catch the wind or easily trap snow and rain. More common is to crisscross the poles as an exoskeleton over the outside body, attached using external fabric sleeves or suspension clips. The pole tips normally clip into grommets in webbing tabs sewn to the tent floor. The fly is draped over this assembly and oftentimes clips to buckles on webbing extending from the pole attachment points at the tent floor. Defying this description of "freestanding," the flys on these tents generally need guying to create adequate space between canopy and fly, minimize flapping in the wind or sagging in the rain and snow, and keep the whole works from blowing off the lip of that ridge. Freestanding tents filled with gear take flight surprisingly often.

Hoop tents

Hoop tents are a variation of the canvas covering on a Conestoga wagon. A series of hoops, usually two or three, runs essentially parallel to one another. In a tapered design, the pole at the foot will be the shortest. If a double-wall tent, the fly extends beyond the door to create a vestibule and to keep rain off the inner door itself. Recent hoop tents often have a front door that's along one side, rather than dead center of the head end. This arrangement can help reduce the rain or snow that gets inside when entering or leaving.

Solo tents

The solo traveler has several small tents to choose among, but at a fairly high PPS. Some one-man designs exceed 5 pounds of trail weight. Most ultralight models are coming in at 2.5–3.5 PPS. Thus, a tent seldom offers the best PPS for the solo hiker, but can compare favorably for parties of two or more. In addition to a high PPS value, most solo tents severely cramp living space. They are best suited for those who hike all day and only need a place to sleep at night, rather than to hang out and camp. Spending a few days hunkered down in a tiny tunnel solo tent while waiting out a storm will certainly cause you to come back to this book and star the margin here.

FOOTPRINTS

Nearly every tent made offers a companion *footprint*, a piece of coated nylon that goes under the tent's floor. The rationale is that the tent floor needs protection from the ground, lest it spring leaks from punctures and wear spots. Costing from $30 to $50, these footprints beg the questions: Is the tent floor strong enough? And if not, why?

The extra weight and expense can be avoided two ways. Keep the tent floor healthy by carefully selecting tent sites and not wearing shoes inside. Or take along a thin sheet of plastic, perhaps a painting dropcloth or Mylar rescue blanket, and fashion your own lightweight footprint. In areas where sharp rock or thorns can't be avoided, this second floor might be necessary. Trim the sheet to be smaller than the tent so that it doesn't funnel water underneath.

Another possible reason to opt for the footprint is that certain tents can be pitched using the fly, poles, and footprint only. In some cases leaving the tent body at home can save several pounds. How well this arrangement works depends on the tent's design.

CHOOSING A TENT

How do we choose among the hundreds of tents on the market? Because of our focus on weight, most of them will fall off the list right away. Many have PPS weights of 4–6 pounds, with that solo-tent PPS among the highest of all.

There are two issues:

- Creative manufacturer weights
- The packed/minimum weight paradox

As with the other major pieces of gear, tent weights are frequently misstated, so they turn out to be heavier than claimed. Also, the interpretation of "packed" and "minimum" weights vary from manufacturer to manufacturer. "Packed" can include tent, fly, poles, lines, stakes, and sacks, or it can include all that plus instructions, seam sealer, hang tags — everything that ships with a new tent. "Minimum" weight is even more confusing, ranging from just the tent, fly, lines, and poles, to just the fly, poles, and (optional) footprint.

If your head is swimming, you know what you have to do. Take your own scales to your local gear emporium and weigh the candidates yourself. Once you have some finalists, have them set up and climb inside. You need room to sleep and live. However many occupants you're planning for need to fit inside along with their sleeping gear and at least a few extras.

Hammock shelters allow you to spend the night in places no one sleeping on the ground would even think about. Here, a Hennessy Adventure Racing Hammock is pitched on a steep forested slope. The stock silnylon fly has been replaced by a Bozeman Mountain Works Stealth 1, which adds space, offers more flexible pitching options, and saves weight. The total package shown here, which includes the hammock, tarp, six titanium tent stakes, and Spectra guylines weighs less than 1 pound.

You may also want to bring in your gear or leave it protected under a vestibule. If so, make sure your tent can do it.

- Can you sit up without your head grazing the ceiling?
- Can you stretch out without your sleeping bag touching any tent walls?
- Can you hang clothing, a flashlight, or lantern from the ceiling?
- How is the door(s) configured?
- Can two or more people get in and out without climbing over their tentmates or without letting rain or snow inside?
- Can you scoot in backward, take off your shoes out of the weather, and leave them outside still protected from the rain?

Next, ask yourself what the ventilation is like. Look for the ability to take in fresh air at ground level and exhaust it above. This flow will help reduce the accumulation of moisture. Some tents vent well even with the fly configured to fend off rain. Others don't and become veritable saunas that will soak the occupants. In hot, dry weather, a tent that opens wide while keeping bugs away is best.

And, for many ultralighters, perhaps the best reason for never bringing a tent should be the top priority when selecting yours: How are the views? Forget about plastic windows. They fog with condensation and lack optical clarity after only a short time of use. Look for flys that can be rolled back and pitched open and voluminous mesh bodies that allow you to enjoy the surroundings in the absence of bad weather and in the presence of swarms of mosquitoes.

HAMMOCKS

"I'm swingin' in the rain. . . ." There's nothing new about hammocks. Tropical dwellers have used them for centuries, perhaps millennia. They've never been an especially popular option for backpackers, perhaps because nobody had taken the time to sort through and overcome their limitations. That's changed.

First, to state the obvious, a hammock has to attach on either end. So high-alpine, desert, and tundra hikers will probably have to take a pass. But where there are trees, or even sturdy bushes, stringing a hammock is a legitimate bedroom option. The simple and elegant Hennessy Hammock is a two-piece miracle of fabric and line. The body strings between two trees a few paces apart. Two sidelines spread the body and prevent excessive sway. A rainfly covers the works, attaching to the mainline and sidelines. The fabric body and a surprisingly slender ridgeline provide its strength.

To get inside, you enter headfirst through an opening slit in the bottom that extends from the end about a third of the way to the center. You sit on the floor and bring your feet up and in, swinging them away from the opening, which snaps shut. Other hammock brands offer a more traditional configuration, including entrance from the side. They are generally heavier and more complex than the Hennessy. But more innovation is likely to come in the hammock arena.

A hammock seldom allows for gear storage. Your gear can either stay directly underneath, protected by the fly overhead, or perhaps be hung from one of the supporting trees.

Keeping warm on cold nights in a hammock is a challenge. It hasn't been well quantified how much more heat is lost while suspended in air compared to sleeping on the ground with a pad. If heat loss is through a combination of conduction, convection, radiation, and evaporation, it's likely that hammocking significantly increases convection. The body is exposed to free-flowing air all around. By comparison, the ground directly under an earthbound sleeper slowly warms and probably carries away less total heat. Because the hammock fabric presses both from underneath and the sides, an insulating pad should wrap around the torso where the sleeping bag insulation is compressed. An added radiant barrier in the form of an emergency blanket or other reflective fabric can preserve more of the sleeper's body heat. Hammocks seem to match well to blanket-and-pad combinations, such as the Rab, Golite, Nunatak, or Big Agnes.

Pyramid shelters like the Black Diamond Megalite and Oware Alphamid (both shown in this photo on a backcountry ski and snowshoe trek in the Montana Beartooths) provide adequate shelter for mild winter storms, but attention needs to be paid during heavy snows (digging is required to keep the shelters from collapsing) and setup takes some time due to the high number of snow stakes required for a taut pitch.

TEEPEES AND OTHER ODDITIES

There are still shelters that don't fall into the other categories we've discussed. Teepees are single-wall and usually floorless, with a single center pole. They are equipped with a simple door and some sort of vents near the top. Made of waterproof-coated material, usually nylon, teepees rely on venting to clear out moisture. In fair weather, many teepee designs allow the floor to be raised above ground level, allowing good airflow but admitting critters. In anticipation, some have a netting skirt. Others, targeted at wintertime camping, have fabric skirts upon which snow can be heaped to provide a shield from the wind and weather. Curiously, teepee doors never seem to be fitted with netting backing to allow for bug-free ventilation in hot weather. At least one, however, offers a netting door insert as an optional accessory.

And another offers a fully enclosed, netted, inner-teepee tent with a floor.

Teepees are useful year round. In winter, quite the living space can be excavated underneath with sleeping platforms, etc. You just need to accommodate the center pole with some sort of support that won't allow it to sink into the snow. Something like a small plywood disk will do. The Megamid by Black Diamond is a popular floorless teepee, but lighter ones are available, including Black Diamond's MegaLite, the GoLite Hex, and other models from Oware and Tipi Kifaru.

There are other fabric shelters. Some are tentlike but you supply the frame, or they're suspended from a ridgeline and spread out with lines and stakes. The Six Moon Designs Lunar Solo shelter is an example. Created by lightweight backpacking enthusiast Ron Moak, the Lunar Solo is a silnylon-and-netting tent that relies on trekking poles for support and large vents and awnings for minimizing condensation. It provides effective shelter for 1.5–2.0 pounds. The Integral Designs Silshelter is a floorless tentlike shelter that relies on trekking poles for support and weighs about a pound. A series of fully enclosed shelters with netted doors are also available from the likes of TarpTent, TrailQuest, GoLite, and Six Moon Designs.

BIVY SACKS

Covered previously, bivy sacks deserve mention in this shelter discussion too. First, there are bivy sacks that blur the line between bivy and tent. They have one or more hoop poles, and some even have open head areas and netting-backed, zippered doors. All are single walled and made of waterproof-breathable fabric, some with coated nylon floors. These are for folks who don't suffer from the merest hint of claustrophobia and who aren't interested in bringing much gear or doing much more than sleeping inside. In the event of long stretches of bad weather, the bivy should probably be paired with a small tarp to protect gear, the bivy entrance, and cooking out of the weather.

Maybe the bivy's biggest appeal is its ability to occupy the smallest possible bit of real estate, miniscule campsites that everybody else has to pass by. A spot in a tiny mountainside meadow that faces east can reward the lucky bivouac'er with a sunrise to remember forever. In addition, a bivy takes little pack space. Many, but not all, are quite light. Some of the more complex designs are well over 2 pounds.

In the case of the simpler overbag-style bivy, their sheltering qualities keep away wind and wind-driven rain and snows, making tarp camping in nasty weather far less risky.

Trail Shelters & Structures

Some parts of the US offer the option of trail shelters, cabins, or lean-tos. These range from the most basic of accommodations—a roof and a spot to sleep—to a multi-room cabin. Significant stretches of the Appalachian Trail can be hiked without carrying any sort of tent or tarp. The shelters are abundant. The same is true of New Zealand's Great Tracks and many hiking areas of Asia, Europe, and the United Kingdom. Clearly, for those minimizing pack weight, planning to stay in manmade shelters means having to carry no shelter at all.

As appealing as this may sound, they are sometimes full, meaning a hike to the next one or perhaps even backtracking to the last. Crowded into a shelter with several strangers isn't always a recipe for a good night's sleep or a practice in exercising social graces. And some shelters are overrun by vermin. You can spend the night fending off mice or rats. But to some, there's an appeal to solid walls and a roof, a fireplace and a kitchen, and a place to dry wet clothes. Granted, many ultralight backpackers call these places their "house" or "apartment"—the very place they're trying to escape from.

Shelters that are staffed and managed usually operate on a reservation system so that they are, in fact, dependable. Some backcountry shelters can also be reserved, including a great many US Forest Service cabins and fire lookouts. In many parts of the Western US, trail shelters were once common, but many have been removed over the last couple of decades by the National Park and Forest Services, making the shelter option just a memory.

SNOW SHELTERS

Sleeping in the snow requires special preparation and care. The shelter's job remains staving off the cold and wet. Typical four-season and mountaineering tents are bombproof and bomb heavy, often sporting a PPS of 4–5 pounds. What alternatives are there for the lightweight hiker?

Two options that come to mind are the igloo and the snow cave. Igloos are walled domes made from snow blocks that you cut yourself from the floor area and surrounding snow pack. You'll need a snow saw, snow shovel, time, practice, and snow with a reasonable amount of water content.

Snow caves are caverns dug into a very deep and thick snow bank. They require snow shovels, time, waterproof clothing, and practice.

The positives of igloos and snow caves are many. They are shelters made of available materials, freeing the camper of carrying a tent. A snow shovel is generally carried anyway, and a snow saw for igloo making along with a ground tarp are it—perhaps 2 pounds versus 10. Neither of these options are a casual shelter. You don't pull into camp at 4:00 and crawl into bed by 5:00. Igloos and snow caves take hours to construct, and residents are tempted to tweak the interiors for hours more. They're not for sleep-quick-and-split winter fastpacking.

If you supply the roof, you can fairly quickly dig a living space in the snow. A teepee, a tarp stretched over a line or pole can be used in an emergency.

Stakes and Guylines

Myriad tent stakes exist on the market, with only three types that distinguish themselves from the rest and are actually worth considering.

The first type is the titanium skewer, usually 1/8 inch or so in diameter and 6 inches in length. At less than a 0.25 ounces apiece, they are far and away the lightest stakes you can buy. They are strong enough for most soils. Considering that you can carry double the amount of titanium stakes for the same weight of cheaper stakes, they are very popular among tarp campers who like to dance with foul weather and need plenty of additional guy-out points to secure their shelter. The primary disadvantage with titanium stakes is that they are expensive: $2.50 to $3.00 apiece, but are available to BackpackingLight.com website subscribers for as little as $1.75 each. And in a natural color that can only be described as stealth gray, they're easy to lose. Bozeman Mountain Works addresses the issue with an even more expensive option by offering hi-visibility orange coatings on their 0.22-ounce titanium stakes. Hikers buy them on the theory that money invested up front in loss protection is money saved in the long run.

The other type of stake that works well in a wider variety of snow conditions and offers greater strength is the nail stake. Budget hikers claim the performance of an aluminum gutter nail purchased from the hardware store is sufficient, but our experience tells us differently. Anodized aluminum nail pegs with rectangular cross sections, as distributed with MSR (US) and Lightwave (UK) tents are superior. They weigh only 0.5 ounces apiece. For serious pegging in rocky environments, 0.5-ounce titanium nail pegs from both Snow Peak and Vargo Outdoors are available.

The third type of stake that is popular comes with the tent you purchase. Quality, size, strength, and weight vary widely. You may perceive that you are getting a free set of pegs with your tent. Soon enough the quality will reflect that and you'll seek replacements.

Snow and sand stakes tend to be heavier (1+ ounces apiece) and come in two primary designs: *flukes*, such as the SMC T-Anchor that work well in soft snow, and *crescent moon pegs*, which have a semicircular cross section that works better in harder snow. Sand and snow anchors can be as simple as a small, silnylon stuff sack filled with sand or snow, and weigh less than 0.1 ounces apiece.

Virtually any thin (1–2mm) cord material works well enough for guylines, but weights, strengths, handling properties, water absorption, and stretch varies widely. The gold standard for lightweight hiking has long been Kelty Triptease. At $15 per 50 feet, it is an expensive ounce of equipment. On par, but with higher strength/weight ratios, are pure braided Spectra lines, such as those available from Gossamer Gear and Bozeman Mountain Works (AirCore 1 and 2). From a weight standpoint, these guylines are the lightest you can buy. But they suffer from tangling in long lengths, especially during storage. Also, they absorb some water into the core of the braid, and they are only available in white. To address these issues, Bozeman Mountain Works offers AirCore Pro, a urethane-coated, 100-percent Dyneema guyline dyed bright yellow for visibility.

Conclusion

At the end of the day, backpackers need to find shelter to get out of the weather, rest, and refuel. Hopefully, they will stay comfortable during the wilderness night. Shelter can take on many forms, but for the lightweight backpacker, it's a three-part challenge: selecting the right shelter, mastering how to use that shelter in a wide range of conditions, and choosing the right place to set up camp—all while maintaining the minimalist approach to weight and bulk.

Part 3:

Eating, Drinking, and Hygiene

Chapter 9: **Hydration**

By George Cole

The Physiology of Hydration

You've made it this far, and you've been exposed to a great deal of technical and detailed information on the high points of lightweight backpacking. So in starting this chapter with a discussion of the physiology of hydration, we're going to be less technical, less specific, and probably a wee bit less accurate, depending on which "expert" you pay homage to.

If you accept the theory that all life on earth evolved from single-celled organisms that lived in a primordial sea, you probably are not too uncomfortable with the fact that your body consists of millions of individual cells filled and surrounded by a fluid much like seawater. In fact, about 70 percent of the total weight of the body is fluid weight. Ninety percent of that fluid is good old H_2O. The rest is mostly dissolved salts.

"Big deal," you say. "What does that have to do with backpacking?"

Following a hearty meal of trail mix, often called *gorp* (usually raisins, peanuts, and chocolate chips), we immediately go to work breaking down all the foods into their constituent sugars, carbohydrates, proteins, and fats. This process starts in the fluid environment of the stomach and continues in the slightly less fluid environment of the small intestine. The resulting nutrient molecules, dissolved in fluid, get passed through the walls of the stomach and intestine and end up floating in another fluid — blood.

Nutrients are carried throughout the body by the bloodstream. Eventually, they are dropped off at the various resident cells that need fuel in order to do the work that we will ask them to do tomorrow, such as carrying us and our pots, pans, and GPS units further up the side of Mount Soreknees. Nutrients get into various resident cells in various ways, and all of those ways depend on some method of fluid transport through cell walls.

Once in a cell, nutrients move about in the fluid that fills the cell, called the *intra-cellular fluid*, until they are taken up and transformed by the cell's motors, or *mitochondria*, into energy. This process is actually composed of various chemical reactions that together are referred to as *metabolism*. Many of these reactions depend upon molecular water (H_2O) to work properly.

What's left of a nutrient after it's been metabolized does not have to remain inside the cell in order for the cell to do its job. In fact, it takes up valuable space. So in a dissolved state, it is transported out of the cell and back into the blood, where eventually it is removed by the kidneys and stored in another fluid until it gets peed into a little hole in the side of old Mount Soreknees.

At the same time, we're sucking in large quantities of thin mountain air while trying to get some oxygen to our cells so that they can make those M&Ms in our gorp go to work for us. The oxygen gets dissolved in the fluid on the surface of the lung. In its dissolved state it passes through the surface of the lung into the bloodstream, where it hitches a ride on a red blood cell. It then gets washed up against the wall of a waiting resident cell and diffuses through the cell wall into the intra-cellular fluid. Eventually, while lending its unique properties to the metabolism of an M&M by a mitochondrion, the oxygen combines with one of the byproducts of backpacker metabolism, carbonized peanut butter, and returns to the bloodstream for its journey back to the lungs, where it ends its journey as bad breath.

Further, all the metabolizing we're doing to get up Mount Soreknees produces heat. Since our cells don't want to end up boiling in their own juice, they allow some of it to leak out onto the surface of the skin, where it evaporates and cools us down. At the same time, our muscles are contracting, rubbing up against one another, and causing the ends of our bones to pivot, slide, and twist in our joints. A type of water-based WD-40 is used to lubricate all the potential points of friction.

Finally, while our body depends upon its skeleton for its axial structure, kind of like a flag does a flagpole, it depends upon the pressure of the intra- and extra-cellular fluid to keep us firmly inflated. Otherwise, we'd flap. So, fluid is not only important to backpackers in the activity of backpacking; it's important to backpackers in the act of being backpackers, as opposed to being flags.

Basically, what this all means is that we have to stay hydrated, maintaining just the right amount of fluid in and between our cells and circulating in our bloodstream. If we don't, the moisture that escapes through our pores, breath, urine, and feces will result in the body rapidly losing its ability to sustain itself. We can slow the process of fluid loss by reducing our activity level and covering our skin with a vapor barrier. But without replenishing body fluids, we will die within days. All things considered, that means that backpackers must drink water, or a reasonable facsimile thereof.

And herein lies the problem: Water is heavy.

Water Weight

For the amount of space it takes up, water is the heaviest survival item that backpackers carry. One liter of water weighs about 35 ounces. Whether it's summer or winter, while working hard getting to the top of Mount Soreknees our body *needs* 4–5 liters or more in a day. That's at least ten pounds of water.[1]

Refer back to the chapter devoted to pack weight and energy expenditure and do the math. Do you really want to carry 10 pounds of water while walking ten miles and climbing three thousand feet? What if you plan to be out there for more than a day?[2] It just makes sense that we would want to make use of the water that we find on the face of Mount Soreknees, even if it did start out in little cat holes. But, as Calvin once said to Hobbes, "Eeeeyewwww, there's cooties in that stuff!" Well, maybe and maybe not, but you're not going to know until several days after you scoop it up in your Sierra cup and try to strain the chunks out of it as they're going past your teeth. And, if there are cooties in it, you're probably not going to enjoy what they do to you later on.

Water Cooties

Water cooties, as we refer to them here, is the collective term we use for the single- and multi-cellular organisms known as waterborne pathogenic viruses, bacteria, and protozoa. The protozoa paranoia includes, most commonly, amoeba, Cryptosporidium, and Giardia. The latter is probably fueling more hype than howl outside of rangeland waterways, and the former provides real threats to water quality, especially in Asia, South America, and Africa.

Viruses can be associated on occasion with carcasses in the US wilderness, but are more likely to be a threat in developing countries where you're sipping downstream of yak crossings and village sewage farms. Bacteria are probably the most serious US threat. Notable organisms include Campylobacter, Enterobacter, Enterococcus, and E. Coli and result from both human and animal defecation and animal matter decay. The former three organisms are found in areas frequented by stock parties.

There are numerous pathogenic bacteria and protozoa that *might* be living in natural water sources while waiting for you to happen by. Most viruses don't survive very long outside of a host. But if animals or humans are defecating in our source or there's a carcass upstream, there may be a virus or two in the water. Protozoan pathogens are more likely to be associated with the pond scum of stagnant waters rather than rapidly flowing mountain creeks, which typically harbor less sophisticated food chains.

We know of a number of backpackers who drink straight from highland springs, savoring the cold, unadulterated taste of water emerging fresh from the rock. They believe it's highly unlikely that this water will have had time to be infected by any nasty bugs. We also know of backpackers who drink small amounts of water from suspect sources, believing that they can vaccinate themselves by ingesting small numbers of pathogens.

We admit, some of these brave souls have never gotten sick, or say they haven't, or don't recognize that the symptoms they're having this winter stem from the contaminated water they drank last spring. However, pathogenic microorganisms can be present in any natural water source, including ice and snow, no matter how far up the side of Mount Soreknees you find it. And even if your hiking buddy is a full-bore PhD, water-quality analyst with a lab in his pack, he may not be able to identify all of the little cooties swimming around in your Sierra cup. So how are you going to know?

"OK, OK, enough already," you say. "Big deal. How bad can it be?"

The Cootie Boogie

As indicated above, in one way or another, these little guys either eat our cells or they turn our cells into cloning factories. And not unlike our own cells, bacteria and protozoa pee in our blood. If enough of these micro-assassins get inside us to defeat our natural pest control mechanisms, also called our immune system, the extent of cell destruction, blood loss, or the toxic effect of their wastes can make us sick, sometimes very sick. We usually won't know that we've been infected until a lot of damage has already been done. Two early signs are fever and, if you really were Jack the Ripper in a former life, the Cootie Boogie.[3] Besides being a pain in the butt (stomach, intestines, and colon), the Boogie can result in rapid dehydration. That is not a good thing up on Mount Soreknees, where clean water is absent for washing and the only natural toilet paper consists of rocky scree shards.

In anticipation of having to dance the Boogie while on the trail, some backpackers carry anti-diarrhea medications. However, these medications have the disadvantage of allowing offending nasties to stay in the gut longer. They probably shouldn't be used except when diarrhea is severe, more than ten episodes a day.

There are broad-spectrum prescription antibiotics that can knock down bacterial or protozoan infections. If the offending cootie is a virus, our immune system is going to have deal with it on its own, although we may need medical help to control the symptoms and alleviate discomfort. But again, how will we know what's eating us? Even a sober doctor is not going to be able to figure out who our little dinner guests are without access to a lab.

So what are you supposed to do? It's better to keep the little monsters out in the first place. Given the present state of water treatment technology, that's really not difficult to do.

Overview of Water Treatment Technology

Basically, there are three ways to make sure that the water we get from a natural source is safe to drink.

1. Kill all or most of the microorganisms that might be in it by sterilizing the water
2. Prevent active microorganisms from getting inside us by filtering or purifying the water
3. Both sterilize and filter the water

All three methods have disadvantages, but they're all better than the Boogie.

DISINFECTION—THE LETHAL OPTION

No known microorganism can live longer than five minutes in water that has been heated to 212°F. Therefore, the oldest and surest way to kill waterborne microbes is to boil the water. Even this simple solution can be a challenge. Backpackers often go high, where the air pressure is low. At lower air pressures, less heat is required to bring water to a boil. At 14,000 feet water will boil at 187°F. At this temperature it will take more than five minutes to absolutely, positively kill all the microbial residents. The conservative rule of thumb is to boil water for ten minutes when in the mountains. However, water takes a while to cool after being brought to a boil, so most of the backpackers we know wait only until a boil is reached. Most of them are still alive.

Another challenge for boiling water is that we've got to have a stove, pot, and probably a windscreen. And we're going to have to pack enough fuel to cook our food and boil our drinking water. Although it will depend on where and with what we boil it, let's say that it takes about thirty grams, or 1 fluid ounce, of fuel to boil a liter of water. If we need five liters of drinking water a day, we'll have to carry 5 extra ounces of fuel for every day that we plan to be out. For a three-day trip that means about a pound of fuel.

Then, there's the issue of water that is chunky, silty, slimy, scummy, or otherwise tainted with visibly disconcerting matter you'd rather not have in your gut. If there are chunks in the water, most of them can be removed by pouring the water through a bandanna and by letting silt settle out in the bottom of a pot. But the hassle of screening the water, setting up the stove, boiling the water, letting it cool down, and then repacking the stove is probably why most three-season backpackers carry filtering devices. On the other hand, winter backpackers may have to melt snow or ice for drinking water anyway, so it just makes sense for them to leave the filtering devices at home and let the water come to a boil before bottling it. Winter backpackers usually do this routine twice a day, preparing two liters of drinking water at each camp sitting—morning and evening. They simply accept that a little dehydration is going to occur through the course of the day.

CHEMICAL TREATMENTS

Another method of killing is to dissolve some sort of toxic substance in the water and wait until the cootie screams stop! If you're too civilized to recognize cootie screams, just follow the directions in the side of the toxic substance package. The recommended "killing" period varies by water temperature but averages about twenty minutes at 70 degrees. The most widely used substance is tetraglycine hydroperiodide and can be found in products such as Polar Pure and Potable Aqua.

Tetraglycine hydroperiodide is always packaged in crystalline form and must be dissolved in the suspect water, where it releases iodine. Used as directed, the amount of iodine dissolved in the water does not pose a health hazard, although we don't find it very tasty. In order to kill the taste, sodium disulfate or vitamin C can be added to the water after the recommended killing period has passed.

A newer substance is chlorine dioxide. Chlorine dioxide can be found in McNett Aquamira (US) or Pristine (Canada). Both are packaged as two separate liquids—a stabilized chlorine dioxide solution and a phosphoric acid activation solution. When the solutions are mixed in equal quantities and the resulting chemical reaction is allowed to progress for a few minutes, the chlorine dioxide solution is activated and becomes a potent disinfectant.

Chlorine dioxide is quite toxic to cells. Rather than interrupting cellular metabolism, as in the case of some antibiotics, chlorine dioxide (and iodine and chlorine) interrupt the cell membrane and prevent the flow of nutrients into and out of the cell. Essentially, these chemicals oxidize, or bleach, the cooties to death. It would you, too, if you were only a couple microns in diameter. Don't drink the stuff straight. However, chlorine dioxide is generally considered safer than iodine or chlorine bleach when used as directed, and it doesn't seem to add much taste to water compared to chlorine bleach or iodine. The reason might be that lower dosages of chlorine dioxide are required to have the killing power suitable for backcountry water disinfection.

Laboratory testing by real scientists suggest that, at least under field-simulated laboratory conditions, chlorine dioxide kills a wider variety of cooties than tetraglycine hydroperiodide or chlorine bleach. This includes viruses, bacterial spores, and protozoan cysts, which are the forms of microbes most resistant to killing. Nearly every backcountry walker we know who is also a water scientist or engineer prefers Aquamira to Potable Aqua, especially in the less benign environments

Aquamira kit, by McNett of Bellingham, WA. Contrary to manufacturer recommendations, this Aquamira kit was repacked into smaller, lighter dropper bottles, available from BackpackingLight.com.

of Central America, Central Africa, and the Himalaya. Those three areas are famous for their awful water quality.

No matter what chemical you use, make sure that you let it get at the threads and cap of the container you treat your water in. Slosh the treated water around until some of it leaks out past a loosened cap. And, for heaven's sake, decontaminate your hands before either drinking or eating. Alcohol hand gel, such as Purell, is good for this and may serve as a dandy backup fire starter. Several brands of alcohol gel are packaged in small plastic squeeze bottles and can be found in drug stores.

All of the water treatment chemicals that we know of come in small packages and treat substantial quantities of water, anywhere from thirty to two thousand liters. Therefore, as many thru-hikers have discovered, chemical treatment is a space and weight-efficient treatment strategy. That is, of course, unless "chunky" water grosses you out so bad you have trouble getting it down without drinking a liter of Irish coffee first. The big downside of chemical treatment is the time it takes to work, especially at low water temperatures.

The newer cootie killers on the market are battery-powered devices that use either ultraviolet light (the SteriPEN) or electrochemically-activated mixed oxidants (MSR Miox) as its lethal mechanism. These devices cost $100 to $200 and weigh 3–6 ounces with batteries.

Both devices are lightweight, elegant, and simple to use, but neither is without its problems. The SteriPEN requires an awfully long time to treat several liters of water. It's designed for glass-at-a-time volumes. The MSR Miox Water Purifier is notably better suited for backcountry use, but our initial usability tests indicate that strong dosing is required in order to maintain an adequate free chlorine residual (as measured by the included test strips) in murky waters, resulting in odiferous water reminiscent of a swimming pool.

FILTRATION—THE (SORT OF) HUMANE OPTION

Earth-friendly backpackers would never actively kill cooties. They just don't want them moving into their neighborhoods, which is why many of them strain sus-

The MSR Miox weighs 3 oz, but requires batteries, supplemental salt, and careful attention paid to dosage requirements. It is lighter, simpler, and faster than most water filters weighing twice as much — or more.

pect water through a variety of materials that are designed to let only the water through. Devices known as water filters mechanically remove submicron particulate matter. As most, but certainly not all, common pathogenic protozoa and bacteria are bigger than a micron, a properly functioning filter keeps them out of our drinking water. Viruses are much smaller and usually found only where there's a carcass or human fecal matter in the water. So filters work pretty well for most North American water sources.

Devices known as water *purifiers* are certified by the manufacturer to meet the Environmental Protection Agency standard that requires the removal of 99.99 percent of all identifiable bacteria, protozoa and viruses. Some, like the First Need purifiers, do this with a laboratory-grade mechanical filter element. Others do it using a mechanical filter in combination with some type of tetraglycine hydroperiodide element (e.g., only the viruses and smallest bacteria are killed outright by the iodine, so a purifier with this type of element is "sort of" humane). The problem with purifiers is that they are more expensive than simple filters. Some also work slower than filters and, not surprisingly, clog quicker.

The knock on all these devices is that you eventually have to change or clean the filter element, depending on what type of material the element is made of. And, since these devices invariably clog in the backcountry, you have to be prepared to change or clean them in the field. Second, while none of the devices made specifically for backpacking are all that heavy when dry, they can absorb up to 25 percent or more of their weight in water. And most of the time, you are carrying them wet. Third, bacteria and protozoa can colonize a filter element unless it is specially treated. They will act as a source for massive contamination if the filter fails by cracking or allowing unfiltered water past its seals. Fourth, when storing the device, it's hard not to allow water from the dirty (inflow) side of a filter to contaminate the apparatus that is devoted to the clean (outflow) water. Fifth, all but one type of device use muscle power to pump water through the filter element. Some pump filters and purifiers can require a good bit of effort. Last, they can freeze if it gets cold enough, causing the filter element to crack.

The current favorite filter type of the ultralight backpacking community seems to be the gravity filter, popularized by Ray Jardine in *Beyond Backpacking* and sold in various configurations by Seychelle and ULA Equipment. The filter element of a gravity filter is typically a proprietary charcoal matrix block that is housed in a small, oblong plastic case. The block may contain silver iodide to retard bacterial colonization. Input and output hose barbs on either end of the filter casing allow you to splice the filter into the drinking tube of a hydration bladder, and water is moved through the block when you suck water through the tube or hang the bladder on a tree limb and let it drip into a clean water bottle. These filters are typically disposable (treating up to about 100 gallons of water), weigh about 3 ounces and cost about $30. Some are field maintainable.

OVERKILL?

One ultralight backpacker we know of is not content with either filtration or chemical treatment alone. He combines three stages of mechanical filtration with both chemical and ultraviolet treatment. He uses an inline Sweetwater Siltstopper II pre-filter in front of an inline carbon filter in the drinking tube of his Platypus Big Zip hydration bladder. He pours untreated water into the Platypus through a homemade silk muck filter (a silk coffee filter cone). And before sucking the water through the filters, he treats it with Aqua Mira. When he gets to camp he hangs the transparent bladder in the sun. He says it's cleaner, better tasting water than he can get at home, and the whole kit, including an extra pre-filter element, weighs 11 ounces, wet. The bladder also serves to carry his water.

Is he being paranoid or just obsessively careful? He says, "What if I run into some of those military experiment cooties?" We have absolutely no idea what he's talking about. He's otherwise a pretty nice guy, and we've never seen him Boogie. Regardless, such a system might be suitable for treating water for infant children, the elderly, and other immune-compromised individuals.

Even if you're not paranoid, it's probably a good idea to pre-filter your water if you procure it regularly from mucky sources. Not only will it result in your filter working longer before it clogs, it will remove many of the suspended particles on which bacteria reside in large numbers. This can be done as simply as using a rubber band to secure a piece of coffee filter paper over the end of your filter's intake tube. Or you can buy a silt pre-filter, the likes of which are distributed by Cascade Designs and others.

Trip Analysis

Of course, all of this high-tech chemistry and gadgetry only works to save you weight when water is readily available. Otherwise, you have to carry enough clean water to safely make it from one source to another. How do you know how much to carry?

Start by recognizing that you're going to need at least 4 liters a day. Depending on your genetics and physical condition, you may need more or less. So this is probably a lower limit for most of the population. Few have ever taken the time to quantify the amount of water needed to drink in order to stay hydrated. However, in preparation for becoming a skilled and knowledgeable ultralight backpacker, we recommend that you take the time.

For one week, while carrying out your normal activities, count the number of ounces of water that you must drink every day in order to keep your urine *clear*. If it's not clear, you're not getting enough to drink — unless you have a chronic medical condition, are exercising very hard, are overdosing on vitamins, or are coming down with or fighting an illness.

Add up the total number of ounces and divide by seven. That's your basic daily need. When you're backpacking you're going to need more, unless your normal day involves climbing three thousand feet while walking ten miles and carrying a pack. Experiment with different levels of activity in different environmental conditions until you can estimate your need during a typical day of backpacking. Alternatively, while backpacking you can carry more than you think you'll need and keep a record of how much you actually drink, what the air temperature is, what the terrain is like, etc.

Next, gather the following information about each upcoming backpacking trip:

- What is the terrain like?
- How high will you be climbing each day?
- How hot will it get?
- How far will you walk each day?
- Where are the water sources for each day?
- In what condition are the water sources — clarity, potential for microbial contamination?
- What amount and type of precipitation is anticipated?

This is not rocket science, but knowing these things can help you figure out how much water you should carry between sources on any given day. For instance, if the terrain is rugged, you will need to drink more. If it's hot, you will need to drink more. If you're high up (the air is drier), you'll need to drink more. And since you'll know how widely spaced the sources are, what condition they're in, how far you're going each day, and whether or not you can count on rain or snow at any point, you can guesstimate your needs. Then, you can decide on a daily water consumption strategy.

Daily Water Consumption Strategy

To develop a daily water consumption strategy is to predict the timing and quantity of water intake so that you can carry less between sources. Since water is easier to carry and does you more good when it's inside of you instead of on your back in a bottle, what we're really talking about is a lightweight water intake strategy referred to as "tanking up" at sources.

When there's at least one reliable source every several miles or so and it's not particularly hot, drink as much as possible first thing in the morning and before starting to hike.

Then carry no more than 1 liter of water to the next source. At each source, drink any clean water you have left. Then drink a liter of newly filtered water and carry no more than 1 liter to the next stop.

An added benefit to tanking up early and often is how much better you'll feel and how much more energy you'll have throughout the day. The downside is you'll have to stop to pee more often. Some ultralight backpackers take this strategy to its logical extreme, drinking only at sources and carrying none. This approach is okay if you're absolutely sure where the next reliable source is and believe you can make it there comfortably, but it doesn't leave you with much room for error. As with everything in backpacking, you'll have to figure out what works best for you.

Water Storage

We can't leave the chapter without discussing the basic rudiments of backcountry water gear: bottles.

Few ultralight backpackers carry hard-sided water bottles anymore. Even lightweight winter backpackers use wide-mouth, soft-sided bottles, such as Nalgene Cantenes. The wide cap can be opened and closed with mittens and is far more resistant to freezing than narrow mouth caps. Nalgene Cantene bladders take boiling water well, and when stuffed in a sock, make terrific nighttime warming bottles in a sleeping bag.

Three-season water storage containers are typically divided into two categories: hydration bladders and non-hydration bladders. The distinction between the two is simple: Hydration bladders include a hose and bite valve, so water can be consumed hands-free (sort of) while walking. Non-hydration bladders are secured with only a small cap and/or zip closure.

The advantage to hydration bladders is that they give you ready access to water while hiking, eliminating the need to stop and retrieve a water bottle from your pack. There is also some physiological benefit to consuming small quantities of water regularly, rather than tanking up, although those benefits are more important as the level of endurance and exertion rates are increased. Thus, hydration bladders are popular among ultrarunners, adventure racers, and fastpackers hiking 30–50 miles per day.

One disadvantage of hydration bladders is that they are heavier than non-hydration bladders because of the tubing and bite valve configuration. In addition, most hydration bladders are made with heavier plastics. A typical 2- or 3-liter hydration bladder will weigh between 6–9 ounces. That's quite a lot heavier than a 3-liter Cascade Designs Platypus Bottle, which weighs only 2 ounces. And the Platypus Bottle can be converted into a lightweight hydration bladder as well. However, even the heavy hydration bladders are lighter than the backpacker's gold standard: three 1-liter Lexan Nalgene bottles will tip the scales at nearly a pound.

Conclusion

The human body needs to stay hydrated in order to work properly. This means that backpackers must drink water. Given this, backpackers must either carry all their water—a very heavy solution—or find sources as they go. If you're sticking to the ultralight ethic, you'll opt to find water sources on the trail. And there are three ways to make sure it is safe to drink: sterilization, filtering, or purifying the water. All methods have advantages and disadvantages. But when all things are considered, any method is better than the boogie.

Chapter 10: **Trail Food,**
Backcountry Cooking, and Nutrition

By Dave Schultz, Lee Van Horn, and Ryan Jordan

Other than the integration of clothing, shelter, and sleep systems, the synthesis of backcountry menu planning and cooking kit design is one of the more complex challenges faced by the ultralight hiker.

The components and weight of your kitchen will ultimately depend on your cooking style and menu design. Likewise, the limitations of your backcountry menu will likely be governed by your choice of stove and cookware.

This chapter does not provide a treatise on backcountry cooking. Nor does it provide a comprehensive overview of all cooking gear available to the hiking community. Rather, we hope to illustrate the ultralight philosophy as it applies specifically to designing a wilderness menu and cook kit that focuses on simplicity, efficiency, and of course, minimum weight for the solo hiker.

Food and Nutrition

The author Henry Fielding wrote, "We must eat to live and live to eat." Nowhere does this concept ring more true than on the trail. After a long day on the trail, your body needs fuel. Few things can make you forget the weariness in your limbs like a good meal. The challenge comes in trying to keep weight and bulk to a minimum while keeping nutrition and good taste to a maximum. As if this were not hard enough, we also place a high premium on ease of preparation and clean up. In the context of this chapter, we recognize what is the dominant ethic among ultralight hikers and others who focus more on walking than on camping. When cooking on the trail, meals are designed such that the most difficult preparation step is boiling water and pouring it in a bag. Yes, ultralight hikers can practice more sophisticated culinary arts and engage in multi-course meals that require complex preparation, but that is the topic of another volume.

Now we know what you are thinking, *Another treatise on which brand of freeze dried meal tastes the least like sawdust.* Au contraire, reader. Those freeze-dried meals, while extraordinarily convenient, can range from $4–$7 each. Thus, they are an expensive option for the long-distance walker or hiker on a more restricted budget.

Price, however, is not the only downside to using commercially prepared freeze-dried backpacking meals. They tend to be packaged in bulky and heavy materials. The portions are sometimes on the meager side for a hungry hiker, so it may require the purchase a two-person meal to satisfy the caloric needs of a solo hiker. The quality of taste is inconsistent among the different brands, and they often lack real nutritional value. The process of precooking and then freeze drying is thought to inactivate many key nutrients and vitamins. Some manufacturers are recognizing this and adding nutrient supplements to the freeze-dried mix after lyophilization.

Quite honestly, some hikers simply enjoy the art of food preparation and cooking with their own hands. There is great satisfaction, especially among the ultralight hiking community, to be gained in shopping for primary ingredients, experimenting with recipes, and crafting easy-to-cook backcountry meals suitable for royalty. For some, the pursuance of these types of emotional rewards will prevent many hikers from spending a dime on a commercially prepared meal. Therefore, the first part of this chapter is for the do-it-yourself backpacker looking to make their own tasty, lightweight, caloric- and nutrient-rich, and easy-to-prepare trail meals.

CALORIES

Unless you are a long-distance hiker who will be eating on the trail for many weeks in a row, the most important nutritional goal is to maximize the caloric density (calories per volume or weight of food) of your food within the limits of your personal preferences for variety and taste. Caloric density is an important metric because calories are required for energy, and food weight and bulk must be kept to a minimum.

A few days without the proper ratios of vitamins and minerals in our diet will not harm most of us. A few days without sufficient calories can cause your energy levels to dive. Your ability to walk, perform normal functions, and stay warm may come to a grinding halt. This doesn't mean that you should ignore vitamins and minerals in your meal planning. It simply means that calories are king. A few days of hiking at a significant caloric deficit won't kill you, and most of us, by invoking some mental fortitude, can survive a few days without food with no long-term effects. However, running low on caloric fuel will make you miserable and put emotional and physical dampers on what might have otherwise been an enjoyable trip.

Going ultralight means that you can go farther and faster than you were able to with your old heavy pack. Hikers walking twenty or more miles per day are not uncommon among the ultralight community. This is true even among hikers who wouldn't have dreamed of hiking a twenty-mile day in their pre-ultralight days, where five to ten miles might have been the norm.

While this newfound freedom is made possible by shedding pounds, the temptation to hike all day, every day, may cause a penalty in increased energy usage. It takes more energy to walk, even with a light pack, than to hang around camp.

In his book *Factors and Formulas for Computing Respiratory Exchange and Biological Transformations of Energy*, T. M. Carpenter lists the caloric expenditure of almost every activity imaginable, including sleeping and hiking. He suggests that a 225-pound man can burn in excess of 6,500 Calories[4] during an 18-mile day of hiking that includes three-thousand feet of elevation gain.

This estimate warrants a disclaimer. There are many methods and variables involved in the calculation of caloric expenditure. The best can only provide you with an estimate. Use them as a starting point for menu planning and depend on the data with cautious reliance at best. The most valuable data is that which you collect in the field as you gain experience. It would be foolish to pack food for a two-week trip based solely on an untested calculation of caloric expenditure.

Based on the estimate of 6,500 Calories required to hike an 18-mile day, and assuming an average caloric density of 100 Calories per ounce, our 225-pound hiker would require an astonishing four pounds of food per day—a ridiculous amount by any standards, even among long-distance hikers with elevated metabolisms from months on the trail.

To put this caloric expenditure in perspective, it takes about eleven Big Macs to get in the neighborhood of 6300 Calories, and that would weigh about 5 pounds. Can you imagine a five-day trip with fifty-five Big Macs? Not only would this much food fill up a good portion of a heavy expedition backpack, it could weigh more than the rest of your equipment—even if you weren't packing ultralight gear! Thus, the objective of this discussion is to consider trail foods that are more caloric dense than a Big Mac. With any luck our trail food will taste better as well.

Butter has roughly 200 Calories per ounce. Contrast this to a Big Mac, which offers about 80 Calories per ounce. We have heard of some ultralight hiking diets that approach 150 Calories per ounce of food. However, that diet would, of necessity, be very high in fats—oils and nuts—and not be terribly interesting with respect to flavor or variety. Such diets are great for emergency rations or short trips but do little to enhance the morale of a long-distance hiker.

A generally accepted target among the ultralight community is an average of 125 Calories per ounce of food. The

USDA Nutrient Data Laboratory website has a searchable database of just about every food imaginable. And it lists, among other things, the Calories per 100 grams of a given food. This database can offer invaluable insight into menu planning for hikers with an interest in optimizing the caloric density of their homemade meals.

Menu Planning

After reviewing a variety of foods you will notice that it isn't easy to make an interesting meal only from foods that have a caloric density in excess of 125 Calories per ounce. The secret here is to remember that we are talking about an *average* of 125 Calories per ounce in your diet. For example, an ounce of raisins contains only 82 Calories. But when that ounce of raisins is combined with an ounce of goldfish crackers (141 Calories) and an ounce of cashews (160 Calories), the resulting trail mix contains an average of 127 Calories per ounce.

Consider a typical dinner meal of 190 grams of dry instant rice (enough to make 2 cups cooked). It contains only 107 Calories per dry ounce, but when some tomato powder, dried vegetables, spices and an ounce of butter- or pepper-flavored oil is added, the resulting Spanish Rice mixture contains about 125 Calories per ounce of dry weight.

The key to making a tasty diet with a high caloric density is stacking the deck with foods having an ultra-high caloric density (over 140 Calories/ounce). Such foods include nuts, peanut butter, chocolate, butter, oils, fried or dry snack chips and crackers, pepperoni, and precooked bacon.

When planning meals, a good place to start is to estimate your daily caloric needs. Then divide those calories between packages for breakfast, lunch, and dinner. Such meal separation is more common among hikers that spend more time in camp and less time on the trail. Other long-distance hikers simply enjoy snacking all day on the trail, with no formal morning or evening meal cooking. These hikers wake up, pack, walk/eat, stop walking, setup camp, go to bed, and repeat the next day. A fair rule of thumb for ultralight hikers that spend most of the day on the trail is to split their caloric needs between in-camp or on-trail meals.

- Breakfast, 20%–25% of daily Calories
- Lunch, 50%–60% as a series of snacks eaten on the trail while hiking
- Dinner, 20%–25% as a late on-trail or in-camp meal

BREAKFAST AND LUNCH

Many long-distance walkers do not eat a formal breakfast. Others require a hot breakfast, commonly oatmeal or muesli, before hitting the trail. Still others enjoy a hot breakfast, but choose to hike for an hour or two while eating a granola bar before stopping on the trail to cook the morning meal. Which style you prefer will be dictated more by your own hiking style rather than by some particular need to optimize energy performance.

It is said that lunch is a hiker's most important meal. Hiking requires a significant amount of exertion. Maintaining frequent and adequate fuel intake throughout the day is vital to hiking longer distances without experiencing the all-too-common "caloric crash," which occurs after hiking for a few hours without eating. To combat this, many hikers recognize the need to eat small snacks at regular intervals throughout the day, rather than eat their "lunch" all at once at high noon.

The art of no-mess, no-fuss dinner meals

Few hikers, on the other hand, skip dinner. For many, dinner is the main meal, a ritual of relaxation with hot, well-flavored food that rewards a long day of hiking. Even those who walk regularly in grizzly bear country enjoy hot and aromatic evening meals. They just cook them while still on the trail or several hundred yards away from camp.

Dinner is not a meal that is often rushed, but many ultralight hikers still disdain the practice of preparing complex evening meals and cleaning up their sometimes equally complex messes. Having the opportunity to enjoy the fabulous taste of a well-cooked evening meal that requires only boiling water be poured into a disposable bag (no cleanup) is consistent with the long-distance hiker's primary end-of-day needs: unwind and savor their repast.

So-called one-pot meals (remember "camper's stew"?) can be prepared in single-serving plastic bags. They only require that you add boiling water and wait for several minutes while the food rehydrates and "cooks." Then the meal can be eaten straight from the bag. When through, simply zip the bag back up and pack it out.

Finding plastic bags that accept boiling water and are durable enough for meal storage can be tricky. The Glad Stand-and-Zip bags were a favorite among ultralight hikers for several years, until the quart-sized bags were taken off the market for lack of demand. Their primary advantage was the bellowed bottom that allowed the bag to stand up, even with boiling water inside. We've made and eaten soups in such bags. Other similarly sized options include the new 9"-x-7" OP-Sak zip-closure bags by Watchful Eye Designs. They have a bellows bottom, stand up nicely, hold enough food for a hungry hiker, and have the additional benefit of being odor proof. That's a useful feature when trying to minimize the odors of uncooked foods or uneaten residues in bear country.

The base ingredient for a dinner meal is typically grain or starch-based pasta, rice, or potato flakes. Often a prepackaged rice or noodle side dish (Lipton

Boil-in-a-Bag Dinner
in a 9" x 7" OP Sak:
Vegetable Chili.

noodle dinner or Thai noodle soup) is the foundation. To that, you can add whatever suits your taste: dehydrated vegetables, dehydrated or freeze-dried meats or soy chunks, textured vegetable protein (TVP), tofu crumbles, or spices.

Some hikers write the caloric content on the outside of the bag with a water-insoluble marker, such as a Sharpie felt pen, and the amount of water and oil (*ghee*) needed. Doing this saves some guesswork in food preparation on the trail but requires some experimentation when meal planning. A reasonable rule of thumb is that one cup of water is required for every cup of dry ingredients. Writing down the caloric content of the meal allows you to plan meals based on distance hiked in a given day and your caloric needs required for recovery and replenishment at the end of a day.

To prepare such a meal, simply

1. Boil water
2. Pour it in the bag
3. Zip the bag shut
4. Mix the contents well by kneading the bag with your hands
5. Let it stand until the food is fully rehydrated and cooked

In cold conditions, or for meals containing more robust grains and longer rehydration times, wrap the bag in some unused clothing to insulate it. Even foods containing slower-cooking grains such as dry elbow macaroni and larger soy chunks require only ten to fifteen minutes of standing time. Using quick-cook rice, potato flakes, ramen noodles, or angel hair pasta can get your meal cooking times down to five minutes.

The primary advantage of this cooking method is not always obvious, but the ultralight hiker is acutely aware of it. Passive cooking requires only that you boil water and not actually simmer on the stove. In addition to saving a food mess in your cookpot, this technique saves a significant quantity of fuel. In the end, weight is saved by bringing less fuel and less sophisticated (and often lighter) stoves that do not require the ability to simmer.

Sourcing ingredients

Your local supermarket can provide most of the foods for your hiking pantry. Specialty food stores—health, ethnic, and bulk outlets—can be invaluable sources of ingredients for backpackers. Here is a list of some things that typically go into easy-cook hiking meals:

- Prepackaged rice or noodle side dishes or bulk rice/pasta. Look for those that have real cooking times of less than eight minutes. Examples include Thai and ramen noodles, quick-cook rices, angel hair pasta, egg noodles, small shell pasta, couscous, and elbow macaroni.
- Instant potatoes. Typically sold as flakes that cook faster, or "chips", which have a more palatable texture.
- Instant soups and legume mixtures. These often include pre-spiced mixtures and are available in a seemingly infinite number of varieties. Mixed with a rice, pasta, or potato base, a soup or legume mixture such as refried bean flakes can result in a complete meal with minimal preparatory investment.
- Dehydrated or freeze-dried vegetables. Most vegetables can be easily dehydrated in several hours in a conventional oven. Freeze dried and dehydrated varieties are available from a number of specialty health-food markets and online sources.
- Spices. For simplicity, look for all-in-one spice mixtures, such as chicken or beef broth or jerk-style seasonings. For a little heat, try crushed red pepper, a tiny bottle of Tabasco, or Dave's Insanity Sauce—use sparingly and at your own risk!
- Powdered gravy or sauce mix. Typical options include conventional chicken or turkey gravies but also include sauces one might use in alfredo or marinara pasta dishes.

- Oil. A great way to boost calories, especially in the winter. For a particularly delightful indulgence, look for butter-flavor oils in the popcorn section of your supermarket.
- Clarified butter or ghee. You can make ghee at home. Ghee can also be purchased in stores that sell East Indian foods. As long as no moisture is introduced to the ghee, it does not require refrigeration and is a useful staple for long-distance, remote adventures.
- Dry cheeses. Try grated Parmesan. In colder weather, try fresh shredded Parmesan or Romano.
- Sour cream powder. This is available from specialty health-food and outdoor food outlets. It's an excellent sauce/soup thickener and adds significant flavor.
- Dehydrated precooked ground beef, chicken, or tuna. Some freeze-dried meats are available commercially, but they aren't cheap. For a vegetarian option, try dehydrating fresh Tofu crumbles.
- Textured vegetable protein (TVP) or soy flakes/chunks. These are available in most specialty health stores. TVP and soy flakes are an excellent means of boosting protein content in your foods. Soy chunks are an easy meat alternative that adds body to your meals.

Few hikers, with the exception of winter snowshoers and skiers in northern climates, cook hot lunches. The focus is on ingredients that are pocketable or otherwise extremely easy to prepare. Common lunch/snack foods include

- Dry or dense meats — beef jerky, pepperoni sticks, and liverwurst
- Spreads — peanut butter or honey
- Grains — crackers, pound cake, flat bread, melba toast, rye crisp bread, or pilot biscuits
- Fresh cheeses — dry cheddar or single-packaged string cheeses or sticks
- Dried fruit — unsulphured apples or mangoes, dehydrated bananas, raisins

- Nuts—almonds, pine nuts, sunflower seeds, cashews
- Candy—chocolate or licorice; primarily morale food
- Gorp—raisins, peanuts, M&Ms, chocolate chips, etc.
- Nutrition bars—Clif Bars, Power Bars, Luna Bars, Pemmican bars, fig bars

Little Debbies snack foods, and especially the caloric-rich Nutty Bars, have a cult following among ultralight hikers.

LIQUID FOODS

"Flavored hydration" comes in various forms, and can be an important part of a hiker's menu. In the summer, when water bottles get warm on the trail and water becomes less palatable in the sweltering heat of midday, diluted electrolyte drinks can provide flavor to keep a hiker drinking on a regular basis and avoid dehydration. Drink mixes from the grocery store, such as sweetened Kool-Aid or Crystal Light, are popular among hikers as are specialty sports drink mixes, such as Gu_2O, CytoMax, and PowerMax. To avoid excessive sweetness and make them more drinkable, dilute by at least 25 percent more than what the manufacturer recommends. In the case of drinks containing natural sugar as opposed to artificial sweeteners, such as Nutra-Sweet, flavored drinks can be a viable Calorie source as well. One of the advantages of balanced electrolyte drinks is that they increase the effectiveness of water absorption. You require less water to remain successfully hydrated.

Some hikers, particularly those with an endurance training background, find that a shake made with a dry protein-based powder consumed at the end of a long day can help the body recover more quickly from strenuous activity.

Hot drinks are usually a luxury item for a hiker. But again, they offer an excuse to consume added water and remain hydrated. On cold mornings and evenings, a hot drink can do wonders for morale if the weather is particularly foul. Hot tea, coffee, or warm Scotch whiskey are among more popular choices. There is quite a lot of debate about the utility of coffee and alcohol on the trail, most of it focusing on their contributing to dehydration. As with coffee and alcohol off the trail, moderation is in order. Few hikers with any objective sense will find that a morning cup of coffee or evening toddy will affect their performance. To each his own, of course. And those that do consume small amounts of either on the trail certainly seem to skip along a little happier in the morning and retire a little more relaxed in the evening!

Tea can be made fresh with a tea ball or from prepackaged bags. Small tea balls, about the size of a golf ball and made of stainless steel, weigh less than an ounce. Coffee drinkers have more options, from cowboy coffee—fresh grounds boiled for a few minutes in the cup and strained through the teeth, a common technique in the Rocky Mountain states—to single-use coffee servings in tea-bag style packets (e.g., Folgers and Senseo, most common on the East Coast), to lightweight French presses (made of Lexan or Titanium, 4–6 oz) and mini-espresso makers (6 oz or so)—the favorite of Starbucks addicts from Seattle to San Diego.

Beer and wine tend to be not so popular with ultralight hikers on the trail, since single servings weigh 3–12 ounces, not including the container. Harder drink, with a proof content in excess of 40, is more common, and can be repackaged successfully in soft-sided water bladders. A Platypus Lil' Nipper holds a pint of alcohol and weighs only 0.7 ounces. For an ultralight cocktail on the fly, mix a half ounce of 190-proof grain spirits (e.g., Everclear) and 3 ounces of vitamin fortified Crystal Light drink mix powder. Add a small snowball, and shake or stir as required by your own style. The high-proof spirits offer the strength of a full shot at half the weight. And they are consistent with the ultralight multi-use philosophy: They serve double duty as stove fuel for alcohol stove users and as an effective disinfectant for first-aid crises.

WHO NEEDS COOKED FOOD?

There are several different approaches to building a cook kit for food preparation. The lightest option is to take food that requires no cooking. This eliminates the need for a pot, eating utensil, stove, and fuel—a potential savings that can be measured in pounds of cooking gear left at home. Ironically, most hikers that buy into the no-cook philosophy carry a heavier food weight, so the savings may not be that significant. Many no-cook hikers do so to avoid the hassle of cooking rather than to save weight, as they tend to include more fresh fruit, vegetables, and breads in lieu of dehydrated and freeze dried items. In addition, the no-cook gig is best exercised while hiking solo. Sniffing the deliciously spicy simmering stew of a hiking companion on a cold and rainy evening while you are gnawing on a dry bagel is no easy situation to handle gracefully.

COOKING FIRES

A second option, and one that has been exercised by a great many long-distance hikers, is to cook over small open fires. Because open-fire cooking is prohibited in some wilderness areas, especially in alpine regions and during the late summer when fire restrictions are in place, open-fire cooking requires careful planning. In addition, the hiker relying exclusively on open fires must be confident and experienced in building fires reliably in wet conditions. Unfortunately, few hikers of today's generation are competent firebuilders. The advent of lightweight backpacking stoves, paranoia over violating leave-no-trace camping ethics, and the paradigm of staying on established and well-mapped trails near roads has all but sent the survival and sustenance skill of firebuilding into hiking history. Still, cooking over open fire is the lightest way to travel and circumvents the need to carry stove or fuel. As for no-trace firebuilding, that too is a learned and practiced skill. The accomplished firebuilder with an appreciation for the minimum-impact camping ethic can do so with no visible or meaningful environmental impact. Finally, the experienced firebuilder knows where to find dry tinder and maintain a cooking fire in the wettest conditions.

Less practiced firebuilders can save weight while enhancing their success by including a few solid fuel tablets (e.g., Esbit brand) or preconditioned firestarters (e.g., Spark-Lite Tinder-Quik) in their firestarting kit.

A comprehensive guide to firebuilding is beyond the scope of this book, but three core principles guide the building of low-impact cooking fires:

1. Use exceptionally dry tinder or material to start your fire. Dry tinder is found most often under thick brush, tree cover, or fallen logs. It should have a diameter or thickness less than that of a sewing needle. Dry tinder, when loosely balled up, should be lightable with a single match or brief lighter flame and burn with a baseball-sized or larger flame for at least sixty seconds.
2. Kindling for the fire should consist of dry twigs no larger than 1/8-inch in diameter.
3. Fuel wood should remain the size of a pencil, perhaps slightly larger. Fast-burning fuels are essential to a hot cooking fire. Fast-burning fuels also increase the chance that the fire will burn completely to ash, an essential principle for minimum impact.

In spite of the allure of building fires, which is mostly rooted in man's quest to tame the wilderness, backpacking stoves are still faster, cleaner, simpler, and remain the choice for food cooking by most backpackers.

Because fires are sensitive to wind, some hikers use "fire cans" or hobo stoves, which simply consist of quart-sized coffee cans with ventilation holes cut along the top and bottom rims to promote chimney venting. The cans serve as a pot support as well. The fire is built inside the can with fuel twigs fed through an opening in the side near the bottom. Most solo-sized hobo stoves weigh in the range of 4–8 ounces.

Another fire stove is the Sierra Zip Stove, a double-walled hobo stove with a battery operated fan that works exceptionally well with a variety of less-than-optimal fuel sources. Zip stoves come in standard and titanium models weighing 10–16 ounces. Its weight, which is quite a bit heavier than most ultralight backpacking stove kits, somewhat limits its utility to long-distance hikes that have little opportunity for resupply. However, it has gained a following among fire aficionados that don't hike more than a few miles from a trailhead, and it is more popular among canoeists, sea kayakers, and hunters, who tend to build campfires more often than modern backpackers.

Backpacking stoves

So, you've decided that cold water and trail mix on a snowy morning isn't your idea of a delicious breakfast? Perhaps your idea of a camping fire is a Presto log and a half gallon of gasoline. Or, maybe you've realized that your 1.5-pound white gas stove kit is anything but light.

After a shelter, sleeping system, and backpack, new cooking gear may offer the biggest weight savings for your dollar. There are three basic types of ultralight stoves, distinguished primarily by their fuel type:

- Solid fuel stoves that burn tablets (e.g., Esbit or hexamine). The folding-box style weigh in the neighborhood of 3 ounces, and collapsible "wing" stoves are around 1 ounce.
- Alcohol stoves that burn denatured alcohol. They range in weights from 0.2–3.0 ounces, and come in both homemade and commercial versions.
- Canister stoves that burn compressed gas (usually isobutane/propane mixtures). They weigh 2.5–4.0 ounces.

Solid fuel stoves burn the coldest flames and are the most sensitive to wind. A good windscreen is vital if the stove is to be used for serious cooking needs. Most single tablets weigh around 0.5 ounces and are suitable for boiling up to 12 ounces of cold water in cool weather using a good windscreen. Tablets don't require any special fuel storage container needs, but they are odiferous, subject to crushing, and some are sensitive to moisture. Aloksak zip-closure storage bags are tough, totally waterproof, and becoming popular for storing and transporting solid fuel tablets on the trail.

Generally, most hikers plan fuel needs based on a 0.5-ounce tablet per pint of water that needs heated/boiled.

Alcohol stoves burn hotter than solid fuel stoves, and thus, can be used for larger water volumes. Most homemade alcohol stoves are cheap to make and are popular among Boy Scouts, the budget conscious, and born tinkerers. They are typically made by forming one of dozens of bowl-like configurations using soda or food cans. Search online for instructions on making a variety of can-based alcohol stoves. The more popular ones include the Cat Stove, the Photon Stove, and the Pepsi Stove. Commercially available alcohol stoves are made by Brasslite, Trangia, Vargo, Hike-Lite, and Anti Gravity Gear.

The Brasslite Turbo F Alcohol Stove, at only 0.8 oz, has a fuel capacity of 1 oz, boils a pint of cold water in less than five minutes, and requires less than 0.75 oz of fuel to do so. As such, it complements a cook kit nicely, shown here with a 14-oz titanium mug and other minor accoutrements of an ultralight backcountry kitchen, including a titanium foil mug lid and windscreen. Total cook kit weight, including the fuel bottle (not shown, a Platypus Lil' Nipper), is less than 5 oz.

All alcohol stoves can be successfully fueled by denatured alcohol, ethanol, Heet, or Everclear. Thus, one of their main advantages is readily available fuel in trail towns across the world (hardware stores, liquor stores, auto repair shops, gas stations, etc.). However, these fuels have a lower caloric heat density than the long-chained hydrocarbon fuels of canister stoves. So they are less efficient. Because alcohol stoves are generally lighter than canister stoves, they end up comprising lighter cook kits on short trips or for hikers that don't cook often.

Alcohol fuel can be stored in virtually any lightweight plastic container. Most important is the quality of the seal. The lightest containers are soft-sided bladders used for water bottles, such as those made by Cascade Designs (Platypus) and Nalgene (Cantenes). Brasslite offers a nifty bottle in various sizes that allows you to precisely meter the fuel quantity into the stove. Old mouth rinse (e.g., Act brand) bottles work in this manner as well. Many hikers simply buy a bottle of gas-line antifreeze (e.g., Heet) and use the original bottle for on-trail fuel storage.

In general, alcohol stoves will consume 0.7–1.0 ounces of fuel per pint of water boiled under normal three-season field conditions.

Recent demand for ultralight high-performance gear has led to the development of lightweight canister stoves using non-refillable gas (e.g., isobutane/propane) canisters. Popular brands include MSR, Primus, Snow Peak, Brunton, Vaude, and Coleman.

The fuel canisters for these stoves are offered in 110-, 220-, or 450-gram net weights (fuel weight only), while the empty canisters themselves weigh 4.0, 5.0, and 8.0 ounces each, respectively. Consider that if you run the stove at its optimum efficiency — windless conditions and throttled at about 2/3 of maximum heat output — it will consume as little as 0.25 ounces of fuel to boil a pint of water. Thus, even with the added weight of an empty canister, such stove kits are easily the most efficient for hikes longer than a weekend or where significant cooking is involved.

Unlike solid fuel stoves and many alcohol stoves, canister stoves provide excellent simmering control for hikers that

The Brunton Crux Canister Stove, at only 3.0 oz, offers features of heavier stoves, including a high BTU output, wide burner head, and a wide pot support diameter for good pot stability.

like their pancakes golden and their stir fry tender.

Windscreens

Even in windless conditions, a windscreen makes any stove more efficient. It not only acts as a windscreen, but also as a heat exchanger that keeps a layer of hot air around the sides of the cookpot. The bottom line: Make a windscreen for your cook kit and use it. You'll save fuel. A caveat: Canister stove manufacturers won't endorse windscreen use because of the risk of overheating a canister and causing it to explode. Search BackpackingLight.com for "Homemade Canister Stove Windscreen" by Ryan Jordan. You'll find instructions and guidelines for circumventing this issue.

The cookpot

Boy Scout cook kits for solo hikers, as distributed by the BSA, are made of aluminum, weigh about 9 ounces, and include a small pot, fry pan/lid, and plastic cup. Solo aluminum or stainless cookpots from major manufacturers (e.g., MSR, Backpacker's Pantry) can weigh as much as 12 ounces for equivalent functionality. We think this is pretty heavy.

Thin-walled aluminum and titanium are the cookware materials of choice for ultralight backpackers. There are disadvantages for each. Thin-walled aluminum dents easily, and titanium is expensive. Both are very light. A liter-size pot will weigh in the range of 4.5–6.0 ounces with a lid. Popular brands include Antigravity Gear (aluminum), Snow Peak (aluminum and titanium), Evernew (titanium), and MSR (titanium).

Some ultralight hikers paint the outside of their pots with black stove paint, using the theoretically sound basis that less radiant heat is lost and greater fuel efficiency is realized. Unfortunately, radiant heat loss is very small while cooking. The dominant heat loss mechanism in windy conditions is convection, and in cold conditions it's conduction. Field tests performed by several parties indicate that black pots don't afford much additional efficiency outside the confines of an indoor testing laboratory.

More commonly, we are seeing solo ultralight hikers move to smaller and smaller cookpots. Popular choices now focus on titanium mug-shaped pots — taller than wider. These are less efficient shapes for fuel efficiency but provide more stowable containers in small backpacks. The Snow Peak Model 700 (0.7L capacity) and Model 600 (0.6L) mugs, and the MSR Titan Kettle (0.85L) are popular choices. The Model 700 includes a thin lid and weighs 4.2 ounces. The Model 600 requires that you make a homemade lid from aluminum foil or flashing material and weighs 2.8–3.2 ounces with such a lid. The MSR Titan Kettle weighs 4.5 ounces with lid. Bridging the gap between mugs and one-liter pots is the immensely popular Evernew Titanium Pot at 0.9L with foldaway handles and a lid made with thin-walled titanium to a 4.3 ounce specification. It's an excellent choice for the solo ultralighter.

Fringe ultralighters are using large beer cans (e.g., 24-oz capacity and wide bottoms) with the tops cut off as cookpots. With an aluminum-foil lid and a thin wire handle, the result is a fragile pot that weighs less than an ounce. Yes, it works. Quite well, in fact.

Drinking cup

Do you really need a mug? Why not share your coffee from the pot? If you want to drink coffee with your oatmeal, the cheapest and lightest option is the green plastic mug that came with the Boy Scout cooking kit, a 1-cup plastic mug that weighs about 1 ounce. A titanium mug weighs 1–2 ounces with a capacity ranging from 10–16 ounces. Fringe ultralighters use less conventional cups, including yogurt containers and aluminum cans with the top cut off and lip folded in.

Many ultralighters simply mix their drinks in their water bottles, or drink hot drinks straight from their cookpot.

Eating utensils

Since you're not hauling your grandmother's silver into the wilderness, you probably won't save much weight here. But you don't need a spoon, fork, and a knife for each person. A spoon is usually enough, and a *spork* is luxury. Some hardcore ultralighters use cheap plastic picnic flatware that won't last long in the hands of a clumsy person, but is very light. Lexan spoons and sporks weigh 0.3–0.4 ounces apiece, and their titanium equivalents weigh 0.5–0.6 ounces apiece. The advantage of a titanium spork is that it serves as a spoon and a fork, is durable, and may be bent to shape repeatedly for easy stowage in a small cooking pot or cup. It's the clear performance choice here.

Bear resistant food storage

While few hikers become sustenance for larger carnivores, their food is often attractive. Take measures to protect the food you bring from bears. "A fed bear is a dead bear." Without getting into the politics of bear conservation, simply remember: In addition to wildlife management headaches resulting from human-habituated bears, a bear that gets your food ends your trip.

The primary problem with conventional backcountry food storage systems is weight. Bear canisters made with plastic (e.g., BearVault BV200 or Garcia Backpacker's Cache) or carbon fiber (Wild Ideas Bearikade) generally weigh 2–3 pounds. As such, most lightweight backpackers only consider taking them in wilderness areas that require hard-sided food storage canisters. Reinforced fabric stow bags made of Spectra or Kevlar (e.g., Ursack) weigh in the range of 5–10 ounces. Even with the added weight of a hanging rope, the bag system weighs a lot less than hard-sided counterparts. We recommend products like the Ursack for climbers and alpine hikers who camp above the treeline and need to protect their food from aggressive rodents and the passing bear.

Traditional bear bagging

Most backpackers visiting wilderness areas and camping below the treeline where bears are either not particularly habituated or canisters are not required employ some sort of bear-bag hanging system. It usually consists of a stuff sack and a rope. The most common method theoretically described in many backpacking books may go something like this in real life:

1. Put your food in a stuff sack.
2. Tie one end of the rope to the stuff sack.
3. Tie the other end of the rope around a rock you find on the ground that happens to be the only rock within a three-mile radius, is perfectly spherical, and with a coefficient of friction akin to Body Glide.
4. Select your tree of choice, which Murphy's Law dictates is at least four miles from the nearest comfortable campsite and has only two limbs that can support your food weight. One is at eye level — high enough to keep mice and beetles at bay — and the other high enough that if you hung an orange stuff sack up there, it would serve as an emergency signaling device, visible by spy satellites.
5. Find another tree with a sturdy branch about 15 feet off the ground.
6. Throw the rock toward the branch. Line gets tangled around your ankle and rock makes it only six feet high before slamming back into the ground with a thud.
7. Retie your complex knot. Then lash the rope around the slippery, spherical rock, and try your throw again. This time the rock sails successfully over the branch, but the end of the rope has slipped off and remains in a crumpled pile at your feet. Your rock ends up in the next county, never to be seen again.
8. Find a new rock.
9. Repeat step 7 until the rope is successfully hung over the tree. This could take several hours. Have your headlamp ready, and maybe your cooking supplies, so you can take a dinner break.

10. Pull your food up over the branch, tie the other end of the rope to the tree trunk, and go to bed exhausted but proud of your significant accomplishment.
11. Wake up in the morning and learn that a black bear has chewed through the rope, dropped your bag, and had a feast, leaving you three days from the nearest road with a Clif Bar wrapper and some peanut butter on the inside of your now shredded stuff sack.
12. Make a commitment to learn the counterbalance method of hanging when you get home.

COUNTERBALANCE METHOD

And so, the counterbalance method solves these problems, right? Well, at least it solves the problem of having an animal untie (raccoons are quite good at this) or chew through the cord attached to the tree trunk.

The counterbalance method depends on throwing a rope over a tree branch (as in steps 1–9 above). Then, to one end of the rope you tie a stuff sack full of food and pull it up to the branch. Then tie another stuff sack as high as possible on the other end of the line. Using a long, stout stick/trekking pole/ partner on your shoulders, raise the bag and let gravity drop the other one until the two are equal in height. Admire your work: two precisely balanced food bags hanging equidistant from the limb. Then the counterbalance neophyte also comes to the realization that both bags are now hanging between the level of your waist and neck. Once again, you have performed a hang that will only protect your food from beetles.

A proper bear-bag hang requires that your food be suspended at least 10 feet above the ground. So the counterbalance method requires a branch that is as much as 25 feet up, depending on how tall you are, to what extent you can tie the second food bag to the rope while holding it over your head, the degree of stretch in your rope, the weight of your food, and the sturdiness of the branch.

Retrieving your food involves reversing the process by pushing one of the stuff sacks — again, with a stick/trekking pole/shoulder-standing partner — to the height of the branch so you can retrieve the other, lower bag. You remove it from the cord, release the cord, and let the first bag fall to the ground. Elegant in theory, but in practice it is not always that easy, especially toward the end of your trip when food bags are lighter and gravity can't overcome the friction of the rope on the tree branch.

An effective counterbalance system requires two stuff sacks, no less than 50 feet of rope, and a method for counterbalancing *and* retrieving your food. Of all the bear-bagging techniques, counterbalancing requires the most judicious branch selection, careful distribution of food between two sacks, and more complexity in retrieving and hanging your food. Bottom line: Counterbalancing is not exactly favored by the fast-and-light crowd seeking simplicity in their backcountry experience.

If you really want to add time, complexity, and weight to your bear-bag system, check out the Marrison bear-bag haul system online. It uses the mechanical advantage of a trucker's hitch with two carabiners or pulleys to make pulling your food up a little easier. In reality, unless you are hauling up the group supply of food for a NOLS course, pulling the bag up is the least of your worries as an ultralight backpacker out for a weekend or weeklong trip.

PCT METHOD

Affectionately known by the lightweight hiking underground as the "PCT method," presumably because it was first used by long-distance hikers on the Pacific Crest Trail, a bear-bag hanging method exists that is lighter, requires less rope, offers the benefits of counterbalancing, is easier to set up, and allows simple and quick hanging and retrieval of your food.

You can make your own system quite easily by assembling the following components:

- Food storage bag
- 40 feet of hanging rope
- Keychain carabiner
- Small stuff sack for a rock (rock sack)
- Pencil-sized twig about 4–6 inches long

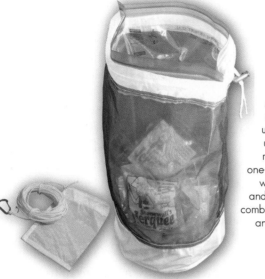

A system that combines the "bear" essentials for hanging a bear bag using **the PCT method**. Here, an ultralight 600 ci food storage sack made with noseeum mesh and sub-one-ounce silicone coated nylon (lined with an odor proof zip-closure bag) and a rock sack of the same material, combined with 40 feet of Spectra rope, and a micro wiregate carabiner can weigh as little as 3 oz.

Using 1.4-ounce, silicone-coated nylon waterproof stuff sacks for the rock sack and food storage bag, 1/8-inch parachute cord for the hanging rope, and a two-inch carabiner from Wal-Mart, you can achieve a system weight of about 5–6 ounces. The Bozeman Mountain Works Ursalite System for bear bag hanging using the PCT method weighs a scant 2 ounces and includes an odor-proof stuff sack liner for food storage.

The system is used as follows:

1. Tie one end of the rope to the drawcord of the rock sack.
2. Tie a loop (e.g., bowline) into the other end of the rope and clip the carabiner through it.
3. Insert a rock into the rock sack, cinch it closed, and throw it over a branch that is 15–20 feet high.
4. Remove the rock from the rock sack.
5. Attach the food sack drawcord to the carabiner.
6. Clip the rock sack end of the rope into the carabiner so that it can run freely.
7. Pull the rock sack end of the rope until the food bag is at the height of the branch.
8. Take the twig and reach as far as possible up the rock sack end of the rope (about 6 feet for the average man) and tie a clove hitch around the twig.

9. Let the rock sack end of the rope go. The twig will catch on the carabiner and keep the food sack at least 10 feet above the ground.

This system leaves extra rope hanging freely below the food bag. Unlike conventional hanging systems where the spare end of the rope is tied to a tree trunk, this eliminates the possibility of an animal untying or chewing the rope in an effort to bring the food bag down.

In addition, the PCT method requires less skill. Thus, it is faster to deploy than the counterbalance method. Finally, it requires a system of equipment that is lighter than the counterbalance method because it uses less rope and only one food sack.

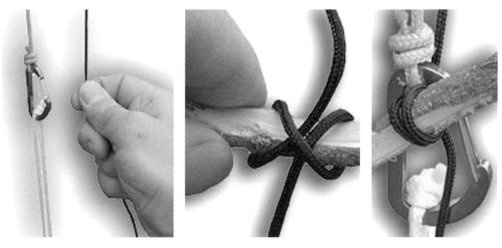

This three-panel image set shows the process of hanging a food bag using the PCT method: **(LEFT)** The rope is thrown over a tree limb at least 15 feet high (with the aid of the rock sack, which in this panel, is tied to the bottom of the black cord). The food sack drawstring is then clipped into the carabiner, and the food raised by pulling on the rock sack end of the cord until the carabiner reaches the top of the limb. **(CENTER)** The hiker reaches as high up the rock sack end of the rope and ties a two-loop clove hitch and inserts a pencil-sized twig into the loops, then tightens the knot. **(RIGHT)** The rock sack end of the rope (now containing a twig tied in as high up as possible) is then slackened, allowing the twig to come to rest against the carabiner, stopping the sack high enough above the ground for a good bear hang (at least 10 feet). To retrieve your food, simply pull the rock sack end of the cord and reverse the process.

Conclusion

As you have seen, the ultralight philosophy focuses on simplicity, efficiency, and minimum weight. These can be accomplished even with a backcountry menu. Unless you are a long-distance hiker who will be eating on the trail for many weeks in a row, the most important nutritional goal is to maximize the caloric density. The components and weight of your cook kit will ultimately depend on your cooking style and menu design. With some experimentation, you will likely find a menu that suits your taste and allows some rest at the end of a day's hike. Of course, none of this matters if the bears make a snack out of your pack.

Chapter 11: **Hygiene**

By George Cole and Ryan Jordan

Your Skin

Do you remember the obsessive backpacker, the one who filters his drinking water three times? It's amazing that after he finishes repacking his chemistry set and carefully hanging his clinically sterile Platy on a limb, he dives into the water he just spent twenty minutes purifying.

"Gotta stay clean," he says. "Lots of bacteria in dirt."

Uh, . . . yeah. That's true. But, dude, don't you realize that you're exposing your eyes and the mucous membranes of your nose, mouth, and at least two other orifices to whatever bacteria is in that water? Poor guy. We suspect he also believes that the food you steal off someone else's plate won't make you fat.

It's not that his underlying philosophy on backcountry hygiene is flawed. There are bacteria, protozoa, and viruses in dirt that can cause us serious problems. However, skin is an excellent barrier against the incursion of potentially harmful microbes. Problems arise when pathogenic microorganisms are allowed to enter the body through natural or accidental openings in the skin. Swimming in contaminated water is one way to do that. Another is to eat with or rub our eyes with dirty hands. A third is to allow contaminated water or soil to get into a wound.

If somehow we open the door to enough of the little buggers, we can be in for a bad time. One of the authors of this book is immune-compromised due to a motorcycle accident. On two occasions he has ignored the itching of athlete's foot to the point of allowing lesions to develop between his toes. The results were Staphylococcal infections that quickly raged through his bloodstream. Lucky for him, medical help was close by or he probably would have died.

Most of us have healthy immune systems and more than half a brain. So why take a chance with something as dangerous as a Staph infection, especially when in the backcountry medical help can be days away? Even so, we all have to eat and drink. Sooner or later we're all going to get a cut, scrape or blister. Fortunately, staying clean doesn't carry much of a packbag weight penalty. Even a full, 16-ounce bottle of Dr. Bronner's Peppermint Soap weighs only a pound or so. But there are lighter ways of keeping our skin clean enough to avoid infections.

We say "clean enough" because we don't believe that it's necessary to get every inch of skin antiseptically clean. Unbroken skin provides a lot of protection in itself. If you're going to backpack regularly, you need to get used to sweat and some selectively placed grime. But at a minimum, you should disinfect your hands after filtering water or toileting and before eating or snacking. It also does no harm to keep the skin around your eyes, nose, and mouth free from dirt. Because your private parts are covered (except on naked hiking days), they usually stay dirt-free.

CLEANING

For critical cleaning and disinfecting chores we use one or a combination of the following tools:

- Liquid antibacterial soap
- Piece of cloth
- Moist towelettes
- Alcohol gel

Major grime can be removed from less critical portions of your body with a piece of damp towel. Generally, untreated water is used for this, although make sure you have no open wounds, sterilize your hands afterward, and use soap the next time you use the same cloth on your face or rear end. Also, you can use a still-moist towelette after cleansing critical parts with it. These little things can remove amazing amounts of grime.

ANTIBACTERIAL SOAP

Dr. Bronner is probably the most famous maker of liquid antibacterial soap for campers. Dr. Bronner's soaps are well-suited for lightweight backpacking because they are packaged in an extremely concentrated form, requiring you to carry less to make the same amount of suds. Any brand of drug or food store antibacterial soap will do. And since ultralight backpackers use only the smallest amount of it at each cleansing, its environmental impact should be minimal. However, we buy only an unscented variety and hang it up with our food, lest the sensitive noses of bears find it appealing.

Liquid antibacterial soap can be repackaged in lightweight plastic containers as small as a few drams. Camping and backpacking stores usually carry 0.5-ounce containers in packages that also contain other sizes of containers. BackpackingLight.com has a plethora of micro-sized bottles and containers that hold as little as 0.1 fluid ounce of product (the MicroDrop Bottle), which is ideally sized for a week's worth of Dr. Bronner's soap.

Likewise, any piece of cloth can serve as a washcloth. Some ultralight backpackers use a bandana. Others use a small piece of the non-woven, hydrophobic fabric that is advertised to be "90 percent dry" when wrung out. This fabric can be found in camping specialty stores but is also sold by auto supply stores for a good bit less money. We make it do triple-duty by also using it to clean up tent spills and sponging rainwater off a tarp or tent fly. Since rainwater is generally pretty clean, we wash with it when we can.

MOIST TOWELETTES

Most of us first encountered Handi Wipes on summer vacations with our parents. This brand of moist towelette is still around, along with a whole slew of others. Most brands can now be purchased in individual foil packages. Virtually all brands use an antibacterial cleaning solution, and some are advertised to be gentle enough for private parts. Some are even unscented.

The benefit of these towelettes is that you can take exactly the number you need for any length trip. Although, for long trips the weight of the foil packages may offset any advantage they have over liquid soap. They vary in size and cost, so look around until you find ones you like. If you're going into bear country, always buy unscented and hang them at night in your food bag.

ALCOHOL GEL

It seems that even the camping specialty stores are selling alcohol gel as a disinfectant for hands. It's usually inexpensive, can be found in small squeeze containers, and can also be used as an emergency fire starter, so it qualifies as a multifunctional ultralight item.

Feet

Feet are a special case. When dry and free of openings, the skin on our feet is about as good as any other skin at keeping microorganisms at bay. However, moist skin on a foot swollen from a day of backpacking can quickly lose its integrity. A blister can form and rupture without much warning, and a bleeding blister can provide opportunistic microbes with access to our insides.

Also, fungi love the warm, moist environment inside a shoe or boot, especially when there are delicious skin cells to snack on. A fungal infection can quickly penetrate moist skin and result in a deep lesion. Therefore, as a prophylactic measure, keep your feet as clean as your face and hands.

As an additional step, at least one of the authors applies liquid antiperspirant to his feet every morning for three days prior to, and each morning of, a hike. This helps to keep his feet dry and reduces the tendency of his feet to sweat during the hike. The antibacterial and antifungal properties of the antiperspirant help suppress microbes. While nothing can completely stop feet from getting swampy, they're less swampy and therefore less susceptible to blisters and fungal infections. He says his feet thank him. We do, too, when we have to sleep next to him in a crowded shelter.

Liquid antiperspirants can be rebottled in the same tiny containers as liquid soaps. Experiment with different brands of antiperspirant until you find a brand that doesn't irritate your skin. And use only an unscented variety.

Teeth

Most of us first heard about ultralight backpacking when we were told about that crazy thru-hiker who drilled holes in his toothbrush. We're certainly not that obsessive. Just buy a child's brush and cut the handle short. Or pick up a fingertip toothbrush, common among prisoners and pets, from GossamerGear.com. A few drops of Dr. Bronner's soap (peppermint) makes for an invogorating and effective tooth-cleansing experience as well, and is Ryan's toothpaste du normale.

At any rate, we do brush our teeth, if for no other reason than to maintain regular rituals that are important to staying safe and sane in the backcountry. Clean teeth make us feel good. And if we remember to brush our teeth, we also remember to wash our faces and rub antiperspirant into our feet. And while anointing our feet, we can check them for any areas that might be developing blisters or lesions.

We don't use commercial toothpaste for backpacking. Good old baking soda and salt is perfect. Unlike commercial products, this concoction doesn't require rinsing and spitting, is unscented, and a 0.5-ounce vial can contain enough to last two weeks. Add a few grains of rice to absorb moisture. If you can't stand the thought of swallowing all that yucky baking soda and salt, try to spray the solution around when you spit it out. That way no unfortunate slug or snail that happens to be in the way will get a full dose. (We'd like to tell you that we carefully check for slugs or snails before we spit, but most of the time we don't.)

Laundry

Sooner or later, we all have to do something about the shirt that announces our presence ten minutes before we arrive at a shelter. Or the shorts that have accumulated so much salt that deer nibble on them when hung on a limb to air out. Generally, soaking and wringing a garment in plain water is sufficient. But if you've been wallowing in smelly organic mud, then some soap may be in order.

No matter how we do our laundry, we are compelled to minimize the effect it has on the environment. In fact, it's not just laundry; it's the effort to keep us and the environment clean. The good news is that it's not difficult to be a low-impact backpacker. You just have to remember to be one.

Low-Impact Practices

Let's start with clothing. Almost all hikers carry a pot of some sort. Those who don't, usually carry a spare Ziploc bag or two. Put the offending garment in the pot or Ziploc, add clear but untreated clean water, and massage the garment until the water gets cloudy. Then empty the container under a tree, bush, or shrub that's well away from the water source. If needed, do it again, and maybe once more.

If soap has been added to the water, the doused water is actually feeding the plants. If there are no plants, then it's feeding the micro flora. If the container is emptied into snow, the wash water will be well diluted by the time the snow melts and joins a water source.

The washcloth used to cleanse critical parts doesn't need rinsing every time a hiker freshens up. Hanging it to dry is sufficient. However, when it does need rinsing, avoid rinsing it out in a water source. At that point, treat it just like a dirty garment. In fact, if there's soap in it, wash it with a dirty garment so both come out clean.

Low-impact hikers carry their trash out of woods. If you use moist towelettes, take it out with the rest of the trash. Foil does not burn. However, the towelette itself, after it's been allowed to dry, makes pretty decent tinder. If there's no campfire, then add it to the trash as well.

La Toilet

Controlling the impact of bodily wastes takes a bit more care. First of all, most hikers use privies where they're available. And even then a carefully regimented strategy is employed. Have biodegradable toilet paper in hand when you open the door. Then yell at the top of your lungs to drive the 15-pound privy spiders back into their webs. Immediately on hearing the telltale patter of little pincers, drop your trousers while turning around and backing over the hole. In a continuation of the same movement, do your business, wipe once, and leap half-naked out the door.

Frankly, we're perfectly happy when we don't find a privy, because it makes us feel less guilty when we use a cat hole. To be honest, we may not even use a cat hole when the waste is liquid. Cat hole or no hole, waste placement is critical. The old rule of thumb is to locate a drop site at least 300 feet from any water source. For that reason, try not to toilet within five minutes of arriving at or leaving a known source. You won't always know where all the sources are and you may not always get 300 feet away, but do the best you can. Also, try to get at least 100 feet off trail. If the waste is just liquid, and if you're appropriately equipped, try to spray it around a bit. If you're not equipped for directed spraying, or if the waste is solid or semi-liquid, scoop out a hole for it.

Cat-hole construction is an art. You may not claim to be an artist (we don't, either), but the crucial design parameter is to get the hole deep enough to cover the contents with three inches of soil but not so deep as to go below the biologically active top layer of soil. Six inches is too deep. However, here's another good rule of thumb: If the soil is too hard to dig out with your heel, cross your legs until you find a softer spot. If you're not adept at completing the hole with your heel, or you wear sandals, use a tent stake to finish the digging.

After making your drop, stir the contents of the hole with a stick, mixing solid, liquid, paper, and oxygen together with soil. This speeds up the process of decomposition quite a bit. When closing the hole with soil, leave the stick in it with the business end down. That way, the next time you're looking for the spot, you might find a little upright memento of your previous visit. It's actually kind of homey.

"Hold, on," you say,. "What do you do when you're above the treeline and there's no soil?"

When there's no soil, or when there's only sand (solid waste doesn't break down in sand), use what Buck Tilton of the Wilderness Medicine Institute calls the "smear technique." Think of spreading peanut butter as thinly as possible on an exposed surface, then leaving it to desiccate and sterilize in the sun and open air. As unappealing as Buck's smear technique sounds, it really is the least potentially harmful when in the desert or on a rocky surface.

However, be prepared. Local regulations may require you to pack your solid wastes out. If so, use plastic baggies within plastic baggies within trash bags. We've heard that packaging coffee grounds with the waste masks its odor somewhat. Nonetheless, you'll know when you're in a pack-it-out area because most folks will be carrying curiously lumpy trash bags on the outside of their packs.

Insect Protection

There are two major schools of thought on this one. Some despise putting chemicals on their skin, and would rather defend themselves with clothing. Others like to get as naked as possible and have no problem with lathering themselves with bug goo. Essentially, it's up to you. You can either burn up under layers of recycled soda bottles or you can run the risk of glowing in the dark.

Some hike in running shorts, shirt, and shoes in spring, summer, and fall. They swear by a base layer of waterproof gel sunscreen followed by a layer of time-release DEET. Waterproof sunscreens bond with the upper layers of skin. Not only do they afford protection from the sun, they help prevent the absorption of DEET. Further, microencapsulated time-release DEET products do not penetrate the skin as readily as other DEET formulations. At any rate, DEET is not anywhere near as bad as some people would have you believe.

"Oh, yeah?" you say. "My sister's college roommate's great aunt's butt fell off after her neighbor opened a bottle of DEET in the next yard."

Um, well, she must not have reported it. In the four decades that DEET has been available to the public, there have been only forty documented cases of DEET toxicity in adults. And, while there's reason to suspect that some of these folks must have ingested the stuff in order to get so much of it into their systems, none of them suffered serious after effects—including butt separation. Further, no other synthetic or natural repellant has been found to deter biting insects for as long or as effectively as DEET . Of course, give every chemical the backyard test for sensitivity before going into the backcountry with it. It's hard to carry a pack without a butt.

The current Department of Defense Insect Repellant System calls for DEET to be used in conjunction with Permethrin, a synthetic copy of a natural insecticide that is applied to clothing. A 35 percent concentration of time-release DEET, used in conjunction with Permetrhin-soaked uniforms, has been found to provide 99.9-percent protection from Alaskan mosquitoes over an eight-hour period. If you've ever encountered a cloud of Alaskan mosquitoes, you'll recognize what an amazing statistic this is.

Permethrin quickly loses its toxicity when it comes in contact with the skin, but it's deadly to biting insects, including ticks, for at least two weeks after being applied to clothing.

If you choose clothing over chemicals, you'll have to experiment until you find garments that will prevent the little fangs and probosci from getting through to your skin. However, you'll still have to deal with the exposed skin on your hands and faces. There are mesh gloves and head nets available for this purpose, but perhaps the ultimate bug armor is full-body mesh clothing. We've found this material to be warmer than you might think, but for cooler climes and bugs that aren't deterred by DEET (e.g., Northeastern blackflies), it can be a real trip-saver.

Whatever method of insect protection you choose, give this issue plenty of thought before you head into the woods. Biting insects can ruin the enjoyment of a beautiful view, and some insects can transmit serious diseases. For example, ticks are known carriers of Lyme disease and Rocky Mounted Spotted Fever. So, for heaven's sake, use some type of bug protection. If you backpack in tick country, make a habit of checking your skin every night, and carry a tick extractor tool in your first-aid kit. Finally, if you're camping in the desert, check your shoes or boots before you put them on in the morning. We're pretty sure that scorpions and big, hairy land spiders have discovered that DEET just adds a little flavor to toes.

Conclusion

So what it all comes down to is taking care of yourself and following the hygiene lessons you learned as a kid. Even in the pristine backcountry where few humans have traveled there are bacteria, protozoa, and viruses that can cause serious problems. At the minimum, you should disinfect your hands after filtering water or toileting and before eating or snacking. And don't rub your eyes with dirty hands. To stay with the ultralight and low-impact principles, carry items that will do double duty on the trail. And carry your trash out of the woods. You'll not only be happier and cleaner, you'll leave little trace behind for the next guy.

Part 4:

First Aid and Emergency Preparedness

Chapter 12: **Risk Management**

By George Cole

We often see novice backpackers carrying first-aid kits
and emergency medical supplies that would make a
search and rescue team proud. When asked, most of these
folks allude to the comfort they derive from knowing that
they are prepared for any medical crisis, even though they
can't identify half of the items in their kit, have never treated
anything worse than a headache, and have no emergency
medical training.

For all intents and purposes, these folks would be better off trading their first-aid kits for a vial of Valium. Few
of us return from a backpacking trip without a bug bite or
a patch of sunburn. From time to time, we've all suffered
a bruise, scrape, sore muscle, or blister. However, most of
us have never experienced a serious ailment while in the
backcountry. Maybe on one or two occasions we've limped
slowly back to a trailhead while trying to keep the weight
off a sprained ankle. But even a sprained ankle is relatively
rare, and more serious injuries and illnesses are rarer still. A
1992 study found that soft-tissue injuries—such as sprains,
strains, abrasions, contusions, and lacerations—account
for 80 percent of reported wilderness injuries ("Wilderness

Injuries and Illnesses" Ann Emerg Med. 1992; 21:853–861). Dislocations or fractures, most of which occur in the lower limbs, may account for less than 5 percent of those injuries (research by Zell and Goodman), and injuries to backpackers resulting from encounters with wild animals are so rare as to be almost nonexistent (research by Freer and colleagues). Most minor injuries are never reported. However, they are reported three times more often than illnesses, and 60 percent of reported illnesses are non-specific or diarrheal in nature (Gentile et al; Zell and Goodman).

It should be said that backpackers without training in wilderness medicine should not attempt to diagnose and treat illness or injury in the backcountry, no matter how sophisticated their supplies. Our standard is this: If you're not competent to practice medicine on the sidewalk, don't do it on the trail. And if you don't know how to use first-aid or medical supplies and equipment, don't take them with you.

This does not mean that backpackers should go into the woods blissfully unconcerned and unequipped. All back-packers should know how to get a person breathing, get a heart beating, stop serious bleeding, and stabilize a broken bone, especially since instruction on doing so is readily available from the Red Cross and wilderness first-aid educators. Prevention and preparation are the keys to staying healthy in the backcountry. You can anticipate and attempt to prevent the things that are most likely to happen, and carry supplies to deal with those things if they do happen. For less likely but potentially more serious events, prevention is the only way to go. However, if prevention fails and a serious event occurs, be prepared to keep someone alive until trained professionals can deal with the consequences of the event. This means you should know when and how to get an injured or sick person out of the backcountry and into the care of the pros.

Following these principles, there is no need to carry more than a pound of first-aid and emergency medical supplies, including whatever device seems to be the most appropriate for getting professional help in the aftermath of a serious event. However, carry at least 50 pounds of knowledge about where you're going, what you're likely to encounter, and how you intend to deal with what you encounter.

Pre-Trip Risk Analysis

Start accumulating the knowledge you want to take into the backcountry with a pre-trip risk analysis. For several weeks before a trip (or months, if the trip is going to be long or in a foreign country), gather and record information on the following characteristics.

ANTICIPATED MILEAGE AND PACE (MAPS, MAPPING SOFTWARE, AND TRAIL GUIDES)

- Total miles walked
- Miles walked per day
- Hours walked per day
- Miles walked per hour
- Terrain and elevation (maps, mapping software, and trail guides)
- Starting elevation each day
- Ending elevation each day
- Total elevation gain each day
- Surface and conditions encountered each day (maps, mapping software, trail guides, local and national authorities, authority informational websites, local trail maintenance clubs and websites, and Internet chat groups)
- Type of surface
- Approximate most severe slope of surface
- Width and boundaries of surface
- Exposure of surface
- Surface covering, coating, or condition
- Location and type of water barriers, and how water barriers must be crossed
- Season, region, and anticipated weather (maps, mapping software, trail guides, local and national

authorities, authority informational websites, local trail maintenance clubs and websites, and Internet chat groups)

- Anticipated temperature averages and extremes — day and night
- Recent historical temperature averages and extremes — day and night
- Anticipated precipitation amounts and type
- Recent historical precipitation amounts and type
- Anticipated wind speed averages and extremes, with associated wind chill estimations — day and night
- Recent historical wind speed averages and extremes, with associated wind chill estimations — day and night
- Insects, wildlife, and poisonous plants
- Human encounter trouble spots, such as trailhead parking lots or campsites
- Location and condition of drinking water sources
- Location and method of contacting evacuation assistance
- Location and method of contacting medical assistance
- Assessment of personal health and pre-trip fitness
- Assessment of personal backpacking experience/knowledge for this type of trip
- Assessment of backpacking experience/knowledge of companions

Risk-specific Prevention Strategy

Once you've accumulated the above information, it will be easier to assess the risk of the hike.

Essentially, take only what you're likely to need given the conditions you expect to encounter. If you perceive there to be a reasonable risk of any of the following events, initiate the following preventive strategies:

PRESSURE BLISTERS

- Use new shoes or boots under load for at least a month before the trip. If shoes or boots are leather, treat with leather softener
- Sweat reduction/skin toughening
- Pre-treat feet with alcohol for at least a week before the trip. This helps to prevent blisters by toughening the skin while minimizing overhydration of the pores and softening of the skin
- Pre-treat feet with a liquid antiperspirant for three days before the trip, and then pack and use the anti-perspirant daily.
- Apply coating of Tuff-skin to soles of feet immediately before trip
- Tape "hot spots" during the trip
- Pack and use alcohol wipes for cleansing and degreasing
- Pack and use duct tape or waterproof tape on hot spots. A foot or two wound around a hiking pole or pill bottle should be sufficient for this purpose. Inspect feet every couple of hours while walking

SUNBURN AND "EYEBURN"

- Pack and use sufficient clothing for adequate skin coverage, or pack and use a sufficient amount of a sunscreen preparation rebottled into a small container
- Pack and use billed headwear and sunglasses, especially at high altitudes

DEHYDRATION

- Treat and drink 8 to 16 ounces of water per hour during trip

HYPOTHERMIA

- Pack and use sufficient, appropriate clothing.
- If your clothing is insufficient, use your shelter and sleeping bag for unanticipated conditions

HYPERTHERMIA

- During trip, wear a hat when in direct sunlight
- Treat and drink 16 to 24 ounces of water per hour during trip
- When temperatures exceed 90 degrees, find shade and rest at least once per hour during trip

INSECT BITES

- Apply DEET every day of trip and pre-treat clothing with Permethrin
- Mesh clothing
- Self-inspection
- After consulting with a physician, pack and use a non-sedating oral antihistamine daily. For example, take one Allegra tablet or its equivalent each morning of the trip.

CHRONIC / UNIQUE AILMENTS, INCLUDING ALLERGIES AND IMMUNE-DEFICIENCIES

- Pack and use appropriate medications. Consult physician

ALLERGIC REACTIONS TO POISONOUS PLANTS

- Learn to identify the poisonous plants that you will encounter on the trip. Avoid them
- Pack and use a plant-oil-blocking preparation, such as Ivy Block
- Pack and use appropriate clothing (covering the lower legs). Learn how to dress and undress without contaminating your skin
- If skin comes in contact with poisonous plants, immediately cleanse affected areas with alcohol wipes
- After consulting with physician, pack and use a non-sedating oral antihistamine daily. For example, take one Allegra tablet or its equivalent each morning of the trip

ILLNESSES

- Before the trip, make sure you are current on all immunizations, especially Tetanus toxoid.
- During the trip, practice proper hygiene and pack sufficient hygiene supplies.
- During the trip, treat drinking water.

INJURIES DUE TO EXCESSIVE PACK LOAD

- For heaven's sake, lighten up

INJURIES DUE TO SLIPS AND FALLS

- Before the trip, consult with your physician and then condition yourself for backpacking. If you can't walk daily in rugged terrain with a loaded pack, purchase a weight vest and climb the stairs at your local high school football stadium
- Before the trip, reduce your pack weight and its attendant fatiguing effects
- During the trip, pay attention to where you're walking and where you place your feet. Ensure that you have adequate traction on slippery surfaces. Wear footwear with lugged, wet-traction rubber soles that you've tested before the trip
- If you're going to encounter especially slippery surfaces, such as wet, mossy, or submerged rocks or logs, etc., pack and use a set of traction devices
- Pack and use crampons where surfaces are icy
- Use hiking poles for balance and support

INJURIES FROM TWO- AND FOUR-LEGGED WILDLIFE

- Avoid and escape — when appropriate. For example, don't run from wild animals
- Pack and use pepper spray
- Fend off wildlife with hiking poles
- Pack and use legal weapons

Specific First-aid Strategy / Kit

Once you have a prevention strategy, pack a first-aid kit with the supplies you'll need to deal with the minor events you are not able to prevent. While stocking the kit, think about how and when you'll use each item and where it needs to be in your pack for best access during stress or inclement conditions.

Specific Evacuation Strategy

There's always a little distress when you hear a self-proclaimed expert backpacker say something like, "It's sacrilegious to take cell phones into the backcountry. If you need a cell phone, you shouldn't be out there. Why, back in '72, I stitched myself up with a fishhook, splinted both legs with saplings I gnawed off at the root, and dragged myself 50 miles back to a trailhead, in the dark, leading a troop of lost Girl Scouts on the way."

Having gone to the aid of such an "expert" after he camped under a dead limb and got a dent in his brain, we can report that he didn't seem terribly distressed when we called for help on our weenie 4-ounce Motorola. We can also report that he got real quiet after the Emergency Medical Tech (EMT) told him that when people do get seriously hurt in the backcountry, mortality rates vary due to the time it takes to get professional help.

Nothing replaces knowledge, but even experts can have a really bad day. When they do, you should be prepared to evacuate them. An evacuation strategy will include the following elements:

PRIOR TO THE TRIP

- Prepare and distribute a detailed trip plan. Include estimated arrival times at landmarks
- Pack notes indicating the location and two methods of contacting evacuation assistance
- Pack notes indicting the location and two methods of contacting emergency medical assistance

- Pack a working communication device that is appropriate for the locale of the trip
  - Cell phone, or
  - Satellite phone, or
  - UHF/VHF radio, and
  - Signal mirror, or
  - Flares and/or fire starters, or
  - Notes on the construction of passive signals

You've Got to Be Kidding Me!

While all this planning and preparation hardly seems worth the effort, we can promise you that going through the process will increase your sense of safety, reduce your anxiety, and lighten your pack. More importantly, we're convinced that it will reduce the probability that something catastrophic will happen during your trip. However, if something does happen, you'll be ready for it. Further, after you go through the process several times, it will become second nature. You'll find yourself quickly developing into a knowledgeable and skilled ultralight risk manager.

Chapter 13: **First Aid**

By Dave Schultz and Ryan Jordan

For most people, first aid means the first, basic care given to a victim of an accident or sickness. These basic medical skills are vitally important for all people to know. They can prevent permanent damage and death from occurring during the short period of time it takes for professional medical help to be obtained.

Hikers, however, find themselves in a unique situation. The period of time that can pass between injury and professional help can be several hours or even days. Also, hikers do not always have a way to signal for help and may have to travel for many hours to reach medical assistance. For hikers, appropriate medical skills go well beyond first aid and into the area of wilderness medicine.

Just as backpackers adapt the processes of eating, sleeping, staying warm, and traveling, wilderness medicine is really just the adaptation of standard medical practices. The lightweight hiker makes further adaptations to wilderness medicine, and in doing so substitutes knowledge, ingenuity, and preparation for many ounces or pounds of gear.

An adequate treatment of wilderness medicine for the layman is well beyond the scope of this chapter and could easily fill several hundred pages. What we intend to accomplish in this space is

- Basic theory and techniques to handle a few common situations
- How to choose specialized gear to handle medical situations while on the trail
- Emphasize the importance of researching additional information on wilderness medicine

There are many excellent volumes on wilderness medicine. Classes on first aid are available in most areas.

Common Situations

To begin, we will discuss how to handle a few of the more common trail situations. Before we begin, however, there are a few things you should consider. For example, your anxiety over a situation can easily lead to bad decisions. Always tend to the safety of the group first, and to the injured second. When it comes to the injured, deal with the most life-threatening situation first. The frostbite on the victim's hands might look bad, but the hypothermia will kill him. And above all, do nothing that will make the situation worse. Risky rescues tend to create more victims, and poor aid can be worse than no aid at all.

If you do nothing else, learn basic CPR and first aid. Classes and books on this material abound. The American Red Cross, community colleges, local libraries, and local bookstores are all good sources of information on CPR and basic first aid.

CUTS AND ABRASIONS

Bleeding

Most bleeding can be stopped by applying direct pressure to the wound. Cover the wound with the cleanest material immediately available and apply firm direct pressure. Hold the pressure without release for at least a full 10 minutes, and up to 30 minutes if necessary.

Cleansing

The most important part of managing a wound is getting it clean and keeping it that way. Aggressively cleaning out a wound through irrigation and vigorous scrubbing removes as many harmful bacteria as possible. This cleaning also removes much of the damaged tissue that bacteria feed on.

For many cuts, the best way to clean the wound is through irrigation. Simply put, irrigating a wound involves spraying a stream of disinfected water (0.5 ounces of 10-percent Povidone iodine mixed with 16 ounces of clean water works better than plain water) into the wound with enough force to flush out germs and debris and without harming healthy tissue. One lightweight method uses a 20-cc syringe with a catheter tip. These weigh 0.25 ounces and can be purchased in the medical supply section of mountaineering stores. If you do not have a syringe, you can use a clean plastic bag with a pinhole in it. Place the solution in the bag and squeeze the bag to force a jet of solution into the wound. After the irrigation, if any debris is still present, either pick it out with a sterile tweezers or scrub it out as described below.

If the injury is an abrasion, where the outer layers of skin are scraped off, dirt and debris are likely to be embedded in the wound. Irrigation will probably be insufficient to clean it. In this case, the wound must be scrubbed clean. This process is very painful and messy. The scrubbing process should be done vigorously and quickly, as the injured person will not stand for it for very long.

1. Aggressively irrigate the area.
2. To help deaden the pain, it may help to apply pads to the area soaked with a solution of 2.5-percent lidocaine (e.g., Bactine) 10–15 minutes prior to the scrubbing. To prevent lidocaine toxicity, do not apply lidocaine to over 5 percent of the victim's body.
3. Pick out any large pieces of debris with a sterile tweezers.

4. Quickly scrub out the wound with a clean pad soaked with the irrigation solution.
5. Irrigate again.
6. Cover the wound with a non-adherent protective dressing. This can be made by applying a thin coat of triple-antibiotic ointment over a clean gauze pad.

Wound Closure

After cleansing a cut, bleeding may start again. Bleeding should stop with the application of direct pressure to the wound. Close the wound with wound-closure strips — thin strips of material that have an adhesive backing used to "tape" the wound shut. These are available at drug stores. Before you begin, make sure the surrounding skin is thoroughly dry so that the strips will stick. Then start by matching up the edges of the wound and placing one closure strip across the middle of the wound to tape the edges of the wound together. Place additional strips every half inch along the rest of wound.

After Closure

Check the wound daily for signs of infection

- Pus or a pink, green, or cream colored, cloudy discharge from the wound
- Fever
- Increasing tenderness
- Redness or swelling
- Red streaks that radiate from the wound toward the trunk

If an infection develops, open the wound and irrigate. Pack the wound with clean bandages without bringing the edges of the wound together. Apply warm, moist compresses four times a day to promote local circulation. Seek immediate professional medical help, as antibiotics are probably needed.

BLISTERS

Prevention is the best way to handle blisters. Condition your feet in the same shoes that you are going to wear before a long hike. This will toughen your feet and make sure that your shoes and your feet are broken in together. Wet skin blisters more easily, so remember to change into dry socks regularly on the trail. And attend to "hot spots" early on by covering them with tape, moleskin, etc., to stop them from progressing to blisters.

Even with careful preventative measures, blisters can still form. If the blister is small and unbroken, apply one of the new blister-care bandages. These are made by several manufacturers and have a gel-like inner surface that eliminates friction and feels very soothing.

If the blister is large, disinfect the skin around the blister, puncture it at its edge with a sterile needle or knife point and then work out the fluid. Cover the blister with a blister-care bandage and continue on your journey. Check the wound for infection daily. If the drained blister shows signs of infection, trim away the loose layer of skin, disinfect the area, apply a light layer of triple-antibiotic cream, cover with a blister-care bandage, let the area drain frequently, and consult a physician.

BURNS

Determining severity is extremely important in treating burn victims. The severity of a burn is determined by the surface area and the depth of the burned tissue. A rule of thumb used to determine the percentage of a body that is burned is called the rule of palms. A person's palm (not including fingers) covers an area approximately equal to 1.0–1.5 percent of the surface of that person's body. Thus, a burn that covers 10 times the area of a person's palm would cover 10–15 percent of that person's body.

The depth of a burn is grouped into one of three categories:

- First-degree burns, or superficial burns, involve only the outermost layer of the skin (the epidermis).

- Second-degree burns are those that damage not only the top layer of skin, but also some lower layers of skin (the dermis).
- Third-degree burns involve all layers of the skin and can extend into muscle, bone, etc.

First-Degree Burns

The common sunburn is usually a first-degree burn. It typically extends only into the uppermost layer of skin. First-degree burns can be treated with a cool, moist compress and a non-analgesic anti-inflammatory, such as ibuprofen, to relieve the pain and inflammation. This type of burn rarely requires evacuation. If it covers a large area of the body and is accompanied by fever or vomiting, a physician should be consulted.

Second-Degree Burns

These burns, which extend deeper into the skin, are more painful than first-degree burns and are accompanied by blisters. Because they extend into the dermis, which contains sweat glands and small blood vessels, these burns can hinder the body's ability to control its temperature and moisture levels, especially if they cover more than 15 percent of the body. Victims with large second-degree burns are prone to dehydration, hypothermia, and shock. Drinking fluids should be encouraged, and the victim should be kept warm. To treat the burn area, cover it with a cool, moist, non-adherent covering. Use a dry covering if the victim appears hypothermic.

Second-degree burns that cover more than 5 percent of the body or become infected require a consultation with a physician. Second-degree burns that cover more than 15 percent of the body require evacuation.

Third-Degree Burns

Surprisingly, third-degree burns may not be as painful as other burns, because the burn extends deeper into the body and there may be nerve damage. The skin on a third-degree burn may appear dry, leathery, hard, or charred.

Immediately treat the wound by covering it with a clean, dry, non-adherent dressing. A physician should be consulted for all third-degree burns. Evacuation is required if the burn covers over 10 percent of the body. Third-degree burns almost always require skin grafting.

SPRAINS AND STRAINS

Sprains and strains are injuries to muscles, tendons, and ligaments caused by stretching, tearing, twisting, over exertion, and blunt trauma. The symptoms can include pain, swelling, bruising, and decreased range of motion. The most common examples of sprains or strains on the trail are twisted ankles and knees. If an injury of this type occurs in the field, use the RICE method (rest, ice, compression, elevation) for treatment. Medications such as Ibuprofen can help with both the pain and inflammation associated with these injuries.

- *Rest.* Stop using the injured part of the body if possible. Further use can lead to further damage.
- *Ice.* Cooling the injured area reduces circulation at the site of the injury and will help reduce pain, swelling, and bleeding. This is important. Since ice is often a rare commodity in the field, soak the injured area in a cold stream or make a cold pack by placing cold stream water in a Ziploc bag. The cold pack should be applied for at least 20 minutes and as long as 45 minutes. If ice is used, take care not to cause a freeze injury. This can be done simply by placing a bandana or other piece of dry material between the ice pack and the skin. If a soak in a cold stream is used, remove the injured area from the water every few minutes when the cold gets uncomfortable. The cold treatment should be applied every two hours if possible, or at least four times per day. The sooner the cold treatments are started after the injury, the more effective they will be.
- Compression wraps reduce swelling and provide support. A compression wrap can be made by placing

spare clothes, sleeping pad material, or other padding around the injured area and then wrapping the area very snugly with bandages, pack straps, rope, etc. If the area becomes numb or painful, loosen the wrap.
- Elevating the injured area above the level of the heart helps reduce swelling by slowing the circulation to the injured area.

If complete rest for the injured area is not realistic, it should be wrapped to provide as much support as possible. After the injury is wrapped, the victim may be able to travel under his/her own power without a pack. During travel, a cane, walking stick, or other such device should be used to take as much pressure off of the injured area as possible.

HYPOTHERMIA

Hypothermia is the abnormal lowering of the body's core temperature. This condition is generally divided into three degrees of severity depending upon the body's temperature.

Mild

Mild hypothermia occurs when the body's core temperature drops as low as 95°F. (The average body temperature is 98.6°F.) During this stage, a person feels very cold and will shiver. Mental ability is not yet impaired, but coordination may be slightly impaired. Treatment includes sheltering and insulating the victim. Warmed water bottles may be placed in areas of high heat transfer, such as in the groin, armpit, and neck. Make sure that any heat is adequately insulated so that it does not burn the victim. Warm fluids, preferably those containing sugar, should be administered as soon as possible. Avoid drinks with caffeine.

Moderate

Moderate hypothermia occurs when the body's core temperature falls between 90 and 95°F. During this stage, mental ability will be impaired and the victim may display poor judgment, apathy, and confusion. Speech may be slurred, and the victim will often be clumsy and stumbling. Treatment for this stage of hypothermia is much the same as for mild cases, but care should be given when administering fluids. An incoherent victim has an increased danger of choking and aspirating on vomit.

Profound

Profound hypothermia occurs when the body's core temperature falls below 90 degrees. During this stage the victim will have obvious mental degradation and exhibit confusion and irrational behavior, or even fall into a coma. Shivering will stop. Weakness and stumbling will become more pronounced. Eventually, all voluntary motion will cease. The pupils will dilate. Breathing and heart rate will decrease to at least half their normal rates, and eventually will become so shallow as to make the victim appear dead. Treatment of profound hypothermia is much the same as for moderate hypothermia, involving stabilization and the prevention of further cooling. There are, however, a few additional things to know.

- The victim needs to be handled extremely gently. Rough handling—such as jostling, vigorous rubbing, or walking—can easily lead to heart failure.
- Experts disagree as to whether adding heat to the victim in the field is helpful or harmful, due to the complications inherent in rewarming.
- Evacuating victims of profound hypothermia will require the assistance of medical professionals. After stabilizing the victim, your first priority should be to seek help.

FROSTNIP AND FROSTBITE

Frostnip and frostbite are two degrees of the same malady. Frostnip is the early stage where exposed skin experiences superficial freezing but no permanent damage. The affected area will turn pale or whitish and may feel numb. The most commonly affected areas are the tip of the nose, ears, and fingers. Treatment of frostnip involves the immediate re-warming of the affected area. This is often accomplished by simply blowing warm breath into cupped hands to warm your cold nose, placing your warm hands over your cold ears, or putting your cold fingers inside your jacket next to your warm torso. If not tended to immediately, frostbite will follow with more permanent damage to the area.

Frostbite is the freezing of the skin and surrounding tissue. Frostbitten skin will appear waxy with a whitish, grayish, or yellowish color. The affected area may also be hard to the touch.

To treat frostbite, the affected area should be rapidly rewarmed with warm water — that is, water heated to 108°F. Remember, if the water is too hot, the victim will not be able to sense it and a burn may occur. On the other hand, the victim's cold skin will immediately lower the temperature of the rewarming bath. Have plenty of hot water available and replenish as needed. The thawing process can take 20–45 minutes and will be extremely painful. Pain medication administered prior to the rewarming process will help. The anti-inflammatory effect of ibuprofen may also be helpful. The thawing process is complete when the skin is soft and has turned a red or pink color. Do not rub the skin during the thawing process; the frozen tissue is easily damaged once it starts to thaw. Even thawed tissue is fragile and can be very easily damaged. Aloe Vera gel is helpful in protecting the affected area. Blisters will likely form on the affected area after several hours. Avoid opening these blisters. Infection can easily set in — a dangerous complication of frostbite. If a blister ruptures, carefully trim away the loose skin and apply an antiseptic ointment. Pad frostbitten areas with a soft and sterile dressing, especially between the fingers and toes. Elevating the area above the heart is also beneficial. Seek the help of a medical professional on all cases of frostbite.

The faster the rewarming process is started, the smaller the loss of tissue. note: It is imperative that once the affected area has been thawed, it must not be allowed to refreeze. If the area refreezes, large amounts of tissue will be lost. It is far better to walk on a frozen foot, than to walk on a foot that has been thawed and allowed to refreeze.

HEAT ILLNESS

When we hike, our bodies produce as much as 10 times the amount of heat as when we rest. To further fuel the flame when we hike in a sunny environment, we absorb additional heat from the sun. The body's temperature could easily increase by over 15°F in an hour of hard hiking. Such an increase in body temperature, without some sort of release, would be fatal.

Luckily, we do have mechanisms that allow our bodies to rid themselves of excess heat. As we sense that we are becoming overheated, our bodies dilate surface blood vessels to increase blood flow near the surface of our skin. Our blood moves heat from our body's core to the surface of our skin, where it can be radiated away. Additional heat is lost from the skin through evaporation, as our bodies sweat in response to increases in our core temperature. Over 70 percent of the energy we expend is released in the form of heat Normally, 65 percent of that is radiated from our skin.

However, if the temperature of our environment is over 95°F, we no longer lose heat through radiation. As the humidity of our environment increases, evaporative heat loss slows. Thus, as the temperature and humidity of our environment increases, our body's ability to lose heat from radiation and evaporation decreases. The National Weather Service has developed a chart that shows the apparent temperature at different combinations of air temperature and relative humidity. To find it, visit the National Weather Service website (www.nws.noaa.gov) and search for "wind chill chart."

As our core temperature rises, so does the rate of our metabolism. The rate of metabolic increase, however, is not linear. It accelerates as our core temperature increases. Therefore, as our core temperature rises, our metabolism produces even more heat, fueling a vicious cycle.

Heat exhaustion and heat stroke (sun stroke) are different levels of the same basic problem: a body's inability to dissipate excess heat. In trying to deal with the increase of its core temperature, the body dilates blood vessels and loses fluid through profuse sweating. As this happens, the volume of fluid and blood pressure drop. This drop in blood pressure can leave the brain and other organs with an inadequate level of blood flow — the first stage of shock in heat illness.

Heat exhaustion is the less serious of heat-related illness. While it generally does not result in permanent damage, it can develop into a fatal heat stroke quickly. The victim's core temperature can be as high as 104°F. Victims of heat exhaustion may exhibit weakness, minor confusion, irrational behavior, and dizziness. They may also have a rapid pulse, headache, and nausea. (Vomiting is not uncommon.) Contrary to the popular myth that heat exhaustion victims always have clammy skin, the victim may or may not be sweating. Skin temperature can feel cool even of the core temperature is at a fatal level. Core temperature can only be properly assessed with an appropriate thermometer.

To treat heat exhaustion, all physical activity should be stopped and the body must be cooled. Liquid should be applied to the skin and vigorously fanned to promote evaporative cooling. (Urine could be used if water is in short supply.) A bath in a cool stream or pond will cool the body even faster. If a water bath is used, massage the arms and legs to help circulate the blood. Rapid cooling of the skin may cause vasoconstriction, which hampers the movement of cooler blood to the body's core. If the victim is conscious and able to swallow, administer fluids. Elevation of the feet above the head will help to keep blood circulating to the brain. Do not use aspirin or acetaminophen (Tylenol) to try to reduce the victim's elevated temperature. These medications will not be effective in this situation and may make the condition worse.

Heat stroke is an advanced degree of heat illness. It represents a grave medical emergency. The victim's core temperature will be in excess of 105°F. The heat stroke victim will exhibit a severely altered mental state with belligerent behavior, extreme confusion, and seizures. Often, a coma will result. Rapid heart rate, low blood pressure, rapid respiration, and vomiting are also common. The treatment of heat stroke is much the same as for heat exhaustion, but it is more urgently needed. Once the victim's temperature is reduced to a normal level, monitor the core temperature every 15 minutes. The temperature can continue to rise and fall unpredictably for several hours. Victims of heat stroke must be evacuated for professional medical attention as soon as possible.

Hydration is an important factor in heat related illness. When we are dehydrated, our blood vessels do not dilate as well and we produce less sweat. This means that our body's main mechanisms lose efficiency for thermoregulation. To combat heat illness, drink four quarts of water in a moderately hard day of hiking. In fact, a quart an hour is appropriate if the hike is strenuous and the temperature is hot. A good way to gauge adequate water intake is by examining the color of your urine. It should be clear or light yellow in color. If it is dark or a rich yellow color, you are not drinking enough water.

SHOCK

Shock is a potentially deadly condition in which the blood flow to the brain and other organs is insufficient enough to provide an adequate supply of oxygen. Shock can be caused by many serious injuries and illnesses. The treatment for shock involves not only tending to the shock itself, but also tending to the medical conditions that lead to shock—e.g., hypothermia, hyperthermia, and bleeding. Shock can progress rapidly from its early stages to death.

Shock victims may have a rapid but weak or undetectable pulse. Breathing may also be irregular, weak, and rapid. The victim's mental state may range from normal to confused to unconscious.

To treat shock, lay the victim down and keep him calm, warm, and comfortable. Try to identify and treat the underlying cause of the shock. If the shock is caused by visible bleeding, stop the bleeding first. If you're sure there is no severe head injury or internal bleeding, elevate the victim's legs to assist the blood flow to the head. Closely monitor the victims pulse and respiration. Be ready to begin rescue breathing or CPR if appropriate.

Training

If the preceding material on common wilderness health problems was new to you, consider further study of the subject. Because of space considerations, we have briefly outlined only eight conditions that we feel are important to ultralight hikers. There are a great many other conditions that can, and do, occur on the trail—e.g., dislocations, fractures, dental problems, eye problems, head injuries, heart conditions, poisoning, abdominal injuries, etc. Ask yourself: Do I know specifically what to do if I, or someone that I am hiking with, is suffering from any of these conditions? If your answer is no, consider further study of the subject.

Sample First-Aid Kit

Equipment is no substitute for knowledge in health issues. For the majority of hikers, the single most useful item in a first-aid kit would be a small booklet on wilderness medicine. While there are several first-aid guides available, I am partial to the compact and excellent book, A Comprehensive Guide to Wilderness and Travel Medicine by Eric A. Weiss, M.D.

This wilderness medicine text is far superior to others in that it focuses on issues common to backcountry travelers, is extremely thorough considering its small size, and is filled with ways to improvise equipment for use in wilderness medical situations. It is as though Dr. Weiss wrote this book with the ultralight hiker in mind. This guide weighs in at 4.75 ounces. If you remove the book covers and the sections on international travel medicine and diving medicine, another 0.5 ounces can be saved.

The other items packed in your first-aid kit will depend on:

- Your wilderness medical knowledge. Someone with advanced training would have a greater chance of getting along with less gear than a novice. Conversely, someone with advanced training might include some items that would be of little use or even counterproductive in the hands of a novice.

- The length of your hike. If the trip length is a simple overnight jaunt, less gear is needed than if you are going for an extended trek deep into an isolated wilderness.
- The number of people in your group. If you are carrying the first-aid kit for your group of six hikers, you may want to carry greater amounts and different items than if you are traveling solo.
- Pre-existing conditions in your group. For example, Dave knows that his wife is prone to indigestion and knee pain, so he carries antacids and material to stabilize her knee when he hikes with her.
- The degree of preparedness that you wish to maintain, which will determine the size and weight of your first-aid kit. After having discussed the contents of first-aid kits with the other authors of this book, I have come to realize that this is a very personal decision. At the end of the day, you will have to take responsibility for your choices and their consequences.

For comprehensive lists of items that you could carry, look in any of the wilderness medicine books referenced at the end of this chapter. Whatever you decide to carry, ask the following questions about each item:

- Can some other item be substituted? For example, would you feel comfortable improvising a splint or bandage if you did not have these items with you?
- Can you get by with a smaller version or amount? Do you really need a 1-ounce tube of antibiotic ointment, or will a few single-use blister packs do?
- What are the consequences of not having this item if someone in your party needs it? If you skip taking an anti-diarrheal, are you willing to live with the condition until it clears up?
- Do you have the skills needed to use this item? Do you know how to suture a wound, or would you be better served by taping a wound closed? Do you know when not to use the medications that you are packing?

Sample First-Aid Gear List

The following are the contents of the first-aid kit that that might be carried by a lightweight backpacker experienced at treating minor injuries.

CONTAINER	WEIGHT	ITEM	PURPOSE	DOSE	QTY	NOTE
Film canister with instructions	0.75 oz	Ibuprofen	For pain and to reduce inflammation	200mg tablets	32	4 days of the maximum non-RX dosage. Larger dosages of the drug can be helpful for severe inflammation, but that is between you and your doctor.
Film canister with instructions	0.5 oz	Decongestant Actifed (Pseudoephedrine)	For congestion and sinus pressure	60mg tablets	8	Enough for the maximum non-RX dosage for 2 days.
		Antihistamine Benadryl (Diphenhydramine)	For allergic reactions, insect stings, rashes, and as a cough suppressant	25mg tablets	8	2 days of the maximum recommended non-RX dosage.
Film canister with instructions	0.5 oz	Imodium A-D (Loperamide Hydrochloride)	For diarrhea	Tablets	8	
		Pepcid AC (Famotidine)	For heartburn	Tablets	6	
Heavy-duty Ziploc bag with instructions	2.0 oz	0.5 fl oz of 10% povidone iodine solution to mix with 16 oz of water. To flush the solution into wound, a 20cc syringe with a catheter tip.	For sterile irrigating solution			Bag doubles as a mixing container for the irrigation solution.

CONTAINER	WEIGHT	ITEM	PURPOSE	DOSE	QTY	NOTE
Small Ziploc bag	0.75 oz	Iodine	For cleaning around blisters and wounds	Prep pads	12	
		Double antibiotic ointment	For prevention of wound infection	Squeeze packets	4	
Small Ziploc bag	1.25 oz	Bioclusive transparent dressing pads	Cover and protect non-seeping wounds	2" x 3"	3	
		Blister care pads	For blisters		4	
Small Ziploc bag	1.5 oz	Spenco adhesive knit bandage	For covering hot spots before they blister	2" x 4"	2	Better than moleskin
		Sterile gauze sponges	Wound dressing	4" x 4"	6	
Small Ziploc bag	0.75 oz	Tincture of benzoin	To help tape stick to skin	Swabs	2	
		Wound closure strips	For closing wounds		20	
		Butterfly bandages		Medium	6	
Small Ziploc bag	4.5 oz	A Comprehensive Guide to Wilderness and Travel Medicine by Eric A. Weiss, M.D.,				
		Small nub of a pencil	To write			
Total	**12.5 oz**					

Suggested Reading List

Weiss, Eric A. *A Comprehensive Guide to Wilderness and Travel Medicine* (Oakland, CA: Adventure Medical Kits, 1997)
- Unless you have done a great deal of wilderness medical study, carry this book.

Auerbach, Paul S. *Medicine for the Outdoors* (New York: The Lyons Press, 1999)
- An excellent and comprehensive guide to wilderness medicine for the layman.

Forgey, William. *Wilderness Medicine: Beyond First Aid* (Merrillville, IN; ICS Books Inc., 1994)
- An excellent and comprehensive guide to wilderness medicine for the layman.

Auerbach, Paul S., editor. *Wilderness Medicine* (St. Louis, MO: Mosby, Inc., 2001)
- With over 2,000 pages and over 1,200 photos and illustrations, this is easily the most comprehensive volume on the subject available. While much of the text can be understood by the layman, it is not an easy read. Most of the book is more suitable for medical professionals and others with a great deal of advanced study.

Tilton, Buck and Hubbell, Frank. *Medicine for the Backcountry* (Merrillville, IN: ICS Books, Inc. 1994)
- An excellent and comprehensive guide to wilderness medicine for the layman.

Resources for First-Aid and Wilderness Medicine Training

WILDERNESS MEDICINE INSTITUTE

PO Box 9
Pitkin, CO 81241
970-641-3572
wmi.nols.edu

NATIONAL SAFETY COUNCIL

1121 Spring Lake Drive
Itasca, IL 60143
800-621-7619
www.nsc.org

WILDERNESS MEDICAL SOCIETY

3595 East Fountain Blvd., Suite A1
Colorado Springs, CO 80910
719-572-9255
www.wms.org

AMERICAN RED CROSS

Look in the telephone directory for your local chapter of
the American Red Cross, or check their website at www.
redcross.org

Supply Resources

Local outdoor equipment stores, drug stores, and surgical
supply retailers can provide you with most of the first-aid
equipment that you need. Below are three mail-order businesses that have a complete selection of wilderness medical
supplies.

WILDERNESS MEDICINE OUTFITTERS

2477 County Road 132
Elizabeth, CO 80107
303-688-5176
www.wildernessmedicine.com

CHINOOK MEDICAL GEAR INC.

3455 Main Avenue
Durango, Colorado 81301
800-766-1365
www.chinookmed.com

ADVENTURE MEDICAL KITS

PO Box 43309
Oakland, CA 94624
800-324-3517
www.adventuremedicalkits.com

Part 5:

Proven **Lightweight Solutions**

An encore collection of **fan favorites**
from BackpackingLight.com

Chapter 14:
Advanced Tarp Camping
Techniques for Inclement Conditions

By Ryan Jordan

The biggest gripes I hear from tent-tethered hikers about tarps are:

1. "A tent is warmer!"
2. "They offer no protection from bugs!"
3. "They're worthless above the treeline, especially in inclement weather."

Most seasoned ultralight backpackers admit to the first but choose to invest weight where it counts the most: high fill down in a sleeping bag.

Most have also figured out a variety of solutions to the second, ranging from the Spartan's choice—a headnet—to the more secure and roomier offerings of nest-like shrouds of noseeum mesh, such as those offered by GoLite; or a mesh perimeter sewn to the edge of the tarp, as in Henry Shire's Tarptent. Combined with some strategically applied DEET and/or Permethrin, avoiding insanity from buzzing is not difficult.

Thus, the first two proclaimed disadvantages of tarp camping for three-season backpacking are weak arguments.

However, when it comes to the third, too many veterans — even experienced lightweight hikers — scamper down to the treeline to avoid having to face the rock music of tarp camping in a tempest. And, hey, I'll admit it: When I'm carrying a poncho and leaving my tent at home, pitching a bombproof tarp in a gale force storm at 11,000 feet is not high on my list of things to do when dusk is approaching and I'm craving my evening soup.

However, being able to pitch your tarp properly under inclement conditions is a skill that opens up new avenues of very light high-mountain travel, including alpinism, ridge hiking, and alpine high routes. Above the treeline, you are immersed in a mountain range's full glory — and sometimes, her wrath — en route to a richer experience with better-than-IMAX views, planetarium-quality stargazing, and an intimacy with the alpine realm that cannot be appreciated by spending the night in the arbor cathedrals of lower elevations.

And so, this article will focus on more advanced considerations for tarp camping above the treeline in inclement weather.

Resistance to Inclement Weather: Panel Size and Tension

The two biggest mistakes novice lightweight mountain travelers make when tarping above the treeline is thinking that a larger tarp provides better weather protection, and that stakes and guylines provide opportunities for weight savings.

Consider two tarps side by side. One measures 10′ x 12′ and the other 5′ x 8′, both staked as A-frames in similar configurations, with each corner staked to the ground, broadside to a stiff wind. Now consider the rule that deflection of the normal surface of a panel in tension is proportional to:

1. The surface area of the panel
2. The degree of tension in the panel

You can begin to appreciate the two most important factors that go into properly pitching a shelter in inclement conditions.

First let's consider the surface area of the panel. A larger surface exposed to wind will deflect more in response to wind than a smaller surface exposed, given that tension across both surfaces is the same. conclusion: Use a smaller tarp if you are going to be exposed to high winds. If you don't buy into this philosophy, then consider that the world's strongest mountain tents are those that

- Have the smallest sized panels (visualize a geodesic dome tent with eight criss-crossing poles vs. only two or four), or
- Are low in height, width, and length (like the Integral Designs MK1XL, the de facto standard of blizzard-ready mountain tents)

Small Tarps for Inclement Weather

The SpinTarp X, an ultralight silicone-coated 4.25″-x-7.75″ tarp by Bozeman Mountain Works (4.15 oz) is designed to be used in conjunction with a bivy sack to provide overhead rain

High Uintas, UT: This tarp is actually **two Integral Design Sil Ponchos**, snapped together to form the ridgeline of a tarp pitch 8' in length and 10' in width. The low end is into the wind, which spilled down from a 12,000-foot ridge during the night. Panel tension and a tight pitch were maintained by using a total of 14 titanium skewer stakes and fine-diameter guylines.

protection. Combined with plenty of tent stakes and guylines, it is well suited to exposed conditions above the treeline.

Second, let's consider the tension in the panel. Since we don't have the option of using tent poles to reduce panel tension, we are simply left with stakes and guylines. As you add stakes and guylines to the sides of your tarp, you effectively create more and more (smaller) tension panels in the structure. The result: higher tension forces across the panel resulting from smaller panel surface area. Stakes and guylines don't weigh much. A set of 12 titanium skewer stakes and a set of Spectra guylines can weigh less than 3.25 ounces, while providing your tarp with the structural integrity required for weathering storms above the treeline. conclusion: Don't skimp on stakes and guylines if you are going to be exposed to high winds.

Precipitation Protection: The Breathable Bivy Sack

We've addressed the need to deal with high winds already, but what about precipitation? Using a smaller tarp means a greater risk of getting wet from sideways blowing rain, snow, or spindrift.

Pitching windward edges close to the ground is one way to minimize the effects of wind and windblown precipitation on your sleep system. Beaks, such as those found on the front of Tarptents and the ends of the GoLite Cave series of tarps, also help. However, swirling winds that change direction are the high-mountain norm. Tarp design and pitching options can only take you so far.

The mainstream mountain tarp aficionado recognizes these limitations, and often complements the tarp with a synthetic sleeping bag, a down bag with a nearly waterproof-breathable shell (e.g., Gore DryLoft or Pertex Endurance), or a waterproof-breathable bivy sack. However, there are a few problems with these:

1. Synthetic bags are heavier than high-fill down bags of comparable warmth — by up to 40% or more!

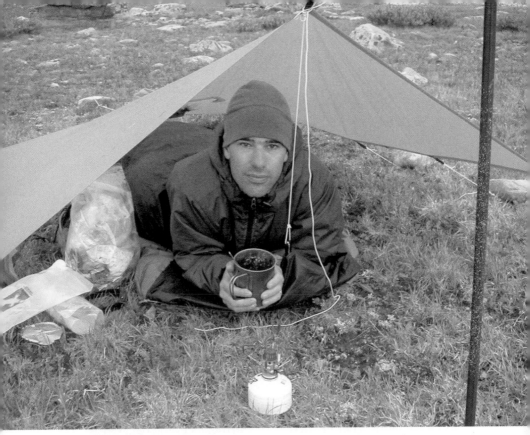

Staying Warmer with a Bivy. This photo was taken the morning after a subfreezing night in the High Uintas with winds in excess of 40 mph. The solution was simply to pitch the tarp (an Integral Designs Sil Poncho) low enough to spill wind effectively with plenty of stakes and guylines to maintain panel tension. The bivy sack, with a Pertex Quantum top (6.5 oz), was essential to staying warm in conjunction with an ultralight, 16-ounce down sleeping bag.

2. A down bag shelled with a low-breathability shell, such as DryLoft or Endurance, doesn't pass moisture vapor well enough to maintain its insulation on longer trips.
3. Waterproof-breathable bivy sacks: ditto. They don't pass moisture vapor well.

Thus, I'm a strong advocate of bivy sacks that have a waterproof bottom—so you can leave a ground cloth at home—and a highly breathable, water-resistant top that can pass perspired moisture vapor quickly. An uncompromised DWR finish for the bivy top is a must for precipitation to bead up on the fabric and roll off without penetrating into the rest of the sleep system. I've been successfully using bivy sacks with Pertex Microlight, Pertex Quantum, and Nextec Epic Malibu tops for nearly three years with great success in terrible weather. This approach works especially well in the winter, when condensation retained inside a Gore-Tex bivy sack can cripple your sleep system in a matter of only a day or two.

Other benefits of a bivy sack (not unique to those with breathable tops) are additional warmth due to the entrapment of insulating air between the bivy sack and the sleeping bag (improves resistance to conductive heat loss), additional warmth due to inhibited exchange of warm with cool air inside the bivy (improves convective heat loss due to the bellows effect of air exchange), and the additional warmth afforded by wind resistance from the bivy sack (improves convective heat loss by maintaining boundary layer thickness through which the inside-outside temperature gradient is defined).

Arguments against such a system are that a bivy is heavier, and the weight is better spent on a warmer sleeping bag. (Also consider that a wet down bag is less warm—and heavier!) Epic Malibu bivy sacks weigh in the range of 9–12 ounces, while Pertex Microlight bivies range from 8–10 ounces. The Bozeman Mountain Works Vapr Bivy (silnylon floor and Pertex Quantum top) reduces the weight to 6.5 ounces. This almost closes the gap between bivy sacks and ground sheets (remember that half of that bivy weight is a groundsheet you'd take anyway). conclusion: a sub 12-ounce, breathable bivy sack affords tremendous wind and rain protection that cannot be provided by adding insulation (like down fill) to a sleep system.

Trekking Poles, Stakes, and Guylines

Pitching a tarp above the treeline requires a bit of innovation at times. Trekking poles give you the opportunity to strike camp virtually anywhere, because they provide you with strong supports for the ridgeline. Those who do not use trekking poles to rig the ridgeline sometimes carry dedicated collapsible tent poles (e.g., carbon fiber poles from Fibraplex) and take advantage of equipment or natural features, such as sticks, large boulders, or ice axes.

Tent stakes for alpine camping should be thin, strong, and short. They need to be thin because the alpine realm is a rocky place. Thin stakes snake their way through rocky ground better than thick ones. Stakes should be strong for the same reason: They need to resist a bit of driving force into the ground as the point deflects off rocks. Finally, they should be short — and thus, light and easy to place and remove. Six inches is plenty. My recommendation: titanium skewer-style stakes 1/8 inch in diameter. There are stronger stakes — including those made with high-strength aluminum in tube, T-, or V-shaped cross sections — but they are heavier (0.5 oz or more). The difference between a set of twelve 1/8"-x-6" skewer-type titanium stakes (0.25 oz each) and the other is 3 ounces — significant when you consider that this could be 3 extra ounces of down fill in your sleeping bag (to boost its rating 5–10 degrees) or 375 calories of extra food energy. Furthermore, the T- and V-shaped stakes are difficult — and painful — to place and remove with bare hands in hard ground.

Guylines for tarp camping should be strong, light, short, and plentiful. I've tarp camped with other ultralighters that use fishing line or dental floss for their guylines. I've also watched the slightest breeze snap these guylines. I wouldn't trust them above the treeline. Search for guylines that have high strength/weight ratios. Those made with pure Spectra (AirCore) or Spectra cores with nylon sheaths (Kelty Trip-Tease) make great guylines for fiercely windy conditions.

Guylines can be pre-tied with overhand, figure-eight, or bowline loops in each end. They should be about two or three feet in length to minimize tangling during storage). Longer guylines can be made by girth hitching multiple short pieces together. This gives you a very flexible system for pitching in a variety of configurations. Once your guyline length is set, simply girth hitch one end loop to the tarp's guyline tie-outs, insert the stake in the other end loop, tension the guyline, and set the stake. Tension is adjusted by resetting the stake, rather than fiddling around with a tautline hitch, that artistic adjustable knot so prominently showcased by the Boy Scouts as an essential skill. This is where the benefit of titanium skewer stakes really shines. They are easier to place and remove relative to other types of stakes, so this guyline-and-stake system used for tarp adjustment is simple, fast, and effective.

Conclusion

This chapter focused on three key points:

1. How well a tarp sheds high winds depends on its panel size and degree of tension in those panels, both of which can be optimized by increasing the number of guy-out points used. In short, don't skimp on tent stakes or guylines.
2. Use of a water-resistant, breathable bivy sack can increase the warmth, wind resistance, and driving rain/snow protection of your sleep system.
3. The tarping life is kept simple with short guylines and skewer-style tent stakes.

Tarp camping above the treeline in inclement weather is not an essential skill for the average backpacker. However, for the lightweight hiker that likes to travel above the treeline for long distances, having the flexibility to pitch a camp anywhere you like, and knowing that you are going to have a shelter and sleep system that can handle high winds and driving rain, opens up new possibilities in your backcountry explorations. With this skill you'll achieve a level of intimacy with the mountains that cannot be enjoyed from beneath a canopy of trees.

Citation

This chapter was originally published as an article in the online magazine BackpackingLight.com (ISSN 1537-0364) in September 2003.

Chapter 15: **Superultralight**, Breaking the Five-Pound Barrier

By Ryan Jordan

The ability to carry a pack that is not just light (12–20 lbs base weight) or ultralight (6–11 lbs), but ridiculously light (< 5 lbs) and still maintain a level of comfort and safety suitable for hiking in the high mountain ranges of the lower 48 states requires a bit of innovation, some compromise in durability, and most importantly, an advanced set of backcountry skills that allows you to remain warm and dry in inclement weather with a kit of gear that offers little margin for safety.

Thus, herein I make no attempt to define a new standard for lightweight backpacking, but instead offer you some insight for pushing the sub-5-pound barrier at the ultralight fringe.

Although some skill is needed to use this kit in inclement weather, my intention is to build a kit that doesn't sacrifice a lot of function.

- I don't leave the toothbrush at home
- I use a pack with a hip belt
- I'm not using a bivy sack as sole shelter
- I'm not starving myself on cold food

- I'm treating my water
- I'm not wiping with pine cones
- I'm not using good vibes to disperse mosquito clouds
- I'm successfully using this kit in rain and snow and wind at high elevations with nighttime temperatures below freezing in the mountains.
- I even advocate a synthetic insulating layer over a down vest or jacket, as a measure of insurance against wet weather.

When I was researching this topic, I found less than ten people — in the US and Europe — that actually practice sub-5-pound backpacking on a consistent basis. After interviewing dozens of ultralight backpackers, I've come to the conclusion that the reason the fringe isn't being explored is simple: It's the fringe. And there is not a lot of gear or education to help people explore it.

I've found that achieving light loads can be accomplished in one of two ways. Herein, I discuss careful selection of individual ultralight items that can be used together as a system without sacrificing a great deal of comfort or functionality. The alternative is to start throwing items out of your pack, which is the subject of another article perhaps. But that philosophy eventually results in the emergence out of traditional backpacking and into wilderness survival.

Base weight is herein defined as the dry weight of gear and nonconsumable supplies in your pack. It excludes food, fuel, water, clothing worn, and items normally carried (like trekking poles). We don't claim that this is the most accurate representation of one's pack weight, but it is the most popular. We use it herein to maintain consistency with what most perceive to be their pack weight.

Rethinking the Big Three

Most self-proclaimed lightweight backpackers carry less than 6 pounds of equipment for their shelter, sleeping bag, and backpack, allocating approximately 2 pounds for each item.

Ryan Jordan holding his loaded backpack at 12,000 feet on day 2 of a four-day trek through the Uinta Wilderness near the Utah-Wyoming border. His pack weight including food and a liter of water at the trailhead at the beginning of the trek: just over 11 pounds.

The superultralighter must reduce this weight to a maximum of 2–3 pounds if they hope to reduce the total weight of their gear list to less than 5 pounds.

SLEEPING BAG

You need to remain comfortable at temperatures near freezing, even midsummer, if you are going to be hiking in the Tetons, Wind Rivers, Sierras, Glacier National Park, Yellowstone, or North Cascades. Limit yourself to a sleeping bag that weighs no more than a pound. Perhaps a few ounces heavier if you're tall. That limits your options to sleeping bags using ultralight fabrics, such as Pertex Quantum and high-quality down fill, so you can at least maintain an inch and a half of single layer loft over you. Combining your sleeping bag with a smart clothing selection will allow you to remain comfortable on those freezing or sub-freezing nights.

My sleeping bag choice is a custom 15.2-ounce variable girth bag with a Pertex Quantum shell and 800+ fill down offering 2.25 inches of single-layer loft that tapers to 7 inches in the footbox. Other possibilities include

- Nunatak Ghost
- Western Mountaineering HighLite
- Feathered Friends Vireo
- Rab Quantum Top Bag
- PhD Minimus Bag

Don't forget about a waterproof stow bag to protect your precious down. My choice is a homemade spinnaker cloth stuff sack, 400 cubic inches, 0.5 ounces.

Finally, you need a sleeping pad for ground insulation. Skip the Therm-a-Rest and go for closed-cell foam with a cured surface so it doesn't absorb water. A 3/8-inch foam pad cut to torso size costs only 2.0–3.5 ounces.

SHELTER

Tents are out. Tarp tents are out. Big tarps are out. A sub-12-ounce waterproof bivy sack is a possibility, but awfully uncomfortable in inclement weather. You've got to think multi-use here and take a hard look at a poncho tarp that serves as both raingear and shelter. Silicone-coated nylon is the only material to consider. Check out poncho-tarp offerings from GoLite, Integral Designs, and Equinox, and you'll get by with something less than 10 ounces. Add six 1/8"-x-6" titanium skewer stakes (1.5 oz) and about 35 feet of Spectra guylines (0.5 oz).

In addition, a poncho tarp is not going to provide you with enough coverage during the severe storms that make the Wind Rivers or Tetons famous. If you want some additional warmth and insect protection, consider a bivy sack with a breathable but water-resistant top and a waterproof bottom, so that it serves sufficiently as a ground cloth as well as minimizing condensation in the bivy by blocking evaporated moisture transport from wet ground. Equinox makes a 6.5-ounce nylon/silnylon bivy of this type — without hood — that must be paired with a 1-oz noseeum headnet for bug protection. Or go to an Epic/Silnylon bivy like that from Oware for 10 ounces or so. And there's the Bozeman Mountain Works Vapr Bivy that weighs 6.5 ounces.

My shelter system consists of a 0.9-ounce spinnaker cloth poncho-tarp (5´ x 8´, 6.3 oz), six titanium stakes (1.5 oz), 35 feet of Spectra guylines (0.5 oz), and a Pertex Quantum/Silnylon bivy sack (6.9 oz). This 15.2-ounce package provides additional sleeping bag warmth (bivy), inclement weather protection (tarp and bivy), bug protection at night (bivy), overhead shelter protection (poncho), and rain protection (poncho). You'll be hard pressed to find a lighter system that provides this much functionality.

PACK

With a 5-pound base weight, forget about frame support. Even with a week's worth of food and 3 liters of water (the maximum amount ever carried by a thru-hiker or recreational backpacker), you're not going to break over 20 pounds very often, if at all. Most of the time, you're going to be packing less than 12–15 pounds. And often, less than 10. Start thinking about unconventional packs to address your superultralight needs. You don't need much more than a bag with straps. Granite Gear makes a 10.5-ounce compression pack that holds 1,500 (medium) to 1,900 (large) cubic inches, which is plenty of space for this type of load. For serious weight reduction, check out the 3.7-ounce G6 Whisper Ultralight Backpack, or simply make your own sub-10-ounce pack in the 2000 cubic inch range, using silicone-coated nylon for the body, simple padded shoulder straps, and a 1″ webbing belt to help out with those "heavy" 15–20 pound loads.

My superultralight pack choice for short trips is a Bozeman Mountain Works G6 Whisper. It weighs only 3.7 ounces, has a 2000 cubic inch main compartment, single rear pocket, and shoulder straps that accomodate socks or gloves for padding. (See the G6 Whisper in the front cover photo of this book.) For trips longer than a weekend, I prefer the more robust 15.5-ounce GoLite Dawn (2400 cubic inch main compartment), which carries heavier loads a little better than the G6 and is more durable.

Clothing

BASE LAYERS

As you increase your level of skill, you can decrease the number of pieces of clothing you bring. The superultralight philosophy requires rigid adherence to the mantra of "no duplicate item." Your base layers must function over as wide of a temperature range as possible. For the torso, a very thin wicking knit base layer, such as silkweight capilene or fine merino wool (treated with Permethrin for mosquito protection) is essential. It will keep you as warm as possible if your clothing gets wet. My choice is a Smartwool lightweight long-sleeve crew top. If I'm going into colder conditions, I prefer the Cloudveil Rodeo pullover, an 8.5-ounce stretch woven shirt with a deep neck zip for ventilation. For pants, a stretch woven fabric provides insect and sun protection, warmth, wicking, wind resistance, and enough rain protection when coupled with a poncho that additional rain pants or wicking pants are unnecessary. Schoeller Dynamic pants are a good choice, but for even lighter protection, check out Cloudveil's Prospector pants: 9.25 ounces (men's medium). Add to this a pair of trail-running socks and your hiking shoes, a sun hat, and a bandana, and you are dressed to cover a tremendous comfort range.

WINDSHIRT

The addition of a 3-ounce breathable windshirt extends the comfort range of your clothing in high winds, cool temperatures, and light rain like no other layer. A poncho, windshirt, and your base layers provide you with enough warmth and protection to cover 90 percent of the inclement weather you'll encounter during summers in the Continental US mountain ranges. My choice is the GoLite Whisp HP at 2.8 ounces.

INSULATING JACKET

This is our safety piece. We probably won't need to hike in it. If we need this to remain warm while hiking, then maybe we should stop hiking and pitch our shelter! The insulating jacket extends the temperature range of our sleeping system significantly and offers some insurance if (God forbid) our sleeping bag gets wet. Synthetic jackets are the safest and provide a level of insurance in wet conditions that can't be matched by down. But ultralight offerings are limited for these types of garments. One of the best is the 15.3-ounce hooded EP (Epic-Primaloft) jacket from Wild Things. My choice for wet conditions is the Cocoon pullover from Bozeman Mountain Works (8.0 ounces), which offers a Pertex Quantum shell, partial neck zipper, and Polarguard Delta insulation. Also, Western Mountaineering has a nice 5-ounce down vest that complements their Flight jacket (10 ounces), and MontBell makes an 8-ounce quilted down sweater. But if you are hiking in inclement conditions, carefully consider whether or not you want *all* of your insulation to be down.

EXTRAS

An extra pair of socks buys you the ability to continuously hike long-distance days with freshly washed and lofted socks, making sure you have a dry pair every night for sleeping. A simple fleece beenie hat or thin polyester (e.g., PowerStretch) balaclava gives you a lot of comfort for hiking in cold conditions and cutting some head chill while sleeping. Finally, unless you like hiking with those stinky extra socks on your hands, you better throw in a thin pair of gloves. My choice of a beanie hat and gloves are made by PossumDown Knitwear of New Zealand.

Kitchen

Going superultralight doesn't mean going superultra*hungry* or eating superultra*cold* food. The best way to reduce your kitchen weight is to minimize the amount of water boiled that you really need. Skip the two cups of hot tea at night, Cream of Wheat breakfasts, and those streamside trout lunches, in lieu of a single hot meal in the evening. Reducing your fuel needs means you can go to the lightest stoves available. In addition, plan your meals so that they can be made with as little water as possible, so you can reduce your pot size. If you use boil-in-a-bag packaging, you can probably get away with a 12-ounce titanium cup for boiling water. You'll need more pot volume if you mix food and water in the pot, rather than a bag.

Water treatment is a must for most hikers. Aquamira repackaged in small eyedropper bottles makes a very light and effective system. It gets you through five to seven days for an ounce. There is no room for filtration systems on this list. For water storage, hard containers are out. I like to have a 2-liter Platypus for water storage during long dry stretches of trail and for collecting water in the evening if I'm going to be in a dry camp. But most of my drinking is done from a 1-quart Platypus bottle that weighs 1.2 ounces with a push-pull squirt top.

Food storage is critical in most mountainous areas of the country where bears are present. Bear canisters in the Sierras aside, most wilderness areas let you get away with bear bagging. A simple, silicone-coated nylon stuff sack weighs only an ounce. Combined with 35–50 feet of braided Spectra, it gives you enough to rig a simple bear-bagging system that is effective enough for most areas of the country.

Miscellaneous Items

You are now walking very close to the 5-pound barrier. Don't go over by adding a bunch of useless items. Be very critical with your essentials list here. Take only what is absolutely necessary.

LIGHT

A Photon Freedom (0.3 oz) worn around a lanyard on your neck provides plenty of light for nighttime trail walking and camp chores.

BUG PROTECTION

A tiny MicroDrop Bottle full of DEET will last two weeks and weigh less than 0.2 ounces. A 1-ounce noseeum headnet may be required for hanging out during the peak of mosquito season.

SUN PROTECTION

A $300 pair of titanium sunglasses that weigh 0.2 oz does you no good if you have to house them in a hard case that weighs 3–4 ounces. Stick with basic, cheap sunglasses (0.5 oz) with plastic lenses that you can just toss into your pack without fear of breakage. Since you are wearing a long-sleeve shirt and long pants, a bandana for the neck, and a wide-brimmed hat for sun protection, your need for sunscreen is now limited to your nose, cheeks, and backs of your hands. A Dermatone stick fits the bill, and provides lip protection to boot for 0.5 oz.

TOILET

You can save TP weight by invoking a sense of raw wilderness skill in your quest for "natural" wiping methods. However, the skilled superultralighter will plan their diet with enough fiber to ensure "clean" feces that result in minimizing the number of TP squares you need. A 0.5-ounce bottle of alcohol hand gel gives you some hygiene insurance if your TP is a little on the thin side (1-inch aspen leaves come to mind) or you miscalculate your prune intake. For mouth hygiene, a prison-type finger toothbrush is only 0.05 ounces, and Dr. Bronner's provides a month's supply of toothpaste if packaged into a tiny eyedropper bottle.

FIRST AID AND EMERGENCY

As your skill increases, the size and weight of your first-aid kit decreases. The only items I carry anymore as *critical* include some blister treatment (for long-distance days), a few painkillers, and some butterfly bandages to stop bleeding from large cuts. A whistle worn around the neck gives you signaling insurance in populated areas, and some waterproof storm matches and an Esbit tab for a firestarter might get you through a surprisingly cold and wet night if all of your stuff is soaked.

Assemble Your Kit. Then Do It!

The superultralight fringe is not an exclusive club for freaks, Marines, or veteran hikers. Nor is it wilderness survival. Nor is it intended only for summertime hiking in Southwest Texas.

Review this list carefully. Many of you are already achieving the same functionality in your gear lists (e.g., using a poncho-tarp for both shelter and raingear). If you possess some basic skills, such as keeping your stuff dry, dealing with a poncho-tarp in rainy conditions, pitching a tarp, locating your camp in inclement weather, etc., then you can certainly explore this fringe.

However, understand that we are bringing less stuff here. Thus, there is little room for error. Going superultralight requires that you pay careful attention to every detail and evaluate the consequences of each choice you make while walking. You must have the ability to forecast challenging scenarios, develop contingency plans, and implement those plans when things go awry. Practice! Use this kit on fair-weather overnighters where the security of a car heater is only a few feet or few miles away. Then try it on foul-weather overnighters. Finally, begin to extend your mileage into the wilderness and the number of days you remain out. Eventually, you will have logged enough foul-weather nights to wonder why you ever carried that tremendously heavy 15-pound pack!

Ryan's Superultralight List

I've now had the opportunity to explore this fringe for three years during conditions of heavy rain, spring snow, high winds, and fierce mosquitoes. It has required some iterative fiddling. In fact, it still does. But I'm comfortable enough using the gear here that I can wholeheartedly recommend every item on the list to those wishing to explore lightweight, long-distance backpacking on a new level.

PACK, SHELTER, SLEEPING

- 6 Whisper (3.7 oz) or GoLite Dawn (15.5 oz)
- 3/8" foam torso-sized sleeping pad (1.9 oz)
- SpinPoncho spinnaker cloth poncho-tarp, 5' x 8' (6.3 oz)
- Six (6) Lazr 1/8" x 6" titanium skewer stakes (1.3 oz)
- Eight 3-foot lengths of AirCore 1 Spectra guylines (0.2 oz)
- Pertex Quantum variable girth down sleeping bag (15.2 oz) SpinSack stuff sack for sleeping bag (0.5 oz)
- Vapr Quantum/Silnylon bivy sack (6.2 oz)

CLOTHING WORN AND ITEMS CARRIED

- Smartwool Lightweight long-sleeve crew shirt (8.0 oz, worn)
- Spandex shorts (3.0 oz, worn)
- Cloudveil Prospector Pants (9.3 oz, worn)
- Smartwool trail-running socks (1.4 oz, worn)
- Inov-8 Terroc shoes with carbon fiber orthotics (24 oz, worn)
- Tilley LT hat (3.0 oz, worn)

- Cotton bandana (1.0 oz, worn)
- Bozeman Mountain Works Stix Pro carbon fiber trekking poles (6.0 oz, carried)
- Emergency whistle and Photon Freedom microlight worn on Spectra cord lanyard (0.5 oz, worn)

EXTRA CLOTHING PACKED

- GoLite Wisp HP Windshirt (2.8 oz)
- Bozeman Mountain Works Cocoon pullover (8.0 oz)
- Spare pair of Smartwool trail-running socks (1.4 oz)
- PossumDown Beanie Cap (1.4 oz)
- PossumDown Gloves (1.2 oz)
- SpinSack clothing stuff sack (0.5 oz)

KITCHEN

- Mini-Pepsi stove with wire pot support (0.35 oz)
- Titanium foil windscreen (0.2 oz)
- Platypus Lil' Nipper bottle with fine spout cap for fuel (0.7 oz)
- Box of wooden matches in Ziploc (0.3 oz)
- Snow Peak 450 mug, no handles (2.0 oz)
- Titanium foil lid for mug (0.05 oz)
- Titanium mini-spork (0.4 oz)
- UrsaLite bear bag system (2.0 oz)
- 2L Platypus bag, 1L pop-top Platypus bottle (2.3 oz)
- Aquamira repackaged in eyedropper bottles, with mixing cap (1.1 oz)

MISCELLANY

- Noseeum mesh headnet (0.7 oz)
- MicroDrop bottle of DEET (0.2 oz)
- Dermatone stick (0.5 oz)
- Sunglasses (0.2 oz)
- Finger toothbrush (0.05 oz)
- Dr. Bronner's in MicroDrop bottle (0.2 oz)
- Alcohol hand gel in small bottle (0.5 oz)
- TP: 4" x 4" blue shop towel squares, 1 per day (0.5 oz)

- Blister & minor wound care supplies (1.0 oz)
- Small stuff sack for organizing these essentials (0.5 oz)

Total Pack Weight: 4.03 pounds with G6 pack (4.77 lbs with GoLite Dawn pack)

Total Weight Worn or Carried: 3.51 pounds

Total Weight (less food, fuel, and water): 7.54 pounds with G6 pack (8.28 lbs with GoLite Dawn pack)

Citation

This chapter was originally published as an article in the online magazine Backpacking-Light.com (ISSN 1537-0364) in August 2003, and has been updated to reflect changes in the author's "superultralight" style at the time this book went to press.

Chapter 16: **Hiking Efficiency**
A Day in the Life of an Ultralight Hiker

By Ryan Jordan

Often people comment to me, "I'd love to be a mouse in your pocket on an ultralight backpacking trip!" At first, I wondered why. After conducting more than fifty ultralight backpacking seminars in the past few years, I now understand. Participants tell me that the number one seminar benefit has been learning how to hike efficiently.

Hiking Efficiency

Hiking efficiently is one of the most difficult skills to learn over the course of a few days, or by reading an article. Perhaps as much as any backpacking skill, hiking and camping efficiency is borne more out of the experience that cements habits through repetition (conditioning) than by conscious practice. However, the effort required to practice and repeat those habits initially is real and requires profound effort.

In short, hiking efficiency is accomplished in three phases:

1. Habit Assessment. Critically analyzing your current practices
2. Habit Reformation. Consciously altering your hiking and camping habits so that maximum output is achieved with minimum effort

3. Habit Cementation. Repeating step 2 until the action is performed with less conscious effort

Habit Assessment

One of the most effective tools that I use in my ultralight backpacking seminars to teach hiking efficiency is a habit assessment exercise that I call "Too Slow Joe." This features a character called Too Slow Joe, a very slow backpacker and inefficient camper. Joe covers little distance per day, requires an inordinate amount of time setting up camp, and is always cooking his dinner after everyone else has gone to bed. Is this you?

In the exercise, I show videos of backpackers (Too Slow Joes and a few Janes) conducting a variety of tasks. They may be as "complicated" as pitching a tarp or cooking a meal, or as "simple" as accessing a trail snack or using a map and compass while hiking.

Then I replay the video in stepped increments of individual actions, and record those actions on a white board. As a group, we then begin re-piecing the actions together to achieve the final goal of the task. We recreate the task in a workflow chart not unlike those used by the project managers of Dilbert corporations. In the end, we realize the amount of time and effort wasted in performing nonessential actions.

The action list from one video illustrates the inefficiency of Too Slow Joe trying to access his water bottle (a 1L Platypus) from the side pocket of his pack (Granite Gear Virga):

1. While hiking, Too Slow Joe places both trekking poles in one hand.
2. Too Slow Joe reaches around to access water bottle from side pocket of pack, but cannot reach the bottle effectively.
3. Too Slow Joe stops hiking.
4. Too Slow Joe again reaches around to access water bottle from side pocket of pack, but still cannot access it.
5. Too Slow Joe disengages chest strap buckle.
6. Too Slow Joe disengages hip belt buckle.

7. Too Slow Joe takes off pack.
8. Too Slow Joe places pack on ground.
9. Too Slow Joe reaches down to pocket area.
10. Too Slow Joe loosens side compression strap covering the water bottle pocket.
11. Too Slow Joe removes water bottle from pocket.
12. Too Slow Joe unscrews cap from water bottle.
13. Too Slow Joe lifts water bottle to mouth.
14. Too Slow Joe drinks from water bottle.
15. Too Slow Joe drops water bottle away from mouth.
16. Too Slow Joe replaces cap on water bottle.
17. Too Slow Joe places water bottle back into side pocket.
18. Too Slow Joe tightens side compression strap.
19. Too Slow Joe lifts pack and puts it back on.
20. Too Slow Joe re-engages hip belt buckle.
21. Too Slow Joe re-engages chest strap buckle.
22. Too Slow Joe starts hiking again.

Imagine that! Twenty-two distinct actions simply to get a drink of water on the trail! You can probably appreciate the number of actions that goes into more complex tasks like cooking a meal or pitching a tarp.

Habit Reformation

Reforming habits is not always easy. Often, it requires a change in conscious thinking about the order in which you perform certain actions or simply the elimination of certain (superfluous) actions as you complete a task.

However, habit reformation can be accomplished in simple ways as well, such as by carefully selecting your gear to suit a more efficient hiking style. For the illustration of Too Slow Joe above, habit reformation could have been achieved in one of several ways. The three primary options that were considered include:

1. Replacing his pack with a model that allowed for easier side pocket access.

2. Modifying one side pocket on the pack to allow for easier side pocket access.
3. Replacing a conventional water bottle with a hydration system.

After analyzing the impact that each of these three options had on efficiently drinking water while on the trail, as well as other tasks (such as collecting water for purification or dispensing water into a cookpot for a meal), option 2 was chosen. The solution involved replacing one elastic side pocket on the pack with one made with non-elastic fabric in a roomier shape, and with a shorter height, allowing for easy access to the bottle while hiking. The key to the redesign of the pocket was making sure the compression strap remained functional but did not interfere with pocket access. Thus, the compression strap was threaded in a sleeve behind the pocket. It remained adjustable by providing access behind the pocket to the ladder-locking adjustment buckle. One additional adjustment was made: We replaced a screw-off cap with a pop-top cap that could be opened and closed easily with his teeth.

The result was a dramatic increase in the efficiency of this task without significantly affecting the performance of the rest of the hiker's gear system or technique:

1. Joe reaches around to access his water bottle from side pocket of pack.
2. Joe removes water bottle from pocket.
3. Joe lifts water bottle to mouth.
4. Joe pops top of water bottle cap open with teeth.
5. Joe drinks from water bottle.
6. Joe pushes the water bottle cap closed with teeth.
7. Joe lowers water bottle.
8. Joe places water bottle back into side pocket.

Thus, with minor changes Too Slow Joe was able to reduce the number of steps involved in carrying out the task by more than 60%. Because the task was now able to be performed while hiking, it may have saved a significant amount of time over the course of the day by eliminating the need to stop, take off the pack, and drink. In actual practice, Too Slow Joe found that his previous difficulty in accessing the water bottle resulted in him drinking less. By making these changes in his hiking gear and style, he was able to drink more often and hike in a more hydrated state to increase his well being on the trail.

Habit Cementation

Habit cementation requires repetition of the newly formed habit until the conscious effort required to perform the action is minimized. The only way to cement habits is through experience. Just get out there and do it. Even if you practice on day hikes and backyard campouts, any experience you gain will be invaluable.

A Day in the Life

Here is another valuable exercise we require from all of our course participants. In this session, we ask everyone to write a detailed essay that describes the actions (in not quite as much detail as above) they perform from the moment they wake up in the morning to the moment they fall asleep. The essay details their perceptions of themselves at a level of efficiency that is much higher than their current practice. The essays are valuable tools. They are idealistic models of hiking efficiency that serve as a point of reference for reshaping hiking habits as outlined above (assessment, reformation, and cementation).

What follows is one of my own essays, written in the summer of 2003. It approximates the actual events of one very wet April morning in the backcountry of Montana's Madison Range.

The first memory I have of today is waking up two hours before dawn to the din of hard rain pounding against the roof of my poncho tarp, and feeling the rain spray hitting my face. I zipped up my bivy sack hood, rolled over to lay on my other side, and fell back asleep.

I wake up and open my eyes. It's still dark, and still raining. I roll over to lie on my back, and look at my watch: 5:25 AM. I reach down to my right pants pocket, pull out a tiny dropper bottle containing ophthalmic saline solution, and place a drop in each eye to lubricate my contact lenses. After screwing the dropper cap back on, I put the bottle into my essentials bag, which is lying in the hood of my bivy sack, and now gets tossed outside the bivy sack into what will become the nucleus of a "to pack" pile. This bag contains all of my essentials — first aid, toilet items, firestarting kit, water treatment chemicals — i.e., anything that is not clothing, sleeping, shelter, food, or cooking gear.

I pull my lighter out of my pants pocket, unzip the bivy about eight inches, reach a hand out, and light my alcohol stove, on which is already sitting a mug full of water. After dropping the windscreen cylinder over the pot and stove, I return the lighter back to my pants pocket and enjoy the gradually building symphony of the creaking titanium cup as it heats up. I retrieve a teabag from an odor-proof sack sitting in the head of my bivy with the rest of my breakfast and savor its rich aroma! When I peek out of the bivy to see water boiling, I reach out and drop the teabag into the pot, letting the alcohol burn out as the tea steeps. Finally, I unzip the rest of the bivy, turn over on my stomach, place my breakfast sack outside the bivy, and enjoy the glorious warmth of the day's first gulp. I savor the hot tea over the course of the next few minutes, uninterrupted by anything but my own contemplation as to what challenges lie ahead today. After the last gulp of tea, my wakeup ritual is complete.

I return the teabag to the breakfast sack. Within reach is my fuel bladder, which I use to refill the stove. I toss the bladder into the "to pack" pile. I grab my water bottle and fill the cook cup half full, toss the bottle into the "to pack" pile, place the pot on the stove, light the stove, set the windscreen in place again, and put the lighter into the essentials bag.

While waiting for my next pot of water to boil, I turn over on my back again, bring my knees up while wriggling my sleeping quilt down, and stuff the sleeping bag into its stow sack while in the bivy. When I'm done, I sit up, retrieve my empty backpack from underneath the foot of my bivy sack, and stow the bag immediately into the bottom of my backpack, which is then set aside next to my "to pack" pile.

I withdraw my legs from the bivy sack and swing them around to put my shoes on. I remove my sleeping pad from the bivy sack, and stow the bivy into the backpack, loosely on top of the sleeping bag. The sleeping pad is placed under the tarp as a sit pad.

I am wearing my hiking clothes (long pants, socks, and base layer shirt), followed by a windshirt and a synthetic insulating layer, wool hat, and wool gloves. It is raining hard and the DWR on my clothing can only withstand so much. Plus, my raingear is currently pitched as shelter. So I stand up and purposefully walk to where my bear bag is hanging. After taking my morning pee, I retrieve the bag, stow the cord into the bag, and walk back to my tarp. I place the bear bag in my "to pack" pile and sit down on the sleeping pad under the tarp, where it is dry.

The water has now boiled, so I take the pot off the stove, withdraw a bag of muesli from my breakfast sack, and add its contents to the pot and stir with the spoon that has been lying beside the stove since last night. Then I return the bag to the breakfast sack, which is now all garbage. I set the pot aside to let the cereal soften a bit.

I stuff my breakfast garbage down into the bottom of the bear bag and pull out my prepackaged lunch sack. I close the bear bag and place it inside the backpack on top of the sleeping bag and bivy sack. I withdraw a packet of carbohydrate gel and a breakfast bar from the lunch sack and put them in my pocket. The remaining contents, in the lunch sack, go into one of my pack's side pockets.

While eating my cereal, I watch the pale dark gray of a rainstorm sunrise begin to work its way on the horizon. When I finish eating, I fill my cup up with Cytomax (made the night before) from my other water bottle, and place that bottle into a side pocket. I drink it while scraping the sides of the cup. I roll my windscreen up and insert it into the cup, followed by the stove and spoon. I then stow the cook kit into a backpack side pocket with the fuel bottle.

I take off my insulating top and stow it in my clothing stow bag from my "to pack" pile, and place it inside the backpack. I will start hiking while wearing my hiking clothing, windshirt, hat, and gloves and, after I take it down, my poncho tarp.

The final items that are packed in the main packbag are my essentials bag and clean water bottle. I follow with my Cytomax water bottle (side pocket). I then squat under the tarp, fold up my torso pad, and place it into the pack's pad pocket. The pack stays under the tarp. It's still raining very hard.

While still under the poncho tarp, I drop the trekking poles supporting the poncho tarp and reset their lengths for hiking, placing them next to the pack under the tarp. I'm still dry! I exit the tarp, remove all of the tent stakes and undo the poncho hood. I slide back under the tarp, place the tent stakes in the bottom of the pack's rear pocket, and put the pack on (only the shoulder straps for now). Finally, I slide the hood opening of the poncho over my head, and buckle the hip belt of my pack. I now take my time and remove the guylines from the corners and sides of the tarp, and stuff them into the back pocket of my pants.

I snap the sides of the poncho together, tie its rear drawcord around my waist to secure it around the backpack as a pack cover, and off I go.

It is 5:50 AM.

Conclusion

The benefits of hiking efficiently are real.

- By purposefully considering the efficiency of actions required to complete a task, you can save significant time. Such time may be spent increasing the distance you walk or decreasing the time you spend hiking and increasing the time you spend in camp (according to your preference and style). For the long-distance hiker, efficiency is a prerequisite to completing maximum distances in minimum times, which ultimately can result in more mileage between resupply points, or less time spent covering a given distance.
- Hiking efficiently can save significant mental and emotional energy, increase your free time, and minimize frustration borne from using inefficient gear or practicing inefficient technique.

In conclusion, hiking efficiently requires some effort on your part to assess old habits, and reform and cement new ones. It is an advanced skill that is not easily taught or learned. It requires experience, a careful assessment of hiking gear and how it is best used, and knowledge of the full spectrum of lightweight (and efficient) hiking and camping techniques.

Citation

This chapter was originally published as an article in the online magazine Backpacking-Light.com (ISSN 1537-0364) in May 2004.

Chapter 17:
Lightweight Backpacking
with Young Children

By Stephanie and Ryan Jordan

Introducing your child to the wonders of nature is one thing. Helping them enjoy themselves while preserving your own sanity on a backpacking trip is quite another.

Most parents view backpacking with a child as an arduous, masochistic experience by which Mom carries her screaming infant or drags her whining toddler (or both!) up a dusty trail, while Dad shoulders a 100-pound pack containing gear for the entire family. While this style of family hiking may not lead directly to divorce, it's certainly going to be unpleasant.

So, let's do it a different way. We'd like to offer some ideas and insights for parents that have not yet made the plunge into backpacking with their kids and are still blessed with naiveté. At the same time, maybe we can help those that have already experienced the pain and rage of doing it the hard way. And hopefully, even you moms and dads capable of planning and executing flawless adventures with your kids can extract some tidbits to help you on your next hike. (Note: if you fall into this last category, don't tell anybody. They won't believe you).

Backpacking with kids offers an opportunity for bonding, teaching, and escape from a world littered with too much social stimuli.

Hiking Considerations

PACE

Infants can't walk, and letting them crawl to your destination is neither timely nor hygienic. So that means Mom's going to carry the baby in a backpack and Dad's going to shoulder the rest of the gear. Dad may be shocked at the realization that he's not going to get to carry the same sub-20-pound pack that he gets to carry on a summer trip with his buddies, but rules are rules! The bottom line: You're both going to be shouldering some weight, so slow down, take it easy, and lower your mileage expectations.

Toddlers, on the other hand, can walk. There are two major problems when hiking with toddlers. First, they hike slower and tire more quickly than adults. Second, they have ideas of their own about the route you carefully planned at the kitchen table. Distractions like bugs, moss, and maybe even decaying animal carcasses can all cause deviations from your path.

Our experience is that as a result of these issues, you can only count on hiking about 2–4 miles per day, a little more for school-age children or if you are carrying your infant on your back. Perhaps a little less for preschoolers.

More important than the number of miles you hike is the amount of time you spend on the trail.

If your family can walk 5 or 8 miles a day, great! Realistically, however, you probably should try to limit your time on the trail. You don't want to rush to flee camp in the mornings, and you don't want to be setting up camp and cooking dinner in the dark. Give your kids the time to enjoy camping and playing in the wilderness, not just hiking in it. A good rule of thumb for summer: Spend about four to five hours on the trail, with plenty of trail time built in for breaks and play.

PACKS FOR PARENTS AND KIDS

Face the facts, Dad. You aren't going to fit your family's load into the latest 30-liter fastpacking rucksack, nor should you be shouldering all that weight with a frameless pack. But all is not lost. There are plenty of large-enough capacity backpacks that weigh less than 4 pounds and easily carry a 40–50 pound load. Try a Granite Gear Nimbus Ozone (60L and 48 oz), the GoLite Infinity (50L and 37 oz), or a custom-fitted and made-to-order pack from the McHale Pack Company (50–80L at 40–60 oz).

When hiking with an infant, Mom will usually carry the baby in a backpack. The most popular models are made by Madden and Kelty and are absurdly heavy at 7–9 pounds. Unfortunately, this remains one of the last uncharted markets for lightweight gear, so your choices are limited. Get a baby pack with enough additional capacity for a few extras, like diapers, baby wipes, and a water bottle for Mom. Plush models have room for a sleeping bag stowed into a lower compartment, which frees up a lot of space from Dad's pack for denser (and heavier!) items.

Toddlers aren't going to be too enthusiastic about carrying a "fair share" of gear for the family, and you're not going to be enthused if they poop out a quarter mile from the car and refuse to carry their pack or walk one more step! So, give the little ones a break and set them up with tiny packs like the CamelBak Skeeter, a hydration pack with a 35-ounce capacity ideally suited for preschoolers and kindergartners. For younger school-age children, step up to something with some cargo capacity like the CamelBak Scout (10L and 35 oz). Older kids can graduate to a 20L rucksack and carry their own sleeping gear and clothing with a liter of water and some snacks, usually not to exceed 10 pounds.

My Favorite Things about Backpacking
AN INTERVIEW WITH CHASE JORDAN

RJ: Chase, I need to ask you some questions about an article we're writing for BackpackingLight.com.

CHASE: Oh.

RJ: I want to chat with you about lightweight backpacking.

CHASE: OK. Are you going to take my picture and show the Internet?

RJ: Sure, buddy. Whatever you want.

CHASE: OK. I want it to be a big picture.

RJ: How old are you, Chase?

CHASE: I'm five.

RJ: Do you like backpacking?

CHASE: Oh, yes!

RJ: What is your favorite place to go in the wilderness?

CHASE: Yellowstone National Park. I love to see buffalo by my tent.

RJ: What is your favorite thing to do when you go backpacking?

CHASE: Roast marshmallows!

RJ: What do you like to do when it's raining?

CHASE: Get in the tent. I like to read stories and play with my trucks in the tent with my dad.

RJ: Do you have a rain jacket?

CHASE: I have a poncho, but I don't really like it. It's black.

My dad made it. Black was all he had. I like my winter snow coat the best. It's red.

RJ: Do you like it when it snows on backpacking trips?

CHASE: Yeah. I like making snowmen and igloos!

RJ: What's your favorite food that you like to eat while hiking?

CHASE: Let's see here . . . peanuts and raisins, I think.

RJ: What's your favorite dinner food when you are in camp?

CHASE: Macaroni and cheese, with no hot sauce.

RJ: Do you carry a backpack?

CHASE: Yeah—a water backpack.

RJ: What kind of stuff is in your backpack?

CHASE: Water and stuff. But I like to carry one of my dad's trekking poles—they're really superlight—and my whistle around my neck. That's my favorite thing to put around my neck because the scarf my mom and dad make me wear is way too itchy.

RJ: Wow, all that stuff sounds heavy. Is it heavy?

CHASE: Yeah, but my dad carries all the really heavy stuff, like the tent and food and, um . . . oh yeah, my trucks.

RJ: I suppose you think you need some new lightweight backpacking gear, right?

CHASE: Oh yes! I would like a new water pack—a big one. I'm going to put water in it, and also my snacks, my notepad (I bring just a little one), and maybe a can of pop. Does a new pack cost a lot of money?

RJ: It depends, buddy. You see, there are Spectra fabrics that tend to be rather expensive due to the cost of fiber construction, difficulty in cutting and sewing, etc. And then, you have ultralight silnylon, which is very slippery, and that can drive up the cost. Or you can go to a new high-tech X-Pac from Dimension-Polyant that offers unparalleled rip resistance and very good abrasion resistance at a paltry 4 ounces a yard. But I think you need a custom McHale, which can run upward of $600 by the time you add shovel pockets, ski slots, fanny-compatible top pockets, multiple frames for different loads, and several hip belts to suit a particular trip style. And you may want to consider a sewn-in hydration pocket, rather than a removable one since —

CHASE: Do they have red ones?

RJ: Oh, yes!

Trip Planning and Navigation

It's important to involve your children in trip planning. Bring out the maps, show them some photos, and let them select some options (that you have previously screened, of course). Give them some ownership in the itinerary. For toddlers and older kids, destinations are very important. They give the child a sense of accomplishment. Destinations involving water (streams, lakes, or swamps) can save a parent's sanity by giving the child endless opportunities for exploration of aquatic life, rock throwing targets, and sailboat races. Always remember, of course, that parents must pay special attention to the safety of their children around any water body.

On the trail, involve your children in navigation decisions. If they know the difference between right and left, then show them trail junctions on the map as you reach them on the trail, and help them figure out the right way to go based on the route. It is helpful to trace your route with a highlighter on the map prior to the trip. As your child reaches the age of five or six, you can begin introducing the use of a compass. Orient the map for them, and help them choose between obvious directions, like east and west. Best of all, whether your children know how to use a compass or not, arm them with small compasses on their wrists or around their necks. They will feel like hikers.

INCLEMENT CONDITIONS

When we talk to other parents about backpacking with children, their greatest fear, by a large margin, is always, "What do we do if it rains?!" Prior to backpacking trips, many moms are often glued to the Weather Channel, secretly hoping for a hurricane-class forecast so they can justify cancellation of the trip, rather than face the challenges that come with cold and wet conditions.

These fears are rational. It can be difficult enough staying warm and dry in inclement conditions without having to worry about your kids. Parents' protective instincts instill a sense of responsibility to make sure your kids remain warm and dry, which can be very challenging. In this section, we offer some advice to deal with wet and cold conditions, as well as the midday heat of summer.

DEALING WITH RAIN

Hiking in the rain can be a wonderful experience for a child. Rain brings out wildlife of all sorts, from big game to slimy worms. But being wet and cold can be a miserable experience for a child. A little preparation and an understanding of a child's low tolerance for discomfort can improve everyone's disposition dramatically.

First, dress to get wet. Combined with a fleece balaclava and some waterproof mittens, a hooded poncho (nylon is far more durable than plastic) worn over a fleece jacket and long underwear can keep a child warm and dry for hours. On the bottoms, synthetic long underwear and waterproof or water-resistant pants are usually sufficient. For the feet, a pair of thick wool socks for warmth and some water-resistant (not mesh) shoes are a far better alternative than rubber boots, especially while hiking.

Try to encourage your children to minimize their natural sprint-and-stop technique. Hiking slowly and continuously will minimize sweating and the subsequent chilling that results when taking a break. If you are taking longer breaks in inclement conditions—a lunch break or simply to wait out a storm—consider setting up a tent or tarp, and even the child's sleeping bag, to give them a warm and safe refuge that minimizes their discomfort.

When camping, nothing provides better refuge from the elements than a tent. Most children (and parents) feel safer and more secure when surrounded by fabric. During an intense storm with high winds, a tent will keep your little campers happy.

Above all, when the weather turns bad, small children shouldn't be expected to just "deal with" being uncomfortable. You bear 100 percent of the responsibility to keep them warm, dry, and comfortable.

DEALING WITH COLD

Dealing with cold requires that your child has proper clothing and a warm sleeping bag. Consistent with lightweight backpacking principles, there is no reason not to combine the two while sleeping, to take advantage of available insulation at the lightest weight. We've come up with a recommended list of summer clothing and sleep gear that will keep most children warm in conditions down to freezing.

Clothing Worn While Hiking

- Supplex nylon shirt (long sleeve) and long pants to protect them from sun, brush, and wind
- Wool socks with comfortable shoes
- Wide-brimmed hat for sun protection
- Sunglasses

Base Layer

- Lightweight synthetic long underwear, top and bottoms
- Consider doubling up on these two items if your kids have bed-wetting challenges or you are expecting extra cold or wet conditions

Mid Layers

- Fleece jacket, 200 or 300 weight
- Consider 100–200 weight fleece pants for cold conditions
- An additional mid layer to give you the flexibility to adjust warmth according to expected temperatures

and can be from a 100-weight fleece vest to a high-loft synthetic insulating jacket

Outer Layer

- Nylon rain jacket with waterproof pants, or
- Poncho with water-resistant pants

Sleeping Bag

- Synthetic bag (e.g., Polarguard, PrimaLoft), at least 2 inches of loft for conditions down to freezing.
- Our choice? The Integral Designs Assiniboine.

If temperatures drop dramatically, parents can further increase the comfort of their kids by using their sleeping bags as quilts and sharing body heat.

DEALING WITH HEAT

One experience that may have a higher misery factor than dealing with a child that is cold and wet is dealing with one that is hot, tired, thirsty, and cranky!

One item that can help is a hydration bladder, complete with a hose and bite valve. (For safety reasons, be sure to follow manufacturer recommendations about age appropriateness). Kids love to drink out of their own container. If they carry it themselves, you can be assured that they will get plenty to drink. Add some flavor to that drink, such as presweetened Kool-Aid, Crystal Light, or Flavors2Go drops, and they'll thank you for it. Not a fan of sweetened drinks at home? Some products also come in unsweetened varieties. But consider making an exception while backpacking. The additional calories and flavors will motivate your child to remain hydrated, far outweighing the disadvantages of the sugar.

In the previous gear list, we recommended long-sleeve shirts and long pants for clothing. We are big advocates of keeping your kids' skin exposure to the harmful rays of UV light at a bare minimum, especially in the thin air of the mountains. If temperatures are too hot and your child is uncomfortable wearing this type of clothing, then maybe you should consider shadier trails, cloudier weather, or some hardcore sunscreen, frequently applied. Regardless of your hiking clothing choices, make sure your child has a wide-brimmed sun hat and a pair of sunglasses.

Some other tips for hiking in the heat:

- Let them cool off in a creek or lakeside at midday.
- Arm family members with spray bottles or squirt guns and have occasional water fights along the trail. Getting your clothing and skin wet will aid evaporative cooling.

Meal Planning and Cooking

One of the great challenges of backpacking with kids is ensuring that they consume plenty of nutritional calories. For anything shorter than a weeklong excursion, place more emphasis on calories than nutrition. Like adults, children need to maintain steady caloric intake to offset their daily activity and fuel their metabolic engines.

Only experience will tell you about the food quantities to pack, types of food your child will eat on the trail (a safe bet is to bring what they like at home as well), and timing of meals. Emphasize frequent snacks, rather than three squares served rigidly at 8:00 am, noon, and 6:00 pm.

For parents new to hiking with children, a good rule of thumb for quantity is to bring

- 12–16 ounces of food per day (dry weight) for toddlers ages 3–6
- 20 ounces/day for young children age 7–10
- 24 ounces/day (or more) for children in rapid growth spurts that commonly occur between the ages 11–13.
- All bets are off for teenagers, who can seemingly fast for days and then eat 3 pounds of food at the drop of a hat.

As far as types of food to pack, err on the side of maximum variety, rather than gamble on the improbability that your child will be able to extract his entire caloric needs from a huge bag of gorp. Likewise, as much as you want your children to consume organic foods, whole grains, and hormone-free dry milk, cut them some slack and toss in some red licorice or Jolly Ranchers. They will thank you for it with their wide eyes, and you will thank yourself for their good morale.

As for timing, go with small meals for breakfast and dinner, with plenty of variety snacks that the child can freely access throughout the day. Children burn calories in spurts. Likewise, they tend to eat in spurts.

Parents with infants have to deal with other issues. Breast-feeding moms have it best (although some may argue) with ready-to-eat food that doesn't have to be packed! For infants eating soft foods, parents are limited to baby foods sold in very heavy jars. For short trips, these foods can be repackaged into small plastic containers that are far lighter. For maximum weight savings, repackage the foods in zip-closure bags (e.g., O.P. Saks), but keep in mind that repackaging baby foods compromises their sterility and shouldn't be practiced for trips longer than a weekend in warm temperatures.

For bottle-fed babies, parents have two options: washable bottles or bottles with disposable liners. Bottle "cages" with enough disposable liners for a weekend trip are lighter than regular bottles by 50 percent. Better yet, disposable liners can be pre-filled with formula or dry milk at home, so mealtime—and cleanup—is about as simple as can be.

WATER PURIFICATION AND HYDRATION

We tend to be more cautious about the quality of water that our children drink than the quality of water we drink. Children have immune systems that tend to be more susceptible to foreign organisms simply because of their lack of previous exposure to them. Parents should not allow their children to drink untreated water in the wilderness.

The safest and most effective form of water treatment technology for immuno-compromised patients continues to be ceramic-element filtration. Only two companies make water filters that offer uncompromised performance: MSR

(WaterWorks II) and Katadyn (Pocket Filter). Combined with low doses of chlorine dioxide (Aquamira) on post-filtered water, one ends up with water quality that often exceeds that coming out of your tap at home. We recommend this form of treatment for infants.

As children get older, their immune response strengthens. Thus, chemical treatment alone may be sufficient in mountain areas with good wilderness water quality (low organic and silt content). Our recommendation is Aquamira over iodine-based solutions. It has greater efficacy against bacteria and lower incidence of harmful byproduct creation. Both chlorine bleach and iodine can form these byproducts — some of them carcinogenic — through oxidation of organic matter.

Many parents are lured into buying so-called water purification products that are promoted by the health food industry. These are sold under the description of "stabilized oxygen" and marketed under the premise that they are "chemical-free treatment alternatives for safe drinking water." After extensive research, we have been unable to find any reasonable scientific evidence from a credible research institution to support the claim that they are appropriate for wilderness water quality treatment, and cannot recommend them as a viable water treatment alternative, especially for immuno-compromised patients, infants, or children.

Personal Hygiene

DIAPERS

Parents of infants are often stricken with backcountry diaper terror when faced with the prospect of family backpacking. In reality, however, dealing with diapers can be a rather simple affair.

The choice between cloth and disposable diapers is the primary issue. Cloth diapers require washing, rinsing, and drying. That's often problematic and time consuming when faced with your own underwear — not to mention a pair that's been covered in fecal matter! It doesn't take long to realize that the time required to properly deal with washing a dirty cloth diaper while minimizing the environmental impact of disposing of the wash water is worth it only for those parents that ascribe to a stringent philosophy that, for one reason or another, prevents them from purchasing and throwing away disposables.

For us, the choice was a matter of convenience and hygiene. Fecal matter is simply cat-holed like your own, and then the disposable diapers are set out for a few hours each day to allow moisture to evaporate, thus reducing their weight. Transport is accomplished by placing the diapers in an odor-proof plastic bag with a secure zip-closure. We recommend 12-x-15 inch O.P. Saks from Watchful Eye Designs. The process of using disposables in the backcountry is a no-mess, no-fuss, low-impact, and healthy process for both baby and parents.

TREPIDATIONS OF WILDERNESS TOILETS

As children get older, they get to pee and poop like us big kids. For our son (and we are told, for most boys), there is little trepidation involved in letting it rip in the backcountry. Dad and son can make it competitive with distance contests. And the prospect of pooping in a hole that you dug with your foot, toy backhoe, or sand shovel, is high on the list of very cool things to do as a young boy.

We are told by other parents, however, that some boys and many girls experience a bit of performance anxiety when it comes to wilderness toileting. For these kids, some parents have even resorted to bringing potty chairs with a real toilet seat and plastic bag for the catch basin. At up to 4 pounds apiece, such chairs aren't high on the list of things lightweight backpacking parents like to bring into the backcountry. The alternative: some psychological skill in dealing with children, and a whole lot of patience. Barring rewards of chewable candy by the pound and promises of extra toys at Christmas, we've heard parents having good success by doing the side by side thing with Mom or Dad, which may give rise to a new axiom: "The family that poops together, stays together."

The Magic of Purell

There is an increasing body of evidence that suggests that more incidents of gastrointestinal illness in the backcountry can be attributed to poor hygiene than to inadequate water treatment. We would logically infer, then, that children are more susceptible to illnesses resulting from poor hygiene than adults, simply because hygiene is not ingrained in a child's daily habit! Consequently, we recommend that parents frequently ensure that their child's face and hands are clean, especially after using the toilet and before meals. While soap and water is most effective at removing dirt, alcohol hand gels (e.g., Purell) provide more effective disinfection of microorganisms, can be used anywhere—even in the absence of water—and air dry effectively. Most parents will find some combination of washing with soap and using alcohol hand gels useful. We use alcohol during the day, and then have a hands-and-face (and sometimes, whole body) wash while having access to water in camp in the evening.

Baby Wipes, Washcloths, and Other Towels

Baby wipes are a godsend to parents with infants. For diaper changing, wiping up food messes, dealing with spit-up, and cleaning up other liquefied masses well known to baby-parents, moist baby wipes are an ideal solution to cleanup. Because they are water-saturated, however, they tend to be heavy. Lighten the load by repackaging them in a zip-closure plastic bag. The upside is that they can be dried or burned while on the trail, and thus, can be considered a consumable. The biggest advantage of baby wipes are that they can be treated as a disposable, and thus, are consistent with good hygiene practices.

Dry wash towels that can be moistened and used for more rigorous cleanup chores can also be useful. Fortunately, those made of microfiber or viscose are very light and dry quickly. Check out the Pack-Towl line from Cascade Designs, or our favorites: the 0.5-ounce ultralight towels available from Light-load Towels.

Shelter Considerations

Most parents, even those who normally practice what we consider lightweight backpacking techniques, would never consider taking their kids into the backcountry without a tent. Let's take a closer look at the rationale for this decision and assess whether or not tarp camping is something that can be appropriate for parents with young children.

Parents possess a natural protective instinct that engages whenever cold, wet, windy, or snowy weather comes within miles of the warmth of a car heater. Consequently, the walls of a tent provide a sense of security and home for a backpacking family that gives them a tiny environment in which they can be safe, warm, dry, and content. Having backpacked with our son in both tents and tarps, I can recommend without reservation that a lightweight tent should be the first choice for beginning parents or parents of infants and/or small children traveling in backcountry areas with the potential for foul weather.

TARP CAMPING WITH KIDS

Unless you have an exceptional level of skill and experience tarp camping yourself, please do not consider subjecting infants and young children to the rigors of exposure to wind, blowing rain, and drifting snow while camping in a tarp. If you and your kids are tarp-camping aficionados (and we certainly are), do so in the midst of a fair weather forecast, with the opportunity to bail out readily available. There is no worse misery while camping with kids than having them be cold, wet, and cranky because wind and rain are blowing into the protective space that should provide complete comfort and shelter.

A Small Tarp for Refuge

During prolonged periods of inclement weather, both parents and kids can go a little "shacky wacky" in the confines of a tent. A light tarp, brought as a supplement to the primary shelter, can provide some fresh air during rainy periods, as well as some refuge for cooking or playing. We have often brought a 5´-x-7´ silnylon tarp in addition to our lightweight tent when we knew there would be a good chance for foul weather. Set up as a vestibule across the front of our tent, it served as an ideal "porch" for refuge from the rain.

Sleeping Pads

Some naïve parents believe that a sleeping pad no thinner than a toddler bed is required for backcountry camping. Common sense, however, dictates that children lose heat to the ground similarly to their bigger counterparts, and that no additional insulation from conductive heat loss to the ground surface is necessarily needed. In fact, there is some scientific evidence that supports a higher level of cold tolerance in children than in adults—attributed to something akin to a survival mechanism. For the lightweight backpacking family, this is all good news. Further, smaller pads are needed for smaller people, so there is weight savings to be made in this department as well!

The choice between inflatable sleeping pads (e.g., Therm-A-Rest brand) and closed-cell foam pads is more a matter of parent's desire for children's comfort than a matter of safety or warmth. We tend to compromise between the two, using a thicker (0.5 inch) closed-cell foam pad for our son, after learning that nighttime migratory behavior inherent in children means that they easily slip off the slick nylon surfaces of inflatable mattresses. You can alleviate some slippage by adding stripes or dots of McNett SilNet or SeamGrip, but such measures are not likely going to arrest the migration of your child throughout the night unless she sleeps between you.

Camping Activities

Stockpiling an arsenal of lightweight activities to keep children busy in camp is not as hard as it sounds. Parents often think that they have to bring their home to the wilderness by packing a multitude of toys, favorite stories, and handheld games for the purpose of ensuring constant entertainment for their children. For most backpacking families, however, children are often entranced by what nature has to offer and are creative enough on their own (perhaps with some parent facilitation) to make the outdoors an ideal playground sans props.

Collecting leaves, bugs, and rocks has probably entertained more children visiting the backcountry than any other activity. As children grow older, you have an opportunity to teach them about the natural world that can help them appreciate their collecting habit even more.

Looking for animal tracks is one of our favorite activities, and a plaster of Paris cast kit weighs only a few ounces and provides a memento from the trip. After the plaster has dried, it can even be painted in the backcountry—or you can wait until you get home.

If you are near running water, a great way to spend creative time is to make sailboats from natural materials. We sometimes bring along some extra string or wire and a few 6-piece sections from an egg carton to serve as the hull. This activity can occupy our son for hours, as he builds a boat and sends it down the "rushing" waters of a tiny brook.

For school-age children, photography can be a great way for a child to record their own trip. Combined with their own paper journal and pencil, encouraging them to write about, draw, and photograph their memories helps them appreciate their backpacking adventure more fully. Disposable cameras and cheap, hand-me-down digital cameras are our lightweight favorites for kids.

Fishing a lake or creek in camp that is filled with mountain brook or cutthroat trout, of course, can require little more gear than a stick, a six-foot section of line, and a bushy fly. The simplicity of such a fishing kit means that young children can operate it by themselves, and you won't be burdened carrying large amounts of heavy fishing gear if your child loses interest.

We still love to read to our son when away from home. We often let him bring his choice of one book, and we supplement that with a small field guide to local flora and fauna. During the day, we can use the field book to identify flowers, insects, or birds. Then before bedtime, we review what we saw by looking at pictures in the book—and often, redrawing them in his own "notebook."

Campfires, of course, provide great security for children. Where permitted, and when conditions warrant, a campfire before bedtime helps the family unwind from a long day with a relaxing way to share their favorite things about the trip, stargaze, and perhaps roast a few marshmallows.

Safety Considerations

Safety need not be compromised while taking your children into the backcountry, and thus, lightweight equipment is just as applicable for backpacking with kids as it is for backpacking with adults. However, safety must always be considered first. Don't use the same standards for safety with kids that you would use for yourself.

Preparation for inclement weather is perhaps the most important consideration when backpacking with kids. You, as parents, are solely responsible for your child's safety and appropriate use of their clothing. Parents having no experience dealing with inclement weather on their own should not gain those first experiences with their children without a suitable "bailout" option (e.g., backyard or car camping).

THE WHISTLE

Arm your child with a loud whistle, worn at all times on a lanyard around her neck, and instruct her on how to use it. We have ingrained in our son what it means to be lost (when you can't find Mom or Dad), and what to do: Stop, blow your whistle three times, and listen for a response from our whistle — then repeat.

BEAR COUNTRY

Hiking in grizzly country with young children who cannot defend themselves — or are unable to defend you — is not recommended. Grizzlies are simply too unpredictable. When is a child old enough to hike in grizzly country? This question is impossible to answer, as there are plenty of ignorant adults out there that are unprepared for hiking in grizzly country! Our rule for hiking with others that want to bring their kids into grizzly country: Both parents and children have to be well-practiced in the use of bear spray, and the parents have to be able to trust their child's skills enough to defend them in case of an attack. In our experience, the age at which this occurs is usually between 12 and 15.

BACKYARD AND CAR CAMPING PRACTICE

The best way for families to learn how to backpack is to get out and do it. When reducing your pack weight and evaluating lighter gear, you may want to practice using it, especially in inclement conditions, while car camping or in your backyard. Most children who enjoy backcountry camping get a kick out of backyard and car camping, as well. It offers the family an additional outlet for outdoor enjoyment without the commitment and logistics associated with entering the backcountry.

Conclusion

This chapter cannot hope to deal with all of the issues involved in backpacking with young children. We hope that we've offered you a framework that encourages you to introduce your kids to the backcountry using lightweight gear and techniques that do not sacrifice your family's safety. Further, we are confident that with experience, you will develop your own style and make smart decisions about your gear.

Our final rule of thumb for hiking with kids: Know when to bail. Whether you are camping in your backyard, out of the trunk of your car, or are at 10,000 feet in the Sierra wilderness, you're bound to encounter conditions, situations, weather, and environment that contribute to the demise of morale. If nobody's having a good time, go home, regroup, and try again. Family backpacking should be fun. Lighter weight gear can make it even more fun — especially the hiking part. But the key is to enjoy the wilderness together, not just endure it.

Citation

This chapter was originally published as an article in the online magazine BackpackingLight.com (ISSN 1537-0364) in October 2003.

Chapter 18:
Lightweight Backpacking
for Couples

By Alison Simon and Alan Dixon

Most of us do not venture into the backcountry alone. Sharing the outdoors with another person heightens our outdoor experience. That person can be a spouse, friend, parent, brother, sister, or child. Going into the wilderness with a spouse may be the ultimate expression of togetherness. This chapter will focus on the delights and challenges of going into the backcountry with that special person in your life.

OK, so this is about ultralight backpacking and you're expecting this article to jump right into the good stuff — gear selection — right? And yes, there are a lot of cool things you can do with ultralight gear for two, but you'll need to wait a few paragraphs while we cover the true basics of couples backpacking.

First, we'll cover the most important thing about traveling with two: Traveling together is a partnership.

Nothing can make a trip better or worse than the dynamics between two close people. Nothing is more delightful than when you and your partner are in sync together. When you're in a groove, even a rainy day's hike can be a delight. But nothing is less fun than when you and your partner are in a funk. When you are irritated and squabbling with each other, no amount of natural beauty, clement weather, or fancy ultralight gear can do much to improve the situation.

To keep the joy in our backcountry travel we have one simple rule, "If either of us is not having fun, we stop and make a new plan." Each of us has the unilateral right to invoke it. Each of us has trust in the other to know that the request will be gracefully honored. This rule has stood the test of time. Nobody is in charge and nobody abdicates responsibility. Backpacking is a joint effort that requires flexible and synchronized input from both of us. If one of us is having a slow day, doesn't want to do that class-three, 13,000-foot col, or maybe one of us wants to bag an unplanned summit; or possibly we just need a day to swim, fish, and relax; we stop what we are doing and come up with a new plan. Without exception, the new plan is much better than what we were doing before. Not every trip is what we expected from the

Jubilation. Alan Dixon and Alison Simon at the top of a 13,000 foot summit. Not much suffering here – just jubilation. Note our light windshirts. Even at noon in full sunlight it was windy and cold enough that we needed them to stay warm while climbing up the mountain.

start, but each trip ends up being the best trip we could have.

Other Couples

Herein, we offer only one of many ways to backpack as a couple. We thought readers would like to look at some other approaches, so we've invited perspectives from other experienced backpacking couples: Jim and Amy Lauterbach, and Ryan and Stephanie Jordan. We've received excellent advice from them. Much of what we do originated from these sage veterans, who offer a combined 34 years of experience backpacking as couples. You will find a section on each of them at the end of this article.

Overview and Gear Selection

Enough philosophizing on traveling together! On to gear and technique. One of our biggest shared pleasures is doing the gear thing. Both of us enjoy researching, testing, and selecting just the right gear for a trip. For example, we spent a whole afternoon setting up different shelters at a local playing field before picking just the right one for our last trip. Our criterion for equipment is that it must be as light as possible, but also keep us happy and comfortable. Neither of us is remotely interested in going on a suffer fest.

Our combined base pack weight is usually less than 16 pounds. For a five-day trip in the mountains, loaded with fuel, food, GPS, camera, fishing stuff, and miscellany, Alison's pack weighs less than 15 pounds. Alan's weighs less than 18. With this gear, we expect to be warm, comfortable, amply equipped to cover difficult cross-country terrain, and capable of camping above the treeline in inclement conditions. We can even catch fish for dinner. We always have a great time and do not lack for much in safety, comfort, or enjoyment.

We selected our gear for a typical summer to early fall trip in the Sierra Nevada Mountains of California. We like to do as much higher elevation cross-country travel as possible — especially through high cols and over peaks — but we

The **benefits of a light pack**. Alan on his way to the summit. Since the mountain was on our way to the next drainage, we carried our full packs to the top. No sweat!

stop short of technical climbing that requires ropes! We love to camp above treeline, enjoying the exposure to the winds and cooler temperatures of higher elevations. As such, we do like warm clothing and a lofty sleeping bag. But because it's the Sierras in the summer, we don't expect much rain. The most likely precipitation is a strong afternoon thunderstorm and we're equipped accordingly. We have enough clothing and gear to stay warm overnight and hike out the next day if we get a freak summer snowstorm. Also, since one of us has a very low tolerance for bugs, our shelter has to be a mosquito proof haven for our lower elevation camps.

SLEEPING BAG

On our first backpacking trip together we took two single-person sleeping bags, but eventually migrated to a single narrow mummy bag (Western Mountaineering Ultralight) used quilt-style, which proved to be an adequate arrangement for a close couple down to about 40 degrees. A small mummy bag like this might not be the best choice at cooler temperatures, due to its inability to control drafts.

After that trip, we considered getting a wider semi-rectangular bag that unzipped all the way around the bottom to make a flat quilt. After some research we got a 45-ounce, 600-fill-power, semi-rectangular down bag with about 3.5 inches of loft, a North Face Chrysalis (sadly, no longer in production). This arrangement works out to less than 1.5 pounds per person. We purchased the bag on closeout for $150, which kept our wallet shrinkage to a minimum. The Chrysalis keeps us warm in below freezing temperatures, at over 11,000 feet, under a tarp, and in windy conditions. What more can you ask from a couples bag?

Our sleeping system. A semi-rectangular bag spread out as a quilt. A Therm-A-Rest pad and a Mt. Washington foam pad linked by Therm-A-Rest Couplers, and a Campmor Emergency blanket as a ground pad. Warm, light, and comfortable.

An option that should be considered by any serious back-packing couple is the 26-ounce down Back Country Blanket from Nunatak. It can shave a pound or more — each — off your sleep system and would cost about $315. For a more couples-friendly, semi-custom blanket that is wider (approximately 32 ounces), you could expect to pay $400 and wait three months, so plan early! Nunatak also makes a more traditional two-person bag, the Dual-Person Alpinist, which weighs 50 ounces and costs $533. Yet another Nunatak bag is the lighter Dual-Person Arc-Alpinist, which could easily come in at under two pounds.

For those of you looking for a bargain, Campmor's +20-degree semi-rectangular bag is only $125. Be warned that it has less loft than the Chrysalis and probably will not meet its +20°F specification unless you and your partner are hardy sleepers. Some couples have used a Western Mountaineering semi-rectangular bag and sewn a simple 1.1-ounce nylon sheet on the bottom. There are plenty of other semi-rectangular mummy bags on the market. One of them may work for you. Try to stay clear of zipping two bags together, unless they are very light bags. Most zip-together bags tend to be heavy, and you'll have the expense of two bags instead of one. Obviously, there are even more options if you want to get creative and are handy sewing baffles or dealing with eiderdown clusters all over your house.

SLEEPING PADS AND GROUNDSHEETS

Couples will immediately notice that ground pads tend to slowly drift apart during the night. One or both of you will end up in the cold, hard rift between the pads. Cascade Designs has a simple solution: Therm-A-Rest Couplers. A pair of these light and simple straps will keep most 20-inch wide pads closely attached. You can mix and match pads, including Therm-A-Rests, Ridgerests, Z-Rests, and most other 20-inch pads on the market. Other people have sewn special pockets and holders onto the bottom of their sleeping bags. Yet a third option is to use two Link Rests. These pads lock together with puzzle-shaped edges and require no straps. They are, however, a bit heavier than most foam pads.

Pad selection depends primarily on an individual's tolerance for comfort. Some can sleep fine on a 3/8-inch thick foamie the size of a jockey's torso (< 3 oz) while others demand the comfort of a full-length inflatable (20+ ounces). After Alison bruised both hips sleeping on a foam pad, she selected the new 3/4-length Therm-A-Rest ProLite 3 (13 oz). An even lighter inflatable solution: Bozeman Mountain Works Torsolite (10 oz). Alan still loves his now-discontinued 7-ounce Mt. Washington foam pad. The Therm-A-Rest Couplers do a great job of keeping our disparate pads together.

Since we use a floorless shelter, our groundsheet needs to be wide and reasonably water resistant. We use Campmor's Emergency Blanket. This huge groundsheet weighs only 5 ounces and has proved over numerous trips to be extremely tough. Another benefit is that it is soft, flexible, and stows to a small size.

SHELTER

In addition to their obvious protections, shelters provide privacy and a sense of home in the backcountry. We are keen on simple and light shelters. On our first trip, we used a floorless shelter with a center pole (GoLite Hex 2). Structurally, a center pole is a great idea and provides tremendous wind resistance for the shelter. However, the center pole is a curse for couples who like to sleep close. We ended up angling the bottom of the offending pole toward one side of the tent and sleeping cramped together on the wider side, placing our gear on the narrower side.

A bit wiser now, we use the Henry Shires Squall Tarptent. This shelter, at 1.5 pounds including stakes and guy lines, is almost as light as some two-person tarps but offers more advantages. The Squall has room for our packs and us, gives us sufficient privacy, provides adequate (as opposed to stellar) protection from a mountain thunderstorm, pitches more easily than a tarp, and offers excellent mosquito protection. The Squall is more stable in the wind than a tarp and does not rely on trekking poles or sticks to pitch. Since the shelter has no floor, we use the 5-ounce Campmor Emergency Blanket under our pad and bags. Shires' larger Cloudburst, at 33 ounces, with more room and rain protection, would be our choice for trips in climates with more rain and wind than the Sierras.

You can save a lot of weight if you use a tarp. An 8´-x-10´ tarp is airy and roomy. If you don't think you'll be in driving rain and can handle a few mosquitoes, it may be an ideal choice. GoLite's Cave 2 is the cult favorite of couples tarps,

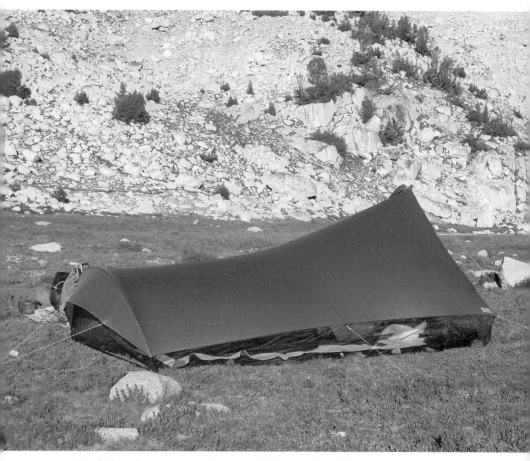

Our beloved nest, a Henry Shires Squall Tarptent. Only 90 seconds were required to get this catalog photo pitch. As you can see from the tautness of the pitch (in part due to a catenary's cut ridgeline), the tarp spills wind well. The mosquito netting preserved our sanity on the previous night when darkness forced us to camp in a lower, wetter, and bug-infested valley.

offering plenty of room with great protection from inclement weather for the skilled tarp pitcher. We are excited about some catenary-cut tarp designs (e.g., Oware and Granite Gear) as well. Another intriguing option is to take two poncho tarps and use them together to make one 8´-x-10´ tarp. Use your ponchos for both rainwear and shelter to save even more weight. Sleeping under the paired tarps is the Ritz of two-person tarping.

There are many other options for couple's shelters. Six Moon Designs makes the Europa II, a 33-ounce, single-wall tent. (Add a bit more weight for stakes and a front pole, unless you carry trekking poles.) It gets high marks from reviewers at BackpackingLight.com for its storm resistance and livability. GoLite's Den 2 and Trig 2 are additional options.

Double-wall tents for two haven't reached the sweet spot for light weight yet, but look for tents that weigh less than 5 pounds. When we interviewed other couples on this topic, we found that most enjoyed the added rain protection, resistance to high winds, and simplicity of a single-wall tent over the proposed major benefits of a double-wall tent — breathability and condensation resistance — which are highly debatable.

New single-wall tents made with lightweight breathable fabric, like Black Diamond's EPIC Firstlight, are closing the weight gap. At a bit over 2 pounds (with custom aftermarket carbon fiber poles) this tent provides the living space and storm resistance of some double-wall dome tents.

PACKS

Since we often travel cross-country above the treeline, there's a good possibility of a pack ripping in an accidental "butt slide" down scree or talus, or any other manner of mishap with sharp granite. We need packs that can take some abuse and still hold their contents. For instance, the thinner fabrics of ultralight packs may not survive close encounters with sharp granite. Of late, we have been evaluating Granite Gear's ultralight packs for our more rugged backpacking endeavors.

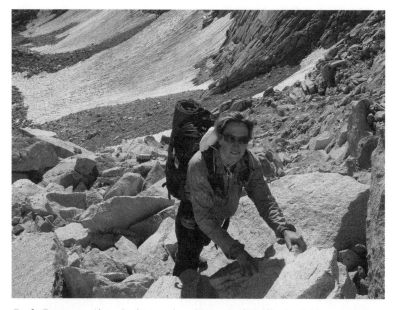

Pack Features. Alison finishing a class 3 section of a difficult col. A great place for a light pack to help you keep your balance. Also a good place to concentrate on where you put your hands and feet. And not the place you want to worry about babying your pack. Her light and rugged pack was a winner on all counts.

Alison, like many women, has tender shoulders and hips. She needs well-padded shoulder straps and a hip belt in order to comfortably carry the weight of the pack (even a lightweight one). She also needs enough of a frame to her pack so she can distribute most of the load to her hips. Grantite Gear's Vapor trail pack (2 lbs) works well. The pack has a good compression system that allows the pack to remain stable toward the end of multi-day trips as load volume decreases, and it has tough fabric in most areas prone to encounters with granite. Alison has a short torso (but a tall personality) and the small size Vapor Trail provides a good fit. Another benefit is the external hydration pocket between the pack frame and pack bag. Easy access to plenty of water improves relationship dynamics on hot, dry days!

Alan has tough shoulders and has successfully, but not necessarily comfortably, carried close to 30 pounds all day in his hip-beltless GoLite Breeze pack. (Yeah, it was a long day in the desert!). The Granite Gear Virga at 21 ounces is considerably more durable, has more comfortable shoulder straps, and a simple web hip belt. The pack's good compression system, when wrapped around his rolled ground pad inside the pack, provides excellent structure for a frameless rucksack. Alan admits that for carrying over 20 pounds, the Virga is more comfortable than his Breeze. Even so, for lighter loads and more moderate terrain, of if he is just plain feeling lucky, Alan may still opt for his Breeze.

CLOTHING

We both run a bit cold and have colder than normal hands and feet. Since we expect to be at high elevations where it is cold and windy we bring plenty of clothes to stay warm. The warmest pieces of gear we carry are our very light down jackets. The other piece of gear that you'd have a hard time prying from our cold dead torsi, is a very light windshirt. For 90 percent of cold dry weather above treeline, we'll hike in our base layer and a windshirt. If it's really cold, we'll add our fleece layer. No combination is better for keeping you warm and sweat free.

Since down is useless when wet, we use our wicking, top base layer and a fleece layer under a rain jacket in the unlikely case of precipitation. Also, we don't expect to be in the rain all that long. In foul weather we intend to quit hiking and pitch a shelter at the earliest opportunity. We have soft shell pants that shed rain reasonably well and have a napped inner surface for added wicking and warmth. The pants are warm enough that we don't bring a bottom base layer or rain pants for summer trips.

For colder and/or wetter climates than the Sierras we might switch to a synthetic parka like GoLite's Coal and bring a more substantial rain jacket and pants.

Cooking, Food, and Water

For us, cooking is an integral part of the mutual mountain experience. Sharing a hot cup of tea in the morning or a warm homemade dinner is a crucial part of the esprit de corps.

Also, since both of us are fond of fish, we bring a fly rod, intending to catch some mountain trout for lunch or dinner. So no skimping on cooking equipment or fuel for us! We take a 3-ounce canister stove, a pair of titanium mugs, a 1.5-liter titanium pot, and plenty of fuel.

From experience, we know that Alan needs about 1.7 pounds of food a day, and Alison about 1.5 pounds. We both aim for around 120 to 125 calories/ounce from our food. When we pack this much food we usually have enough breakfast to make it out on the last day by early afternoon — not starving, but with a healthy appetite for a hearty restaurant dinner.

Alan can pretty much eat the same food day in and out. Alison enjoys a much greater variety of foods. We each pack our own breakfasts and lunches but carefully plan our shared dinners to have enough variety to please us both. Tea in the morning and hot chocolate at night is a must for us.

We carefully choose our food to be compact so that we can store our food in a single bear storage device (canister or Ursack, depending on land agency regulations). Getting all of our food into one container saves 2–3 pounds and volume. In areas that do not require a bear canister, we use an Ursack TKO food sack that weighs only 5.8 ounces. It's far easier to tie the Ursack to a tree than to fiddle around bearbagging late in the evening when we camp below the treeline.

We sometimes carry up to 7 liters of water between us. We find this amount adequate even for the driest sections of the Sierras. Alison likes to drink a lot of water. For her, a hydration system is an essential piece of gear. Alison carries a 3-liter Zip Platypus with a hydration hose and drinks smaller quantities more frequently. Alan is something of a camel and is fine with taking large (up to 1 liter) swigs from his Platypus from time to time.

The Zip Platypus makes for easy collection and treatment of water. Alan carries two 2-liter Platypus bags, but has been known to take a few hits from Alison's hydration hose. We use the 3-liter Zip Platypus or our mugs to fill the narrow opening of the 2-liter Platys. We chemically treat with Aquamira and have given up on water filters a long time ago.

Aquamira excels for its light weight, ease of use, good taste, lack of maintenance, and effectiveness.

Navigation

Both of us enjoy route planning on our trips. For us, figuring out just how we'll make it over some remote 13,000-foot col is one of our favorite parts of the trip. We always do our best navigating when we put our heads together.

We use mapping software (e.g., National Geographic Topo! 1:2400 state series) to plan many of our trips. This software is a boon to the cross-country traveler. With it we can get reasonably accurate mileages and elevation profiles for our routes. We can print up to a few days of travel on a single side of an 8.5″-x-11″ sheet of waterproof map paper. This saves a lot of weight from carrying a complete set of USGS 7.5 minute series maps in a waterproof container. As a backup, and in case our plans change, we usually carry a USGS 15 minute series map of the area we'll hike in.

An admitted luxury, we carry a GPS receiver, the Garmin eTrex Legend. We started using one in Scotland and found it to be so much fun and so useful navigating to two summits in complete whiteout that we've carried it on all of our trips since. Yes, we could save weight and navigate just fine with maps and a compass, and have done so for years. But for now, we like all the benefits of a GPS. We know exactly where we are and just how far it is to the next waypoint or location. This helps us make better decisions, like how far we'll comfortably go in a day and where we'll most likely camp at night. We think we gain back more than the weight of the unit in good decisions and trip logistics.

To be safe, the person not carrying the detailed maps and GPS receiver usually carries a 15 minute USGS map and a small compass. Each of us is capable of independently navigating without the other's help, maps, or navigation equipment.

Garmin's lighter Geko series of GPS units have limited screen resolution and a reduced feature set, but can be useful as well.

Shared Miscellany

We've already covered the obvious ways to share equipment and save weight, sleeping bag, shelter, cooking equipment, water storage, and navigation equipment. When there are two of you it makes sense to share as much equipment as possible and save even more weight.

We love to take pictures on our trips. A recent purchase was a high-resolution digital camera that is compact and weighs only 8.1 ounces. In our experience, it runs for four or more days on a single lithium-ion battery. Alison usually carries the camera and extra battery. Alan carries the GPS unit, its extra batteries, and the detailed maps. We also share a single 1-ounce LED headlamp (each of us also has a button light) and of course, the fishing equipment.

Routines

If you're like us, you'll find that each has tasks during the day that they like. These routines make the trip efficient and fun. In setting up camp for the night, we both pitch the tent. Alison finishes putting the pads and bags in the shelter and getting everything arranged inside and outside. At the same time, Alan gets and treats water, cooks dinner, and makes our evening hot chocolate. We finish our tasks in time to enjoy our cocoa and meal together. If there's scouting to be done for the next day's route, Alan usually goes out while Alison cleans up and gets things ready for bed. Both of us find the best spot to view alpenglow before settling in for the night. In rare instances alpenglow and moonrise happen simultaneously!

Perspectives: Jim and Amy Lauterbach

Jim and Amy Lauterbach have been backpacking together for 20 years. Most weekends, they take an all-day hike together. As such, they are in great shape to pull long (sometimes 20+-mile) days in the high Sierras with some cross-country trekking mixed in. Jim and Amy are self-admitted, hardcore backcountry travelers. They like to do difficult routes that get them off trail and into remote places. On their southern Utah canyoneering trips, it's not uncommon for them to do a bit of class 5 climbing.

Their routes are hard on equipment. You'll notice sometimes they have to make the difficult decision between lightweight and durability. For example, in southern Utah they take heavier packs to withstand the abuse of being dragged across slickrock. Jim and Amy also take a 4-pound double-wall tent to withstand the extreme weather of their trips. Finally, they do not sleep happily on foam pads, so they take Therm-A-Rest 3/4 Ultralight pads. They like comfort and a good nights sleep.

Jim and Amy enjoy longer trips than most couples. A normal trip is 8 to 10 days without resupply. They don't cook on their trips, so they save weight on cooking gear and fuel. At a 2 mph pace they are extremely efficient and don't need more than 1.5 pounds of food each per day, even on 20-mile days.

Of special note, Jim and Amy use a Nunatak semi-custom Back Country Blanket (BCB). Their BCB is 67 inches wide at the shoulder, has 3-inch high baffles (2.5 inches is standard), 5-inch baffle spacing, and 6 ounces of extra down to give it 3+ inches of loft. They ordered the BCB with a custom down draft flap at their shoulders. In addition, Amy sewed a nylon liner/footbox on the bottom half of the BCB. They use Velcro straps to secure the upper half of the bag to their Therm-A-Rest pad couplers. These straps keep the bag edges near the ground to control drafts well.

Jim and Amy are avid birders and wouldn't dream of hiking anywhere without their fancy full-size German binoculars. We've tried to convince them to look at some of the newer compact binocs with asymmetrical lenses, but no dice. They want the best optical performance possible for their avian pursuit.

Perspectives: Ryan and Stephanie Jordan

Stephanie and Ryan have been backpacking together since 1989. Their couples experience was incubated on Washington's

Olympic Peninsula. Their travels took them alpine climbing on the glaciers of Mt. Olympus, beachhead scrambling along the wilderness coast of the Pacific Northwest, and trail hiking into the remote alpine beauty of Enchanted Valley. Since migrating to Montana, of course, their backcountry travels have been ocean starved, but mountain rich.

Stephanie suffers from lower back anomalies that seriously limit her ability to travel long distances or carry much weight. She has two herniated disks, spondylolesthesis, and osteoarthritis along her spine. For Stephanie, lightweight hiking is not a style of choice, but of necessity.

Stephanie and Ryan's typical backcountry outing is a three-day weekend trip. Unintentionally, nearly 90 percent of the trips they have taken together, even in summer, have been under the throes of lightning, rain, or snow. "How Ryan manages to go hiking solo and bring back these beautiful photographs of blue sky in the mountains is beyond me," says Stephanie. "But I'm now pretty much tuned into the fact that he might actually be taking me on these inclement weather trips as a covert means of testing new gear, like rain jackets and waterproof stuff sacks. . . ."

In June 2001, Ryan and Stephanie took a weekend backpacking trip to a little known Montana alpine lake. They started the trip in heavy rain and ended it in sub-freezing conditions with snow and a crazy hip-deep ford of a stream that had risen during the storm. "Remarkably, we stayed warm and comfortable. We've developed a level of trust between each other that allows us to tackle challenging situations together and come out on top," Ryan says.

Stephanie follows, "That was one of my favorite trips, even though we ignored the winter storm warning on the Weather Channel and tackled the elements anyways." By the time they reached the trailhead, the storm was in full force with nearly 30 inches of snowfall accumulated.

Ryan and Stephanie are small people — 5′ 8″ and 5′ 6″ — and are lucky enough to get away with a single 2-pound sleeping bag between them (Western Mountaineering VersaLite). They complement this with high-loft insulating jackets (Stephanie, a GoLite Coal; and Ryan, a Western Mountaineering Flight) and sleep in a tarp tent. In winter weather, they sleep in a Stephenson 2RS tent. In buggy conditions they like the comfort of a tent, but stick to a single-wall silnylon shelter, such as a Tarptent Rainshadow or Stephenson 2X.

Stephanie tries to limit her pack weight to 15 pounds carried in a lightweight internal frame pack that provides uncompromising stability to her load, even on rough terrain, so as not to put undue stress on her spinal musculature. Her choice: a custom-fitted McHale Subpop. Dual frame stays keep the pressure off her spine, and the wide hip belt helps distribute weight. A Therma-Rest ProLite Long is her sleeping pad of choice, while Ryan's is a torso-sized foam pad. On a typical 3-day weekend, Stephanie carries between 10–12 pounds, including her water, tent, the sleeping bags, and clothing.

Ryan carries the balance of the weight for them, which usually totals about 15 pounds, including clothing, cooking equipment, food, and remaining gear.

Ryan and Stephanie share a 1.3-liter titanium cookpot, along with a set of titanium mugs and sporks for eating. They usually cook over a small canister stove. For water treatment, they are diehard Aquamira fans, and simply filter murky waters through a bandana and their own silt filter homemade with open-cell foam.

Montana winters can get pretty long, so the Jordans have adapted to snow travel well. In the winter, they use an MSR Simmerlite white gas stove and a 2-liter titanium pot in conjunction with larger titanium mugs for meals and drinks. A GoLite Hex custom made with Epic fabric is their shelter of choice, which cuts the biting evening winds so common in the mountains of the Northern Rockies and eliminates blowing spindrift from Montana's cold smoke. They travel on Northern Lites snowshoes, using summer weight footwear (fabric boots give more kick leverage when snowshoeing than trail runners) in conjunction with neoprene overboots for warmth and waterproofing, and RBH Designs fleece socks for warmth and vapor barrier protection.

For winter sleeping bags, they replace their Spartan single VersaLite with a pair of mating-zip North Face Cat's Meows and Patagonia DAS parkas. Ryan adds a long Ridge Rest Deluxe for a pad, with Stephanie putting a torso-sized Ridge Rest under her Therma-Rest UltraLite Long pad for additional insulation. They go totally synthetic for clothing and sleeping bags in the winter because, as Ryan says, "We get wet after a day of snowshoeing."

And as Stephanie says, "We get wet because of this 'hike-with-Ryan-means-inclement-weather' phenomenon."

When asked what advice they had for new couples learning to backpack together, Ryan and Stephanie gave us a top ten list:

10. Schedule a night at a bed and breakfast after the trip.
9. Turn a memorable photograph from a trip into a postcard and mail it to your spouse the next time you travel and have to be apart.
8. Always give the girl the warmer jacket.
7. If she wants to bring Wet Ones for hygiene, don't argue.
6. Most satin in women's lingerie weighs about 1.6 oz/yd2, but real silk can weigh as little as 0.8 oz/yd2.
5. Don't try to split the weight equally or turn weight distribution between the two of you into a formula. Men, carry the heavier pack. It's been that way for thousands of years. Don't try to fight the system.
4. Be flexible. This is an exercise to allow you to enjoy your relationship, not accomplish mileage records.
3. Clear a sitting area of pine cones and sticks before your wife sits down at a rest break.
2. Pick a bundle of wildflowers and use a rubber band to secure them to a titanium tent stake. An instant dinner bouquet.
1. Have a sense of humor. The weatherman is not always right. And your spouse may never be.

Conclusion

Sharing the outdoors with a spouse can be a pinnacle experience. Unfortunately, normal heavy packing (carrying 40–50 pounds of gear each) sucks the pleasure out of backcountry travel and turns what should be fun into a long and miserable trudge. With ultralight backpacking equipment, the strain and discomfort go away. For us, ultralight backpacking puts a spring in our step and brings the joy back to sharing the outdoors. We hope it will do the same for you. Just remember the most important axiom that we introduced at the beginning of this article: Traveling together is a partnership.

Citation

This chapter was originally published as an article in the online magazine BackpackingLight.com (ISSN 1537-0364) in September 2003.

Chapter 19: **Face Off**
First Aid and Emergency Gear

By Bill Thorneloe, David Schultz, and Ryan Jordan

There are a few categories of equipment that can be the subject of hostile discussion around a campfire. First aid and emergency equipment are certainly among them. We've met hikers with first-aid kits ranging from a baggie full of band-aids to 5-pound expedition kits.

The purpose of this article is to highlight some of the differences in first aid and emergency equipment selection among three self-proclaimed lightweight hikers and reflect opinions on the subject that span a broad spectrum between conservative and "Why the heck do I need this?"

We'll start with Bill and Dave critiquing each other until Ryan joins in, no longer able to tolerate the banter.

Dave's Rationale

Over the last several years, my business has taken me all over the United States. On these trips, I have been lucky enough to find the opportunity to hike extensively in areas that were totally new to me. Unfortunately, I also tend to push my personal envelope a bit and have a unique talent for getting lost. When I go hiking with other folks, they are usually newbies who don't have a lot of outdoor skills, don't always have the best equipment, and often push themselves a bit harder than they should. Being well prepared is essential for where and how I hike, so I carry 25 ounces of preparedness for those times when things don't go smoothly.

These items, along with my general equipment, help me handle a wide range of medical problems. My goals in selection are:

1. Management of the little ailments that can spoil a trip—e.g., blisters, diarrhea, stings, cuts, minor pains, etc.
2. Treatment for moderate problems and control of major pain so that a walk out is possible
3. Stabilization of larger problems and control of major pain until a rescue can occur

Dave's List

FIRST-AID SUPPLIES

- Pain meds in a film canister with instructions
  - o Ibuprofen
  - o Percogesic (325 mg acetaminophen and 30 mg phenyltoloxamine citrate)
  - o Percocet
- Decongestant and antihistamine tablets in a film canister with instructions
  - o Benadryl, pseudoephedrine
- Digestive system meds in a film canister with instructions
  - o Imodium
  - o Tums
- Topical Meds
  - o Alcohol prep pads
  - o Iodine prep pads
  - o Triple antibiotic ointment
  - o Ophthalmic ointment
  - o Burn ointment
  - o 20% benzocaine gel

- Blister kit in a small Ziploc
  - o Spenco adhesive knit (moleskin)
  - o Knife w/scissors
  - o Bioclusive breathable dressing
  - o Curad Blistercare pads
- Closure kit
  - o Coverstrip closures
  - o Band-aids
  - o Small straight hemostats
  - o Sutures (#3 and #5 in gut and nylon)
- Sterile gauze pads, 1″ breathable plastic tape, 3-oz bulb irrigation syringe, 0.5-oz 10% povidone-iodine solution, pencil
- Pair latex gloves

SURVIVAL EQUIPMENT

- Two 1-gallon freezer ziploc bags
- Fire starters in a waterproof wrapping
  - o Lighter
  - o Matches
  - o Tinder
- Signal mirror, marine-type signal whistle, LED light
- Water purifying tabs
- Large garden trash bag

REPAIR SUPPLIES

- Duct tape
- Hot patch repair kit , needle, dental floss, 4 large nylon wire ties, 4 small nylon wire ties
- Two AAA batteries
- Pouch for carrying emergency/first-aid kit

BILL: Dave, your list is excellent and quite reasonable, particularly given the weight. I suspect that our kits look quite similar, but this kit may be closer to the contents of my top compartment Ziploc bag. This would serve someone very well, but I suspect that there is duplication and some outdated equipment here.

DAVE: It could be that my relative inexperience in the healing arts leads me to be overly cautious. I know that if I mishandle a small problem, my lack of skill and experience means that I have a higher chance of failure if the condition worsens. This is why I emphasize items needed to clean and disinfect a wound.

BILL: Why carry moleskin and Bioclusive dressings and Curad blister pads? Why not just the Bioclusive dressings?

DAVE: While the Bioclusive dressings are very useful in that they are waterproof and breathable, they are relatively fragile and do not breathe well when compared to the non-waterproof but tougher Spenco Adhesive knit. So for ultra-heavy sweaters like myself, I find that the Adhesive knit works better. For low perspiring folks, like my wife, Bioclusive dressing keeps the blister clean in a relatively dirty environment. I also use the Bioclusive dressing for covering cuts and other non-weeping wounds.

BILL: Why carry both Percogesic and Percocet, neither of which will treat major pain? I carry two 20-mg OxyContin tabs?

DAVE: The only reason I carry the Percogesic (over-the-counter or OTC med), is that my wife tends to get an upset stomach from Ibuprofen. I have found Percocet (prescription or RX med containing acetaminophen and the narcotic oxycodone) to be quite effective on moderate to severe pain and far more effective than any non-RX meds available. Certainly there are stronger alternatives (OxyContin 40, MS Contin 30, etc.), but not being a medical professional, I have limited access to RX meds. Before moving, I had a long relationship with my family physician and getting a few RX meds was not such a problem. Now I must use a large and impersonal managed care group and can no longer acquire RX meds for a field kit.

BILL: Why carry iodine prep pads, alcohol pads, povidone-iodine solutions, and water treatment tabs? I can see the povidone to help adhesion of skin closures, but the rest?

DAVE: It is far easier to use a prep pad to disinfect a small area than it is to mix up some povidone-iodine solution. But if I had to clean or irrigate a larger wound, the prep pads would not be sufficient, so I carry both. I am intrigued with the idea of using the water treatment tabs to mix up a batch of wound irrigant/disinfectant. This deserves exploration. Omiting the povidone-iodine will save about an ounce.

BILL: Why carry the extra and non-waterproof packaging of sterile gauze pads, instead of a plastic wrapped Kling roll gauze?

DAVE: Ease of use and sterility.

BILL: Why breathable tape and duct tape and skin closures?

DAVE: You've got a good point here, Bill. I could lose the breathable tape. I'll keep the Cover Strips though. They are quick and easy to use.

BILL: Why carry gut sutures? Any stitches will be removed and revised on arrival at the emergency room. I suspect the nylon or silk suture I carry (but did not list) would be more visible and also useful for gear repairs. Heck, a curved needle and dental floss could service in a crisis.

DAVE: Again, good point. The main reason that I carry a few gut sutures is that I learned that they were preferable for use in severe mouth lacerations. Granted, I have never run into such an injury. I imagine this could be very tricky.

BILL: Why carry a heavy first-aid kit package when you have 2-gallon Ziplocs as well as latex gloves (e.g., for an emergency water container)?

DAVE: I used to use Ziplocs, but found that they were beat up so much that they were often replaced.

BILL: Why bring an irrigation bulb? I would use my Platypus and tubing to direct the flow, and squeeze the bag for more pressure.

DAVE: Excellent idea for when I am in a group. It will save 3 ounces. When I go solo, however, I usually only carry one bladder and no backup water container.

BILL: Have you considered orthopedic injuries and means of splinting or otherwise stabilizing a fracture?

DAVE: I considered carrying a SAM splint, but figured I could improvise by cutting up my closed-cell foam pad and using duct tape, poles from my shelter, sticks, etc.

BILL: Overall, I believe I am picking nits on these questions. I suspect our real gear is identical, and that the choices of medications, wound treatments, and such are solely personal preferences.

Bill's Rationale

My first-aid kit responds to three questions.

1. What happens if I lose all or part of my gear?
2. What are the most likely medical problems I will encounter?
3. What am I carrying that can be used for more than its intended use?

I should know my gear and be able to accurately assess a wound or emergency. If I do not understand a piece of gear, it should be left at home. Without understanding the hazard, I am likely to make the situation worse by trying to intervene blindly. The most likely acute emergency will be trauma. I anticipate falls, fractures, bruises, abrasions, stings, and bites. Burns may happen, but preparation for other trauma provides gear for this. Digestive tract (GI) distress with upset stomach, nausea, vomiting and diarrhea are likely to impede my walk. I prepare for dehydration, hypothermia, and hyperthermia. Infection concerns come next, addressed by water purification, hand cleaning, toilet hygiene, and wound cleansing. Finally, I consider comfort issues like sunburn.

What would happen if I lost everything by the trail while I go for water? If I broke my ankle slipping on a mud bank by a creek bed, I would need to be able to alert someone of my location, stay warm, and avoid bleeding and shock. Hence, my lanyard kit. A lanyard or pocket kit, always with me, provides for splinting and allows scrambling back to the trail. If I wandered away from a shelter wearing my fanny pack from the top of my pack, the contents of the top pocket would make a similar injury easier to manage. I also have the beginnings of good treatment for other problems, including temperature regulation and dehydration. Unfortunately, dehydration and temperature problems are often first detected by confusion and cognitive deterioration. I have not figured out a reliable means for a solo hiker to recognize when their brain is going south, much less how to intervene. The closest I have found is attention to the UMBLES—grumble, mumble, fumble, and stumble—treated initially with sitting down in the shade, drinking water, and assessing the circumstances.

My clothing and backpack are integral to trauma care. I can fashion slings and braces for a variety of upper extremity injuries, dislocations, and lacerations (cuts and scrapes) with clothing and well placed diaper pins. I can rig a splint with backpack stays and trekking poles using the closed-cell mat or clothing to cushion the splint. I could even rig a litter with trekking poles or available sticks, clothing, and diaper pins. My tent and sleeping bag are excellent for treatment of hypothermia, along with a warm cup of Jell-O. My water treatment and Platypus bags give me disinfectant and a means to irrigate and cleanse a wound or foreign body in an eye. There are few GI problems that do not respond to Pepto Bismol, unless they demand a visit to a local emergency room. I carry much more on a canoe trip, especially medications and allergy treatments. When desert hiking, a larger mirror for signaling comes along.

I don't carry a Sawyer Extractor, as I have not been exposed to either severe bee stings or snake bite. Poisonous snake bites require immobilization of the area bitten and evacuation of the patient by the quickest means possible. I don't carry Epinephrine, as I have no history of anaphylaxis (shock) in response to allergy. Anyone with this susceptibility should provide their own and be able to use it immediately.

Bill's List

LANYARD KIT (WORN AT ALL TIMES)

- laminated photo ID
- whistle
- Swiss Army clone pen knife, scissors, tweezers
- compass with mirror
- Photon light (red)
- Magnesium block and steel
- 3 feet of nylon cord

PRIMARY FIRST-AID AND EMERGENCY ITEMS (IN TOP POCKET OF PACK, STORED IN A 1-QUART ZIPLOC BAG)

- 1 emergency mylar blanket
- 3 pairs of latex gloves, with the following stored in the fingers:
  - One 20-gram tube of Silvadene
  - 3 band-aids for child use
  - 1 roll of Kling gauze (4 inch by 4 yards)
- 1 tin
  - 8 tabs aspirin
  - 2 tabs slow release oral narcotic
- 1 roll of TUMS
- 6 tabs Pepto Bismol in foil
- Laminated ID card with inventory, phone numbers, insurance info, and medical history info
- Envelope of electrolyte replacement powder and 1 pack of nutrasweet (in weather below 40 degrees)
- 1 pack of Jell-O
- 1-oz tin of bag balm or petroleum jelly
- 1 bottle of Polar Pure (water treatment and wound disinfectant)
- 4 packs of Bioclude dressings
- 4-oz bottle of Purell alcohol hand sanitizer—stored outside of the Ziploc
- 8-oz bottle of honey (excellent sugar source and topical antibiotic)

- Paper and pencil—to record chronology of an emergency
- Fire starter—long-handled lighter, which is easier for cold and tired hands)
- Silicon-based GOOP adhesive
- 8 waterproof matches and striker

DAVE: Well Bill, it looks like you've got all the bases covered. In comparing each of the items in my kit with their functional equivalent in your kit, my only question is: What do you do if you get a really bad case of the trots? Pepto Bismol just doesn't have enough stopping power, in my experience.

BILL: Severe diarrhea in the backcountry can be deadly, with attendant risks of dehydration and electrolyte disturbances. Sure, Pepto Bismol has limited cork potential, but is effective for most mild to moderate events, and should help slow the flow of a severe diarrhea. I aggressively push Pepto until symptoms begin to fade. I expect to use copious water and electrolyte replacement with Nutrasweet to help treat the dehydration, and Gatorade once that is exhausted. I would consider a narcotic, especially if I were already immobilized by diarrhea. Severe diarrhea is like a fracture: It takes us off the trail and on the way to an ER.

DAVE: The main differences I see in our approaches to emergency kits are that mine has a bit more emphasis on convenience and I try to make up for lack of experience with 4–5 ounces of additional gear.

BILL: I agree with the observation that our kits vary only in convenience and compartmentalization. I depend much more on making do with items originally designed for other uses. I carry a bit more than needed as I anticipate providing attention to others when on my own walks. This goes with the job. I expect that a first-aid kit of a couple of band-aids and a waterproof match would be plenty for many, but too little for my confidence.

RYAN: You two are a piece of work. I assumed that I could put two opinionated souls together, give you free license to hammer each other, and you end up getting cozy and complimentary. What's up with that? Are you guys really serious about bringing an entire pound, or pound and a half, of first-aid and emergency equipment? So I say, rid yourselves of all the nonessentials, use your head, and what the heck — roll the dice a bit. My kit weighs a paltry 5 ounces.

Ryan's Rationale

I prepare primarily for two things: minor ailments and light weight. Period. I'll try to use my brain for the big stuff. Sure, that might be risky, but that's what going light is about.

Ryan's List

BLISTER TREATMENT AND WOUND CARE SUPPLIES

- Spenco 2nd Skin dressing and adhesive knit — 3 square inches of each, primarily for blisters
- Tincture of benzoin for a tape adherent
- A few feet of duct tape
- Two needles
- Kevlar thread
- tweezers and one tiny pair of scissors from a Swiss Army classic pocketknife
  o   Tweezers for splinters and ticks
  o   Scissors for tape cutting
- 2 iodine-impregnated wipes for wound sterilization
- triple antibiotic ointment, about 1/3 oz

MEDICINES

- Ibuprofen, 8 caps
- Acetominophen, 6 caps
- Acetaminophen with codeine, 4 caps
- Immodium, 4 caps

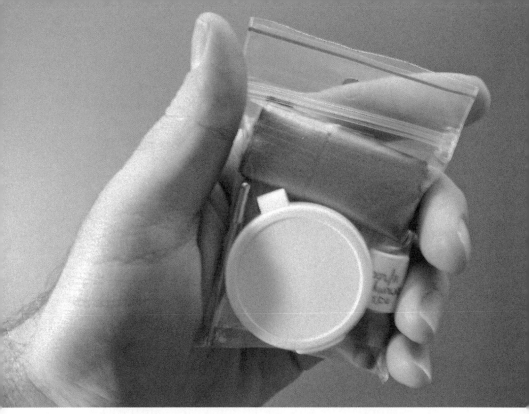

A first-aid kit need not be heavy, or bulky for that matter. This one fits in the palm of your hand and is easily packaged in a 2" x 3" zip closure plastic bag.

- Benadryl, 4 caps
- Menthol throat lozenges, 4

Emergency Survival Equipment

I limit this primarily to a firestarting kit, storm matches, birthday candles, and a mini-Bic lighter in a cardboard match box with extra strikers, vacuum sealed in a heavy waterproof plastic. Also a single mini-LED light (0.3 oz) and a tiny waterproof whistle (0.1 oz) for emergency signaling.

RYAN: That's it. All of these supplies weigh 5 oz and are stored in a 2″-x 4″-x 6″ bright yellow silnylon stuff sack.

BILL: You have really trimmed your stuff down in the medicine department. Are you willing to rot in place without means of alerting rescue for significant trauma?

RYAN: What do you mean? I carry a Photon single-LED mini-light for signaling (smile). The advertisements say that it's visible for a mile.

DAVE: Now Ry, I agree that a decrease in weight can lead to an increase in risk, but with all of the wild stuff that you do (much of it solo as I understand), you ought to consider a bit more preparedness.

RYAN: "All that wild stuff?" It's a matter of perspective. I really toned it down after I became a father! I think it's high time you explored your wild side, my friend.

BILL: Dave?

DAVE: Bill?

BILL & DAVE: "Git a rope."

BILL: OK, Ryan, why would you want iodine wipes unless you fail to bring iodine for water purification?

RYAN: What is it with you guys and your iodine? It's time to get with the program and use something that actually works for water disinfection. While iodine is still appropriate for virus protection, viruses are the least of your problems, at least here in the US. Bacteria and protozoan cysts (Giardia and Crypto) pose a more serious threat to backcountry water. I opt for a chlorine dioxide chemical kit (e.g., Aquamira) due to its greater efficacy toward microorganisms. Hey, thousands of city water treatment plants around the world that are using chlorine dioxide can't all be wrong. But the bottom line for iodine wipes is this: simplicity of use. Hassling to make a concentrated solution of iodine using Potable Aqua tablets is not my idea of a great time. In addition, with iodine crystals, you also run the risk of incompletely dissolving the crystals when preparing a topical solution. If an undissolved crystal comes into direct contact with flesh, it can cause damage to the tissue via a pretty aggressive oxidation reaction. But that should be just fine with you guys, since y'all are also carrying burn ointment!

BILL: What's the point of triple antibiotic ointment? Triple is useless and potentially dangerous for open wounds.

Vaseline or bag balm or skin lotion/sunscreen would be more practical, along with 20 grams of Silvadene for a burn or real infection.

RYAN: The primary purpose of the cream is to provide a barrier to outside contamination — not unlike Vaseline or bag balm as you suggest. The secondary purpose is to disinfect the skin surrounding the wound and prevent these bacteria (e.g., Staphylococcus epidermidis) from colonizing the wound. Most OTC antibiotic creams are ineffective at treating massive wound infections. That is not the purpose here. But they are indeed effective at preventing the onslaught of a wound infection. Remember, the goal with these ointments is preventative treatment, not reactive treatment. As for danger, the antibiotic components of triple antibiotic ointments (which vary somewhat, but may include neomycin, bacitracin, or polymyxin B) can cause kidney damage or renal failure. In most cases, this is only an issue when administered orally, as is commonly done to treat intestinal infections in pets. Applied topically (e.g., to the eye as part of an opthalmic infection treatment strategy) or to superficial skin-deep wounds, the chance that the antibiotics will be absorbed into the bloodstream at a high enough concentration to induce a life-threatening condition is extremely low. I do agree with you, though, that application of this ointment into a deep open wound is probably not a wise decision, since you'll have a rapid and direct path to the bloodstream. I do like your suggestion for Silvadene when faced with having to treat a serious wound infection that has already exploded.

BILL: Why so much Ibuprofen, Tylenol, and Tylenol with codeine?

RYAN: I don't take meds on the trail for routine conditions like muscle aches. Thus, eight caps of Ibuprofen provide two healthy doses to control serious inflammation, as might occur for a sprained ankle. Six caps of Tylenol provide three doses to help tolerate such common problems as severe headache caused by dehydration or acute mountain sickness. Sure, we can be careful and drink our water at regular intervals, or acclimatize by only climbing 1,000 feet per day, but that's simply not a reality in the mountains.

BILL: The variety of meds you carry enhances the risk of misidentification.

RYAN: Fair enough, but I eat wild mushrooms, too.

BILL: And codeine? It's too mild and short term and too frequently allergenic to be used reasonably in the backcountry.

RYAN: Each of us reacts differently to narcotics. I respond well (hey, calm down, I'm a clean-livin' good old boy). Tylenol 3 was successful at quenching the pain of a jumping molar nerve (which subsequently required an emergency root canal) while on a hike. Two years ago, I hiked 40 miles out of an extremely remote area on a broken talus bone (foot) using Tylenol 3. Emergency extrication was an option, but I chose to take the responsibility myself, since the injury wasn't life-threatening. The fact that Tylenol 3 is mild is the very reason I use it; it provides a nice balance between desensitizing myself to the pain and keeping my head clear enough to make reasonable decisions. Of course, I'm not allergic to it, and I certainly don't administer it to others while in the woods for fear of an allergic reaction.

BILL: Immodium is useful only if diarrhea is the only GI event expected. Why not Pepto tabs?

RYAN: Immodium is a more aggressive plugger-upper than Pepto, and has the power to arrest diarrhea before it begins to severely dehydrate you, which Pepto won't do in a short time frame. I also had adverse reactions to it in the past, where it has induced vomiting on several occasions, something that appears to be unique to me, unfortunately.

BILL: Throat lozenges? How about some honey or hard candy?

RYAN: You bet. Any of the above. I just like the menthol high that comes with some throat lozenges. The real purpose here is to fend off the Russian Army Hat Tongue and sore throat that often accompany dehydration at altitude. The addition of menthol clears sinuses and nasal passages and for this hay fever-prone hiker, really helps breathing when working hard.

BILL: And Benadryl? For what real purpose?

RYAN: Benadryl offers a few massive (prescription strength) doses for a bee sting allergy. I've not responded well to Epi-pens in the past, but have done great with Benadryl.

DAVE: So, Ryan, what do you do when you slip off of one of those big rocks that you are so fond of climbing in your cross country treks and tear an eight inch chunk of meat out of your (fill in the body part)? If this is not bad enough, you also abrade a good patch of skin off of your (pick another part). Sure you could just pack the void that used to be filled with flesh with gauze (if you had any) and wrap it up all neat with duct tape. But, how are you going to get the crud out and disinfect that wound? Your iodine wipes just ain't going to be enough. Adequate cleansing is the most important aspect of wound management.

RYAN: I agree wholeheartedly with the cleansing part. The scenario you describe is similar to one I experienced while hiking near Cimarron, New Mexico, in 1986. I had just climbed a peak and was descending a steep talus slope, lost my footing and tore quite a lot of flesh from my upper thigh in the fall. Treatment required thorough cleansing—it was a very dirty wound—and took about 3 hours. My immediate approach was to flush the wound with my remaining water, which was about a liter. I then packed it with toilet paper (TP), wrapped a bandana around it, and high-tailed it down into the valley with access to a stream. Then I sterilized about a gallon of stream water (using iodine tablets) and used tweezers to pick every piece of grit I could find out of the wound, all the while rinsing with water and letting the wound bleed itself to prevent clotting while I was cleaning. I used triple antibiotic ointment on the outside edge of the wound, dressed it with some TP that had been soaked in some triple antibiotic creme (my barrier to outside infection), more TP on top, followed by six layers of a cotton t-shirt that I cut up, with duct tape to hold it all in place. This was an agonizing process for someone who is normally pretty impatient, but you do what you must. I hiked out the next day and within 36 hours after the injury was at a health clinic where I received kudos for wound cleansing and treatment but a lamenting lecture about hiking down talus slopes in sneakers.

DAVE: — except that you also had a bad case of the runs early on in the trip and you only brought four Immodium tablets, so your TP has long since been used up.

RYAN: I actually only use TP to polish things up, relying instead on more natural sources for doing the dirty work. This becomes even more important when you have the trots. It's amazing how much comfort a prickly alpine spruce bough provides—if you wipe with the needles facing the proper direction. I've also long since replaced normal TP with those tough blue shop towels. They make great TP for loose bowel movements because they are so absorbent, and are also ideally suited for wound dressings.

DAVE: If you knew that you would be found in a darn quick hurry, all of this might not be quite so bad. I notice though, that you don't have much signaling equipment so you might be hanging out for a while.

RYAN: In addition to the whistle and see-for-a-mile-LED-mini-light in my kit, I often carry a LED headlamp and a mirror in my toiletry kit (used primarily for grooming and tick checks). Finally, what happened to the power of fire? Three fires arranged in a large triangle can't be beat for night signaling. In daytime, a big wet smoky fire has the power to attract attention from miles away.

DAVE: OK, so your light runs out of juice in the middle of one of your night hikes. What do you do? You don't have any extra batteries.

RYAN: This is why I've gone to LED headlamps. I install fresh batteries, lasting between 40–120 hours, for any hike of more than a few days and use lithium batteries if the light will take them. I've yet to run out of juice, even on an all-night winter escape from a Teton summit, where the low temps can really suck the life out of batteries. But if worse came to worst, and I didn't have the luxury of a moon or sixth sense to rely on, I'd just stop and camp.

DAVE: You are hiking deep into an area that has little water. While cooking dinner you accidentally knock your burning canister stove into the water bag on your hydration/filtration system. Now, not only can you not filter the small amount of water that you can scoop from the hoof prints that you find around the dry watering hole, but you can't carry any of the putrid water with you. A couple of Ziploc bags and some water purifying tabs could come in handy here.

RYAN: All of my food is packaged in Ziplock bags, either sandwich-sized or gallon-sized. I don't burn my garbage. I have enough Ziplocs in a weeklong food supply to carry a few gallons of water. As for filtering, I always carry some kind of backup — usually, a chlorine dioxide chemical kit. And as a last resort, you can always boil the water to treat it, even using a fire if your stove fuel is gone.

BILL: Why is your firestarting kit vacuum sealed? You need fire starters anyway. I'd carry the matches on me and leave the Bic in the first-aid kit.

RYAN: I vacuum seal it for total waterproofness. The matches and lighter in this kit are to remain untouched except in an emergency — absolutely no exceptions. The fire is the last line of defense between you and hypothermia. When all of your equipment has failed, it is the only source of heat, other than your body, available in the backcountry. I carry a few backup matches in my stove kit, although my stove uses a piezo ignition. The only other reason for a lighter is sterilizing a needle to pop blisters. On those rare occasions I use a match from my stove kit stash.

BILL: By the way, where are your ID and your medical history? The search-and-rescue (SAR) folks who find you rotting away will be curious about who you were.

RYAN: Under the crown of my Tilley hat in a waterproof Ziploc with business cards that read: "If I'm alive, I'm a Backpacking Light subscriber. If found dead, please cancel my Backpacker subscription."

BILL: Ryan, you may want to throw your organ donor card in that Tilley hat of yours.

DAVE: As well as your term life and disability insurance policies.

Conclusion

What can be learned from this discussion? Four overriding themes stand out:

1. It may be impossible to compartmentalize a first aid and emergency kit as there are many dual-use items in your other gear that can be used in a first-aid or emergency situation.

2. No amount of equipment can substitute for the knowledge required to actually use it in an emergency situation.

3. Your creativity and resourcefulness with a solid base of knowledge about first aid and emergency assessment are the most important components of your kit. The weight? Zero. It's all in your brain.

4. Your choice of equipment reflects your style and approach to backcountry travel. If you want to peer into the soul of a backpacker, check out their first aid kit. And always look in the crown of their Tilley Hat.

Editor's Note: Since this article was first published at BackpackingLight. com, all three of the authors have continued to reduce the weight of their first-aid kits. For more detailed information about what's in Dave's first-aid kit, please review chapter 13. In the past few years, Ryan has been carrying a first-aid kit that weighs less than 2 ounces for more than 1,000 miles of alpine hiking in the Northern Rockies. The most severe injury he's had to deal with was a two-inch long seed husk that became stuck in his throat in a remote valley of the northwestern Teton Range, far from a road. The seed husk had entered into the water he used for his dinner meal, and became stuck while eating dinner. Sharing camp with 5 other people, no one carried any device that was capable of responding to this emergency. Inducing vomiting did not dislodge the husk. John O'Mahoney coming at Ryan with a titanium spork handle was enough to initiate the gag reflex before the implement could even approach the mouth. The most useful item used was a signal mirror, which Ryan used to guide two of his own fingers, in a state of panic, deep down his throat to extricate the husk. The trauma induced by the procedure damaged throat tissues but did not end Ryan's hike. He began a course of antibiotics, one of the key meds Ryan has learned to take with him for infection control on long, remote journeys.

Citation

This chapter was originally published as an article in the online magazine Back-packingLight.com (ISSN 1537-0364) in August 2001.

Chapter 20:
Especially for Women

By Ellen Zaslaw

Probably no single demographic group stands to benefit as much from the advent of lightweight backpacking as women. In the past, women were somewhat foreclosed from backpacking, in good part because it was beyond the strength of many to carry the heavy packs that used to be standard, at least any distance with any ease. Since the typical young American woman weighs 133 pounds and the old packs weighed perhaps 50 pounds fully loaded, many women rightly felt that backpacking was not a healthful, enjoyable recreation for them. If nature designed women to carry little more than 25 pounds of pregnancy weight, she probably didn't design them to carry those heavy packs.

No doubt there have also been certain psychological issues keeping women from backpacking, perhaps a feeling that rough, sweaty, dirty physical activity is unfeminine; or that the backcountry is populated by predatory men, in the face of whom they would be helpless; or that husbands couldn't possibly run things at home while they took a turn on the trail. But all these impediments ought to give way as men's and women's attitudes about themselves and their place in the world evolve. Women are more physically active

Women in Winter

Historically, winter in the backcountry has been the domain of mountain men, extreme skiers, or testosterone-juiced snowmobilers. Women can enjoy winter as much as men. In spite of real physiological and emotional differences in a woman's needs for warmth, nutrition, and privacy, women can thrive in the winter—even on a trip with a bunch of men!

Throughout this chapter, you'll see photographs from a trip to the Montana Beartooths that included at its core testosterone junkies looking to dance with winter's chill, but graced by the presence of two women passionate about extending their ultralight backpacking experience to the winter realm. As a group, we enjoyed campsites at 10,000 feet in the shadows of hostile peaks, traveling cross country in winter storms, and real beef hamburgers in a Cooke City diner.

Ellen Zaslaw, the author of this chapter, gives new meaning to the phrase, "Let's give it a whirl." As both a woman and a senior citizen, she has proven that lightweight gear can allow anyone to enjoy the wilderness in any season.

Carol Crooker, BackpackingLight.com editor, lives in Phoenix. Transplanting her into a land of snow and cold with a pair of lightweight snowshoes and a can-do-anything attitude indicates that some women actually travel from Phoenix to vacation in the winter, rather than the other way around.

nowadays, working out in gyms and participating in sports and garnering recognition as competitive athletes. They are an increasing presence in physically demanding occupations such as firefighting and police work. They're taking classes in self-defense and learning martial arts. Their husbands are co-parenting more equally than in times past. Women, of course, are legion in the workforce, to a greater extent than decades ago, making their allotments of vacation time — and a chance to breathe fresh air — precious as never before. Vigorous women have been learning to speak up and act up, and to regard their bodies more as equipment for experiencing the world and less as adornment. All of this would suggest that the time is ripe for women to explode onto the trails in huge numbers. But is this happening?

Interestingly, the US National Park Service's bureau of statistics keeps no records as to the numbers of men and women issued backcountry permits. The statistics it does keep are ones of consequence to its budgets. Its officers reason that backpackers make the same demands on park maintenance regardless of sex. So how are we to know how well women are represented among backpackers? One measure, possibly an optimistic one, might be their numbers in a major online Yahoo! discussion group devoted to lightweight backpacking, BackpackingLight — some 5000 strong by late 2005. This group ought to be well populated with women if any group is. Yet at last estimate (based on a large sample) women comprised only 15 percent of the membership.

Even if one were to consider another online Yahoo! group, the 600+-member WomenHikers, together as if the two were a single group, the resulting assembly would appear to be 27 percent women. Not a very grand showing, and furthermore an overestimate since many in the women's group also belong to BackpackingLight and so are counted twice this way.

We can consider estimates of other sorts as well. *Backpacker* magazine has done a survey of its audience for marketing purposes, and it counts three times as many men as women. BackpackingLight.com has performed similar demographic surveys on its readership with quite contradictory results: 43

Carol Crooker and Ellen Zaslaw trying to understand why water is freezing in their Nalgene bottles at a snowy camp near Lake of the Woods, Montana Beartooths. "I left Phoenix for this?"

percent of their readers are women. Perhaps the lightweight philosophy indeed draws women to backpacking.

The Appalachian Long Distance Hikers Association (ALDHA) maintains a website that gives links to online trail journals. Among the 150 or so journal writers embarked on PCT or AT thru-hikes early in 2002, women represented as much as 32 percent. Yet an eyewitness to the parade of AT through- and section-hikers at Trail Days 2002 reckoned that women were only about one in ten of those marching. Between these extremes, by the estimate of officials of the

Appalachian Trail Conference, women have been a constant 20 percent of thru-hikers for many years. A specialty manufacturer of lightweight hiking gear keen to attract the female market confides on condition of anonymity (because it seems so embarrassing) that so far only 30 percent of its customer base is women. But whose embarrassment is this? There seem not to be more women out on the trail.

The picture is different in New Zealand. Various correspondents from there, some working for the national park service and some affiliated with hiking clubs, have assured me that women have taken up backpacking in great numbers, much like the numbers of men. The country's lush, mountainous landscape and an abundance of spectacular trails make backpacking an obvious recreation. There are thriving clubs in localities, schools, and universities that promote the activity. There seems general agreement that women don't worry about being assaulted in remote places there, nor do they fear dangerous animals and poisonous insects or snakes, since New Zealand doesn't have any.

For all of that, there are the following intriguing statistics. On the famous "tracks" (multi-day routes where the trails are unmistakable and manicured), women are 60 percent of the hikers in the so-called guided mode, which offers at the end of each day a rustic inn where they will have a bedroom, a hot shower, and prepared meals. Somewhat fewer women but still a full complement—48 percent—walk these same tracks independently, staying at huts that provide mattresses or bunk beds in dormitory rooms, gas burners, privies, and cold running water. As independents they must carry food, cookware, clothing, personal items, and sleeping bags, but not more. Yet even in the face of such participation figures, one study shows that women are only 12 percent of those who go into the more remote backcountry, where they must carry the full array of backpacking gear.

I conclude from the New Zealand statistics that women delight in long-distance hiking, and the less they have to carry, the more they like it. If they also like their comforts, or if, as one correspondent put it, they hesitate to find themselves "cold, wet, and scared," I don't know how large a part these considerations may play; but they are after all quite negotiable with appropriate lightweight gear and good technique. In short, I believe that women have the interest and can greatly extend their range.

Here in the United States, given the conflicting figures, we don't know exactly what proportion of backpackers women may be. But from the evidence we can safely say this much: Whatever their numbers in the entire universe of backpackers, whether they are 10 percent, 20 percent, 30 percent or some other proportion, women are clearly in the minority. No one who has spent much time in the backcountry is likely to dispute this. So for now, if you're a woman reading this book, or if you're a man looking to tempt your wife, sister, or girlfriend (or mother or grandmother for that matter) into backpacking, you're in the vanguard.

The Sexes Weigh In

As to why a heavy pack might discourage a woman, consider the following:

Women are, on average, smaller than men. The average young woman in the US is about 5´4˝ tall while her male counterpart is 5´9˝. Not surprisingly, women are also lighter, weighing 133 pounds (at the median) in their twenties while men weigh 165. (For all women and men ages 20–59 those figures are 144 and 176 pounds — which is to say, people spread with age, though regular hikers may well stay leaner.) These figures come from the US National Health and Nutrition Examination Survey. Even among men and women of the same height and weight, women are less strong, since a larger proportion of their body weight is fat — half again as much, in fact — and a smaller proportion is muscle. Androgen (male hormone) promotes the development of muscle, a fact well known to unscrupulous athletes who beef up their muscle mass with help from the pharmacy. If women could compete equally with men in sports, sooner or later they would find themselves on the same playing fields, and sooner or later they would shatter some of their records. This has not happened.

Because of their differences in strength, a man and woman will not view a monster pack with the same equanimity. But let us fast forward to a futuristic time — the present! — when trail-ready packs are much lighter for everyone. A base weight of 15 pounds for three-season backpacking is not especially noteworthy, not even low enough to be called ultralight. It is achievable without hardship on the trail and without outlandish expense beforehand. Add well-considered food for a week and water for half a day and carrying such a pack is still within virtually every woman's capabilities. So is it that simple? Now that lightweight gear is available is it exactly the same for women as for men?

No. But that is not the end of the story.

Women coexisting with men at 10,000 feet in shadow of the Sawtooth Range, Montana Beartooths, Winter 2003. (L to R) Don Johnston, Carol Crooker, Dave Schultz, Ellen Zaslaw, and Alan Dixon.

Components of Pack Weight

You might suppose that women will overcome much of their pack-weight disadvantage because a good deal of what they carry will be proportional to their size. After all, don't outfitters now carry gear in a variety of sizes? Smaller pack, smaller sleeping bag, smaller clothes — these could begin to add up to some real weight savings, you reason. Let's look inside the pack and see.

First off, we must acknowledge many unisex pieces of gear: navigation equipment, map, chemicals, flashlight or headlamp, stove, hydration system, cookpot, cup and bowl, tools, first aid, shelter, bear canister or bag, bear spray, camera, sunglasses, and so on. These sorts of things comprise a substantial portion of pack weight and will of course weigh the same in a woman's pack as in a man's. Then there are some items that *add* weight for the woman: she may need a cushiony sleeping pad to accommodate her curves against hard, flat ground. She may need sanitary supplies (and she may have used ones to pack out). She'll carry more toilet paper, fresh and used. She's likely to tolerate cold less than a man, so she'll need warmer clothing and perhaps a warmer sleeping bag. She's much likelier to need a structured pack with a hipbelt and well-padded shoulders (though some experts in body mechanics would argue that men need this too).

Ah yes, but, as we were saying, since she's smaller, isn't her clothing lighter, and doesn't she use a shorter sleeping bag, and isn't her pack itself smaller and lighter? The answer is that these things may be smaller and therefore lighter for a smaller person, but the difference accounts for less pack weight than you might think.

One manufacturer of ultralight packs lists a difference of one ounce between small and medium or medium and large packs — and these are packs with a solid suspension. The difference may even be smaller in the case of some frameless packs.

How about the sleeping bag? A sampling of specifications for lightweight bags of different lengths in the 20–30°F range yielded weight differences from 0–4 ounces, more typically less than 2 ounces for a given model. And it should be remembered that many bags do not come with size options at all, like those of at least one manufacturer much favored by the lightweight crowd. Their bags would of course weigh the same for men and women, larger people and smaller ones. Finally, some manufacturers make bags especially proportioned for women, wider in the hips, narrower in the shoulders, and loftier at the foot. But these different proportions don't make the women's bags any lighter. Only when a small person can select a small bag is there a break in weight.

And the pad? Self-inflating pads do not come in increments of 5 inches, the difference in height between average men and women. And even a short woman will lap over the end of a three-quarter-length pad. My best guess is that hikers don't make sex-linked choices of inflatable pads. Closed-cell foam pads, on the other hand, can be cut down, and slicing 5 inches off a full-length pad would save between half an ounce and a little more than 1 ounce, depending on the type of pad. The *torso*-length pad of a typical woman would have an even smaller weight advantage over a man's.

You can see that a few extra ounces for the weight of the pack, sleeping bag, and pad do not begin to add up to a proportionally greater load for a man, especially if you consider that women may have some special weights of their own to carry plus all the unisex items. Clothing, then? Food?

Clothing is heavier for a larger person. However, it isn't heavier in proportion to the difference in people's sizes. A surprising amount of the weight comes from zippers, pockets, elastics, bits of hardware, hoods, and such, and relatively little from extra inches of lightweight fabric in the sleeve or pants leg. Pants and long-sleeved shirts of different sizes made of lightweight wicking nylon may not differ in weight at all; insulating pants or expedition-weight long johns may differ by an ounce or two between, say, a women's medium and a man's. Ironically, identical insulating garments are often filled more generously in larger sizes, so that a smaller person may need to layer more items to keep comparably warm, when fewer ones with more fill would be more weight-efficient.

Finally there is the matter of food. Here at last women have a compelling advantage, at least on the trail. The caloric needs of people of different sizes are fairly proportional to the difference in their weights and levels of activity. Moreover, men and women metabolize somewhat differently. It takes fewer calories to sustain a woman than a man of identical height and weight, something on the order of 10–20 percent fewer. The difference is more dramatic when a woman and a man are physically active and differ in size, as they typically do. So on the trail a typical woman may need 25–30 percent fewer calories than a typical man. That means less food for the woman to carry — at the start of a week-long backpacking trip, perhaps 4 pounds less. Many women may not be pleased at their physiological differences off the trail, where they put on weight more readily than men and take it off with greater difficulty. But on the trail, their metabolic efficiency is pure advantage.

Hauling the Load

So what does all this add up to in terms of pack weight? Estimating conservatively from the above figures (and not counting footwear as part of pack weight), we might guess that the average lightweight pack for a woman might be at most one eighth lighter than a man's pack equipped similarly. That would be on a week-long backpacking trip potentially entailing some freezing weather. On a shorter trip, or one in warmer temperatures, the difference between the two would be smaller or perhaps even trivial. On an overnight trip in summer, the most common sort of backpacking outing, the difference between his pack and hers might not be much more than a pound. Meanwhile, as I have said, women weigh on average roughly one fifth less than men, and they are less muscular and strong besides. There's no escaping the fact that most women will carry packs that are a larger proportion of their body weight and they will work harder to carry them.

All the same, carrying a fully outfitted pack should be well within a woman's capacity. Even equipped for that week-long trip with some freezing weather, a woman needn't carry more than about 25 pounds total. And if she's rigorously ultralight, she can carry much less. As I've noted, this is the amount of weight a woman gains by the end of a typical healthy pregnancy. She, of course, acquires the strength to carry this load gradually as her pregnancy progresses. With training, the strength of muscles can increase 200 percent and more. Thus with a pack as with pregnancy weight a woman can come, little by little, to carry her load with ease. There is no fixed limit to how far training may take her.

From the start a woman has certain advantages in carrying a pack. One is her relatively broad pelvis, which provides an excellent platform for supporting and distributing pack weight. Whereas a potbellied man must tighten his hipbelt around his abdomen (or forgo one) and hope for the best, even a roundish woman can support the pack's weight largely on her pelvis. With a hipbelt and a good suspension, the pack should transfer substantial weight to the lower torso, and this is ideal from an ergonomic point of view, decreasing stress on the back and stomach muscles and increasing endurance, radically in some cases. It's a matter of simple physics that the farther from the pelvis an item is stowed, the more leverage it exerts and the more the muscles must work to carry it along. If the pack weight hangs off the shoulders, it impacts a good foot and a half higher than if it is lodged at the pelvis. Both because of the transfer of pack weight to the pelvis (with the right pack) and because of a woman's physique—her broad hips and narrow shoulders relative to a man's—a woman hiker has a low center of gravity, which aids not just endurance but also balance and forward propulsion.

While on the subject of packs, let's take a moment to reflect on the overall fit. Packs are being made these days that are highly suitable for women—a recent development. Some packs are even designed especially for them, with hipbelts that flare outward as their hips do and harnesses that are appropriately narrow at the shoulders so that they don't impede the motion of the arms. Shoulder straps that are S-shaped sit well at the top and give comfortable clearance for breasts. Many unisex packs can achieve this sort of fit as well. A sternum strap is valuable, too, in fitting the harness to the wearer and in helping to distribute weight away from the shoulder blades and onto the entire rib cage and torso. This matter of weight distribution is even more critical for women than for men because they have less upper body strength to begin with. This difference becomes more pronounced after age 35.

A woman who would like to backpack but is initially daunted by the load should consider that she can regulate her pack weight simply by planning her hikes with this in mind. Since food can be such a major share of the weight, she can opt for trips whose provisions she cares to carry, namely, ones of an acceptable length. Similarly, she can backpack in climates and seasons she finds congenial, given the heavier weight of clothing and shelter for colder weather. And she can choose routes where water is plentiful and she needn't carry much. In short, she can keep the physical challenge well within her comfort range.

If a woman is backpacking with another person, the pair will do well to view the hike not as a contest, but rather as a cooperative venture in which the communal load is distributed to best advantage. By trial and error, the hikers can figure out how much each can carry, so that they move at a similar speed with similar effort. It does not make for companionable or efficient hiking for one member of the pair—either one—to be struggling to keep up, slowing their progress and perhaps succumbing to fatigue at an early hour. Many hikers haven't considered the extent to which their difficulty or ease of hiking relative to someone else is really a function of the different loads they are carrying.

As I said at the start, the lightweight way makes it possible for all sorts of women to backpack comfortably the first time. These days a woman of average size, even a small one or a heavy one, one of no great strength or athleticism—such an utterly ordinary woman—can travel in the wilderness for days on end, long hours every day, carrying with ease everything she is likely to need.

Managing the Fears

Pack weight is not all that makes women hesitate. Many American women are afraid of encountering dangerous men in the backcountry, far from defenders or rescuers, as improbable as this might seem to some who have hiked a lifetime and never seen anyone remotely unsavory. At the time of this writing, the women's section of an online forum at Backpacker.com contained more archived posts on this than on any other substantive topic. The title of the thread: "Creepy Guys on the Trail."

How realistic are such fears? In 2001, over 3 million visitors spent at least some time on the Appalachian Trail. Yet it has been several years since the last report of a violent crime against a woman. The last murder took place in 1990, though there was one on an intersecting trail in 1996. The last reported rape also took place in the early 1990s. This is with millions of visitors every year, within easy reach of many of the most populous areas of the country. Where else in a congregation of millions of people can one imagine so *little* violent crime?

The National Park Service maintains crime statistics but unfortunately doesn't differentiate urban incidents from ones in the great outdoor expanses: the Service oversees many urban parklands and national monuments as well as wilderness-type parks. Even so, the NPS (with a typical 279 million visitors in 2001) has reported only three or four dozen rapes or attempted rapes in each of the past several years. That means, if as many as half the visitors and all rape victims were female, a given female's chance of facing such a crime in a given year on any national park property anywhere are at most 0.0000003 percent. Her chances of being murdered are about a third as high, or of being assaulted in some other fashion about twelve to sixteen times higher. If women are only a quarter of park visitors, then we can estimate that these minuscule risks are twice as great — and still minuscule. Scant as they are, these figures vastly overestimate the probability of facing such a crime in the backcountry, which sees only a tiny minority of all visitors and surely disproportionately few violent types. Thought of this way, violence really shouldn't be much of a worry.

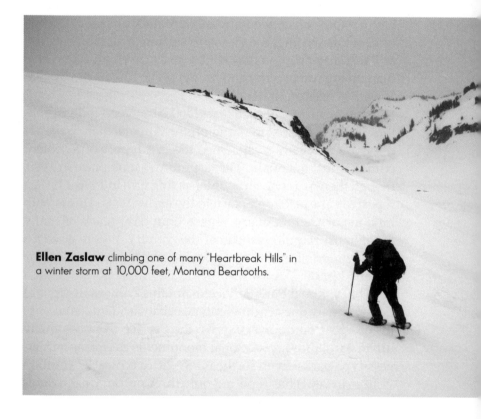

Ellen Zaslaw climbing one of many "Heartbreak Hills" in a winter storm at 10,000 feet, Montana Beartooths.

Some hikers carry firearms as a last-resort defense against animal attacks and as a deterrent against human ones. This is a highly controversial practice. In any event, it's illegal in state and national parks and many other areas hikers frequent. The figures above may give a measure of security to a woman who wonders if she's safe unarmed.

Still, if a woman is looking for extra margins of safety against the crimes that almost certainly will not occur, she can increase her confidence by taking a course in self-defense. She can read the book *Trail Safe* by Michael Bane, commissioned by the Appalachian Trail Conference. She can think of her bear spray as a defense not just against bears. She can travel

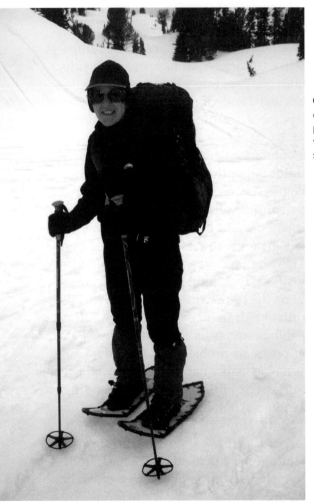

Close-up of The author carrying a lightweight pack (ULA Equipment) and walking on lightweight snowshoes (Northern Lites).

in the wilderness with others. None of these things will (at least in bear country) add an ounce to her pack weight, and if they lighten the load on her mind, that's a good thing.

Sleeping on the Ground

We come now to a variety of matters of practical concern to the female backpacker, and where better to start than with a good night's sleep? A woman's hourglass figure is not well suited to lying on the ground, particularly when she is lying on her side, unless she finds an exceptional "sweet spot", where curves on the ground exactly meet hers or she camps on something springy like tundra. What happens with side sleeping is that the spine collapses into a bent position, sinking into the gap between waist and ground, so that ligaments may be stretched to the point of disturbing normal alignments at the joints.

Many women will opt for a cushiony sleeping pad, even though it will cost weight, rather than wake up with aching hipbones on which she has balanced all night, or an aching back. There are lighter solutions, however. One would be to pin a rolled-up garment around her waist at bedtime, so that it fills the hollow even as she turns from side to side or rests on her back. This may be support enough. Another is to learn some sleeping positions that nights on her innerspring never drove her to. Flat on the back works surprisingly well, especially with the buttocks drawn back a bit so that the spine, rather than the silhouette, is as straight as possible. And stomach sleeping poses no problem. As well, the rear pants-pocket surface is a reasonably flat plane to place flush on the ground. The result is a position midway between side sleeping and back sleeping. Another excellent position is the commando crawl, on the stomach but a quarter-turn off horizontal, as if the sleeper is actually going to crawl low to the ground. This puts the spine in an ideal position, straight and not curled. Finally, a choice solution, when a woman is camping on friable soil, duff, or snow, is for her to scoop out her own hip hollow for the night (replacing the dirt when she decamps).

Whatever arrangements the woman tries, she should understand that the object of the game is to sleep comfortably and wake up with nothing hurting. It can be done.

Sports Bras

The women who need these know who they are. In everyday life, their bra straps leave ruts in their shoulders, and they are keenly aware of carrying a load on their chest. They will need firm support for long hours in motion, and they will want that support anchored over a wide area. A sports bra with wide straps that cross in back is best. Among other things it reinforces the posture that is most sustainable without fatigue. The bra should be of a cool and comfortable wicking fabric, lightweight of course. Happily, a sports bra serves nicely as swimsuit top, and here a fabric that dries quickly is often essential.

Even a woman who does not need extra support has options to consider. Ordinary lingerie (without lace or other abrasive decorations) is generally lightest and coolest, yet a minimalist sports bra or bare-midriff tank top might be worth the weight for a swimmer. As with other garments for the backcountry, cotton is to be avoided.

Cosmetics and Coifs

The female backpacker knows better than to fill her pack with pencils and brushes and crèmes and whatnot. These have no place in the backcountry, where naturalness and simplicity are the order of the day and where fragrances can invite visits from bears and other animals better left uninvited. Furthermore, nonessentials add unnecessary weight. Besides, the blush of healthy outdoor living will lend a radiance that cannot be daubed on from a pot.

Still, she might have a need or two. If lipstick (or any particular item) feels essential, she should study the products available and choose one that is fragrance free, offers sun protection, and is super lightweight. Ordinary neighborhood drugstores and chain stores carry such things. Lip balm may appear in the guise of colorless lipstick. She should hold out for lipstick or balm no thicker than a pencil, weighing half what the usual ones weigh. There are tinted sunscreens, if she feels the need.

I'll say even less about hairdos than about cosmetics. Practicality is all in the backcountry, so pony tails, braids, short bobs, and even buzz cuts are good options, among others. A woman won't make life changes in preparation for a week or two in the Rockies, but someone anticipating several weeks or months on the trail might think differently. In this connection, if she intends to cut off long hair, she might consider donating it so that it can be made into a wig for a sick child undergoing chemotherapy. Two organizations receiving such donations are called Wigs for Kids and Locks of Love.

To Pee or Not to Pee
(and Other Existential Questions)

Willy nilly, women hikers find their female plumbing a force to be reckoned with in the backcountry. It can be managed, just as water purification and other sanitary matters can. What follows is a survey of the management issues.

First a small excursion into the matter of how to urinate. Every woman who has spent more than a couple of hours on the trail has figured out a way to do this, but not every woman has thought of her best option. The least satisfactory approach, believe it or not one exercised by some experienced hikers, is to squat incompletely in such a way that urine at times dribbles onto clothes and perhaps into boots. This is unpleasant and (in terms of our particular focus) adds weight to the gear.

A common technique for urinating, guaranteed to be successful for all toileting, is the thoroughgoing squat. The best position is one that has the feet far forward of the business end, so that the hiker is in much the same position she's in on a toilet. If there's a branch or tree trunk or rock to grab onto, so much the better. It helps with balance and may even enable the woman to keep her pack on (with the belt open).

Many women find that aiming the stream downhill helps keep things under control, averting splashes and puddles at the feet.

Some women are blessed with an anatomy that enables them to urinate standing up, legs spread fairly well apart, in a fairly coherent stream. Some first investigate whether they may have this talent in the shower. (Keeping downhanging hairs well trimmed seems to be part of the technique.) This ability isn't of much use unless they are hiking in skirts, but as luck would have it, a few gear manufacturers are now making hiking skirts out of materials like Supplex, replete with cargo pockets. And of course many ordinary skirts can fit the bill as well. Miniskirts are lightweight but exposed. (I suggest dark underwear). Longer skirts are heavier but protect better from sun and abrasion. Minis can be teamed up with long johns or tights when the air cools down. Most women who have tried skirts still favor pants for bushwhacking or scrambling. Wind poses a challenge for skirts, especially billowy ones, but for trail hiking under the right conditions, skirts can be comfortable and they afford a measure of privacy in toilet situations that pants cannot match. For just such reasons, skirts are time-honored apparel for women hiking in the open landscape of the Himalaya. Actually, skirts merit consideration whatever a woman's toileting technique. They're cool and comfortable to hike in and, depending on their design, they may be lighter than pants.

It so happens that m'lady, in heeding the cries of her bladder, has much on her mind besides privacy and aim. She's also concerned about baring large amounts of flesh when it's cold outside or when she's likely to be assailed by biting insects. The obvious solution here is to anoint her bottom with insect repellent, just as she anoints her more public parts. One way of limiting exposure is to wear long pants with a snap or zip crotch, just like a baby's, so that the pants are not so much removed as parted when the need arises. At least one gear manufacturer (Wild Roses) makes such a thing — and tights constructed similarly. It would not be difficult for a hiker (or her tailor) to convert any pair of pants to this purpose.

NIGHT DUTY

What about those dreaded nighttime excursions out into the freezing air? The hiker has been very still for a very long time. She isn't flushed from exercise as she is during the day. She may need to leave her cozy nest, her sleeping bag and whatever shelters it, and maybe it's 15°F out there.

There are at least three possible approaches. One is the polar bear approach. She's gotta do what she's gotta do, so she goes out there and does it. It's a chance to prove what stern stuff she's made of. She needn't prove it all that far from the tent (unless she's in a designated camping spot). Nobody's looking, and some say that marking the campsite with urine will fend off bears and pacify mountain goats.

A second approach is the Ziploc approach. This approach assumes that she's in a tent, one in which it's possible to sit up and indeed squat, for that's what she's going to do. A Ziploc bag is going to be her chamber pot, and then she's going to close it very, very well. This technique has some potential for messiness, but like all techniques it improves with practice.

The third approach is for the Freudian. There are flexible plastic gizmos, suitably lightweight, the Freshette and the TravelMate by name, that cup around a woman's labia minora and collect urine into a tube that opens at the far end, enabling her to shoot it in the direction of her choosing — just like a man. Or she can attach a dedicated hose and collection bag and relieve herself tidily inside her tent. These products, managed adroitly, are said to reduce the need for toilet paper. They can certainly have their nighttime uses, and even some daytime ones: privacy and cover, operating through an unzipped fly. The downsides are that such a tool will need rinsing and storing in the meanwhile. To the extent that it can reduce the need for toilet paper, as it does for some, it may reduce pack weight.

Almost certainly the polar bears outnumber the Ziplocs and Freudians in this pursuit, and on really cold nights some of those polar bears are reluctant ones. Absolutely not to be recommended is severe limitation of fluids in the evening —

for example, leaving thirst unsatisfied in hopes of limiting the nighttime traffic. Even slight dehydration will reduce the hiker's capacity for thermoregulation, the very thing she's concerned about in the first place. At altitude it can increase the danger of acute mountain sickness or worse. Still, the hiker can be prudent rather than self-indulgent about fluids late in the day. And she can do one more thing: She can learn the difference between a seriously insistent bladder and one that is merely reporting in. She can learn to go back to sleep in the face of the latter.

The Tissue Issue

If a hiker is too casual about personal hygiene, the price may be soreness, or worse, infection. Urine, though sterile in the bladder, picks up pathogens as it passes through channels exiting the female body. In any event, it is acid, and a buildup of unblotted, air-dried urine is likely to cause irritation in a woman's tender parts. Thus, provisions have to be made.

Toilet paper is not a wholly trivial component of pack weight for women, who use it in multiples of the amounts men require. And the used product, now wet, is heavier than before. Nonetheless, it must be packed out or otherwise properly disposed of in a suitable cat hole in the conscientious application of LNT principles. So every female backpacker will be keen to minimize the amount she uses. Some women find that they can manage using it only every two or three times they urinate, perhaps washing themselves off at such times with toilet paper moistened with water and even a drop of soap (which neutralizes the acid in any urine residue and, if well chosen, can have antibacterial properties). In between times they might just shake off or else use leaves or stones for impromptu toilet paper, although lacking absorbency these are not ideal. Other women may economize on toilet paper by learning certain virtuoso techniques for urinating such as those explained on the TravelMate website, accomplished with or without the tool. Another way a woman can reduce the need for toilet paper is to use instead a squirt of clean water to her external parts from a tiny water pistol or squirt bottle. This can be a weight saver where water is plentiful but not where water has to be carried long distances. For the very brave, snow when available is a perfectly good cleanser.

Cleanliness and management of waste are every bit as important with regard to defecation, but here women's needs converge with men's, and so the reader may consult the chapter on hygiene for further advice.

Menstruation

Women of childbearing age, unless pregnant or pausing for lactation, will need to take their menses into account in planning backpacking trips. Even if they plan carefully for trips to fall between periods — clearly, we aren't speaking of thru-hikers here — they must prepare for the unexpected because travel involving changes of latitude, altitude, activity, and diet can bring on a period ahead of schedule.

Outdoorspeople may have heard that it is dangerous for a menstruating woman to be in bear country — that bears, with their uncanny sense of smell, fix on the aroma of menstrual blood from great distances and prowl in pursuit. If that were so, it could be a life-or-death imperative to avoid the backcountry at that time of month. Fortunately, as far as we know, this turns out to be an urban legend. Although research in this area is far from extensive and more would be welcome, a pair of studies has shown that black bears much prefer garbage or suet-soaked tampons to tampons soaked with menstrual blood or drawn blood. A perusal of books on grizzlies finds no evidence of preference for menstruating women on their part either. And a survey of bear maulings in US and Canadian national parks confirms the same thing: They have not involved menstruating women disproportionately. So fortunately, I am speaking of hygiene and comfort, not survival.

The lightest and tidiest possible solution to the matter of menstruation is the guarantee of none for months at a time. For women inclined to use oral contraceptives there actually may be such a solution, a formulation newly released in

2003 called Seasonale. The active pills are actually the same combination of low-dose estrogen and progestin used in many versions of the Pill already long in use. What makes Seasonale different is the packaging, placing a week's worth of dummy pills (to induce a period) after twelve full weeks of active ones. Do the arithmetic: This would result in only about four periods a year. Many doctors have prescribed this sort of regimen off label (or even the continuous use of active pills) for decades. Seasonale merely formalizes the practice. About 8 percent of women attempting to use it drop out because of unacceptable levels of breakthrough bleeding. However, this undesirable side effect declines with each cycle.

From time to time most women will have to deal with the menstrual flow in the backcountry one way or another. It is perfectly possible to use tampons or pads, and that is what most do. The requirement to pack the used products out adds weight, but fortunately food stores will go down faster than this weight will go up. It also creates a nighttime storage problem, but backpackers know all about stowing food out of reach of animals. It will be the same with menstrual waste. Crushed aspirin or a black tea bag mixed in with the refuse will minimize odor. Some have suggested a scented sheet of fabric softener as a mask, but these scents are often intense. In bear country there are wiser plans.

There is a unique piece of gear that may appeal to some women, and that is The Keeper (a.k.a. Instead), a small dome that is placed over the cervix, much as a diaphragm would be. This cup can collect menstrual fluid—perhaps only a couple of hours' worth on a day of heavy flow—and then can be emptied (away from water sources), washed, and reinserted. A menstrual sponge would offer similar benefits. Worn internally, it collects menstrual blood and, after being squeezed out and then washed, it can be reinserted. In either case, in return for minimizing the weight and bulk of supplies carried, the woman has extra duties to perform in order to maintain a hygienic environment. They should—I cannot emphasize too strongly—be performed with treated water and, at least once a day, soap as well.

Backpacking During Pregnancy

There is no reason why a pregnant woman cannot backpack. She should use good sense—and her body will warn her—about hiking if she is not meeting her nutritional needs due to nausea. She should also use good sense about how far into the backcountry to go if it's late enough in the pregnancy that she's in any danger of delivering. Those two caveats aside, she's free to backpack just as she has done before.

The expectant mother will contend with certain challenges as the pregnancy progresses, namely, her weight and her shape. Actually both of these lead to the same conclusion: that her pack weight must diminish as her pregnancy weight increases. Before long it ought to be no more than 15 pounds, or 10 percent of her body weight, if that is less. With a light enough load, it should then be possible for her to wear a belt-less pack, which by virtue of the geometry of the situation (and the delicacy of the changing uterus) will have become something of a necessity. She will enjoy a pleasant balancing of payload fore and aft, something not often given to hikers. It will fall to her hiking companions to carry portions of her usual pack contents. They should not forget that she is carrying the weightiest and most precious cargo of all.

Backpacking with Baby

Valuable books have been written on the subject of outdoor experiences with the very young, and they teach much about managing logistics and imparting a love of these activities to the children. I'll pause only briefly to note that aspect most intimately connected to a woman's body, breastfeeding. Breast milk is of course the perfect trail food for baby: always ready, always sanitary, never in need of warming. It's lightweight in that it requires no special equipment. On the other hand, bottle-feeding parents are not badly off. Powdered formula carried in disposable plastic bags is perfectly lightweight. With the use of a lightweight plastic nurser, there will be nipples to wash and perhaps sterilize and emptied bags to carry, but that's all. Unlike mother's milk, formula travels in dehydrated form. The nursing mom and the bottle feeder can, one day when they have time on their hands, sit down together and calculate whose load is really lighter, given the enlargement and extra weight of lactating breasts.

Conclusion

In the space of a chapter we have sampled moments along a woman's lifespan, from her reedy youth to her fuller womanhood, and from her hikes with friends and lovers to her time on the trail during pregnancy walking alongside the husband or partner who will see her through. Finally we peeked at a woman hiker as a mother, introducing her child in tenderest youth to the outdoors. The story of a woman's life of course continues on from there. She grows into middle age and her children (if she has them) grow up, having grown all the while in their outdoor skills and in their appreciation for the natural world she has visited with them again and again. I don't know how many people think of their grandmothers when they think of women who backpack, and I'm in no position to vouch for the eccentric Grandma Gatewood. But I can tell you that increasing numbers of grandmas wearing backpacks will appear in people's picture frames in the future, and quite a few already do. Without the lightweight revolution this would not have been possible.

Acknowledgements: For their valuable assistance, I wish to thank Stuart Bilby, Kay Brown, Carol Crooker, Jackie Davidson, Carol (Coosa) Donaldson, Katherine Flegal, Brian King, Don Ladigan, Roz Lasker, Lisa Lee-Johnson, David McCune, John O'Mahoney, Robert Reid, Robert Romauch, Glen Van Peski, Neal Zaslaw, and an anonymous gear manufacturer.

Appendix A:
Gear Lists

Lightweight backpacking enthusiasts entertain various degrees of obsession with spreadsheets, postal scales with tenth-ounce accuracy, and other activities central to gear planning. Here are a few practical checklists to get you started.

Generic Checklist for Summer Ultralight Backpacking in Temperate Mountain Ranges

By Ryan Jordan

The purpose of this list is simple: to provide a framework for developing your own checklist. With all of the optional gear, this list is entirely suitable for virtually any wilderness location in the lower 48 states between Memorial Day and Labor Day, with the exception, possibly, of the highest slopes of Washington's Mount Rainier. With some care in gear selection and only moderate expense, anyone should be able to outfit themselves with a complete off-the-shelf lightweight gear kit that costs between $300 and $1,000 and easily weighs less than 12 pounds. Additional expenditures will buy you more luxury in items that have a higher performance-to-weight ratio—such as high-quality down fill sleeping bags—and will allow you to pack less than 10 pounds of equipment (not including food and water) while remaining safe and comfortable.

HIKING GEAR

- ☐ Trail-running shoes
- ☐ Ankle-length merino wool socks (2 pair)
- ☐ Collapsible trekking poles

CLOTHING WORN WHILE HIKING

- ☐ Underwear
- ☐ Breathable stretch-woven hiking pants
- ☐ Long-sleeve lightweight merino wool crew shirt
- ☐ Wide-brimmed hat for sun
- ☐ Cotton bandana for neck shade (optional)

OTHER CLOTHING PACKED

- ☐ Ultralight windshirt
- ☐ Synthetic or down insulating sweater
- ☐ Lightweight rain jacket and pants
- ☐ Fleece or wool gloves
- ☐ Fleece or wool beanie cap

SHELTER AND SLEEP SYSTEM

- ☐ 700-900 fill down sleeping bag rated to 30 degrees
- ☐ Torso-sized inflatable or closed-cell foam sleeping pad
- ☐ Waterproof ground cloth
- ☐ 8´-x-10´ silnylon tarp (sleeps 1–2)
- ☐ 12 titanium tent stakes
- ☐ Spectra guylines

COOKING AND HYDRATION SYSTEMS

- ☐ Alcohol stove & pot support
- ☐ Windscreen
- ☐ 1-liter titanium cookpot (for solo cooking) or 1.5–2.0 liter (for couples)
- ☐ 16-oz capacity titanium mug
- ☐ Titanium spork
- ☐ Two collapsible water bottles, 3L+ total capacity
- ☐ Chorine dioxide (Aquamira) chemical water treatment kit
- ☐ Box of matches and 1 lighter
- ☐ Silnylon stuff sack and Spectra rope for hanging a bear bag

PACKING SYSTEMS

- ☐ Internal frame or frameless backpack, 40L capacity < 2.0 lbs
- ☐ Silnylon stuff sacks for sleeping bag and clothing, and to organize small items in pack
- ☐ Trash compactor bag liner for use inside pack to keep contents dry

NAVIGATION SYSTEMS

- ☐ Maps printed on waterproof paper
- ☐ Watch with compass-altimeter functions
- ☐ LED Headlamp with Lithium AA or Lithium AAA batteries

OTHER GEAR

- ☐ DEET insect repellent & noseeum mesh headnet
- ☐ SPF 30+ sunblock repackaged in a small balm jar
- ☐ Firestarting tinder & firestarter sealed in a waterproof zip-closure bag
- ☐ First-aid supplies for blister and wound treatment and medications for pain, diarrhea, allergies, and other ailments as appropriate

- ☐ UV blocking sunglasses
- ☐ Assorted toilet items as appropriate: toothbrush, toothpaste or castile soap, alcohol hand gel, feminine hygiene supplies, and small microfiber washcloth or towel

ADDITIONS AND SUBSTITUTIONS TO CONSIDER FOR INCLEMENT CONDITIONS

- ☐ Single-wall tent instead of a tarp and groundcloth *or* water-resistant/breathable bivy sack instead of a groundcloth
- ☐ Hooded parka instead of a sweater
- ☐ Fleece vest & balaclava
- ☐ Silkweight synthetic long underwear bottoms
- ☐ Waterproof mitt shells
- ☐ Short, breathable gaiters
- ☐ Canister stove instead of alcohol

SUBTRACTIONS AND SUBSTITUTIONS TO LIGHTEN YOUR LOAD IN MID-SUMMER

- ☐ Poncho tarp instead of a flat tarp and rain jacket
- ☐ Use cook fires instead of a stove
- ☐ Insulated vest instead of a sweater
- ☐ Down quilt instead of a sleeping bag

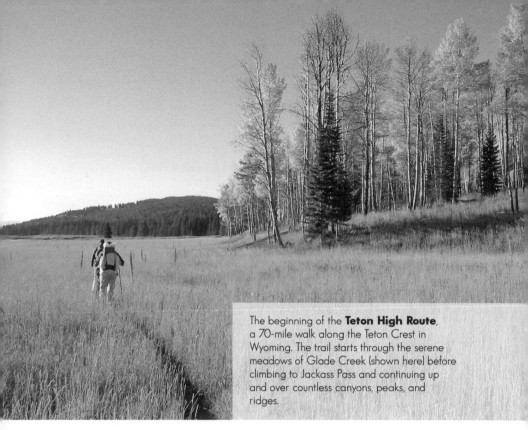

The beginning of the **Teton High Route**, a 70-mile walk along the Teton Crest in Wyoming. The trail starts through the serene meadows of Glade Creek (shown here) before climbing to Jackass Pass and continuing up and over countless canyons, peaks, and ridges.

3-Season, 3-Day Gear List

By Ryan Jordan

The gear list provided below is merely an example of how one lightweight backpacker might select equipment for a 3-day weekend outing. Generally, the choices below are suitable for most three-season conditions (spring, summer, fall) in the mountain ranges of continental US, recognizing that some level of skill and experience is required to successfully use this equipment kit in inclement conditions. More experienced backpackers can trim weight even further from this list. Less experienced backpackers will find that a few extra pounds of clothing, shelter, and/or food will give them a more acceptable level of comfort and safety.

Some examples of brands and models/styles are listed below for reference only. They neither represent an endorsement of that particular product, nor a suggestion that the product listed is the best choice in the context of any particular situation.

Clothing Worn

FUNCTION	STYLE	EXAMPLE	WEIGHT
Hat With Brim	Wide-brimmed, Water-resistant Nylon Hat	Tilley Lt	3.0 oz (85 g)
Hiking Shirt	Lightweight Merino Wool Long-sleeve Crew	Smartwool Aero	7.0 oz (198 g)
Underwear	Trim-fitting Support Shorts, Boxer-style	Nike Spandex Running Short Tights	3.0 oz (85 g)
Hiking Pants	Soft Shell Stretchwoven Long Pants	Cloudveil Prospector	9.0 oz (255 g)
Hiking Socks	Merino Wool Trail Running Socks	Smartwool Trail Runner Ii	1.5 oz (43 g)
Hiking Shoes	Breathable Synthetic Trail Running Shoes	Montrail Vitesse Ii	26.0 oz (737 g)

Other Items Worn/Carried

FUNCTION	STYLE	EXAMPLE	WEIGHT
Trekking Poles	One Piece, Carbon Fiber	Stix Pro	6.0 oz (170 g)
Whistle	Pealess Whistle On Spectra Cord	ACR Mini Whistle, Aircore Plus Lanyard	1.0 oz (28 g)
Watch	Compass/altimeter Watch	Suunto S6	1.3 oz (37 g)

Other Clothing

FUNCTION	STYLE	EXAMPLE	WEIGHT
Windshirt	Thin, Breathable Pullover-style Windshirt	GoLite Wisp HP	3.0 oz (85 g)
Insulation Layer	Synthetic High Loft Insulation Pullover	Bozeman Mountain Works Cocoon	8.5 oz (241 g)
Rain Jacket	Waterproof-breathable, Simple Jacket	Montane Superfly	8.0 oz (227 g)
Rain Pants	Waterproof-breathable, Simple Pull-on	Golite Reed	5.0 oz (142 g)
Warm Hat	Wool Beanie Cap	Possumdown Beanie	1.5 oz (43 g)
Warm Gloves	Wool Liner Gloves	Possumdown Gloves	1.3 oz (37 g)
Rain Mitts	Waterproof-breathable Shell Mitts	Outdoor Research Rain Mitts	1.1 oz (31 g)

Citation:

This list was originally published in the online magazine BackpackingLight.com (ISSN 1537-0364) in December 2003.

Sleep System

FUNCTION	STYLE	EXAMPLE	WEIGHT
Overhead Shelter	One Person Tarp	Bozeman Mountain Works 7' X 9' Catenary Spintarp	7.5 oz (213 g)
Tent Stakes	Titanium Skewer Style	Bozeman Mountain Works Hi-vis Ti Stakes (8)	2.2 oz (62 g)
Guylines	25 Feet, Thin Diameter Spectra	Bozeman Mountain Works Aircore 1	0.1 oz (3 g)
Bivy Sack	Waterproof Bottom, Breathable Top	Bozeman Mountain Works Vapr Bivy	6.5 oz (184 g)
Sleeping Bag	Variable Girth Down Bag	Nunatak Arc Ghost	16.0 oz (454 g)
Sleeping Pad	Torso Sized Inflatable Mattress	Bozeman Mountain Works Torsolite	10.0 oz (284 g)

Packing

FUNCTION	STYLE	EXAMPLE	WEIGHT
Backpack	Lightweight Frameless Pack	Six Moon Designs Moonlight	16.0 oz (454 g)
Stuff Sack	250 Ci For Clothing	Bozeman Mountain Works Spinsack	0.25 oz (7 g)
Stuff Sack	250 Ci For Clothing	Bozeman Mountain Works Spinsack	0.25 oz (7 g)
Stuff Sack	500 Ci For Sleeping Gear	Bozeman Mountain Works Spinsack	0.35 oz (10 g)

Cooking and Water

FUNCTION	STYLE	EXAMPLE	WEIGHT
Stove	Canister	Vargo Jet-Ti	2.5 oz (71 g)
Fuel Container	Canister, Small Size	Snow Peak Giga Power 110g Fuel Canister (Empty)	3.5 oz (99 g)
Cook Pot	21 Oz Titanium Mug/pot	Snow Peak 600 Mug	2.8 oz (79 g)
Cook Pot Lid	Foil	To Fit Mug	0.1 oz (3 g)
Wind Screen	Foil	Heavy Duty Aluminum Foil	0.5 oz (14 g)
Utensil	Spoon	Backpacking Light Long-Handled Titanium Spoon	0.6 oz (17 g)
Lighting	Matches & Lighter	Bic Lighter & Matches In 4" X 7" Aloksak	1.0 oz (28 g)
Water Bottles	1l Soft Side Bladders	Platypus 1l (Two)	1.8 oz (51 g)
Water Treatment	Chlorine Dioxide	Aquamira Kit Repackaged In Dropper Bottles	1.1 Oz (31 G)

Cooking and Water (con't)

FUNCTION	STYLE	EXAMPLE	WEIGHT
Food Storage	Bear Bag	Ursalite Bear Bag Hanging System	3.0 oz (85 g)

Other Essentials

FUNCTION	STYLE	EXAMPLE	WEIGHT
Maps	Custom Printed On Waterproof Paper	National Geographic Topo!	2.0 oz (57 g)
Light	LED Headlamp	Photon Freedom Microlights (3) on Aircore Spectra Lanyard	1.2 oz (34 g)
First Aid	Minor Wound Care & Meds	Assorted Wound & Blister Care And Medicines	2.0 oz (57 g)
Firestarting	Emergency Firestarting - Waterproof	Sparklite & Firestarter In 4"x7" Aloksak	1.0 oz (28 g)
Sunglasses	100% Uv Blocking, Plastic Lenses/frames	Julbo	1.0 oz (28 g)
Sunscreen	100% Uv Blocking, Waterproof, Paste	Dermatone	1.0 oz (28 g)
Insect Repellent	100% Deet	Repackaged in MicroDrop Bottle	0.5 oz (14 g)
Personal Hygiene	Assorted Toiletries	Toothbrush, Soap, Toilet Paper, Alcohol Hand Gel, In 4" X 7" Aloksak	2.0 oz (47 g)

Consumables

FUNCTION	STYLE	EXAMPLE	WEIGHT
Fuel	Canister, Small Size	Snow Peak Giga Power, 110g	3.8 oz (108 g)
Food	2.5 Days	20 oz/day	50.0 oz (1418 g)
Water	Average Carried	Half Quart	16.0 oz (454 g)

WEIGHT SUMMARY		
(1)	Total Weight Worn or Carried	3.61 lb (1.64 kg)
(2)	Total Base Weight in Pack	7.20 lb (3.27 kg)
(3)	Total Weight of Consumables	4.36 lb (1.98 kg)
(4)	Total Initial Pack Weight (2) + (3)	11.56 lb (5.25 kg)
(5)	Full Skin Out Weight (1) + (2) + (3)	16.22 lb (7.37 kg)

Ultralight Snow Cave Camping

By Ryan Jordan

The gear list provided below is one example of how a lightweight backpacker might select equipment for a 3-day weekend outing in temperate mountain ranges in the winter. Inherent assumptions in this list include:

- Several feet of unconsolidated snowcover on the ground
- Overnight low temperatures of 0–15 degrees
- Daytime highs not above freezing

This list focuses on camping inside a snow cave. With enough snow cover, snow caves are the fastest, warmest types of snow shelters available. Properly built, a snow cave gives you the flexibility to use three-season gear to remain warm, which can save a tremendous amount of weight. However, this approach requires an exceptional level of skill in locating a site and properly building a snow cave. In addition, snow caves can be wet enough to warrant the use of a highly water-resistant sleeping bag shell or bivy sack for a down sleeping bag. Finally, digging a snow cave is wet business: waterproof raingear or all-synthetic insulating clothing is warranted.

IMPORTANT DISCLAIMER

IF YOU ARE CAUGHT WITH AN EQUIPMENT KIT LIKE THIS AND ARE UNABLE TO BUILD A SNOW CAVE, OR YOU BUILD ONE IMPROPERLY, YOU WILL SUBJECT YOURSELF TO SEVERE RISK OF HYPOTHERMIA.

In context, it is important to note what constitutes an improperly built snow cave. Primarily, a properly built snow cave is one that is just large enough for the number of occupants (less volume to maintain a thermal mini-climate), has thick enough walls for proper insulation (generally, 2 feet), has a properly located entrance (below the level of the ground surface so warmed air doesn't escape), and proper blocking of the entrance (with packs or a hung jacket to minimize cold air exchange).

In a snow cave, conditions are very damp. They tend to be quite humid, gear has no ability to dry, and dripping walls tend to get sleeping gear wet. Consequently, we have selected synthetic insulation in our clothing and sleeping bag, and have added a water resistant bivy sack to shed some of the external moisture. We have specified an insulated clothing and sleep system that will allow the user to survive a night outside the snow cave, if one cannot be built. This system has been used to comfortably sleep at winter temperatures down to minus 10 degrees outside of a tent. If the risk of spending a night in the open is very small, and the user is a competent snow cave builder, we recommend that the user save further weight with a lighter sleeping bag. We have spent nights down to 0 degrees using the clothing specified in this list in combination with a 2-pound synthetic bag rated to 40 degrees F (Integral Designs Andromeda Strain).

We have elected to bring a white gas stove over a canister or alcohol stove, for the improved efficiency in melting snow. Snow cave environments are usually warm enough such that both white gas and alcohol stoves work well. However, a white gas stove has the power to melt several liters of snow quickly. If you need to melt snow while traveling at midday and conditions are cold, you'll appreciate the power of a white gas system.

We have selected wide mouth water bottles for their ability to resist freezing in the opening, and the wide mouth caps are easy to handle with gloves or mittens. We've chosen a hybrid LED headlamp with a high-power (1-watt) LED to give us the flexibility of navigating after dark, which is not uncommon in the winter.

Some examples of brands and models/styles are listed below for reference only. They neither represent an endorsement of that particular product, nor a suggestion that the product listed is the best choice in the context of any particular situation.

Clothing Worn

FUNCTION	STYLE	EXAMPLE	WEIGHT
Thin Hat	Thermal Headwear For Active Conditions	Thin Powerstretch Balaclava	1.5 oz
Active Shirt	Bicomponent Windshirt	Rab V-trail Top	12.0 oz
Underwear	Trim-fitting Support Shorts, Boxer-style	Nike Spandex Running Short Tights	3.0 oz
Active Pants	Soft Shell Stretchwoven Long Pants	Arc'teryx Gamma Mx	18.0 oz
Gloves	Windproof, Insulated Gloves	Cloudveil Icefloe Gloves	5.0 oz
Snow Socks	Ultralight Thin, Ski-style Sock	Smartwool Ultralight Ski Socks	4.0 oz
Gaiters	Breathable Gaiters	Outdoor Research Flex-tex	4.5 oz
Boots	Insulated Snow Boots	Baffin Tundra	48.0 oz

Other Items Worn/Carried

FUNCTION	STYLE	EXAMPLE	WEIGHT
Ski Poles	One Piece, Carbon Fiber, With Snow Baskets	Stix Pro with Snow Baskets	8.0 oz
Snowshoes	Large Deck Model For Deep Snow	Northern Lites Backcountry 30"	43.0 oz
Whistle	Pealess Whistle On Spectra Cord	ACR Mini Whistle, Aircore Plus Lanyard	1.0 oz
Watch	Compass/altimeter Watch	Suunto S6	1.3 oz

Other Clothing

FUNCTION	STYLE	EXAMPLE	WEIGHT
Storm Jacket	Soft Shell Stretchwoven Jacket	Cloudveil Icefloe	20.0 oz
Insulating Jacket	Synthetic High Loft Insulating, Hooded Pullover	Integral Designs Dolomitti Parka	23.0 oz
Insulating Pants	Synthetic High Loft Insulating Pants With Side-zips	Integral Designs Denali Pants	20.0 oz
Warm Hat	Wool Beanie Cap	Possumdown Beanie	1.5 oz
Warm Mitts	Insulated Mitts	Integral Designs Down Mitts	5.0 oz

Sleep System

FUNCTION	STYLE	EXAMPLE	WEIGHT
Snow Shovel	Suitable For Digging A Snow Cave	Snowclaw Backcountry Snow Shovel	5.4 oz
Bivy Sack	Waterproof Bottom, Breathable Top	Bozeman Mountain Works Vapr Bivy	6.5 oz
Sleeping Bag	Synthetic, Rated To 10 °f	Integral Designs North Twin Primaloft Sleeping Bag	56.0 oz
Sleeping Pad	Full Length Closed-cell Foam Pad	Cascade Designs Ridge Rest Sleeping Pad, Full Length	14.0 oz
Sleeping Pad	Torso Sized Inflatable Mattress	Bozeman Mountain Works TorsoLite	10.0 oz

Packing

FUNCTION	STYLE	EXAMPLE	WEIGHT
Backpack	Backpack With 30-lb Carry Capacity	Granite Gear Vapor Trail	32.0 oz
Stuff Sack	250 Ci For Clothing	Bozeman Mountain Works Spinsack S	0.25 oz
Stuff Sack	250 Ci For Clothing	Bozeman Mountain Works Spinsack S	0.25 oz
Stuff Sack	500 Ci For Sleeping Gear	Bozeman Mountain Works Spinsack M	0.45 oz

Cooking and Water

FUNCTION	STYLE	EXAMPLE	WEIGHT
Stove	White Gas	Msr Simmerlite With Pump And Windscreen	11.0 oz
Fuel Container	Titanium	Msr Titan Fuel Bottle, 0.6l	3.5 oz
Cook Pot	2l Cookpot (Large Enough For Melting Snow)	Antigravitygear 2l Pot With Lid & Cozy	8.0 oz
Drinking Mug	16+ Oz Capacity Drinking Mug	Snow Peak 2l Oz Titanium Mug	2.8 oz
Utensil	Spoon	Backpacking Light Long-Handled Titanium Spoon	0.5 oz
Lighting	Matches & 2 Lighters	Bic Lighters (2) & Storm Matches In 4" X 7" Aloksak	1.5 oz
Water Bottles	1.5l Soft Bottles With Wide Mouth Lids	Two 48-oz Nalgene Cantenes	5.0 oz
Food Storage	Waterproof Bag	12" X 15" Aloksak	2.0 oz

Other Essentials

FUNCTION	STYLE	EXAMPLE	WEIGHT
Maps	Custom Printed On Waterproof Paper	National Geographic Topo!	2.0 oz
Light	Led Headlamp, Suitable For Nightime Navigation	Princeton Tec Yukon HI With Lithium Aa Batteries	7.0 oz
First Aid	Minor Wound Care & Meds	Assorted Wound & Blister Care And Medicines	2.0 oz
Firestarting	Emergency Firestarting - Waterproof	Sparklite & Firestarter In 4"x7" Aloksak	1.0 oz
Sunglasses	100 Percent Uv Blocking, Plastic Lenses/frames	Julbo	1.0 oz
Goggles	Lightweight Ski Goggles For Blizzard Travel	Bolle Zoopla	3.0 oz
Anti-fog	For Glasses & Goggle Care	Anti-fog Balm, Cleaning Cloth	1.0 oz
Sunscreen	100% Uv Blocking, Waterproof, Paste	Dermatone	1.0 oz
Personal Hygiene	Assorted Toiletries	Toothbrush, Soap, Toilet Paper, Alcohol Hand Gel, In 4" X 7" Aloksak	2.0 oz

Consumables

FUNCTION	STYLE	EXAMPLE	WEIGHT
Fuel	White Gas, 2.5 Days	6 oz/day	15 oz
Food	2.5 Days	32 oz/day	80 oz
Water	Average Carried	1.5 quarts	48 oz

WEIGHT SUMMARY

(1)	Total Weight Worn or Carried	9.33 lb
(2)	Total Base Weight in Pack	15.53 lb
(3)	Total Weight of Consumables	8.94 lb
(4)	Total Initial Pack Weight (2) + (3)	24.47 lb
(5)	Full Skin Out Weight (1) + (2) + (3)	33.70 lb

Citation:

This list was originally published in the online magazine BackpackingLight.com (ISSN 1537-0364) in January 2004.

Desert Hiking Gear List

By Carol Crooker

The desert hiking gear list provided below is one example of how a lightweight backpacking enthusiast might select equipment for a 3-day weekend outing in benign desert conditions in the spring through fall. Deep summer conditions (the monsoon season), when torrential rains threaten and temperatures exceed 105°F (41°C), are excluded.

The list is designed for the southwest United States desert. Vegetation is of the prickly variety, and trails are generally rocky. Trees, if any, are normally small and thorny. Water is available, but scarce. Three-season temperatures range from about 25°–105°F (-4° to 41°C) and can be quite variable. A single trip into the Grand Canyon in May can see temperatures from freezing to the 90s (low 30s C), with intense sun in the inner canyon, and snow, rain, and hail near the rim.

This list is aimed at the cooler end of the above range. For a trip where the expected low is 60°F (16°C), both insulation layers, the warm hat, and the sleeping bag could be left at home. For a trip at the very lowest end of the range, a warmer sleeping bag might be added.

It is assumed that water is not available along the trail, and that campsites are located near reliable water sources. A water sack could be added if a dry camp is planned. Rain is possible, but not expected.

An inflatable mattress was selected since it provides some extra cushion on the sometimes rock hard ground. Although there is some danger of the vegetation pricking a hole in an inflatable, the Bozeman Mountain Works TorsoLite inflatable sleeping pad offers a tougher cover than other ultralight sleeping pads. A repair kit can be added to the pack for an extended trip.

Bear bagging rope was not included because suitable trees for hanging are rare.

Crew-length socks were chosen to provide some protection from ankle attacking vegetation.

A wide-brimmed hat protects the face and neck from desert sun. The airy mesh panels in the Rail Riders Adventure shirt provide excellent ventilation in the heat. The Salomon Tech Amphibian shoes were selected for the versatility needed for hiking in the heat as well as wading canyons.

Some examples of brands and models/styles are listed below for reference only. They neither represent an endorsement of that particular product, nor a suggestion that the product listed is the best choice in the context of any particular situation.

Clothing Worn

FUNCTION	STYLE	EXAMPLE	WEIGHT
Hat With Brim	Wide-brimmed Hat	Tilley Lt3	3.0 oz (85g)
Hiking Shirt	Long Sleeved Sun Protection Shirt	Rail Riders Adventure Shirt	6.1 oz (173g)
Sport Top	Minimal, Breathable	Patagonia Mesh Sport Top	2.1 oz (60 g)
Underwear	Synthetic Briefs	Moving Comfort Microbrief	1.3 oz (37 g)
Hiking Pants	Lightweight Sun Protection Pants	Solumbra Active Pants	6.3 oz (179 g)
Hiking Socks	Lightweight Merino Wool Blend, Crew	Smartwool Light Hiker	2.7 oz (77 g)
Hiking Shoes	Breathable Synthetic Trail Running Shoes	Salomon Tech Amphibians	24.2 oz (686 g)

Other Items Worn/Carried

FUNCTION	STYLE	EXAMPLE	WEIGHT
Trekking Poles	One Piece, Carbon Fiber	Stix Pro Trekking Poles	6.0 oz (170 g)
Watch	Thermometer Watch	Casio Women's Pathfinder With Band Removed On Bozeman Mountain Works Ursalite Micro Carabiner	0.9 oz (26 g)

Other Clothing

FUNCTION	STYLE	EXAMPLE	WEIGHT
Windshirt	Thin, Breathable Windshirt	GoLite Wisp HP	2.9 oz (82 g)
Insulation Layer	Lightweight Merino Wool Long Sleeve Crew	Smartwool Lightweight Merino Crew	7.5 oz (213 g)

Other Clothing (con't)

FUNCTION	STYLE	EXAMPLE	WEIGHT
Insulation Layer	Lightweight Down Long Sleeve Top	Montbell Ultra Lite Down Inner Jacket	7.2 oz (204 g)
Rain Jacket	Lightweight Poncho/tarp	See Overhead Shelter Below	0.0 oz (0 g)
Warm Hat	Beanie Hat	PossumDown Fleece Beanie	1.2 oz (34 g)

Sleep System

FUNCTION	STYLE	EXAMPLE	WEIGHT
Overhead Shelter	One Person Poncho/tarp	Bozeman Mountain Works Spinponcho	6.5 oz (184 g)
Tent Stakes	Native	Rocks	0.0 oz (0 g)
Guylines	50 Feet, Thin Cord Able To Hold A Tautline Hitch	Kelty Triptease	1.0 oz (28 g)
Bivy Sack	Waterproof Bottom, Breathable Top	Bozeman Mountain Works Vapr Bivy	6.5 oz (184 g)
Sleeping Bag	Variable Girth Down Bag	Nunatak Arc Edge	11.0 oz (312 g)
Sleeping Pad	Torso Sized Inflatable Mattress	Bozeman Mountain Works Torsolite	10.0 oz (283 g)

Packing

FUNCTION	STYLE	EXAMPLE	WEIGHT
Backpack	Lightweight Frameless Pack	Gossamer Gear G5 with Padded Harness	7.6 oz (215 g)
Stuff Sack	250 Ci For Clothing	Bozeman Mountain Works Spinsack (S)	0.25 oz (7 g)
Stuff Sack	500 Ci For Sleeping Gear	Bozeman Mountain Works Spinsack (M)	0.35 oz (10 g)

Cooking and Water

FUNCTION	STYLE	EXAMPLE	WEIGHT
Stove	Esbit Solid Fuel	Bottom Quarter Inch Of V-8 Juice Can	0.1 oz (3 g)
Cook Pot	21 Fl Oz Titanium Mug/pot	Snow Peak 600 Mug	2.8 oz (79 g)
Cook Pot Lid	Foil	To Fit Mug	0.1 oz (3 g)

Cooking and Water (con't)

FUNCTION	STYLE	EXAMPLE	WEIGHT
Wind Screen	Wind Screen/pot Support	Cut Down Vienna Sausage Can With Vents	0.4 oz (11 g)
Utensil	Spork	Backpacking Light Titanium Mini Spork	0.4 oz (11 g)
Lighting	Lighter	Scripto	0.6 oz (17 g)
Water Bottles	2l Soft Sided Bladders	Platypus 2 L Zip Hoser (2) With Caps And 1 Hose	5.3 oz (150 g)
Water Treatment	Chlorine Dioxide	Aquamira Kit Repackaged In Dropper Bottles	1.1 oz (31 g)
Food Storage	Odor Proof Bag	12	1.0 oz (28 g)

Other Essentials

FUNCTION	STYLE	EXAMPLE	WEIGHT
Maps	Trail Map	Superstition Mountains Trail Map	2.0 oz (57 g)
Light	Led	Princeton Tec Scout Without Headband	1.0 oz (28 g)
Ditty Bag	Medical, Emergency, And Miscellaneous	Waterproof Sunblock, 100 Percent Deet, Compass, Uv Blocking Lip Balm, Aspirin, Paper Cutter, Duct Tape, Whistle In Mesh Bag	2.8 oz (79 g)
Firestarting	Emergency Firestarting, Waterproof	No-blow Out Birthday Candles (3), Storm Matches (3) And Striker In 4	1.1 oz (31 g)
Sunglasses	Clip On	Clip On Sunglasses In Flat Leather Case	0.6 oz (17 g)
Insect Netting	Mosquito Headnet	Adventure 16	0.8 oz (23 g)
Personal Hygiene	Toilet Kit	Toilet Paper, Alcohol Hand Gel, Zip Bag For Used Tp, Antibiotic Cream With Pain Relief In 4"x7" Aloksak	2.0 oz (57 g)
Personal Hygiene	Teeth Cleaning Kit	Toothbrush, Floss, Baking Soda In Tiny Zip Bag, In Zip Bag	1.1 oz (31 g)

Consumables

FUNCTION	STYLE	EXAMPLE	WEIGHT
Fuel	Solid Fuel	Esbit Tablets, One 0.5 oz Tablet For Each Dinner	1.0 oz (28 g)
Food	2.5 Days	20 Oz/day	50.0 oz (1417 g)
Water	Average Carried	3 Quarts	96.0 oz (2722 g)

WEIGHT SUMMARY

(1)	Total Weight Worn or Carried	3.29 lb (1.49 kg)
(2)	Total Base Weight in Pack	5.33 lb (2.42 kg)
(3)	Total Weight of Consumables	9.19 lb (4.17 kg)
(4)	Total Initial Pack Weight (2) + (3)	14.52 lb (6.59 kg)
(5)	Full Skin Out Weight (1) + (2) + (3)	17.81 lb (8.08 kg)

Citation:

This list was originally published in the online magazine BackpackingLight.com (ISSN 1537-0364) in May 2004.

Appendix B:
Gear Manufacturers
Referenced in This Book

BACKPACKS

Bozeman Mountain Works
Dan McHale, Seattle, WA
Go Lite
Gossamer Gear

CAMERAS AND OPTICS

Cameras

Canon
Contax
Contax
Hasselblad
Konica
Leica
Minox
Nikon
Olympus
Pentax
Rollei
Voigtlander

**MONO/BINOCULARS
AND TELESCOPES**

Bushnell
Canon
Celestron
Leica
Meade
Minolta
Nikon
Orion
Pentax
Steiner
Swarovski
Zeiss

CLOTHING

BaseWear
Black Diamond
Bozeman Mountain Works
Buffalo Clothing Systems
Capilene
Cloudveil, WY

Coolmax
Early Winters Company
Feathered Friends
GoLite
Ibex
Inego
Lifa
Marmot
Montane
Paramo Directional Clothing
Systems
Patagonia
Perseverance Mills, UK
Polartec
Rab Carrington, UK
Railriders
Schoeller
Smartwool
Wild Things

RAIN WEAR: JACKETS, SHELLS, AND PONCHOS

Bozeman Mountain Works
Dancing Light Gear of Georgia
DriDucks
Equinox of Pennsylvania
Frogg Toggs
Haglöfs
Hilleberg
Integral Designs
Marmot
Moonbow Gear, NH
Oware USA
Patagonia
Rainshield
Sierra Designs
Stephenson's of New Hampshire

Vapor Barrier Clothing

Integral Designs
RBH Designs
Stephenson's of New Hampshire
Wild Country

COOKING AND EATING

Mountain Safety Research (MSR)
Antigravity Gear
Backpacker's Pantry
Evernew
Nalgene Lexan
Snow Peak

Coffee & Tea

Folgers
Senseo
Starbucks

Drink Mixes

Crystal Light
CytoMax
Gu_2O
Kool-Aid
PowerMax

Firestarters & Fuel

Esbit
Everclear
Heet
Purell
Spark-Lite

Food Storage Systems

BearVault
Bozeman Mountain Works
Garcia Backpacker's Cache
Wild Ideas

Food Storage Saks

Aloksak
Glad
Watchful Eye Designs

Nutrition and Snack Bars

Clif Bars
Little Debbies
Luna Bars
Pemmican Bars
Power Bars

Stoves

Brasslite
Brunton
Coleman
Hike-Lite
Mountain Safety Research
(MSR)
Primus
Sierra Designs
Snow Peak
Trangia
Vargo
Vaude

Water Disinfectants and Purifiers

First Need
McNett AquaMira (US)
Mountain Safety Research
(MSR)
Polar Pure
Potable Aqua
Pristine (Canada)
Safewater Anywhere (now
defunct)
Seychelle
Steri-Pen
Sweetwater
ULA Equipment

Water Storage

Cascade Designs
Nalgene Lexan

Fabric Manufacturers

Brynje, Norway
Cloudveil, WY
Dupont (Tyvek, polyethylene
tarp)
Gore
Inego
Nextec
Paramo Directional Clothing
Systems
Patagonia
Perseverance Mills, UK

Pertex
Schoeller, Switzerland

FOOTWEAR

Aftermarket Insoles

Superfeet
La Sportiva

Shoes, Boots, and Camp Booties

Brasher
Merrill
Montrail
New Balance
Salomon
La Sportiva
Forty Below
Neos
Outdoor Research
Nunatak USA
Sierra Designs

Socks

GoLite
Integral Designs
RBH Designs
CoolMax
Smartwool

Snowshoes

Mountain Safety Research
(MSR)
Northern Lites Company

Hygiene and First Aid

Actifed
Benadryl
Dr. Bronner
Imodium A-D
Pepcid AC
Purell

Navigation Equipment

Brunton
Garmin
Lightwave
National Geographic
Suunto
Teslin
Zeiss

Shelter

HAMMOCKS

Big Agnes
Golite
Hennessy
Nunatak USA, Twisp, WA
Rab Carrington, UK

SEAM SEALANT

McNett

STAKES, NAIL PEGS, AND CORDING

Bozeman Mountain Works
Gossamer Gear
Kelty Triptease
Lightwave, UK
Mountain Safety Research (MSR)
Snow Peak
Vargo Outdoors

TENTS, TEPEES, AND OTHER ODDITIES

Black Diamond
Early Winters
GoLite
Integral Designs
Outdoor Research
Oware USA
Six Moon Designs

TarpTent
Tipi Kifaru
TrailQuest
Wanderlust Nomad

SLEEP SYSTEMS

Bivy Sacks
Bibler
Bozeman Mountain Works
Equinox
Outdoor Research
Oware USA

MATTRESSES AND PADS

Big Agnes
Bozeman Mountain Works
Cascade Designs
Exped
Gossamer Gear
Pacific Outdoor Equipment
Slumberjack
Stephenson's of New Hampshire

SLEEPING BAGS

Big Agnes
Fanatic Fringe
GoLite
Macpac of New Zealand
Nunatak USA
Rab Carrington, UK
Sierra Designs
Western Mountaineering

Appendix C:
Resources

BOOKS

- Auerbach, Paul S. *Medicine for the Outdoors* (New York: The Lyons Press, 1999)
- Auerbach, Paul S., editor. *Wilderness Medicine* (St. Louis, MO: Mosby, Inc., 2001)
- Carpenter, T. M. *Tables, Factors, and Formulas for Computing Respiratory Exchange and Biological Transformations* (Washington, DC: Carnegie Institution of Washington, 1939)
- Curtis, Rick. *The Backpacker's Field Manual: A Comprehensive Guide to Mastering Backcountry Skills* (Three Rivers Press, 1998)
- Fletcher, Colin and Rawlins, Chip. *The Complete Walker IV* (Knopf, 2002)
- Forgey, Wm. *Wilderness Medicine* (Merrillville, IN; ICS Books Inc., 1994)
- Jardine, Ray. *The Ray Way Tarp Book* (Adventurelore Press, 2003)
- Jardine, Ray. *Beyond Backpacking* (Adventure Lore, 1999)

- Jordan, Ryan; Nelson, Jim; and Dixon, Alan. *Clothing and Sleep Systems* (Beartooth Mountain Press, 2004)
- Jordan, Ryan (editor). *Lightweight Backpacking 101* (Beartooth Mountain Press, 2001)
- Kephart, Horace. *Camping and Woodcraft*, (University of Tennessee Press)
- Ladigin, Don and Clelland, Mike. *Lighten Up!* (Falcon Press, 2005)
- O'Bannon, Allen and Clelland, Mike. *Allen and Mike's Really Cool Backpackin' Book* (Falcon Press, 2001)
- Tilton, Buck and Hubbell, Frank. *Medicine for the Backcountry* (Merrillville, IN: ICS Books, Inc. 1994)
- Townsend, Chris. *The Backpacker's Handbook* (Ragged Mountain Press, 2004)
- Vonhof, John. *Fixing Your Feet: Third Edition* (Wilderness Press, 2004)
- Weiss, Eric A. *A Comprehensive Guide to Wilderness and Travel Medicine* (Oakland, CA: Adventure Medical Kits, 1997)
- Weis, Hal. *Secrets of Warmth* (The Mountaineers, 1992).
- *Hiking Light Handbook: Carry Less, Enjoy More* (*Backpacker Magazine*, Mountaineers Books, 2004)

PERIODICAL ARTICLES

- "Waterproof Breathable Fabric Technologies: A Comprehensive Primer and State of the Market Technology Review" (Alan Dixon. *Backpacking Light Magazine*. ISSN 1537-0364, February 10, 2004. www.backpackinglight.com/).
- "The Arc Bag Concept: Saving Weight with Variable Girth Sleeping Bags Having an 'Arc' Shaped Cross Section," (Ryan Jordan, *Backpacking Light Magazine*, April 29, 2001. www.backpackinglight.com/).

ONLINE RESOURCES

- Backpacker.com
- BackpackingLight.com
- Backpacking.net
- Thru-hiker.com
- WhiteBlaze.com
- PCTA.com
- AppalachianTrail.com
- CDTrail.com
- ALDHA.org
- ALDHAWest.org
- YahooGroups.com/group/BackpackingLight
- House of Nutrition: www.houseofnutrition.com/
- USDA Nutrient Data Laboratory: www.nal.usda. gov/fnic/foodcomp

OTHER RESOURCES

- American Red Cross
  www.redcross.org
- Chinook Medical Gear Inc.
  3455 Main Avenue
  Durango, Colorado 81301
  800-766-1365
  www.chinookmed.com
- The National Outdoor Leadership School (NOLS)
  www.nols.edu/
- National Safety Council
  1121 Spring Lake Drive
  Itasca, IL 60143
  800-621-7619
  www.nsc.org
- Wilderness Medical Society
  3595 East Fountain Blvd., Ste. A1
  Colorado Springs, CO 80910
  719-572-9255
  www.wms.org

- Wilderness Medicine Institute
  P.O. Box 9
  Pitkin, CO 81241
  970-641-3572
  http//wmi.nols.edu/
- Wilderness Medicine Outfitters
  2477 County Road 132
  Elizabeth, CO 80107
  303-688-5176
  www.wildernessmedicine.com
- US Forestry Service
  www.fs.fed.us

"There is nothing a man of good sense dreads in a hiking companion so much as his having a lighter pack than himself."

Ryan Jordan to Glen Van Peski as he begins removing essential items of nutrition and emergency gear from his pack in a Pinedale motel the night before a backpack weigh-in that will start their traverse along the Wind River High Route.

(Adapted from a Henry Fielding quote)